www.routledgesw.com

D0144508

Alice A. Lieberman, The University of Kansas, Series Editor

An authentic breakthrough in social work education . . .

New Directions in Social Work is an innovative, integrated series of texts, web site, and interactive case studies for generalist courses in the Social Work curriculum at both undergraduate and graduate levels. Instructors will find everything they need to build a comprehensive course that allows students to meet course outcomes, with these unique features:

- All texts, interactive cases, and test materials are **linked to the 2008 CSWE Policy and Accreditation Standards (EPAS).**

- **One Web portal with easy access** for instructors and students from any computer—no codes, no CDs, no restrictions. Go to www.routledgesw.com and discover.

- **The Series is flexible and can be easily adapted for use in online distance-learning courses as well as hybrid and bricks-and-mortar courses.**

- Each Text and the Web site can be used **individually** or as an **entire Series** to meet the needs of any social work program.

TITLES IN THE SERIES

Social Work and Social Welfare: An Invitation, Third Edition by Marla Berg-Weger
Human Behavior in the Social Environment, Third Edition by Anissa Taun Rogers
Research for Effective Social Work Practice, Third Edition by Judy L. Krysik and Jerry Finn
Social Policy for Effective Practice: A Strengths Approach, Third Edition by Rosemary K. Chapin
The Practice of Generalist Social Work, Third Edition by Julie Birkenmaier, Marla Berg-Weger and Martha P. Dewees

The Practice of Generalist Social Work

Third Edition
by Julie Birkenmaier and Marla Berg-Weger, Saint Louis University, and Martha P. Dewees, University of Vermont

To access the innovative digital materials integral to this text and completely FREE to your students, go to www.routledgesw.com/practice

In this book and companion custom website you will find:

- Complete coverage of the range of social work generalist practice within the framework of planned change, encompassing engagement, assessment, intervention, and evaluation and termination—for work with individuals, families, groups, organizations, and communities. This edition features expanded coverage of practice with individuals, families, groups, organizations, and communities.

- Consistent and in-depth use of key theoretical perspectives and case examples to demonstrate essential knowledge, values, and skills for generalist social work practice. But the text does not overwhelm the student reader with a plethora of nuances of intervention and other skills that will occur in a variety of practice settings and roles. *Instead, this book presents clearly the core competencies for general social work practice.*

- Six *unique*, in-depth, interactive, easy-to-access cases, which students can easily reach from *any* computer, provide a "learning by doing" format unavailable with any other text(s). Your students will have an advantage unlike any other they will experience in their social work education. One case, Brickville, is brand new to this book. Go to www.routledgesw.com/ cases to see each of these cases on the free website.

- In addition, *four* streaming videos relate to competencies and skills discussed in the book at the three client system levels—individuals and families, groups, and communities. The videos depict social workers demonstrating skills discussed in the chapters, and offer instructors numerous possibilities for classroom instruction. In the video for the new case, "Brickville," a social worker combines individual and family practice skills with multicultural community engagement as he works with an African American family about to be displaced by redevelopment and facing multiple stressors. Go to http://routledgesw.com//sanchez/ engage/video, http://routledgesw.com//

riverton/engage/video, and http://routledgesw.com//washburn/engage/video, and http://routledgesw.com//brickville/engage/video to see *each* of these videos that are included within *each* of the web-based cases.

- At least 10 exercises at the end of each chapter provide you with the means to insure that your students can *demonstrate their mastery* of the theoretical frameworks, skills, and core competencies of generalist social work practice as presented *not just* in the text, but in the free web-based cases as well. Instructors can choose from among the approximately 5 exercises that relate to relevant practice issues, and 5 relate specifically to one of the on-line cases.

- A wealth of instructor-only resources also available at www.routledgesw.com/practice provide: full-text readings that link to the concepts presented in each of the chapters; a complete bank of objective and essay-type test items, all linked to current CSWE EPAS standards; PowerPoint presentations to help students master key concepts; a sample syllabus; annotated links to a treasure trove of social work assets on the Internet and teaching tips on how to use them in your practice sequence of courses.

- A clear focus on generalist social work practice, informed by the authors' decades of real-world practice experience, at *all* levels of engagement and intervention.

ADAPTING THE THIRD EDITION TO YOUR COURSE NEEDS

CUSTOM OPTIONS FOR THE TEXT ARE AVAILABLE: if an instructor or social work program wishes to assign *only a portion* of the text for a micro-level practice course, or a course focused on group practice, they may do so. Smaller units of the text are available in modular formats from the publisher. Please contact orders@taylorandfrancis.com if you would like to pursue this option.

The Practice of Generalist Social Work

Third Edition

Julie Birkenmaier
Saint Louis University

Marla Berg-Weger
Saint Louis University

Martha P. Dewees
University of Vermont

 Routledge
Taylor & Francis Group

NEW YORK AND LONDON

Third edition published 2014
by Routledge
711 Third Avenue, New York, NY 10017

and by Routledge
2 Park Square, Milton Park, Abingdon, Oxon OX14 4RN

Routledge is an imprint of the Taylor & Francis Group, an informa business

© 2014 Taylor & Francis

The right of Julie Birkenmaier, Marla Berg-Weger and Martha P. Dewees to be identified as authors of this work has been asserted by them in accordance with sections 77 and 78 of the Copyright, Designs and Patents Act 1988.

Second edition published 2011 by Routledge

Trademark notice: Product or corporate names may be trademarks or registered trademarks, and are used only for identification and explanation without intent to infringe.

Library of Congress Cataloging in Publication Data
Dewees, Martha.
  [Contemporary social work practice]
  The practice of generalist social work / by Julie Birkenmaier, Marla Berg-Weger, and Martha Dewees. – [Third edition].
    pages cm. – (New directions in social work)
  Includes bibliographical references and index.
  1. Social service. 2. Social service–United States.   I. Birkenmaier, Julie.   II. Berg–Weger, Marla, 1956-   III. Title.
  HV40.D534 2014
  361.3'20973--dc23
  2013020892

ISBN: 978–0–415–51988–5 (hbk)
ISBN: 978–0–415–51989–2 (pbk)
ISBN: 978–0–203–07098–7 (ebk)

Typeset in Stone Serif
by RefineCatch Limited, Bungay, Suffolk, UK
Printed and bound by Courier in Westford, MA

SUSTAINABLE FORESTRY INITIATIVE

Certified Chain of Custody
Promoting Sustainable Forestry

www.sfiprogram.org
SFI-00712

This SFI label applies to the text and cover papers.

BRIEF CONTENTS

DETAILED CONTENTS

CHAPTER 3

PREFACE

MAJOR CHANGES TO THE THIRD EDITION

Like the previous editions, this new edition of *The Practice of Generalist Social Work* provides detailed coverage of the knowledge, skills, values, competencies, and practice behaviors needed for contemporary generalist social work practice. Using a strengths-based perspective, students are given a comprehensive overview of the major areas relevant for social work practice, including: theoretical frameworks; values and ethics; expanded coverage of communication skills for all client systems; and extensive coverage of practice with all client systems through all phases of the change process. *The Practice of Generalist Social Work* offers a comprehensive discussion of practice with individuals, families, groups, communities, and organizations within the concepts of planned change, encompassing engagement, assessment, intervention, evaluation, and termination. Students have the opportunity to learn about generalist practice through in-depth case studies, examples, and exercises integrated throughout the text.

This edition expands greatly on the previous edition to provide all the material necessary and relevant for a two or three course sequence. This third edition provides additional contemporary case studies and applications of theory and knowledge for all client system levels. New exhibits provide in-depth information relevant to practice, summarize pertinent facts from the chapter, and give practical examples of the application of key chapter content. The Quick Guides provide students with brief guidelines for practice and sample documents used in practice. These expanded resources contain up-to-date individual, family, group, community and organizational guidance for the beginning practitioner. New and expanded end-of-chapter exercises, and online supplemental material, including videos, podcasts, and other web-based resources with teaching tips give the instructor additional avenues to challenge students to integrate and expand on chapter content.

For the new editions of all five books in the New Directions in Social Work series, each addressing a foundational course in the social work curriculum, the publisher has created a brand-new, distinctive teaching strategy that revolves around the print book but offers much more than the traditional text experience. Quick Guides within the text offer students guidance for their field experiences. Book-specific websites are accessible through the series website, www.routledgesw.com, and offer a variety of features to support your integration of the many facets of an education in social work.

At www.routledgesw.com/, you will find a wealth of resources to help you create a dynamic, experiential introduction to social work for your students:

- Companion readings linked to key concepts in each chapter, along with questions to encourage further thought and discussion.

- Six interactive fictional cases (three new for this edition) with accompanying exercises that bring to life the concepts covered in the book, readings, and classroom discussions.

- A bank of exam questions (both objective and open-ended).

- PowerPoint presentations, which can serve as a starting point for class discussions.

- Sample syllabi demonstrating how the text and website, when used together through the course, satisfy the 2008 Council on Social Work Educational Policy and Accreditation Standards (EPAS).

- Quick Guides from the books offered online for students to copy and take into the field for guidance.

- Annotated links to a treasure trove of articles and other readings, videos, podcasts, and internet sites.

ORGANIZATION OF THE BOOK

The following paragraphs serve to briefly introduce each of the chapters included in this book with emphasis on the updated content. All chapters have updated and expanded end-of-chapter exercises that use online resources.

Chapter 1

Understanding Social Work Practice provides an overview of social work practice by grounding students in the purpose of social work, social work competencies, types of client grouping, and the practice framework of engagement, assessment, intervention, termination, and evaluation. A discussion of the ethics that guide social work practice, licensure of social work, client populations that social workers work with, and the tensions in social work provides students with real-world information about the profession. Students are also introduced to major theoretical perspectives for social work practice, including the ecosystems, social justice, human rights, strengths, and postmodern perspectives. In this third edition, Chapter 1 features five new exhibits and two new quick guides to highlight key content and summarize material, including a summary of social work approaches.

Chapter 2

In contrast to a straightforward overview of values and ethics, **Applying Values and Ethics to Practice** provides a brief history of social work ethics and the NASW *Code of Ethics* (2008), then contrasts the *Code of Ethics* with the International Federation of Social Workers' Ethical Statement, and also discusses the limits of ethical codes. A discussion of the intersection of ethics and the law gives students information about the interplay between the two, followed by a discussion of ethical dilemmas and processes for resolving them. Extensive discussion about common practice dilemmas gives students exposure to situations that they may encounter in practice, followed by an emphasis on risk management. Expanded coverage of ethics violations and state sanctions round-out the discussion. New content in Chapter 2 includes expanded coverage of ethics violations and state sanctions.

Chapter 3

Individual Engagement: Relationship Skills for Practice at All Levels provides students with the characteristics of core relationships qualities, as well as a description of the specific skills for dialogue with clients at all system levels, including coverage of common communication pitfalls. As the helping relationship includes the dimension of power, the chapter provides extensive coverage of sources of power within relationships, and provides guidance on the use of power through a case study of "Jasmine and the Social Worker." Practical questions guide students toward active listening. Students are also provided with strategies and skills for promoting social justice and human rights within helping relationships. New content in this third edition includes an exhibit on nonverbal behavior guidelines, a quick guide that helps students discover their listening skills, and content about using children as translators.

Chapter 4

Social Work Practice with Individuals: Assessment and Planning includes a focus on the assessment and planning process within the global environment in which practicing social workers live and practice. The chapter begins with a discussion of the history of assessment and moves to an overview of theoretical approaches to social work practice, both classic and contemporary (strengths, narrative, and solution-focused). The application of evidence-based practice approaches is highlighted. The need for practice knowledge and behaviors in the area of diversity within the assessment and planning phases emphasizes the need for cultural competence. The chapter concludes with a discussion of the relevant skills and practice behaviors in the assessment and planning phases of the social work intervention process, including skills needed for strengths-based, narrative, and solution-focused approaches, documentation, and self-care for the social worker. This edition offers more content on narrative and solution-focused approaches, documentation, self-care, and suicide risk assessment with vulnerable populations with more examples on applications of knowledge and theory.

Chapter 5

Social Work Practice with Individuals: Intervention, Termination, and Evaluation introduces students to key areas of social work practice that will impact virtually every dimension of their professional lives. With an emphasis on theoretical perspectives, students learn to apply various intervention, termination, and evaluation practice behaviors. Traditional and contemporary social work roles are highlighted and discussed. Documentation and record-keeping for social work interventions is explained. Interventions with individuals are also framed within an empowerment practice approach. Framed within theoretical perspectives for understanding diversity, students are offered an overview of the skills required to be a culturally competent social work practitioner. New features in Chapter 5 include additional content on cognitive behavioral treatment and expanded content on motivational interviewing, documentation, and empowerment.

Chapter 6

Social Work Practice with Families: Engagement, Assessment, and Planning The chapter begins with a history of social work practice with families, grounded within a systems framework. Theoretical perspectives, including narrative and solution-focused, are discussed within the context of the engagement and assessment phases of interventions with families with emphasis on empowerment. Students encounter a broad range of family constellations as they read about contemporary family social work. Practice behaviors and skills are presented for achieving engagement and assessment with families and documentation strategies are included. This newest version of Chapter 6 offers more content on documentation, empowerment, and more in-depth discussion about solution-focused and narrative assessment and planning.

Chapter 7

Social Work Practice with Families: Intervention, Termination, and Evaluation conceptualizes generalist social work practice interventions with families. Continuing with the theoretical perspectives discussed in Chapter 6, this chapter develops interventions with families using strengths and empowerment, narrative, and solution-focused approaches. Skills and practice behaviors for intervening, terminating, evaluating, and documenting family-focused interventions are discussed in detail. New to this edition is more in-depth content on empowerment and resiliency, and extended exploration of narrative and solution-focused family interventions.

Chapter 8

Social Work Practice with Groups: Engagement, Assessment, and Planning provides students with up-to-date perspectives on social work practice with groups. The chapter opens with an overview of the role of groups within our communities and profession followed by a historical and contemporary perspective on the use of groups for change. The dimensions of group practice are presented within the framework of theoretical perspectives (i.e., narrative and solution-focused). Planning for group interventions, including the engagement and assessment of group members, is emphasized from a practice behaviors perspective along with the importance of cultural competence in the group setting. With this edition, Chapter 8 now includes expanded coverage on cultural competence in group work.

Chapter 9

Social Work Practice with Groups: Intervention, Termination, and Evaluation Developing and implementing interventions with various types of groups is the emphasis of this chapter. Continuing the framing of skills and techniques within theoretical perspectives, the use of evidence-based interventions with groups is introduced using the strengths, narrative, and solution-focused frameworks. Models for group intervention are described along with an in-depth examination of the roles, skills, and practice behaviors required for carrying out a group-level intervention. Termination and evaluation of group interventions are also covered. New to Chapter 9 is additional content on narrative group work, social worker roles, group member behaviors, and evaluation.

Chapter 10

Social Work Practice with Communities: Engagement, Assessment, and Planning introduces students to the concept of community. The chapter defines and discusses types and functions of communities. Students learn about various theoretical perspectives, including contemporary perspectives for community practice. Engagement and assessment concepts, including community-based analysis, evidence-based practice, and community needs assessments, are extensively discussed. Examples of types of needs assessments, surveys used in needs assessments, and needs assessment summaries provide additional practice guidance. Community practice skills are thoroughly covered, as are the implications of global interdependence for community practice in the United States. This edition contains expanded content on needs assessments, including types, examples, and surveys used to collect needs assessment data.

Chapter 11

Social Work Practice with Communities: Intervention, Termination, and Evaluation builds on the engagement and assessment content of Chapter 10 to present strategies and techniques for community practice. Using the insights gained about practice at the individual, family, and group levels, this chapter expands the students' awareness of social work practice with communities through a discussion of today's trends and skills for intervention, including community social and economic development, and community organizing. Included in this discussion is coverage of international community practice. Examples of public and private efforts to promote evidence-based community practice assist students in applying the material. Additional guidance on advocacy efforts and asset based development are presented. Students also learn the knowledge and skills needed for termination and evaluation of community practice. The third edition offers a host of examples of contemporary community interventions, with a special focus on community development and community organizing examples, as well as quick guides that offer students concrete tools to use in community interventions, termination, and evaluation.

Chapter 12

Social Work Practice with Organizations: Engagement, Assessment, and Planning covers a challenging client system for beginning practitioners—the organization. Students learn a wealth of practical and theoretical aspects of organizations, including a discussion about the purpose and structure of organizations, power relations within organizations, and social work within host organizational settings. The chapter provides discussion about the elements of an internal assessment of organizations, to include organizational culture, and external assessments as well. Material about organizational policy advocacy and nonprofit partnerships help guide practice. The many new, recent examples of organizational engagement and assessment provide students with contemporary illustrations of key content in Chapter 12. Three new quick guides offer handy tools to assist students in their efforts to contribute to organizational engagement and assessment work.

Chapter 13

Social Work Practice with Organizations: Intervention, Termination, and Evaluation uses the foundation built in Chapter 12 to discuss approaches, perspectives, and models for intervening with organizations. This chapter provides extensive coverage of the relationship between theoretical perspectives and organizational change, as well as a practical framework for thinking about generating change and the needed knowledge for a social work generalist in this endeavor. Termination and evaluation of change efforts within organizations, including a discussion about the role of the generalist practitioner in this process, help students see their potential role in a change effort with organizations. Content about the challenges of implementing organizational change, and persuasion skills to assist in these efforts, provide direction for the practitioner. In this edition, Chapter 13 has expanded content that includes examples of intervention at the organizational level that includes developing and refining new programming, as well as the associated challenges.

INTERACTIVE CASES

The website www.routledgesw.com/cases presents six unique, in-depth, interactive, fictional cases with dynamic characters and real-life situations. Three of them—the RAINN, Hudson City, and Brickville cases—are entirely new to this edition of the series. Your students can easily access the cases from any computer. The cases provide a "learning by doing" format unavailable with any other book, and the experience will be unlike any other your students will experience in their social work training.

Each of the interactive cases uses text, graphics, and video to help students learn about engagement, assessment, intervention, and evaluation and termination at multiple levels of social work practice. The "My Notebook" feature allows students to take and save notes, type in written responses to tasks, and share their work with classmates and instructors by e-mail. Through these interactive cases, you can integrate the readings and classroom discussions:

The Sanchez Family: Systems, Strengths, and Stressors   The 10 individuals in this extended Latino family have numerous strengths but are faced with a variety of challenges. Students will have the opportunity to experience the phases of the social work intervention, grapple with ethical dilemmas, and identify strategies for addressing issues of diversity.

Riverton: A Community Conundrum   Riverton is a small Midwest city in which the social worker lives and works. The social worker identifies an issue that presents her community with a challenge. Students and instructors can work together to develop strategies for engaging, assessing, and intervening with the citizens of the social worker's neighborhood.

Carla Washburn: Loss, Aging, and Social Support   Students will get to know Carla Washburn, an older African American woman who finds herself living alone after the loss of her grandson and in considerable pain from a recent accident. In this case, less complex than the Sanchez family case, students can apply their growing knowledge of gerontology and exercise the skills of culturally competent practice at the individual, family, and group levels.

RAINN Based on the first online hotline for delivering sexual assault services, this interactive case includes a variety of exercises to enable students to gain knowledge and skills related to the provision of services to persons in crisis. With a focus on social work practice at all levels, exercises provide insight into program services and evaluation, interactions with volunteers and clients, and research.

Hudson City: An Urban Community Affected by Disaster A natural disaster in the form of Hurricane Diane has hit Hudson City, a large metropolitan area on the northeastern coast of the United States. This interactive case will provide students with insights into the complexities of experiencing a disaster, including the phases of the human response to disaster and the social work role in responding to natural disasters.

Brickville A real estate developer has big plans to redevelop Brickville, an area of a major metropolitan area that has suffered from generations of disinvestment and decay. The redevelopment plans have stirred major controversy among community residents, neighborhood service providers, politicians, faith communities, and invested outsiders. This case is a "community case" in which a "family case" is embedded; the case is multi-layered and detailed. Students will be challenged to think about two levels of client systems, and the ways in which they influence and are influenced by one another.

IN SUM

We have written this book with the purpose of providing you and your students with the information needed to learn the knowledge, skills, values, competencies, and practice behaviors that are required for a competent and effective generalist social work practice. The multiple options for supporting your teaching of this content are intended to help you address the diverse range of student learning styles and needs. The design of this text and the instructor support materials are aimed at optimizing the experiential options for learning about generalist practice. We hope this book and the support materials will be of help to you and your students as they embark on their journey toward social work practice.

ACKNOWLEDGEMENTS

We would like to thank the many colleagues who helped to make this book and previous editions possible. To Alice Lieberman, we are grateful for your innovation and vision that has resulted in this series and the web-based supplements that bring the material alive. We appreciate the camaraderie and support of the authors of the other books in this series—Rosemary Chapin, Anissa Rogers, Judy Kryzik, and Jerry Finn. A special thank you to Anissa Rogers and Shannon Cooper-Sadlo, and Andrea Seper whose creativity makes the exercises, test questions, and PowerPoint slides enticing and easy to use. We want to thank the group who participated in the production of the video vignettes: actors John Abram, Patti Rosenthal, Beverly Sporleder, Sabrina Tyuse, Kristi Sobbe, Myrtis Spencer, Phil Minden, Katie Terrell, and Shannon Cooper-Sadlo and videographers, Tom Meuser and Elizabeth Yaeger. A special thanks goes to Sue Tebb, for her careful review and invaluable feedback, and Andrea Seper, graduate student assistant, for her extensive assistance with this edition and supplemental materials. Thanks also goes to social work graduate student assistants, Michelle Siroko and Luxiaofei Li, for their help with research, writing and editing. We also want to thank:

Toni Johnson	University of Kansas
Lara Vanderhoof	Tabor College
Chrys C. Ramirez Barranti	Sacramento State University
Kameri Christy	University of Arkansas
Robin Bonifas	Arizona State University
Bill Milford	Thomas University
Martha Haley-Bowling	Ferrum College
Mary Clay Thomas	Mary Baldwin College
Armon Perry	University of Louisville

for their reviews of the book as it was evolving. Finally, we are most appreciative to the staff of Routledge for their support and encouragement for making this book a reality. It takes a village . . . .

ABOUT THE AUTHORS

Julie Birkenmaier is an Associate Professor in the School of Social Work at Saint Louis University, Missouri. Dr. Birkenmaier's practice experience includes community organizing, community development, and nonprofit administration. Her research and writing focuses on financial capability, financial credit, community development, and asset development. With colleagues, she co-edited *Financial Capability and Asset Development: Research, Education, Policy and Practice*. With Marla Berg-Weger, she also co-authored the textbook, *The Practicum Companion for Social Work: Integrating Class and Field Work* (3rd edition).

Marla Berg-Weger is a Professor in the School of Social Work at Saint Louis University, Missouri and Executive Director of the Geriatric Education Center. Dr. Berg-Weger holds social work degrees at the bachelor's, master's, and doctoral levels. Her social work practice experience includes public social welfare services, intimate partner violence services, mental health, medical social work, and gerontological social work. Her research and writing focuses on gerontological social work and social work practice. She is the author of *Social Work and Social Welfare: An Invitation* (3rd edition). With Julie Birkenmaier, she co-authored the textbook, *The Practicum Companion for Social Work: Integrating Class and Field Work* (3rd edition). She is the Past President of the Association of Gerontology in Social Work and currently serves as the Chair of the *Journal of Gerontological Social Work* Editorial Board Executive Committee and is a fellow in the Gerontological Society of America.

Martha P. Dewees, Associate Professor Emerita of the University of Vermont, made her way into social work through counseling and then focused on mental health work at the state psychiatric facility. Her inclusion on the faculty at the University of Vermont provided the impetus for looking at social work practice through the lenses of human rights, social justice, strengths, and social construction. These are reflected in her previous publications and in the first edition of this book.

CHAPTER 1

Understanding Social Work Practice

Debbie, Joan, Marcy, and Kate felt as if the whole cosmos had just opened up for them. As a group they had already shared their experiences as women who had experienced intimate partner violence. Their social worker had explained how they could use their stories to help educate children in schools about violence at home. Their collective power felt liberating to them.

Chan, an 11-year-old orphaned child in Southeast Asia, hung on every word the community development worker uttered. She spoke of human rights that he had in his workplace. He had never imagined that he had any rights.

Jamie was very relieved after the hospital social worker provided information about potential rehab centers for his father, who was struggling with physical and mental health issues. Jamie's father could not be cared for at home, and Jamie now knew how his father would be cared for during his recovery.

At their annual meeting, the neighborhood association expressed gratitude for the work of the community social worker. Her efforts, along with her colleagues', had resulted in neighbors who were more connected to job opportunities, teens involved in working for a new community park, and additional city funding made available to the neighborhood by local elected officials.

Key Questions for Chapter 1

(1) How can I prepare to engage, assess, intervene, and evaluate with client systems (EPAS 2.1.10(a)–(d))?
(2) How do you define the practice of social work? (EPAS 2.1.1)
(3) How does theory relate to social work practice? (EPAS 2.1.7)

WELCOME TO THE WORLD OF SOCIAL work practice. This world is sometimes exhilarating, sometimes frustrating, and sometimes heartbreaking. It is nearly always challenging, offers a deep sense of purpose, and once you have entered it, you may find it impossible to imagine doing any other kind of work.

This chapter examines the professional competence that the social worker offers and the ways in which the profession's mission has taken shape. You will explore ways to think about social work practice, types of client groupings and processes, tensions in social work, a brief account of the way the profession has dealt with theory, and contemporary practice commitments. The brief vignettes you have just read describe only a few of the many types of social work practice and client systems.

PURPOSE OF SOCIAL WORK

What is social work trying to accomplish? The primary mission of social work, according to the National Association of Social Workers (NASW) *Code of Ethics* is "to enhance human well-being and help meet the basic human needs of all people, with particular attention to the needs and empowerment of people who are vulnerable, oppressed, and living in poverty" (2008). This mission can be narrowly defined as tied to a particular type of system (e.g., mental health, correction, and child welfare). Alternatively, the mission can be defined as tied to a specific method (e.g., behavioral or cognitive change), a particular problem-solving process or the elimination of a problem-focus (e.g., through the strengths perspective). The mission can also be defined as trying to achieve goals, such as adaptation, sobriety, or a clean criminal record. Although these endpoints are real examples of social work purpose, they are embedded in the deeper and broader mission. The purpose of social work is expressed generally and somewhat vaguely in the *Code of Ethics*, and therefore leaves much open to interpretation. Tensions, therefore, have arisen within the profession about the identity of the profession, some of which are discussed below.

PRACTICING SOCIAL WORK

Social work practice can be conceptualized in several different ways, including: (1) type of practice or range of practice settings; (2) set of activities; (3) set of roles; (4) set of competencies and practice behaviors; (5) types of client grouping; (6) practice framework; (7) a profession that is licensed by states; (8) by purpose (as mentioned above); and (9) by the tensions experienced in the profession. Self-knowledge is also a critical component of effective practice. These concepts are described below, and some are described in depth in this chapter.

Generalist social work practice, included in the curricula of undergraduate social work programs and in the foundation coursework in social work graduate programs, prepares students to work with a range of systems, from direct, one-to-one practice to group-level practice to local and global community development work and work in international settings. Advanced social work practice, taught in the concentration curriculum of graduate school, focuses on more specialized practice, such as social work within a medical setting, family therapy, and administration of social service organizations. The range of generalist and advanced practice settings includes psychiatric facilities, schools, community organizations, family service organizations, legislatures, correctional settings, and a host of others.

Social work practice is also framed as a set of activities, often associated with particular agencies and the functions they carry out in the community. Examples of these include: (1) advocating for policy change regarding the rights of older adults to services from an area agency on aging; (2) facilitating an empowerment group in a domestic violence program, such as the group in which Debbie, Joan, Marcy, and Kate belong; (3) mentoring students in a neighborhood school; (4) developing a psycho-educational group in a mental health agency; (5) supporting families in an emergency housing shelter; (6) implementing human rights policies in another culture by learning a new language and traveling to another part of the world to assist children like Chan; (7) advocating with public officials, companies, and corporations; (8) working with a group of adolescents; and (9) fundraising from government and foundation sources to assist in the empowerment of disadvantaged neighborhoods.

Another way to look at generalist social work practice emphasizes the role of the social worker and the relationship between social worker and client. In the helping process, the generalist social worker working in direct practice with individuals may take on the role of *case manager* (i.e., assisting clients to assess for, arrange, and coordinate needed goods and services), *counselor* (i.e., providing suggestions to assist clients to reach their goals), *broker* (i.e., referring clients to appropriate needed goods and services), *mediator* (i.e., assisting two parties to mutually resolve a dispute), *educator* (i.e., providing relevant information to client systems), and *client advocate* (i.e., working with or on behalf of a client to obtain goods and services). Some definitions of role relationships are driven largely by theoretical perspectives. These roles are discussed in great detail in Chapter 5. All social worker functions are associated with roles that clarify the nature of the interaction between a social worker and the client system. These roles are fluid, and can change from interaction to interaction, and even within interactions. The roles define responsibilities for both the client system and the social worker. Social work practice involves a wide variety of roles because social work is involved in the breadth of human experience.

Social work is a complex and multifaceted profession, with practitioners found in virtually every setting from health clinics to housing programs. Social workers are also engaged in a wide variety of activities. The idea of social work practice is defined by competencies and practice behaviors, client populations, practice frameworks, as a licensed profession, and by the purpose of social work. These various ways of defining and describing the profession are discussed in the following section.

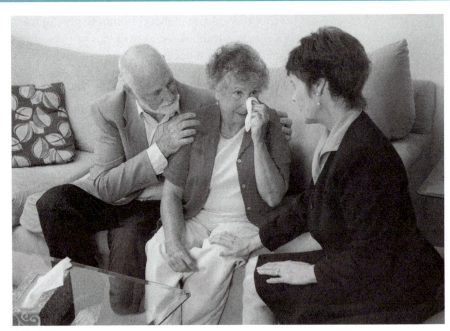

© Lisa F. Young

SOCIAL WORK COMPETENCIES

Generalist social work practitioners bring a set of competencies and practice behaviors to serve client systems. These competencies, or "... measureable practice behaviors that comprise knowledge, values and skills" (Council on Social Work Education (CSWE), 2012, p. 3), are defined by the Council on Social Work Education's Educational Policy and Accreditation Standards (EPAS) to guide social work education, and therefore influence social work practice. The 10 competencies define practice elements, as well as address the practice structure of engagement, assessment, intervention, and termination and evaluation. Each competency consists of several descriptive practice behaviors that social workers should competently be able to demonstrate in practice settings. These competencies encompass knowledge, values, and skills, and are the attributes that social workers bring to the interaction with the client system of individuals, families, groups, organizations, and communities.

Knowledge, Values, and Skills

The trio of knowledge, values, and skills is the core of social work education and training. As an integrated whole, these elements can be considered the tools that a practitioner brings to the work, as they reflect personal aspects and attributes acquired by—and some scholars think inherent to—the social worker. Each is necessary for effective service delivery.

Knowledge   Facts and research findings comprise professional knowledge along with broader topics such as intuition and cultural awareness. A practice-based example may include the need for social workers to know facts, histories, theories, and trends about human development, policy, research, and practice, which are often combined and labeled "biopsychosocial" knowledge. Knowledge of many theories of human behavior and the social environment is central to generalist social work practice. This knowledge is needed to understand normal (or expected) behavior for an adolescent under stress, or the likely dynamics in an agency when a policy change is initiated from the administration. This arena also assumes that the knowledge required is largely agreed upon and that it is attainable through study, discussion, research experimentation, and related activities. According to the EPAS competencies, social workers should also know the history of social work, the value base and ethical standards of the profession, and the history and current structures of social policies and services (CSWE, 2012). Knowledge may also include your experience of utilizing theory and ideas, and even the knowledge emanating from the first-hand experience of seasoned practitioners, or "practice wisdom." This form of practice knowledge may elude traditional empirical measurement, an ongoing challenge both in the field and in social work education. This practice knowledge is the integration of knowledge learned "on the job" with knowledge from other sources, such as prior education and continuing education. Practice wisdom is an invaluable part of social work practice.

Two other critical areas of knowledge are culture and spirituality. First, social workers must understand the broad ways in which a culture's structure and values may create or enhance privilege and power for certain groups in society, and to eliminate the influence of personal biases and values in working with diverse clients (Council on Social Work Education, 2008). Cultural competence refers to the "process by which individuals and systems respond respectfully and effectively to people of all cultures, languages, classes, races, ethnic backgrounds, religions, and other diversity factors in a manner that recognizes, affirms, and values the worth of individuals, families, and communities, and protects and preserves the dignity of each" ("Indicators for the Achievement of the NASW Standards for Cultural Competence in Social Work Practice," 2008). The notion of spirituality is also included in models of both human development and social work education. Spirituality is integrally connected with culture and therefore gives practitioners access to knowledge about important dimensions of their clients. For example, recognizing a Navajo child's spiritual affirmation of harmony may help a social worker understand the child's reluctance to engage in aggressive competition in school. In some areas of practice, such as end of life, a biopsychosocial-spiritual model is being utilized to serve the needs of clients as whole persons (Buck, Overcash, & McMillan, 2009).

Values   Social work has always strongly identified itself as a profession of values, which are strongly held beliefs about preferred conditions of life. The values of the social work profession articulate several key elements, such as (1) the inherent worth of people; (2) the need for open and honest communication to build relationships; and (3) respect for the unique characteristics of diverse populations (to name just a few of the values of the social work profession). Although the social work profession has clearly stated values, you may hear spirited discussion about the ways to implement these values in practice. Consideration of values and ethics will present many challenges to social workers, and will often look different in complicated practice contexts from the way they do in isolation. Through the professional organization, the National Association of Social Workers' (NASW), *Code of Ethics* (NASW, 2008) plays a significant role in sorting out complex situations in which values and ethical conflicts are at issue. While values, as beliefs, guide professional thinking about behavior and judgments about conduct, ethics are the rules, or prescriptions, for behavior that reflect those values. For example, one of the cardinal values held by the social work profession is that all human life is worthy. From that value arises the ethical principle that human life should be protected in social work practice, which means that social workers actively try to prevent any harm that might occur to another person. Ethical dilemmas arise when ethical principles conflict, such as the case when trying to prevent harm to one person puts another at risk. The National Association of Social Workers developed a *Code of Ethics* to clarify the principles of ethical practice. The role of values provides critical criteria for the ways in which the profession shapes itself and the professional rules of conduct.

Skills   The third element the social worker brings to the professional work is skills, or the implementation of the knowledge, theoretical perspectives, and values the social worker brings to her or his work with client systems. Social workers need a wide range of skills, from traditional communication skills and individual assessment skills, to skills in working with families, groups, communities, and organizations. The range of skills will be discussed in subsequent chapters of this book, and the skills mentioned in the EPAS core competencies (CSWE, 2012) will be emphasized.

EXHIBIT 1.1

The full NASW Code of Ethics is available in English and Spanish here:

http://www.socialworkers.org/pubs/code/code.asp

NASW has also published a series of publications that articulate standards for social work in various practice settings (e.g., school social work) and with various populations (e.g., family caregivers of older adults). See the listing of standards publications here:

http://www.socialworkers.org/practice/

Types of Client Groupings

Competencies to practice social work may be viewed within the context of client groupings; social workers work with individuals, couples, families of all types, groups, communities, and organizations, both domestically and internationally. These client groups often overlap, as in the need for group work within community practice, and the need to engage in community work to assist families. These groupings define the constellation of the service beneficiaries involved in the interaction. The more recent expansion of global awareness has resulted in the inclusion of international and global social work, extending the arena in which social work practice is both relevant and critical. Social work education frequently uses this

EXHIBIT 1.2

Types of client groupings

- *Individual work, family work, or casework:* This face-to-face focus, or individual work, family work, or casework, spans all fields of practice, populations, and settings. Casework may include working with an adolescent struggling with sexuality issues, a mother concerned with her child's development, an older adult who is facing an inability to care for himself, or a five-year-old who does not pay attention in school. The nature of the work will be heavily influenced by the agency's purpose, the practice perspective, the personal characteristics of the client (individual or family), and your skills and theoretical perspective. Cultural context, social and political influences, and current community concerns will also affect client relationships.
- *Group work:* Social workers frequently practice with groups. The focus of group work may be on helping the group members make individual changes, the group as a whole make changes, or for the group to make changes in the environment. Group-level social work practice is conceptually social, and embodies the relationship emphasis of the profession. Group work can be a powerful tool for change, and has similarities and differences in the many different practice settings and contexts within which it is implemented. Social work with groups is one of the most distinctive practices of the profession.
- *Community practice:* The method of practice known as community practice usually involves a common locality, such as a city neighborhood, small town, or rural area. Beyond locality, however, *community* also refers to a common concern, interest, or identification. For example, you might consider yourself a member of a hometown as well as a community of gay men or Jewish women or people of Irish descent. Social work practice has historical work in community practice, and aspires toward inclusive participation of community citizens in addressing their self-defined concerns.
- *International work:* An emerging focus of practice is international social work. International social work is a broad concept that can include many facets, including: 1) a worldview; 2) a domestic practice and/or action informed by knowledge of international issues; 3) participation in international professional associations; and 4) development and human rights (Healy & Link, 2012).

organizational scheme in the layout of its curriculum by specific course content or emphasis.

The social work profession increasingly integrates a global, transnational perspective into local issues, such as employment, homelessness and health. Such a perspective provides a full account of the challenges faced by client systems.

An organizational scheme based on client groupings contains a number of underlying assumptions rooted in culture about social work skill development. For example, many U.S. social workers agree that one-to-one practice work is the natural starting place for social work practice, and other types of practice refer back to one-to-one methods. However, in other cultures in which family or community is the major organizing structure or reference point, this assumption may not fit. For example, a social worker providing mental health services may be accustomed to seeing clients individually. However, it may be more culturally appropriate to work with a Latino client's entire family, rather than just the individual client, in order to best assist the client (Conan, 2012). Although the distinctions between types of groupings continue to be a useful way of thinking about social work, generalist practice emphasizes an integration of knowledge and skills across all system levels and sizes.

Practice Framework

The practice framework views social work practice as it relates to the progression of the work. The most commonly used practice framework describes the activities of the social worker and the client system as they proceed together through relatively standard phases. Although these phases are described here in a linear progression, the social worker and client frequently loop back and forth between phases as necessary. The phases described below are more fully discussed relative to client systems in Chapters 3–13.

Engagement   Building a relationship among the social worker, the client, and the client's environment is referred to as engagement. Successful engagement involves establishing a degree of trust and a sense that the work ahead will be helpful to the client system and professionally rewarding and satisfying to the social worker. Engaging a client system requires effective communication and engagement skills with individuals, as well as establishing significant and collaborative connections with the client system's environment and the relevant service systems that will impact your work and the client's goals. For example, your client has asked for your help in negotiating and advocating within her disabled child's school system. You carefully develop a relationship with her so that you may understand the issues and her experiences. You will also need to engage with the client's network (in this case, the school system), to learn about the system constraints and challenges, in order to effectively facilitate a more productive relationship between your client and the school.

Without a successful engagement, the effectiveness or helpfulness of the work that follows may be compromised or more challenging. Engagement may not be effective for a variety of reasons: for instance, the client may lose investment in a process due to a lack of significant meaningful connection to the work, or the critical network contacts in the environment may feel that their role is neither appreciated nor fully understood. In the situation just described, if the school staff thinks that you do not understand the difficulties of providing extensive services with shrinking resources, they may actually become less willing to work on improving their relationship with your client.

Assessment and Planning   Assessment encompasses recognition of the parameters of the practice situation and the way in which the participant is affected. The client's goals are central to the process of assessment and planning for an intervention. Through mutual exploration of the issues, the client and social worker decide the best ways to address the client's goals. Assessment focuses on the analysis of the major area for work; the aspects of the client environment that can offer support

© Lisa F. Young

A social worker engages in a child welfare assessment

for a solution; the client knowledge, skills, and values that can be applied to the situation; and ways in which the client can meet her or his goals.

The social worker's theoretical perspective guides the selection of assessment styles and planning approaches. The overall mission of the agency also plays an important, perhaps defining role in the activity. For example, the assessments conducted in foster care agencies may vary, but they are all likely to be focused on children and parenting, rather than vocational development or personal growth counseling.

Planning is an integral part of the assessment process. Developing the plan will require the client and social worker to assess or evaluate the options, the resources, the barriers, client preferences, and the agreed-upon goals, along with the established methods of achieving them. The plan should also include consideration of the less-than-obvious or unexpected outcomes of reaching a goal. For example, a social worker may assist a couple in adopting a child for whom they provided foster care. Another child in the family may have accepted the temporary nature of the foster care arrangement but suddenly feels threatened by the permanency of foster care turning into an adoption. The complexity of human emotion frequently appears in unexpected places and times in social work practice.

Intervention   The next stage in this sequence, intervention, refers to the action—the doing of the work that will enable the client and the practitioner to accomplish the goals decided upon in the assessment. Generalist practice interventions vary widely, from helping an older adult tenants' union organize a rent strike to helping a family receiving Medicaid benefits receive health care for an ill child. Intervention is the joint activity of the client system and the social worker. In some cases, the intervention may involve the social worker listening to and reflecting on the client's situation, helping the client think about the situation and her or his role in it, and facilitating an opportunity to create a different, more preferable situation. The intervention process is also influenced by the theoretical and/or practice perspective of the social worker. In some practice models, the social worker is very active in determining the client's best interests and initiating action to achieve a specific outcome. In other models, the planning and intervention is a more collaborative process with shared responsibility for actions, and together deciding on the best course. As with other aspects of practice, the type, level, and focus of the intervention vary widely.

Termination   Ending with client systems, or termination, is a long-standing area of focus for social workers. Many clients have experienced abrupt, sometimes violent or completely disconcerting endings to relationships or arrangements; therefore, the profession is committed to facilitating appropriate and effective termination with client systems. In general, the termination process includes reviewing the work and accomplishments, discussing the development of the working relationship, and planning the future to sustain the changes that have been achieved. To many social workers, termination is one of the most difficult as well as one of the most important aspects of the work. Those who want to focus more on the future sometimes call it "consolidation" or "graduation."

Evaluation   Although many social workers are pressed for time to complete other tasks, present and future clients benefit from evaluation to determine the effectiveness of the practice intervention. The social work *Code of Ethics* (NASW, 2008) mandates social workers engage in and utilize research to improve practice, which can include program evaluation and research on individual effectiveness, as well as using research findings to inform their practice. CSWE accreditation guidelines require social workers to "engage in research-informed practice and practice-informed research" (CSWE, 2012, EPAS, 2.1.6). At the same time, the profession has put increasing emphasis on evidence-based practice, defined as "an educational and practice paradigm that includes a series of predetermined steps aimed at helping practitioners and agency administrators identify, select, and implement efficacious interventions for clients" (Jensen & Howard, 2008). Use of evidence-based practice facilitates the integration of research findings, client values and preferences, practitioner knowledge and expertise, and other factors to make practice, policy, and research decisions.

Research on practice may involve evaluation tools that assess the progress of a program, and may provide encouragement for a reflective approach by individual workers on the quality of their work. Others see an important link between research activities and effective client advocacy. For example, if you want to advocate for persons who are homeless by demonstrating that existing services are inadequate or are not directed effectively, an understanding of the demographics of the homeless population, the number of homeless, and previous research findings about effective services for homeless populations (among other items) is imperative.

There are many kinds of evaluation, including quantitative, qualitative, subjective, objective, formative (during the work), summative (at the end of the work), self-report, reflection, and standardized tests. The prevailing trend within the various funding and accountability arrangements associated with social work practice is to require more evaluative activity both to demonstrate effectiveness and to justify continued or increased financial support for practice initiatives and policy programs.

Licensure of Social Work

Another way to conceptualize social work is as a helping profession that is licensed by states to protect the public. Social work, as a profession, is regulated within and by all 50 states, the District of Columbia, Puerto Rico, the Virgin Islands, and 10 Canadian provinces. Regulation protects the public by establishing: (1) the qualifications that a professional must possess; (2) a means of holding professionals accountable; and (3) a system for the public to make complaints against incompetent or unethical practitioners and have them investigated and adjudicated. Today, there are almost 400,000 licensed social workers practicing in the United States and Canada (Randall & DeAngelis, 2008).

The social work profession has four types of licensure available: BSW (usually upon graduation); MSW (one type upon graduation, and a second type, independent, after two years of supervised general experience); and clinical (after two years of

EXHIBIT 1.3	A variety of on-line and face-to-face options are available for CE credit for social workers. Below are some examples of resources for social work CEs:
Continuing Education	From NASW: http://www.naswwebed.org/
	From NASW California: http://www.socialworkweb.com/nasw/
	Rutgers School of Social Work: http://ssw-web.rutgers.edu/ssw/ce/

supervised clinical experience). Most jurisdictions license social workers at two or more of these categories. While the requirements vary from jurisdiction to jurisdiction, the general requirements for licensure are a specific level of education, supervised experience by a social worker, and demonstration of knowledge and minimum competence by passing an exam, providing references, and demonstrating evidence of good moral character. Some locales require more than two years of supervised clinical experience, or proof of a minimum number of hours in a clinical field placement, or proof of specific clinical coursework. After licensure, many states require that licensed social workers complete ongoing professional continuing education units (CEUs) through professional workshops or conferences that provide skills training for new situations, new populations, and new ways of thinking about the work (Randall & DeAngelis, 2008).

Tensions in Social Work

Almost since its inception, the social work profession has been challenged by a set of tensions that have sometimes seemed to obscure the identity of the profession. The most significant tensions (discussed below) are those that strongly shape the identity of the social work profession and the way in which social workers practice. They are:

- Whether to promote a clinical or nonclinical approach to working with clients

- The extent to which social workers exercise social control or promote social change

- The extent to which social workers promote change or acceptance of their clients

- The struggle between encouraging clients to adjust to their circumstances or challenge their circumstances

- Whether social workers promote their expert position or share power with their clients

- The profession's adjustment to globalization.

Clinical and Nonclinical Approaches   A central tension involves the question of whether practitioners should focus primarily on clinical or nonclinical work. The word *clinical* has many meanings, and can represent a code for a medically based private practice model that involves such concepts as diagnosis and managed care. *Clinical* can be associated with cold, calculated, stiff, or impersonal interchanges that are driven by the expert and received by the patient.

In this book, *clinical work* encompasses social work with individuals, groups, and/or families that is not only direct practice, or direct work (face-to-face), but also designed to change behaviors, solve problems, or resolve emotional or psychological issues (Grant, 2008). For example, clinical work can include intervening individually with a young woman to address her self-harming behavior, facilitating a series of groups for children who have experienced the death of a parent, and assisting a family to redefine the communication patterns among the three generations of its members. Clinical work can extend into many practice arenas such as physical and mental health, substance abuse treatment, school social work, gerontological social work, and some child welfare work. Some states define clinical work explicitly and require a master's degree. For example, West Virginia has separate levels of licensure for new MSW graduates, MSWs with over two years experience, and MSW clinical social workers with over two years of experience (West Virginia Board of Social Work Examiners, n.d.). Additional or different credentials may be required to work in some areas (e.g., an addictions certificate for substance abuse work).

Nonclinical work usually implies that the work addresses the environment. Macro, or indirect, practice addresses social problems in community, organizations, institutional, and society systems. Nonclinical, or macro, practice social workers, achieve social change through neighborhood organizing, community planning, locality development, public education, policy development, administration, and social action. Nonclinical work can also include social work that is political or focused on social reform efforts. These efforts involve such activities as working for improved institutional responses or changing or supporting laws, policies, and social structures relating to various dimensions of diversity, such as class, gender, ability, and cultural ethnicity. This field of work, policy practice, focuses specifically on ensuring that policies are more responsive to client needs and rights. Nonclinical work focuses less on the internal dynamics of an individual's experience and more on opportunity and change in the environment. While tension can exist between clinical and nonclinical work, thoughtful and principled efforts can connect the approaches. For example, clinical social workers can identify and communicate client needs to administrators and other nonclinical social workers, so that policy practice efforts are appropriately channeled to the client needs that are the most significant. In another example, clinical social workers can be involved in and refer clients to neighborhood organizing efforts to make social connections with others concerned about similar topics. The following discussion considers some dimensions of this tension.

Developmental Socialization and Resocialization The late Harry Specht, a social work policy educator, distinguished between "developmental socialization" and "resocialization" (Specht, 1990). Specht defined developmental socialization as the attempt, through providing support, information, and opportunities, to help people enhance their environments by making the most of their roles. Developmental socialization also involves confronting obstacles such as abuse or oppression that impede people's attempts to make the most of their roles. Developmental socialization was the natural domain of social work, and is basically nonclinical. In contrast, Specht defined resocialization as the attempt to help people with feelings and inner perceptions that relate primarily to the self. Specht purported that psychotherapeutic approaches associated with psychology and psychiatry, rather than social work, should deal with such issues. Significantly, Specht argued that social work had been seduced from its original mission by clinical psychotherapy, which many people characterize as a higher-status activity. As an advocate for an emphasis on the social environment, rather than inner psychological life, Specht called for social work to build its professional core in public, rather than private, services and institutions and to replace all its clinical training with adult education, community work, and group work. His last major co-written publication was tellingly called *Unfaithful Angels: How Social Work Has Abandoned Its Mission* (Haynes, 1998).

Many social workers are committed to the kind of work that Specht rejects as inappropriate. These practitioners view social work as providing useful perspectives for dealing with clinical, interactional, interpersonal, and sometimes intrapersonal issues. Many practitioners view these perspectives as appropriate tools in the realms of individual counseling, family intervention, and a host of other areas that might be called clinical, or therapeutic. This location of social work's appropriate domain has been a prevalent controversy since Mary Richmond's day. In more recent times, some social workers who are committed to environmental or structural intervention have seen the movement to license social workers as a negative continuation of the move into professionalism, which in this context usually means individual psychotherapy and, often, private-pay practice. Clinical practitioners, however, report values, ethical principles, and practices consistent with social work's mission to improve human well-being and promote social justice, and promoting wellness over pathology (Bradley, Maschi, O'Brien, Morgan, & Ward, 2012).

The perceived polarity between clinical and nonclinical practice is a challenge in contemporary social work. The *Code of Ethics* (NASW, 2008) provides some guidance by requiring social workers to engage in work that supports socially equitable allocations of opportunity, which by definition is environmental and political. When clinical practice focuses entirely on individual issues and ignores or excludes the nonclinical work of advocacy and power analysis inherent in the pursuit of social justice, it comes into conflict with the *Code*. The proximity of some clinical practice settings (such as mental health and substance abuse) to the health care delivery world and its requirements for individualized, de-contextualized labels of pathology, sometimes discourages or diverts social workers from entering into social justice pursuits.

Integrating Approaches for Clinical and Indirect (Macro) Practice   The debate between an individual, clinical focus and a nonclinical, or macro, environmental focus can be reconciled through integrating approaches. For example, Gitterman and Germain (2008b) argue that social work professionals must be prepared to work with all types of client systems, as situations require. Many methods and skills are common across all client systems. The historical loyalties to both the individual and to the macro advocacy pursuits to match client needs with environmental resources are a strength of the profession. The Educational Policy and Accreditation Standards (EPAS) (CSWE, 2012) for social work education underscore the commitment of social work to work with all client systems, with competencies and practice behaviors that require mastery of knowledge, skills, and values across all client systems.

There are many contemporary and generally complementary efforts to connect clinical practice with social justice issues. One approach expands the definition of clinical work to include "case management, advocacy, teamwork, mediation, and prevention roles, as well as therapeutic and counseling roles" (Swenson, 1998, p. 527). The clinician also uses self-reflection to consider her or his privilege. This in turn addresses the worker's accountability to clients, clearly an important component of a social justice approach. Newer areas of contemporary practice, such as environmental social work, also propel social workers to connect individual work with work at a systems level (Gray, Coates, & Hetherington, 2012).

A second way to integrate approaches is through the use of theory, perspectives, and methods that guide social workers through working with client systems. For example, a generalist, empowerment perspective (discussed below) also bridges the clinical and indirect practice tension. Within this perspective, social work practice is both clinical and indirect, and is at the intersection of private troubles and public issues. According to the empowerment perspective, social work employs an integrated view of humans in the context of their physical and social environments. Social workers using the empowerment perspective seek to promote a mutually beneficial interaction between individuals and society (Parsons, 2008). Narrative approaches (discussed in more detail in Chapters 4 and 6) provide an example of the way in which the issue of clinical practice and nonclinical pursuit of social justice occurs. A narrative approach to working with clients focuses on empowerment, collaboration, and viewing problems in social context. A narrative-oriented practitioner addresses the societal injustices individuals and families encounter in the client intervention (Kelley, 2008). The issues that individuals and families bring to the work are always put into the contextual arena of the social and power relations in the client's experience. Although narrative approaches began in family therapy work, narrative approaches have also been applied to work at the individual, group, and community levels (Kelley, 2008).

The use of the concept of social construction also blurs the distinction between clinical and nonclinical work. Social construction emphasizes the power of agency, a person's ability to affect her or his own circumstances that human beings exercise in creating their social locations. The focus of the work involves helping the client to create a new identity that is more empowering (Dybicz, 2012). In this view, people shape their environments, which in turn (or recursively) influence them. For example, you are a member of a community, and as such, you respond to other members of the community. However, you also take a part in creating your community, a process that goes beyond simply reacting to various individuals. By focusing on the client as a participant in the creation of the environment, this approach blurs the distinction between clinical work with the person and nonclinical work with the environment. Finally, a highly integrative model bridges individual, clinical work and environmental practice concerns through the use of deconstruction (Vodde & Gallant, 2002). In this conceptualization, the social worker moves from helping the client conquer the internal ramifications of the problem (such as clinical depression) to helping the client connect with others who are experiencing and resisting the same kind of oppression. Georgia's story will help demonstrate many of these points about deconstruction.

> *Georgia is a 25-year-old woman from the southern United States. She has come to a large city in the Midwest to see a different world and another part of the country. Very early in her stay, she met and fell in love with Tom, a native to the Midwest. Georgia and Tom developed a serious relationship, and Georgia moved into his apartment when she discovered that she was pregnant. From that time on, things did not go well for Georgia. Tom began to resent her interest in the coming birth, and at times he was verbally abusive, insulting her southern background and degrading every personal aspect he could find wrong with her. He then started to be physically rough with her when they had any difference of opinion. Eventually he began to shove her into the wall, slap her, and kick at her belly. Georgia was disillusioned and frightened both for her own safety and that of her child. She could not understand how she had failed Tom, or what she had done to become so disgusting to him, or how she had become so hard for him to be around. When Georgia finally believed she could no longer manage this situation, she contacted a local women's shelter. She was devastated. By this time she believed herself to be entirely worthless and thoroughly unlovable due to Tom's labeling her as ugly and stupid. Georgia was at a very low point and was fearful for her future.*

Georgia's social worker, over time and with the use of her professional skills, helped her to see that Tom's battering was not a function of her personality or unworthiness but rather of his own impulses. Tom, not Georgia, was responsible for Tom's abusive behavior. With support, Georgia began to regain her sense of worth and resilience and to feel stronger about her own capacities. Gradually she felt less in need of intense work on her esteem. She began to explore how our society supports violence. She met with other women at the shelter and joined in their resistance to societal violence through advocating for education in the schools and providing personal testimonies to groups of women.

This work empowered Georgia by enabling her to take control of her own emotions while addressing an environmental issue in a meaningful manner. The scenario presented here demonstrates the integrated approaches described earlier that address both clinical issues and social justice concerns. The approach spans the inner psychological turmoil that Georgia experienced as it began to become more political and facilitates Georgia's role in influencing her environment. In this way the work has gone from an individual clinical focus to a nonclinical, integrated political focus without sacrificing either, as each supports the other.

Social Control and Social Change   Social work is part of the society that it tries to change. Some of the regulatory bodies in which social workers practice, such as child protection, criminal justice, and mental health, carry an authoritative sanction for social control. In some circumstances this control appears to be at odds with the commitment of the social work profession to social change, a process in which social workers attempt to alter basic social structures. The two functions—control and change—are not inherently irreconcilable, but the ways in which they play out in their respective practice arenas tend to make them appear incompatible at times.

Change social structures.

Change and Acceptance   Another tension involves how much the goal of social work is to implement change—either in individual or environmental—or to help a client accept their status as "good enough." As you would expect, the particular circumstances and settings associated with each situation strongly influence the social worker's approach to this issue. In fact, although the pull between acceptance and change occupies a place in the historical tensions of the profession, it may prove to be so contextually influenced that it will never be fully put to rest as long as individuals continue to evaluate social contexts, based on their own idiosyncrasies, in different ways.

how much change is nessesary

Adjustment and Challenge   The dilemma of helping people to adjust to their circumstances or helping people challenge their circumstances is another historical tension in social work. This question must be answered in context according to factors relating to social justice. For example, many practitioners might support a female client who feels angry, distressed, and overburdened in a marital relationship and struggles with the sociological realities of contemporary families. These realities might include the expectations of partners, employers, and society at large that most mothers, even those working full time outside the home, should assume more responsibility than fathers for child care and home life. In this situation the social worker would offer support to bolster the client's existing coping mechanisms rather than facilitating a change within the client.

Adjust circumstances or challenge them

The social worker (who could possibly see herself in the same scenario) may offer suggestions for child care respite, recreation, or self-care that would help mitigate the client's sense of injustice in the arrangement, but not address an overall change in a significant or structural way, while other clients and practitioners would respond differently. They may not be willing to wait until parenting and homemaking become more equitable but instead demand or at least work for substantial change, both within the marriage and in the larger society. The possible stances that either client or practitioners take are not polarized but can be thought of as situated on a continuum, meaning that both the client and social worker may wish for large-scale social change, and both may believe that they need personally to make peace with the current reality of an individual situation.

The question becomes, are their respective positions compatible enough so they can agree on the goal of the work? If the social worker has a strong position that the client needs to change the situation, and the client really wants to learn to accept the situation, setting mutually agreeable goals will be challenging. There may be situations in which the tension of adjustment or challenge involves a significant concern for personal safety of an adult. The response to such a situation is not clear. You may suggest that to overcome this relationship stress, the client can work through its internal dynamics in some interpersonal work rather than through overt activism. Others may suggest that practitioners need to respond to any available opening for services, even if a woman cannot or will not separate from her partner. This is a controversial issue, in part because of the differences of opinion about what is tolerable, and the larger or political ramifications of inequitable relationships.

Experts and Shared Power   The relationship between the ideas of expertise and shared power has recently created a tension within the social work profession. The history and development of both the educational and professional systems in U.S. culture have revolved around the idea of expertise, or expert knowledge. Social workers are educated and socialized in professional programs to become respected members of a profession in which there are others with the same or similar expertise. In contrast, the idea of shared power is relatively recent in professional culture and challenges the claims of expert power. In shared power, the individual is the expert on her or his life, culture, dreams, experience, and goals. This creates a mandate in the work for social work practitioners to assume power only over limited activities in which they are trained while the client retains the power to direct the work. For example, if you are working in a college setting as an advocate for an African American student who experienced discrimination in housing options on campus, you may claim expertise on the process of advocacy, but your client would retain control regarding those issues that require your focus and the goals to be met through the advocacy. In this way, the power is shared.

Shifting your views of your expertise and interest in sharing power may not come easily; the U.S. population is socialized to value expertise, thus, we may interpret our own value and contributions through the lens of expertise. Given the competition that can develop between complex specialization on the one hand and client empowerment on the other, this tension is likely to persist. Some clients may want social workers to be the expert on their lives and relationships in the same way people want their dentist to be an expert on dental care.

Like much of U.S. culture, the social work profession has been caught up in the status and perceived legitimacy of being scientific and thus tends to take on the same metaphors of expertise. Social workers have spent decades trying to "prove" the effectiveness of their interventions, and have fought for professional prestige through this "expert" label. However, social workers have come to recognize that the expertise on the experience of any particular relationship, oppression, or phenomenological event belongs to the person who has lived it, and social workers can honor this wisdom by sharing power within the professional relationship. In the contemporary world, many strong client voices in the realm of human service interchanges, situations, and relationships have made it known that adopting the role of expert is not necessarily helpful, particularly when it obscures their own ownership or participation in the work. Social workers recognize the disillusionment and anger in people, such as people with disabilities, women, and people of color, who have experienced service systems that rely on expertise as humiliating, insulting, or patronizing. The development of many contemporary social work perspectives reflects this reality in their deliberate attempt to reduce the centrality of expertise and to substitute an enhanced commitment to partnership, or shared power.

Minimization of Distance   Such theoretical perspectives as the strengths perspective, nearly all feminist approaches, and empowerment approaches make a conscious effort to minimize the rigid boundaries of expertise between social worker and client. The client is seen as the expert on her or his life, whereas the social worker is seen as skilled in various arenas that will help the client get to a client-defined destination. This shift is played out in practice approaches that involve visiting clients' homes or meeting in community facilities like coffee shops, houses of worship, and community centers. These approaches emphasize client comfort in familiar surroundings, in contrast to the 50-minute clinical hour in the agency office, which tends to send a message of worker authority and increased distance between social worker and client.

This trend toward more fluid relationships represents a deliberate shift in thinking and a transformation of values. For some theoreticians, the shift signals a new way to respect the experiences and views of people who previously had never been listened to closely. For others it is a critical response to a power analysis that results in the elimination of abusive or oppressive authority relationships. In broader terms, this shift to a more egalitarian relationship affirms the right of the client to enter into a relationship of shared power in which the assets of both the client and the worker are recognized, valued, and used. Accordingly, in this conception, one person does not have power over the other; rather, a collective power is facilitated through sharing.

One of many Native American views of shared power has much to offer contemporary practitioners (Lowery & Mattaini, 2001). This approach conceptualizes shared power as shared responsibility allocated according to the particular strengths of each participant. It does not mean equality of responsibility, but recognizes that skill levels differ and emphasizes the worth of all contributions. Social workers are responsible for maintaining professional ethics, and clients are responsible for making changes in their lives. For example, in a situation of client substance abuse, social workers would ask questions such as, "How does your drinking affect your children?" rather than making a statement such as, "You need to quit drinking" (p. 116). The relationship created by this approach discourages hierarchies in the client–worker relationship and encourages a sense of joint investment in both the process and the results.

Global Citizenship and the Local Community   The final tension considered here, between local and global investments of effort, is now more relevant for social work practitioners than ever. Traditionally, U.S. social workers have carried out most of their activities in local or neighborhood contexts and have regarded global developments as remote. The social and cultural history, geography, and resource wealth of the United States have all contributed to national and professional insularity. The tendency to judge U.S. culture as preferable is shaped by and reflected in such devaluing language as "third world" or "underdeveloped" that is almost exclusively based on the U.S.-defined dimensions of economy in any given culture. Traditional Western markers are primarily limited to economic assets that are important for all people but are not the totality of life for any person.

Globalization is a "set of social processes that appear to transform our present social condition of weakening nationality to one of globality" (Steger, 2009, p. 9). It consists of a complex of economic, social, and technological processes that have resulted in the formation of a single world community in which we are all citizens. The essence of globalization is the flow of information, ideas, knowledge, technology, capital, labor, artifacts, and cultural norms and values across national borders. The impact of global occurrences, such as terrorism and wars, have a direct and compelling influence on the environment and practice of social work at home and require workers to develop new skills and devise new perspectives. Social problems such as homelessness, neglect and exploitation of children, poverty, violence, health and aging issues, and epidemic infections are worldwide issues that impact all nations (Sowers & Rowe 2009; Steger, 2009).

The process of globalization facilitates the recognition of the signs of U.S. economic dominance. For example, the availability of Coca-Cola in Bangkok or the presence of Pizza Huts in Manila are signals that the U.S. economy dominates many world markets. The outsourcing of many U.S. jobs to countries in which much cheaper labor can be located has resulted in high rates of unemployment domestically as well as exploitation abroad. Yet many U.S. and other Western-based companies are thriving. These dimensions of globalization are part of the reality of expanding international trade in the Global South (Payne & Askeland, 2008).

Factors Promoting Globalization   International financial institutions, such as the World Bank, the International Monetary Fund (IMF), and the World Trade Organization (WTO) have promoted and facilitated globalization, which has been accompanied with significant challenges and questions. These organizations were originally instituted to promote economic stability and growth and to help individual countries as they experience economic crises, but the strategies they have adopted to achieve these objectives have been problematic and counterproductive. Many question the policies of these international financial institutions, as they have disproportionately benefited wealthy people around the world, failed to address concerns about the environment from worldwide development, led to abuses in human rights, and provided significant setbacks to those promoting social justice. Globalization agreements and efforts have not incorporated regard for employment creation, expanded or improved health, or educational or social services for the poor, or promoted progressive land reform. Critics charge that decision-making within these international financial institutions lacks transparency and often reflects the interests of wealthier countries (Head, 2008; World Health Organization, 2012).

As an example, the WTO has been the primary promoter of free trade policies. Although free trade policies were ostensibly designed to encourage the development of market economies, the policies often require receiving nations to accept particular conditions thought to foster trade and economic growth, including privatization of resources and restrictions on imports and exports, as well as cutbacks in many social programs such as health, education, and housing and income assistance. In many cases these conditions have had the effect of abolishing welfare entitlement programs and social safety nets, debilitating local economies, altering or eliminating substantial aspects of indigenous ways of life, and eroding the autonomy of national governments. In their place, large multinational corporations have been free to build enormous industries whose purposes relate entirely to profit, with little regard to environmental or other concerns. Globalization policies have been associated with a substantial increase in worldwide poverty, misery, violence, HIV/AIDS cases, drug addiction, and economic stratification (to name a few), as well as the exploitation of the land and other important environmental resources (Payne & Askeland, 2008).

In such a context, social work as a profession is developing models of understanding that are global in context. For example, social workers in domestic settings are working with diverse populations, including immigrants and refugees, in this country, and gaining knowledge of non-Western ideas and perceptions. Rather than focus on strictly clinical work, social workers in international settings may also be called to assist with economic and social change to change situations of economic inequality and poverty (Payne & Askeland, 2008). While globalization provides both challenges and opportunities for social work, social workers can advocate and work toward a process of globalization that has a strong social dimension and is accountable for improving such global issues as poverty, environmental degradation, unemployment, and human rights (Hong & Song, 2010).

At the individual practitioner level, a commitment to reciprocity, interdependence, human rights, and social justice in practice is one way to incorporate globalization into practice. Social workers must be familiar with global events through media sources, as well as the ways in which events that occur within the U.S. impact individuals within other countries and other nations. The implications of globalization for social work practice are likely to increase in number and in impact, and social workers must be involved in helping to strengthen local structures within communities, such as nonprofit organizations to ensure civil rights (Hong & Song, 2010). Ironically, increased localization has been one of the important responses to globalization (Payne & Askeland, 2008) as people seek local alternatives that are appropriate for their particular circumstances. Social work, therefore, must focus on both global and local perspectives and make meaningful connections between global inequities and domestic social justice issues that will discourage any artificial local/global polarity (Hong & Song, 2010), as well as initiate educational and political initiatives to ensure respect for human rights, democratic decision-making, environmental protection, and meaningful benefits to local populations.

Perspectives on the Conceptualizations of the Social Work Profession   Although each of these conceptualizations provides a useful way of thinking about social work practice, each also has limitations. To use them for the best interests of the client system, the models must be used flexibly. For example, knowledge, values, and skills can overlap, and over-focusing on one dimension, such as factual knowledge, may lead practitioners to apply knowledge without adequate consideration of the appropriate skill level and social work values. The integration of many kinds of knowledge, values, and skills as applied through competencies is the goal of social work education. Likewise, dividing the work into constituent groups of beneficiaries may suggest that the background, values, and skills necessary for each kind of practice vary more significantly than the reality of practice.

Generalist social work practice requires that the social worker be proficient at all levels of client groupings, as the competencies can be applied to all system levels. The similarities far surpass their differences; work in any of them is grounded in the practitioner's consistent set of values, theoretical perspectives, and goals. Similarly, a social worker does not build a relationship, then cease utilizing engagement skills (i.e., become "all business") because she or he has moved on to the assessment phase. Like all relationships, the professional connection between social worker and client must be attended to, nurtured, and encouraged to grow throughout the time of their work together, or it will wither. Likewise, assessment occurs throughout the course of the work, beginning with the first interaction and continuing through the last. The phases of helping are highly connected, with special emphasis paid to one phase at any given time during the work. The tensions discussed in social work, while useful, may fall short of describing the full, day-to-day realities of social work practice within specific practice settings and with specific populations. Therefore, while the structures are helpful, flexibility in the application is important.

Importance of Self-Knowledge   To practice competently, social workers must have a clear understanding of themselves, including their own biases. One type of bias that can impact practice is bias about socioeconomic class. For example, you may notice that you respond differently to people who are living in poverty than to people who are socioeconomically middle-class. To grow in cultural competence, you can explore the reasons for this difference; perhaps you learned as a child that "poor people" are somehow less worthy than affluent people, or that they are not hard-working. Your family and/or the wider culture may have supported these views. To uncover your biases, you can ponder the following questions: How does this view clash with the view that people living in poverty are resilient in the face of debilitating exploitation? How is your view implemented in your practice? Are you less empathic, energetic, or invested when you work with people living in poverty? Are you less likely to advocate or seek out resources? Do you have an opinion about a client that is a "truth" in your mind, or do you treat it as one interpretation out of many?

Practice decisions are shaped by our experiences, motivations, values, attitudes, and other factors. Sometimes practitioners are unaware of influences on practice decision. Therefore, social workers need to continually explore the ways their values are prioritized, the patterns they develop in making decisions and exhibiting practice behaviors. This exploration may include recognizing idiosyncratic approaches, quick responses, and patterns of reaction. Are you patient and likely to stand by your client, even when things do not go well? Are you quick to assume someone is judging you or wants to bring you harm? Are you likely to blow off steam or sulk when you are rebuffed? Do you assume that you are competent to deal with any crisis? Are you inclined to address an interpersonal problem privately and quietly? Are you more likely to "sound off" in a meeting? All of us have idiosyncratic ways of dealing with relationships, stresses, and social interactions that are personality variations. Social workers must recognize their behavioral patterns, understand how they impact their work, and identify those responses that, if changed, would help them to develop a higher degree of competency and skill.

Culture has a strong influence on social work practitioner biases. For example, culture may impact practitioner beliefs and attitudes about a situation in which an adolescent's choice of vocation may clash with the family's ideas about suitable professions. In another example, cultural bias may influence a practitioner belief that, in social relationships, participants are equal and all should speak out honestly about tension in the relationship. These two examples are part of mainstream U.S. culture, and are cultural variants that are not necessarily shared by all people and therefore do not represent a universal truth. The emphasis on individual drive and ambition as well as equality and forthrightness are Western beliefs, and clash with other cultures. In another example, an Asian client, who is 20 years older than a practitioner, may relate in very formal terms with the practitioner and appear reluctant to share details about her family life, even though she has been referred for parent support. Rather than labeling her "resistant" or "closed," the practitioner can recognize potential bias in the

QUICK GUIDE 1

Social workers work with many different types of client populations. Examples include:

LGBTQ youth, adults, and older adults
Range of religions (such as Jehovah's Witnesses, Jews, Catholics, Mormans, and Muslims)
People with Disabilities (Physical, emotional, behavioral, developmental)
Minority Ethnicities (such as Native Americans, Hispanics, African Americans, Asian Americans, and
   Pacific Islanders)
Immigrants (from such countries as Mexico, India, China, Vietnam, and African nations)
Refugees (from such areas as Africa, the Middle East, and Asia)
Older Adults, Active Military and Veterans
Rural Populations
People in Poverty
Children, Adolescents, and Youth

Questions to explore your self-knowledge about diversity

- What is my race, ethnicity, religious affiliation, and socioeconomic status?
- How does my background related to diversity impact my knowledge about this client's background?
- How is "family" defined by my culture? Other cultures?
- Do I assume my culture is the worldwide norm?
- To what degree do I understand the ideas of other cultures other than my own?
- To what degree is my language respectful about other cultures?
- Do I think that I will be less empathic or energetic when working with persons from one or more particular populations?
- Do I acknowledge that cultural differences exist?
- Do I recognize the thought patterns of other groups as equally valid as mine?
- What is diverse within my culture? What diversity exists between my culture and others?

Questions to ponder about building cultural competency

- How might my biases impact my practice?
- Do I think that I will be less likely to advocate for or seek out resources for particular types of clients?
- Do I think that I will advocate for effective services that differ by culture?
- Do I stereotype client from specific groups?
- Am I aware that some clients may not relate closely to their cultural group?
- Am I aware of different types of natural support systems that differ from my own (e.g., folk healers and religious leaders)? Do I understand how to utilize natural support systems in practice?
- Do I know how to respectfully obtain personal and family background information from clients to determine their ethnic/community sense of identity, rather than making assumptions?
- Will I look for working environments that positively impact my cultural competence?

Sources: Lum, 2011; Mason, 1995; NASW, 2001

perspective applied about such relationships and style and evaluate the "fit" of the practitioner and client perspectives.

The emphasis on our own biases and assumptions is closely related to values and how these values influence our ideas of ethical practices. These constructs are critical to social work practice. The next chapter will deal more explicitly with the ideas and contexts relating to values and ethical frameworks and the emphases placed on them in social work practice.

THEORETICAL PERSPECTIVES FOR SOCIAL WORK PRACTICE

Social work has a history of adopting, adapting, formulating, and integrating various theoretical perspectives. A theory is an explanation of some event or phenomenon. Theories usually have clear principles and propositions that provide a framework for predicting events and a supporting body of empirically-based evidence. Theory assists social workers by providing the flexibility to see client systems and social problems from many points of view, anticipating outcomes of different interventions, and in applying the results to future situations (McNutt & Floersch, 2008). Theories can bring order and coherence to practice situations so that activities are based on a logical assessment of the fit between a client system situation and the assertions of the theory. Theories about the social world evolve and adjust in order to fit new ideas or to accommodate further evidence that adds or contradicts theories. Consequently, some theories are discarded when they are no longer acceptable to the professional community (for example, theories asserting that some races are superior to others) or when they are unable to be grounded in reliable research. Other theories evolve to incorporate additional refinements or methods, such as the contemporary interpretations of Freud's 19th-century psychoanalytic theory.

A perspective is a view or lens through which to observe and interpret the world. A perspective is generally less structured than theory but is similar in that it is often based on values and beliefs about the nature of the world. For example, a belief that people are generally good is a perspective that will guide practice and interpretations of client system situations. In that way the ideas behind theory and perspective are similar. In social work practice, the terms theory and perspective are often viewed as synonymous and may also be called theoretical perspectives. These three terms are used interchangeably throughout this book.

The theoretical positions of the social work profession have received important contributions from biology, ecology, sociology, anthropology, psychology, and many of the humanities and human service professions. More recently, social work scholars have expanded the development of the profession's own understandings of practice to create theories specific to the provision of social work services. Some of these theories focus on psychosocial systems, problem-solving, ecological/ecosystems, and empowerment, as they represent uniquely social work emphases on the interface between a person and her or his environment.

Theories are important to the social work profession, as they are driven by values. The ways social workers select, implement, and evaluate a theory or theoretical perspective will be highly influenced by their value orientations. For example, creating an alliance with a client that results in complete dependence on the social worker could be the result of an adherence to a theory that supports "reparenting," because the theory allows for directing the client's goals to carrying out the will of the social worker. On the other hand, using a theory in which autonomy and self-determination are prioritized will result in a different outcome. The role of theory in this scenario would be critical in directing the work of the practitioner.

This book presents five practice perspectives that guide the focus and are central to the content. They are: (1) the ecosystems perspective; (2) the social justice perspective; (3) the human rights perspective; (4) the strengths perspective; and (5) postmodern perspective approaches, including critical social construction, narrative theory, and solution-focused interventions. Other perspectives are included in subsequent chapters as they relate to specific levels of practice. Some of these perspectives have a longstanding history within social work education and practice (such as social justice), and others are more contemporary (such as postmodern approaches).

Ecosystems Perspective

Using concepts from systems theory and ecology, the ecosystems perspective is an often-used framework for generalist practice. This perspective examines the exchanges between individuals, families, groups, and communities and their environment. Systems theory utilizes constructs to organize complex activity in the social environment, while ecology seeks to explain how people adapt to and influence their environment. Taken together, these two concepts describe the functioning and adaptation of human systems in a dynamic interchange with each other. Interactions or transactions between the two help explain how people influence their environment, and vice versa. The ecosystems perspective is very useful for social work practice because it encourages increasing the degree to which people and their environments fit one another. Increasing the degree of fit between the two can lead the social worker toward direct services with individuals, families, and groups to mobilize and draw on personal and environmental resources for effective coping. Increasing the degree of fit between human needs and environment can also lead the social worker to influence the client system's social and physical environment to adequately address human needs. Influencing the environment can include working to influence organizations to develop more responsive policies and programs, as well as working to influence legislation, regulation, and implementation of laws (Gitterman & Germain, 2008a).

Social Justice Perspective Social justice refers to the manner in which society distributes resources among its members, including material goods and social benefits, rights, and protections. Although there are various theories of social justice regarding the criteria for the distribution of wealth, the profession of social work generally accepts an egalitarian focus that is concerned with the fair distribution of both material and nonmaterial resources (Rawls, 1971) and equal access for all people (Reichert, 2011). From this perspective, developing or distributing social and natural resources based on political or social power rather than social justice or human need is unacceptable (Saleebey, 2012). The social justice perspective has important implications for social workers and their practice as it requires a response to the injustice that is status quo in our society.

As required by the National Association of Social Workers *Code of Ethics* (NASW, 2008), social workers invest a significant amount of time and effort in championing individual, group and community rights, working toward more effective institutional responses, and influencing major social policy shifts. Social work is, therefore, a political profession. Social workers identify individual, family, group, and community needs, and seek to address the areas of injustice that have a negative impact on people. For example, if a social worker is working at the community level with a group of older adults who have been wrongfully denied access to services or government support programs, it is the social worker's responsibility to confront that injustice either directly or indirectly by using community resources to address the issue. The issue can be addressed individually, or, if the problem rests in policy or procedures, at the group-level.

Human Rights Perspective

The United Nations describes human rights as rights that are inherent in our nature and without which we cannot live as full human beings. Human rights and fundamental freedoms allow us to completely develop and use our human qualities, our intelligence, our talents and our conscience, and to satisfy our spiritual and other needs. They are basic for humankind's increasing demand for a life in which the inherent dignity and worth of each human being will receive respect and protection (Lundy, 2011: United Nations, 1997).

The principle of human rights offers a powerful and comprehensive framework for social work practice; it not only recognizes needs but strives to satisfy those needs (Lundy, 2011). The human rights perspective provides a moral grounding for social work practice and reflects an ongoing commitment to the belief that all people should have basic rights and access to the broad benefits of their societies. Many social workers evaluate their practice based on its contribution to an environment in which universal human rights are honored.

Contemporary perspectives on human rights emphasize the social understandings of our commonality rather than the rigid assertions about specific human rights. Accordingly, human rights can be viewed as socially constructed, reflecting differing contexts, ideas, and cultures (Gregg, 2012). Ife (2000) likewise suggests that the human rights discourse should de-emphasize the focus on legalistic,

EXHIBIT 1.4

A summary of the Universal Declaration of Human Rights

1. Everyone is free and we should all be treated in the same way.
2. Everyone is equal despite differences in skin colour, sex, religion, language for example.
3. Everyone has the right to life and to live in freedom and safety.
4. No one has the right to treat you as a slave nor should you make anyone your slave.
5. No one has the right to hurt you or to torture you.
6. Everyone has the right to be treated equally by the law.
7. The law is the same for everyone, it should be applied in the same way to all.
8. Everyone has the right to ask for legal help when their rights are not respected.
9. No one has the right to imprison you unjustly or expel you from your own country.
10. Everyone has the right to a fair and public trial.
11. Everyone should be considered innocent until guilt is proved.
12. Everyone has the right to ask for help if someone tries to harm you, but no-one can enter your home, open your letters or bother you or your family without a good reason.
13. Everyone has the right to travel as they wish.
14. Everyone has the right to go to another country and ask for protection if they are being persecuted or are in danger of being persecuted.
15. Everyone has the right to belong to a country. No one has the right to prevent you from belonging to another country if you wish to.
16. Everyone has the right to marry and have a family.
17. Everyone has the right to own property and possessions.
18. Everyone has the right to practise and observe all aspects of their own religion and change their religion if they want to.
19. Everyone has the right to say what they think and to give and receive information.
20. Everyone has the right to take part in meetings and to join associations in a peaceful way.
21. Everyone has the right to help choose and take part in the government of their country.
22. Everyone has the right to social security and to opportunities to develop their skills.
23. Everyone has the right to work for a fair wage in a safe environment and to join a trade union.
24. Everyone has the right to rest and leisure.
25. Everyone has the right to an adequate standard of living and medical help if they are ill.
26. Everyone has the right to go to school.
27. Everyone has the right to share in their community's cultural life.
28. Everyone must respect the 'social order' that is necessary for all these rights to be available.
29. Everyone must respect the rights of others, the community and public property.
30. No one has the right to take away any of the rights in this declaration.

Source: Human Rights Education Association (n.d.).

Western views of entitlements in favor of a more reflective dialogue among the world's peoples. This dialogue would center on exploring the meaning of human existence, and how humans want to recognize our interdependence, protect our futures, and safeguard our survival in the current and future global era. This focus is consistent with social work's emphasis on community, quality of relationship, and concern for the future of the world's inhabitants. It also recognizes the dynamic nature of living one's principles, such as those inherent in human rights, as they continuously evolve to remain meaningful.

Human rights have the potential to occupy a central place in social work practice and can provide a focal point in the evolution of people's understanding of their place on the planet. Viewed as a set of dynamic principles that can provide a substantive contribution to guidelines on international relations as well as community-based practice, human rights constitutes a vital focus for work with people. Social work as a profession can take up the lead started by many of our global colleagues in making human rights a central discourse and in exploring its relevance more thoroughly to our everyday work (Healy & Link, 2011).

The Strengths Perspective

An increasingly widespread approach in social work practice, the strengths perspective is explicit in its emphasis on affirming and working with the strengths found both in people seeking help and in their environments. Like human rights practice, this perspective emphasizes basic dignity and the resilience of people in overcoming challenging obstacles. Contemporary advocates have established some significant breaks with social workers' historical and cultural tendency to focus their work and energies on problems and pathology (Kim, 2008a).

Principles of the Strengths Perspective Saleebey (2012) identified six key principles for the strengths perspective (pp. 17–21):

1. *Every individual, group, family, and community has strengths.* Social workers must view their clients as competent and possessing skills and strengths that may not be initially visible. In addition, clients may have family and community resources that need to be explored and utilized.
2. *Trauma and abuse, illness and struggle may be injurious, but they may also be sources of challenge and opportunity.* Clients can not only overcome very difficult situations, but also learn new skills and develop positive protective factors. Individuals exposed to a variety of trauma are not always helpless victims or damaged beyond repair.
3. *Assume that you do not know the upper limits of the capacity to grow and change, and take individual, group, and community aspirations seriously.* Too often professional "experts" hinder their clients' potential for growth by viewing clients' identified goals as unrealistic. Instead, social workers need to set high expectations for

their clients so that the clients believe they can recover and that their hopes are tangible.

4. *We best serve clients by collaborating with them.* Playing the role of expert or professional with all the answers does not allow social workers to appreciate their clients' strengths and resources. The strengths perspective emphasizes collaboration between the social worker and the client.

5. *Every environment is full of resources.* Every community, regardless of how impoverished or disadvantaged, has something to offer in terms of knowledge, support, mentorship, and tangible resources. These resources go beyond the general social service agencies in the communities and can serve as a great resource for clients.

6. *Caring, caretaking, and context.* Strength perspective recognizes the importance of community and inclusion of all its members in society and working for social justice. This is built on the basic premise that caring for each other is a basic form of civic participation.

Although these key principles may evolve and be refined, the focus of the strengths perspective is on clients' personal assets along with their environmental resources rather than on their pathology and limitations is a core element. Using the strengths perspective, social work interventions are centered on helping the client system to achieve their goals, affirming and developing values and commitments, and making and finding membership in or as a community. The strengths perspective does not preclude the need to validate the suffering and pain of the client system (i.e., the physical, emotional, or existential) nor the seriousness of the situation or distress. Rather, the strengths perspective seeks to acknowledge clients' expertise regarding their own lives and to focus on their resilience and capacities to survive and to confront such seemingly overwhelming obstacles.

Postmodern Perspective and the Social Construction Approach

Any contemporary perspective that questions the way in which knowledge is attained and valued, and distinguishes belief from truth, comes under the broad heading of postmodernism. Postmodern approaches invite examination of the cultural assumptions that underlie many of the arrangements of power and politics, and it tends to be critical of assumptions or theories that claim absolute or authoritative truth. To illustrate, the contention that "all people in the United States can get ahead if they work hard enough; therefore, all poor people are lazy" is an example of an assumption or belief that is asserted as truth. Postmodernism invites people to challenge the truth of such claims (Logan, Rasheed, & Rasheed, 2008).

Social Construction   A useful postmodern perspective for understanding the social realities of the lives of the people served by social workers, social construction suggests that people construct reality based on experiences in the social world, which occur within the context of culture, society, history, and language. Practicing from this perspective means that rather than being a product of an objective external world, or the result of the individual mind, social realities are actually beliefs formed through social interchanges (usually starting with the family) that regulate learning to make sense of things and, often, to form judgments. For example, when children experience people as good-hearted and the world as a kind place throughout their youth, this social experience informs their adult belief that the world is a relatively decent place. On the other hand, when their social experiences tell them that the world is full of evil, hurtful people, their view of reality is often very different. This observation of how people decide the nature of their world is meaningful for social workers when they work with people who have lived in a different reality than one then they experienced (Lee & Greene, 2009).

Noticing your social location in this way is consistent with postmodernism and social construction. Recognizing that a person's reality is based on her or his perceptions and experiences in the social world and that there can be more than one reality of an experience because each person perceives the world differently and has different experiences is one way to implement postmodernism and social construction. Social workers, using these approaches, approach clients from their realities, rather than the reality of the practitioner. For example, if a client appears to have little ambition to financially support themselves or to participate in civic life, an understanding of the reality of the client's culture and environment may help you to understand the realities of institutionalized racism that may leave clients bitter and non-participatory, with little vision of what their life might be. Recognition of this postmodern principle of multiple realities impacts the purpose of practice and may expand one's practice to advocate for or take up the causes of people who have little power. In practice, postmodernism and social construction approaches require acknowledgment of the practitioner's boundaries and allow practitioners to enter the world of the client system.

Deconstruction   Constructionist thinking opens the way to explore particular beliefs, such as that the world is a kind place, through a process of taking those beliefs apart to examine the way they developed, or deconstruction. Through the process of deconstruction, you can explore the factors that helped these beliefs to develop and determine which ideas that had power and dominated. The following is an example of both social construction and deconstruction.

For many years in the 20th century it was a "reality" that adults with severe disabilities were neither capable of negotiating nor entitled to engage in adult relationships, particularly sexual ones. Institutions and community-based facilities worked diligently to prevent relationships and sometimes even kept couples with disabilities from being together alone in the same room. That particular social

EXHIBIT 1.5	Some of the many assumptions by those practicing eugenics were:
Eugenics Assumptions	• People with severe disabilities are like children who should not enter into adult relationships. • People with severe disabilities are not adequate as human beings and should not have children. • People with severe disabilities are not entitled to define their needs or desires. • People with severe disabilities do not have the capacity for love.

understanding and sense of reality contributed to the infamous practice of eugenics, which sought to eliminate the reproduction of people who were seen as genetically deficient. As advocates for the rights of persons with disabilities began to decon-struct and debunk the assumptions of the social construction that supported this callous practice, eugenics became less acceptable.

Although these assumptions are by no means extinct now, they are situated in a specific economic, historical, and cultural setting that is no longer dominant. The concept of contextual setting, or social location, refers to the time, place, and prevailing ideas or discourse that influence standards, particularly about what is considered "right." All ideas emerge from within a context that includes attitudes or beliefs, and ideas must be recognized as contextual rather than as absolute, moral truths for all situations and contexts (Kelley, 2009). Consider, for example, a new social worker who is judged and silenced if she or he counters the so-called truth regarding persons with disabilities and, based on human rights or social justice concerns, objects to such social restrictions. You might consider those beliefs or customs that are so strongly held in your own community or agency that deviance from them has significant professional or personal consequences and is interpreted morally.

Questions that expose the attitudes and beliefs that underlie ideas often have the effect of creating opportunities and visions for people. Using social construc-tion, social workers are likely to question arrangements that bring harm to people and to be suspicious or wary of presumed expertise that denies people their own experience. For example, a social worker may advocate for an older adult whose acute medical distress is being dismissed by a physician as insignificant. The social worker, with support from a supervisor or others, may even need to challenge the adequacy of the medical care offered to the client. In this way, the social worker refutes the idea that any particular set of assumptions or positions cannot be challenged, and operates on the idea that all beliefs, ideas, and arrangements can be respectfully questioned.

Narrative Theory Consistent with postmodernism are narrative and solution-focused interventions (Kelley, 2008). Narrative theory guides practitioners to utilize "stories" to understand the lived experience of clients. A therapeutic theory founded on the notion that people's sense of their identity consists of interacting narratives, a social worker using narrative theory would use a conversational approach to surface the cultural discourses about identity and power that have shaped the client. This approach involves helping clients make sense of the meanings they give to events in their lives. A narrative is the thread that binds disparate events together. Stories involve events linked together in a time sequence and have a plot. Narrative approaches view problems as separate from people, and people possess the qualities and skills needed to change their relationship with the problem(s) they are facing in life (Madigan, 2010).

Solution-Focused In contrast, a solution-focused approach invites clients to explore and determine the concrete change desired in their lives and the resources and strengths clients possess to make the change occur. Using a solution-focused approach, clients identify a specific goal that they believe will make their lives better in some fashion, and to attach specific strengths to a plan to reach that goal. Often clients are asked to think about an exception, times in which the challenge did not exist, and to identify the condition under which the challenge did not exist, as indicators of potential ways to address the problem. For example, if a child is struggling to focus in school, a discussion of the exceptions to this situation, or conditions under which the child is ever able to focus on schoolwork, may shed light on the factors on which to focus. Is the child able to focus early in the school day? When seated with specific classmates or away from specific classmates?

Critical Social Construction The *critical* in critical social construction is derived from a contemporary analysis of power, which recognizes that any social group can shape its beliefs to its own benefit at the expense of other groups. The critical dimension then allows the social worker to question power arrangements, especially if many people's voices have been silenced or "subjugated" (Hartman, 1994). Those who were able to arrange such systems as slavery had the power to privilege themselves, while oppressing others. In this way the privileged group not only benefits from but also perpetuates the privilege by using their power to assert their beliefs, which come to be regarded as truth. Although many groups today who benefit from privilege would not consciously choose such advantage if presented with a choice, such groups as whites, heterosexuals, Christians and those who are able bodied, benefit from privilege (Diller, 2011).

Critical social construction can be utilized in social work practice through critical viewing of power relations and dominance of specific beliefs that result, which especially impacts non-privileged groups with whom social workers often work. This critical viewing has significant repercussions for social work practice, which will be addressed throughout the book.

QUICK GUIDE 2   SUMMARY OF APPROACHES

Ecosystems perspective – Examines the exchanges between individuals, families, groups, and communities and their environment.

Social justice perspective – Focuses on the manner in which society distributes resources among its members, including material goods and social benefits, rights, and protections.

Human rights perspective – Reflects an ongoing commitment to the belief that all people should have basic rights and access to the broad benefits of their societies.

Strengths perspective – Affirms and works with the strengths found both in people seeking help and in their environments.

Postmodern approaches – Examines the cultural assumptions that underlie many of the arrangements of power and politics, and is critical of assumptions or theories that claim absolute or authoritative truth.

> *Critical social construction* – As people construct reality based on their experiences in the social world, examines power relations and dominance of specific beliefs that result, which especially impacts non-privileged groups with whom social workers often work.
>
> *Narrative theory* – Through telling "stories," helps clients make sense of the meanings they give to events in their lives.
>
> *Solution-focused interventions* – Explore and determine the concrete change desired in their lives and the resources and strengths clients possess to make the change occur.

Complementary Aspects of the Theoretical Perspectives

Each of the five perspectives—ecosystems, social justice, human rights, the strengths perspective, and the postmodern perspectives—offers the social worker unique and complex challenges. In many respects they complement each other by placing a slightly different emphasis on the work that fits well with the other views. The strengths perspective, for example, is used in the service of bringing social justice to people who have experienced inequities. Human rights, in turn, may be seen as the moral grounding for undertaking justice-oriented work. The constructionist ideas regarding the influence of historical and cultural standpoints allow the social worker to question previously unexamined ideas and approaches that marginalize people and characterize them as pathological or undeserving. Taken together these perspectives provide a comprehensive and compelling approach to social work.

STRAIGHT TALK ABOUT THE TRANSLATION OF PERSPECTIVES INTO PRACTICE

The relevance of theoretical perspectives to actual practice situations has always raised questions from students and social work educators. Some of the frameworks and perspectives may seem abstract or far removed from client systems, such as a destitute older adult, or a politically active group of adults with psychiatric disabilities. On the other hand, when perspectives reflect and honor the experience of people and fit the situation, they can be a critical guide to social work practice. For example, using the strengths perspective may mean focusing on the support networks and clean-up efforts of a struggling, poverty-stricken neighborhood to focus on the capabilities and assets, rather than focusing on the dilapidated housing, trash, and abandoned cars that line the streets. While using the frameworks and perspectives and integrating theory and practice can be very challenging, the frameworks and perspectives offer guides and a foundation for social work practice.

CONCLUSION

This chapter has presented several different perspectives with which to view social work practice. Social work practice is defined in the following ways: (1) by type of practice or range of practice settings; (2) as a set of activities; (3) as a set of roles; (4) as a set of competencies and practice behaviors; (5) by types of client grouping; (6) by practice frameworks; (7) as a licensed profession; (8) by purpose; and (9) by the tensions experienced in the profession. Self-knowledge is also a critical component of effective social work practice.

Exploring social work practice through this array of methods allows for many interpretations of situations and various foci of attention, some of which will be discussed in subsequent chapters. Coverage of the tensions experienced by the profession allows you to consider the profession in its ongoing concerns and have a sense of reference and context. Also discussed were five explicit theoretical perspectives, and you are encouraged to use them flexibly to offer an empowering and liberating approach to people who have lived their lives in the margin of society. Although the challenge of translating these approaches into ethical, sustainable, effective social work competencies will always be present in your practice, it will also sustain your growth. Building on this frame, Chapter 2 will delve into the role these values and ethics play in social work practice.

MAIN POINTS

- Social work practice can be conceptualized in at least nine different ways, to include by type of practice or range of practice settings, by the activities of the profession, as a set of roles, and as a licensed profession.

- Tensions that persist in contemporary practice include those between social control and social change, acceptance and change, clinical and nonclinical perspectives, experts and shared power, and global citizenship and the local community.

- Effective social work practice requires questioning your assumptions, understanding the impact they have on your work, and framing your methods.

- Theoretical perspectives play a significant role in guiding practice activities.

  The five perspectives, or frames, presented in this book are ecosystem perspective, the social justice perspective, the human rights perspective, the strengths perspective, and postmodern approaches, such as narrative and solution-focused, and critical social constructionism.

- The ecosystems perspective provides a frame for generalist practice, and examines the fit between individuals and their environment.

- The social justice perspective addresses the manner in which resources are allocated.

- Guided by the United Nations Universal Declaration of Human Rights, the human rights perspective is a frame that encompasses the conviction that all people have civil, political, social, economic, and cultural rights simply because they are human beings.

- The strengths perspective is a practice approach that highlights and works with individual, family, group, and community resilience and assets, honoring the client system's goals and dreams, and asserts that all communities possess resources.

- Critical social constructionism is a contemporary, postmodern frame based on the assertion that social truths are agreed-upon beliefs shaped in a common history and culture and perpetuated through assumptions, language, and stories. It also notes the power arrangements responsible for the prevalence of such truths.

- The translation of perspectives into practice is challenging and necessary for effective social work to maintain its mission, integrity, and consistency.

EXERCISES

a. Case Exercises

1. Go to www.routledgesw.com/cases and explore the Sanchez family interactive case study by reviewing the introduction and the tasks of each of the four phases. Click on the "Start this Case" button (under the Engage Tab), and complete Tasks #1, 2, and 3.

2. After completing Exercise #1, imagine that you are working with the Sanchez family as a social worker employed by the U.S. Bureau of Citizenship and Immigration Service. You are assigned to Celia and Hector Sanchez as they

receive their permanent resident cards, or "green cards," which authorize them to live and work legally in the U.S. Your role is to help them understand their new rights and responsibilities. What knowledge, values, and skills do you think would be particularly important for your work with the couple? Identify at least one *specific* area of knowledge, one value, and one skill. What challenges might result from emphasizing one (i.e., knowledge, value, or skill) over the other two?

3. After completing Exercise #1 and #2, consider the social justice issues involved in the family's permanent resident status and the ways in which the issues are related to human rights. Respond to the following:

    a. From your knowledge of human rights and the Sanchez family, identify two human rights that apply particularly to Hector and Celia as immigrants.

    b. How might you expect that having a green card would impact the family?

4. Consider the consequences of different social work practice discourses, and respond to the following:

    a. Describe the ways in which a social work discourse of strengths differs from a discourse of pathology when applied to the Sanchez family.

    b. Describe the way in which the strengths-based social worker would approach the family. How would you describe the professional relationship? How would you describe the focus of the work? Be as specific as possible.

5. Go to www.routledgesw.com/cases. Click on the Sanchez family, then "Start this Case," then review the case file for Emilia Sanchez (including Client History, Client Concerns, and Goals for the Client). Click on "Mapping this Case" (under "Case Study Tools"). Explore Emilia's relationship with her relatives by reviewing the family genogram. Also review Emilia's ecomap, and interaction matrix (under "Case Study Tools"). Answer Emilia's critical thinking questions.

6. After completing Exercise #5, consider the following case, which occurs prior to the time depicted on the website:

    You are employed as a hospital social worker, and have been assigned to Emilia Sanchez. Emilia is 24 years old and has just given birth to Joey. She used crack cocaine during her pregnancy, and Joey tested positive for the drug. A child protection social worker assigned to the case believes that Joey will likely be taken into the custody of the state, and probably placed with Celia and Hector, who have already indicated their willingness to take him as a foster child. As Emilia's social worker, your specific responsibility is to work with her on a plan to address her substance abuse and to adjust to the placement of Joey in foster care with her parents. You have been told by the nursing staff that she has just had an angry outburst and is now quietly sullen. You are currently heading to her hospital room.

    a. What do you notice about your own responses to the information you have received about Emilia? How will they influence your attitude about her? How will your attitude influence your work with her?

      b. What are you thinking as you walk to her room to meet with her? What emotions, if any, are you bringing with you?

      c. From the information you have at this point, what areas of strengths can see in Emilia?

      d. Balancing the safety of the child with the rights of the parent, would you suggest that Emilia have interaction with Joey while in foster care? If so, under what circumstances?

      e. You are anticipating that Emilia will be sullen when you first meet with her. What will you say to her? If she later expresses anger at the situation, what might you say then? What might be the next step in this situation?

7. Go to www.routledgesw.com/cases. Click on the Sanchez family. Go to the "Assess" menu, then click on "My Values." Take the Values and Ethics assessment.

b. Other exercises:

8. Write a two paragraph reflection journal entry to answer the question, "Why do I want to be in the helping profession?"

9. Reflect on three concerns that you have about being an effective helper. How can those also be strengths? (For example, Concern: "I am afraid that I will become too attached to my clients." Strength: "I am capable of developing strong relationships.")

10. Imagine a scenario in which a friend or family member is expressing doubts that social work is really a profession (She says "a person without a college degree can be a social worker"). Write a one-two page paper summarizing the reasons that social work can be considered a profession, using the main points from this chapter.

CHAPTER 2

Applying Values and Ethics to Practice

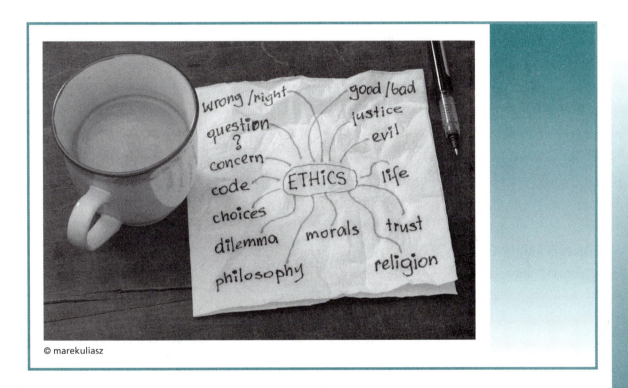

© marekuliasz

Deeply earnest and thoughtful people stand on shaky footing with the public.

Johann Wolfgang von Goethe

Key Questions for Chapter 2

(1) How can I identify as a professional social worker and conduct myself accordingly (EPAS 2.1.1)?

(2) How can I apply social work ethical principles to guide my professional practice (EPAS 2.1.2)?

(3) How can I apply critical thinking to inform and communicate professional judgments (2.1.3)?

(4) How can I advance human rights and social and economic justice through my professional practice (EPAS 2.1.5)?

CONSIDER THE DEGREE TO WHICH YOU AGREE WITH the following statements related to social work practice:

- People who choose to smoke cigarettes or cigars, chew tobacco, or drink excessive amounts of alcohol are responsible for resolving and paying for their own health problems, since the risks of these behaviors are widely known.

- Under some conditions, physical discipline of children is acceptable.

- Children who are sexually abused should never be returned to the residence of the person who abused them.

- Social workers who agree to an agency's terms of employment do not have the right to criticize the agency's practices.

- Most homeless people want to live out on the streets.

- Under particular circumstances, suicide is an acceptable strategy.

- All world citizens, regardless of what they have done, deserve to be free from hunger.

- HIV-positive people should be tattooed on the heel so potential sexual partners can take precautions.

- Perpetrators and victims of crime are equally deserving of social work services.

Social work is a value-laden profession. While social workers may not agree about all values, the importance of professional values is central to the practice of social work.

Values are best defined as beliefs, while *ethics* are the rules of conduct that embody those beliefs. This chapter focuses on the way that social work values shape professional ethics; specifically, ethical codes and their application to practice; the relationship between ethics and the law; and the ways social workers manage ethical conflicts and dilemmas.

A BRIEF HISTORY OF SOCIAL WORK ETHICS

When social work first became a profession in 1917, social workers were more concerned about their clients' morals than about the conduct of individual social workers (Reamer, 2006). In the first two decades of the 20th century, the emphasis on social reform shifted to address social problems, such as those related to health, employment, and poverty (Reamer, 2008). In the late 1940s and early 1950s, social workers made several attempts to develop an official, written code that articulated the current, collective thinking of the profession. In 1947, the American Association of Social Workers (a predecessor of the National Association of Social Workers) adopted the profession's first formal code that established guidelines and standards for its ethical conduct (Reamer, 2006). The National Association of Social Workers adopted the first formal code of ethics in 1960 (Reamer, 2008).

The second wave of ethical development occurred in the late 1970s and early 1980s. Advances in biotechnology (such as organ and bone marrow transplants) changed the medical profession. These advances were especially influential in sensitizing social workers (and other human service workers) to the importance of their values and the relationship between their values and their professional decisions. New concerns about decision-making developed: Who could make certain decisions? For example, who decides whether a dying relative is taken off life support? Which decisions were acceptable? Was it all right to abort a fetus diagnosed with a severe developmental disability? Other societal changes, such as developments in computer technology, globalized ecopolitics, and growing interest in human rights, also shaped and intensified the concern for values in ethical practice (Reamer, 2008).

Recently, social work ethics have been concerned with risk management. Ethical standards guide conduct with a concern for liability risk and professional malpractice. A body of literature has developed around risk-management strategies that protect clients and prevent ethics problems (Reamer, 2008). Over time, social work has developed standards to guide workers, prioritize principles, affirm its values, and distinguish social workers' responsibilities. The *Code of Ethics* (NASW, 2008) (referred to hereafter as "*Code of Ethics*") reflects the profession's official views on appropriate conduct with clients, with one another, with organizations, and society at large.

PROFESSIONAL CODES OF ETHICS

The social work *Code of Ethics* (2008) is a comprehensive code of ethical standards and guidelines that serves to: (1) affirm social work as a legitimate profession; (2) provide guidance for practice circumstances; and (3) explicate the standards to which the public may hold the profession accountable. Social work practitioners generally appreciate the structure the *Code of Ethics* provides in today's increasingly complex practice situations.

The *Code of Ethics* is the official code of the social work profession in the United States. This chapter will review the *Code of Ethics*, discuss the *Code* as a tool of

EXHIBIT 2.1 *Other Subgroups' Ethical Codes*	Sub-groups of the social work profession, such as those working with specific populations, have developed their own ethical codes, including (Reamer, 2008): • National Association for Black Social Workers • Clinical Social Work Federation • International Federation of Social Workers (IFSW) • Canadian Association of Social Workers

practice, and highlight the most recent International Federation of Social Workers (IFSW) code.

The NASW *Code of Ethics*

The six core values in the preamble form the basis of the *Code of Ethics* (see Exhibit 2.2). The core values represent a mix of the worker's activities, skills, principles, character, and attitudes. The ethical standards cover and are organized according to the following six relationship categories or standards:

1. Social workers' ethical responsibilities to clients.
2. Social workers' ethical responsibilities to colleagues.
3. Social workers' ethical responsibilities in practice settings.
4. Social workers' ethical responsibilities as professionals.
5. Social workers' ethical responsibilities to the social work profession.
6. Social workers' ethical responsibilities to the broader society.

Within each of these categories the *Code of Ethics* contains from two (category five) to 16 standards (category one), along with varying substandards to total 155

EXHIBIT 2.2 *The Foundation of the Social Work Perspective*	CORE VALUES	ETHICAL PRINCIPLES
	Service	Social workers' primary goal is to help people in need and to address social problems.
	Social justice	Social workers challenge social injustice.
	Dignity and worth of the person	Social workers respect the inherent dignity and worth of the person.
	Importance of human relationships	Social workers recognize the central importance of human relationships.
	Integrity	Social workers behave in a trustworthy manner.
	Competence	Social workers practice within their areas of competence and develop and enhance their professional expertise.

> ## 6. SOCIAL WORKERS' ETHICAL RESPONSIBILITIES TO THE BROADER SOCIETY
>
> **6.01 Social Welfare**
> Social workers should promote the general welfare of society, from local to global levels, and the development of people, their communities, and their environments. Social workers should advocate for living conditions conducive to the fulfillment of basic human needs and should promote social, economic, political, and cultural values and institutions that are compatible with the realization of social justice.
>
> **6.02 Public Participation**
> Social workers should facilitate informed participation by the public in shaping social policies and institutions.
>
> **6.03 Public Emergencies**
> Social workers should provide appropriate professional services in public emergencies to the greatest extent possible.
>
> **6.04 Social and Political Action**
> (a) Social workers should engage in social and political action that seeks to ensure that all people have equal access to the resources, employment, services, and opportunities they require to meet their basic human needs and to develop fully. Social workers should be aware of the impact of the political arena on practice and should advocate for changes in policy and legislation to improve social conditions in order to meet basic human needs and promote social justice.

EXHIBIT 2.3

Sample of the NASW Code of Ethics

standards. These substandards explain the appropriate conduct for social workers (see Exhibit 2.3 for a sample of the *Code of Ethics*). Social workers may deviate from these expected norms when appropriate ethical justification is available (Barsky, 2010).

International Federation of Social Workers Ethical Statement

The International Federation of Social Workers (IFSW), a worldwide professional organization of social work organizations and individuals, documents its position on ethical practice in a statement that reflects concerns that are similar but not identical to the NASW *Code*. The IFSW document, *Ethics in Social Work: Statement of Principles ("Statement of Principles")* was approved jointly by International Federation of Social Workers and the International Association of Schools of Social Work in 2001. This document contains a more explicit and pervasive emphasis on human rights than the *Code of Ethics*. For example (IFSW, 2012, para. 3):

Definition of Social Work: The social work profession promotes social change, problem solving in human relationships, and the empowerment and liberation of people to enhance well-being. Utilising theories of human behaviour and social systems, social work intervenes at the points where people interact with their environments. Principles of human rights and social justice are fundamental to social work.

As a federation, IFSW assumes that member organizations, including the National Association of Social Workers (NASW), adhere to the standards in the *Statement of Principles*. Therefore, a comparison between the *Code of Ethics* and the *Statement of Principles* reveals some of the different emphases of the U.S. and international ethical practice. The following section of the *Statement of Principles* highlights seven international conventions that form "common standards of achievement and recognise rights that are accepted by the global community" (IFSW, 2012, para. 4). These include the Universal Declaration of Human Rights (1948), the International Covenant on Civil and Political Rights (1965), and the International Covenant on Economic, Social, and Cultural Rights (1965), as well as some conventions that the U.S. has not yet ratified.

The next two sections in the IFSW statement, on human rights and social justice, are the equivalent of the first two principles in the *Code of Ethics*. These address social work's commitment to human rights and human dignity. The full text of the Principles is shown in Exhibit 2.2. The values in these statements are similar to those in the *Code of Ethics*. However, the Universal Declaration of Human Rights, which is central to the IFSW statement, includes emphases on a global (rather than national) perspective and on the importance of economic, social, and cultural rights for all people.

Limits of Ethical Codes

Although the *Code of Ethics* offers helpful guidance to social work practitioners wrestling with difficult situations, the code is often difficult to apply because it offers general statements, can be difficult to interpret, and may offer unrealistic guidance given a social worker's situation (Strom-Gottfried, 2008). As discussed through examples in this chapter, issues of context, risk taking and creativity, and diversity also provide challenges to ethical codes.

The Role of Context Ethical decisions are made within a practice context, which may shape the decision-making process in subtle ways. For example, if a social worker is unaware of attributing negative qualities to a client because of missed appointments, the social worker may believe that the client does not want services, is unable to take full advantage of scarce resources, or that the client does not deserve these resources. If the social worker is in a position to choose the clients who have access to a limited service, she or he may disqualify the client without further reflection. On the one hand, this could be viewed as using good judgment as the social worker is seeking to maximize the effectiveness of the scarce service. On the other hand, the decision reflects a decision-making process that is not transparent, that is influenced by one interpretation of client behavior, and is

Human rights and human dignity: Social work is based on respect for the inherent worth and dignity of all people, and the rights that follow from this. Social workers should uphold and defend each person's physical, psychological, emotional, and spiritual integrity and well-being. This means:

1. Respecting the right to self-determination—social workers should respect people's rights to make their own choices and decisions, irrespective of their values and life choices, providing this does not threaten the rights and interests of others.
2. Promoting the right to participation—social workers should promote the full involvement and participation of people using their services in ways that enable them to be empowered in all aspects of decisions and actions affecting their lives.
3. Treating each person as a whole—social workers should be concerned with the whole person, within the family and the community, and should seek to recognise all aspects of a person's life.
4. Identifying and developing strengths—social workers should focus on the strengths of all individuals, groups and communities and thus promote their empowerment.

Social justice: Social workers have a responsibility to promote social justice, in relation to society generally, and in relation to the people with whom they work. This means:

1. Challenging negative discrimination—social workers have a responsibility to challenge negative discrimination on the basis of irrelevant characteristics such as ability, age, culture, gender or sex, marital status, political opinions, skin color or other physical characteristics, sexual orientation, or spiritual beliefs.
2. Recognizing diversity—social workers should recognize and respect the racial and cultural diversity of societies in which they practice, taking account of individual, family, group, and community differences.
3. Distributing resources equitably—social workers should ensure that resources at their disposal are distributed fairly, according to need.
4. Challenging unjust policies and practices—social workers have a duty to bring to the attention of policy makers, politicians and the general public situations where resources are inadequate or where policies and practices are unfair or harmful.
5. Working in solidarity—social workers have an obligation to challenge social conditions that contribute to social exclusion, stigmatization or subjugation, and to work towards an inclusive society.

Source: IFSW & IASSW, 2004

EXHIBIT 2.4

Final Proposal for New IFSW Ethical Document 2004

perhaps inaccurate. For example, if the client did not have reliable transportation to appointments, had an unstable home life, or had a medically needy child, the decision-making process may have resulted in a different outcome. Such judgments may not only be inaccurate but also present an ethical question relating to the professional discretion and impartial judgment that the *Code of Ethics* requires. Therefore, an ethical code provides guidance that is decontextualized.

Professionals must be aware of their perspectives and judgments as important influences in making ethical decisions (Barsky, 2010). Thoughtful social workers frequently come to the conclusion that a resolution of an ethical question depends on many factors, in recognition of the importance of the surrounding circumstances, social location, and current pressures (Harrington & Dolgoff, 2008). Ethical decisions also benefit from consulting with knowledgeable colleagues (Reamer 2006). An in-depth conversation between professionals and their colleagues regarding their thinking, the implications of varying choices, and an analysis of their values can be very helpful. For example, many health care facilities have committees that review situations that involve ethical questions. In other situations, social workers engage in a discussion with a knowledgeable colleague or supervisor about a situation, and arrive at a decision through dialogue (also discussed later in this chapter).

Risk Taking and Creativity   Another concern about rigid interpretation of ethical rules is the potential for oversimplification. Social workers may rely on the *Code of Ethics* to avoid using their creativity and professional judgment. Using critical thinking to inform professional judgment is a valuable component of social work practice and sometimes requires risk taking (Strom-Gottfried, 2008). There is rarely one correct answer to an ethical dilemma. Social workers must have a tolerance for ambiguity, and work to apply ethical principles in practice (Dolgoff, Harrington, & Lowenberg, 2012).

The following case vignette illustrates this idea:

A school social worker named Cora, in strict adherence to the ethical principle of practicing only within her area of competency (Code Standard 4.01a), at first declined to see a young student who clearly was struggling with substance abuse. Cora felt competent to work with adolescents with developmental issues, but she was not educated to treat those struggling with substance abuse, so she decided it would be unethical to work with the student. The student, however, was in great need of assistance and was ready to work on the problem, and had no other obvious or realistic options for services in her rural community. The substance use issue was intertwined with other challenges related to growing up in difficult circumstances, and developmental issues were involved. When the student asked her to reconsider, Cora decided to discuss the matter with a colleague. The colleague reminded Cora that she had skills and experience that would directly benefit the student. For example, she knew about adolescent development, had strong relationship skills with adolescents, and was committed to a hopeful, resilience-based perspective. Cora's colleague also advised that she might find a resource in her former supervisor, who was a certified substance abuse counselor. Cora contacted her former supervisor, who was recommended available training and the supervision of a clinician who also was a certified substance abuse counselor.

Substance abuse in school populations is a common, yet a potentially life-changing issue for youth. Cora was able to negotiate with the school administration for time and reimbursement to obtain training that would allow her to better serve her clients, and the school population in general. Cora was creative and willing to explore options in response to important needs, and her client(s) were likely to receive competent services from an experienced worker who sought both training and supervision. There is some risk in Cora's assumption of the role of providing substance abuse treatment; however, taking on the issue is more closely aligned with social work's values than denying help to the student.

Strict and nonreflective adherence to a standard code can help preserve the current social order, which may be in direct conflict with the profession's commitment to confront social injustice and oppression (Witkin, 2000). If the student's family in the example was limited financially and belonged to an ethnic population that experienced oppression, the student would likely experience more barriers to receiving needed services than students in other families without these characteristics. The student's access to needed resources would be constricted, a situation of social injustice. Cora's commitment to responding to the student's need and providing services embodies social work's obligation to confront injustices.

While Cora made a decision using the *Code of Ethics*, colleague advice, and critical thinking, not everyone will agree that her solution was the best solution. For example, advocates for diversity empowerment might view Cora's effort as perpetuating social injustice because the situation involves non-white people receiving substandard services with a worker without the appropriate credentials. While there may be different, well-informed opinions about the best course of action in this situation, a too-narrow interpretation of the *Code of Ethics* that precludes critical thinking and creativity should be avoided. Resolving issues like Cora's is seldom easy; it is not hard to overlook worthwhile concerns, such as competency of the worker. Practitioners are encouraged to consider the *Code of Ethics*, and talk to colleagues to fully explore issues. This decision-making process contributes to the ongoing development of the profession's larger ethical stance.

Diversity A postmodern recognition of diversity and multiple realities raises another concern about the use of codes. Universal codes meant to apply to everyone in all situations can fail to address the contexts of both social workers and clients, or to recognize differences among people and cultures. For example, the ethical mandate for confidentiality, which refers to the social worker's obligation to keep information about clients from becoming public in any way, is often regarded as absolutely critical in maintaining a professional relationship. However, a universal application of confidentiality as an ethical mandate may present an obstacle in cultures less individualistic than that in the U.S., in which the community may be both the reference point and a rich source of resources that may assist individual clients. In such communities, maintaining confidentiality can be experienced as secretive, alienating, divisive, and harmful. For example, some Latino families may not be receptive to individual work with a social worker, but become engaged and respond to family systems work (Diller, 2011).

Briskman and Noble (1999) suggest that social work needs an ethical model that is more affirming of difference. One possibility is to develop multiple codes, grounded in client-based and service delivery schemes. For example, the authors cite an organization that works to prevent and treat sexual assault in Melbourne, Australia, that shapes its code based on the perspective that sexual assault is a violation of human rights (p. 64). This is an example of a specific code tailored to the organization's commitments to a particular client population. Another way to recognize difference is to develop constituency-based codes founded on specific concerns, such as tolerance for sexual orientation in schools. In this case, norms would develop with specific reference to the issues raised by gay, lesbian, bisexual, transgendered, and questioning groups. The development of specialized codes for different groups departs from the universal application of U.S. and Canadian codes.

In some cases a bicultural code of practice may work best. For example, the Aotearoa New Zealand Association of Social Work (ANZASW) currently uses a Bicultural Code that reflects an effort to deal justly with its native Maori people through recognition of the independence guaranteed to them in a treaty negotiated in 1840. The historical emphasis on the Maori people's independence has led New Zealander social workers to recognize the contemporary demands that this principle places on their work with Maori people. This code is based on the IFSW code and explicitly requires a bicultural focus for all of New Zealand's social workers. See Exhibit 2.5 for an excerpt from the ANZASW Code of Ethics.

Despite the challenges discussed above, the NASW *Code of Ethics* provides a valuable structure for the social work profession. The *Code* articulates expectations and provides overall guidance about conduct so that social workers have clear expectations and can identify points of departure from the norms. The *Code of Ethics* is value-based and is consistent with social work history. Like all ethical codes, the *Code of Ethics* has limitations and is framed in consideration of experiences outside of the mainstream. As such, the *Code of Ethics* addresses growing concerns for recognition and affirmation of diverse peoples worldwide. Codes are evolving documents that reflect the consensus of the profession at the time of adoption, a consensus that can change as contexts change. Social workers are encouraged to be involved in the professional dialogue about the *Code* through professional organizations, and to contribute to its evolution.

ETHICS AND THE LAW

International, federal, state, and local laws have a significant impact on social work practice, and its constant changes create a complex, sometimes bewildering climate in which to practice (Strom-Gottfried, 2008). Ethics and the law are related and sometimes overlap, yet there are clear distinctions between the two. The following

In New Zealand, the Treaty of Waitangi, negotiated in 1840 between the occupying British and the native Maori chiefs, recognized the native Maori people as Tangata Whanua and guaranteed their right to independence. This treaty is an integral part of contemporary ethics in New Zealand social work, and it reflects an active commitment for the promotion of indigenous identity. The following is an excerpt from Section C, the Bicultural Code of the Code of Ethics of the New Zealand Association of Social Work.

Independence

1.1 Social work organisations and agencies and individual social workers should acknowledge and support the whanau [here, Maori clients] as the primary source of care and nurturing of their members.

1.2 Social workers are expected to work in ways that recognise the independence of the whanau and its members, by empowering the whanau and its members to handle their own lives and living conditions, and by enabling them to take care of themselves and to develop autonomously and collectively.

1.3 NZASW [New Zealand Association of Social Workers] recognises the right of Maori clients to have a Maori worker. Social work agencies and organisations should ensure that Maori clients have access to Maori workers at all levels, and social workers are expected to open up access to Maori workers. If no Maori worker is available, appropriate referral may be made if that is requested by the client. During their social work education Maori social workers should receive appropriate training in Maori models and methods.

Liberation through Solidarity

2.1 Social workers should work with agencies and organisations whose policies, procedures and practices are based on the Treaty of Waitangi, and actively and constructively

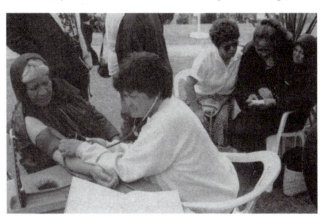

promote changes in those agencies and organisations that operate from a mono-cultural base.

Non Discrimination

3.1 All social workers are expected to participate in Treaty of Waitangi education as part of their entry into social work and on an ongoing basis. This should include a

Cultural solidarity: Maori address health issues.

knowledge and understanding of their own ethnicity and the actual history of Aotearoa New Zealand.

NZASW, 1993

EXHIBIT 2.5

Sample Bicultural Code of Practice

EXHIBIT 2.6

Changes to the NASW Code of Ethics

The first NASW Code of Ethics, adopted in 1960, was only one page long with 14 brief declarations, such as "to give appropriate service in public emergencies." In 1979, the second NASW Code was adopted, including six sections of brief principles and a preamble. This Code was revised twice, eventually containing around 80 principles. For example, statements about solicitation of referrals, fees for referral, and dual relationships were added.

A third Code was approved by the NASW in 1996, and included four major sections: a preamble, the purpose of the NASW Code of Ethics, Ethical Principles, and Ethical Standards. There were many changes from the previous Code, including the addition of a mission statement, a section on the uses of codes, a list of social work values and principles, and almost twice the amount of practice standards from the 1979 Code. This third Code also contained standards about confidentiality limits, avoiding conflict of interest, and emphasizing social justice and social change (Brill, 1998; Reamer, 2009). The 2008 version of the Code includes new standards regarding cultural competence and social diversity, respect, discrimination, and social and political action (NASW, 2008).

discussion highlights parallels and distinctions between social work ethics and the law, as well as the potential for, and benefit of, collaboration between social workers and lawyers.

Parallels between Ethics and the Law

Many parallels exist between social work ethics and the laws that impact practitioners. For example, social workers who make derogatory comments to colleagues about clients who are living in poverty may be accused of actually violating the *Code of Ethics* (Section 1.12), as well as the spirit of the profession by expressing oppressive attitudes. In many states, clients could initiate a complaint with the state licensing board that a social worker has violated the *Code of Ethics*. If the client's culture differed from that of the social worker, a complaint could be added regarding a violation of *Code of Ethics* Section 1.05b, which requires the social worker to understand the function of culture and recognize the strengths of all cultures. State licensing boards can impose sanctions or require various forms of corrective action, such as license suspension or revocation (Reamer, 2008). NASW can also sanction social workers through a process by an ethics committee, and can impose a range of penalties such as suspension from NASW, mandated supervision or consultation, censure, or others (Reamer, 2008), which includes publishing the names of those sanctioned. While NASW's process is professional—rather than legal—sanctions can still harm a social worker's career.

Conflicts between Ethics and the Law

Social workers may experience practice situations in which there is an overt conflict between ethical practice and the law. The next section considers two legal duties: the duty to report and the duty to protect. Both of these legal mandates support ethical practice in most contexts, and create conflicts in others. These duties will be discussed more fully in Chapter 4.

Duty to Report: Child Protection   Social workers operating in the arena of child protection frequently find themselves in a contentious environment. Like many types of helping professionals, social workers have a legal duty to report their suspicions of child abuse or neglect to child protection authorities or law enforcement.

A common sequence of events leading to a report of suspected child abuse or neglect begins with a child telling a teacher, school nurse, or another school-related adult that she or he has been abused or neglected. Alternatively, a nurse or doctor may suspect abuse or neglect based on physical signs. In either situation, the professional reports these allegations to the proper authorities. The charges are then investigated by a child protection worker, who often interviews the parents/guardians as well as the child, and determines whether the charges are substantiated and further action is required. The person making the referral may be convinced that the child is being abused or neglected, but she or he may also suspect that the abuse or neglect is going to be difficult to substantiate. In such a case, reporting the abuse might place the child at much greater risk, because the parent/guardian will learn about the accusation, become angry and take out the anger on the child. Where there is no obvious way to protect the child, the referring professional may be tempted not to obey the reporting law.

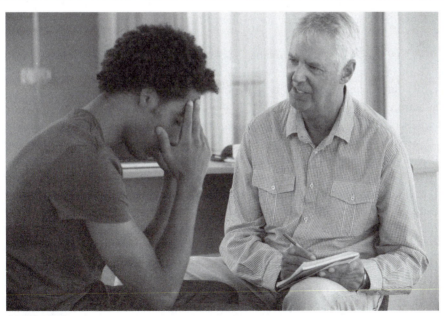

A discussion of abuse or neglect can elicit strong emotions

© Mark Bowden

A similar situation may occur if the social worker is cynical about the adequacy, timeliness, or effectiveness of the response of child protection agencies. For example, a social worker who experiences an unreasonably long response time from a child protection agency due to inadequate department staffing may be reluctant to report again.

Social workers may encounter other practice situations in which compliance with the law may create more harm than good. For example, a social worker may work through a 15-year-old pregnant client's options about her pregnancy. In a discussion with the client, the social worker discovers that the client knows who the father of the baby is, and the father is terribly frightened about the possible reaction of his family to the pregnancy. The client is under 18, and legally a child; therefore, the pregnancy becomes a matter of child abuse and, by law, must be reported. However, the social worker views the reporting possibility as nonproductive: the client claims that the sexual activity was consensual; reporting will not assist the client; the father is under 18 years old; reporting will possibly alienate the baby's father, who might otherwise participate in the decision-making process; and reporting could put the baby's father at risk of a violent reaction from his family.

Duty to Report: Adult Protection   All states have reporting laws designed to protect older adults from abuse, neglect, and exploitation; however, each state has its own definition of reportable acts, those responsible for reporting, and the entity that is responsible for accepting the report and investigating (Barsky, 2010). Social workers may experience similar challenges between the law and ethical duties with situations involving suspected abuse of older adults.

Duty to Protect: Threats of Violence   Social workers also have an ethical obligation to protect people from serious, foreseeable, and imminent harm (Barsky, 2010). This ethical and legal responsibility emerged from a court case resulting from a tragic situation. In 1969, Tatiana Tarasoff, a young student at the University of California at Berkeley, had a casual dating relationship with a graduate student from India. He apparently did not understand dating customs in the U.S., and consequently was despondent that Tatiana was simultaneously dating several men. Depressed, he went to a psychologist at the University Health Services and told the psychologist that he intended to kill Tatiana with a gun. The psychologist wrote a letter to the campus police and asked that the graduate student be detained in a psychiatric hospital. The police interviewed the young man but did not feel there was evidence to prove that he was dangerous. The police required him to promise that he would not contact Tatiana. When Tatiana returned from a summer visit abroad, the man stalked her, and finally stabbed her to death. Tatiana's family sued the campus police, the University Health Services, and the Regents of the University of California for failing to warn them that their daughter's life was in danger. The trial court dismissed the case because although there was precedence for notifying the victim, there was no precedence for warning a third party (which, in this situation, would have been Tatiana's parents). The appeals court supported the dismissal, and an appeal was taken to the California Supreme Court, which overturned the dismissal, citing the therapist's responsibility to warn people who have been threatened as Tatiana had been. This case is *Tarasoff I* of 1974 and is often called the Duty to Warn decision.

This ruling opened the way for the family to sue the police and the therapist. A massive outcry from members of both police and treatment-related groups led to the decision by the California Supreme Court to hear the case again. The 1976 court decision, *Tarasoff II*, stressed that when a therapist has determined that her or his client presents serious danger of violence to another, the therapist must "use reasonable care to protect the intended victim against such danger." The court's position was that the therapist might have to take any of several steps to ensure the safety of the person threatened by the client, and the emphasis was on the Duty to Protect rather than the warning emphasized in *Tarasoff I*. Although the Tarasoff decisions were based on the work of a clinical psychologist, social workers, as well as other human service professionals, are subject in most states to the same legal precedents.

Social workers must now carefully consider any threats of violence they learn about in the course of practice. For example, if a client with a history of violence threatens to "belt" his girlfriend after discharge from a hospital, an assessment of the seriousness of the threat must be completed. Additionally, social workers must practice with consideration of protection against legal charges. A situation of this type is complex, and social workers must respond with several considerations in mind, including their employer's policies, the legal obligation of Duty to Protect, and the *Code of Ethics*. In the case of the Tarasoff decisions, the courts, not the ethics board of the profession, defined the parameters of responsibility.

Practice situations at various client system levels can involve the legal system. U.S. society has become increasingly litigious, and social workers may encounter practice situations with legal questions in policy practice, research, and community and direct practice (Barksy, 2010). For example, a social worker may encounter ethical challenges at the policy level if a new law requires adoption workers to provide the "adoption triad" (i.e., birth parents, adoptive parents, and adopted children) with access to all information about the adoption. If a birth mother had been guaranteed confidentiality at the time of the adoption, she, along with her social worker, may be distraught by this sudden breach of the document that she signed, which she considered a binding legal agreement. Another example is a social worker faced with maintaining a city zoning ordinance against a group home for those leaving prison, an establishment that she believes is critically needed in the community. Social workers working at the community level can experience ethical challenges in supporting community initiatives. For example, a community group may work toward an ordinance which would result in discouraging individuals who are not documented from residing in the community. Social workers can discover challenges in attempting to practice within the constraints of the law and the *Code of Ethics*.

Collaboration between Ethics and the Law

In the best scenarios, the law and social work professions can work together to empower people whose legal and social rights are frequently violated. There are many examples of this kind of collaboration in joint law and social work degree programs; for example, collaborations occur in legal clinics for refugee and immigrant peoples, and in family law and social work partnerships. In the U.S., the law drives much of the complex social welfare system, as well as the structures for shaping income and benefits distribution. A joint effort between the professions of social work and the law, based on common goals, can benefit a great number of people, with each profession enhancing and enriching the work of the other.

The law also places external pressure on all of the helping professions to hold one another accountable within their professions. The law protects the general public from the possibility that helping professionals can collude to cover up or obscure unethical conduct within their profession. Although the incidence of covering up unethical behavior is relatively low, all professionals may be tempted to minimize the seriousness of any offense raised. Child abuse allegations and convictions involving priests from the Roman Catholic Church, and a scandal involving the abuse of developmentally disabled in state care in New York state unveiled by the New York Times in 2012 are tragic reminders of the potential dangers to vulnerable populations of unethical behavior by people in helping professions.

DILEMMAS AND CRITICAL PROCESSES

The complex context of real client system situations often highlights the potential for competition between social work values, and/or between ethical standards in a given situation. This complexity can make it difficult to identify the appropriate ethical decision. The next section addresses the distinction between ethical conflicts and dilemmas, the idea of an ethical screen, various models for resolving dilemmas, and some examples of common dilemmas in social work practice.

The Distinction between Value Conflicts and Ethical Dilemmas

Value conflicts occur when an individual's personal values clash with those of another person or system. In contrast, ethical dilemmas occur when a social worker must choose between two or more relevant, but contradictory, ethical directives. An ethical dilemma exists when there is no clear single response that satisfies all ethical directives in a situation (Dolgoff et al., 2012).

Many practice situations involve ethical dilemmas. For example, social workers may learn that their clients are having affairs or using prostitutes, and struggle with contrasting ethical and legal obligations to maintain confidentiality and notify client partners of physical harm. In another example, clients may demonstrate racism toward their social worker, who would then struggle with weighing an ethical mandate against abandoning clients with confidentiality, client self-determination and other ethical obligations. Another situation involving an ethical dilemma is when a relative of a suicidal person asks a social worker to help their relative, but the person has not sought services.

In all of these situations, no one response is clearly the correct, ethical way to handle the situation. Social workers must struggle with their ethical and legal mandates, consult with colleagues, and engage in other activities to arrive at a decision. In the next section, structures to assist with the decision-making process are discussed.

The Ethical Principles Screen

A useful tool in considering ethical priorities is the ethical principle screen (Dolgoff et al., 2012). This screen assists in the decision-making process by highlighting the relative significance of values and the likely results of particular decisions. The elements in the screen, listed in Quick Guide 3, are reflected and prioritized in professional social work values, and are rank ordered so that Principle 1 has the

QUICK GUIDE 3   ELEMENTS OF THE ETHICAL PRINCIPLES SCREEN

- **Principle 1: Protection of Life** This principle refers to guarding against death, starvation, violence, neglect, and any other event or phenomenon that endangers a person's life.
- **Principle 2: Equality and Inequality** This principle reflects a commitment to equal and fair access to services and basic treatment.
- **Principle 3: Freedom and Autonomy** This principle affirms the notion of self-determination and supports people's right to make free choices regarding their lives.
- **Principle 4: Least Harm** This principle supports the idea of protecting people from harm; when harm seems likely in any event, it asserts that people have the right to experience the least amount possible.
- **Principle 5: Quality of Life** This principle confirms that people, families, and communities all have the right to define and pursue the quality of life they desire.
- **Principle 6: Privacy and Confidentiality** This principle supports the right of people to be protected from having their personal information made public. Maintaining confidentiality means the social worker must not share client circumstances, struggles, or decisions without the client's explicit (generally written and signed) permission. Information revealing any identifying characteristics (such as name and physical description) must also be kept confidential.
- **Principle 7: Truthfulness and Full Disclosure** This principle directs social workers to tell clients the full truth of any information pertaining to them, and explain whatever is needed to ensure understanding.

Source: Dolgoff, Loewenberg, & Harrington, 2009

highest priority and Principle 7 the lowest. The screen is constructed to reflect socially constructed priorities that involve values.

The following scenario demonstrates the use of the ethical principle screen. A social worker believes that a child on her caseload is at risk because his father regularly beats him. This case clearly reflects Principle 1 regarding threats of bodily harm. A competing concern is a violation of confidentiality and the continuing trust of the child that is threatened if the abuse is reported. Thus, the case also involves Principle 6. To resolve the dilemma, the ethical questions involved are identified: the protection of life versus confidentiality. These questions are prioritized by applying the ethical priorities screen, the priorities are rank ordered. In this situation, the life of the child provides a more urgent and compelling principle to guide actions than does a desire to maintain silence so that the child will continue to trust the social worker.

While not all social workers would agree with the prioritizations in the ethical screen in this situation, the screen offers a tool for decision-making. However, the principles address very broad concepts that are subject to interpretation, and their relative evaluation in the real practice world often invites critical thinking skills. The next section explores other models for resolving ethical dilemmas.

Models for Resolution of Ethical Dilemmas

Different models for resolving ethical dilemmas structure decision-making in other ways, reflecting a different ordering of social work values. Here are two examples.

Reamer (2006) suggests that social workers follow several steps to enhance the quality of their ethical decision-making:

1. Identify the ethical issues, including the social work values and duties that conflict.
2. Identify the individuals, groups, and organizations that are likely to be affected by the ethical decision.
3. Tentatively identify all possible courses of action and the participants involved in each, along with the possible benefits and risks for each.
4. Thoroughly examine the reasons in favor of and opposed to each possible course of action.
5. Consult with colleagues and appropriate experts (i.e., professional colleagues, supervisors, agency administrators, and attorneys).
6. Make the decision and document the decision-making process.
7. Monitor and evaluate the decision.

Strom-Gottfried (2008) adds several options for addressing ethical dilemmas, including researching the literature, relevant laws, and policies, consulting formally with established committees, obtaining supervision, and consulting peers. Strom-Gottfield (2003) also suggests the following strategies for solving ethical dilemmas:

1. Consider the "worst case scenario" of each option.
2. Consider the principles of least harm, justice, fairness, and the level of publicity that will result.
3. Consider clinical and ethical implications.
4. Consider the process.
5. Consider barriers to acting on the principal identified power relationships.

Both Reamer's and Strom-Gottfried's approaches help analyze the issues involved in any particular dilemma. While Reamer's model is more methodical than Strom-Gottfried's because it prescribes a specific sequence of analysis, the Strom-Gottfried model allows for a creative strategy that can accommodate specifics of the client system situation. Like codes of ethics, neither can produce an infallible result, and flexibility is needed in applying models to the specifics of the individual context.

Representative Examples of Practice Dilemmas

Of the many potential dilemmas, three types are common in social work: dual relationships, professional versus private tensions, and struggles between paternalism and client self-determination.

Dual Relationships   Relationships between social workers and clients that exist in addition to and distinct from their professional contacts create dual relationships. Such relationships are often only publically known in extreme circumstances, such as when the worker has a sexual relationship with the client. Sexual relationships, although an egregious affront to the profession, are fairly easy to resolve because there is a clear prohibition against them.

Nonsexual dual relationships pose another set of questions. For example, consider the situation of Lara, a new social worker.

> Lara works in a local community health center with young adults whom legal authorities have identified as delinquent. Her responsibility is to support their integration into the community's work-study program that the center sponsors. Lara finds her work interesting and rewarding, and particularly enjoys working with one client, Joe, who is progressing in the program. Lara's 20-year-old sister recently called her to tell her about her new boyfriend. Lara realized that her sister's new boyfriend is her client, Joe.

The dilemma created by this dual relationship is between personal values and professional responsibilities. There are many reasons for Lara to maintain the current situation. Lara enjoys her job, values her work with Joe, and does not want to resign. On the other hand, Lara also wants to participate in her family gatherings, which are likely to include her sister's new boyfriend. The *Code of Ethics*, however, cautions against dual relationships, which includes a professional and a personal relationship. Because of the ethical mandate about confidentiality, Lara is not free to tell her family that Joe is a client, or reveal anything about his situation.

Specifically, Section 1.06c of the *Code of Ethics* stresses that social workers should not engage in dual relationships with clients or former clients in which there is a risk of exploitation or potential harm to the client. Reamer (2003) classifies dual relationships as unethical when they

- Interfere with the social worker's exercise of professional discretion.

- Interfere with the social worker's exercise of impartial judgment.

- Exploit clients, colleagues, or third parties to further the social worker's personal interests.

- Harm clients, colleagues, or third parties (p. 129).

In this scenario, the dual relationship Lara has with Joe has the potential to affect her professional discretion and impartial judgment. For example, if Lara discovers personal information about Joe that suggests he might not be a viable candidate for marriage, Lara may experience difficulty conducting herself in a professional manner.

In some situations, the social worker may have justification for a dual relationship with a client. For example, in rural areas dual relationships may be very difficult to avoid, given the small number of service providers (Dolgoff et al., 2012). In a rural area, clients may have worked for a member of a social worker's family, attend the same faith community as a social worker, or be behind the social worker in the checkout line at the local grocery store. In a world characterized by expanding notions of community and multicultural experiences, social workers may find that they are asked to maintain relationships in several domains with others and to perform multiple roles. For example, in some cultures, social workers would risk insulting a family by refusing an invitation to a family dinner party.

Some social workers disagree that rigid boundaries are necessary or desirable. Zur and Lazarus (2002) maintain that some aspects of dual relationships—such as greater connectedness and an increase in the client's self-determination—can actually benefit rather than harm the client. They discuss a specific framework that separates the idea of exploitation into more manageable components to determine whether a certain aspect is potentially beneficial or hurtful in any particular relationship. The continuum, displayed in Exhibit 2.7, allows the social worker to explore the areas and degrees to which a specific relationship's dimension (for example, a social relationship with a client) might benefit or harm a client.

Applying this to the situation described earlier, Lara might evaluate the risk of exploiting Joe rather than empowering him if she were to continue working with him. Lara might also consider the likelihood of increasing Joe's vulnerability through her knowledge of his past struggles. Some variables, such as control of resources, might not be applicable; unless, of course, Lara favored Joe as a potential

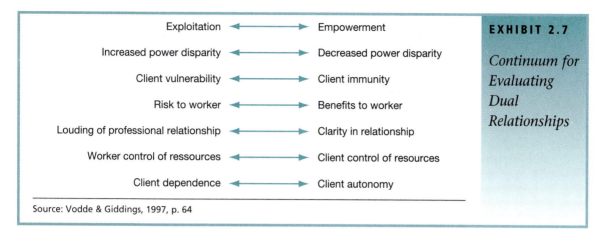

Exploitation ←——————→ Empowerment	**EXHIBIT 2.7**
Increased power disparity ←——————→ Decreased power disparity	*Continuum for*
Client vulnerability ←——————→ Client immunity	*Evaluating*
Risk to worker ←——————→ Benefits to worker	*Dual*
Louding of professional relationship ←——————→ Clarity in relationship	*Relationships*
Worker control of ressources ←——————→ Client control of resources	
Client dependence ←——————→ Client autonomy	

Source: Vodde & Giddings, 1997, p. 64

brother-in-law by allocating an unfair share of resources, such as work stipends. Lara may be at high risk for clouding the professional relationship by working with him while he is dating her sister. Lara will need to evaluate whether the level of risk is too high to continue working with him.

A second framework that includes the idea of "boundary crossing" as different than "boundary violation" (Zur & Lazarus, 2002, p. 6) allows the social worker to decide if the dual relationship occurs naturally (with no intention of the social worker) or is contrived (arranged by the social worker for her or his own purposes). The framework also allows the social worker to examine whether the relationship is exploitive (for the worker's benefit), essential (for survival in the community), or enhancing (beneficial to the client). Returning to Lara's situation, although her relationship with Joe is naturally occurring (she did not arrange for the relationship), the dual relationship is neither essential for the community's well-being, nor empowering for Joe. The dual relationship has the potential to be exploitive. Analysis using this framework can be helpful in situations in which dual relationships are impossible to avoid; this framework uses the specific content of the case rather than applying a one-size-fits-all model that simply prohibits dual relationships.

Responsibility to the Larger Society and Client Well-Being Relationships that involve child or elder abuse or neglect, exploitation of older adults, and intimate partner violence were once considered private family issues outside the jurisdiction of the law or of any public sector interest. Through the legal and social welfare systems, the larger society has wrestled with the question of whether certain events are private matters or public issues that impact society. While social workers often tend to value the private experience of families to recognize and acknowledge clients' perspectives on their experiences, social workers are also obligated to intervene with the client's environment to the extent that public issues impact and reflect the quality of lives of all citizens. The dilemma in this situation arises when the social worker values both the client's right to privacy and the potential benefit to the community of making the issues public.

For example, a social worker might struggle with his or her obligation to encourage a rape survivor to report the incident to the police (Dombo, 2011). Authorities often treat survivors of rape or sexual assault poorly. Survivors are reluctant to pursue legal recourse for many reasons. These may include: (1) wanting to heal and to avoid dredging up the past through legal proceedings; (2) fear of rejection if their experiences are made public; and (3) fear that actions of the authorities could re-traumatize them by implying that they are the guilty parties. Due to these reasons and more, rape is often underreported. Many social workers encourage reporting, so the crime is reported and appropriate resources can be devoted to the issue. This benefit to society of reporting the crime must be balanced with the experiences and wishes of individuals who have been raped. Attempting to force a person to report an experience of rape to the authorities may jeopardize mental and physical wellbeing. Striking a balance between promoting the public's general welfare and honoring the wishes of individuals is very challenging in practice, and must be the result of critical thinking and practice experience. When making decisions, social workers must consider the following questions: What is a public issue and clearly a private issue? Is violence against people an individual event or a violation of a larger social order as well? Does violence affect the entire community? Does a zealous social worker have the right to raise a public issue that could exploit the client's pain?

Paternalism and Client Self-Determination Long a cornerstone of social work, self-determination is the right of a client to make choices and exercise control over her or his life. In the *Code of Ethics*, self-determination is listed in Section 1.02, second only to a general commitment to clients. In contrast, paternalism refers to a process of interfering with clients' self-determination because the social worker believes she or he has a better understanding of what is in the clients' best interests. Reamer (2006) identifies three different forms of paternalism: (1) withholding information from clients for their own good (for example, not communicating a medical prognosis or the extent of injury in an accident); (2) deliberately lying to clients, which is more overt than withholding information (for example, assuring a distraught family member that a dying client will improve); and (3) intervening to prevent clients' behavior by controlling their physical placement (for example, facilitating involuntary hospitalizations). A paternalistic approach is also when social workers provide too much assistance to clients who avoid developing their problem-solving skills, give too many suggestions, or interact in a controlling manner. For example, a social worker who contacts a resource for a client, when the client is capable of making the contact, is acting in a paternalistic manner.

Questions about what rights and responsibilities social workers have to interfere in client situations have been debated since the profession began. In some situations, social worker rights and responsibilities are dictated by the law. However, social workers are sometimes asked to make an ethical decision concerning client self-determination without such a clear-cut guide, such as intervening with a client who is disorderly or does not adhere to social norms in public. Another example is whether a client should be forced to conform to mainstream standards of cleanliness in a residential setting, or whether a social worker must facilitate the involuntary hospitalization of a person with a mental illness who is not adequate in her or his self-care. In such a case, someone must make a judgment about the standards of "adequate." In another example, some social workers may struggle with the question of whether to intervene with clients who are eating in an unhealthy manner, and who have a health condition that is exacerbated by the eating habits. Situations in which social workers question whether to intervene are questions involving social control and social change, and raise the broader issues about the degree to which U.S. society tolerates eccentricities or even mere differences. Social workers are obliged to "promote the well-being of clients" (Section 1.01 of the *Code of Ethics*), and must decide about the balance between responsible caretaking and excessive interference with client self-determination.

A subtler variation of this dilemma occurs when the social worker urges clients to engage in an activity that the worker values. Reamer (2006) has called this "pseudopaternalism" because the paternalistic interference does not arise out of professional values but from personal self-interest, even if the social worker has good intentions. For example, most social workers would agree that it is consistent with the profession's values to encourage a young person to achieve the highest level of education possible. At the same time, most social workers also value education personally. If a social worker encourages an adolescent with great academic potential to achieve scholastically beyond the goals of her or his family, the social worker could be acting paternalistically if the client is not interested in such achievement. The social worker could be imposing her or his dreams and goals on the client. In contrast, accepting the adolescent's limited view of life may not be upholding the social worker's commitment to promote an individual's well-being. In another example, a social worker could encourage a community to enact a community-wide recycling program, when the community is not interested in recycling currently. The social worker could again be imposing his or her values about environmentalism on the client – in this case, the community. The issue of client system self-determination versus paternalism occurs frequently in social work practice; social workers must be constantly aware of this dilemma and make decisions based on critical thinking.

STRAIGHT TALK ABOUT EXPECTATIONS AND STANDARDS IN A LITIGIOUS WORLD

Many issues concerning ethics and values are complicated by context and are difficult to resolve in real practice situations. Social workers must consider values and ethics thoughtfully throughout their practice career. The following sections consider ethical social work practice in terms of postmodernism and in the context of a litigious environment for professionals. While different, social workers must navigate social work practice with consideration of both perspectives.

Thoughtful Practice in a Postmodern World

The current substance of professional ethical inquiry tends to be focused on ethics enforcement and risk management (Reamer, 2008). Rather than serious client issues, such as poverty, or the collective responsibilities of the social work profession, the *Code of Ethics* and most ethical inquiries focus on the individual conduct of the practitioner. Social workers, however, can explore other dimensions to enrich the professional discourse about ethical practice. For example, Walz and Ritchie (2000) suggest that Gandhian principles (based on the work of Mahatma Gandhi), could make a valuable contribution to Western thinking about ethical issues in social work practice. These principles include service, social justice, nonviolence, priority to the disadvantaged, and the notion of the heart as unifier of all things. Social workers interested in expanding the notion of ethical practice might examine the degree to which their practice is consistent with nonviolence, maintaining material simplicity, or prioritizing the needs of the disadvantaged.

Risk Management in a Litigious World

Some situations require social workers to be concrete and decisive about their actions. U.S. society is increasingly litigious, particularly in the helping professions. Licensed social workers are obligated by a state regulating body to uphold the *Code of Ethics*, even if practitioners question certain aspects and/or challenge the *Code of Ethics* to encourage change. While an uncommon occurrence, social workers face risks of censure and lawsuits charging malpractice or negligence. Social workers are held accountable for upholding the *Code of Ethics* by the profession through the NASW ethics complaints process, and by the courts through lawsuits and state licensing boards. In a very small number of cases, social workers are also indicted on criminal charges about ethical misconduct (such as an allegation of fraudulent billing) (Reamer, 2008). Boland-Prom (2009), in a study of 27 state regulatory boards about their actions against 874 certified and licensed social workers found that the most frequent violations were dual relationships, license-related problems, problems with basic practice, crimes, and practice below specific standards of care. State regulatory boards typically sanctioned social workers with letters of reprimand, revoked certificates or licenses, imposed probation or instituted the supervision of practice, and accepted the social workers' surrender of their licenses. Strom-Gottfried (2000), in an examination of 781 ethics violations, discovered that boundary violations (with sexual relationships as the most numerous) composed the greatest number of ethics violations (254). "Poor practice" (160) was the second, and "Competence" (86) was the third most common violation, with "Record keeping," "Honesty," "Breach of confidentiality," "Informed consent," "Collegial violations," "Billing," and "Conflicts of interest" accounting for the remainder violations.

Social workers are encouraged to take advantage of the knowledge and experiences of other competent and concerned social workers through supervision when wrestling with decisions that have an ethical component. Strategic thinking and planning with another professional, particularly one with more experience in recognizing various perspectives and aspects of the situation, can be an invaluable decision-making aid. Further, receiving input on practice through regular social work supervision can assist in the prevention of inadvertent ethical violations.

Social work practice occurs within a context of reflective, contextual practice, in which values are explored and rules about them are challenged, and the litigious structure of absolute rights and wrongs of ethical violations. The ability of social workers to transition from a postmodern perspective to one in which the legal and professional obligations are clear requires that social workers be "bilingual" in a sense. Social workers must be aware of the expectations of the law and the profession, as well as maintaining a personal obligation to engage in critical thinking.

CONCLUSION

This chapter has examined many governing morals and values rules. Consistent with the postmodern ideas of challenging taken-for-granted precepts, social workers are encouraged to explore the implications of the profession's values and ethics.

As social workers gain skills in ethical decision-making, they encounter increasingly complex ethical dilemmas. Although social workers strengthen the profession through active participation in questioning the values and ethics principles, social workers must also understand contemporary concerns about ethical violations, and the need for critical thinking about societal expectations.

MAIN POINTS

- Ethical codes are useful in providing standards of professional conduct, but may also restrict creativity when dealing with different contexts and multiple realities.

- Social workers have an ethical responsibility to contemplate, challenge, and work to change the profession's ethical awareness.

- Social work ethics and the law are different, although they have parallels and offer the potential for interdisciplinary collaboration. Ethics and law can conflict when legal duties, such as the duty to report, come into question in certain contexts.

- Ethical dilemmas arise out of competing values—for example, dilemmas involving dual relationships, privacy versus public issues, and paternalism versus self-determination.

- Social workers need to develop sophistication in risk management practices that protect them from ethical violations by learning from others' experiences and familiarizing themselves with basic legal mandates.

EXERCISES

a. Case Exercises

1. Go to www.routledgesw.com/cases and select the Sanchez family case. Review the client history of Celia and Hector Sanchez. Imagine that you are a social worker employed by Our Lady of Guadelupe Church, where the Sanchezes are parishioners. You have noticed that when Celia comes to pick up commodities, she talks about the desperation of her family. When asked about food stamps, she replies that her husband will not allow her to enroll in the program, even though she thinks it would be a good idea, and is considering enrolling despite her husband's wishes, if she could think of a way to do this. You have helped other families access the program, even when one member does not wish to enroll. Should you encourage Celia to use your assistance to enroll? What social work values are involved in this situation? Is it an ethical dilemma? How might you resolve the situation? What might be the implications?

2. Go to www.routledgesw.com/cases and select and become familiar with the Riverton case. Under the "Engage" tab, answer the Critical Thinking Question #1.

3. Go to www.routledgesw.com/cases and select and become familiar with the Riverton case. Under the "Assess" tab, take the Values and Ethics Assessment (under the "My Values" option).

4. Go to www.routledgesw.com/cases and select and become familiar with the RAINN case. Under the "Engage" tab, answer Critical Thinking Question #2. Also consider the following question: The RAINN website combines services and fundraising. Using the NASW Code of Ethics as a guide, do you believe that it is ethical to combine these activities on the same website? Explain.

5. Go to www.routledgesw.com/cases and select and become familiar with the Hudson City case. Under the Engage tab, answer the Critical Thinking Questions.

6. Go to the www.routledgesw.com/cases and select and become familiar with the Brickville case. Under the "Assess" tab, "My Values" option, take the Values and Ethics Assessment.

b. Other Exercises

7. You are a social worker in a psychiatric hospital setting. While most patients are discharged from the hospital setting after only a few days, some patients are able to stay for longer periods of time. Due to the mandate from insurance companies

to discharge patients as soon as possible, discharge planning begins as patients are admitted.

Your client, Bea, was admitted for psychiatric reasons and is terrified to leave the hospital after a stay of over three weeks. Your responsibility is to locate long-term housing and outpatient care for her in the community. As you meet with her one morning, you find her tearfully pleading with you to be allowed to stay longer, as she does not feel able to live independently. You are not sure that she is ready either, although the medical staff state that she is ready for discharge. You feel caught between the demands of your organization and the wishes of Bea.

    a. What three primary values are represented in your thinking about Bea's situation?

    b. Is this an ethical dilemma? Justify your answer.

    c. In what section of the *Code of Ethics* would you look for guidance?

    d. Apply one strategy for resolving ethical dilemmas discussed in the chapter to Bea's situation.

    e. How will you go about resolving this situation?

    f. Compare your response with other students. Do using different strategies lead to different resolutions?

8. After reading the following scenarios, consider these questions:

    a. What is the ethical issue?

    b. What are the values of the client system?

    c. Are they in conflict with your values? Society's?

    d. What strategy would you use for resolving the situation?

    e. What would you do?

After answering these questions, discuss findings with classmates.

Scenario A In a public setting over lunch, one of your co-workers begins speaking disparagingly about a challenging client. The co-worker does not use the client's full name.

Scenario B You are new to the area in which you have taken a job. Your new client, a hairdresser, offers to cut your hair.

Scenario C You are seeing a couple for marriage counseling. Both parties report that they are committed to remaining in the marriage. While you are out socially, you see the wife holding hands with someone other than her husband.

Scenario D While out with friends at a restaurant, you notice one of your clients is sitting at the next table.

Scenario E You are working with a teenage girl in a youth shelter. She reveals to you that she was raped by her neighbor, who is involved with gangs and drugs. She reports that she told her father and they agreed not to press charges due to fear of retaliation.

Scenario F Your client of six months reveals that he/she has begun to experience romantic feelings for you.

Scenario G One of your clients reports symptoms of a mental illness to you. She reports that she wanders around her neighborhood at night in the winter without appropriate clothing, is hearing voices, and refuses to take her medication or go to the hospital. You are concerned about her safety.

Scenario H You are working with a family in a family preservation program. In the home, the teenage daughter is violent towards her mother. During an altercation, the mother hit the daughter, presumably in self-defense, leaving a mark.

Scenario I You are leaving the agency for another position. On your last day, a client brings you a goodbye gift and asks if you will still call her.

Scenario J You receive an emergency call from your client. He reports to you that he just got fired from his job. He states, "I am not going to let him get away with this. He is going to be sorry. He has not seen the last of me." You know that this client has access to firearms and a history of assault.

Scenario K You receive a call from the spouse of your client. He wants to discuss his wife's case with you. The wife's chart does not contain a release of information.

Scenario L One of your adolescent clients invites you to his graduation and family party.

Scenario M A client's insurance benefits have ended but you feel she needs continued care.

Scenario N You are working with a teenage client. She reports to you that she is having sex with her boyfriend when her parents are not at home. She asks you not to tell her parents, and if you do, that she will feel as though you have betrayed her trust.

9. In a journal entry, reflect on a time when you faced a situation that challenged your personal values. What did you do? Why? How did you decide what to do? What were the results of your decision? If you could re-live the situation, would you handle it differently?

10. In a journal entry, reflect on a time where you observed a person doing something that was unethical, according to the NASW Code of Ethics. Describe the situation, and the part(s) of the Code that was violated. What did you do? Why? How did you decide what to do? What were the results of your decision? If you could re-live the situation, would you handle it differently?

CHAPTER 3

Individual Engagement: Relationship Skills for Practice at All Levels

What do I need out of a relationship? What can I give in a relationship? I am no different than any of you out there today. I have the same heart, I have the same feelings, I have the same aches and pains and the same hope and dreams that you do. I have suffered disappointment in relationships, as have you. I have been hurt too, but through all of this I have grown . . .

Resa Hayes, disability activist, in Mackelprang & Salsgiver, 2009, p. 284

Key Questions for Chapter 3

(1) How can I prepare for action with all client systems? (EPAS 2.1.10(a))
(2) What are the key interpersonal skills and techniques that I need to know to work with any client system? (EPAS 2.1.10(a))
(3) What communication mistakes can I avoid? (EPAS 2.1.10(b))
(4) How do I utilize a social justice and a human rights perspective when working with client systems? (EPAS 2.1.5)

THE ABILITY TO CREATE A RELATIONSHIP is at the very heart of social work practice. The idea of building relationships with people was probably a big part of what attracted you to social work in the first place and will likely be an abiding component that sustains your commitment. Social work scholars and practitioners have long recognized relationship as a crucial element of the profession's work with all types of client systems. Relationship building, or engagement, is the first step in the professional helping process and leads to the other processes of assessment, intervention, and evaluation.

When you think of relationships, you may first think of one-to-one partnerships that characterize much of direct practice. These relationships, however, rarely stand alone and are usually enhanced by other connections in the client system, which can include teachers, landlords, therapists, case managers, clergy, friends, and family, and anyone helping the client to reach her or his goals. Relationships are also as critical in group, family, organization, and community development work as it is in interventions with individuals. At the community and global level, relationship skills are necessary for work with decision-makers, community members, coalition partners and funders.

This chapter explores aspects of engagement, the process of building relationships across direct and indirect practice settings, and its importance to the overall success of social work practice. The first section examines the importance of listening to the situation and perspective of a client system (i.e., individual, family, group, community or organization). You will learn about interviewing skills and approaches that will both help your client share with you and help you enlist the assistance of others. This section also includes skill combinations that will help you establish productive connections with your clients. Later sections in the chapter show the engagement process through the lenses of strengths-based, social justice, and human rights practice as the perspectives that ground the work.

HEARING THE CLIENT'S SITUATION AND PERSPECTIVE

The most important moments of a social work relationship often occur at the beginning. Regardless of your agency's focus or your theoretical perspective, you first want to hear the client's situation and perspective. The length and the type of listening that you do will vary from practice setting to practice setting and agency to agency. For example, some agencies will expect you to complete a comprehensive psychosocial history that details a client's whole life, which may seem much more focused on the past than on the present. Despite this focus, you will want to prepare for your intervention work with the client system by carefully listening to them first. Quick Guide 4 provides questions to consider as you first listen to the client system.

QUICK GUIDE 4 LISTENING TO A CLIENT SYSTEM

As you listen to a client system, ask yourself the following questions:
- What brings the client system here today?
- How does the client system describe the situations, and what meaning do these situations have for them?
- What will life look like when the situation is better?
- What strengths and talents do they have?
- What are their expectations of me?
- What do they want to happen in their work with me?
- What can we accomplish together?

Although these may seem like general considerations, they are helpful in establishing the respect and affiliation that lead to successful work together. Rather than asking questions in a rote manner, you will want to demonstrate genuine curiosity in questioning, as well as your overall approach to the relationship with the client. Seeking understanding of the client's situation and perspective helps keep the conversation fresh and honest, as you are less likely to ask questions designed to confirm what you already think. You personally may have experienced frustration with people who assume they understand your thoughts or situation because they knew a lot about others' thoughts and situations in a similar situation, or have pre-formed opinions about people in your situation. It is challenging to remain open to and hear the story of your client if you have made conclusions mid-conversation based on information in a textbook or from your experience.

The ability to carefully listen is a critical social work skill because you want to hear the client's situation as she or he has experienced it, which may be different from your expectations. Relationship and listening skills are essential to a genuine approach to working with people, and are just as meaningful for work with client family members, community members, and staff as they are with clients.

For example, you may have made a connection with a client because you have heard their situation and perspective, conveyed professional and warm acceptance, demonstrated confidence and hope, and worked with your client to set tasks and goals. If one of those tasks is to help the client locate and secure housing that better suits her needs, you may want or need to work with a reluctant landlord. In such a situation you might perceive the scenario only in the client's terms—that is, you might be inclined to criticize a landlord who resists renting to your client. For this reason, in your beginning contacts with the landlord, you want to use the same relationship approach and listening skills that you used with your client. You will work to avoid stereotyping the landlord by entering the conversation with an open mind and avoid jumping to conclusions about "slumlords." You will avoid assuming that you know about the rental business based on your experience working with other landlords, and try to understand the difficulties the landlord has in maintaining rental properties in a profitable manner.

Social workers are often so invested in clients' rights that they are sometimes tempted to leap to unfounded conclusions about perceived adversaries. In some cases, that person may be the only person who can help the client; therefore, you need to put effort into developing an effective relationship. The social worker's role is to be fair, articulate, and open with all parties concerned. You will need to recognize your own biases and understand the client population.

Core Relationship Qualities

In a seminal work that still applies to social work practice, Carl Rogers (1957) defined unconditional positive regard and empathy as necessary to forming and maintaining effective professional relationships. Later, genuineness and warmth were added as essential items. These core attitudes or conditions are the basis for caring, and assist in forming a positive, non-possessive relationship with a client system.

Warmth   The demonstration of **warmth** is "non-possessive caring" (Shebib, 2003, p. 72). The expression of warmth entails the expression of caring and concern without expectations for the individual or relationship, as well as goodwill by the social worker. Examples of warmth are caring facial expressions, soothing tone of voice, and appropriate pacing of verbal interaction. Social workers also show their concern and warmth through extending courtesies, such as making sure that the client system is physically comfortable, offering them something to drink, making eye contact, and offering well-timed, appropriate humor. However, social workers will want to consider ethnic and cultural considerations about the expression of warmth, and offer flexibility in the amount of warmth demonstrated to coincide with the comfort level of the client system.

Empathy   is the "act of perceiving, understanding, experiencing, and responding to the emotional state and ideas of another person" (Barker, 2003, p. 141). **Empathy** is a core condition for all helping relationships, and social workers must develop a capacity for working with feelings, even intense feelings, without changing the subject, offering quick solutions, or moving the dialogue to the intellectual level. An empathic attitude is characterized by a willingness to learn about the emotional world of another. Suspending judgment by controlling personal biases, assumptions and reactions is a first step toward adopting empathic attitude. An essential element to empathy is the ability to enter into the emotional state of another person without actually feeling the same feelings as the person. For example, if the client has experienced a death in the family, rather than making assumptions about how the client feels and the intensity of the feeling, an empathetic stance toward the client is to attempt to understand the nature and intensity of the client's feelings about the situation. The client may have a number of reactions to the death, such as being grief-stricken, relieved, or satisfied at some sense of justice being served. A social worker can also express empathy to a colleague who experienced significant challenges in his/her work through attempting to understand the colleague's feelings about the situation. Also important is the ability to make an empathetic response by putting into words the feelings as expressed by the client. You will learn more about this later in the chapter.

Genuineness   Sincerity and honesty are essential elements of **genuineness**. Developing an effective relationship requires these elements, as well as being unpretentious, acknowledging your limitations, and providing only sincere reassurances (Barker, 2003). Being authentic and reliable provides the basis for a trusting relationship, which is the core of a helping relationship. Social workers who are genuine provide information that is timely, helpful, and accurate, and avoid hidden agendas and games with client systems (Shebib, 2003).

Unconditional Positive Regard   Each human being is considered to be "of worth whose rights and dignity are to be respected without reservation" (Barker, 2003, p. 445). **Unconditional positive regard** requires acceptance and nonjudgmentalness of client systems, regardless of whether a social worker approves or accepts individual or collective client system actions.

While these qualities must exist for a positive relationship, these qualities do not guarantee that client systems will always respond positively. That is, social workers should expect to be rejected by clients at times, despite their best efforts. For example, clients may interpret empathy as manipulation, and view genuineness as fake. A mature acceptance of the limits of possibilities will help social workers avoid burnout.

Specific Skills for the Dialogue

Communication is complex, and demonstrating oral communication skills is important to professional practice. In this section, you will learn about approaches and skills that are useful in purposeful communication with your clients. This includes both nonverbal and verbal communication skills that facilitate professional relationships with clients. Consistent with the strengths approach, the discussion below will emphasize skills used in facilitation of a dialogue with clients (Saleebey, 2013) rather than interviewing skills.

Preparing to Listen   **Attending** is a term used to describe a method of conveying interest in communicating with clients to promote exploration of ideas and challenges. Attending involves verbal and nonverbal components such as verbal following, eye contact, posture, and disciplined attention (Barker, 2003).

Prior to meeting with clients, you need to ensure that you have a physical and psychological commitment to a professional conversation in the best interest of the client. This can mean ensuring that any psychological needs you may have do not interfere with your listening to the client system. Additionally, attending means that you fully disengage from prior interactions with others before engaging with a new client system. You also need to mentally prepare yourself to avoid reacting to client system communication in a verbal or nonverbal way that conveys judgment or impatience. Third, ensure that you practice nonverbal behaviors that facilitate dialogue. See Exhibit 3.1 for nonverbal behavior guidelines.

While these are general guidelines, you will need to alter your nonverbal behaviors to match the comfort level of your client. In most cases you will want to sit relatively close to the client. When the client is not upright (i.e., the client is in a hospital bed), the social worker will usually want to minimize the height differential by sitting on a low chair at an angle to empower the client to control the amount of eye contact and full face contact.

EXHIBIT 3.1

Nonverbal behavior guidelines

Culturally competent social workers will utilize verbal and nonverbal behavior consistent with the cultural expectations of their clients (NASW, 2007b). Some modifications of these general guidelines may be needed, depending on the culture of the client.

- Turn your shoulders and legs toward the client.
- Sit with an open body position, with uncrossed arms and legs.
- Slightly lean toward the client.
- Smile and use head nodding to provide positive reinforcement.
- Maintain eye contact, within the comfort and cultural norms of the client.
- Use responsive facial expressions.
- Speak in a warm, pleasant tone.
- Give brief, encouraging comments
- Avoid the presence of large objects and heavy furniture between you and the client.

Professional working with a client at eye level

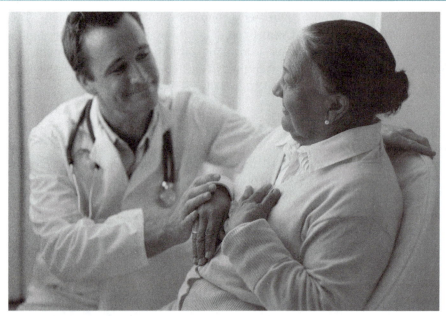

© Yuri Arcurs

A facet of the interchange that can be both highly variable and powerful is the degree of eye contact that you maintain with the client. In most cases you will make strong intermittent contact to indicate interest and connection. For clients of almost any culture, eye contact that is too constant and intense may be acutely uncomfortable; to some clients, even minimal amounts may seem intrusive. Individualizing your eye contact to maintain client comfort is an important practice skill.

Other important aspects of client interaction include dress and time of day of meeting. In general, your dress will be guided by the policies of your agency. Some agencies ask their staff to dress formally or "business casual," while others ask that staff match the style of dress of the clients, which may be informal. Clothes that are relatively modest in nature facilitate the interaction focus to be on the client, rather than on the social worker. Social workers work different sets of hours (i.e., day, evening, overnight, and weekend), depending on the nature of the work. If meeting clients in a community setting outside of the office, social workers must exercise some flexibility because there is less control over the environment of the interaction than in an office setting. In settings outside of offices, such as in client homes, community centers, and public locations, social workers must maintain professional verbal and nonverbal communication, or work to minimize distractions.

Diversity Considerations   Your preparation will include consideration of elements of culture or style—both yours and your client's—to which you need to attend. Supervision, peer consultation, and a general assessment of the particular culture in which you work will be helpful. Weigh whether your dress, posture, and language are appropriate to the person you are working with and the setting in which that work takes place. In general, the goal is to communicate respect for your client and for the nature of the event in which you are accompanying her or him. For example, in most practice contexts do not wear jeans to a courtroom appearance or use "dorm room" slang to the judge. Conversely, you might dress more informally in making an outreach home visit to a client and family, or while engaging in community organizing or community outreach. Continually be aware of the customs and contexts of the client system with whom you are working, and work to match the nonverbal behavior of the client.

Specific Interviewing Skills

Discovery-Oriented Questions   In general, your role is to hear the client's situation and perspective in the way in which she or he wants to tell it, without making assumptions and filling in information gaps yourself. **Discovery-oriented questions** are designed to invite your client to communicate her or his purposes in communicating with you and to express goals for the relationship. Discovery-oriented questions assist you in getting to know the client, and they can put the client at ease. Such a process may mean waiting a minute after you make welcoming introductions to allow your client an opportunity to begin. If she or he does not take that cue, you can invite her or him with such phrases as, "Where would you like to begin?" or, "Can you tell me what brings you here?" Some clients may be prepared for a much more directive stance on your part, so you may need gently to encourage their ownership of the dialogue.

Silence   As you dialogue with a client, moments of silence should be permitted. There are many interpretations of silence, and some people feel more comfortable with silence than others. While some practitioners and clients struggle with their ability to allow silence in a dialogue, you will want to develop a comfort with silence. Exhibit 3.2 describes the possible meanings of silence.

During silence, you can attend to the silence through the use of eye contact, maintaining your psychological focus on the client, maintaining strong nonverbal focus (i.e., avoid shifting your body, checking your watch, or other means of communicating discomfort), and using self-discipline to minimize external and internal distraction. Conversely, some silences should be broken by the social worker to discern the meaning of the silence or to shift to another topic. Silence during your dialogue can be encouraged to allow for self-reflection and for slowing the pace of the conversation. Use of silence can also lead clients to answer their own

---

EXHIBIT 3.2

Meanings of silence

There are at least six meanings to silence:

1. *The client is thinking.* Some clients need more time than others to gather and organize their thoughts. Allowing time for this helps clients feel empowered, and worthy of the patience of the social worker.
2. *The client is confused.* Your questions may be unclear, or clients are unsure what you expect from them. If you suspect this, you might try asking whether the client is confused and needs the explanation or question again. Clients may demonstrate confusion or uncertainty during the beginning stages of the relationship or time together.
3. *The client is experiencing uncomfortable thoughts and/or feelings.* Providing silence gives the client time to process pain or anxiety, and consider proceeding further in the discussion. If you think the client is silent because of powerful emotions, you may wish to provide empathy. A statement such as, "I sense that the topic of your daughter's life provokes some strong feelings," provides support for the client and conveys understanding.
4. *The client is working to develop trust with you.* Silence provides clients with a sense of dignity and control over their lives, a way to avoid rejection, and a way to maintain control over the conversation. To move the relationship toward more openness, you could proceed slowly with a discussion of less personal matters, or you might choose to raise the issue of trust directly with clients.
5. *The client is a quiet person.* You might utilize open-ended questions to draw out the client, or, in a supportive manner, discuss her or his silence directly in terms of your working relationship. Consider using other methods for the discussion, as some clients are more expressive when combining an activity with a discussion, journaling or when using the arts.
6. *The client has achieved closure.* If you think this may explain the client's silence, you can ask the client if there is anything else to discuss at the moment.

questions and discover their own next steps toward a resolution (Shebib, 2003). The appropriate length of silence between the social worker and the client must be determined by the situation and context. If, for example, a client is giving extensive thought to a question asked by the social worker, a long silence may be appropriate. Long silences may not be appropriate in settings where the social worker may only have a few minutes with each client, such as some hospital or school settings, or when a client is clearly suicidal or homicidal. Ultimately, professional judgment must be the guide to interpreting and responding to silence.

Example:

Social Worker: *You mentioned that your daughter was really angry at you the other morning, and you had a fight before she left for school. What was the argument about?*

Client: *Well, I think she and I. . . . .(lapses into silence for a minute). (The client begins to cry).*

Social Worker: (After a few minutes). *This argument really upset you.*

Following Responses This type of response gives clients immediate feedback that their message has been heard and understood. This immediate feedback can be conveyed through paraphrasing, summarizing, conveying empathy, and showing attentiveness through short verbal statements and questions such as "Go on," "I see," and "Can you tell me more?" (Barker, 2003). You will use **following responses** to provide only enough response to inspire the client to continue speaking. Providing a more complete response at the time may interrupt the client's direction and distract the client from fully sharing her or his situation and/or perspective.

Paraphrasing Expressing an idea of the relevant points of the immediate past statement of the client in your own words is **paraphrasing**. When the social worker states the essence of the client statement, clients are assured that the social worker heard and understood them accurately. Paraphrasing can also assist clients to clarify their own thoughts to them (Barker, 2003). After paraphrasing, you can invite the client to correct you if you are mistaken. An invitation to correct can communicate both that you care enough about them to want to accurately understand their situation and perspective, and that you recognize that you may have the wrong understanding of the specific issues at hand. Paraphrasing is presented without judgment and without an attempt to solve any issues. There is no attempt to add meaning to or change the meaning of the client's statement (Shebib, 2003).

Example:

Client: *I don't really get what is going on. I mean, I put food on the table, keep a roof over our heads, and try to keep her going to school. I don't understand what her problem is!*

Social Worker: *You are working really hard to provide for her, and cannot understand what your daughter is talking about.*

Client: *Yeah! She is skipping school, running off, and now I am in trouble!*

Social Worker: *In other words, she is not grateful for everything you are doing for her. In fact, she is getting you in hot water with the law.*

To avoid monotony, social workers can use a variety of lead-ins for paraphrasing, to include the following:

As I understand it . . .

It sounds a little like . . . As I hear it . . .

The picture I am seeing is . . .

Clarifying   **Clarifying** is closely related to paraphrasing, but the social worker is directly asking for client feedback to clarify a point. Clarifying could be used at the end of a paraphrase. For example, the worker might say, "What I understand you to be saying is. . . . Is that right?" Clarification contributes to understanding the uniqueness of the client's message rather than generalizing or framing it in a way that matches your own perceptions. Clarifying increases the accuracy of your assessment while communicating a respect for the complexity of the client. Clarification may be needed at any point in the planned change process, especially to clarify each other's intent, interpretations, and meanings. For example, a client may demonstrate tearfulness or giddiness that you might assume is joy, but the tears may also be a sign of regret, loss, or confusion. Clarifying the meaning of a client's communication is an important component of the work.

Example:

Client: *The last time she ran off, she told me that she was never coming back, and that she hated me. Can you believe that?*

Social Worker: *Did I get this right? You are saying that she refuses to ever come back home?*

Client: *Yeah. What does she think, that she can live at a friend's house forever?*

Summarizing   A summary can provide closure and consensus either after a segment of the session is complete or at the conclusion of the whole session. A summary is a way of confirming your understanding of the client's message thus far and checking the validity of your assumptions. **Summarizing** can also help to establish organization for the entirety of your work together as well as frame a particular interaction or series of interactions. In situations in which the issues evoke significant client emotion, or in which the work is directed at some complex task, summing up the interaction can demonstrate manageability and hopefulness. Summing up can provide both you and your client with a snapshot of the topics discussed thus far, which can help to clarify the future direction of the dialogue. Summarizing can also assist to focus a conversation that wanders off topic.

Examples:

Social Worker to Client: *So far we have talked about your job responsibilities and my responsibilities, and how they overlap. We have discussed this vaguely in prior staff meetings, but no one has really picked up on the idea that this is a problem because we are wasting some time. Do you agree with this?*

Social Worker to Client: *Let me try to sum up our discussion so far. Your daughter has run away many times, and refuses now to come home. As far as you can tell, you have not done anything to cause her to run away and skip school. No one at the school believes that you are trying to fix the problem. Is that a fair summary so far?*

Social Worker to Client: *You have been working to get this street fair organized, but you are really in need of some people from the business community to get involved in the organizing and recruiting phase. Do you agree?*

Direct, Closed Questions   Direct [closed questions] encourage the client to provide factual information in a concise manner, and can be helpful in gaining specifics about behaviors, such as frequency, duration, and intensity. This type of question can be answered "yes" or "no," or with a numerical answer. While such questions do not encourage clients to open up and share, they are useful in situations in which precise information is needed. These situations include times when you will need a numerical number to get a sense of the situation, or involve dangerous conduct or some imminent threat of harm that must be dealt with directly in order to ensure safety. An example of a situation in which you would seek concrete information is a situation in which a client is expressing an intention of hurting her or himself or someone else and you need to know if the client has a real plan to engage in the dangerous behavior (for example, suicide) and the means to carry out the plan (Shebib, 2003).

Examples:

Client: *I have not eaten in quite a while.*

Social Worker: *How many days has it been since you had a meal?*

Community Member: *We had a community organizer working on health care in this neighborhood a while back.*

Social Worker: *For how many years did the organizer work in this neighborhood?*

Open-Ended Questions   Open-ended questions are designed to elicit extensive answers (Barker, 2003). While both open- and closed-ended questions are useful for social workers, open-ended questions are especially helpful at the beginning of a dialogue to encourage client systems to share their experiences and perceptions in the manner which is most comfortable to them, and in the way that makes the most sense to them.

Examples:

Client: *My brother and I always fight after school.*

Social Worker: *What are your fights like?*

Community Member: *We are trying to push the drug dealers out of our community.*

Social Worker: *How do the drug dealers affect the neighborhood?*

Indirect Questions   **Indirect questions** are questions phrased as sentences, rather than questions. Indirect questions allow clients the freedom to choose to respond or not, as well as provide flexibility in the type of response. In a conversation, mixing direct and indirect questions can help clients to feel less pressured and avoid monotony in the types of questions asked (Barker, 2003).

Examples:

Client: *I would like to save some money to buy a house some day.*

Social Worker: *I wonder how you would be able to save money, given all of your responsibilities.*

Client: *My teacher is picking on me! She punishes me for things that other kids get away with!*

Social Worker: *Wow! That sounds really upsetting. It must be so hard to try to get your work done in class while you are worrying about your teacher looking over your shoulder all of the time.*

Empathic Communication   **Empathic communications** assist client systems to identify and label their feelings, as well as provide the support to process feelings that previously were overwhelming. Social workers must, therefore, gain familiarity with the range of feelings, and become skilled at accepting feelings at face value, rather than placing judgments on feelings or demonstrating disapproval about client feelings (Shebib, 2003). To demonstrate empathy, social workers identify the feelings expressed as well as communicate their understanding of the feelings to the client. Social workers also must be aware of their own emotional state at the start of a relationship, so that the social worker is aware of the potential impact of her or his emotional state on the interaction with the client (Shulman, 2009a).

Three types of empathy are: (a) basic empathy, in which the social worker mirrors clients' statements; (b) inferred empathy, in which the social worker makes guesses about feelings based on clues in clients' statements; and (c) invitational empathy, in which the social worker encourages clients to talk about their feelings. Invitational empathy provides an opening for the clients to talk about feelings, without making a demand to do so (Shebib, 2003).

Example of basic empathy:

Client: *I am ready to kill my daughter. This whole thing is very embarrassing. I have not done anything wrong!*

Social Worker: *So you are angry with your daughter for putting you in this situation where you have to defend yourself.*

Example of inferred empathy:

Client: *My husband tells me that I am no good, and beats me all the time. But last week, he started beating my daughter too!*

Social Worker: *This is a really tough situation. I suspect that you might have been scared at what he might do to her.*

Example of invitational empathy: Client: *My son died in a fire last week.*

Social Worker: *Oh, I am so sorry for your loss! A lot of people in your situation might feel in shock about their sudden loss.*

A common challenging scenario with beginning social workers and the use of empathic communication is the challenge of working with clients who are older than they are who have had different types of life experiences. For example, a young social worker who does not have children may be working with a mother of several children. If the social worker is asked whether she has any children, the social worker may be tempted to respond defensively by talking about her training, or suggest that they are not here to talk about her background, but instead about the situation with the mother. Instead, this scenario provides the opportunity to utilize inferred empathy by thinking about the likelihood that the client might be wondering about her ability to understand the client's situation. A response of, "No, I do not have any children. Are you wondering whether I am going to be able to understand what it is like for you to raise your children? I am wondering that too, and I am wondering if you will explain it to me so I can understand?" might help to uncover the true concern that underlies the question (Shulman, 2009a).

As mentioned earlier, when clients experience or verbalize emotions, sometimes the use of silence is the best response. When you sit with a person who is experiencing powerful emotions and simply wait until that person is ready to speak, you are respecting her or his pace of processing feelings. In a profession characterized by verbal purposefulness, respecting your client's silence can be a challenge. Clients generally experience this process as non-pressuring, accepting, and highly respectful. This silence can be needed at any point in the planned change process (i.e., engagement, assessment, intervention, or termination and evaluation).

Avoiding Communication Pitfalls

Communication is an art and a skill. When dialoguing with client systems, social workers need to keep in mind the possibility of creating communication errors. Some of the more common errors are described below:

Jargon   Social workers, like most professionals, have their own **jargon**, or verbal shortcuts, to describe their activities that can be confusing to clients. Jargon can include abbreviations, distinctive words, and routines. You are encouraged to keep your communication with clients as free from jargon as possible (Shebib, 2003).

Examples of jargon:

Social Worker: *After the intake process, you will be on level one for a week. Then your DJO will assess you, and decide whether you can go to level two or you need to go back to court.*

Social Worker: *We have been discussing my ecomap and genogram for some time, so I am now redirecting the discussion.*

Leading Questions   The way in which a question is asked can shape the response. **Leading questions** manipulate client systems to choose the preferred answer. Leading questions can mask the preferred approach of the social worker. Clients who have a need to be liked and/or those who are compliant are especially vulnerable to leading questions (Shebib, 2003).

Example of leading questions:

Social Worker: *Given all that you have tried in the past, don't you think it is time to call the police to get the drug dealers out of the neighborhood?*

Client: *Well, I guess so.*

Social Worker: *Do you want to call now to report what you just saw?*

Excessive Questioning   While questions are an essential part of the helping dialogue, the asking of questions also puts the social worker in control of the dialogue. Client systems can feel resentful of answering questions, which can interfere with the relationship. Employing a diversity of responses can avoid a situation where clients feel interrogated. When dialoging with client systems, mixing different types of questions with empathic communication, summarizing, silence, and other types of approaches may help to avoid defensiveness, frustration, avoidance, and other responses that interfere with building a relationship. In those situations in which the social worker must ask many questions, it may be helpful to have a periodic break to check in with the client to convey respect and recognition that the questioning may be taxing (Shebib, 2003).

Example of check-in:

Social Worker: *I have asked a lot of questions of you today. How are you doing so far?*

Multiple Questions   Asking two or more questions at the same time, or **multiple questions**, can be problematic, because the client can become confused. If the questions are complementary, or the second question clarifies or adds to the first question, the multiple questions are not a problem.

Example of complementary multiple questions:

Social Worker: *What happened after the police arrived? What did the police do?*

Irrelevant Questions   Social workers need to have a clear idea of the purpose of the dialogue, and avoid asking **irrelevant questions**, which are questions that do not relate to the topic at hand. While you might be curious about details of situations or perceptions, you must consider the relevancy of the information before asking a question.

> Examples of irrelevant question:
>
> Client: *My boyfriend broke up with me for the second time this week. He already asked my friend out!*
>
> Social Worker: *How did he tell you that he wanted to break up?*
>
> Client: *My husband and I have been swingers for several years, and now he tells me that he wants to stop. I don't want to stop – I really enjoy swinging.*
>
> Social Worker: *How often do you two swing?*
>
> Client: *My mother wants me to wear clothes that are so out of style and boring. I don't want to wear her stupid clothes!*
>
> Social Worker: *Exactly what type of clothes does she want you to wear?*

Using Children or Neighbors as Interpreters or Translators   In an effort to communicate respectfully and effectively with clients from all ethnic, cultural and linguistic backgrounds, social workers have a responsibility to provide services in the language chosen by the client, which may include the use of qualified language interpreters (for example, certified or registered sign language interpreters). Interpreters generally need proficiency in both English and the other language, as well as orientation and training. At a minimum, social workers also have a responsibility to ensure that interpreters maintain confidentiality, are properly trained to the ethics of interpreting in a helping situation, and understand key terms and concepts specific to agency programs. Therefore, the use of children or neighbors as translators is problematic, and should be avoided. Social workers may need to prepare themselves for work with various populations by learning at least the basics of another language and customs of another culture, and completing training about how to work with professional interpreters who are linguistically and culturally competent (NASW, 2007b).

Integrating the Core Qualities and Skills in Dialogue and Interviewing

Social work practice activates the core qualities and skills through dialogue and interviews. Interviews are "purposeful conversations between social workers and clients . . ." (De Jong, 2008, p. 539). While many skills are important to social work, meta-analysis of controlled research studies indicate that relationship factors may be more important to positive client change than specific practice models used. Social workers spend more time in dialogue and interviewing client systems than any other professional activity, including individuals, couples, families, small groups, in supervision, organizational task groups, and with colleagues in other organizations (De Jong, 2008).

ARTICULATING PURPOSE: SOCIAL WORKER ROLE AND AGENDA

In addition to demonstrating the core qualities and basic skills, social workers must be able to articulate the purpose of their involvement with the client. Transparency refers to social workers' communication about the intention of their involvement, and displays a lack of an agenda for the client (Miller, 2011). More specifically, transparency can be demonstrated through a social worker's openness in discussing the reason why a particular question or line of questioning was asked. This kind of openness can help the client understand the social worker's thought process about the client's situation and address possible obstacles in the working relationship. Transparency helps to remove the mystery from the work and lessen the distance and power difference that may exist between the worker and client. Social workers who are transparent with their clients can, if asked, acknowledge that they are a student who will leave at the end of the year, or are young and have no children, or are not a person of color.

The beginning of the professional relationship is often the most appropriate time to articulate your purpose through a clear, concrete description of roles or job responsibilities, as well as describe the types of activities that are outside of your roles and responsibilities. For example, if you are a court advocate for a family violence shelter, you will want to be clear with your clients about the type of work that you do as an advocate, and that you cannot provide counseling, medication, or other types of services for them or their children.

On a more subtle level, the **overall purpose** of the work should also be transparent and explicit. It is sometimes tempting to engage the client in work on one issue and attempt, somewhat surreptitiously, to work on other issues you may think are more worthy. For example, if you and your client agree to work on the client's troubling relationship with school authorities regarding her child, you will focus on this task without trying to covertly intervene in her parenting style, or her negative relationships with men or any other issue. To maintain a genuine and honest relationship with clients requires that you are open about the jointly agreed-upon direction of the work, the methods you are employing, and the goal of your intervention. If you believe that another construction of the issue is more relevant or that the goals should be different, you should raise this issue early as a tentative point of negotiation about the nature and scope of the work. You would then take your cue from the client's response. Avoiding secret agendas is important to enhance the overall genuineness of the initial engagement, which will make a great deal of difference to the client's sense of being valued and accepted in the relationship.

This respectful stance regarding the client is one way to demonstrate a strengths-based approach. The following section will elaborate on the strengths approach in the engagement process.

MOVING FROM SPOTTING DEFICIENCY TO RECOGNIZING STRENGTHS

A central hallmark of the profession is the **strengths perspective**, or an orientation that emphasizes client systems' resources, capabilities, support systems, and motivations to meet challenges and overcome adversity to achieve well-being (Barker, 2003). The strengths approach to engagement can be challenging due to the need to identify and intervene in practice-based challenges. Social work as a profession developed during the late 1800s, in which moral conversion was a focal point. Poverty was often seen as a reflection of moral deficiency or laziness rather than as a structural failing that places and maintains people in adversity. As professional fields of helping, including psychology, developed more sophisticated and complicated assessment schemes (including the *Diagnostic and Statistical Manual of Mental Disorders DSM IV-TR Fourth Edition,* the first edition of which was published in 1958), the focus on pathology became more pervasive. Although social workers have a long history of recognizing their clients' strengths, this emphasis on pathology, problems, or dysfunction is deeply embedded in the culture and the traditions of the helping professions. An emphasis on pathology also persists in the current social service delivery system. Agencies often offer services around specific types of problems (for example, substance abuse or major mental illnesses), and these problems define the focus of the agency. Given the agency's purpose and milieu, developing the ability to focus on strengths when meeting a client may seem like an enormous challenge.

Nevertheless, when there is support for, and commitment to, a departure from illness-based models, social workers can implement strategies based on client strengths rather than deficiencies. For example, an increasingly visible body of literature reflects a different perspective from the various models of deficit, damage, or blame. Much of this literature focuses on **resiliency**, or "the human capacity to deal with crises, stressors, and normal experiences in an emotionally and physically healthy way" (Barker, 2003). Resiliency is an important area of potential strength in client systems, and social workers consider resiliency in assessing the coping skills of their client systems. Most people raised or living in the most daunting of circumstances survive, and sometimes even thrive. Communities can demonstrate resiliency after a traumatic event or natural disaster by processing grief and shock through utilizing the resources of community systems and assets to hold events and rituals, help victims, and demonstrate the ability to cope and function as a community. Resilient client systems can generate strengths and coping capacities even in some of the most oppressive and compromising scenarios.

In the first encounter with a social worker, client systems are often wondering about several aspects of the social worker, such as whether the social worker will be trustworthy, whether the social worker will be understanding or judgmental, and whether the social worker will be able to help. Clients are also often unsure whether they really need or want any assistance (Shulman, 2009a). Strong engagement skills and methods, discussed below, will assist to build an effective professional relationship and overcome these complex challenges to working together. For example, sending a clear nonverbal and verbal message that you will not make negative judgments or try to change the client as a person, but rather will affirm their aspirations and work to make them a reality can help build client trust. Engaging in enjoyable activities together, when possible, and seeking to incorporate humor, joy, and laughter into the helping process is another strengths-based approach. Lastly, being sensitive to cultural factors, honoring diversity, and seeking to assist people in activities and involvements that hold meaning for them will serve you well in a great variety of practice settings (Kisthardt, 2013).

Skills and Methods

Rapp and Goscha (2006) identify a series of methods for building a strengths-based relationship. Beyond exhibiting the core conditions described earlier, they suggest mirroring, contextualizing, self-disclosure, accompaniment, reinforcement, and celebration.

Mirroring   Reflecting the client's talents and capabilities so that the client can see himself or herself from a strengths perspective is called **mirroring**. The worker focuses on these strengths, emphasizing their presence in the client's daily life and stressing their importance. This metaphor counters the negative reflections many clients have of their own value and worth. While all mirrors distort images to some degree, the social worker uses a mirror that is more positively focused while building the relationship and throughout work with the client. For example, if family members identify specific issues that they experience with one another, the social worker might reflect on the care that they are demonstrating for one another by wanting to improve their family functioning, rather than split up the family.

Contextualizing   Social workers use **contextualizing** to put clients' issues into the wider community, society, and/or global context in order to discourage them from blaming themselves for their problems, and encourage them to take environmental and structural roots of their challenges. For example, when landlords discriminate against clients of the mental health system simply because they do not want "those people" to live in their building, some clients blame themselves for somehow being undesirable. In such a situation, the social worker can explore with the clients the effects of stigma in an intolerant society or provide evidence that they are acceptable to other, more positive landlords. In another example, a social worker might point out to a community group experiencing drug dealing and violence that their community is struggling with funding cuts to city social and community services. Rather than blaming themselves completely for their problems, community residents must also consider that their security challenges are at least partly rooted in lack of sufficient city-sponsored security resources and a lack of sufficient job opportunities. The goal of contextualizing is to point out the environmental roots, causes, and contributions of client system challenges, while working with clients to maximize their strengths and take advantage of their opportunities and resources toward addressing their specific challenges.

Self-Disclosure   The extent to which social workers should reveal their feelings, values, and personal information to their clients remains a controversial issue in social work practice and is called **self-disclosure** (Barker, 2003). Rapp and Goscha (2006) point to the inequities of expecting clients to disclose the most personal and profound aspects of their hearts and souls, while professionals sit back and reveal little about themselves. A strengths-based approach, based on normalizing the relationship in genuine ways, calls for some degree of worker self-disclosure to establish trust, validate the quality of the relationship, and model effective ways of managing emotions for the benefit of the client. Although there are no accepted standards governing the amount and nature of the disclosure, social workers should only reveal themselves to clients to assist to achieve a client goal. Social workers should carefully consider the purpose of self-disclosure, and avoid self-disclosure that strictly meets their personal needs and goals, such as for expressing strong feelings about something. For example, the social worker might share a story from her or his life to demonstrate appropriate behavior in a specific situation to meet a client goal of learning this skill, rather than for bragging about how well they handled a certain situation.

While caution should be exercised about self-disclosure, social workers can strive to foster open communication and a caring relationship, which may mean sharing relatively unimportant aspects of one's life routinely with clients, while maintaining a focus on the client. You can, for example, converse with clients by talking about your hobbies and interests, or share information about your familial or parenting status if asked. Social workers are warm and genuine with client systems and avoid strict formality by sharing information about themselves to further the relationship, yet avoid self-disclosure of significant information unless it serves a therapeutic purpose or is designed to achieve a client goal.

Accompaniment   Rapp and Goscha (2006) advocate for accompanying a client in the performance of a task. This can be **accompaniment** in the literal sense of going with a client to court or to a landlord's office, and/or in a metaphorical sense, as in joining the client in her or his journey of change. Rapp and Goscha (2006) acknowledge the concern for dependence on the social worker that can emerge when accompanying clients. Social workers may wonder whether helping a client through a task is serving the best interests of the client in the long-term, or whether clients should be encouraged to complete tasks on their own most of the time. The need or desirability for accompaniment should be assessed critically according to the specifics of the situation. Social workers should take into account such aspects of the situation as the emotional, physical, and intellectual capabilities of the client, as well as the working relationship with the client, when making decisions about accompaniment. Social workers should be careful to take cultural considerations into account as well, and avoid making decisions about clients based on *their* cultural or personal sense of the optimal level of independence, especially when the client either does not share or cannot attain their ideal. When literal accompaniment is not appropriate, the metaphor of accompaniment can be vital to the working relationship and resonate with the client long after the work is over.

Reinforcement and Celebration   To carry out a strengths-based approach successfully, the social worker needs to understand the meanings the client attaches to such behaviors as praise or recognition of particular events or accomplishments. **Reinforcement**, a procedure that strengthens the tendency of a response to recur, can assist in building a strong working relationship, but the social worker cannot make assumptions about the client system's view of reinforcement (Barker, 2003). Some expressions of support, for example, can affirm one person and embarrass another. By the same token, indiscriminate praise can be insulting, whereas purposeful, immediate, and specific positive feedback may be highly valued and strengthening. Although nearly everyone wants to feel appreciated, the worker needs to anticipate client responses in a particular context.

Logistics and Activities

To establish a collaborative relationship with the client, the strengths-based social worker will give the client the choice of the location, day, and time to meet, and, if possible, offer the option of meeting in a community location, rather than an office setting. Some clients may request that the meeting be held at their home, either because they have small children, they lack transportation, or they are simply more comfortable in this setting. As is true of much of social work, the client's choice of location depends on the nature of the contact, the context of the interaction, concerns regarding confidentiality, and the agency purpose.

Incorporating recreational or fun activities can also help the client to engage and feel comfortable. Some clients, such as children, adolescents, immigrants, and others, may struggle with sharing aspects of themselves in an office, face-to-face setting, and may be more comfortable in another setting, or talking while engaged in another activity. For this reason, playing basketball with an adolescent, playing a board game with a group of children, or walking in the woods with a client struggling with mental health issues can create an environment that is much less intense (and therefore more tolerable for some clients) than an interview-type meeting in an office.

An interesting variation on this theme is a strategy of using metaphors (Sims, 2003). This approach assumes that some clients will use metaphors as a way to communicate without exposing the specific details of their own lives until they are ready to do so. For example:

Client: (Her small business has recently failed) *Have you ever thought about how trying new activities is kind of like wearing a new pair of shoes?*

Social Worker: *With new shoes, you are never really sure whether they are going to fit or be comfortable.*

Client: (looking at the social worker while biting her lip and nodding).

Social Worker: *Wearing new shoes can make you feel maybe a little vulnerable.*

Client: *I just want to wear my old slippers! I know they fit me.*

Social Worker: (Nodding in agreement) (Gives her a chance to be more direct if she is ready to be)

Client: *It does not always feel good to feel vulnerable.*

(Sims, 2003).

As you can see, the social worker responds by using the same metaphors that the client suggests, and is sensitive to the client's readiness to be more direct. The purpose of using and encouraging metaphors is to respect the client's communications rather than seeing them as a form of resistance. The social worker can use the information conveyed by the client to support the client's efforts to communicate the depth of her or his experience. This strategy honors the client's meaning and validates her or his approach to engagement in the work.

RECOGNIZING AND ARTICULATING POWER

Social work practice almost always involves issues related to power. The relationship of power, or the possession of resources that enable a client system to accomplish a task or to exercise influence and control over others (Barker, 2003), may not be readily apparent to you. Because you are eager to engage with clients in their struggles and help them achieve their goals, you may not immediately see why a discussion about power is relevant. In most instances, the obstacles clients face involve power, and the effective management of power can benefit the client. Power is a component in many types of social work relationships, from political advocacy to one-to-one counseling.

Sources of Power

There are four sources of power with which social workers engage: agency resources, expert knowledge, interpersonal power, and legitimate power (Hartman, 1994).

Agency Resources Social service agencies have access to and control over a number of resources. These include **tangible resources**, such as clothing or money for emergency housing, and **intangible resources**, such as individual counseling and education groups. Traditionally, social workers and administrators have allocated resources to client groups or individuals depending upon their evaluation of the fit with agency purposes and funding source(s) guidelines and constraints. However, some contemporary organizations, and even some federal programs, have experimented with arrangements that empower clients to determine and control the resources they receive. For example, an agency that serves children with disabilities might encourage the child's family members to identify the services they need, both within and outside the agency, rather than undergoing an agency-driven assessment in which a professional tells them what they need. By the same token, some Medicaid provisions include a waiver that permits a family member (usually a parent) to act as case manager, thereby coordinating services for the child and eliminating the costs of professional case management. Services that the family chooses and obtains with assistance are called **client-directed resources**. The concepts of power sharing and client-consumer advocacy threaten the notion that social workers and administrators should continue to control the disposition of agency resources. Most agencies struggle with the idea of giving up their authority in this arena.

Expert Knowledge Many social workers find that some clients see them as possessing **expert knowledge** because they have credentials and experience. Social workers can counter that assumption in part by using the strengths perspective to clearly articulate that clients are the experts on their own lives, and work to develop a partnership with clients that focuses on reaching client-defined goals.

Interpersonal Power The personal attribute characterized by the ability to build strong relationships, develop rapport, and persuade people is known as **interpersonal power**. Both social workers and clients may have this type of personal power, which is closely related to charisma. Although the social worker's interpersonal power can benefit clients when used to attain resources or access to services, the social worker's interpersonal power can also perpetuate the power imbalance between the client and social worker by diminishing the client's efforts to reclaim power. Social workers must strive to reduce their interpersonal power by establishing more egalitarian relations and genuine collaboration with clients (Hartman, 1994).

Legitimate Power The term **legitimate power** refers to legal power to perform actions to control the behavior of others. Social workers need to be very careful about this power. The responsibility to protect clients and others (as in cases of child or elder abuse) must be acknowledged, but social workers must also recognize that legitimate power must be exercised very carefully, and have limits. Social workers must be careful not to replicate the power abuses of the past by exercising legitimate power beyond what is absolutely necessary to protect clients. Although social workers may choose to retain their various powers to use for individual, family, group, or community client benefit, they may alternatively try to work to change structures that impact client systems at the policy and organizational levels to empower clients.

Power in Client Lives: Jasmine Johnson

There are many other ways to think about power with clients. One approach focuses on the power relationships with which the client system is struggling that are external to the social worker relationship, either in interpersonal, community, policy, or larger cultural terms. For example, a community may be struggling to convince their local government to allocate and spend city funds on trash pickup in their area. The second involves power issues experienced directly between the social worker and the client. This vignette about Jasmine Johnson provides examples of the types of power.

Jasmine's Situation   You work in a family support agency.

> *Your client, Jasmine Johnson, is an African American mother who comes to you with a concern about parenting. Her teenage son is difficult to manage behaviorally both at home and, increasingly, at school, and Jasmine is unsure how to deal with him. He often does not seem to respect her authority, and ignores her attempts to discipline him. He is "sassy," talks back, and is occasionally quite rude to her. He ignores the limits she sets, and he does not obey school-night curfews or help with any household chores. Jasmine struggles financially to support him with only sporadic help from his father. Her job pays poorly, carries little status in the work world, and does not provide extra money for either her or her son to enjoy any recreational activities. Overall, Jasmine struggles with low self-esteem.*

Jasmine and Power Relationships   At first glance, Jasmine's challenges appear to be strictly personal. Jasmine knows that she does not feel good about herself or her situation, and she assumes she needs to improve at something. You might assume that she needs to address her self-esteem issues, or you might even conclude that she is depressed and needs medical attention. Yet, from another vantage point, it is likely that power, or lack of it, plays an important role in her experience. She is a woman who performs many interpersonal roles (i.e., ex-wife, single mother, daughter, worker, friend, and neighbor) and a member of a cultural group that has experienced pervasive and persistent oppression in our culture for more than 300 years.

These external conditions and stressors can be deconstructed and examined toward the goal of empowerment (Broussard, Joseph, & Thompson, 2012). Although

Jasmine may have interpreted her experiences as signs of her own deficiencies, she has also exhibited remarkable resilience in dealing with disadvantage and oppression. She has managed to survive in trying circumstances that have had a far-reaching political repercussion in her life. If she is to be empowered, she will need to recognize those political events in which her life is embedded. You can bring these events to her consciousness through purposeful (and skillful) articulation.

This does not mean that Jasmine's own sense of her problem is erroneous and that the real problems are racism and sexism. Rather, as a social worker, you want to validate her experience and recognize the meaning she makes of it. However, Jasmine has genuine feelings of inadequacy, and she has experienced the negative side of the power differential. That realization can open many doors. For example, Jasmine may begin to separate her feelings of inadequacy from her sense of identity and start to look at her experiences as a function of her social location. In turn, this new perspective might inspire her to engage in some action, such as forming an informal support group for single, African American mothers. This group can share stories and experiences, provide day care arrangements for one another, or coordinate grocery shopping. Adopting a different outlook also might encourage Jasmine to become a spokesperson for more stringent requirements regarding child support payments or increased benefits for working women with children. The possibilities for Jasmine's roles and activities are endless, and these types of activities may affirm Jasmine's experience even as they are instrumental in changing the quality of life for her and others.

Jasmine and the Social Worker   There are nearly always noticeable differences between social workers and clients. As long as the profession sustains the concept of the social worker as the expert, there will be a felt power differential based solely on distinct roles in the social worker-client relationship. There are also likely to be additional differences related to gender, age, race, socio-economic status, and other dimensions of diversity. These differences, if perceived as problems, can complicate the engagement process.

For example, Jasmine may find it challenging to think of social work students or younger workers in general as a genuine source of help to her. Students may come from a different cultural or ethnic background, and they may not have partners or children. They may also seem to her to be so privileged by their race and education that she thinks that they cannot relate to any experiences in her life. Yet, social workers are supposed to be experts, and as such they have some level of power that she may resent, admire, or barely recognize. In most cases, these differences related to worker and client roles or attributes are, at the core, about power and power differences. It is necessary, then, to discuss these differences openly when they get in the way of the work. Simply raising them can open up the whole relationship. For example, in the early stages of the relationship, a social worker working with Jasmine might ask whether she has any hesitation about working together.

"Look, Mr. Cook, I know you think I'm a nice kid and that you like me," I said.

"I do like you," he confirmed.

"But you know I'm too young to have experienced what you go through every day!" I said.

Silence.

"And you may even figure that a kid like me can't help you."

Silence.

"Right?" I continued.

A nod.

"But you want to get out of this depression real bad, don't you." I said.

"I sure do," he said. Then he sighed and added, "I'm probably being foolish. You

 youngsters are right out of school with the latest techniques. I guess I'd just be more comfortable talking to someone closer to my own age. But here I am already talking to you, aren't I? So I guess I already decided to try it out with you."

I nodded. "How about if anytime you feel uncomfortable, you say so and every time I think you may be a little uncomfortable I'll say so?" I suggested.

"It's a deal," he said.

Source: Middleman & Wood, p. 163

EXHIBIT 3.3

Recognizing and Articulating Power

The social worker might acknowledge that the two of them have experienced different life circumstances in the past and present, and ask that Jasmine be willing to tell her about her background and current life situation so that the social worker can try to help her. Asking the client to share this type of information, and giving the client the opportunity to talk about any hesitations that they may have in working together, provides the client with the opportunity to talk about differences, and the impact they may have on the relationship.

Jasmine Johnson: Conclusions Situations that involve power differentials are sometimes awkward or even embarrassing to confront, particularly for you as a student or an otherwise humble person. You may understand that the client sees you as having power simply because of your role as a helping person, an employee, or a student. At the same time, you may secretly wonder yourself about the extent to which you can help an exasperated parent who might be of a different race and remote social class, when you might not even be a parent yourself. You may feel some hesitation at working with an oppressed client when you have enjoyed so much privilege. Thus, the concept of power in the relationship can become quite complex and problematic.

When these situations arise, you might hope that the concern will pass or that clients will just trust that you know what you're doing in spite of these differences. Unfortunately, once these issues are perceived as problematic, they will not simply go away. You and your client should confront them directly through open acknowledgment and exploration. Exhibit 3.3 provides an additional case example. In this excerpt, consider the ways in which the worker addresses the issue at hand. What impact do you think this approach will have on the future of the relationship?

This vignette in Exhibit 3.3 conveys an extended message. First, the social worker addresses the immediate obstacle, namely, that the social worker is both much younger than the client and comparatively inexperienced. The social worker also paves the way for ongoing honesty in the relationship by addressing the obstacle openly and directly. The scenario is a relatively complex one in which both participants seem to feel an initial lack of power that is subsequently alleviated by open acknowledgment. Ultimately, the case suggests that there is a broader context for the work than the one-on-one issues that emerge between the social worker and client, leading to recognition of social justice and human rights issues in client stories.

VIEWING THE CLIENT SYSTEM SITUATION AND PERSPECTIVE FROM SOCIAL JUSTICE AND HUMAN RIGHTS PERSPECTIVES

When clients describe a situation that involves hardship or oppression, or is emotionally challenging, social workers use their professional skills and methods to respond to the client. However, social workers are human, and are often personally moved by the situation as well. There is something very powerful about talking directly to an individual who is sharing a powerful story with you. This experience typically creates a bond. In such circumstances, the larger perspectives of social justice and human rights may seem like remote, intellectual concepts in the face of the personal pain that your client is experiencing. Nevertheless, these perspectives provide the rationale for your practice, and they help to connect client system experiences together. The perspectives thus provide an organizing frame for your work so that your practice transcends the parameters of individual emotional responses or simple sympathy. Instead, your practice consists of carefully planned and cohesive activities in response to clear, principled commitments.

Although you will always want to recognize personal pain and respond on a human level, you will also want to go beyond the intensity of the direct relationship and see your client's experiences as social justice and human rights issues as well.

Full Participation in Culture

As discussed previously, work toward social justice is a cornerstone of social work practice and is mandated in the NASW *Code of Ethics* (2008). A number of "isms"—racism, elitism, sexism, heterosexism, ageism, and others—that you have probably already studied reflect the degree of social injustice that is prevalent in our culture. These prejudicial attitudes toward the "other" are generated by our society and suggest a discriminatory standpoint that most social workers find profoundly distasteful. The attitudes also carry concrete repercussions for individuals, families, groups, and communities that take many forms of exclusion, including exclusion from resources and limited class mobility within society. The term "exclusion from society" refers to the process through which people are unable to participate in the benefits of public and cultural resources. This inability can be felt quite literally (for example, when there is no access ramp to the public library for people with disabilities) or more indirectly (for example, when policies and poverty limit public investment in public schools). Clearly, these exclusions are injustices because they represent arbitrary allocation of access to public benefits, and are violations of the principles of human rights. Such exclusion tends to be pervasive and on all levels—individual, organizational, and structural. Quick Guide 5 examines these three levels of social and cultural exclusion. Considering client situations relative to all three levels is necessary for the practitioner's work to have an impact on larger systems, such as policies, communities, organizations, and societies. Although many practitioners see their labors in terms of individual, one-by-one achievements, the collective achievements make a difference in the larger environment. Social workers respond to clients on a personal, one-to-one level while acknowledging and addressing social injustices and human rights violations that exist on a variety of levels.

Strategies and Skills for Promoting Social Justice and Human Rights

Social justice and human rights issues call for well-organized strategies and skill sets that usually fall within the realm of policy practice. The following strategies are particularly applicable in such situations.

- Understanding the repercussions of social injustices on clients, and helping clients understand.

- Helping clients gain access to their legal entitlements through social advocacy.

- Convincing legislative bodies to adopt, amend, or repeal laws when such changes would benefit clients.

QUICK GUIDE 5

Individual Exclusion

During your dialogue, clients may make an explicit reference to the way exclusion has influenced their situation. Individual exclusion refers to the perception of being left out of or barred from participation in interpersonal situations. This situation could include, for example, that your client was a victim of racist harassment by peers in school or was dismissed by teachers as having no future because of her or his ethnicity or ability status. Other clients may not give voice to any strong or concrete sense of their own exclusion or the violation of their human rights but rather describe it as "fate" or the "way things are."

Organizational Exclusion

Like individual exclusion, organizational exclusion, the phenomenon of being prevented from participation in activities by an organization, can be obvious to clients (and others), or obscure. For example, even hiring practices that appear to be fair may actually favor some groups over others through their written or unwritten rules, regulations regarding promotions, or subtle differences in work assignments. In fact, many battles over such efforts as affirmative action arise from a concern for the organizational structures in which unjust practices and advantages have taken hold. For example, given that there is no equality in access to this country's top-rated educational institutions, the organization that automatically hires the candidate with the most prestigious degree—even when the requirements of the job do not mandate it—is engaging in preferential practices that are rooted in injustice.

Just as Jasmine Johnson interpreted her difficulties as individual failings, your clients may not be sensitized to the role that discrimination plays in their place of work. It is important in connecting and engaging with clients to recognize manifestations of organizational exclusion and work with clients regarding the meanings they attach to these life events. In some situations, this alone can be a liberating activity.

Structural Exclusion

Institutionalized arrangements such as poverty tend to maintain and perpetuate themselves. Structural exclusion refers to the interconnecting role of institutions and societal forces in preventing participation or limiting access, such as the connections among poverty, poor schools, limited achievement, limited employment options, restricted housing, poor health care, and shortened life expectancy. Recognizing poverty as a structural problem directly conflicts with presumptions about equal opportunity and the myth that anyone can get ahead. Social workers may need to work with client systems over a period of time before clients and others can begin to see the roots of their personal challenges as stemming from structural exclusion.

- Educating the community regarding certain populations, for example, giving a talk on the needs of refugee children or families with disabilities.

- Developing resources (this involves identifying and procuring resources that are needed but do not exist currently).

- Facilitating the redistribution of resources.

- Testifying in court hearings regarding issues that affect clients.

This list is by no means exhaustive, but it suggests the flavor of work focused on systems larger than the individual. These strategies do not negate the importance of individual connections with human beings on a personal level, but enrich the engagement and the worker's understanding in a way that is consistent with the complexities of people in the contemporary world.

STRAIGHT TALK ABOUT THE RELATIONSHIP: INTERPERSONAL PERSPECTIVES

Being transparent, or explicit about your work, means being clear about the restrictions you encounter as a practitioner. A goal of the work is to establish a meaningful and trusting relationship with the client system, and the tasks of discussing constraints or inviting critical evaluation may not seem very appealing. In fact, the social worker may tend to postpone or avoid them altogether. Nevertheless, attending to the boundaries of your role early in the development of the professional relationship, along with confidentiality and maintaining client privacy as discussed below, is important to developing a trusting relationship.

Confidentiality

There are at least three areas in which social workers may be required to break confidentiality, including cases of child abuse/neglect/exploitation, older adult abuse/neglect/exploitation, and when a client threatens harm to another person. First, as mandated reporters, social workers, among many human service professionals, are legally required to report cases of child abuse, neglect, or exploitation. Second, most states have mandated reporting laws for adult protective services for older adults and persons with disabilities. Third, as mentioned in Chapter 2, social workers in many states have a duty to protect as a result of the *Tarasoff II* court ruling. Legal ramifications regarding these reporting requirements may vary somewhat by state or locality; however, social workers must report incidents of abuse, neglect, or exploitation that are witnessed or described to them, and must consider taking steps to ensure the safety of a person threatened by a client.

Depending on the setting of the work, the mandate to break confidentiality can appear to be a significant obstacle to establishing a relationship of trust. For example, you may be concerned that clients will not share any information with you if told that you must call the authorities. Although this concern is legitimate, to represent yourself fairly, you must communicate your responsibility in that area early in the work. Informing clients of the limits of your confidentiality may affect the relationship in unexpected ways. Clients may understand that they need help from authorities. For example, consider the social worker who worked with a woman who struggled with substance abuse and had a difficult time keeping track of her five children, for whom she was the single caretaking parent. During the sixth meeting, she told the social worker that she felt sure she was grossly neglecting the younger children and that she often struck the oldest child "hard" when he "mouthed off" to her. After discussing this situation, she informed the social worker that she had finally confided the information *because* the social worker was a mandated reporter and she knew she could get help.

Social workers must be honest with clients about their roles and not assume that an adversarial relationship will evolve simply because of the mandated reporter obligations. Most clients who struggle with caring for their children want to be good parents. Even if the client is guarded about what she or he tells you (which you might expect), you still have significant opportunities to build a relationship. You can address the obstacles to the client's successful parenting (or caretaking for an older adult), model a genuine relationship in which you support the client's parenting competence rather than search to discover deficits, and build the foundation for further work. Adopting this approach does not suggest that the imminent safety of a child or adult should be compromised. Rather, it is a strategy of beginning to work in those countless scenarios in which there is concern but no clear mandate for legal intervention.

Privacy

Client privacy can be challenging for many reasons; for one, actions that some people consider invasive can seem caring to others. When negotiating with clients about the nature and parameters of the work during engagement, you and your client should address the issues of privacy and invasiveness. For example, a client who perceives your care and enthusiasm for the work may get the impression that you want to know everything about her or his life and become an active participant in it. If this is not your intention, you should make the client aware of this. Similarly, in a group setting, you will want to discuss plans for allowing individuals to maintain some information about themselves as private, while sharing pertinent information of their choice with the group. Being straightforward about your involvement and the parameters of privacy is important to avoid the client system feeling disappointed and perhaps even betrayed. For example, if your role involves monitoring client activities and you have established a mutual, client-driven relationship, you will likely be the initiator in situations that the client may not expect. For instance, if you have suggested that the client call you when she wants to meet again, but you then drop in unannounced "just to see how she's doing" (or to see how the children seem or if they have eaten that day), she may rightly perceive your visit as an invasion of privacy.

On a deeper level, as a practitioner in your particular role and setting, you might consider the extent of privacy to which clients are entitled. For example, in a residential or correctional setting, what is important to know? If your work involves a social control function, do your clients deserve less privacy? How does your agency's purpose affect the degree of privacy granted? These questions all relate to the importance of knowing yourself and the values, skills, and roles that you bring to the setting, and noticing how you (and/or your agency) may or may not be influenced by predominant social norms about the rights (or lack thereof) of clients.

Ongoing Evaluation

All through the engagement process, you have invested your energy and skills in establishing a solid initial connection with your client that will grow as your work together progresses. Another task you must undertake in this early stage, and throughout the work, is evaluation of the effectiveness of your efforts. Relationships can be easily misunderstood. You may be concerned that your client is hesitant to be as open as you would like, or that she or he seems uneasy in some way. Conversely, you may feel wonderful about the productive beginning of a professional relationship. In either case, it is important to find out how your client feels about your relationship and to make any needed changes in your approach that are indicated by your client's feedback. Although you are not likely to use formalized tools at this point, you will want to ask your client about how the work is going. For example, you might ask an individual client whether he or she is comfortable talking about the issues discussed thus far. How does it work for him that you are a Hispanic woman and he is a black man? Is the process of meeting with you similar to, or different from, what he thought it would be? If it's different, how does he feel about it? What can you do to be more supportive or clearer or helpful? For group work, you might ask the group for feedback about your role as facilitator or teacher. At the community level, seeking feedback from individuals and colleagues in the community as well as from committees can elicit important suggestions.

At the individual level, the process of continuously monitoring your work also applies to your engagement with the people who are significant in your client's life. You will want to validate your understanding of their role in helping to achieve your client's goals and to check for any misunderstandings. This strategy will be particularly important in situations that involve contentious feelings, such as the reluctant landlord considered earlier in this chapter. While landlords might assume that you will take sides with your client, you will want to take care not to alienate them from your client's goals.

CONCLUSION

Now that you have explored the importance of various aspects of engagement and building relationships in social work practice, you are well prepared to support your connection with your client system as you enter into the assessment arena of the work. Although you are not likely to have addressed all the issues presented here in the first interactions with client system, you have the framework to go beyond the initial connections and respond to an ongoing, dynamic association. You have taken care to anticipate the meaning for the client of your particular work together, and you will find that this dimension grows and is shaped by the nature of your shared activities and experiences.

One further caveat about skills: At first you may feel that thinking about and trying to use them interferes with your spontaneity and/or responsiveness. However, as you use the skills and develop your practice style, you will become much more relaxed in using and personalizing the skills, and develop your own style. While the engagement stage is often thought of as the beginning stage, engagement is a process that will occur throughout your work with client systems. You will continue to notice engagement dynamics, your own growth as a worker in establishing engagement, and how engagement assists your client as the work continues into the assessment, planning, and implementation of the work. In particular, the next step, assessment, will build on the relationship foundation that you build during the engagement phase.

MAIN POINTS

- The social worker's first and probably most important activity in the engagement process is careful listening to the client's situation and perspective. This activity requires the worker to initiate a skilled, purposeful dialogue that nurtures the relationship.

- Negotiating the purpose and direction of the work enhances the trust between the practitioner and client. For this process to be successful, the agenda must be open and must not contain any hidden aspects.

- Using the core relationship qualities of warmth, empathy, genuineness, and unconditional positive regard, along with strong interviewing skills, will assist the social worker to establish a strong, professional working relationship with the client system.

- Respecting the strengths and resilience of the client system has an enormous impact on the work. Respect for strength is critical in establishing the relationship, and must be pervasive throughout the relationship.

- Power and its relationship to social work practice present both obstacles and potential. The various sources of worker power, the power in client lives, and the power between the worker and the client are all part of the relationship. These sources should be recognized and articulated as explicitly as possible.

- Although client stories may appear to be private and are certainly unique, they can always be seen from the perspective of social justice and human rights. This perspective gives the entirety of the work meaning and frames your commitments.

- The worker and client should discuss the issues of confidentiality and privacy openly and directly, even if these topics make them uncomfortable. The client may not welcome some of these constraints on practice, but the worker owes it to her or him to be respectful and clear about them from the beginning.

- Evaluation of the work, including the relationship, should occur at all stages, beginning with engagement.

EXERCISES

a. Case Exercises

1. Go to www.routledgesw.com/cases. Select the Sanchez case and review the Engagement phase on the interactive case study of the Sanchez family and the tasks of that phase. With classmates, discuss the needs of the Sanchez family.
2. After completing Exercise #1, review the Client History, Client Concerns, and Goals for the Client for Alejandro Sanchez. Next, click on the "Explore the Town" (under "Case Study Tools") to review the neighborhood, review Alejandro's Critical Thinking Questions, and explore his Interactional Matrix. Consider the following scenario:

    Alejandro is one of your clients. He presents as melancholy although pleasant and respectful. He says he is "unhappy" and seems to carry with him an existential sort of sadness that relates to his family. He notes on the first interview that his father Hector was also 19 when he came to this country as an undocumented worker.

    With a classmate assuming the role of Alejandro, role-play for 10–15 minutes the scenario that you are meeting Alejandro for the first time. In the session, you attempt to engage Alejandro and begin an assessment. (The classmate who is playing the role of Alejandro should prepare by reviewing his concerns and goals, as well as his strengths.) Other classmates should observe, and consult during the role-play as needed. Afterwards, the entire class can debrief by considering the following questions:
    a. Which attending skills were used? Which were not used?
    b. Were empathic responses used? What were they? What was most challenging to you about the use of empathy?
    c. Was the social worker in the role-play able to validate his feelings of unhappiness, and identify strengths and verbally share those strengths with Alejandro? Were there other strengths that were not mentioned? How can a

social worker emphasize a client's strengths when the client is not receptive to hearing them?

d. What was the experience of the student who played the role of Alejandro? Did the student, in character, feel that the social worker demonstrated specific listening skills? Which skills?

e. What elements of Alejandro's experiences reflect social justice and human rights concerns?

3. Go to www.routledgesw.com/cases and, under the Sanchez family case, watch the videotaped interview with Emilia and the social worker. While watching the interview, note where in the interview each of the following skills were demonstrated:

a. Open-ended question

b. Closed-ended question

c. Reframing

d. Paraphrasing

e. Attending

f. Nonverbal communication

g. Clarifying

h. Summarizing

i. Empathic communication

What were the strengths of the interview and what could the social worker have done differently?

4. Go to www.routledgesw.com/cases and become familiar with the Riverton case file (under the "Assess" tab). Using the questions provided by Quick Guide 4, consider the scenario of a client coming to her first appointment with you at the Alvadora Community Mental Health Center when she is clearly drunk. In a one-two page paper, describe which of the questions might be more significant than others. Would you use some of the questions to guide your interaction? Why or why not?

b. Other Exercises

5. You are a social worker in a neighborhood community mental health center. You are awaiting the arrival of a new client, Jasmine Johnson (discussed in this chapter), who lives near the center. After you introduce yourself and she relaxes somewhat, she states, "My life is a mess; nothing I ever do is right; sometimes I think I can't go on."

Using relationship building and interviewing skills, indicate how you would respond to her statement by giving a very brief verbal (one sentence or less if possible) or a behavioral example (if appropriate) if you were:

a. Attending

b. Responding nonverbally

c. Responding with minimal verbalization

    d. Paraphrasing

    e. Clarifying

    f. Summarizing (make any needed assumptions about information provided prior to the statement above)

       What other skills do you think are important for this situation?

6. For these role-playing exercises, create groups of three students so that one is the client, one is the social worker, and one is an observer.

    a. Set a stopwatch for three minutes. The client tells the social worker a peculiar story. The social worker may not speak for three minutes. However, the social worker conveys nonverbally that the client is being heard. At the end of the three minutes, the observer provides feedback to the social worker, and the social worker and client share their perspective on the process. Each student should have the opportunity to play each role.

    b. Set a stopwatch for three minutes. The client will tell the social worker about a serious concern in their life. The social worker reacts in each of the following ways:

       1. Disinterested

       2. Inappropriate affect (forced smile, blank stare)

       3. Distracting behaviors (e.g., foot tapping, excessive gesturing, fidgeting, head nodding)

After three minutes, the client provides feedback regarding the process. Each student should have the opportunity to play each role.

7. Review the following case to prepare for a role-play: Gina is your 16-year-old female client at a local teen drop in center. Gina is usually talkative and outgoing with staff and other participants. Today you notice that Gina is sitting in the corner alone and she looks as though she has been crying. When you approach Gina and inquire about her day she wipes her eyes and says in a quiet voice, "I can't do this anymore. My parents are always fighting and I just can't take it. I am not going back there."

       For the role-playing, create groups of three students so that one is the client, one is the social worker, and one is an observer. Using the above case, the client begins the interview. The observer will buzz the social worker whenever he/she becomes aware of the social worker using the following:

    a. Excessive questions

    b. Closed-ended questions

    c. Jargon

    d. Leading questions

    e. Multiple questions

    f. Irrelevant questions

Each student should have the opportunity to play each role.

8. Using the case about Gina (provided in Exercise #7), the class instructor will take the role as Gina. Various students fulfill the role as a social worker. Each social worker will demonstrate appropriate skills for the interview. When the

helper has a point when he/she feels stuck, s/he may return to the class and the next student begins where the previous student left.

9. The instructor creates flashcards with various interviewing skills. For the roleplaying, create groups of three students so that one is the client, one is the social worker, and one is an observer. Using the case of Gina (provided in Exercise #5), during the interaction between Gina and the social worker, the observer randomly presents a card with a skill listed on it to the social worker, who must demonstrate the skill in the interaction. Each student has the opportunity to play each role. After a 10–15 minute role-play, discuss the degree to which the skills were utilized appropriately.

10. The instructor creates flashcards with various interviewing skills. For the roleplaying, create groups of three students so that one is the client, one is the social worker, and one is an observer. Using the case of Gina (provided in Exercise #7), during the interaction between Gina and the social worker, the observer selects the card on which the skill presently being used is written and creates a pile. At the end of the role-play (10–15 minutes), a pile of cards that state the skills that were used is compared to the pile of cards that state the skills that were not used. The client, social worker, and observer engage in discussion about how the skills were used, and whether any skills not used may have been appropriately used during the interaction. Each students has the opportunity to play each role.

Social Work Practice with Individuals: Assessment and Planning

Barbara, a sixteen-year-old mother of a baby, is on public assistance, and lives alone in one room. She dropped out of school when she became pregnant, her family and the father of the baby have abandoned her, and her only social contact is a neighbor who works during the day. One afternoon the young mother, lonesome and depressed, went out for an hour and left the baby alone. The baby fell off the bed and cut his head on an object, seriously injuring himself. When Barbara returned home she took him to the hospital, where the doctor in the emergency room, suspecting child abuse (maybe neglect?), referred her to the child welfare agency.

Carol Meyer, 1993, p. 22.

Key Questions for Chapter 4

(1) How can I prepare for assessment with individual client systems? (EPAS 2.1.10(b))
(2) What are the evidence-based theoretical perspectives that I will use to guide my assessment and planning with individual client systems? (EPAS 2.1.6)
(3) What are the skills that I need to have to work with an individual? (EPAS 2.1.10(b))
(4) How can I ensure that I engage in appropriate professional and personal self-care activities? (EPAS 2.1.1)

IN HER CLASSIC 1993 WORK *ASSESSMENT IN SOCIAL WORK PRACTICE,* Meyer notes that the way social workers think about such situations as Barbara's, or the conceptual boundaries they apply to them, includes many dimensions. Consider your conceptual boundaries; as you read about Barbara, what first comes to mind? Do you see her as an unfit mother? As a lonely young woman? What are the major issues you see? What do you want to know more about? Where would an assessment begin?

This chapter considers assessment, the meaning-making process that helps prioritize relevant factors and leads to appropriate action. Assessment is a key social work practice skill that involves collecting information about the client system to determine strengths as well as problems (Jordan, 2008, p. 178). We will also discuss the history of assessment, the importance of the client's goals, and approaches and skills through the lenses of theory, diversity, and diagrams. We will assess resources and explore approaches for when resources are inadequate. The chapter will conclude with a review of the planning process and two areas of challenges.

Consider several questions about Barbara's situation that Meyer (1993) poses: Is hers a case of a mother and child, a teenager without any family, a teenager subject to the rules of social institutions? Would one focus on child abuse? Child neglect? Adolescent acting-out? A teen in need of guidance about romantic relationships? A single parent in need of family planning? Loss of family and social supports? Poverty? (p. 22)

The risk in this situation is in taking too narrow a focus and overlooking key issues. The task then becomes how to acknowledge the complexity of the situation and at the same time focus with enough specificity to intervene in a helpful way. The assessment process, therefore, attempts to identify and gain insight into the situation within the client's context. At the same time, the social worker will want to discover Barbara's goals and keep them central to the process.

When you, as the social worker, begin a relationship with Barbara (or someone like her) through the engagement process, you will also consider many of the preceding questions to shape your focus in the case. Highly interconnected with engaging the client system, the assessment and planning process has already begun as you have taken the time to listen to Barbara's story and consider its meaning. Putting her story into the context of the values of social justice and human rights frames your understanding. As part of your careful listening, you will gain insight into the way in which she views her life, her goals, and ways in which you might help her achieve those goals. You may have reservations about the obstacles that seem to be in the way of the goals and priorities held by Barbara, your agency, or even the legal system. Thinking through these issues, including Barbara's strengths, is the assessment process.

A BRIEF HISTORY OF ASSESSMENT

Since Mary Richmond published her pioneer work, *Social Diagnosis*, in 1917, assessment has been a critical component of social work practice. Many contemporary social workers still consider assessment to be absolutely central to practice because it guides the worker's focus and directs the intervention. However, some criticize the language used in assessment and the implications it carries about the social worker's expertise. The idea of assessment seems to suggest that the social worker has the power to define the client's situation and to impose that definition. In actuality, the assessment of the client's current situation is framed by the client's perception of events, attitudes, and potential outcomes. The social worker's role is to gather and organize the information so she or he, in collaboration with the client, can interpret the meaning and implications of the data. A look at how the profession arrived at the word *assessment* may provide some perspective on this debate.

Since Mary Richmond introduced the term, *diagnosis*, into social work practice, the concept has been a part of the profession's history. However, diagnosis now firmly connotes a medicalized understanding of disease, dysfunction, symptoms, and the authority associated with the declaration of an illness. As the concept of diagnosis is not rooted in a strengths-based perspective, social workers may find it challenging to use the diagnostic term.

Contemporary social workers have adopted the term assessment to represent a more complete understanding of the client's context, one that focuses on strengths and resources as well as challenging areas. Assessment today is also considered a process by which clients can partner with a professional to make informed decisions about the work that can be done together. Client resources include the environment in which the client lives, and the history, culture, and traditions embedded in the life experience of the client system. Treating assessment as an act of client-focused discovery shifts the focus from professional expertise and analysis toward client definitions of the parameters for work. This process is a source of empowerment for clients.

A strengths-based approach is consistent with social work's systemic emphasis on the interface between the client and the environment. A strengths-based systemic perspective invites social workers to examine the whole person, whose many dimensions are never recognized in psychiatric diagnosis. Social workers then stress the importance of dialogue as a way of looking fully at client situations, considering their significance, hearing what goals clients have, and understanding the ways in which clients believe they can achieve these goals. This larger view of assessment assumes that the client, rather than the social worker, directs the decisions about the substance of the work. In essence, assessment has evolved into an integrative collaboration between the social worker and the client system from which the intervention flows (Jordan, 2008). In a scenario such as Barbara's, consider the complexities involved with assessment. As a result of her involvement with child protection services, she may be mandated to participate in services. Working with a client who may be reluctant or resistant requires sensitivity and possibly a longer period of time to establish rapport and build trust.

WHERE DOES THE CLIENT WANT TO GO?

Having established the importance of dialogue between the social worker and client system in the process of gaining a holistic picture of the client's situation and the client's central role in decision-making, initiating assessment then becomes the next step. Many assessment processes begin with long, detailed social histories; these histories have advantages and disadvantages. On the positive side, asking clients to talk about their life events can reveal important issues, such as their great resilience in the face of childhood abuse, that might not emerge right away but that are important to fully understand the client's situation. On the negative side, long accounts can seem intrusive, irrelevant, or even judgmental to clients as they cover personal aspects of a client's life when, for example, a single parent came only to talk about a child care allowance so she can attend a class. Such histories may also seem to emphasize previous difficulties or situations that the client would prefer to leave in the past. Finally, they can appear to be driven by the social worker or agency or even the profession itself, because they seem disconnected and remote from whatever sense of urgency the client brings to the first interaction.

For example, Barbara may find an extensive history-taking process invasive and beside the point, when she is being investigated by child protection services and may be interested only in getting her baby back. At the same time, it is possible to imagine that such a process can reveal aspects of Barbara's life that could assist the social worker in helping her to achieve her goals in her situation through more or better-placed supports. The major requirement in this situation is that you, as the social worker, have effective communication and relationship skills in order to make the client feel comfortable and respected. Providing information to Barbara regarding the reasons for the questions you are asking and maintaining a flexible and patient approach may enable her to comply with your requests. Whether the history is lengthy or brief, it is critical that the work center on the client's goals. The most detailed, painstaking social history will be of little use if the history—and not the goals of the client system—becomes the driving force of the work.

IMPLICATIONS OF THEORETICAL PERSPECTIVES

Despite efforts to minimize prejudices and personal biases about the client's situation, assessments are not neutral gatherings of the facts. The nature of the facts collected and questions asked suggests, at the least, your theoretical biases. For every area on which you focus, there are others on which you do not. For example, if you focus on Barbara's relationship with her baby because you see her as "case of mother and child," and you do not consider her experience as a child herself, you are choosing not to explore an area that could influence the work you do with her. Likewise, if you stress her history of delinquency but not of sexual abuse that you learn about, you are adopting an approach that will affect the nature of your work with her.

In both scenarios, you take a specific approach that is a result of your judgment about what is both relevant and important. This judgment is usually influenced by many personal attributes (for example, who you are, what you believe about the nature of people, and where you work) and by the type of information you believe helps make a story understandable. The theoretical perspective and its assumptions will also influence what you consider useful here, as will the context and function of the agency. All of these components shape the kinds of questions you ask and, therefore, the information you receive. Framed as it is by your perspectives, the client's assumptions, and your own interpretation of a situation, the assessment process is never unbiased.

Classic Theories

The theoretical perspective that you adopt strongly influences the assessment, the client–social worker relationship, and the subsequent work. Three classic theories that have throughout the history of the social work profession influenced assessments are: psychoanalytic theory, attachment theory, and cognitive theory.

Psychoanalytic Theory   Based primarily on the writings of the Austrian physician Sigmund Freud, **psychoanalytic theory** maintains that the unconscious is at the root of human behavior. Freud identified three structures that interact to determine human behavior: the *id, ego, and superego*. Each structure has a distinct function. The id is the repository of unconscious drives such as sex and aggression. In contrast, the ego is the managerial, rational part of the personality, which mediates between drives and perceived obligations. Finally, the superego serves as judge and conscience.

A social worker who believes that inner, unconscious motives and explanations determine the client's choices would orient an assessment toward interpreting the client's unconscious wishes. For example, if Barbara repeatedly describes herself as a "loser," the worker's assessment would likely be directed toward discovering the rewards and gratification she receives from perpetual failure. These rewards might include more concern from previously disinterested parents or protection from the high expectations of others. The first models of assessment were rooted in psycho-analytic theory, but as psychoanalytic theory gave way during the 20th century to more contemporary models based on evidence, approaches began to shift away from psychoanalytic origins (Jordan, 2008).

Attachment Theory   Looking through another lens, the social worker might first want to address Barbara as both a person who was parented and is now parenting. Your assessment might focus on attachment theory, which is currently becoming increasingly pertinent, especially in child welfare work. **Attachment theory**, origin-ally proposed by U.S. psychologist John Bowlby (1969; 1982), holds that very early bonding occurs between a mother and infant and subsequently plays a critical role in the child's future capacity to provide and sustain opportunities for her or his own children to attach. Most of this bonding activity occurs within the first two years of life, and it creates the foundation for the health of all future relationships.

A social worker who uses attachment theory focuses on Barbara's relationships with her early caregivers and the way in which these relationships may have contributed to her current struggles. An assessment of the attachment between Barbara and her child might include experimental observation to identify behavior patterns both child and mother demonstrate when a stranger is introduced into the scene. In stressing these relationships of parental bonding, the social worker would de-emphasize Barbara's other relationships in the environment.

Cognitive Theory   In contrast to psychoanalytic and attachment theories, if the theory guiding the work emphasizes the importance of **cognitions**, or thoughts, then the social worker will see things differently. This approach is consistent with **cognitive theory**, which asserts that thoughts largely shape moods and behaviors. In this approach the focus in assessment is more likely to be on what Barbara thinks about herself, what she subsequently thinks about the way in which she would like to think and act differently to achieve her goals, and the ways in which her thoughts and feelings influence her behavior (Beck, 2011). The cognitive approach assumes that people are thinking beings and if they change their thinking, their emotions will also change. Further, one's feelings influence both specific behaviors and general approaches to life. For example, because Barbara felt depressed, lonely, abandoned, or hopeless, she used poor judgment in leaving her baby. The social work intervention with her might involve helping her appreciate her assets more fully, which in turn would help her feel better about herself and lead her to make caretaking choices that would be safer for her baby.

You may find the assumptions in cognitive theory more similar to your own than those of the psychoanalytic perspective or more hopeful than those concerning attachment. Nevertheless, they are still predicated on assumptions that make a significant difference in the way that the social worker perceives, relates to, and works with the client. The point is not to reject every theory: We are all guided by theories, formal or not. Rather, the point is to recognize that none of them alone is "truth" and that you may use a combination of theories to frame the approach you will select for working with a client.

Contemporary Theoretical Perspectives

The three classic theories illustrate the ways theory can influence social work practice. Next we will look at the implications for assessment approaches and skills of two contemporary approaches, the strengths-based perspective and narrative theory. Like the classic theories, contemporary theoretical approaches influence assessment practice behaviors as the focus is shaped by the worldview inherent in the perspective.

The Strengths Perspective One of the four major perspectives of this book, the strengths perspective is widely discussed in the social work literature on assessment. Strengths-based practitioners uncover client assets, resources, goals, and dreams. A strengths approach also examines the potential of the environment to nurture and support the strengths of individuals. The assessment does not focus on a history of failures but on successes, resources, and goals for the future. The strengths perspective was developed for working with clients receiving mental health services but has since been used with many populations, including families and children, youth at risk, older adults, residents of economically distressed communities, and persons experiencing addictions. Saleebey (2009, pp. 109–111) identifies two elements for strengths-based assessments that are useful with all populations:

The social worker meets the client in the struggle: People have real struggles. There can be a fine line between supporting the positive dimension of a client's personality, skills, or accomplishments and framing the client experiences in terms of negative dimensions (e.g., grief, terror, sorrow, or discouragement). For this reason, it is critical to the relationship that you validate the pain that clients feel. In starting where the client is and listening to the client relate her or his concerns, painful as they may be, it is possible to uncover evidence of potential strengths on which you can build to develop a strengths-based intervention.

The social worker stimulates the discourse and narratives of resilience and strength: A narrative approach can be helpful in eliciting the client system's strengths. This "reframing" is dependent on the social worker supplying the words to help articulate the client's strengths, being affirming, and emphasizing possibilities. With the use of supportive questioning (i.e., questions that emphasize a positive aspect of the situation or a recollection of past successes), you can return the focus to client strengths. Even in the face of repeated, entrenched stories of trouble and pain, you can help clients to recognize their inner capacities for survival and learn the language of strengths in order to uncover a small seed of hope. Quick Guide 6 provides examples of supportive questions in various situations.

Another approach for assessing strengths incorporates guidelines that focus on understanding the client's perceptions of the situation (Anderson, 2013). See Exhibit 4.1 for these guidelines. This set of guidelines are intended to empower the client to share their life stories, acknowledge their strengths and wisdom, and develop greater insight into the complexities of their lives and current situation (Anderson, 2013, p. 187).

In this approach, the assessment includes a two component model in which the social worker first explores a series of questions with the client to define the problem situation (Component 1). The questions will not only help to identify the client's strengths, but also their life experiences (both positive and challenging), and strategies for coping with adversity. Gathering this comprehensive perspective on the client's identity can aid both the social worker and the client in formulating a perception of the client in terms of strengths, versus deficits (Anderson, 2013, p. 191–192). Following this exchange, the social worker and client then together

QUICK GUIDE 6 EXAMPLES OF STRENGTHS-BASED SUPPORTIVE QUESTIONS

Client Situation	Possible Supportive Questions
Middle-aged man who was recently laid off from his job and fears he will not be able to find new employment	"How did you approach the search that resulted in you being offered the position that you just left?" "Who might be a good person or group with whom to network about employment opportunities?"
Single mother with four young children who is feeling overwhelmed with her life	"How have you managed with the demands of your kids?"
Fifteen-year-old teenager who is stressed by the daily arguments with her mother	"Can you recall times when you and your mother had fun together?" "What are those times?"
75-year-old male who is experiencing depression	"How have you handled other challenges in your life?"
33-year-old combat veteran who is experiencing post-traumatic stress disorder and is having difficulty adjusting to civilian life	"What were your best assets as a soldier?" "How might those transfer to this new chapter of your life?"
Middle-aged woman whose mother has dementia is struggling with the decision to seek long term residential care for her mother. She feels that placing her mother would be a betrayal of the deathbed promise she made to her father to always keep her mother with her.	"How has your family traditionally handled difficult decisions?" "If your father were here to help you make this decision, what might his response be?"

EXHIBIT 4.1

The Strengths-Based Perspective in Assessment

Guidelines for a strengths-based assessment include:

- Document the client's story.
- Support and validate the story.
- Honor the client's self-determination.
- Give pre-eminence to the client's understanding of the facts.
- Discover what the client needs.
- Discover uniqueness.
- Reach a mutual agreement on the assessment.
- Avoid blame and blaming.
- Assess; but do not get caught up in labels (i.e., diagnoses).

Source: Anderson et al., 2009, pp. 186–188

---

identify the relevant strengths and obstacles that the client brings to bear. These strengths and obstacles can be charted on the grid in Component 2 to provide visual representation of the assessment results. See Exhibit 4.2 for this model.

In Anderson, Cowger, and Snively's two-component model for assessing client strengths, Component 1 is a process by which the worker and client define the problem situation and clarify how the client wants the worker to help. Component 2 is a graphic representation of the analysis of the problem defined in Component 1 (i.e., the assessment). It invites the worker and client together to chart strengths and obstacles in each of the four quadrants. Quadrant 2 is highlighted and may contain subcategories relating to cognition, emotion, motivation, coping, and interpersonal.

EXHIBIT 4.2

Two-Component Model for Assessing Client Strengths

COMPONENT 1

Defining the Problem Situation: Getting at Why the Client Seeks Assistance

- *Brief summary of the identified problem situation*. This should be in simple language, straightforward, and mutually agreed upon between worker and client.
- *Who* (persons, groups, organization) is involved, including the client(s) seeking assistance?
- *How* or in what way are participants involved?
- *What* happens between the participants before, during, and immediately following activity related to the problem situation?
- *What* meaning does the client ascribe to the problem situation?
- *What* does the client want with regard to the problem situation?
- *What* does the client want/ expect by seeking assistance?
- *What* would the client's life be like if problem was resolved?

COMPONENT 2

Strengths	
Quadrant 3 Social and Political Strengths • Civic engagement • Social networks	**Quadrant 4** Personal and Interpersonal Strengths • Cognition • Emotion • Motivation • Coping • Interpersonal • Physical and physiological
Quadrant 1 Social and Political Obstacles • Systemic oppression • Legitimization of domination and violence	**Quadrant 2** Personal and Interpersonal Obstacles • Powerlessness • Violation • Intense suffering • Isolation • Secrecy/silence
Obstacles	

(Left axis: Environmental Factors; Right axis: Help Seeker Factors)

Adapted from Anderson et al., 2009, p. 192

The assessment process helps clients identify their own strengths, use the resources in their environment, and tell their story about the problem. The approach is also explicitly political in that it recognizes and articulates the power relationships that clients experience and/or in which they participate. In addition, the strengths approach encourages a complex view of the environment as a source of both resources and obstacles. Although this approach seeks to identify obstacles, they are not the primary focus of the assessment.

Narrative Theory   Recall from Chapter 1 that narrative theory, influenced by postmodern thought, focuses on the client's story as the central component in the work. The primary interest for social workers using this approach is in discovering the stories of the people who consult them and in helping them to "re-author" those stories if they wish. A story is defined as events linked in sequence across time according to a plot (Morgan, 2000, p. 5). Narrative theory is consistent with the mission and values of the social work profession as it "focuses on empowerment, collaboration, and viewing problems in social context" (Kelley, 2008, p. 291). Narrative practitioners also subscribe to a person-centered approach to working with clients that embraces the essentials of social justice, a cultural context, and collaboration with and respect for the client system (Kelley, 2008).

Narrative practitioners are interested in helping the client to broaden or "thicken" her or his story. For example, Georgia is a woman who experienced intimate partner violence. Georgia developed a negative self-story response to a pattern of abuse that was perpetrated by her partner. Whereas her story originally was that of a strong and competent young woman, it slowly began to erode, reflecting increasing doubt and finally wholesale dejection as she adopted the persona of an unworthy human being. It became a "thin" story in that it lacked complexity, reflecting only her self-rejection. Georgia's perception of herself as unworthy depicts only one dimension of her person (i.e., self-rejection) while ignoring her strengths, life lessons, and capabilities.

In addition to seeking a more in-depth story, the social worker recognizes the importance of the broader social context of storytellers' lives. In one sense this is a story just about Georgia and her partner. In a broader sense, however, it is also about a pervasive social phenomenon that results in the deaths of thousands of women every year. The intervention with Georgia is to help her rewrite the thin story of worthlessness to one that more accurately reflects her talents, attractiveness as a human being, and competence. The goal of assessment is to discover the alternative story the person seeking help wishes to author and guide the development of a person-centered intervention in which specific tasks and activities will be identified that will enable Georgia to recapture her talents, attractiveness, and competencies.

In Barbara's situation, the social worker using a narrative approach would first want to hear her story. How does she fill the day? What is it like to be mother to this baby? When are the best times? When did her loneliness first interfere with her life? When is she able to conquer it? Who would say she is a good mother?

These are a few of the most basic ideas of narrative theory and ways this approach is used to assess what needs to be done. As you can see, narrative theory differs from many of the more classic theoretical perspectives, but is similar in that the story is the emphasis of the assessment process. Narrative approaches are largely driven by the person seeking assistance, although you, as the social worker, contribute your ideas as well. A narrative approach fits well with the strengths perspective as it assumes that people are the experts on their lives and that they have multiple talents, values, beliefs, and skills for improving their lives. We will look more closely at the applicability of narrative approaches in interventions with families and groups in Chapters 6–9.

Solution-Focused Approach   As introduced in Chapter 1, the solution-focused approach is another example of postmodern-influenced practice in which the client is recognized as the expert on her or his life as well as ways to affect change. Similar to a narrative approach, solution-focused interventions build on a strengths perspective and use solution-related language to empower client systems toward self-initiated change (Lee, 2009). Three primary assumptions and principles guide practitioners using this approach: (1) language is the mechanism for clients and social workers to understand the meanings of the client's life and actions; (2) because clients are the experts on their own lives, they have both the resources and the answers that will guide the solutions; (3) clients, not the professionals, function as the "knowers" within the intervention process and are therefore in the best position to create the solutions.

Solutions to the issues that clients bring to the social worker are developed in stages and created using a series of questions. While posed by the social worker, the content of the questions themselves are rooted in the story that the client has shared during the assessment phase of work. Following on the information presented by the client, the social worker asks questions to fill in historical gaps, identify previous successes and solutions, and explore the client's perceptions for outcomes. The stages of solution-building include: (1) description of the problem; (2) development of well-formed goals; (3) exploration of exceptions; (4) provision of end-of-session feedback; and (5) evaluation of client progress (De Jong & Berg, 2013, pp. 17–18). The questions posed to the client are aimed at eliciting the client's self-evaluation of the meaning of her or his life events and a futuristic exploration of possibilities.

While similar in their strengths-based orientation, client-centered empowerment approach, and commitment to collaboration, narrative and solution-focused approaches are distinct from each other. Proponents of the narrative approach emphasize the importance of "not knowing" and listening for unique outcomes to the client's presenting concerns, while solution-focused adherents delve into the possibility of "exception" questions (i.e., questions aimed at identifying instances in which the problem did not exist) (Kelley, 2008). In pursuing information regarding "exceptions," the social worker can ask the client to describe her or his life before the crisis that brought her or him in contact with the social worker. Gaining information regarding the client's previous coping skills can provide insight into the potential intervention to be developed. With their similarities and differences, both approaches can be successfully integrated with each other as well as coupled with other theoretically driven models (e.g., cognitive behavioral interventions) (Kelley, 2008). Combining approaches requires a skillful and knowledgeable practitioner who is competent in the areas being combined.

Theory and Evidence Matters

The contrast between the *traditional or classic theories* and more contemporary models provides just one example of the ways in which theoretical orientations help to shape and define the assessment processes and skills as well as the roles of the participants. As mentioned, the idea is not that one theory is better than another, but rather that theory matters in assessment and should be consistent with the social worker's basic assumptions and beliefs concerning people.

While theory guides and informs the development of social work practice knowledge, values, and competence, social work practitioners can benefit from using evidence to determine the appropriate skills, competencies, and behaviors to be applied to the social work intervention. In fact, the Council on Social Work Education (CSWE) Educational Policy and Accreditation Standards (2012) calls for social workers to engage in research-informed practice and practice-informed research. **Evidence-based practice** (EBP) is a process that aids practitioners to "systematically integrate evidence about the efficacy of interventions in clinical decision-making" (Jenson & Howard, 2008, p. 158). Within evidence-based practice context, social workers systematically determine, use, and assess interventions based on the consideration and integration of research findings, clinical expertise, client system preferences, values, and presenting issues, and the values and circumstances that will best serve the client system (Thyer, 2009). The five-step process of an evidence-based approach includes: (1) converting practice information needs into answerable questions; (2) locating evidence to answer the questions; (3) appraising the evidence; (4) applying evidence to practice and policy decisions; and (5) evaluating the process of using evidence to guide the practice intervention (Jenson & Howard, 2008).

Using the five-step process evidence-based approach to work with Barbara, where would you begin? Consider the following (Carter & Matthieu, 2010; Jensen & Howard, 2008):

1. Convert practice information into questions about background information, effectiveness of intervention or policy

    - *Information*—Barbara jeopardized her child's safety by leaving him alone.

    - *Question*—What are the risk factors most associated with teenage parent neglect?

- *Information*—Barbara wants to be a good parent.

- *Question*—How can social workers provide assistance to teenage parents at risk of child neglect?

- *Information*—Barbara appears to be experiencing depressive symptoms.

- *Questions*—What assessment tools are most appropriate to assess for depression among teenage parents? What are the most effective intervention strategies to lower depressive symptoms in teenage parents?

2. Locate evidence to answer the questions

- Conduct a search of research and literature on child development, parenting, and assessment of and intervention with depression.

- Consult with social work practitioner(s) who possess(es) knowledge and expertise in the areas of interest and ask for their options of best practices in the areas.

3. Appraise evidence

- Assess the quality of the best available evidence, including the appropriateness of the research design for the question, sponsorship of the research, the similarity of the research subjects to your client system, and other factors.

- Considering the evidence compiled from literature review, your judgment and practitioner discussion and experience, and the client's goals and social context, develop a plan for assessment and intervention.

4. Apply evidence to practice decisions

- Implement assessment and intervention plan.

- Determine the appropriateness of the research methods for the client system situation being explored while maintaining a client-centered approach, cultural humility, and applicability to the practice approach, setting, and client system.

5. Evaluate the process of using evidence to guide practice intervention

- At each step in the change process, conduct an evaluation of the efficacy of the assessment and intervention process. Questions to consider:

- Was the assessment accurate?

- Was the intervention effective?

- Was the information compiled from the literature and practitioner helpful?

- Did ethical questions emerge in the process? How were those resolved?

- What would you have done differently? Why?

Still an evolving area for practitioners, the adoption of an evidence-based practice approach can direct the practitioner to information regarding assessment, intervention, and evaluative strategies and other key resources needed to effectively work with a client system. An increasing number of social workers are accessing evidence to inform and guide their practice, however, students must continue to focus on gaining knowledge and skills to competently evaluate the myriad of evidence that is available from a variety of sources (Pope, Rollins, Chaumba, & Risler, 2011). Effective interventions also include the use of clinical judgment and skills that are required for competent and ethical social work practice. When asked in a recent survey, most social workers were reported to use evidence in a "conceptual" way, that is, to help them better understand information as opposed to using it "instrumentally" (applying directly to practice) (Wharton & Bolland, 2012, p. 162). Each client circumstance is unique and each situation must be assessed individually. Such an approach allows the practitioner to incorporate the complexities of client situations into any practice interventions implemented.

IMPLICATIONS OF DIVERSITY AND CULTURE IN ASSESSMENT

Although theoretical perspectives play a major role in assessment, other lenses are also crucial as well. For example, the impact of diversity and culture on assessment is central. Keeping an emphasis on diversity and cultural influences impacts the approaches and skills this focus implies are critical for competent social work practice. To be a culturally competent practitioner, you must develop a set of practice behaviors—knowledge, skills, values, and actions—that prepare you to address both affective and cognitive domains, and are measurable so you may evaluate your practice (Simmons, Diaz, Jackson, & Takahashi, 2008). Social work as a profession is an institution of culture, affected by the same pressures and forces that influence other aspects of our society's culture. Because of the shifting patterns of diverse populations in U.S. society, social workers must develop appropriate competencies and practice behaviors for different cultures. Consider these diversity-related questions as they may impact your ability to competently work with Barbara: (1) What is Barbara's background, including race, ethnicity, family background, religious/spiritual beliefs, and education?; (2) How might Barbara's experiences related to aspects of diversity impact her knowledge of parenting?; (3) How does your background impact your knowledge of Barbara's ethnic, racial, and cultural background?; (4) What information do you need to work with Barbara in a culturally competent way?; and (5) What culturally competent practice behaviors will be appropriate for working with Barbara?

The social worker who chooses to embrace a strengths-based and or narrative approach must be committed to developing an approach that affirms individuals' strengths and respects their culture. The social worker must also acknowledge the implications of such a commitment on the assessment process, particularly in the areas of: (1) cultural competence; (2) connecting with the spiritual dimensions of culture; and (3) global connections. We will explore each of these areas of cultural competence.

Cultural Humility

Embracing a systemic, strengths-based perspective means including meaningful components of the client's culture in the assessment process. (NASW, 2007b). Known as **cultural competence** (NASW) or "cultural humility" (Clowes, 2005), this practice behavior is defined as "the process by which individuals and systems respond respectfully and effectively to people of all cultures, languages, classes, races, ethnic backgrounds, religions, and other diversity factors in a manner that recognizes, affirms, and values the worth of individuals, families, and communities and practices and preserves the dignity of each" (NASW, 2007b, p. 10). Cultural competence requires that social workers are aware of their limitations and have respect for the unique culturally defined needs of others. As you have learned, assessment involves discovering what is important to the client system, those cultural influences that shape her or his values, how they have affected the client's experience, and how the client's perspectives differ from the worker's.

Clearly, the social worker's ability to approach another culture in this way is predicated upon her or his self-knowledge and knowledge of her or his culture (Schultz, 2004). That is, workers must understand their cultural influences, examine the influences of their own culture on their work, and understand the role culture plays in all of our lives.

An effective assessment process depends on cultural competence; you cannot simply assess the degree to which your client differs from you. Your understanding of the issues that the client brings and the way they are shaped by culture impacts the way you will perceive the presenting "problem." For example, when your client describes communicating with the spirit of his deceased father, you might wonder if he is demonstrating psychosis or hearing voices, unless you have a clear understanding that this kind of spiritual communication is part of his Latino cultural celebration of the Day of the Dead which encourages reaching out and encouraging the spirit of the deceased to come for a moment to hear the prayers and love of the family for them.

Culturally Competent Practice Behaviors

Developing the skills necessary to conduct a culturally competent assessment takes time and effort. Social workers need skills for culturally competent assessment, including the ability to ascertain, through talking to the client, the meaning of their culture, language, cultural norms, and behaviors. You must also be able to see these attributes as strengths on which to build a culturally meaningful intervention (NASW, 2007b).

Social workers who adopt a strengths-based culturally competent model of assessment and planning begin the relationship by initiating friendly yet purposeful conversations. Rather than focusing on long social histories, the worker may consider some aspect of the client's cultural frame that is puzzling or particularly interesting and ask about it through a "global question." For example, consider the situation you encounter as you are working with your client, Emilia Sanchez (refer to www.routledgesw.com/cases for information), a 24-year-old Mexican-American woman with a history of substance abuse and the mother of a four-year-old, Joey, who lives with her parents, Hector and Celia Sanchez. Joey has lived with his grandparents for most of his four years and, while he knows that Emilia is his mother, he considers Hector and Celia as his parents. Emilia has just learned that Hector and Celia are going to take legal action to officially adopt Joey. She is furious and has come to you for your help in preventing the adoption from going forward. As a culturally competent practitioner, you inquire about Emilia's cultural background and work to understand the impact of her background on her beliefs and current situation. As the client/cultural guide answers your questions, you remain highly attuned to the language she uses and inquire about **cover terms**, which are expressions and phrases that seem to carry more meaning than the literal meaning the words would suggest. For instance, your client might respond to the question about what her family thinks with a comment like, "I don't care what those hypocrites think about me; I will never be the person they want me to be!" In this case the cover terms are "hypocrites" and "person they want me to be," because they seem to have a cultural relevance to how she understands her social location.

Although extensive cultural interviewing may seem removed from the main issue, understanding the impact of the client's culture influences the overall success of the work. Of particular importance is the need to identify early on those culturally-related areas that have the potential to become barriers later in the working relationship. For example, given what you have discovered about Emilia, you would make a big mistake if you began by suggesting a family conference with her parents.

Connecting with the Spiritual Aspects of the Client System

In recent years the social work profession has placed greater emphasis on the value of helping people define what gives their life purpose and meaning (see, for example, Hodge, 2005a). Insofar as this effort might be seen as a spiritual quest, it can encourage people to find the most sustaining areas of their lives. Such areas of meaning may be found in religious practices, outdoor activities, and in social connections like volunteering in a hospice, to name only a few. They can also be incorporated into both the assessment and action stages of the work in meaningful ways. For example, your client's volunteer work may be identified as evidence of her or his value to the community, which in turn might reduce her or his sense of isolation. Facilitating a client's connection with her or his spiritual side is likely to be a lasting and significant contribution of the social work intervention.

Global Connections

Social workers have the opportunity to work with a diverse and often international client population. Having competencies in internationally focused social work practice is essential. With the number of foreign-born international migrants currently over 13 percent of the U.S. population and growing (Grieco et al., 2012), social workers may work with individuals who have come to live in the U.S. as non-immigrants (e.g., visitors, students, and temporary workers), legal or undocumented immigrants, or refugees who fled political or religious persecution. At the individual practice level, social workers can work with international migrants in a number of different areas, but the following areas generally encompass many of the interventions social workers will have with international clients: health, mental health, family conflict, language and education, economic well-being, and interethnic relations (Potocky, 2008, p. 445). Social workers can also work with individuals in foreign countries through casework, during times of disaster, and international adoptions (Healy & Hokenstad, 2008).

Whether you are working with clients in your own or another country, you can build on your cultural competence and humility to individualize your skills to the cultural characteristics of the client . . . A strengths-based approach is particularly appropriate when working with a client who has immigrated to the U.S. Given the courage and coping skills required for permanently leaving one's home country, there will be considerable strengths to draw on when aiding the client in their social and cultural adaptation to their new life.

Working in an international area can be a learning experience for both you and your client. To begin your journey toward becoming a culturally competent practitioner, you must gain cultural awareness first about your own cultural heritage, identity, and belief systems (Lum, 2008). Quick Guide 7 offers suggestions for beginning your own cultural heritage journey. After exploring your own cultural make-up you can then begin to gain knowledge and develop skills to work with an international client system. Learn as much as possible about your client's heritage, but exercise caution about making any assumptions about the client's culture, particularly in the areas of beliefs, knowledge of you and your professional value system, language proficiency, familiarity with their new home, or openness to working with a helping professional.

While not presuming to understand the individual client's life experience or goals is important in working with any client system, it is critical with a client who has relocated to a new country. Some clients may have experienced trauma that resulted in their need to flee their country, trauma during relocation, or challenges adjusting to the new culture and environment, or they may have concerns regarding their legal status in their new country. Building rapport and trust is an important element of the social work relationship that may be challenging for a client who is unfamiliar with customs, language, legal issues, or the role of helping professionals. Strategies for developing a trusting working relationship may include: outlining

QUICK GUIDE 7 MY CULTURAL HERITAGE JOURNEY

The cultural heritage journey of both clients and social workers impact their perspectives of life and work. Consider the following:

- Where do my family's roots begin?
- If my family emigrated to the United States, how long has each parent been living here?
- If I am in an adoptive family, what do I know about my biological family's journey to the U.S.?
- What are my family's traditions that have been passed through the generations?
- Do my family's traditions relate to religion or spirituality, holidays, rituals, and or significant events for the family?
- What values have I learned from my family—may be related to ethics, wealth, religion and spirituality, race, ethnicity, health, education, sexual orientation, and image?
- Have I challenged any of my family traditions or values? If so, what challenges have presented themselves and how have I responded?
- What significant life experiences have shaped my view of the world, specifically people who are different from me?
- How will my cultural heritage impact my social work practice?
- Are there changes or additions that I would like to make related to my traditions? How might I start?

your role, boundaries, and limitations as a social worker; asking questions about the client's culture, country of origin, traditions, and beliefs (being mindful not to be overly intrusive); sharing information about the culture of the agency and community, particularly as it relates to the provision of social and or health services; and creating an environment in which the client feels comfortable asking for clarifications regarding the receipt of services.

Approaching the assessment and planning process with a repertoire of strategies will serve both the client and you well. Through research and consultation, arm yourself with culturally appropriate knowledge and skills, be open to learning from the client by asking for the client's help and guidance in understanding her or his culture and experience, and tap into the strengths the client brings.

SKILLS FOR ASSESSMENT AND PLANNING

At this point in the assessment, the social worker will begin to form a view of the future that includes the client's vision and the social worker's own opinions about how they might achieve it. This creates a shared vision between client and social worker. In developing this vision, social workers will help clients articulate the kinds of changes they want to make. The questions that social workers ask will affirm that change is possible and that it can be shaped in a way that makes the client's life better. Building on the foundation of strengths, narrative, and solution-focused perspectives, skills for assessing and planning with the individual client

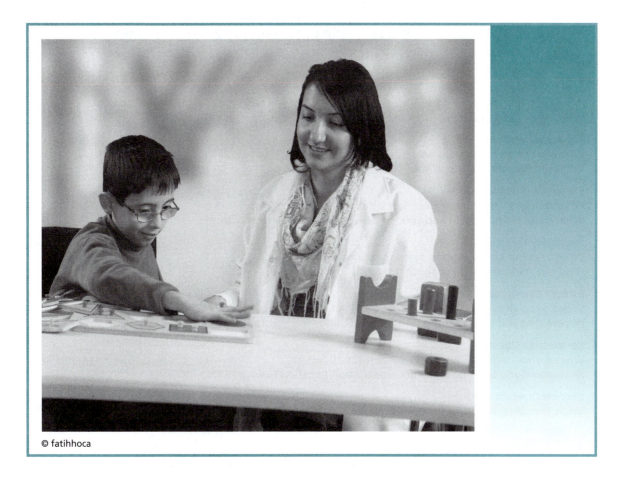

© fatihhoca

emphasize a collaborative, client-focused approach. Skills are shared here that high-light each of these approaches, but first, consider the unique aspects of each approach.

Strengths Perspective

Commitment to being a strengths-based social work practitioner involves begin-ning the social work intervention from that perspective. Establishing a climate during the engagement, assessment, and planning phases in which client strengths are fully explored and acknowledged creates an environment in which both the social worker and the client can identify the strengths the client brings to the inter-vention, those resources that can be mobilized, and those that can evolve.

Earlier in this chapter, the elements of a strengths-based assessment were high-lighted. Consider now a grouping of specific strengths-based questions that you can ask to engage the client in the assessment process. Saleebey (2013) provides a grouping of questions that are designed to elicit information from the client so that

QUICK GUIDE 8   TYPES OF QUESTIONS FOR DISCOVERING STRENGTHS

Survival Questions:
How have you managed to survive this far, given all the challenges you have had to contend with?
What have you learned about yourself and your world during your struggles?

Support Questions:
Who are the special people on whom you can depend?
What did they respond to in you?

Exception Questions:
When things were going well in life, what was different?
What parts of your world and your being would you like to recapture?

Possibility Questions:
What are your hopes, visions, and aspirations?
How can I help you achieve those goals?

Esteem Questions:
When people say good things about you, what are they likely to say? When was it that you began to believe that you might achieve some of the things you wanted in life?

Perspective Questions:
What is your perspective on your current situation?
How would you describe your current situation to others?

Change Questions:
What thoughts do you have about ways your situation could change?
What things have worked well for you in the past? How can I help?

Meaning Questions:
What beliefs do you hold above all others? What gives you a sense of purpose? What are the origins of your beliefs?

Adapted from Saleebey, 2009, pp. 102–103.

both the client and you can work together to identify strengths in order that they may be transformed into planning for an intervention. Quick Guide 8 contains eight questions that can provide the basis for an assessment on which you and your client can collaborate on the development of an intervention plan.

Narrative Theory

Identifying and building on client strengths provides the basis of a narrative approach to assessment. Another of the empowerment-based practice approaches, narrative approaches are distinguished from other similar and overlapping approaches (most notably, solution-focused and strengths-based) in the way in which the perceptions of clients are elicited and interpreted. Narrative practitioners first help clients to share their stories, or "deconstruct," and then through expanding and externalizing perceptions and meanings of the client's words, the stories are "reconstructed" to provide a broader, more effective approach to functioning (Kelley, 2008).

Narrative social work practice may be viewed as a three-stage approach, encompassing: client engagement; exploring and deconstructing pre-conceived client stories and assumptions, and re-authoring new, more empowering stories (Roscoe, Carson, & Madoc-Jones, 2011; Roscoe & Madoc-Jones, 2009). Within a narrative framework, the social worker completing the assessment and planning stages of work will engage the client in reconstructing her or his reality into a new reality. Using a series of strategies and questions, the social worker and client together cast new meaning on the client's life in such a way as to empower the client to interact differently within her or his world. Key to this approach is the social worker's commitment to maintaining a collaborative relationship with the client in which inclusiveness and anti-oppressive views are at the forefront. In the sharing and re-authoring of client stories, both the client and social worker views are of equal importance which serves to empower each of the partners (Roscoe et al., 2011).

Upon gleaning from the client her or his perceptions of current realities, the social worker helps the client to: (1) "externalize" the problem by re-focusing on the outcome rather than the root cause and de-emphasizing *problem-saturated stories* (self-perception in which problems dominate the client's life); (2) discover "exceptions" (i.e., those instances in which the problem or concern did not exist for the client); (3) "re-author" or reconstruct a new reality through mapping of the domain of the issue or problem; and (4) "reinforce" the change by involving others in the client's life and/or sharing the client's change experience to identify unique outcomes (Kelley, 2009; Nichols, 2011). To this end, the social worker poses questions throughout the assessment process that aid the client in reaching her or his desired new reality. Questions are categorized as:

- *Deconstruction questions*—re-focus the issue on an outcome.

- *Opening space questions*—create the possibility for unique outcomes the client may not have considered.

- *Preference questions*—translate the unique outcomes identified through the use of opening space questions into preferred experiences.

- *Story development questions*—move the preference questions to the next stage of change by creating a new reality (or story).

- *Meaning questions*—provide an opportunity for the client to replace negative perceptions with positive interpretations based on strengths identified in the story development.

- *Extending the story into the future*—the client is empowered to see her or himself in future situations. This phase may involve bringing others into the process to support the client as she or he embarks on a new reality.

Solution-Focused Approach

Using overall strategies similar to those described in a narrative-focused assessment and planning process, solution-focused assessment is grounded in the commitment to a focusing on possible solutions as opposed to problems (De Jong & Berg, 2011). Compatible with a strengths-based approach, clients are viewed as not only the experts on their lives but on their challenges and their needs, further accentuating the collaborative nature of the client-social worker relationship (Nichols, 2011).

De Jong & Cronkright (2011) provide this overview of the approach:

- Clients who are able to define what they want to be different in their lives make more progress than those who cannot;

- Clients make greater progress (and do so more quickly) when practitioners spend more time questioning them about what they want to be different than about the details of the problems;

- Clients make more progress, build solutions, and show less resistance when practitioners ask them about exceptions (i.e., their past successes) related to what they want to be different than when practitioners offer advice or confront resistance; and

- Clients make more progress when held accountable for solutions instead of problems (pp. 22–23).

A solution-focused approach incorporates a series of questions to elicit client perception, strengths, resources, and, ultimately, the solution. To facilitate the development of a trusting, collaborative relationship with the client, the first question posed may be "How are you hoping I could help you?" (Nichols, 2011, p. 252). This question invites the client to begin to share her or his story and provide insight into the reasons for seeking your help. Utilizing the ever-important social work skill of starting where the client is, the social worker continues the assessment process by asking the client to share her or his concerns, which is then followed by goal-setting. Solution-focused questions are (Lee, 2009, p. 595; Nichols, 2011):

- *Evaluative questions*—the client engages in an evaluation of the "doing, thinking, and feeling" as it relates to the issue that brought her or him to you.

- *Miracle questions*—the client describes a vision of the future in which the problem or concern no longer exists. Miracle questions promote creativity and hopefulness while, at the same time, promote client self-determination and development of planning for concrete and achievable change.

- *Exception questions*—the client considers a time when the problem or concern was not present, thus allowing the client and social worker to identify existing assets and resources which can be clues of strategies that can be used in the present situation.

- *Scaling questions*—the client is asked to consider her or his situation on a continuum from worst (1) to best (10). Quantifying the issues enables the client and social worker to frame goals, provide feedback, monitor progress, change course, and evaluate outcomes.

Drawing on the similarities of the previously described strengths, narrative, and solution-focused approaches, many practice skills are common to all three philosophical frameworks.

Developing a Shared Vision of Assessment

Preferred reality refers to the client's goal for a changed reality. Preferred reality reflects a postmodern (i.e., client systems are the experts about their lives and situations) and narrative assumption that there are different realities. Long before postmodernism became a common theme in social work theory, however, the profession engaged in efforts to make things different—that is, to work toward a different or preferred reality.

Our discussion of the assessment process has emphasized that the social worker's role is to engage in a dialogue with the client about her or his history, goals, and dreams. This process requires the practitioner to work with the client to develop a picture of what could be. Sometimes this process is difficult for clients, who may feel overwhelmed by the obstacles they face and thus find it quite impossible to be hopeful. Even more challenging, clients may be accustomed to seeing their dreams defeated through their long experience living at the margins of society. In these cases, the social worker has an important job in helping the client see that things can be different, that there are other realities, and that the client can work toward one that she or he prefers.

Being genuinely hopeful and translating that hopefulness to the client can be challenging to social workers as well. When you hear very painful stories, you often feel disheartened. For example, you might feel discouraged after hearing about generations of violence or oppression. However, the idea of preferred realities benefits both the social worker and the client because the idea that the client's reality can be different helps to protect both from a hopeless view of the client's situation.

Remember that working toward a preferred reality does not necessarily require a grand sweeping vision of riches where there was poverty or complete harmony where there was vicious violence. As much as anyone might wish for these long-range dreams, they will appear elusive and unrealistic in many contexts if they are not shared by the client. Social workers need to start with the client's vision of how things should be different, which may only involve small changes in the client's situation. Clients will often frame this vision in clear, small-scale terms when workers are drawn toward a more grandiose transformation.

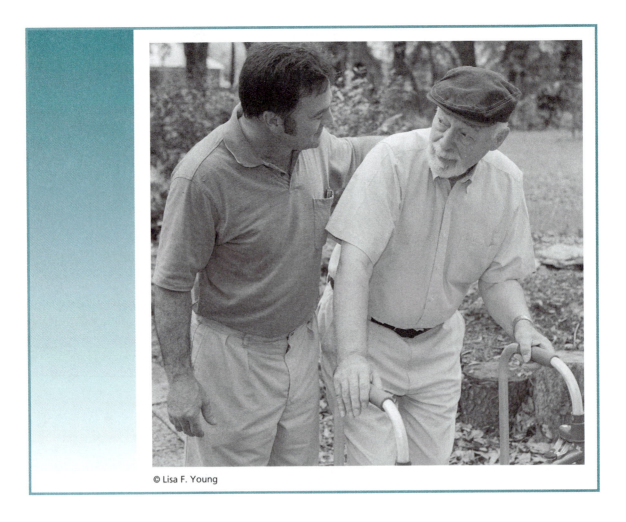

© Lisa F. Young

Support for the Client's Goals and Dreams

As an illustration of the process of moving toward a preferred reality, consider once again the case of Jasmine Johnson, the single mother whom you met in Chapter 3. Recall that Jasmine is concerned because she sometimes hits her son when he speaks disrespectfully to her. Jasmine may verbalize a request to you, as a family support social worker, for help in finding another way to respond to him. Although this request might seem like a relatively concrete goal for behavior change, it can also be thought of as developing a preferred reality because realization of this goal suggests creating a different mother–son relationship, which could have many positive ramifications. Right now Jasmine is asking for help with a behavioral response. Her goal might be simply to avoid child protection charges or to reduce the likelihood that her son will respond violently back to her. Therefore, your work with her might involve exploring her vision of a long-term goal. For example, Jasmine might want to establish a more satisfying emotional connection with the most important person in her life. She may not have allowed that kind of emphasis on feelings to enter into her interpersonal experiences, or she may never have had the time to think that way. It is even possible that she has not known anyone who articulated such a goal or she may simply be disinclined to consider relationships that way. In this scenario, it is important to start with Jasmine's meaning of the situation and then explore it further without imposing your own meanings.

The shared vision in this case will be that Jasmine learns other ways to respond to her son because she has articulated that vision and because you agree that is an appropriate area for work to which you can contribute. As you work together toward achieving this vision, other, more encompassing dreams about the possibilities for her relationship with her son might evolve. Your role in this kind of strengths-based assessment strategy is to support her dream, always affirming its potential for fulfillment. In order to help Jasmine's dream become reality, you will need to engage in a process of specifying both her goals and a plan for the two of you to work together.

Setting Goals   The reason for **setting goals** is to emphasize the usefulness of clarity of purpose and the utility for clients of recognizing the difference between central, current, behavioral concerns, and the longer view of the dream. As emphasized throughout this chapter, a thorough assessment is key to effective and ultimately successful goal-setting. Specifically, prior to establishing short and/or long-term goals *with* the client system, the process includes assessing the level of possible attainment, incorporating resources as well as limitations, and changes needed in order to experience change (Garvin, 2009, p. 309). Depending on the client's goals and needs, work takes on multiple forms. Consider the following goals in the context of your work with Jasmine:

1. Goals that are discrete (single outcome) or continuous (part of an ongoing plan)—a discrete goal is to respond differently when her son speaks to her in a disrespectful way, while a continuous goal may be to improve her relationship with her son.
2. Goals that are framed within different aspects of the client system (individual, family, group, or community)—be viewed by others (e.g., family and co-workers) with greater respect.
3. Goals that are related to various behaviors and behavior changes—get a new job or get her son to speak to her more respectfully.
4. Goals that are dependent on the individual client or need to involve others (e.g., couple or family)—invite her son to participate in family meetings with the social worker. (Garvin, 2009, p. 310)

Jasmine wants to respond differently to her son when he is disrespectful to her. This goal can be measured in a variety of ways. For example, does Jasmine want to "feel better" about their conversations? Does she want to reduce by half the number of times she is tempted to respond physically to him? Does she want to eliminate those episodes altogether? Does she want him to report that things are better? Clearly, the selection of an appropriate measure should reflect Jasmine's priorities. In starting where the client system is, setting priorities will help Jasmine and the social worker sort through expectations to determine the outcomes that are more critical within a particular time frame. For example, what if Jasmine's son is well behaved two times and then rude once, which provokes her inclination to hit him? Does his positive behavior matter in terms of the goal? Is the goal to change Jasmine's behavior or her son's behavior? As you can see, establishing goals and measuring progress toward achieving them can become complicated. Nevertheless, it is worth the effort to clarify how each party defines the goal of the work and how each one will know when the goal is achieved. Unless you are in clear agreement on an end point, Jasmine may believe you will be there to work on her particular situation until she feels it is "fixed." To avoid misunderstandings, you will want to make sure you have a mutual agreement regarding this issue. Setting goals helps both the client and the social worker evaluate the degree to which they are communicating clearly and have similar expectations, and are making progress. It is also true that agencies and organizations need to understand the purpose and goals of the work, often in concrete, measurable terms. This topic is discussed more thoroughly in Chapter 5 as a function of formal evaluation.

Contracting   The process of **contracting** is one in which the client and social worker reach an agreement about what is to happen, who will be responsible, a timeframe, and the priorities. Developing a clear, measurable and achievable contract with the client emphasizes the client's role in the intervention, and recognizes her or his right to self-determination (Rothman, 2009b). Contracts vary greatly depending on practice setting, and they can be formal or informal. A formal contract generally takes the shape of a written document signed by both parties. In contrast, an informal contract can consist simply of a verbal agreement. If a formal contract is used, details should be clarified, including frequency of meetings, goals, individual roles, ways to change the plan, monitoring of progress, and the degree to which each goal needs to be met. Whether formally or informally executed, a contract should include: (1) goals; (2) objectives that emphasize action, time frame, and strategies for determining success (or failure); and (3) proposed intervention specifying "who" is responsible for "what" aspects of the plan (Rothman, 2009a). Of critical importance to both the social worker and the client is clarity regarding the desired outcomes for the intervention. While the assessment and evaluative components of the social work intervention are dynamic, ongoing, and can change, the social worker and client both will be frustrated and unsuccessful if the goals and the path to achieve those goals are not clearly stated (and re-stated). Quick Guide 9 provides an example of a contract that you might find helpful in working with Jasmine Johnson.

QUICK GUIDE 9   SAMPLE CONTRACT WITH JASMINE JOHNSON

Client Name: ____Jasmine Johnson_____

Client Description of Issues to be Addressed:

__Relationship with my son _____

__Deal with my anger toward my son when he is disrespectful to me _____

Goals and Tasks:

Goal	Client Tasks/Timeline	Social Worker Tasks/ Timeline	Three-Month Follow-Up
1. *Improve my relationship with my son*	*Begin attending weekly family therapy with my son as soon as an appointment can be made.*	*Refer Jasmine and her son to a family therapist and communicate regularly with the therapist regarding progress (with Jasmine's informed consent).*	*Social worker made referral and has had three contacts with the therapist. Jasmine and her son are attending therapy regularly.*
2. *Learn better strategies for disciplining my son, particularly when I am angry*	*Participate in weekly parents of teens class and support group (next group begins the first of next month).*	*Refer Jasmine to parenting class and support group and communicate regularly with the group facilitator regarding progress (with Jasmine's informed consent).*	*Social worker made referral and has had one contact with the therapist. Jasmine is attending class/support group regularly and finding it very helpful.*
3. *Get Devon's father to pay child support more consistently*	*As soon as possible, contact Legal Services Child Support Enforcement office to inquire if they can help.*	*Provide Jasmine with Legal Services contact information and eligibility requirements.*	*With information provided by social worker, Jasmine has made an appointment at Legal Services.*

Date Contract will be reviewed: __We will review the contract on a monthly basis for the next three months
_____

I agree with the above stated goals, to complete the contracted tasks, and participate in a review and evlauation of the contract on the specified date.

___Jasmine_____   ___Julie_____
Client   Social Worker

_____   _____
Date   Date
_____

Adapted from Berg-Weger, 2013

Honest Responding

Up to this point you have learned how social workers and clients can identify and work toward a preferred reality. This discussion has emphasized the importance of establishing a shared vision that reflects the client's goals and dreams. However, as a social worker you might find yourself in a situation in which you are inclined to challenge your client's priorities after hearing the story. For example, if your client's overall goal is to avoid being arrested again for selling illegal drugs, you might want to contest that goal as a purpose for the social work intervention. To you, a more healthful goal might be for the client to abstain from using and selling drugs, or to separate from a drug-using peer group. Conflicts over goals raise many difficult questions for social workers. For example, do you have the right to disagree with the client's priorities? Are you inappropriately pushing your values? At the same time, how can you engage enthusiastically to achieve a goal you really do not approve of?

Questions that might serve as guidelines here include:

- Are you able to maintain objectivity about the client's goals?

- Do client goals reflect your priorities, values, or cultural practices?

- What are your legal and professional commitments in this situation?

- Will you violate an ethical principle by not addressing the issue, even if the client would rather not deal with it?

- Do you think the client's goals are either unrealistic or not extensive enough?

Although there are no easy solutions in this kind of scenario, you can respond honestly if you "own" your own biases, which might include more belief in the client's potential than the client seems to possess.

When Confrontation Is Necessary You have probably concluded from the preceding discussion that in some situations in which the goal conflict is particularly acute, the worker has to confront the client system directly. To examine how this process can be conducted, return to the Jasmine Johnson case for a moment. Jasmine has requested your help to change the way she responds when her son, Devon, talks back. However, you have discovered through reliable sources that she may actually be physically abusing him. How will this revelation ethically and/or legally affect the assessment? You may be convinced that you must call the authorities to investigate the serious allegations, with the possible outcome of a temporary separation between Jasmine and her son. This may occur before you can begin to work with her on a different way of relating to him. In this case you may decide that you must establish a new, short-term goal to carry out your professional and legal commitments, and postpone work toward Jasmine's long-term goal. The assessment then moves to an intermediate plateau in which there is a dangerous, or potentially dangerous, situation that requires a more immediate (and ethical) response. You will need to be honest with Jasmine about your understanding of the situation and what you see as your ethical obligations. This process will likely involve some confrontation. In this situation, Jasmine needs to hear that there is an immediate need that must temporarily derail her long-range goals. Exhibit 4.3 provides an example of practice skills that may be helpful when you must face the dilemma of confronting Jasmine and responding with honesty.

You may have noticed in this scenario that any decision to call child welfare authorities, which might lead to a separation between Jasmine and her son, does not necessarily negate her preferred reality of getting along better with him. In fact, a temporary separation may help her achieve this reality. It will be critical in your work with Jasmine to find the common ground and support her dream, even though you must initiate another intervention at the moment. Ideally this respite will improve her chances of working on her original goal after the crisis is past. Your honest dialogue with her will then reassure her that you share her vision, that you want to help her work toward it, and that you can be trusted to tell the truth.

When Alternatives Are Necessary In most cases, people who come to social workers for assistance are realistic about their goals and dreams. Many clients are keenly aware of the level of change that would be required to realize their vision of a more satisfying life. In other cases, social workers must help people expand their vision of what is possible because they have been discouraged, oppressed, or otherwise have had their vision restricted. In such cases the task is to affirm the client's potential and power in changing her or his life.

Occasionally, however, clients will need assistance in clarifying and articulating their goals and their understanding of the situation. Their goals might seem unrealistic or even grandiose to you. These situations are complex, particularly for strengths-based social workers. One strategy for responding in this type of situation is to help clients revise their aspirations, that is, to become more realistic. The argument for establishing realistic goals is that to endorse goals that clients cannot achieve is to set them up for failure, which is a major disservice to them.

At the same time, you are not in the position to determine goals that are realistic or the upper limits of the individual's capacity for growth and change. If social workers are to "hold high our expectations of clients and make allegiance with their hopes, vision, and values" (Saleebey, 2013, p. 19), you should not simply disregard a person's dream as unrealistic. Moreover, many strengths-based social workers insist that clients have the right to fail in the pursuit of their dreams, just like the rest of us. The issue is difficult to resolve and will undoubtedly take on a different look in different contexts.

One option for approaching such a situation is to help clients determine the steps involved in achieving their goals. For example, if you are the high school

EXHIBIT 4.3

*Responding
with Honesty*

During an early meeting with Jasmine Johnson, the social worker learns that Jasmine routinely uses physical punishment to respond to what she perceives as her son's disrespectful behavior. Following is an example of the conversation that the social worker is legally and ethically obligated to have with the client. In the conversation, the social worker balances the goal of honesty with the client about her legal obligation, with an expressed desire to keep working together:

Social Worker: "Jasmine, it is my understanding from another source that when you feel Devon is being disrespectful to you, you hit him. Is that correct?"

Jasmine: "Yes, I just get so mad and he won't listen to me when I tell him he can't talk to me like that. I would never really hurt him though. I just slap him, just to get him to stop mouthing off to me. I haven't even left any bruises or anything."

Social Worker: "I want to thank you for your honesty in confirming the report that I hear about the way in which you respond to Devon when you feel he is being disrespectful to you. Having a complete picture of the relationship you have with him and the way in which you use discipline can help me to help you find alternative strategies for responding to his behaviors."

"Before we can move on to talk about other ways to handle your situation, I would like to talk about the issue of using physical punishment. We have to be certain that the form of punishment that you are using does not constitute physical abuse. I want to make sure that you know that if I have reason to believe that you are physically abusing him, I am required by state law and my social work ethical code to report that to Child Protection Services."

"Once a report is made, the agency will send a social worker to investigate the allegation of physical abuse. If that report is substantiated or found to be true, the agency will decide if they want to recommend that the court remove Devon from your care and place him in foster care. They could also recommend that because you and I are already working together, that they will not pursue removal but they will monitor the situation and get regular reports from me. The other possibility is that they will not substantiate the report and no case will be opened. I want to be very certain that you and I are both clear and comfortable with all this information and the possible outcomes that might occur. So, I will want to talk with Devon about those times when the two of you are having trouble. Using the information I have from the both of you, I will make a decision about making a report."

"I understand that you may be angry with me for even raising these issues and angrier still if I do feel I have to make a report, but I want you to know that I am legally and ethically obligated to ensure the safety of children. I hope that we can continue to work together, but I understand if you don't feel you will be able to continue working with me."

Jasmine: "I know you just got to do what you got to do. I don't think you will find that I have been abusing him, so go ahead and talk with him. If he says I have been, then we'll just deal with that."

social worker and your client states that she wants to be a physician, you and she can consider together what level of education she would require, what it might cost, and how long it would take. You should not use this kind of step-by-step discussion to discourage her, but rather to provide information that she can consider. You may then help her consider alternatives that could serve as stepping-stones. Breaking down goals into workable and achievable sub-goals, or procedural goals, can aid client systems in developing clarity regarding the practical side of the dream and how far they want to take it. This may or may not alter their enthusiasm, but it is an honest response to a sometimes troubling scenario. In this example, you may consider saying to the client whose goal is to be a physician: "Let's put together a plan for you to achieve your goal of becoming a physician. The plan might include gathering information on the educational and training requirements for going to medical school and completing a residency program. Once we know the requirements, we can create a plan that includes strategies for the steps you will need to take to reach each phase of the goal—what you can do while you are still in high school, then the major and experiences you may want to consider for college, and then finally what you can do to make yourself a strong candidate for medical school. What do you think about this plan?"

Using Mapping Skills to Enhance the Dialogue

As you have seen, assessment on any level is influenced by your interpretation of the client's story. This interpretation is shaped by both your own and the client's culture, ethnicity, class, gender, sexual orientation, and age, as well as evidence-based theoretical perspectives, practice skills, and professional knowledge and values. Human stories often have many layers, however, and can be difficult to grasp. Frequently, a visual picture can make the information more accessible. **Mapping** is a technique that represents complex phenomena visually so that they can be absorbed perceptually rather than linguistically. Two fundamental types of mapping—genograms and ecomaps—are discussed next.

Genograms Technically a family tree, the **genogram** usually represents at least three generations and indicates various aspects of the relationships of the individuals included. Exhibit 4.4 presents a sampling of the conventions for indicating these relationships and Exhibit 4.5 is a genogram completed for the Sanchez family interactive case (see routledgesw.com). As you can see from the Sanchez family genogram, when used flexibly, a genogram can portray a broad range of issues and family patterns, such as strained relationships as well as stable marital relationships that can affect individual and family functioning. A review of the family history through the use of a genogram can add important information to the individual assessment, which may inform your work together on a contract. By adding labels to the map that indicate such attributes as life accomplishments or substance uses/

abuses and addictions, and health issues, genograms can be used in a more focused way to address a single issue. For example, a client struggling with a gambling addiction may be able to gain insight into her or his own challenges by identifying an intergenerational pattern of addictions that exists within the family. Patterns can indicate strengths of the family as well (e.g., educational achievements or career choices and longevity).

With client systems that are vulnerable, genograms should be introduced carefully and with sensitivity. The memories evoked and the visual nature of a genogram can result in more intense emotions (e.g., a sense of loss or regret) than mere words can. For example, a couple who review a genogram may become so distraught at the memory of a relative who died by suicide that each may abruptly leave their meeting with their social worker.

Additional concerns about using genograms are that they are frozen in time (that is, they represent relationships at the moment of the map's creation), and that they are sometimes subject to privileged interpretation, making it important to remember that the map represents one person's perception. Most importantly, they may seem deterministic, especially when they exhibit family patterns. For example, if a multigenerational exploration reveals that all or nearly all young male members on one side of a family have had major substance use problems; it may be tempting to see such a pattern as inevitable. When discussing the genogram, the social worker can give clients hope and the assurance that they can change. Therefore, family pattern exploration should never suggest that people are doomed by their familial history. Rather, a family history provides context and can help you locate your most effective intervention points.

EXHIBIT 4.4

Genogram Symbols

People in a genogram are represented by the following symbols:
- Males = □ (occasionally represented by the medical symbol of ♂)
- Females = ○ (occasionally represented by the medical symbol of ♀)
- Unborn or aborted children are triangles (Δ)
- X through a person symbol indicates death (usually accompanied by age or year of death)

Relationships are represented by the following symbols:
- Strong, solid black line = strong, positive relationship _____
- Dotted line = tenuous relationship - - - - - - - - -
- Railroad track line = contentious or strained /-/-/-/-/-/-/-/-/-/-/
- Slanting vertical lines = separation or divorce (on marriage line) //
- Circle enclosing people indicates household
- Arrows along connecting lines indicate the flow of energy, reciprocity ↔
- Jagged line indicates a conflicted relationship with possible estrangement

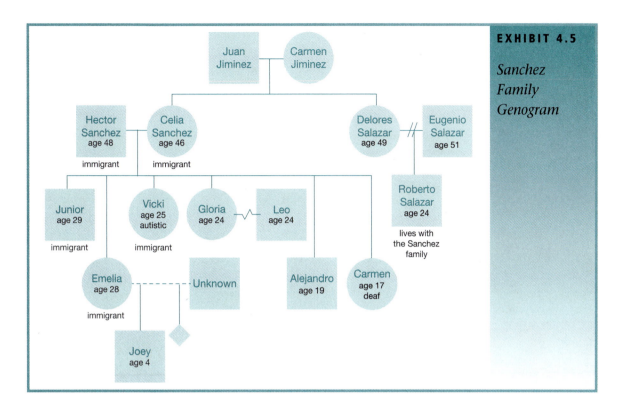

EXHIBIT 4.5

Sanchez Family Genogram

Ecomaps   A diagrammatic representation of the client's world that illustrates the client's levels of connection to such institutions as schools, religious centers or spiritual practices, the workplace, extended family, friends, and recreation is known as an **ecomap**. An ecomap helps clients make sense of their experience by showing them how their day-to-day world looks and the resources and strengths that exist within that world. Ecomaps can also focus on a particular aspect of the client's life. For example, a social worker who is involved with children with special health needs can use an ecomap of medical and social supports relating to the child's health status to help shape the intervention. Some ecomaps include a miniature genogram.

Like all mapping techniques, the ecomap enables your client to explore patterns of everyday living that may or may not be initially accessible in verbal form. For example, your client may complain about being lonely and estranged from his community. An ecomap could reveal that he has very few supports in the community—no satisfying work life, only one friend, no spiritual connections, and no outlet for recreation. Such a diagram would suggest that you expand your dialogue with him into these areas. Here, as always, it is important not to interpret and make conclusions directly from the map without exploring the meaning of the indicators with the client. Consider the Sanchez family ecomap as depicted in Exhibit 4.6 (refer to the Sanchez family case at routledgesw.com for more information). Can you identify the strengths, resources and areas for potential intervention that you

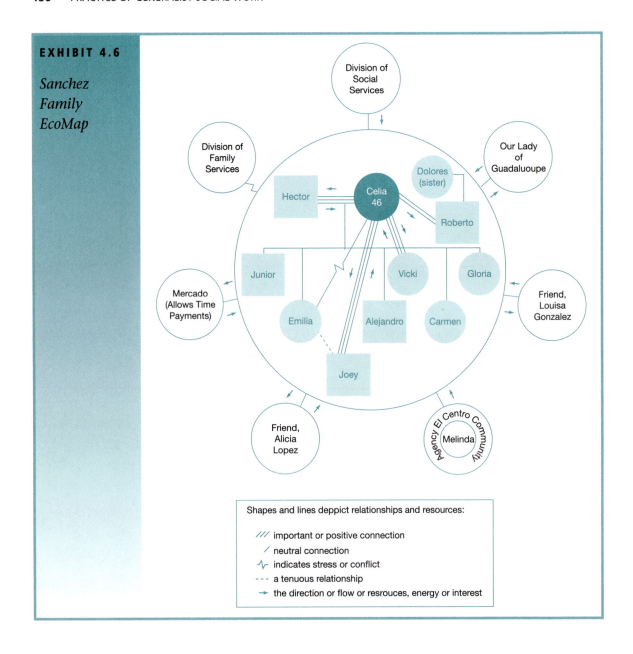

EXHIBIT 4.6

Sanchez Family EcoMap

Division of Social Services

Division of Family Services

Our Lady of Guadaluoupe

Hector

Celia 46

Dolores (sister)

Roberto

Junior

Vicki

Gloria

Mercado (Allows Time Payments)

Emilia

Alejandro

Carmen

Friend, Louisa Gonzalez

Joey

Friend, Alicia Lopez

Agency El Centro Community

Melinda

Shapes and lines deppict relationships and resources:

/// important or positive connection

/ neutral connection

-\/- indicates stress or conflict

--- a tenuous relationship

→ the direction or flow or resrouces, energy or interest

see present in this ecomap? In reviewing the ecomap, you will note that there is a stressful relationship reported between Celia and Emilia, with Celia perceiving that the relationship is not reciprocal (i.e., Celia is devoting more energy to the relationship than she is receiving from the relationship). To fully understand the meaning of that statement, you, as the social worker, can invite Celia to share with you the reasons behind the statement, her emotional response to the relationship, and the implications of her feelings for her relationship with Emilia and others in the family.

Social workers occasionally use a sequence of ecomaps to evaluate the effectiveness and progress (or lack) of the work. For example, if the client mentioned above who is experiencing loneliness wants to expand his social world but feels fearful of that prospect, your work with him might be to develop safe connections, which could be indicated on subsequent ecomaps.

SKILLS FOR ASSESSING RESOURCES

By developing individual skills, such as creating a shared vision, becoming culturally competent, and using social mapping, social workers can work toward an effective assessment. Nevertheless, even the most skilled workers can rarely provide all the assistance that a client needs. Social workers should also familiarize themselves with resources that are available in the larger environment. There are several dimensions to assessing resources that are useful in reaching client goals, from their type and source to their availability.

Formal and Informal Resources

External, structured opportunities for assistance, which usually take the form of services, are **formal resources**. Training in parent education, financial assistance, caregiver respite, and support groups for children in schools are all examples of the hundreds of services you might be able to name that are helpful to clients.

Not all resources are formal, however. **Informal resources** may be people, your own creativity, or naturally occurring social networks, like church groups, neighbors, friends, or families. The informal, internal, or community-based assets can also be mobilized to better serve client systems. Within the practice context, natural helping networks, such as those available from individuals, groups, families, and communities, can be the most important. These resources may endure long past the time that formal resources are involved with a client system. For example, many children benefit from regular contact with an older child who befriends them, understands their troubles, or is just supportive of their abilities. An older adult may benefit from creating networks of friends that are similar age through attendance at a senior center or through volunteer work. It is not necessary in all such situations to hire someone or obtain a service. Some of the most meaningful relationships emerge from informal contexts of community life.

Assessment When Resources Are Available or Unavailable

Your familiarity with both formal and informal resources is an enormous benefit to your clients. Simply locating resources is not adequate. You also need to know enough about the client system and the resources to estimate the fit and likelihood of a successful interaction between them. For instance, your client asks you, as a family support worker, for help in managing an ill infant, and you agree that some supports would help her become more like the effective parent she wants to be. You might recommend some regular time away from the demands of the child and also some assistance in managing the child's challenging behaviors. You would probably then explore the availability of both formal and informal resources. For example, you could investigate formal parent support programs, focusing on the collaborative capacity of the trainers, as well as informal parent support resources such as a child care cooperative and family and friends, and include consideration of concrete issues such as cost and schedule.

Unfortunately, even the more careful social workers cannot locate necessary resources in all situations. At some point, most will have the experience of looking for a particular way to help a client and finding that it does not exist. Even in these situations, you are not powerless. You have at least two options when adequate resources are not available: You can advocate for a change in formal resources, policies, or programs that are not responding adequately (e.g., an older adult day center), or you can create resources where none have been developed. For example, you might assist single parents in a housing complex to organize a network of child care where none existed, or help a community write a grant proposal to fund summer youth employment for neighborhood teens.

These points suggest that social workers do not simply accept, for example, that an uncooperative agency does not respond appropriately to their client, or that a housing project has no child care facilities. Social workers need to remain hopeful and energetic in identifying and developing resources but must also be realistic and careful not to promise more than they can reasonably deliver. In a client's world, where many promises may have been broken, social workers need to maintain trust through an honest approach about the possibilities.

Social Action When Resources Are Inadequate

Many of the cases in which the resources you think necessary are inadequate, nonexistent, or discriminatory are political situations that call for policy practice approaches. Action on behalf of clients is one possible response to an unjust situation. **Social action** is a policy practice method in which the social worker generally aims to shift power structures in order to change an institutional response. The efforts come in many forms and may involve varying degrees of confrontation. For example, if the public health department is slow to investigate a situation of child lead poisoning at a local school, you might assist your client through their formal grievance process, and/or organize a protest with other concerned parents if the health department does not respond to the initial inquiry. Both the actions on behalf of one client and on behalf of many clients are forms of social action. However, the latter is clearly more confrontational than the former. In situations in which this kind of action is contemplated, the assessment will take on the additional dimension of an analysis of the actions that actually should or will happen, who will do it, and what the potential consequences will be. In addition, the assessment must address the client's interest in, and capacity to engage in, the action indicated. The social worker must be completely honest and sensitive to the possible consequences of political action for the client or the client's family. In many ways this last requirement can be considered a dimension of ethics. Read how this might play out in the tenants' story in Exhibit 4.7.

Despite the risks that may be involved, when an understanding is truly reached in partnership, few experiences are more positive or powerful than a successful social action based in client–worker advocacy. Even if the results are somewhat less than hoped for, the process itself can be remarkably empowering for both social worker and client.

Although this scenario expands into the phase of intervention, it points up the importance of assessment throughout the client relationship. The assessment drives the action stage of the work, and therefore, must also address the action inherent in it.

PLANNING

When you and your client have developed a shared vision and specified the goals, means, and end points you envision for the work, you will have addressed the components of a solid, detailed plan. This section will revisit these briefly and then consider the potential impact of two insidious influences—oppression and the emotional impact of change—on the planning process in particular and on the assessment in general.

The key components that influence the concrete plan for work include:

- Setting and prioritizing goals

- Identifying methods of reaching goals

- Developing a clear understanding of responsibilities

- Setting time frames

- Recognizing when an alternative plan is necessary

- Identifying resources

- Identifying an end point for the work.

Incorporating these elements into a plan can enhance the client's understanding of what will happen. The elements then provide a framework that guides the development of the intervention plan that enables the social worker and the client to maintain focus on the identified concerns, priorities, and available and needed resources. Having a structure for creating an intervention provides an opportunity for the social worker and client to collaboratively develop goals and action steps. These

EXHIBIT 4.7

Social Action: The Tenants' Story

In a privately run, not-for-profit housing project in a midsize city, there are several families with young children and some with grandparents. In the past, the housing was kept in marginally acceptable repair, but the residents stayed there because the rent is fixed and relatively low. A change in ownership leads to a distinct deterioration in maintenance, adequate and timely repairs, and the amount of heat allotted to each apartment. Toilets are clogged, rats are visible in the basement, and lead-based paint is beginning to crumble from the walls. The residents are unsure how they can respond to this deteriorating situation so they request that you, as a social worker from the city's housing authority, advocate for them. After discussing the situation with client spokespeople and then asking each client for approval, you sponsor a meeting for residents with the landlord's representatives. Although you have been careful to hear the landlord's side and have used your best engagement skills, the meeting results in a deadlock, and no progress is made.

Convinced that you have exhausted all of the available approaches, you consult with peers who affirm your position. At that point you consider the possibility of organizing your tenants to withhold their rent. You feel for many reasons that this is an appropriate and effective strategy to elicit a more satisfactory response from the landlord. At the same time, however, you know from prior experience that this particular landlord has a history of retaliation against complaining tenants.

You fully recognize the need to collaborate with tenants about the potential plan of withholding their rent. There is some hesitation among them because they too are concerned with the likely consequences of riling a powerful landlord who could throw them out. Some of the residents are people of color, and they are especially concerned with the availability and accessibility of other housing.

Let's consider the following ways the story might play out:

- *Plotline A:* You are so convincing that this is the way to deal with the problem that you are able to engage the tenants in a full-blown movement to withhold their rent. Your clients nervously await the landlord's response.
- *Plotline B:* You hear those who have specific concerns and play out alternative responses. You locate other sources of housing, and you identify legal advocates for those interested in pursuing new housing. You arrange for press coverage and obtain the full support of your agency and supervisor in taking this action.

Social Action: The Moral of the Story

You may fill in the ending of this story. It could be empowering or disastrous or a lot of things in between. The point is that when others live the results of your advocacy attempts, they need to have all the available information about possible consequences, the likelihood of certain outcomes, and the opportunity to choose which path they want to take. You, as the social worker, need to be very clear about who will pay the price of any repercussions. Because the "who" is often the client, the client should enter into such an agreement only when she or he clearly understands the risks and is motivated to follow through with the action consequences. Can you identify an alternative Plotline C?

components have been negotiated as an ongoing feature of your work together and constitute the mutually developed plan.

Although the ideal is that social workers and clients collaborate to plan the process, even the most careful approaches cannot account for all of the potential obstacles that might arise. Many clients face real disabilities. They may have emotional, cognitive, or physical challenges that make it almost impossible for them to participate in planning. Although social workers should never minimize these obstacles, they need to work directly with the client to the greatest extent possible, while bearing in mind that many clients who have experienced lifelong challenges have never been considered as adequate participants in service provision planning. Consequently, clients may be hesitant or even afraid to participate, even though they have the ability to make substantial contributions. Many others who have experienced racial or ethnic oppression will find it difficult to trust the process of mutual assessment and planning.

The transgression of excluding clients from this process has generated two negative consequences. First, service providers have often lost, dismissed, or ignored helpful information that only the person experiencing the context could provide. Second, many of these clients have internalized this kind of oppression and actually have come to believe that they have no right or capacity to participate. The **internalization of oppression**—the process by which individuals come to believe that the external judgments are valid, thus resulting in a devaluing of one's self—is one of the most sinister aspects in the oppression and domination dynamic (Van Soest, 2008) and clearly undermines the spirit of human rights.

Another component of assessment and planning that social workers must keep in mind relates to the impact of emotions. In their zeal to develop a plan, address the issues, mobilize the resources, and engage the contract, social workers may sometimes forget that certain elements of the work (e.g., emotional responses to loss and grief) are not as visible or as easy to categorize as others. By the time social workers have listened to the story and established a preferred reality, they will probably have heard and felt a lot of the emotional content that is related to the client's experience. They may not as easily, however, recognize the power that complicated feelings about change can generate.

For example, whole families are systems that can be organized around one member's addiction to alcohol. In some families, everyone knows how to respond if Dad is drunk and has passed out on the couch. John, the eldest son, may be the one to carry him to bed; everyone else might ignore Dad, step around him, and pretend his drinking does not happen. Mom takes this opportunity to make decisions about the family finances that Dad has always made. The specific patterns may not be as important as the idea of changing them. Although Mom has come to your agency to get help with Dad's addiction because it is obviously destroying his health, their marriage, and their family life, the social worker must be aware that there is a cost to change. Mom may feel uniquely competent when she is so clearly needed to make major decisions, or John may take great pride in being able to manage the chaos. Again, the patterns are not as important as the disruption of them. If Dad successfully withdraws from alcohol, Mom may actually have some regrets because she will have to develop a new role when her husband is more present. John may lose his place as competent caretaker, and all members of the family will need to relate to Dad and each other differently. This need for renegotiating family roles can have some disturbing emotional consequences.

Although there is a risk of over-interpretation, any change that the client is genuinely seeking is embedded in a social context and therefore can generate a powerful emotional response. A change in one part of the system has the potential to change the entire system. This response may take the form of reluctance to engage in ongoing collaboration or hesitation when making progress on specific goals. In such cases, consider engaging in a dialogue that goes beyond the technical or mechanical processes of goal setting and contracting. Specifically, it will be helpful to explore the meaning of the change itself in terms of emotional and logistical outcomes as well as the impact of the change on roles, functioning, and patterns.

STRAIGHT TALK ABOUT ASSESSMENT AND PLANNING: THE AGENCY, THE CLIENT, AND THE SOCIAL WORKER

You have seen that several agency, client system, and professional issues influence your work with clients. From those perspectives, the following discussion will address a range of issues that you will likely encounter as a social worker. Having insights in advance of such encounters can arm you with the knowledge and skills to respond competently and ethically.

The Agency Perspective

From the agency perspective, work methods, schedules, length of the work, documentation, and agency resources all need to be recognized and discussed openly with the client. For example, you need to provide information to the client regarding your schedule, appropriate ways to contact you, ways in which you will be documenting your interactions with her or him, and agency resources that are or are not available to her or him. The social worker needs to inform clients about their work processes from the beginning so that there is no confusion or frustration as the relationship evolves.

Administrative Tasks   With an increasing emphasis being placed on brief, effective, and accountable treatment for individuals, families, and groups, managed care organizations (MCOs) have influenced the assessment and planning process in significant ways (Hopson & Wodarski, 2009). You may be required to complete your assessment, planning, intervention, termination, and evaluation processes within a limited time frame. Standardized, rapid assessment measurement tools have become a mechanism for practitioners to complete assessments in a short period of time while maintaining optimal accuracy. In order to work within the current service delivery environment, your agency may opt to use a rapid assessment process. With numerous rapid assessment instruments (RAIs) available to choose from, the key is to ensure the instrument relates to the issues being presented by the client system and has been empirically validated with that population (Hopson & Wodarski, 2009). In order to have confidence in the efficacy of a standardized assessment tool, the social worker must have evidence that the assessment instrument has been psychometrically and clinically validated on the population with whom it is being administered. Utilizing any assessment tool on a population for which the instrument has not been shown to be effective can produce misleading outcomes in the areas of age, gender, race, ethnicity, and culture. Engaging in such evidence-based practice helps to enhance the potential effectiveness of the intervention.

Other formalities about which to inform the client relate to administrative tasks or financial coverage. For example, if you are required to submit monthly reports to the court, you should discuss this stipulation with your client. Even when clients are not happy with such an idea, they are likely to respect your communicating such information from the outset of the relationship. For another example, if your client will have to file a Medicaid application in order to continue working with you, explain the need for action as early as possible. For many clients, filing for financial assistance for services may be challenging, because it may mean to them that they are admitting defeat, disability, or helplessness. Being sensitive to your client's perspective about the meaning of these aspects of your work together is important.

Another mandate that is becoming increasingly prevalent in community agencies is the requirement for diagnosis as part of the assessment and planning process. As discussed earlier, many institutions now demand a *DSM* (from the American Psychological Association's *Diagnostic and Statistical Manual of Mental Disorders*), diagnosis in order to bill for third-party payment. This mandate can provide uncomfortable moments for social workers who believe strongly in helping clients to identify and use their strengths. The attempt to provide a psychiatric diagnosis requires a focus on deficiencies and can create a stigma. For example, a school social worker who is providing support to a five-year-old whose parents are addicted to heroin may struggle with diagnosing the child with an "adjustment disorder," which will then appear in school records, label the child for years to come, and may be transmitted to other institutions.

Obviously, if your agency requires social workers to make or use diagnoses, then you need to consider your feelings on this issue before you accept a position. Practicum students are not likely to formulate diagnoses, but the use of diagnosis inevitably categorizes clients, which can impact the working environment of a setting and some may object to working in such a setting. Others may find the process tolerable as long as it facilitates service provision. Still others may find the use of diagnosis helpful because they are able to use evidence-based practice to provide the best possible service to clients for their challenges, and collaborate easily with non-social work colleagues who also use the *DSM*. Ethical conduct obliges all social workers to inform their clients when a diagnosis is required to access services. The client can then decide if she or he wants to participate in that exchange. For some clients and social workers the diagnostic process may seem a small price to pay for receiving appropriate services and possibly medication, whereas for others, the benefits do not outweigh the costs involved in using the *DSM* with clients.

Documentation Recording information about your work with clients is both universal and unique. Social work encounters are recorded in virtually every setting, but the requirements and formats are typically specific to the setting. Social workers are required to have competencies to create a variety of documents aimed at diverse audiences to serve a range of purposes. In working with individuals, social workers will complete intake/psychosocial assessments, treatment plans, case notes, case studies, reports to external organizations (e.g., schools and courts) and compose other forms of communications (e.g., memos, letters, recommendations, etc). Social work documentation begins with the first encounter and continues through each phase of the planned change experience. Documentation is important for social work practitioners as recording information from the engagement, assessment, intervention, and termination and evaluation encounters serves a number of key functions, including accountability, supervisory and administrative purposes, practice enhancements, reimbursement, and planning (Kagle, 2008). Kagle and Kopels (2008) provide the profession with fifteen principles of recordkeeping that should be in the forefront of every social worker's practice. Quick Guide 10 provides a summary of those principles for practice.

Despite the need to learn the agency's preferred method for documentation, there are basic components that are likely to be found in the records developed by social workers. Kagle and Kopels (2008, pp. 38–40) suggests the following structure for creating a written record of the social work intervention:

1. opening summary;
2. data gathering and social history;
3. assessment;
4. decisions and actions resulting from initial assessment;
5. service planning, including service options and purpose, goals, and plans of service;
6. interim notes;
7. special materials (e.g., forms, consents, emergencies, and service reviews); and
8. closing summary.

QUICK GUIDE 10   PRINCIPLES OF GOOD RECORDS

- *Client goals* that demonstrate balance in competing goals (e.g., accountability, improving practice, efficiency, and client privacy)
- *Agency mission* guides the documentation
- *Management of risk* for the agency, social worker, and client
- *Accountability* for service decisions, compliance, and legal issues is evident
- *Abridgement*—only information that is needed is included in the record
- *Objectivity* includes observation, sources of information, criteria used in judgment, and appraisal
- *Client involvement* is evident
- *Sources* of information are cited in the record
- *Cultural context* factors are noted as each relates to the client's situation, service delivery, and outcomes
- *Usability* of the record includes organization, cross-referencing, and accessibility
- *Current information* is included in the record and summaries
- *Rationale* for service decisions and actions is evident
- *Urgent* situations are well documented
- Information *excluded* from the record includes information that is unsupported or not relevant to the client's service status

Source: Adapted from Kagle & Kopels, 2008, pp. 10–11

The opening summary portion of the documentation encompasses the engagement phase of your intervention. Information that is typically included in an opening summary relates to the client's demographic characteristics (i.e., name, gender, address, contact information, birth/age, family composition, employment, insurance coverage, etc.), reason for requesting or receiving services, and eligibility status. The assessment portion of the client record should specifically include the social worker's observations and descriptions, sources of the information, criteria used in making the judgments (e.g., formalized measures and information from past history with the agency or referring entity), and inferences and appraisals (Kagle & Kopels, 2008). This may be an appropriate place to record perceptions of strengths, resources, needs, cultural factors, and risks related to services that may be delivered.

While formats are agency or program-dependent, there are elements of social work recording that are common across the profession. Most agencies have a structured format for documenting client encounters or meetings, conducting an intake or eligibility interview, completing a social history, and a treatment/intervention plan. Examples of information to include in client records of these three documentation activities are presented here: (1) Exhibit 4.8 provides an example of information to obtain in a client assessment; (2) Exhibit 4.9 includes examples of information to include in a suicide risk and harm to others assessment; and (3) Exhibit 4.10 is an example of information to include in a treatment/intervention plan (adapted from

EXHIBIT 4.8

Information to Include in a Client Assessment

Demographic Data:

- Name
- Contact information
- Legal status
- All persons participating in assessment
- Presenting need
- Living situation (level of stability and safety)
- Social environment (level of activity, satisfaction, and relationships with others)
- Cultural environment (client satisfaction and view on helping-seeking, and cultural view of help-seeking)
- Religion/spirituality (statement of beliefs and levels of activity and satisfaction)
- Military experience (branch, time in service, discharge status, coping with experience, and view of experience)
- Childhood (supportive, strengths, and significant events, including trauma)
- Family (composition—parents, siblings, spouse/significant other(s), children, and others; level of support; and family history of mental illness)
- Sexual history (activity level, orientation, satisfaction, and concerns)
- Trauma history (physical, sexual, and/or emotional abuse or neglect and experience with perpetrator(s))
- Financial/employment circumstances (employment status, satisfaction, financial stability, areas of concern or change)
- Educational history (highest level achieved, performance, goals, and challenges)
- Legal needs (arrest/conviction history and current legal status)
- Substance use/abuse (history of addictive behaviors—alcohol, drugs, gambling, sexual, or other). Addiction screen (questions include: (1) Have you ever felt you should cut down on your drinking/drug use? (2) Have people annoyed you by criticizing your drinking/drug use? (3) Have you ever felt bad or guilty about your drinking/drug abuse? (4) Have you ever had a drink/used first thing in the morning or to steady your nerves or to get rid of a hangover (eye-opener))?

History of Emotional/Behavioral Functioning:

For each of the following areas, gather information regarding: current status (current, previous, or denies history); description of behavior; onset and duration; and frequency

- Self-mutilation
- Hallucinations
- Delusions or paranoia
- Mood swings
- Recurrent or intrusive recollections of past events
- Lack of interest or pleasure
- Feelings of sadness, hopelessness, isolation or withdrawal
- Decreased concentration, energy, or motivation
- Anxiety
- Crying spells

- Appetite changes
- Sleep changes
- Inability to function at school or work
- Inability to control thoughts or behaviors (impulses)
- Irritability or agitation
- Reckless behavior, fighting, or fire setting
- Stealing, shoplifting, or lying
- Cruelty to animals
- Aggression

Behavioral Health Treatment History:
- Date
- Program or facility
- Provider
- Response to treatment

Mental Status Exam:
- Attention (rate on scale of: good, fair, easily distracted, or highly distractible; and describe behavior)
- Affect (rate on scale of: appropriate, labile, expansive, constrictive, or blunted; and describe behavior)
- Mood (rate on scale of: normal, depressed, anxious, or euphoric; and describe behavior)
- Appearance (rate on scale of: well groomed, disheveled, bizarre, or inappropriate; and describe behavior)
- Motor activity (rate on scale of: calm, hyperactive, agitated, tremors, tics, or muscle spasms; and describe behavior)
- Thought process (rate on scale of: intact, circumstantial, tangential, flight of ideas, or loose associations; and describe behavior)
- Thought content (note: normal, grandiose, phobic, reality, organization, worthless, obsessive, compulsion, guilt, delusional, paranoid, ideas of reference, and hallucinations; and describe behavior)
- Memory (note: normal, recent (good or impaired), past (good or impaired); and describe behavior)
- Intellect (note: normal, above, below, or poor abstraction; and describe behavior)
- Orientation (note: person, place, situation, and time; and describe behavior)
- Judgment and Insight (rate on scale of: good, fair, or poor; and describe behavior)
- Current providers (including psychiatrist, primary care physician, therapist, caseworker, etc.)
- Community resources being used (including support groups, religious, spiritual, other)
- Client goal(s) for treatment
- Summary of social worker's observations and impressions

Adapted from St. Anthony's Medical Center, St. Louis, Missouri

EXHIBIT 4.8

Continued

EXHIBIT 4.9

Information to Include in Assessment of Suicide Risk and Harm to Others

Suicide Risk Assessment:

- Name, date, and time of assessment
- Clinical assessment (include current suicidal thoughts, obsessions with death or indications of putting one's affairs in order, even with no specific plan). If yes to any items, follow-up questions include: is there a plan, is the plan lethal, is there potential access to plan?
- Frequency of thoughts
- Intensity of thought (rate on scale of: (1) no pressure to (5) high pressure)
- Risk level (rate on scale of: negligible, mild, moderate, or severe)

Harm to Others Assessment:

- Name, date, and time of assessment
- Clinical assessment (current thoughts of harming another person). If yes, follow-up questions include: is there a plan, is there a target/victim, and is there potential access to plan?
- Frequency of thoughts
- Intensity of thought (rate on scale of: (1) no pressure to (5) high pressure; and describe plan and victim)
- Risk level (rate on scale of: negligible, mild, moderate, or severe)
- Notify physician
- Complete duty to warn protocol

Adapted from St. Anthony's Medical Center, St. Louis, Missouri

EXHIBIT 4.10

Information to Include in a Treatment/ Intervention Plan

Intervention/Treatment Plan:

- Preliminary assessment/diagnosis
- Preliminary plan for intervention/treatment (to be developed at first visit)
- Interventions for emergency/safety need
- Other interventions needed
- Needs (include date, identified need, status (active, inactive, deferred, or referred), and reason for deferral or referral)
- Strengths
- Facilitating factors for intervention/treatment
- Limitations
- Barriers to intervention/treatment
- Other care providers/referrals and purpose (including plan for service coordination)
- Plan for family involvement (note if client opts for no family involvement)
- Termination criteria/plan
- Planned frequency and duration of intervention/treatment

Adapted from St. Anthony's Medical Center, St. Louis, Missouri

St. Anthony's Medical Center, St. Louis, Missouri). A typical treatment plan will include (Sormanti, 2012):

- brief description of the issues to be address, including client strengths, resources, and challenges;

- theoretical orientation in which the intervention is grounded (may be optional);

- goals for intervention;

- specific and measurable objectives;

- estimated timeline for the intervention;

- planned intervention;

- plans for evaluation and review of progress (p. 117).

A second form of documenting practice that social workers find helpful is referred to as narrative recording. Narrative recording may or may not be a central focus of the agency recordkeeping process but can allow the practitioner to document client-specific process-related information (Kagel & Kopels, 2008). A narrative report might include: nature of the client situation; purpose of the service; service-related decisions and actions; process of the service delivery; and service impact (Kagel & Kopels, 2008, p. 125).

The Client Perspective

Just as agency issues can present challenges for the social worker, there are client situations that can prove to be difficult to address in the assessment phase of work. Client issues that require specialized practice skills can include working with client system situations that involve: involuntary, mandated, and non-voluntary clients; violent situations, including suicidal clients; and the need for crisis intervention skills.

Involuntary, Mandated, and Non-voluntary Clients   When you first considered social work practice, you may have assumed that people would come to you because they wanted your services and believed in the possibility, at least, that you would be helpful. The principles of self-determination and working toward the preferred reality seem the opposite of coercion, and some social workers question the appropriateness of this kind of practice. Yet, because of the constant tension between social work as an agent of social control and an agent of change, a significant proportion of clients (in some settings, *all clients*) are involuntary.

Involuntary has several different meanings. In some sense, all clients are involuntary in that few are happy to receive services as it likely indicates they are experiencing a crisis in their lives (e.g., loss, illness, etc.). Certainly those who seek public sector welfare services are likely to be involuntarily in their current situation. Thus, the distinction between voluntary and involuntary is not always clear cut, but three ways of distinguishing this type of client are accepted in the profession.

Clients are **involuntary** if they have been compelled to receive services, including mandated and non-voluntary client systems (Barker, 2003). **Mandated clients** are typically required by an authority (e.g., legal system, employer, etc.) to receive services in order, for example, to reclaim children, escape criminal charges, or avoid institutionalization. Such mandates occur most often in the systems of care that are heavily shaped and sanctioned by the law in, such as child protection, mental health, and criminal justice. **Non-voluntary** clients are not formally or legally obliged to participate in services, but are pressured into receiving them. For example, persons with substance abuse issues may be "strongly encouraged" by their employers to seek help for their addiction, or a parent "takes" an adolescent to family counseling. In these situations the client is in some way persuaded that she or he needs to get services in order, for example, to keep the peace, or remain married, or stay employed.

There are many, and often unpredictable, patterns of engagement with involuntary clients. Some angry mandated clients become convinced that they can benefit from genuine involvement, whereas others simply wait out their time. Non-voluntary clients may perfunctorily go through the motions to satisfy someone else, or they may work for real change. The whole notion of involuntary clients presents several challenges as well as opportunities.

Challenges in Working with Involuntary Clients For many social workers, whether it is students or more seasoned practitioners, the idea of working with a client who does not want to be there is uncomfortable, if not daunting. In some cases, the issues relate to the interface the social worker needs to maintain with the mandating agency, which may seem rigid or overly authoritarian. In others, social workers might dislike the involuntary client's behavior (for example, negative feelings regarding the client's engagement in child abuse, criminal activity, or substance abuse). In still others, social workers are unsure how to build a relationship in such circumstances. These are understandable concerns, but they put many more limits on the situation than are necessary.

ENGAGEMENT WITH INVOLUNTARY CLIENTS Being well-prepared for your first visit with an involuntary client is the first step. First, prepare *yourself*. In general, you can expect that your client may be angry, hostile, or fearful. If you are assaulted by spiteful or even hateful remarks at the beginning of a meeting, you may feel surprised and hurt, so it is helpful to know how you may react and to think ahead about how to respond. Striving to remain calm and non-reactive are goals for an encounter such as this one. Clients who are emotionally agitated or distressed may seek to shock or outrage the social worker. Having a professional response to the client's outbursts can serve to defuse the potentially volatile situation.

Involuntary clients often take on a perception that they need nothing you have to offer and they may feel they have a valid reason for believing what they believe (De Jong & Berg, 2013). As a result, they do not truly engage with you. Although this seems challenging, it can actually assist you in refraining from taking any angry remarks personally, because the client makes few role demands on you. Another way to prepare for the resentment and negativity of some involuntary clients is to place yourself in the client's position. Remember the times you have felt coerced, invisible, unrecognized, or ignored. You can connect with some part of that scenario that can make you more empathic and help you to understand the client's disinclination to trust anyone, including you.

Not all clients, of course, will barge in with this level of antagonism. Some will be overly polite or seem controlled. The client may perceive that if she or he maintains a complacent or controlled demeanor, you will not be able to break through the exterior to touch them in any significantly emotional way. Some may actually view meeting with you as an opportunity to think about making changes. Since the tendency may be to decide the client is resistant before you start the work, consider remaining as "unknowing" as you can. In any case, the most helpful approach is to listen, as it is in any client situation, to the story. Find out how the client sees the situation. Ask the client how things could have been different, respect the client's reality without challenging it, and assume the client has both strengths and competence in spite of the current predicament. Find out what is important to the client and how she or he wants things to change. This is often an excellent situation for questions that probe for the client's perspective because they can reveal that there is more to the client than the involuntary situation, and that she or he is not just "bad," or a personified crime—for example, "a B & E" (breaking and entering) or a "shoplifter." If the adolescent who is substance-using feels like a "loser" and worthless, you might ask, "What would your best friend say is your greatest strength?" or, "What would your favorite teacher say you're good at?" (De Jong & Berg, 2013). For more on useful approaches with involuntary clients, see Quick Guide 11.

In most cases of mandated services, you will have some externally structured pattern for your work. This can be a set number of sessions (such as 12) or a curriculum to follow. You may need to explain this to your client in order to encourage the engagement process. One of the major ways you can assist your client is to give her or him as much control as possible by emphasizing any choices that are real (for example, you may be able to meet once or twice a week, on Tuesdays or Fridays) and by being as clear as possible regarding requirements. If the court requires you to notify authorities if your client misses a single session, inform her or him of that. Consider that mandated clients typically feel as if control and choice have been taken away from them, and stay attuned to those issues. You will want to provide all the information you can about the contingencies as a respectful gesture of recognition and acknowledge to the client that you are aware that she or he does have choices (e.g., to work with you or not work with you), even if they do not feel they do.

QUICK GUIDE 11   INVOLUNTARY CLIENTS

Guidelines for Interviewing Involuntary Clients

- Assume you will be interviewing someone who probably will start out not wanting anything you might have to offer.
- Assume the client has good reason to think and act as he or she does.
- Suspend your judgment and agree with the client's perceptions that stand behind his or her cautious, protective posture.
- Listen for who and what are important to the client, including when the client is angry and critical.
- When clients are openly angry or critical, ask what the offending person or agency could have done differently to be more useful to them.
- Be sure to ask for the client's perception of what is in his or her best interest; that is, ask for what the client might want.
- Listen for and reflect the client's use of language into your next questions and responses.
- Bring the client's context into the interview by asking questions about her or his relationships with others.
- Respectfully provide information about any nonnegotiable requirements and immediately ask for the client's perceptions regarding these.
- Always stay "not knowing" (i.e., social worker's focus is on the client's frame of reference, not her or his own).

Source: De Jong & Berg, 2013, p. 184

LEGAL ISSUES   In spite of your best efforts to engage your client, mandated or not, you may find yourself having to take a position in the best interests of the client, including children and older adults. This position can become difficult when you have been trying to respect the client's situation and work with their goals and wishes. For example, do not decide prematurely that the single parent in a child protection scenario is not ready to have her children back or that your older adult client cannot live safely in the community. You want to keep working toward the goals of the client system to arrive at a point at which her or his preferred reality can be realized.

Nevertheless, there are times when you may have to take a conscience-driven stand that may seem to work against the client system. For example, if an older adult experiencing dementia has progressed to the point that she is unable to maintain her activities of daily living, including cooking, shopping, and bathing, she may not be able to continue living alone in her home. Your recommendation to the court may be to seek care for your client in a residential setting. The client may be upset about your recommendation and feel you are not supporting her. In such cases, inform the client(s) before any court hearing or other meeting. Avoid any surprises for your client that would further violate trust. For example, initiating an honest dialogue (e.g., "this is the way I see it") conveys respect even if the client does not agree with the assessment. Another way to help the client understand the perspective of others is to ask perspectival questions, such as "What do you think the judge might think about the times when you left the baby alone?" (De Jong & Berg, 2013).

Opportunities in Working with Involuntary Client Systems   Although involuntary situations are not ideal, they are seldom disastrous. Such interactions can present the opportunity to engage people who might never undertake any change without being forced into seeking services. These challenges also present social workers with an opportunity to practice their most cherished social work skills. By hearing and respecting clients' perceptions, assuming they can grow, and believing that their situation is workable, you have an opportunity to engage them in ways that can potentially transform their lives.

INDIVIDUAL SCENARIOS   Consider the man who was adjudicated by the court as a perpetrator of domestic violence, but because he also had a substantial history as a client of mental health services and had just been discharged from a psychiatric facility, you were asked by your supervisor to meet with him individually. This departure from the agency's standard intervention (which was group work for men) was made on the grounds that the client would not respond well in the potential confrontation of a group. He was painfully embarrassed at being singled out as inappropriate for a group process, angry that he was treated like a "common criminal," and exceedingly hostile about meeting with you.

Using a basic approach of respect, a willingness to hear him out, and a position of wanting to understand his life, you can connect with him after several sessions. He then confided that he had never had the opportunity to talk about the challenging issues in his family and that he felt humiliated and stigmatized in receiving mental health services. By the end of the twelve mandated sessions, he wanted to engage in further work, and he had come to believe that he could change his violent behaviors by responding differently to the stresses he felt. This is an example of the way clients respond to an affirming approach that recognizes their strengths even though the client was not initially involved in his treatment decisions.

POWER ISSUES   There is a clear association with power, specifically coercive power, in any kind of involuntary and especially mandated service. Regardless of the relationship or work that transpires, you have considerable power in determining the course of the client's life. In these situations, you need to recognize the power you have, be as comfortable with it as possible, articulate your understanding of the power to your client system and elicit the client's understanding. Transparency about power creates a rich opportunity to demonstrate your genuineness and trustworthiness to clients, and enables the opportunity to discuss power and its meaning to your client. You are presented with an opportunity to struggle with the tension between your role as a person of social control and your role as a person who assists client system who are caught in social control.

Focusing on power provides a context for discussing your client's goals and strategies. For the client, the goal might be as simple as getting authorities "off my back," or it may involve much more complex efforts to change a system that she or he experiences as oppressive. For example, the woman trying to regain custody of her children who has to see you, get clean, get a job, and find a home with no instrumental supports might, for example, want to join with others in an empowerment-focused approach to influence the system in helping her meet her mandates.

Violence   None of us can remain oblivious to the increasing violence in our culture. Violence looms in almost every newspaper, television news story, and on all too many urban street corners and rural crossroads across the country and beyond. From the wars waged overseas to violence in school settings, violence is expressed in ideological as well as interpersonal terms, and is a common theme everywhere. Social workers are frequently in the position of working with the effects of a violent culture and are not immune from direct exposure to violent threats in the work-place. The escalation of violence in our lives has become an insidious component of contemporary experience and should be addressed on personal, agency, and policy levels.

Safety in Social Work Practice   Although it can be comforting to think of violent acts, particularly those related to social work practice, as discrete, chance occur-rences, there is often a difficult-to-deny connection between violence and many historical, political, and cultural processes that reflect a cycle of escalation. Violence in any setting breeds negative, destructive attitudes and relationships that are rein-forced by periodic eruptions in social contexts, but social workers must be know-ledgeable about and prepared for violence within any practice setting. School bullying, interracial taunting, and sexual harassment are just a few pervasive exam-ples that are translated into interpersonal persecution that may occur in social work practice. Occasionally these situations escalate into physical violence on an inter-personal or social level, as witnessed by isolated attacks, school murders, or race-related altercations. Some people resort to violence to get their basic needs met, and our society struggles to eliminate the barriers that prevent people from doing so.

As evidenced by the NASW-issued policy statement calling for the development of organizational policies to address employee safety, the social work profession is committed to minimizing violence in the workplace (NASW, 2012–2014b). Social workers can observe the growing disparities between rich and poor in the United States, consider the wider political components that seem to spur people to hate one another, and renew their efforts to work for a just society. Building on the profes-sion's systemic perspective, social workers can address racist and economic policies of welfare reform that punish people of color and maintain poverty, and can analyze, for example, legal approaches to limiting weapons, their commitment to antiviolence principles, and their positions on war. All of these issues are at the heart of people's lives and as such are in the realm of social justice-oriented social work practice from the most local to the most global levels.

Considering that practitioners are very likely to work with people who are the most affected by the quality of this cultural fabric, it is not surprising that, as symbols of the dominant culture and agents of social control, social workers are increasingly the objects of violence themselves (Jayartne, Croxton, & Mattison, 2004). As early as 1995, Newhill documented that "physical and emotional violence by clients toward social workers is increasing in all settings" (1995, p. 631). A recent survey of NASW members (Whitaker & Arrington, 2008) details specific areas of incidence and risk. Forty-two percent of social workers working in mental health services identify violence as a safety concern, while 43 percent of mental health social workers and 30 percent of social workers working in child welfare settings have actually experienced violence from adult clients in the workplace. Unfortunately, the trend toward violence against human service workers is not abating as workers report being subjected to physical assault, and "all workers were routinely subjected to psychological aggression" (Shields & Kiser, 2003, p. 13), such as outbursts of anger, profanity, or intimidation. As startling as these reports are, social workers can work together to ensure preparedness.

SKILLS FOR WORKING WITH CLIENTS WHO ARE ANGRY   As a social worker in a context of potential violence, you can take reasonable precautions based on common sense and effective communication. See Exhibit 4.11 to consider these strategies. The single most useful tool for working with a client who is angry or hostile may possibly be empathy. Using your knowledge of basic social work engagement skills, you can also speak in a calm, quiet, and impartial manner while maintaining a physical and non-threatening distance (Burry, 2002). Empathic responses to clients demonstrate that you recognize they are upset, would like to understand the reasons for their distress, and want to assist them. In turn, such responses can defuse clients' anger. In addition to this overall compassionate stance, you will want to observe the following:

- Recognize your own tension. Be alert for feelings of defensiveness, and prepare yourself to avoid returning angry or hostile comments.

- Acknowledge the client's strengths as you listen, and include them in your responses when they can be heard as genuine (rather than patronizing).

- Focus on positive and current alternatives that are realistic and open to the client.

- Avoid moralizing or lecturing, no matter how destructive you think the client's conduct has been.

- When necessary, focus on keeping your own control rather than on the client's anger.

WHAT AGENCIES CAN DO   In situations of potential violence, agencies need to assume some of the responsibility to avert danger. Employers can recognize and validate the hazards to which workers are exposed, so that they will report their experiences openly. Policies for handling incidents should be clear and worker-focused. Opportunities for processing and group consultation should be frequent and responsive. Preparation for workers entering possibly dangerous situations and debriefing for those who have experienced aggressive or violent clients should be standard practice and should not require that the worker initiate a formal request. Larger agencies should consider establishing a management team to address violence and should offer training on physical safety and verbal de-escalation procedures that meet worker needs and interests. The majority of social workers surveyed by NASW believe their employers appropriately respond to issues of safety in the workplace (Whitaker & Arrington, 2008). Feeling safe in one's place of work is just one aspect of the social worker as an effective practitioner. The social work profession is committed to ensuring the safety of its members in their places of employment and has a work underway to develop guidelines for social worker safety in the workplace (NASW, 2013a). Read on about issues of self-care and ethical practice.

Crisis Intervention   Crises are an expected part of the social work professional's practice life; all social workers must develop competencies for responding to the range of crises that will present themselves. Events occur in individuals' lives that bring them to social workers as mandated, involuntary, frightened, or hysterical clients. While a life crisis may be the trigger that brings the client system to the social worker, each crisis is uniquely experienced by the client system and should not be considered routine. Crises occur when an intense and stressful event creates disruption in one's life that cannot be resolved using one's usual coping mechanisms, the precipitating event is perceived as meaningful or threatening, or the individual experiences fear, tension, confusion, and/or subjective discomfort following a period of disequilibrium (Roberts, 2008; 2005, p. 13).

Regardless of the origins of the crisis (e.g., forces over which the client has no control or the result of a poor life choice by the client), the trauma felt by the client can be real and devastating. The social worker's ability to quickly and accurately conduct an assessment can support and empower the client in her or his response to the crisis situation. Crisis situations provide the opportunity for the client system (and the social worker) to grow and change, but it is incumbent on the social worker to have a repertoire of practice behaviors that can help the client view what is likely perceived to be a painful experience as the opportunity to strengthen her or his coping skills and even quality of life.

Social workers can benefit from having a theoretically and evidence-based model for responding to crises. Two models that lend themselves particularly well to assessing and intervening in crisis situations are Roberts' seven-stage model of crisis and the solution-focused approach (Roberts, 2005; 2008). Roberts' (2005; 2008) model emphasizes the importance of assessment in the ability to facilitate an

EXHIBIT 4.11

Violence

What Social Workers Can Do in the Context of Violence

- Always inform your client of the time you expect to make a home visit. Keep to that schedule as closely as possible. This is not only respectful, but you are more likely to be safe if you do not surprise anyone with your appearance.
- Consult with others (especially a supervisor) before entering a situation you think may be dangerous. If your client has a history of violence and is highly stressed or is known to have firearms or other weapons, do not make a home visit or an office visit after hours without talking it over with others who may have more experience and can consult with you about your decision.
- When you leave the office to make home visits, always inform someone about your schedule. Check by phone in worrisome (or all) situations.
- Pay attention to your surroundings. If you are on a home visit and you hear fighting or crying from outside the residence, reassess the timing of your visit. If there is activity that seems suspicious and/or is not what you expected, avoid confrontation.
- Do not put yourself physically in a position to be trapped in a potentially violent client's home. Keep a clear path to the door, so you can leave quickly if necessary.
- Make connections with the local police if you work in a dangerous neighborhood, or with local shop owners or residents in rural areas. Alert them of your plans when circumstances warrant and to the extent that confidentiality permits. Know when police should accompany you, and do not hesitate to ask them when appropriate.
- Do not challenge an angry client with rebuttals or consequences. A calm, kind, and reflective presentation can encourage de-escalation.
- If you sense that something is wrong and you are at risk, even if you cannot tell exactly what it is, leave. There is time for analysis later, and if you overreacted, you can explore that in a safe environment.
- Report incidents of any kind to your supervisor, or use an agency-designated process if there is one. This both helps you work through your own reactions and skills and facilitates the agency's effective response to its workers.
- Recognize your own tension. Be alert for feelings of defensiveness, and prepare yourself to avoid returning angry or hostile comments.
- Acknowledge the client's strengths as you listen, and include them in your responses when they can be heard as genuine (rather than patronizing).
- Focus on positive and current alternatives that are realistic and open to the client.
- Avoid moralizing or lecturing, no matter how destructive you think the client's conduct has been.
- When necessary, focus on keeping your own control rather than on the client's anger.

effective intervention plan. Specifically, initiating a rapid and timely response to the client's crisis is a critical first step in working with the client's situation. In reviewing the seven stages of crisis intervention presented here, note the prominent role that assessment plays in the professional's response both in the initial steps and throughout the intervention (Eaton & Roberts, 2009, pp. 210–212):

1. Plan and conduct a crisis assessment including lethality, dangerousness to self or others, and immediate psychosocial needs.
2. Rapidly establish rapport and the therapeutic relationship.
3. Identify the issues pertinent to the client and any precipitants to the client's crisis contact.
4. Deal with feelings and emotions by effectively using active listening skills.
5. Generate and explore alternatives by identifying the strengths of the client as well as previous successful coping mechanisms.
6. Implement the action plan.
7. Establish a follow-up plan and agreement.

Through its emphasis on strengths, solutions, the present and future (as opposed to the past), and short-term intervention, the solution-focused approach is applicable to crisis intervention. Blending well with Roberts' model described here, a solution-based assessment and intervention homes in on the assumption that crisis provides the opportunity for clients to embark on changes; in particular, changes they may have been reluctant or unable to make previously (Roberts, 2005).

Suicide   Whether it is the client who is threatening or has attempted to intentionally take her or his life, the family coping with the suicidal death of a loved one, or the client experiencing depression that you fear is at risk for suicide, the social worker is faced with an individual or a group in crisis. Just as with the other forms of client crises, social workers are ethically bound to identify and assess clients who may be at risk for suicide and take appropriate actions to prevent suicidal attempts.

As with crisis intervention, the key to effectiveness is rapid and timely assessment. An important first step in preventing a suicide attempt or completion is a suicide risk assessment (Freedenthal, 2008). A suicide risk assessment includes questions focused on any thoughts the client may be having about death and suicide. The social worker then inquires if the client has developed a plan, a time frame, and a means for carrying out the suicide. The social worker must then assess the lethality of the client's plan. For example, does the client have access to the means of suicide that she/he has stated will be used, is the plan well formulated, or does the client talk about giving away personal possessions? These are indicators that the client is serious about ending her or his life. Also important is the client or family history with suicide attempts. Exhibit 4.12 provides an example of one agency's suicide risk assessment that you may find helpful in assessing a client's risk for suicide.

When assessing individuals from vulnerable populations for suicidal ideation (e.g., veterans, persons subjected to bullying, and LGBTQ youth), the social worker must have a specialized set of skills to competently and sensitively intervene. Considerations for assessing vulnerable populations include the following (also refer to Exhibit 4.13 for a sample dialogue between a social worker and a youth who expresses suicidal thoughts):

- Recognize that your client is likely to have experienced trauma or victimization for the short-term (veterans) or on a longer term basis (LGBTQ youth), so ensure that you do not re-victimize or traumatize them in your encounter.

- Allow the client to determine the pace of the assessment—they may want to talk or they may not wish to talk during the first meeting.

- Tap into the client's previous coping strategies that she or he feels have been successful in helping them to feel better.

- Understand your client's experience to the extent that generalized information applies or that your client shares, but do not make assumptions or presume to understand their experience even if you have lives something similar.

- Acknowledge that you may have limited time for intervening.

- Do not be overly directive as this may be part of the client's history that was traumatizing.

- The client needs to be in control as the crisis that brought on suicidal thoughts has likely robbed her or him of the sense of control.

- Do not minimize the crisis or offer positive prediction—you cannot know the experience or its outcomes.

- While some clients may find it helpful to share with others who have similar experiences or families, others may not feel comfortable being in a group environment, so do not force the issue.

- Be knowledgeable about the services and resources for clients by familiarizing yourself with evidence-based intervention practices and best practices for intervening with vulnerable groups.

- Above all else, maintain a non-judgmental status.

Critically important for the social worker is knowledge of agency and legal procedures for immediately and appropriately responding to suicidal ideations, threats, or attempts. Mobilizing an emergency response is imperative. Responses may include negotiating a contract in which the client agrees not to attempt suicide, involving members of the client's support network or community, facilitating the prescription of antidepressant medication, and/or seeking hospitalization for the client. Regardless of your response, a thorough and immediate assessment is critically important for your client.

An issue that may arise is the ethical commitment the social work professional makes to honor the client's right to self-determination. However, while advocating for the client's ability to determine her or his own actions is a social work value, preserving life takes priority in the case of threatened or attempted suicide (Freedenthal, 2008). In the practice context, this means that the social worker intervenes to prevent any threat of suicide by contacting authorities or negotiating a no-suicide contract.

The Social Worker Perspective: The Social Worker as a Whole Person

Just as it is necessary to be attuned to safety issues, social workers must be sensitized to their own physical and emotional health. As you have seen, several areas of challenge in social work practice might lead to increasing discouragement and

---

EXHIBIT 4.12

Suicide Risk Assessment

CRISIS WORKER_____   DATE_____   TIME_____

Life Crisis Services, St. Louis   *Suicide Risk Assessment*
Caller Name_____   Phone# _____

1. Are you thinking of suicide? (If yes go immediately to assessment)	2. Have you thought about suicide in the last two months?	3. Have you ever attempted suicide?
Y N	Y N	Y N

RISK FACTORS	RISK LEVELS	LOW	MEDIUM	HIGH	IMMED HIGH

INTENT: *expressed intent to die; availability of means to and opportunity for attempt; specificity of plan; and preparations for attempt.*

	LOW	MEDIUM	HIGH	IMMED HIGH
Attempt in Progress	no	no	no	yes
Plan to hurt self/other	unclear	some plan	well thought out	
– time frame	in the future	>24hrs.	<24hrs	0–12hrs
– method	unclear	some plan	well thought out	
– location	unplanned	unsure	known	
Preparatory steps taken (giving items away, goodbyes, etc.)	none	some	many	
Expressed Intent to die (on a scale of 1–4, with 1 being low and 4 high, when you think about killing yourself, how much do you really want to die?)	1	2	3	4

Details of method:_____
_____

EXHIBIT 4.12

Continued

DESIRE: *no reason for living, wish to die, wish not to carry on, desire for a suicide attempt*

Wants to hurt self/others	no	sometimes	most of the time	now
Hopelessness	none	sometimes	most of the time	always
Helplessness	none	sometimes	most of the time	always
Perceived burden	none	sometimes	most of the time	always
Feeling intolerably alone	not at all	sometimes	most of the time	always
Feeling trapped, no escape	not at all	sometimes	most of the time	always
Psychological pain	1	2	3	4

(on a scale of 1–4, how much hurt, anguish or misery are you feeling right now?)

CAPABILITY: *a sense of fearlessness to make an attempt; a sense of competence to make an attempt*

Means available	have to get	close access	have with	used
History of attempts	none	one	2–3 times	>3
Exposure to suicide	no	know someone	close relative/friend	
Hx of violence to others	none	occasionally	frequently	
Alcohol/drug use/abuse	none	average use	excessive use/abuse	
Currently intoxicated/impaired				yes
Recent dramatic mood swings	none	within last month	within last week	daily
Increased anxiety	none	monthly	weekly	daily
Decreased sleep	none	monthly	weekly	daily
Out of touch with reality	not at all	occasionally	frequently	now
Recent acts/threats of aggression	none	some	many	daily

BUFFERS/CONNECTEDNESS: *how many connectors to meaningful components of life are present?*

Immediate support present	available now	possibly available quickly	not possible
Other social supports	available now	available occasionally	no support
Future plans goals	concrete plans	some plans	no plans
Purpose in life	strong purpose	some purpose	no purpose
Ambivalence about death	much	a little	none
Beliefs about suicide	against belief sys	belief system ambiguous	no belief system
Rapport with Crisis Worker	very engaged	somewhat engaged	not at all engaged

We've been talking for a while now . . . can I ask you about how you're feeling now? On a scale from 1–4, how likely are you to kill yourself?

	1	2	3	4
	low	medium	high	Imm-high
ENDING RISK				

____follow-up scheduled   ____Pager called   ____traced call   ____Police called

Source: Life Crisis Services, St. Louis, MO

EXHIBIT 4.13

Suicide Risk Assessment with Vulnerable Populations: A Dialogue with Christopher

You are a social worker working in a multi-service not-for-profit agency that serves youth who are at risk. Your organization provides crisis intervention, emergency shelter, transitional and independent living, mobile street outreach, educational and employment programs, and individual and family treatment. Christopher arrived at the emergency shelter the previous night and you are conducting an initial intake interview and assessment the following morning. Follow along with the interview below to learn more about assessing a client who is particularly vulnerable:

Social Worker: Christopher, it's good to meet you. What brings you to our shelter?

Christopher: My parents kicked me out a couple of weeks ago. I've been staying with different people, just sleeping on their couches.

Social Worker: How are you feeling today?

Christopher: Ok.

Social Worker: Do you want to talk about your parents kicking you out of the house?

Christopher: They don't like my lifestyle, so they wanted me out of their house.

Social Worker: What is it about your lifestyle that you think they don't like?

Christopher: They found something and flipped out.

Social Worker: What did they find?

Christopher: Well, actually, they saw an email between me and my boyfriend.

Social Worker: What was it about the email they had a problem with?

Christopher: It's that I have a boyfriend. Turns out they didn't know I was gay.

Social Worker: Sounds like they didn't take it well?

Christopher: You could say that. . . .

Social Worker: How are you coping?

Christopher: So, my boyfriend breaks up with me because my parents called his parents and now his parents won't let him see me anymore. They say I'm a bad influence. I'm just done. If my parents don't want me and my boyfriend doesn't want me and I don't have anywhere to go, then I'm just outta here.

Social Worker: When you say you're done, what do you mean?

Christopher: I mean . . . what's the point?

Social Worker: Again, let me ask what you mean.

Christopher: What's the point of living if I don't have a place to stay and nobody cares what happens to me?

Social worker: It's your mention of "point of living" that concerns me. Are you saying you would think of ending your life?

Christopher: Yeah, I guess that's what I'm saying. I don't have anything to live for, do I?

Social Worker: Have you thought how you would do that?

		EXHIBIT 4.13

Christopher:	Yeah, I guess I have. There's a lot of times lately that I've sat at the Metro stop and thought how easy it would be to just step in front of that train. It would just end all the pain, you know, for everybody.
Social Worker:	Do you have a time frame for when you thought you might do that?
Christopher:	No, just been thinking about it sometimes.
Social Worker:	What's keeping you from doing it?
Christopher:	My friend, he saw this flyer at the Metro stop about you guys and he said I should call. So, I did. I don't know what you can do to help though.
Social Worker:	That was a good idea. That took courage for you to call. I'm glad that you came in. Let's talk about how we can help you to deal with some of these feelings you have without you hurting yourself.
Christopher:	{Silence . . . . he begins to cry}.
Social Worker:	I see this is emotional for you. Can you share what's going on?
Christopher:	I don't really want to die. It just seems like it's the easiest choice.
Social Worker:	Let's talk about something that would help you to be able to not follow through with this plan. Would that be ok?
Christopher:	Maybe.
Social Worker:	Let's talk about an agreement that includes some alternatives for when you are feeling bad.
Christopher:	Like what?
Social Worker:	We can both come up with ideas, write them down, and even sign them . . . just like a contract.
Christopher:	What kind of things?
Social Worker:	For instance, what makes you feel good?
Christopher:	Listening to my music.
Social Worker:	What is it about the music that makes you feel better?
Christopher:	I just connect with it.
Social Worker:	How about if you agree that when you are feeling bad, you will listen to your favorite band?
Christopher:	I guess maybe I could agree to that.
Social Worker:	What else do you do that makes you feel good?
Christopher:	Getting high.

At this point, the social worker and the client go on to discuss health and non-healthy coping strategies and long-term consequences of each. Eventually, they agreed on a list of alternatives to suicide which they write down. Each signs the contract, copies are made, and they agree to re-visit the contract within within the week. The social worker offers shelter and makes an appointment to meet within the new few days. Lastly, Christopher agrees to talk with a shelter staff member if he begins to have feelings of harming himself.

ultimately to the emotional and physical exhaustion associated with burnout (Nissly, Barak, & Levin, 2005). Working with clients who experience oppression and trying to help with inadequate resources, engaging involuntary clients who may challenge your capacities, confronting a violent culture and avoiding its direct expression against you, coping with the bureaucratic tensions of managed care—all of these may seem to confound and certainly challenge your best intentions in the practice of social work. Social workers report that the lack of time to complete job tasks is the major stressor, followed by heavy workloads and working with difficult and challenging client situations (Arrington, 2008). When added to the pressure that can be induced by organizational policies and practices (discussed in Chapters 10 and 11), social workers can experience frustration and alienation day after day if effective self-care strategies are not developed.

Therefore, it is important to address two phenomena that are difficult to manage: the incidence of painful events and the occurrence of personal triggers. Social workers need self-care strategies for dealing with the stresses that lead to **secondary trauma**, **burnout**, and **compassion fatigue**. Secondary trauma can occur when helping professions react to pain experienced by client systems, while burnout is a stressful response to the work. When both secondary trauma and burnout occur, the social worker may be experiencing compassion fatigue (Wharton, 2008). Given the intensity of social worker-client relationships and demanding work responsibilities, social workers, particularly in the early stages of their careers, are at risk for negative outcomes, including physical health problems, and should commit to a proactive approach to self-care (Kim, Ji, & Kao, 2011).

Painful Events   Although most of social work practice deals with struggles experienced by client systems, and does so as a routine dimension of the territory, many (probably most) practitioners at one time or another experience a particularly jolting event that shakes their confidence and makes them question their capacity or commitment. This event is often a crisis—for example, a client suicide, a murder, an unspeakable case of child abuse, or an annihilating fire, to name a few. Such events can be experienced as trauma that splits the social worker's world wide open, taking a generally well-balanced human being off guard. Because these occurrences are a departure from the social worker's usual ability to cope, she or he may be reluctant to recognize or acknowledge an unusual reaction. Ignoring the signs can be dangerous for the social worker's own stability and ability to bounce back. Social workers need to allow themselves to be human in this profession, and the experience of overload, contrary to negative connotations, can reflect the traits of a caring, human person.

When isolated situations such as these occur, the social worker should seek and receive as much support as possible. Time away from work, debriefing sessions, or a shift in responsibility may be indicated. The social worker's response should be normalized (i.e., assurance given that her or his response is appropriate to the situation). With appropriate supports and adequate time, most workers will work through such situations and return to their practice as committed as they were before.

Personal Triggers   In a related scenario, the social worker may have some unresolved or not-quite-resolved personal issues that affect her or his capacity to carry out the work of the agency. For example, a social worker who experienced an abusive father in childhood may harbor a great deal of rage. While anger may be understandable and normal, it can be a serious problem if, for example, the worker verbally or physically attacks a client who may be suspected of child abuse. In such cases the agency response is likely to be different from that for a painful event. The event is more likely to become a supervisory issue that is addressed administratively or with corrective action. Here, the social worker can engage in a process (i.e., therapy or education) to effectively change her or his behavior. An extreme reaction can be a difficult experience for someone who is committed to the profession and has the capacity to make a solid contribution. The intensity of the trigger situation can lead a social worker to assess herself or himself as inadequate and not suited to the profession. However, with appropriate consultation with a qualified professional (e.g., supervisor, mentor, or mental health practitioner), many social workers who experience an intense experience can work through the emotional aspects in order to reconcile the personal and the professional. As all helping professionals have areas that can be triggered, this phenomenon can be somewhat normalized. While no professional can claim perfect balance, social workers are obligated to identify and respond to those triggers that may impact personal and professional well-being.

Self-Care   In carrying out the work of the profession, social workers need to learn to care for themselves, even as they care for clients. As in the case of safety, the profession, through a policy statement, has deemed self-care a priority for all social workers from students to individuals to administrators (NASW, 2012–2014b). Although this process will take on different dimensions in different people, strategies that may prove useful include:

- *Learn to use yourself as a resource:* Knowing your own responses, biases, and limits in various processes of your work is a first step in self-care. Self-awareness is critical not only in ethical, culturally sensitive practice but also in taking care of yourself. Appreciating your strengths and accepting your vulnerabilities will help you make good practice connections with clients as well as avoid expecting too much of yourself, which frequently leads to feeling disheartened. In the face of extensive client need, you may expect to save the world and inspire clients to love you while you do it. When you know that about yourself, you can laugh at your own grandiosity, let go of the need for all clients to like you, and continue to strive for competent practice.

- *Understand shared power:* Within a model of planned change that includes engagement, assessment, intervention, and termination/evaluation, the use of the strengths perspective assumes that clients have the ability to control their lives and do not need you to do it for them. Such an approach carries an unexpected benefit of reducing the pressure to be all-knowing and all-delivering, a stance that can be burdensome to clients and professionals as well as harmful to clients. In essence, you do not have to assume responsibility for clients' behaviors; you cannot be responsible for any behavior other than your own.

- *Focus on practical goals:* Related to the impulse to rid the world of all evil, you will always be disappointed and will continue to fail. When you concentrate on the strengths clients have to achieve their own goals and when you stress social justice and human rights in ways the client can relate to, you are more likely to see joint successes more frequently. This in turn will bolster your commitment.

- *Find your own systems for support:* Social workers understand the importance of support for clients but may forget its value to themselves. Support, in and outside of the workplace, is critical for the connectedness discussed throughout this book. Developing a group of peers at work can be helpful and enjoyable. Such a collective can function as a peer supervisory/support network or a strictly social group. Friends outside of work and family are also critical. Spiritual support in the way of religious affiliation or a more informal connection with the dimensions that seem most important in life can help put the occasional but inevitable disappointments and frustrations of the work into a perspective that helps keep you from feeling overwhelmed.

- *Live healthy:* Social work jobs are demanding physically and emotionally. Ensuring that you are caring for your physical health through exercise, adequate sleep, and balanced nutrition is critically important as well (Wharton, 2008).

Although social work will never be an easy job, it need not be overwhelming. Recalling the joys and connections of working with people can fill out the compensation side of the balance sheet. Taking control of your own reactions and caring for yourself will enhance your capacity to stay committed.

Just as social workers emphasize the whole client in context, they need to think of themselves as whole people, too. This means that they are not just social workers. Like clients, they are children, partners, bicycle racers, amateur politicians, musicians, parents, belly dancers, and artists. They are good in some roles and need work in others. They may connect well with involuntary clients and yet steer away from children or older adults. They may be stimulated by institutional settings or find them hopelessly oppressive. They may need to work on how to change urban agency policies effectively or thrive in rural locations where the sole agency has no walls and policy is an on-the-go venture.

Social workers may also be subject to restrictions related to social justice themselves. Their human rights may be violated daily, and it is likely that they—although inadvertently—violate those of others daily. Their identities are privileged in some contexts and devalued in others. When you see yourself as a whole human, belonging in a context, you will be more likely to engage in your human work with enthusiasm and vigor.

Sustaining Ethical Practice in the Face of Challenges   Social workers are bound by the *Code of Ethics* (NASW, 2008) to care for oneself and practice ethically in spite of setbacks and situations that do not go as planned; to keep growing in response to new ideas, perceptions, and client-informed experience; and to keep a vision of what ethical social work practice can be and how you can contribute. The ethical aspects of practice can become obscured by the struggles workers experience. Just as practitioners need to guard against rationalizing funding cuts or avoiding client contact, they need to keep the ethical considerations of omission as much in mind as those of commission. For example, not working for active reform of harmful systems (omission) is as neglectful as committing an outright violation of the *Code of Ethics*. If workers increasingly withdraw, defending themselves against the challenges of dehumanizing contexts, they can slowly lose the spirit of ethical practice without even realizing it.

One of the most effective ways to negotiate troubling practice contexts is to engage fully in a positive, supportive supervisory relationship (Smith, 2005), in which both the supervisor and the social worker can grow. As the social worker, you can contribute to that relationship by bringing something to the process; supervision is not a commodity that is given to you (or done to you), but rather it is an interactive relationship. The term *supervision* conjures up images of a hierarchy. Literally interpreted as "watching from above," it suggests an authoritarian relationship in which one member judges and corrects the other. Fortunately, social work supervision is not limited to that configuration, in spite of the inevitable evaluative nature of the term.

Supervision, then, in all its forms—individual, group, ad hoc, formal case, and peer—has the potential to contribute a great deal to sustaining ethical practice in challenging contexts. Hearing others' beliefs about the issues involved in a challenging practice situation, for example, can expand your thinking and help you work through the places in which you are immobilized or perplexed. Such a dialogic process encompasses a genuine interchange regarding the values and ethics of a case situation. Effective, collaborative supervision can provide technical support, in that it has the potential to increase and improve your practice responses; and emotional support, in that it reduces isolation and increases hopefulness. See Exhibit 4.14 for tips on effectively engaging in supervision.

EXHIBIT 4.14

Tips for Using Supervision Effectively

- Be prepared for each session by reviewing your work and identifying the issues you want to discuss.
- Demonstrate a genuine eagerness about learning more and expanding your knowledge and experience base in practice.
- Take responsibility for your work, your thinking, and your reactions.
- Trust in so far as possible in the supervisory relationship so that you do not need to cover mistakes or deny any struggles you have with the work.
- Assume a willingness to take thoughtful risks.
- Understand the parameters of your work and the expectations your agency/supervisor has of you.
- Respect the difference between the focus of supervision (how an issue affects your work) and the focus of psychotherapy (how an issue affects your emotional life).
- Remain open and non-defensive if/when your supervisor suggests you do things differently.
- Demonstrate a respectful and professional approach to relationships with all colleagues, including your supervisor.

CONCLUSION

In an effort to help you experience the contemporary climate, this chapter has addressed a range of practice behaviors related to assessment (including the very idea of assessment) along with a variety of difficult and challenging issues that exist in social work practice today. Clearly, the process of assessment involves a major combination of efforts and tools. While there are literally hundreds of instruments that social workers can use depending on the practice setting, type of client served, and the range of issues, your agency will use a few instruments that are consistent with the mission and focus of the agency's services.

Assessment is viewed as an integrated activity that arises out of an effective engagement with the client system and progresses into the action-oriented phase of the work. The tone and focus should be consistent with the practice process as a whole. Finally, assessment continues throughout the practice process, sometimes shifting the work slightly and sometimes significantly. It is a fluid activity that fits into an ever-evolving integrated whole.

MAIN POINTS

- Assessment involves dialogue to discover the goals and aspirations of the client system.

- The theoretical perspective used by the social worker has significant implications for the assessment and the intervention. Five theoretical frameworks discussed in this chapter are psychoanalytic, attachment, cognitive, strengths-based perspective, narrative, and solution-focused.

- The social worker develops a shared vision with the client system by respecting the client's preferred reality and responding honestly to it.

- Mapping is a useful addition to verbal assessment. Two types of maps that are widely used within the profession are genograms and ecomaps.

- Assessment evaluates the types of resources, both formal and informal, that the client and the client's environment can bring to bear.

- When resources are not present or adequate or available to client systems, social workers need to respond creatively, appropriately, possibly with social action.

- Assessment and planning move from a shared vision to specific details regarding the intervention. Internalized oppression and the emotional impact of change can influence the entire assessment process and the client's capacity for participation in planning.

- Social workers are ethically bound to be clear and honest with clients about specific agency constraints and requirements that will influence the client's experience of the work.

- The phenomenon of involuntary/mandated/non-voluntary clients creates challenges for social workers that can be met effectively if framed adequately and met with a basic approach of respect and willingness to listen to the client.

- Violence is a pervasive quality in U.S. culture and influences both the work of the social work practitioner and the potential for her or his personal safety. Social workers can engage in social justice-oriented practice to try and minimize societal violence, and they and their agencies can develop skills and policies to deal with situations of potential violence associated with clients.

- Secondary trauma, burnout, and compassion fatigue reflect physical and emotional exhaustion in a complex practice context; it may arise out of painful events and personal triggers and can be mitigated through appropriate agency and social worker response.

- Several aspects of holistic self-care can carry you through difficult moments and are consistent with ethical practice. As in your work with clients, think of yourself as a whole person, with strengths and vulnerabilities and a need for your own systems of support.

- Effective supervision is a useful interactive relationship for negotiating difficult practice contexts.

EXERCISES

a. Case Exercises

1. Go to www.routledgesw.com/cases and review the case file for Emilia Sanchez, including the genogram and ecomap of the family for both its content and form. Click on the Assess tab and view the tasks you will need to complete. To prepare for this exercise, also review "Focus on Strengths" in the Values Inventory.

    Using Emilia as the anchor family member, develop two genograms. The first should reflect her relationships prior to age 14 and the second should be an "update" to her current age of 24. Include as much information as possible while ensuring that the drawing is informative and clear. After completing the first genogram and before completing the second, develop an ecomap that represents your interpretation of the systems and networks supporting Emilia's "change" (her involvement in drugs) that might have led to her estrangement from her family.

    In class, partner with another student and exchange the three drawings. Are they similar? In what respects do they differ? What information is particularly helpful? What facets of Emilia's life are the most effectively represented in a social mapping format? Which ones are the most challenging?

2. Go to www.routledgesw.com/cases and review Emilia's video vignette. After viewing the vignette, complete the following exercise.

    Emilia Sanchez has come to you for help because she has decided she must conquer her substance addiction. Emilia's long history of substance abuse, her family's outrage regarding the out-of-wedlock birth of her son Joey, and the following abortion of another child resulted in her feeling discouraged. Specifically, she is doubtful about her ability to make a place for herself in the family again and to make the changes she wants to make. Using the strengths perspective the social worker can identify and assess Emilia's strengths. Respond to the following:

    a. What was the most challenging aspect of identifying the strengths of someone who has had the number of challenges experienced by Emilia?

    b. How do you as the social worker encourage Emilia to recognize her strengths?

    c. Identify the strengths pointed out by the social worker in the vignette.

3. Go to www.routledgesw.com/cases and review the case of Carla Washburn. Click on Phase 2: Assess the Client System. Review the goals for this phase and complete Tasks 1, 2, and 3.

4. Go to www.routledgesw.com/cases and review the case of Hudson City. Address each of the following areas:

    a. Click on Engage and Discover. Select Case Files and review Your History, Your Concerns, and Your Goals. Respond to the questions posed under Your Goals.

b. Continuing with the engagement phase, click on Critical Thinking Questions. View Your Questions and respond to each of the questions presented.

c. Moving to the assessment and planning phase, click on Assess the Situation. Select Biopsychosocial Perspectives. Review the biological psychological, social, and spiritual lenses and respond to the questions related to each area.

5. Go to www.routledgesw.com/cases and review the Brickville case. Address each of the following areas:

   a. Click on Engage and Discover and complete the Tasks for this section with specific emphasis on strategies for engaging Virginia and other key persons who are relevant in her life.

   b. Review the ecomap centered on Virginia Stone and her family. Identify all relevant linkages Virginia has within her family and community, the character of those relationships, and strengths and areas for changes.

   c. Review the Town Map and develop list of Virginia's needs on the individual, family, group, and community levels.

6. Go to www.routledgesw.com/cases and review the case of Hudson City. Two professional issues are relevant for the social worker depicted in this case: dual relationship and self-care (compassion fatigue). After reviewing the case materials, conduct a literature search regarding one or both of these issues and develop practice strategies that are appropriate for your future as a social worker.

b. Other exercises

7. To begin the process of developing engagement and assessment practice behaviors, complete the following role-playing exercise. Begin by partnering with two other students.

   Using Confrontation: Engage in brief re-enactments of the following scenarios with each student assuming the role of the social worker, the client, or the observer. Use the engagement and assessment practice behaviors highlighted in this chapter to role-play the beginning phases of work with clients in these situations. Upon completion of the role-play, each member of the triad will provide balanced feedback regarding the others' performance of skills. Select from the following list of potential client scenarios:

   a. Client sporadically attends scheduled sessions.

   b. Client reports that when she was angry with her 10-year-old son at the mall she spanked him in public.

   c. Client is having difficulty obtaining employment. You recognize that the client's style of dress and hygiene may be a concern for employers.

   d. Client continues to use language that you find offensive.

   e. Your colleague is not completing tasks and you are experiencing negative consequences.

8. Review and discuss with other students the following situations. Evaluate your level of comfort in them. What makes you comfortable or uncomfortable? Be specific. Upon completion of the discussion, brainstorm with other students strategies for maintaining your safety.
   a. Conducting a home visit
   b. Working after dark at your agency
   c. Driving a client to an appointment
   d. Working with young males (if you are female) or females (if you are male)
   e. Working with individuals with mental illness
   f. Working with individuals with substance abuse issues
   g. Having an initial meeting with a client who is unknown to you
   h. Working with a client with a criminal record

9. In writing, reflect on situations in which you have been involved that resulted in a confrontation between you and another person. If you cannot recall such a situation, remember a situation in which confrontation may have been appropriate, but did not occur. Imagine in that situation that you were confronted by a caring individual in your life. What was your reaction to being confronted? How did you receive feedback? How do you give feedback? What is your level of comfort ability with confronting others? What were the benefits to being confronted?

10. Quick Guide 7 provides questions to consider regarding the cultural heritage journey that each of us takes. To gain insight into your own cultural heritage journey, reflect on the items listed:
    The cultural heritage journey of both clients and social workers impact their perspectives of life and work. Consider the following:
    - Where do my family's roots begin?
    - If my family emigrated to the United States, how long has each parent been living here?
    - If I am in an adoptive family, what do I know about my biological family's journey to the U.S.?
    - What are my family's traditions that have been passed through the generations?
    - Do my family's traditions relate to religion or spirituality, holidays, rituals, and or significant events for the family?
    - What values have I learned from my family—may be related to ethics, wealth, religion and spirituality, race, ethnicity, health, education, sexual orientation, and image?
    - Have I challenged any of my family traditions or values? If so, what challenges have presented themselves and how have I responded?
    - What significant life experiences have shaped my view of the world, specifically people who are different from me?
    - How will my cultural heritage impact my social work practice?
    - Are there changes or additions that I would like to make related to my traditions? How might I start?

Social Work Practice with Individuals: Intervention, Termination, and Evaluation

Where after all, do human rights begin? In small places, close to home—so close and so small that they cannot be seen on any map of the world. Yet, they're the world of individual persons: the neighborhood he lives in; the school or college he attends; the factory, farm, or office where he works.

Eleanor Roosevelt (1958)

Key Questions for Chapter 5

(1) How can I prepare for intervening with and empowering individual client systems? (EPAS 2.1.10(c))

(2) How can I use the strengths-based perspective to guide the development of intervention, termination, and evaluation strategies with individuals? (EPAS 2.1.10 a-d)

(3) What are the social work roles that enable me to effectively intervene, terminate, and evaluate with individuals? (EPAS 2.1.10(c))

(4) How do I determine the appropriate evaluation tool(s) for use with interventions with individual client systems? (EPAS 2.1.10(d))

THIS BOOK EMPHASIZES THE CONTEXT OF THE SOCIAL work intervention as it shapes the meaning of experience for clients and for social workers as they move through the social work intervention. In this chapter, we will explore the impact of context on all aspects of practice. Context both shapes what you do as well as is shaped by what you do. Whether you are working with someone recently diagnosed with a chronic illness such as multiple sclerosis, an adult child who is experiencing stress from caring for an aging parent, or an immigrant who is seeking U.S. citizenship, you interact with the choices and capacities of individuals, the systems in which people are embedded, and the accessibility of existing and potential resources. All of these dimensions contribute to the totality of the social work practice context.

There are multiple ways to intervene. Viewed through a critical constructionist lens (i.e., knowledge is not transmitted, but created, acquired, processed, and relative) (Barker, 2003, p. 93), a useful, direct intervention for one person will not necessarily meet the needs of another person in a similar situation. For example, a single woman with a six-month-old baby may identify job training and finding suitable child care as the goal of the intervention. In contrast, another woman in seemingly the same circumstances may need assistance with locating housing, handling rollercoaster emotions, and keeping a safe environment for her infant. Yet another single mother will need intensive advocacy efforts in order to deal with discriminatory practices in her employment. Social workers must expect differences and advocate against the one-size-fits-all interventions that are sometimes considered optimal by social service organizations and/or public policy.

In recognition of individuals' unique circumstances, you will locate the starting point of your work on the most pressing issue, as defined by each client system. This decision should reflect the priorities for action that are agreed upon in the assessment and planning phase. Each client is the chief negotiator of her or his journey; therefore the work will first assume and then reflect the strengths and capacities to be successful in that journey. From this starting point, the chapter examines the generalist practice competencies and practice behaviors of supporting client strengths within client environments. We will also look at the variety of social work roles and methods that support client–worker relationships, including strengths, narrative, and solution-focused approaches. This chapter also includes a case example focused on Thomas and his road to empowerment that will allow students to bridge the gaps between strengths-based, environmental, social justice, human rights, and social construction perspectives. As do social work interventions, this chapter will end with a discussion of termination and evaluation of the planned change intervention, focusing on strengths-based strategies to help the client to maintain goals they have accomplished.

SUPPORTING CLIENTS' STRENGTHS IN DEVELOPING INTERVENTIONS

Through its theoretical lens, the strengths perspective offers a focused, committed effort for identifying, expanding, and sustaining the resilience and assets that clients bring. Using a strengths-based method suggests that the worker will not only seek out and identify client strengths in the assessment (see Chapter 4) but will also support and maximize them throughout the working relationship. For many practitioners this effort will be the major focus of the work. The strengths-based approach views supporting clients as central to the worker's action. Social workers may need to remind themselves of the client's strengths and centrality as our culture, even for the most strengths-oriented practitioners, focuses on "what needs fixing." Strengths, like all human dimensions, need recognition, validation, and nourishment to remain vital. The following discussion will highlight intervention from the perspectives of strengths, narrative, and solution-focused approaches.

Strengths-Based Perspectives and Intervention

Consider four elements of the strengths-based approach as they apply to the practice context and the action of intervention. Saleebey (2013, pp. 109–111) identifies these as follows:

- *The social worker identifies hints and murmurs of strength even in the struggle:* As the client relates her or his current situation, typically focused on the challenges and stresses, the social worker can "listen" for the strengths and healthy aspects which every client possesses.

- *The social worker stimulates the discourse and narratives of resilience and strength:* Most of us have difficulty recognizing positive aspects about ourselves. The role of the strengths-based social worker is to identify the strengths, affirm positives that are offered by the client, suggest the possibilities that exist for the client, and be grounded in the client's daily life.

- *The social worker acts in context:* Through listening for the strengths as the client shares her or his concerns, the client's competencies become apparent. These competencies can then become the focus of the assessment and intervention process and they guide the development of goals. This "project" results from the social worker and the client collaborating to identify the strengths and plan of action.

- *The social worker can work with the client system to move toward normalizing and capitalizing on one's strengths:* The product of a strengths-based assessment is the intervention in which the articulated strengths and resources are brought together, normalized, and shared with others.

Acting in Context   The social worker's activity centers on helping the client use the strengths she or he is beginning to recognize, as well as those already discovered, and to link them with her or his goals and dreams. That kind of effort might lead, for example, to social worker support for more independence or more assertiveness. Inherent within the strengths-based perspective is the belief that social justice is the "ultimate goal" which requires a commitment to viewing the client-social worker relationship as one of equality (Gray, 2011, p. 8).

Consider a client who has experienced trouble interacting with her landlord and now feels that she cannot negotiate a lease arrangement. The social worker can help her consider the advantages of establishing a positive rental history as they work together to identify appropriate options. The social worker can also encourage the client to recognize her capacity to understand the business-focused details of renting and to negotiate for those specific items or conditions that she feels are important and fair. For example, if she is willing to paint the living room walls, she can ask the landlord to provide the paint and reduce her rent for one month. This endeavor involves some risk taking to stretch beyond her usual comfort zone to initiate change, but the action also offers an unusual opportunity to decide and act on her own behalf. When the venture is successful—the landlord agrees to provide paint and a rental rebate in exchange for painting the living room walls—the client experiences the benefit of adding another competency to her growing list. Conversely, when the effort does not go as planned, she becomes more aware of the specific areas in which she wants to direct her energies to make changes.

Capitalizing on Strengths   To focus on strengths is the consolidation step in which the social worker and client together recognize the successes they have had in establishing and stabilizing the client's competencies. Keeping with the same example, assume that the client found an apartment she likes at a rate she can afford. The social worker would then affirm the skills the client demonstrated, encourage her to generalize those particular skills into other arenas, and support her ability to

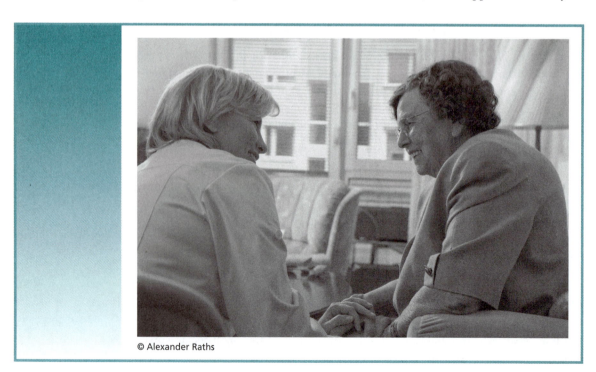

© Alexander Raths

generate new skills. The social worker can also help the client recognize that she is building useful relationships in the community. For example, when she has established a record of reliability in paying her rent on time and maintaining her apartment, her landlord is likely to become a resource if she needs a reference for a job or wants to find a larger apartment across town. In order to help the client grow, the social worker's efforts may include education, advocacy, and support for the client's capacity. Such efforts can enable the client to develop a network that links her accomplishments to her goals. By normalizing the task, in this case, of securing housing, the social worker not only demonstrates the client's capacities, but also reinforces the availability of community resources, and establishes that disengagement, or ending the work, is appropriate once the goal has been achieved. The ultimate normalization is the client's continued development and the recognition that she or he can successfully manage the everyday tasks of living.

Narrative Intervention

Building on the deconstruction of client perceptions that occurred in the assessment process, a narrative-oriented intervention remains focused on the client, her or his strengths, and the meaning that is assigned to current and future realities. Questions posed by the social worker are central to narrative-based intervention. As opposed to eliciting information and interpretation, intervention stage questioning is aimed at helping the client to move toward implementing changes in order to reach her or his goals. Return to Chapter 4 for a review of narrative-focused questioning strategies.

Once the original concern or issue is deconstructed and a plan is conceived, the social worker continues to use strategies (e.g., questions) intended to externalize the client from *being* the problem to having a relationship *with* the problem (Nichols, 2011). As the intervention is underway, the social worker continues to help the client view her or himself from a position of strength and working toward re-authoring the original issue. Upon achieving success, the client can celebrate and share her or his new perceptions by sharing the news about changes with people who are important to her or him. As with many interventions, the path from beginning to end may not be linear. The client-centered nature of a narrative approach may require both the client and the social worker to return periodically to the early discussions of the problem and reconstruct it in light of new insights that unfold throughout the intervention.

Solution-Focused Intervention

Using a solution-focused approach to the intervention provides the client and the social worker with a clear-cut strategy for arriving at the client's goals in a relatively brief, time-limited manner. As you recall from the discussion in Chapter 4 on solution-focused assessment and planning, the client engages in a self-evaluative process (evaluative questions) to learn how she or he views the situation. The client has also envisioned times when the problem did not (exception questions) and will not (miracle questions) exist, thus lending insight into possible strategies for resolving the problem using the client's existing and created strengths and resources. In the intervention phase of change, these questions continue to be important as reminders of the goal and connections to the client's past and future life.

Also used in the assessment and planning phases, scaling questions continue to be a critical aspect of the solution-focused intervention. Prompting the client to regularly assign a numeric value to a particular issue, experience, or behavior can empower her or him to continue to engage in self-evaluation and mutual feedback with you (Lee, 2009). While this practice strategy is evaluative in terms of progress (or lack of), it can also serve to motivate and empower the client and inspire confidence that change can, in fact, be a reality. Being able to acknowledge small, concrete gains can be a powerful motivator for continued work (for both client and social worker). Exhibit 5.1 provides examples of scaling questions and strategies for monitoring scaling questions over the course of the social work intervention.

Due to the emphasis on concrete solutions, the solution-focused intervention can be impactful and empowering for the client. As a social worker using this approach, as the sole approach or in concert with another intervention model (as discussed in Chapter 4), your attention will be directed toward maintaining the client's motivation and focus on solutions and change along with reinforcing your respect and confidence in the client's capacity to reach the desired outcome (Lee, 2009).

EXHIBIT 5.1 *Integrating Scaling Questions into a Social Work Intervention: Virginia Stone*	Virginia Stone of the Brickville neighborhood (www.routledgesw.com/cases) has identified a number of stressors in her life, including caregiving responsibilities for her mother and two grandchildren, redevelopment efforts in her neighborhood that may result in her family losing their home, and unresolved grief over the loss of her daughter and three nieces/nephews in a fire twenty years earlier. Scaling questions can be an effective strategy to help Virginia identify and prioritize areas of concern and strength. Scaling questions can also be infused into the intervention process to frame goals and track and empower Virginia's progress toward her desired goals.

During the engagement and assessment phases of work with Virginia, she identified that she was feeling particularly stressed about the potential loss of her family's home. The following dialogue provides examples of the use of scaling as an interventive strategy during several sessions:

Session #1—Engagement/Assessment phase:

Social Worker: "Virginia, on a scale of 1 to 10 with 1 being the worst and 10 being the best, how would you rate stress today regarding your housing situation?"

Virginia: "I would say my stress level is a 1. I am so worried that we're not going to be able to prove the house belongs to my Grandma Stella. Then, we won't even be able to sell it to that developer if he does move in here and take over."

The social worker and Virginia worked together to develop a goal to reduce her stress by taking action toward obtaining proof of family ownership of the house. They mapped out strategies which the social worker documented both in Virginia's case file and the client contract.

Session #3—Intervention phase:

Social Worker: "Virginia, since we last reviewed your progress toward your goal of reducing your stress, you have been to Legal Services to ask for help in locating a deed to determine ownership of the house and they told you that they believed you have a strong case. Using the same 1-10 scale, how would you rate your stress today related to this issue?"

Virginia: "I am feeling a whole lot better about things today. I would have to say I'm at a 5 right now. It seems there is a chance we will be able to prove Grandma Stella was the rightful owner and that it passes to my mom when Grandma died. I'm still worried, though, that something will go wrong."

The social worker asked Virginia to consider other actions that she could take at this point while she was waiting on the outcome of the legal investigation. Virginia acknowledged that there was little she could actually do, but wait. Once she realized that much was out of her control, she acknowledged that she was feeling better about things. The social worker documented the events and Virginia's perception of her current stress level.

Session #8—Intervention phase (three weeks later):

Virginia: "I heard from Legal Services and they were able to find proof that Grandma Stella is the rightful owner of the house! I can't tell you how much better I feel about this thing."

Social Worker: "Using that 1 to 10 scale, we have used before, where would you rate your stress level on the housing issue today?"

Virginia: "On this one issue, I would say I'm at 8 today! I'm still worried about losing the house to that developer fellow, but at least now, I know that if we do have to sell out, we will get paid a fair price for it so hopefully we can find another place for all of us to live."

With this particular stressor significantly improved for Virginia, the social worker and Virginia were able to turn their full attention to addressing other goals. While the client can certainly pose scaling questions to themselves, doing this exercise with the client may help her to engage in self-assessment and realize the differences even before the social worker has the opportunity to acknowledge the change, leading to a sense of empowerment. Despite the fact that Virginia had been working toward other goals, this stressor was overshadowing her motivation to fully engage in working on the less tangible issues of caregiver stress and unresolved grief.

EXHIBIT 5.1

Continued

Greene and Lee (2011) offer the following suggestions when using a solution-oriented approach:

- Use questions to identify solution-focused patterns that guide the development of client-focused goals.

- Use solution-oriented tasks between meetings to amplify patterns and promote stability and change.

- For clients who are motivated, direct behavioral tasks are developed for completion between meetings (e.g., engaging in a specific activity with client's family members). For clients who acknowledge a problem, but see the cause being external to themselves, observational tasks are best for between-meeting activities (e.g., attending a presentation on parenting).

- At the end of each meeting, provide an end-of-meeting message to affirm the client's work.

- Use client's beliefs, language, metaphors, and figures of speech to guide the tasks to be accomplished.

- Remember, clients have strengths, competencies, and resources to make change (pp. 126–127).

Cognitive Behavioral-Focused Interventions

Considered to be an effective modality for intervening with clients experiencing a range of mental health challenges, cognitive behavioral therapy (CBT) is another approach available to and used by many social workers working in clinical arenas. CBT is based on the premise that thoughts drive one's feelings and actions and changing one's thoughts can lead to changes in one's behaviors (National Association of Cognitive-Behavioral Therapists (NACBT), 2013). CBT has been well-studied over the past four decades and the evidence suggests that this approach is particularly effective with such illnesses as depression, generalized anxiety, panic and phobic disorders, and posttraumatic stress disorder (Butler, Chapman, Forman, & Beck, 2006). The meta-analysis conducted by Butler and colleagues (2006) also determined that CBT has moderate effectiveness within interventions addressing marital stress, anger, childhood somatic conditions, and chronic pain.

As will be evident, CBT shares similarities with other therapeutic approaches. The primary components of CBT include (NABCT, 2013):

Brief and Time-limited format—with a focus on behavior change, the number of meetings with the client can be limited to a specific number with the client continuing to work on change following the formal relationship.

Collaborative relationship—the social worker and client work together to identify and implement goals. The social worker's role is to listen, teach, and support, while the client's focus is on expression and learning.

Structure, Direction, and Education—facilitating change is completed within the context of a structure that includes the social worker creating an agenda with specific techniques being taught during the session and in the form of homework to be completed between sessions that emphasizes learning as well as unlearning behaviors.

While the delivery of CBT requires advanced training and experience, generalist social workers can incorporate aspects of behavioral-oriented strategies into their interventions as well as identify those clients who may benefit from working with a CBT-trained clinician.

Strengths-Oriented Practice Skills and Behaviors

When used effectively, many social work practice skills and behaviors can affirm client strengths and support their underlying position in the work. For example, the familiar "reflection of empathy" has remained a time-honored practice behavior because it mirrors the respect and regard for human beings that is inherent in social work. The practice skills and behaviors discussed in the following sections have also earned their place in social work practice history because they are consistent with the values of social justice and respect and dignity.

Supporting Diversity As discussed in Chapters 3 and 4, a client's cultural background is a potential source of strength rather than an obstacle or deficit. As you strive to become a culturally competent social work practitioner, there are four assumptions on which you can build your skills: 1) reality is social constructed; 2) diverse worldviews need to be appreciated; 3) multiple realities affect individual personalities; and 4) diversity education has a positive impact on the journey to cultural competence (Kohli, Huber, & Faul, 2010, p. 266). Within the social, cultural, political, and historical context, these assumptions can be used to inform the way in which you view not only your client, but yourself.

An appropriate practice behavior is thus to use the traditions or aspects of your client's culture that nourish and give meaning to life. For example, many cultures demonstrate far greater respect for authority or the wisdom of age than U.S. culture has traditionally done. When you work with clients from such a culture, learning the practice behaviors that will support those values is critical because they are assets and can be incorporated as such into the intervention phase of your work. Although you should always confer with your clients regarding your actions, remain especially sensitized to the "fit" of your approach with your client's culturally influenced sense of propriety. Would it be appropriate, for instance, to encourage the client from such a culture to participate in a rent strike aimed at a prominent elder statesman who owns the property, if such an action would likely become highly adversarial?

SUPPORTING CLIENTS' ENVIRONMENTS

Having confirmed the importance of recognizing and supporting client strengths and cultural influences in the intervention process, we will focus now on identifying and intensifying the strengths of clients' environments. This dual emphasis on person and environment is consistent with the traditions of the social work profession. Accordingly, social workers often direct their efforts toward making clients' environments more responsive to client needs. This approach looks to the institutions and policies outside of the client rather than viewing the client's difficulties as a symptom of inner pathology. In maintaining this focus on improving environmental response, the work reflects an underlying commitment to a social justice framework. In the process, clients are assumed to possess the capacity both to identify their difficulties and to participate in the work necessary to alleviate them.

Principles for Taking Environments into Account

In a classic application of a systemic intervention that embraces the client's environment, Wood and Tully (2006) identify six major principles. Consistent with the basic tenets of the social work profession, these principles strongly emphasize a social justice orientation.

The Social Worker Should Be Accountable to the Client System In being accountable to the client system, the social worker responds to the client's perception of the problem or situation despite her or his perception of its accuracy or clarity. At this point in the intervention, the client's perception is the reality that she or he is working with and, as we know, a basic tenet of the social work profession that we "start where the client is." If, for example, an individual client is experiencing substantial difficulty in accessing certain public assistance benefits because he does not speak English fluently, the social worker will direct energies to addressing that need. Strategies may include arranging for an interpreter, requesting an agency worker who is fluent in the client's native language, or simply accompanying the client to advocate for appropriate and equitable treatment.

The Social Worker Should Follow the Demands of the Client Task Creating a "Frame of Reference" is a strategy for conceptualizing the demands of the client task (Wood & Tully, 2006). The Frame of Reference can be illustrated through a quadrant diagram covering the parameters of the social worker's tasks (see Quick Guide 12). This scheme suggests that practitioners may (A) work with client systems on their own behalf, (B) work with client systems on behalf of themselves and others like them, (C) work with others (non-clients) on behalf of client systems, and (D) work with others (non-clients) on behalf of categories of persons at risk. The principle of following the demands of the client stresses that the social worker will look beyond the individual client in order to see if there are others in the same situation. If so, the worker needs to adapt by moving from one quadrant to another or by functioning in multiple quadrants.

To learn how to apply the Frame of Reference into your work, consider the case of a social work practitioner working with the mother of a child with disabilities who has no viable transportation to school. The social worker, with the mother's agreement, can locate a driver, or a person to accompany the child on the regular school bus, or request extended school hours so that the mother can pick up the child after work (working with a client on behalf of the client, **Quadrant** A). However, if the social worker discovers that there are four other children with disabilities in the school who lack adequate transportation, she or he, still working with the mother, might organize and coordinate a team of drivers for all five children in the school (working with the client on behalf of the client and others like her, **Quadrant B**). If the social worker's efforts were directed at enlisting the aid of a community group to help locate and fund a small van that could hold six children, the work would fall in different quadrant (working with others out of concern for specific clients, **Quadrant** C). Finally, if the worker proposes statewide transportation funding to the legislature on behalf of a category of clients—in this case, children with disabilities—the work falls into **Quadrant D**, working with others on behalf of a category of clients. Although the worker's efforts may vary, move from one quadrant to another, and operate simultaneously, the work is always performed on the behalf of clients.

QUICK GUIDE 12   FRAME OF REFERENCE FOR STRUCTURAL APPROACH TO SOCIAL WORK TASKS

INTENDED BENEFICIARY

FOCUS OF INTERVENTION	SINGLE	MULTIPLE
Clients	Work with clients on their own behalf	Work with clients on behalf of themselves and others like them
	Quadrant A	**Quadrant B**
Others	Work with others (nonclients) on behalf of clients	Work with others, such as (nonclients), on behalf of a category of persons at risk
	Quadrant C	**Quadrant D**

Adapted from Wood & Tully, 2006

The Social Worker Should Maximize the Potential Supports in the Client System's Environment This generic principle requires the social worker to identify, access, and, where necessary, modify or even create the supports that a client system needs. These supports might include such resources as temporary housing for a family who is homeless, hospice services for a family dealing with an older member's imminent death, and child care services for a young mother who is employed outside her home. Chapter 3 discussed this aspect of resource development; it remains a central focus for this work phase as well.

The Social Worker Should Proceed from the Assumption of "Least Contest" This tenet holds that the social worker should use the minimal amount of pressure that is required to meet a client's need. For example, a social worker can explore the availability of affordable child care for a client before pressuring the mayor to initiate a city-sponsored child care system. If these early attempts fail, and there is no adequate, affordable child care, the social worker can shift her or his focus to mobilize an effort to facilitate change at the community level.

In a different situation, the "least contest" approach might encourage the social work practitioner to contact another service before engaging in advocacy. For example, a practitioner working with a young woman who was not accepted into a local parent support group might make a referral to a different group. If a series of appropriate referrals does not yield the desired results, the social worker can consider other approaches of greater contest, such as advocating with the person who organized the original group.

The Social Worker Must Help the Client Deconstruct Oppressive Cultural Discourse and Reinterpret Experience from Alternative Perspectives Embracing this principle guides the social worker and client to discuss the larger cultural and societal issues that impact the ways in which the client experiences the world. Exploring the oppression, discrimination, and/or violence that may be a part of the client's life experience can help the client gain insight into the origins of these negative forces and construct alternative perspectives. Creating a different view of oneself can free the individual to develop a new, healthier perspective. Consider the older adult refugee who recently came to the U.S. with her large extended family after fleeing her home country and living for several years in a refugee camp. This client brings with her a lifetime of oppression and discrimination, and she and her family have been victims of violence in their home country. As a social worker, your role can be to help her to create a new perspective on the world in which she now lives. By examining her previous life experiences within the context of her new life, you can work with her to develop an alternative to her earlier life of fear and dread.

The Social Worker Should Identify, Reinforce, and/or Increase the Client System's Repertoire of Strategic Behavior for Minimizing Pain and Maximizing Positive Outcomes and Satisfaction Also known as the **"minimax" principle**, this principle cautions the social worker against holding the client responsible for a lack of community responsiveness in the development of resources or support. The principle recognizes, however, that the client may need assistance in developing behaviors that are likely to elicit cooperation from the community. For example, clients who have been excluded from the community on various levels might present as eager to the point of aggressiveness, and demonstrate a lack of interest in using the grievance process of an organization to file a complaint when they have been treated unfairly. This group of clients will likely improve their chances of being accepted if they curb their enthusiasm somewhat, by speaking in a softer voice and initially using a grievance process, for example.

In applying this principle, social workers are reminded that our culture has led many people to blame themselves for the violence or oppression that they have. Therefore, it is important that social workers, as well as client systems, do not attribute difficulties in accessing resources to our/their own failures by "blaming the victim." Social workers whose clients have adopted this perspective can employ consciousness-raising techniques to challenge these beliefs and transform personal issues such as child abuse and violence against women into political issues. Returning to the earlier example of the older adult woman who has recently arrived in the U.S., a focus of your work with her can be directed at examining the violence that she experienced in her home country. Within the social work intervention, you can help her to recognize that the perpetrators of the violence were responsible for the violence and, despite the pain and guilt she suffers, she and her family are not responsible. Freeing the client from the guilt can aid her in maximizing her opportunity to create a new life with her family in the U.S.

Social Workers Should Apply the Principles to Themselves As well as directing these principles toward the client intervention, social workers can benefit from ensuring they are practicing the same principles they promote to clients. Accordingly, social workers make clear, accountable service and/or therapeutic contracts and explore common practice issues with other social workers. Social workers are also encouraged to apply the principles to their work in agency settings.

Environment-Sensitive Processes and Skills

The groups of skills and behaviors discussed earlier can also be applied to the environment when relevant to supporting clients' effective use of environmental supports. Following is a discussion of practice behaviors that can be used with individual.

Providing Information Client systems often want, need, and ask for information about the environment, which may be their most valuable resource. You may be uneasy that you will over-influence decisions, be too directive, or create dependency. While such concerns are legitimate, they also can be managed. When you consider that information in our society is clearly linked to power, you may become less reluctant to provide it to clients. The challenge with providing information arises when it is confused with advice or is strongly one-sided. This concern becomes more difficult to mitigate with the understanding that you are never able to have all the information related to a particular situation or circumstance. Still, you can offer what you know as a simple proposition, always framed by the limits of your knowledge. Consider again the situation of the older adult refugee with whom you are working on creating a new and healthier perspective. She is concerned about the impact of previous experiences of violence on her younger female family members. She is aware that you have been working with her daughter and granddaughters. She has asked you to share the information that you know about her daughter and granddaughters and to direct them to not discuss their experiences with anyone. While you are sensitive to her concerns, you are ethically bound not to share information about other clients without their consent. Moreover, your commitment to practicing social work in an ethical manner would not allow you to advise any client system in their beliefs or behaviors.

Be clear that you do not hold any expectations about what clients do with the information. Information is typically not yours to be given away only with certain restrictions. For example, you are a social worker working in child welfare helping a young couple to learn more effective methods to care for their three-year-old son who has been diagnosed on the autism spectrum. You may want to generate a compilation of resources you think would be helpful to the parents. You may believe that they would benefit from respite services because you suspect it will be helpful for the mother to develop some trust in a caretaker outside of the family. Therefore, you provide her with the names of several agencies that provide respite services. When she does not follow up on this information, you may become frustrated or even irritated. In this case, your "information" was interpreted by the client as "advice," and the mother is not at a point where she is able to or agrees to act on the information in the way you assumed she would. This simple example illustrates the problematic nature of an investment in giving information. Fortunately, you can process this kind of situation with the client so that your agenda becomes transparent and the client is free to accept or reject it.

Refocusing and Confronting   Bringing the client back to the original focus of the work is known as **refocusing** and can span several possible directions, including two discussed here: referring back to purpose and confronting clients' beliefs, plans, and/or behavior. Social workers frequently use refocusing to assist clients in taking advantage of the potential in their environments.

When clients begin to digress into arenas other than the agreed upon focus area of your work (based on the previously developed contract), a simple reference to the original agreements regarding the focus of the work during the action phase of the work is sometimes all that is necessary. Occasionally the client (or the social worker) will simply become distracted by other compelling issues. Although such diversion is understandable, you are responsible for using your time with the client productively. For example, the social worker may say the following to a client who she or he believes has lost focus on the previously agreed upon goals: "Let us revisit the goals that we developed when we created our contract for working together. I think it would be helpful for both of us to check in with the goals to determine if we are both staying focused on the plan that we laid out. If we feel that the goals are no longer realistic, we can discuss revising our original plans."

In other situations, the client may not carry out the plan or contract as agreed because the plan is not truly embraced by the client as a priority, is proving uncomfortable, or the client is unable to implement the plan for some reason. For example, your client, Jane, established a plan to seek counseling because she had been sexually abused and was experiencing many painful memories. However, initiating that kind of contact involved breaking the culturally and family imposed rule of conduct that she should never discuss anything so personal with an outsider. She finds the effort to initiate this counseling more difficult than she had imagined. An alternative to refocusing is to confront her very gently, even though she may simply need more informal support and acknowledgment from you to manage the unanticipated struggle. You may say to Jane, "Help me to understand your concerns about talking about your painful memories with an outsider." This development might also signal that the plan is not working for Jane and is not likely to lead to the outcome previously anticipated. In situations like these you need to return to the goals, review the client's experience, and make changes as necessary.

Significantly, clients often perceive gentle confrontation of their behavior as not only helpful but supportive. If the social worker carefully contrasts what a client said she or he would do with what she or he actually did, the client might experience this activity as respectful because it affirms her or his capacity to meet the agreed-upon commitments. For example, you may say to the client: "Your goal was to obtain employment and you did not apply for any jobs this week. Please help me understand how your actions will help you reach your goal." Such a process must be carried out sensitively, of course, to prevent the client from experiencing the confrontation as hostile and argumentative. Confrontation is certainly not the first approach to use in working with clients in such situations; rather, referring to purpose (refocusing) should be tried first. When it is used selectively and sensitively, however, gentle confrontation can convey hope and respect.

There will be situations, however, in which a digression from the intended focus of your work with the client system is warranted. You will be called upon to exercise your professional judgment to be able to recognize when a digression warrants a new focus. Returning to the example of Jane, should Jane come to your office with an eviction notice in her hand, the focus of your work related to her addressing the prior sexual abuse would be placed on hold until she could resolve her housing crisis.

Interpreting Client Behavior   Interpretation refers to the social worker's making sense of the client's behavior in ways the client may not perceive or acknowledge.

The goal of interpretation is to inspire the client to consider her or his situation in a new or different way. From a social constructionist view, interpreting can be one of the most challenging practice skills to master.

You may ascribe a different meaning to a client's behavior than the client. Still, there may be a place for interpreting when you are careful to test it out with clients and when you acknowledge that the meaning you take from the situation is only one possibility. Again, returning to the earlier example of Jane, you might, in helping her to use her environmental supports, say "It seems to me as if you do not feel ready to take on the kind of work that this type of counseling is likely to be. Is that correct?" Jane may respond with: "I don't know what you're talking about. You may respond with: "Each time we try to discuss your painful memories, you appear to become uncomfortable and change the subject. I think we might best use our time right now by talking about other aspects of your life. When you feel more comfortable with me, we can revisit your memories. How does this sound to you?"

Although many of us have encountered situations in which the thoughts of others about our behavior were helpful, having others interpret our experience can also be frustrating and alienating, particularly when the interpretation seems judgmental or "expert" (as if someone else possesses the secret of understanding our behavior). Interpreting is a widely applicable process but one that should be used tentatively (after you have established a trusting relationship with the client), checked for accuracy with the client, and with the use of ongoing supervision.

Mapping as an Intervention Strategy   Recall from the discussion in Chapter 4 that incorporating the family and community system within which the client lives is an important aspect of the assessment phase of the social work intervention. Just as mapping the client's family constellation and current living and relationships profile can be a useful strategy for assessment, the same visual depictions of the client's environment can become a component of the intervention itself. As you know, the genogram is a tool used to enable the client system to gain insights into her or his family history and patterns of a wide array of behaviors and issues, including physical and mental health, substance use and abuse, relationship patterns, and estrangements. Ecomaps, on the other hand, provide a visual depiction of the client's current life situation, including relationships, resources, assets, and challenges.

In the development and implementation of the intervention, the same information gathered from both of these tools in the assessment phase can be incorporated into the client's goals and action steps for facilitating behavior and life changes. For example, consider the client who identifies in the course of completing her genogram a multi-generational pattern of intimate partner violence directed toward the women in her family. She has also experienced violence in her own relationships. Understanding the pattern of the abuse can aid your client in understanding the nature of her previous relationships and strategies she can take to enable herself to seek out healthier relationships. The genogram can later be used to help the client determine if the pattern is broken.

In the assessment phase of your work with client systems, the ecomap aided the client in identifying strengths, directionality of her or his energy and benefits, and areas for change. While this information is important for developing the intervention plan, the ecomap can be used as a visioning tool to enable the client to view her or his life after the intervention is implemented. Specific behavior and life changes can be determined as a result of the client's new perspective on her or his current life. Previously unrecognized resources can be mobilized, unhealthy behaviors can be addressed, and dysfunctional relationships can be targeted for change. The ecomap thus becomes a "work in progress" and serves as a mechanism for monitoring progress and outcomes.

TRADITIONAL SOCIAL WORK ROLES IN CONTEMPORARY SOCIAL WORK PRACTICE

In thinking about the preceding descriptions of social work skills and behaviors, consider the specific roles that workers assume in order to support client strengths and environments. As introduced in Chapter 1, social workers engage in practice behaviors associated with roles that can be isolated, highlighted, and deconstructed. The following discussion will focus on the assumptions that underlie these roles and the ways they are actualized in the context of social work practice. Specifically, these roles are:

- Case manager

- Counselor

- Broker

- Mediator

- Educator

- Client advocate

- Collaborator

Together they represent much of social work's activity across the dimensions of supporting both client strengths and client environments.

These seven roles are not mutually exclusive. Rather, there is considerable overlap among them—for example, educating the legislature regarding the needs of foster children may also pave the way for a future effort at advocacy. Such a blending and overlapping of social work roles is common in social work practice, and it can be helpful to be clear about the roles in which you are undertaking with particular practice behaviors. For example, if you were to assume an educator role in presenting useful and relatively unbiased information about adults who have experienced psychiatric hospitalization, you would want to be clear whether you were going to additionally use a client advocate role to advocate for a particular treatment. While education and advocacy are often interlinked, it is important to be clear when you are advocating for a client system and when you are providing education about the client system.

Case Manager

Case management is "a procedure to plan, seek, and monitor services from different social agencies and staff on behalf of a client" (Barker, 2003, p. 58). Clients with multiple challenges and needs particularly benefit from case management. For example, a client with a serious mental health issue, a back injury, and a housing issue may be in need of medication, a referral to vocational rehabilitation, and a referral to a housing resource. This client may be an appropriate candidate for case management. **Case managers** not only coordinate these services but are also responsible for monitoring the responsiveness of services to clients by holding providers accountable, ensuring client participation, and collaborating with others to raise awareness of unmet needs. As mentioned, a case manager may also collaborate with others to advocate for and build needed resources in a community. Case managers are found in settings such as: aging services, behavioral health, substance abuse treatment, child, youth, and family services, corrections, disabilities program, education, employee assistance, health care, housing, immigrant and refugee services, income support programs, military and veterans services, and tribal programs (NASW, 2013b).

Common Components of Case Management While there are multiple case management models, steps that are typically included are: (1) accessing the client system by ensuring eligible people are informed of available services; (2) assessing a client's needs and strengths; (3) developing a plan for intervention; (4) identifying and designing an appropriate network of services to be used; (5) creating a written contract that includes achievable and measurable goals, time limits, agreed-upon actions, and consequences of failure to fulfill the contract (if any); (6) implementing the plan; (7) monitoring of the plan to determine progress or a need to re-evaluate the contract; (8) evaluating the outcomes of the intervention; (9) terminating the case management relationship; (10) following up on the client after termination to determine if the client has maintained the desired change (Roberts-DeGennaro, 2008). The case manager may also serve as an informal, personal support/contact person or even therapist. As the provision of therapy is an advanced-level intervention, the social worker is bound by the *Code of Ethics* (NASW, 2008) to possess an appropriate degree and training. In contrast to brokers, who may match a client to a single service, case managers take responsibility for assessing, monitoring, and evaluating the coordination of all services required by a client.

For more than three decades, the term case management has been used to describe this overall coordinating function, although many scholars believe that modern generalist practice is actually a form of case management. In more recent times, the component of cost containment has become crucial to case management. Accordingly, contemporary versions of case management have two primary—and often conflicting—purposes: to improve the quality of care through coordination of services, and to control the costs of care. While case management was originally conceived to address integration of system-level services, it has been shown to have become an effective practice approach with an array of populations as well as a cost-effective service delivery mechanism. Case management is an accepted strategy for working in family preservation, school attendance and performance, substance abuse treatment, corrections, and health care delivery systems; however, the quality of the services provided and the outcomes for the client systems must be given priority over cost-effectiveness (Rothman, 2009a).

The National Association of Social Workers (NASW) has developed a set of standards for the practice of social work case management. The NASW Standards (2013b) are intended to support the case manager in competently and efficiently serving her or his clients by:

- strengthening the developmental, problem solving, and coping capacities of clients;

- enhancing clients' ability to interact with and participate in their communities, with respect for each client's values and goals;

- linking people with systems that provide them with resources, services, and opportunities;

- increasing the scope and capacity of service delivery systems;

- creating and promoting the effective and humane operation of service systems;

- contributing to the development and improvement of social policy (p. 17).

Counselor

The term **counselor** is used in a variety of ways within the helping professions. Within the social work profession, counseling typically is a specialized clinical social work skill performed by social workers at the graduate level who have advanced training in working in health, mental health, and family service settings. A counselor provides services to individuals, families, groups, and communities that encompass the provision of suggestions and information along with establishing goals (Barker, 2003). Counseling is a term also used to describe volunteers and professionals or paraprofessionals who work in group settings (e.g., camps and residential settings).

While the counseling role can include an array of different activities, the social worker functioning as a counselor typically works with the client system around a specific issue or concern. Dependent on the expertise and training of the practitioner and the needs of the client system, different approaches and strategies are used.

Broker

Social workers typically act as **brokers** by linking clients to a needed service or resource. Needs may range from instrumental assistance (e.g., food, clothing, and children's toys) to intangible services such as counseling, support groups, and advocacy. Consider the functions and context of brokering, the process of building the necessary networks, and making the match of client to service.

Brokering Functions and Context   Five social work functions of brokering are:

- Assess client need

- Assess available resources

- Match and initiate referrals to appropriate services

- Link or network services

- Share information

The brokering role can also include modifying resources and creating new resources where none exist. All of these activities can strengthen the client's environment, or context, as well as to support her or his strengths. These activities also overlap, and they reflect much of what was discussed in Chapter 3 regarding assessment of clients and resources, and the fit between them.

One of the early roles associated with the social work profession, the broker role may have less status today than it once had because of the profession's increased interest in psychological and therapeutic roles and the availability of information through on-line sources. Brokering may also seem fairly simple at times. For example, if your client requests assistance with locating used children's furniture, you simply "refer" her or him to the appropriate agency. It is probably somewhat misleading, though, to think of the brokering role as simple, because it requires the social worker both to be familiar with the resources and to nurture and maintain a network of and relationships with such resources. In the complex world of contemporary, urban social services, the ability to know one service or resource from the next can itself be a feat. In rural areas, where the service system may be much less comprehensive, with fewer choices, knowing and maintaining effective relationships with the available resources becomes even more important.

Building and Maintaining Networks for Brokering   Developing a network will include such activities as making initial and subsequent contacts with appropriate providers in other agencies and organizations, discovering those who will help your clients most effectively, and becoming familiar with eligibility criteria and service elements involved in programs. Effective brokering also involves establishing stable working relationships with people, organizations, and systems that will help your clients. Building an effective working relationship with outside people and systems could involve developing a two-way relationship with network resources, so that you are able to provide referrals that best fit the system of the resource, and able to contribute energy to the relationship in other ways, such as offering to appropriately assist your networks in their service, advocacy, and/or fundraising efforts. For the social worker to build and maintain a network, key elements include reciprocity and open, two-way communication.

To build a network successfully, you must acquire knowledge of the informal aspects of the resource as well as the formal ones. For example, it will be helpful to understand the mission statement of a particular community hospice program—the program's goals and methods of service delivery. Other examples include learning that a program has received a large grant for an additional building, that the local university is about to place a field unit there for student training, or that the board of an affiliated organization has approved funding for a development director. Although you will not have access to all informal developments in the services you use, your attention to, and continuous connections with, both formal and informal aspects of the network you maintain will enrich your understanding of your community's resource environment.

Making the Match in Brokering   As discussed in Chapter 3, knowledge and skills are needed to facilitate the matching of clients and services as you maintain an ongoing and continually growing network of contacts. Developing and maintaining a resource network (or "service system linkage") nearly always requires you to use the skills you first learned about in Chapter 3 in connection with clients—that is, looking with planned emptiness and others. When you understand the purpose of the service, as well as the opportunities and challenges of the service, your ability to use the service for your client will increase.

Following up on your referrals is important, both to determine if the client is participating in and benefiting from the service and to gain insight into the provider's response to your referral. Remember that the match between clients and services is important from the service's point of view as well as from the client's perspective. When you have taken the time and care to learn about an effective and successful referral to a particular service, you will gain the trust of other providers who will respect your competence and skills. Further, when you develop a genuine understanding of, and appreciation for, the work that others do, you are likely to find your own work gratifying, and perhaps more to the point, you will find "the system" more responsive to your client.

Mediator

Mediation has both a formal and informal dimension in the delivery of human services. Mediation as a professional practice has its own identity and is often more associated with the legal system and public policy than it is with social work practice. There are, in fact, social workers who complete specialized mediation training and become mediators in such areas as divorce and child custody. Most social workers, however, engage in some aspects of mediation fairly frequently, if on a less formal basis. **Mediators**, as outsiders to a dispute, try to: (1) establish common ground between disputing parties; (2) help them understand each other's point of view; and (3) establish that each party has an interest in the relationship's stability past the current area of difference.

Finding Common Ground   Locating the points of agreement in the midst of a dispute is a common skill in social work practice. Assume you are working in a youth agency and have just seen Josh, a 15-year-old who has recently run away from home for the first time. After conversation with him, you understand his challenge to be about the relationship between his mother and her new live-in boyfriend. He is upset and scared and is not certain about the ramifications of being on his own. He dislikes his mother's boyfriend and objects to the curfew and other house rules he imposes. Josh also says he misses his mother's companionship the way it was before "he" entered the scene. When you are satisfied that Josh is safe at home (that he is not being abused in any way), you ask him for permission to schedule a meeting with his mother, her boyfriend, and Josh to explore the issues among them. He somewhat reluctantly agrees.

When his mother enters the youth center, she seems exasperated with her son, but she is also relieved to see him. She begins to cry and hugs him. Her boyfriend remains quiet, but when he catches Josh's eye, he smiles at the boy just slightly.

Walking through It   In exploring the process for one possible avenue of mediation in Josh's family, you might do the following:

- Represent yourself warmly and genuinely as one who wants to help resolve this issue without taking sides. Convey to the family that you trust the process of working through the issues and you will walk that journey with them. You might let the members of the family know that you are there to listen, explore options, facilitate, and possibly mediate, but not to direct or advise.

- Attempt to establish common ground. In this case, Josh's present well-being is the immediate point of common interest. You discover that Josh is 15 years old and is not prepared to support himself physically, financially, or emotionally (or legally in most places). He is scared and concerned about his future. At the same time, however, he is vocal about his freedom and does not want to be bound by all the rules imposed upon him by his mother's new boyfriend. His mother cares for him and wants him to be safe. Her boyfriend wants a peaceful household and likes Josh well enough, although he has no strong connection with him. He cares deeply for Josh's mother.

- Help Josh, his mother, and her boyfriend understand and appreciate one another's points of view. Assume that Josh's mother and her boyfriend may have different perspectives and opinions, and acknowledge all points of view. Facilitate their direct dialogue with one another. The skills of planned emptiness and looking from diverse angles will be beneficial to this interaction. A dialogue aimed at establishing a process in which each person is willing to listen to the others' points of view may focus on the following:

    Social Worker: "I would like each of you to be able to share your perspective on the current situation. In order for each of you to be able to hear what the others are saying, it is important that we establish some ground rules for the discussion. For instance, I would like to ask that we each remain silent until the other person is finished speaking. If we have questions or thoughts to share, those should wait until the person has completed her or his statements. I will try to summarize what I am hearing each of you say so that you can confirm or modify our understanding."

- Establish with Josh, his mother, and her boyfriend that it is in the interests of all of them to work together during this interaction so that they can come to a resolution regarding Josh's living arrangements and his general safety.

- Help all parties recognize that each will benefit from an ongoing positive relationship in which they can settle differences that go beyond the current dispute. The quality of Josh's future may depend on their ability to work together, as well as the quality of the relationship between Josh's mother and her boyfriend. These are the abiding points of common interest.

This scenario represents just one way in which this situation might play out. You might make other arguments to reach the same goals of finding common ground and identifying solutions. You will notice that no *particular* solution is implied in this process. Josh, his mother, and her boyfriend might agree that Josh should return home, live with another family member, try to survive on his own on a trial basis, or any number of other possibilities. The major point is that the relationship between Josh and his mother (and her boyfriend) is collaborative and that each has a stake in working out a solution that affirms their mutual benefit.

Educator

There are many ways in which social workers function as educators. While the mission and scope of individual practice settings will determine the nature and level of such an activity, some form of education is commonplace in most social work settings. On an interpersonal and concrete level, as an **educator**, you may teach clients about a range of topics; for example, you might inform clients about services, new programs, completing an application form, or something as basic as the correct bus to take to travel uptown before noon. You may assure an adolescent client that she is indeed normal when she worries that her moodiness indicates she is not, or you might educate clients about the maximum allowable percentage of income charged for rent in public housing. Much of the direct service aspect of acting as educator relates to helping clients to access resources, as well as to make the behavioral changes they want to make.

Developing Client Skills   On a direct practice level, you, as the social worker, can assist clients in developing the skills they need to participate in the intervention and reach their goals. The motivation for this kind of change needs to generate from clients' vision change, rather than from your opinions about needed improvements. You can assist clients in understanding the steps needed to accomplish that change. For example, if your client, Ramon, feels intimidated by his co-workers or supervisor in his job and wants to increase his assertiveness in the workplace, you might help by demonstrating a more assertive (but respectful) stance in a relevant interchange, and/or role-play or assist him to practice the new behavior. In other settings, you can help older adult clients learn to organize their medications to increase their compliance. You can teach parents strategies for supporting their children through positive feedback. You can model clear communication and gradually assist your client in participating more effectively in problem situations. For example, if you are working with an adolescent who is frequently suspended from school for short periods because of her angry outbursts at teachers, you can work with her on appropriate strategies for expressing herself more effectively without alienating adults. Additionally, you might accompany her to her first meeting with the school principal on her return to classes. You can help her describe her situation and support a more focused, direct, and respectful level of discussion based on her goals. Outside of the meeting you can help her process the session, including evaluating what went well and what did not go well, and support her ability to negotiate these relationships with further practice. You may then role-play the next meeting rather than attend yourself to support her goal of self-sufficiency in these types of situations. At the same time, when you use skills with clients, you are modeling skills that they may use on their own in their relationships. In all of these situations the ultimate goal is a more positive sense of strength and agency—a change in clients' thinking about themselves and a greater integration of self and skills into the environment.

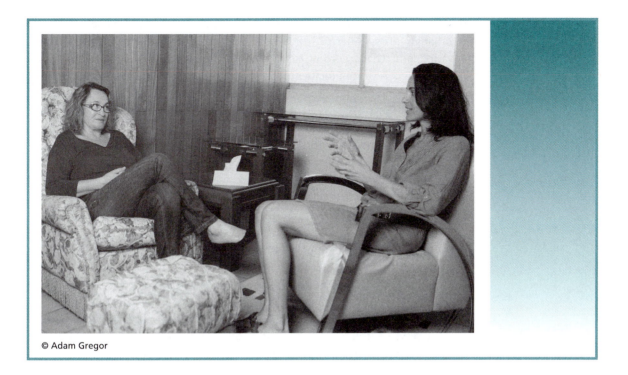

© Adam Gregor

Working with the Public   Social workers frequently are called upon to educate larger groups about issues that affect client systems. In some instances, these efforts take on aspects of primary prevention in that they are designed to prevent the development of a problem. For example, you may teach a parenting class or present a session on ways to support racial tolerance in the classroom to a preschool group. Other education efforts may involve providing testimony in a legislative hearing regarding the cultural needs of a group of refugee children, or speaking to a community group in response to their concerns about a new group home in their neighborhood for discharged clients with psychiatric histories.

Although the activities differ in nature, all of these scenarios involve working in an educator's role. Social work practitioners have a long history of acting as educators when they take on the position of field instructor for students in an academic program leading to a social work degree.

Client Advocate

Advocacy in social work practice is aimed at securing the rights and well-being of clients who are at risk for a negative outcome. The **advocate** may obtain resources, modify existing policies or practices, and promote new policies that will benefit clients. Regardless of the activities involved, advocacy represents a struggle over power, and by definition it seeks to obtain and ensure clients' access to resources.

This role of defending, championing, or otherwise speaking out for clients is one of the original cornerstones of the profession's commitment, although its intensity has varied somewhat according to the political climate (Haynes & Mickelson, 2010). Although advocacy often focuses on the political or civil rights of clients, as a social worker, you frequently have the opportunity and obligation to advocate in informal, everyday situations when a client is treated disrespectfully or inefficiently, or not provided needed services. Advocacy assumes an active role that is not always comfortable or popular with others.

Many social workers distinguish between **case (or client) advocacy**, defined as advocacy on behalf of an individual client or a single group of clients, and **cause (or class) advocacy**, which is initiated on behalf of a category of clients. **Legislative advocacy** is specialized version of cause advocacy in which some aspect of the law is addressed. We will take a brief look at each type.

Case Advocacy   Social workers usually practice case advocacy on an agency or organizational level. For example, if your client has been denied food stamps (Supplemental Nutrition Assistance Program (SNAP)) to which she or he is entitled, you can advocate with the public welfare income support organization that houses the SNAP services. To be an effective advocate, you will need to know a number of variables, such as eligibility requirements, agency appeal policies, regulations, and power structures, as well as contextual variables such as the way in which SNAP fits into the overall welfare organization. You will also want to recognize the situation as one of potential conflict and to enter at the point of least contest so that you do not inspire more resistance than necessary. Therefore, you can address the situation with the worker who originally denied the SNAP application and use the grievance process at the agency before taking any other measures, such as involving powerful outside parties in advocacy, calling the media, or organizing a protest.

Cause Advocacy   More political than case advocacy, cause advocacy involves both larger numbers of people and, by definition, a cause that affects them all, either by imposing obstacles to attaining resources or by directly depriving people of these resources. Cause advocacy involves speaking for a large number of people who are not your clients and who are not likely to be empowered to participate directly in forming either the goals or the preferred advocacy methods related to the cause. Nevertheless, cause advocacy can be effective when you can partner with other concerned organizations, and can spur change that positively impacts many people. It is also helpful when the issue is very clear and does not impose any solution on people who do not choose it. For example, if your community has no adequate facilities for child care after school, there may be agencies, churches, businesses, or other institutions that are concerned and want to develop a facility for parents in need of such a service. Assuming that you will require funding from local public sources, your coalition of interested partners (who are well organized and well-rehearsed) will be in a position to advocate for adequate child care facilities. As in case advocacy, you/your coalition will need to be skillful and to have researched background information regarding the number of children to be served, their needs, the estimated costs of providing the service, the likelihood of participation, the process of getting the issue on the city's agenda, and the benefits to all stakeholders.

Legislative Advocacy   This form of cause advocacy is devoted to adding, amending, changing, or eliminating legislation in order to benefit a large group of clients. For example, when a social worker advocates to lower the legal alcohol limit for driving a moterized vehicle from .08 blood alcohol content (BAC) to .06, that is a case of legislative advocacy designed to benefit a large category—drivers and passengers.

There are many other kinds of scenarios in which a large group of people would benefit from a change in legislation, because nearly all entitlement policies have limitations that may present obstacles to your clients. Controversial resources such as family planning and abortion clinics are likely to have more access constraints (such as age limits or pregnancy duration) than do other less disputed services such as food pantries.

A considerable amount of knowledge, insight, and organization are required to change a law, but it is well within the arena of social work practice to initiate or collaborate in such activity. With careful preparation and diligence in appropriate situations, legislative advocacy can produce the desired results. Legislative advocacy usually requires intensive, cooperative work with one or several organizations.

Thoughts about Power and Advocacy   Social work advocacy is frequently related to the social justice dimension of resource allocation; therefore, it is helpful to recall the assumptions about power. In general, advocates recognize that power is not easily relinquished, not equally distributed, involves conflict, and is necessary to make substantial change. These points may appear harsh if you have not considered power and advocacy within such a context. Familiarity with these concepts can prepare you to enter a more political arena and are beneficial in understanding the social locations of those who have been oppressed and have had little power to exercise in our culture.

Like work with individual clients, advocacy can be a highly rewarding undertaking (Abramowitz, 2005), but can be complex, frustrating, and mysterious. When not executed well, it can be costly to clients, as you will recall from the tenants' story in Chapter 4. See Exhibit 5.2 for a list of cautions and strategies regarding advocacy. More on advocacy and empowerment will be discussed later in this chapter.

Collaborator

Guided by the mission of the social work profession, collaboration is inherent in the daily practice of most social work practitioners. In addition to using collaboration skills in developing plans for change with clients, social workers engage in collaborative relationships with other professions in many different ways. For example, social workers work with health, social service, and legal professionals in the delivery of client services, development of programs and policies, advocacy work, and research. While the terms to describe cooperative practices are sometimes used interchangeably, they do have distinctive connotations. Multidisciplinary practice, for instance, refers to groups of professions working together toward a similar aim, while maintaining their individual interventions (Moxley, 2008). Interdisciplinary practice (also referred to as interprofessional collaboration, collaborative practice, and partnered practice), on the other hand, involves professionals from different disciplines integrating their professional knowledge to work together toward a common goal. In these situations, social workers engage in **interprofessional collaboration**.

Social workers often work in settings in which the primary mission is not the provision of social work services. Known as **host settings**, these include health care facilities and programs, educational institutions, law enforcement or legal systems, military programs, and even financial institutions. While it is essential for social workers working in host settings to understand the philosophies, professional cultures, and language of other professions, social workers will be collaborators in

EXHIBIT 5.2 *Strategies Regarding Advocacy*	• Enter any situation in which you want to advocate at the point of least contest (Wood & Tully, 2006). • When clients are directly involved, ensure they genuinely support your efforts and understand the possible repercussions. • Prepare yourself fully with the knowledge that is relevant to the situation (e.g., eligibility requirements, entitlement limitations, number of people in a given category, history of advocacy on this topic). • Be clear and specific about your goals; a complaint about a policy means little if there is no solution presented. • Begin with simple efforts at persuasion; assume first that there has been a mistake or an oversight. • Be clear when persuasion is not working with the targeted audience and you must enter a new level. • Assess that new level prior to action: Can you be successful? Are your clients still supportive? Do collaborative partners agree on the next step? • Use carefully cultivated social work skills in an advocacy effort, including listening, empathy, clarifying, and firmness. • Use the discourse of collaboration and common ground. • Seek supervision and consultation. You are as vulnerable to "not seeing" in thinking about cause advocacy as you might be in the most intense interpersonal work. • When entering into formal processes (e.g., legislative advocacy), become knowledgeable about the technicalities of the legislative process.

virtually every setting in which they are employed. While effective in enhancing the delivery of services or care, interprofessional collaborations can be complex and, sometimes, frustrating relationships in which to work (will be further explored in Chapter 10). Social workers may find that challenges occur in communicating with other professions who have their own professional "jargon," perceived hierarchy of professional influence, and conflicting opinions on approach, roles, implementation, and outcomes related to the work to be completed.

Social workers can use their training in collaboration and negotiation with client systems to prepare for becoming effective professional collaborators. Abramson (2009) suggests that social workers can become competent collaborators by learning about the other professions with which they will be engaged. Upon learning about your collaborators' professional socialization experience, language, and culture, you can then seek out common ground on which to begin the process of building a professional collaboration. Taking advantage of opportunities to gain interprofessional competence will serve you well as you move into any area of practice.

PUTTING IT ALL TOGETHER

Thus far, this chapter has explored various aspects of social work practice in action. Areas covered include supporting clients' strengths and their environments as well as various actions by workers. Empowerment practice will be used as a model for examining the possible points of integration for social work roles within the context of a strengths-based practice approach.

Empowerment Practice

Social work as a profession has been committed to empowering clients for much of its history. As one of the early scholars of empowerment practice, Simon (1990) asserted that, in its purest sense, empowerment cannot be given to someone else because empowerment is not ours to give. Empowerment resides within the individual and can only be encouraged or perhaps released, but not given, by others. The social worker may be in a position to promote or facilitate empowerment, but ultimately, the change comes from the client her or himself. Best practices in the application of empowerment theory suggest (Parsons, 2008, p. 124):

- A sociopolitical lens is used to frame situations experienced by the client system.

- Power within the helping relationship is couched within the context of client strengths, self-efficacy, and education as opposed to pathology.

- Informal social networks are integral to the empowerment of the client system.

- Collectivity is key to the intervention with a specific emphasis on support, mutual aid, validation, and promotion of social justice.

The practice of empowerment-focused social work establishes a clear theoretical connection among individual client strengths and their environment and the client's capacity to act in a way both to empower her or himself and liberate others. This connection in turn supports intervention in multiple and highly interconnected settings and recognizes the importance of unleashing or strengthening the client's sense of self and agency. Exhibit 5.3 provides an illustrative case example of an appropriate and sensitive empowerment approach.

The concept of empowerment has applicability within each of the roles that a social worker assumes when intervening with a client system. As the social worker serves in the roles of case manager, counselor, broker, mediator, education, client advocate, and collaborator, she or he has the opportunity to use the concepts of empowerment to carry out the tasks associated with each of these roles. Even in situations of crises or tragedies that impact entire communities, regions, or the country, the social worker, working at any level, can approach interventions with an empowerment perspective in mind. If you are working with individuals who have experienced violence (shooting or bombing), a natural disaster, or community-wide crisis, your role can be not only to meet their immediate needs, but to help them become empowered to survive, advocate for themselves or others, or change the system. As Kohli and colleagues (2010) write: "We should appreciate the strengths of individuals that help them to survive in the worst of situations and use their strengths to empower them" (p. 266). Consider the resilience and fortitude of a client who has survived a significant life event and begin the intervention at that starting point.

The social worker working to advocate on behalf of a client system can build the advocacy effort on the strengths of the client, use the client's self-efficacy and life experience in the advocacy, and help the client system become empowered to engage in self-advocacy. Advocacy work that elicits power from clients includes facilitating as strong a role as possible for clients to advocate for themselves. Activities to promote self-advocacy and empowerment include helping them to prepare, providing education and support, and accompanying them during the process. Consider the situation in Brickville in which Virginia Stone is fearful of losing her family's home to a developer. What strengths and experiences do Virginia or her family members possess that might be used in advocacy on her behalf?

Social workers need different strategies to initiate and facilitate a strengths-based intervention that empowers clients. For example, while the narrative approach does not provide specific therapeutic skills, the client can be empowered with the social worker's help in constructing, deconstructing, and finally reconstructing their conceptualizations (i.e., stories) that have previously been used to define their lives. The social worker's role is to help the clients determine if they wish to change their perceptions by challenging and broadening their thinking about their lives.

EXHIBIT 5.3

Thomas's Story

The story takes place in a small New England city in the 1970s. Thomas was born with a neurological disorder, cerebral palsy. His family had little idea of how to deal with his severe physical limitations and had three other children to rear as well. His parents cared about him and did what they could to learn ways to support him and his abilities, as well as cope with his disability. He received the standard medical care of the time and was sent to school with his age group.

Early on it was evident that Thomas's body did not reflect his aptitude for schoolwork. He was, in fact, intellectually capable and did exceedingly well in the subjects in which teachers supported him. His family did not understand, however, the ways in which Thomas's socialization was affected by his physical impairments or how he experienced his life. Although he had only a few friends, he attempted, for several years to maintain a positive outlook, even developing an excellent sense of humor. Nevertheless, he continued to feel excluded by peers and adults alike.

COLLIDING WITH THE WORLD

Over time he became hostile with teachers because he had to prove himself over and over again, every time he entered a new grade or school. Teachers and school administrators first assumed that he was unable to do grade-level work. One teacher questioned his very presence in the regular classroom. His pastor at church advised that he seek supported employment through a public vocational program. Everyone seemed to assume he was unable to do, know, or even feel anything. His medical treatment included the excruciating requirement to walk in physical therapy that was promoted in those days. No one noted Thomas's pain or responded to it.

By the time Thomas was an adolescent, his parents sent him to a psychotherapist to learn the reasons for his intense anger. To Thomas, this was yet another insult to someone who had already suffered so many. His therapist told him he needed to "get the chip off his shoulder" and tend to his schoolwork. There would be no money for college—he would have to earn scholarships if he wanted to do more than sit in the living room until he could be matched to a job he did not want.

MEETING MAURA

Finally, Thomas was in need of a new wheelchair. He was directed to a social worker for assistance when his parents could not pay the required deductible. The social worker, Maura, who worked in the primary care office of Thomas's physician, first spent some time getting to know him and hearing what he had to say about the wheelchair. She assisted him in getting the funding for his new chair and continued to ask about his overall experience. He began to talk about his needs to consider his options regarding school, his family, his anger, and his growing sense of estrangement from the world.

Maura helped Thomas by hearing with an openness and reflexivity that assumed he was the expert on his experience. She heard his story, took him seriously, and helped him look at what his disability meant to him by asking him to talk not only about the physical pain but also about the exclusion that he experienced. She helped him look at his resilience in the face of all he had been through. She did not try to challenge his perception

EXHIBIT 5.3

Continued

of his experience but was completely respectful of it. She asked him to articulate the way he wanted his life to be different in view of his strong capacities. She encouraged him to reflect on his own position and how he might address his goals. As time passed, Maura helped Thomas secure vocational rehabilitation funding for college and validated his, by then, strong commitment to working in human services on disability issues. She also met with Thomas's family to help them understand his choices and the impact these choices would have on the family.

CHANGING DIRECTION

Thomas went on to study for a master's degree in disabilities and is preparing for a career in which he can advocate for others with disabilities as well as himself. He is a full participant in school and in the surrounding context of his family, friends, and culture. He is still angry sometimes, but he is not fearful or alone.

Reading this (almost all) true story, you can see how Maura implemented the empowerment focus identified in the chapter: She assists in liberating Thomas's "potent self" and encourages his interpersonal connections. She supports his understanding of his environment and she helps connect him to a direction in which he can address the more political aspects of his experience. Consider now the connections between Thomas's experiences with other social work perspectives.

Social Justice: Maura works diligently to expand Thomas's access to the benefits of his society by helping him to find funding for education. She does not accept the status quo arrangement in which those with private resources are privileged and those without are not. To complete this role, Maura would work toward reallocation of educational funding for all people, not just Thomas.

Human Rights: Thomas's status as a person with a disability is not accepted as a rationale for discrimination in education, nor does his disability preclude the "full development of the personality" (Article 26, United Nations, 1948) through education. Maura recognizes him as a person who has both needs and abilities and the right to fulfill his life as he chooses.

Strengths Perspective: Maura recognizes Thomas's considerable strengths, validates them, and encourages linking their full expression to his goals. She sees him as a whole human being, with many talents to offer, not as a "victim of cerebral palsy."

Critical Social Construction: Maura sees Thomas's disability as a social construction that results from the prevailing collective meaning given to it by our culture. She questions the limitations imposed by that construction, and she believes Thomas can do what he sets out to do. Maura accepts that there are multiple realities and so honors his experience of exclusion and oppression. Because his experience has developed within the context of his social location, on which he is the expert, she makes no attempt to "correct" his understanding. Her effort goes into changing his future experience in order to make it more consistent with how he wants his life arranged.

Because the narrative approach is consistent with the social work values of strengths and collaboration, and the client as the expert on her or his life, the narrative approach can be integrated with other clinical approaches (solution-focused) and cognitive behavioral approaches (Parsons, 2008).

One practice behavior that can aid social workers in helping clients to redefine their perceptions of their lives is **motivational interviewing (MI)**. Initially developed for practice with clients who are not seeking services voluntarily, motivational interviewing builds on the client's strengths and right to self-determination to implement a plan for change she or he created (Miller & Rollnick, 2013). Aimed at helping clients who are ambivalent or reticent about change, MI is a collaborative process between the social worker and the client in which the practitioner aids the client in becoming more aware of the implications of her or his decision to engage in change process (Lundahl, Kunz, Brownell, Tollefson, & Burke, 2010). A more technical definition of MI can be described as: "... a collaborative, goal-oriented style of communication with particular attention to the language of change. It is designed to strengthen personal motivation for and commitment to a specific goal by eliciting and exploring the person's own reasons for change within an atmosphere of acceptance and compassion" (Miller & Rollnick, 2013, p. 29).

Currently used in a variety of settings with a range of client situations (e.g., child welfare, treatment of substance abuse and other additions, intimate partner violence, and family and group work), motivational interviewing is an evidence-based strategy in which the social worker uses the practice skills of empathy and reflective listening (Wahab, 2005). As the expert on her or his life, the client is responsible for articulating her or his story and developing a motivation for initiating life changes. The underlying perspective (or "spirit") of MI encompasses four interrelated components: partnership, acceptance, compassion, and evocation (Miller & Rollnick, 2013, p. 15). These components along with the principles of MI and skills and strategies for integrating motivational interviewing into practice are further delineated in Quick Guides 13 and 14, including the concepts of change talk, evoking change, and the four processes of MI, known as OARS (Open questions, Affirmation, Reflection, and Summary). MI will be again highlighted in use with families in Chapter 7.

Motivational interviewing is but one of the numerous techniques and skills available to the social work practitioner, but one that is built on a strengths-based, person-centered framework. In determining if MI is an appropriate intervention strategy, consider the following (Miller & Rollnick, 2013, p. 25):

1) Are conversations regarding change occurring?
2) Should conversation regarding change be initiated?
3) Will the client outcomes be influenced by client changes?
4) Is the client ambivalent about change?

The process of implementing an intervention using motivational interviewing encompasses four components (Miller & Rollnick, 2013, pp. 26–29):

- Engaging—establishing a helpful connection with the client to promote a working relationship;

- Focusing—developing a specific agenda for change;

- Evoking—drawing out the client's motivation for change and articulating arguments for making the change; and

- Planning—helping the client to transition from being motivated for change to being ready for change which could be evidenced by the client changing her or his conversation from the "ifs and whys" of change to the "where and how" of change.

The role of the social worker is to maintain a focus on the client and her or his desire to make a change. Specifically, the social worker is engaged in MI when she or he is listening and reflecting, affirming those behaviors/activities that the client is doing well, identifying change talk, drawing out the client's motivation, wisdom,

---

QUICK GUIDE 13 THE SPIRIT AND PRINCIPLES OF MOTIVATIONAL INTERVIEWING

The Spirit of Motivational Interviewing is intended to embrace the following concepts:

Partnership establishes that the client is the expert on her or his life and behavior change is more likely to result from the social worker and the client working together to determine the areas of and strategies for change.

Acceptance is comprised of the social worker's belief that the client has absolute worth, genuinely attempts to understand the client's perspective, respects the client's autonomy, and affirms those strengths and efforts demonstrated by the client.

Compassion is conveyed by the social worker to the client through actively promoting and prioritizing the client's needs.

Evocation is rooted in the idea that the client possesses strengths, wisdom about her or himself, reasons for acting as they have, and have the motivation and resources with which to make desired change.

Stemming from the spirit that guides Motivational Interviewing, Principles on which the strategy is built emphasize the social worker's ability to:

1) **Express empathy** to enhance client rapport and comfort and decrease client resistance.
2) **Develop discrepancy** to enable client to gain insight into the gaps between her or his value system and current behaviors.
3) **Avoid argumentation with client**
4) **Roll with client resistance** to convey to the client that her or his apparent resistance to change is respected and viewed as normal.
5) **Support client self-efficacy** to promote client's confidence in her or his ability to change behavior.

Source: Lundahl, Kunz, Brownell, Tollefson, & Burke; 2010 pp. 137; Miller & Rollnick, 2012, pp. 14–21.

QUICK GUIDE 14   SKILLS AND STRATEGIES FOR MOTIVATIONAL INTERVIEWING

Focused on the person and her or his strengths and resources, three areas of skill related to motivational interviewing include (Miller & Rollnick, 2013):

- **Change Talk** occurs when the client makes statements that relate positively to making a change in her or his life and can be contrasted with **Sustain Talk** which refers to the statements which favor maintaining the status quo (p. 7).
- **Evoking Change Talk** is based on the assumptions that people have wisdom and experience that includes ambivalence about change which can be elicited by the social worker, using a person-centered approach aimed initiating a desired change.
- **OARS** is a pneumonic that embraces four core skills used to facilitate the four processes of MI and includes (pp. 32–34):

  - **Open questions** are intended to engage the client in expanded and reflective discussion about feelings and potential change, such as "how are you feeling about your goal to lose weight?"
  - **Affirmation** enables the social worker to offer positive statements regarding the client's intentions, strengths, efforts, resources, and courage related to the proposed change. For example, the social worker may say to the client who is striving to lose weight: "I admire your commitment to living a healthier life. You will be a good role model for your children."
  - **Reflective Listening** provides the social worker and the client the opportunity to clarify, deepen, and explore the client's previous statements. In working with the client goal of weight loss, the social worker might choose to say: "It seems that you are able to maintain your weight loss plan well, but struggle with compliance when you are going through stressful periods, like the loss of your mother."
  - **Summarizing** allows the social worker to expand on the previous reflections and transition to the next phase of work. Summaries bring together all the aspects of the conversation and aid in the planning of the change process as well as the evaluation of change that has occurred. Summarizing with the client working on weight loss can emphasize: "We have talked about your past efforts to lose weight, the strategies that you feel worked and did not work, and your commitment to being successful this time. We have also explored the triggers that make it more challenging for you to stay on your diet and exercise plan. We have brainstormed some strategies that you can put into place when you are feeling particularly stressed and wanting to revert to your old eating patterns."

and strengths, and resisting the need to offer the "righting reflex" (i.e., advice-giving, confronting, or arguing) (Miller & Rollnick, 2013, p. 324).

As with any practice approach, the social worker is ethically obligated to review the evidence to ensure the efficacy of the intervention. In a 2010 meta-analysis of 119 research studies using MI, Lundahl and colleagues concluded that MI can be effective with an array of issues presented by clients, including: addictions (e.g., substance abuse and gambling); high and low levels of distress; increasing healthy behaviors; decreasing unhealthy behaviors; and enhancing client participation in the intervention process.

STRAIGHT TALK ABOUT INTERVENTIONS: UNEXPECTED EVENTS AND ONGOING EVALUATION

In contrast to other ways to view social work practice, the intervention process may seem orderly. If you practice sensitive engagement, careful assessment of both the players and the environment, and plan consistent methods of taking action on behalf of your clients, you might be seduced into thinking that the work will always go smoothly. This is a mistake.

In the real world, not everything goes as planned. Because social work is completely immersed in people's lives, social workers have only limited control over their work with client systems and need to develop an acceptance (or at least tolerance) for the up-and-down nature of working with clients who are living within their environments. In this real world, people get sick, get into accidents, change their minds, get fired and laid off, become disheartened, move, their kids get into trouble, and they experience violence. On the positive side, people also get promoted, find their strengths, find their voices, fall in love, get jobs, read an inspiring book, discover a new friend, and develop insight. All of these factors and many more have the potential to interrupt, postpone, redirect, or even terminate your work together.

In some cases—for example, if the client becomes discouraged or seems simply to lose interest—you will want to inquire about the role you might have played in contributing to these developments. In many cases your responsibility will be to honor, acknowledge, and explore the meaning of the new situation to the client, and reconfigure your work when indicated. It will generally be helpful for you to *expect the unexpected*. Flexibility is one of the most critical of social work attributes.

Just as you have been consistent in evaluating the progress of your work with your client and others involved throughout the engagement and assessment processes, you will want to evaluate the direction of the intervention periodically as well, particularly if there have been substantial changes or unexpected events in the client's life. You may easily get carried away in the plan that you so carefully put together, even when it may no longer fit very well. Checking and re-checking in with the client will serve you well during the intervention process. In that way you can stay connected to your client throughout and provide more relevant service.

As you recall from Chapter 3, crisis intervention and suicide threats are expected, yet unexpected, aspects of social work practice. The social worker's ability to intervene effectively is contingent upon a timely response and accurate assessment. After ensuring during the engagement and assessment phase that the client is safe, the focus during the intervention phase is on empowering the client to resolve the crisis by reconstructing her or his perceptions of strengths, assets, and resources (Eaton & Roberts, 2009). The social worker and the client collaborate to devise a viable plan for addressing the root causes of the crisis and emphasize concrete action strategies and a clear, agreed-upon plan for follow-up and maintenance.

SUPPORTING CLIENTS' STRENGTHS IN TERMINATION AND EVALUATION

"Important things are almost never easy." This statement captures the real work of the termination phase of planned change. Even when all participants in a relationship agree that it is time to move on, ending can be a wrenching process, often punctuated with doubts about whether you have given or done enough, or wishing, in some vague way, to start over. This is a common experience that you have probably had yourself, perhaps when you left home or ended a significant relationship. Endings tend to raise ambivalence: On the one hand they may be sad, while on the other hand they represent a kind of freedom to be on your own, make a new start, and be who you want to be.

The endings between social workers and client systems often reflect these tensions. Some social workers, as well as clients, will be tempted to minimize any significance in saying goodbye and simply "slip out the back." Others will not even want to talk about it, finding it more comfortable just to be gone. Yet others tend to make scrupulous notes with contact information and schedules and agree to call, text, connect on social networking sites, or email each other. Clients may, in fact, demonstrate both positive and negative feelings about their termination process, viewing termination with a sense of accomplishment or as (possibly another) loss in their lives (Fortune, 2009). People tend to develop patterns about endings, and usually these serve to mitigate the loss that inevitably occurs in all significant relationships. The remainder of this chapter will address the processes of ending a professional relationship with your clients. We will explore strategies for evaluation of the practice intervention on multiple levels. While terminations that occur at the level of the family, group, organization, or community are unique and will be explored in the following chapters, this chapter will emphasize general issues related to terminating and evaluating the social work relationship with the individual client.

ENDINGS AND TERMINATION

There are considerable variations in the way endings occur in social work practice. Factors that play a role include age, gender, ethnicity, socioeconomic status, cultural experience, working style, and personality of both the client and the social worker. The social location of the work, its purpose, the agency, the perspective used, and the organizational pressures surrounding the work also have an impact. Even within this range, however, general planning is necessary and can be helpful to both the client and the social worker in bringing closure to the professional social work intervention.

Planning the Process: Overview

Begin by considering several tasks that relate to endings. These tasks will not apply to all social work relationships and their order need not be rigid. Your theoretical orientation and the specifics of the practice situation will guide much of the timing and ordering, but these tasks are common to a range of relationships and are consistent with ethical practice. They are:

- Negotiate the timing of the termination.
- Review the agreement for work.
- Process successes and shortcomings.
- Develop and clarify plans for termination and maintenance of change.
- Share responses to ending.
- Respect cultural consistency.

Negotiating the Timing   Because termination is a goal that is established at the beginning of the relationship, it should always be before you as you progress through the intervention. In some circumstances your client and you have the opportunity to specify the number of sessions at the beginning of the relationship. The closing date can then be determined during the first meeting. Frequently the same is true of mandated arrangements or managed care situations in which the agency is bound by prearranged guidelines. All of these are, of course, artificial proclamations that the work is done, and they are all externally imposed. In some cases, clients may request an additional number of sessions (as in task-centered models), and social workers may petition for an extended number of sessions (as in managed care).

Predetermined boundaries tend to distract from the ideal timing for ending, which is when the social worker and client have reached the mutually formulated goals. The point at which the goals have been reached may not be clear, particularly if goals have not been clearly established. Even when goals are put in precise behavioral terms (for example, "the client will contact the school social worker"), there is some risk that the established goals and intervention plans may still not be realized. For example, your client may have unsuccessfully attempted to contact the school social worker, or made contact, but was not able to clearly articulate her message; therefore, meeting the goal technically does not meet the spirit of the issue. Nevertheless, you will need to make a reasoned judgment that the client no longer needs your services. Because you and the client may not necessarily agree on the exact moment when that occurs, in many cases you will need to negotiate the timing and criteria, remembering that you are each subject to your own foibles relating to ending relationships.

There are at least three areas for you to consider in your negotiations regarding the termination of the relationship. The first is your responsibility and relates to preventing an unanticipated ending. In many circumstances you will not have control over the timing, but in others you can anticipate, if not change, the conditions. You have a responsibility to provide full information to the client about the possible nature and timing of termination. For example, a state contract or managed care restrictions may determine an ending date that you think is inappropriate. In such a situation you can at least prepare the client for the possibility that your appeal for more sessions may be denied. Other examples of situations in which you need to be straightforward with clients and make the smoothest transition arrangements you can include a situation in which your agency is about to eliminate services or programs, your position is threatened, or you know you are leaving your job or internship on a particular date.

The second issue relates to maintaining an ongoing dialogue with your client regarding her or his status or progress to determine if your work together is helping, and what needs to happen for the client to know she or he has met the goals. Just as you have ongoing discussion with your client about goals, contracts, and progress, you should also discuss termination throughout your relationship. While the agency or the plan you established with the client may determine the ending point, discussion about termination can and should be integral to the work.

The final issue involves predetermined endings. Knowing that you will have a specified number of meetings with the client provides you with the opportunity to regularly check in with the client to ensure that you both share an understanding of the point at which the work will be completed. Some clients may assume you can or will extend the number of sessions as you prefer, and others might expect if they behave well (especially in mandated sessions) that they will be "dismissed" early. Always be as clear as possible about any limits that are imposed on you for the work and be as open as possible to discussing the meaning of those limits to your client. Even when both sides clearly understand the ending date, either the client or you may still experience difficult ending dynamics.

Reviewing the Agreement for Work   In the process of finishing your work together, you and your client should review the formal contract or informal agreement you made for work. You will want again to negotiate the understanding each of you has about the agreement, as it may have changed in view of your completed work, circumstances in the client's life or your life, or due to the agency's ability to offer services.

Processing Successes and Shortcomings   As you precede through the work together, you have discussed and processed the aspects that went well, the things that missed the mark, and any approaches that clearly headed in the wrong direction. This type of assessment should be ongoing and not just take place at the last meeting. Nevertheless, processing a summary of successes at the end is an appropriate strategy to gain perspective on the whole experience and gain insight into the client's view of the work. Sometimes, for example, an experience that seemed difficult at the time, in retrospect, is associated with personal growth (for your client and or you). Recall the example from earlier in the chapter of the client with mental illness who had struggled to locate housing. You may have suggested that she was ready to meet with the landlord on her own, which at the time seemed challenging to her. As your work together progressed, however, she may have seen that it was a useful push that helped her to recognize her strengths. Looking through an empowerment lens, this success suggests your client's ability to act on her own needs, and she no longer views herself as a victim, but as a survivor of the power imbalance experienced by people with labels, such as those given to people with mental illness. It is useful for clients and social workers to process successes based on power and human rights definitions.

At this point in the social work relationship, it is not uncommon for some clients to indicate that they have not made as much progress as you believe they have. The client may point to various criteria to demonstrate her or his own shortcomings or to register some verbal sense of being abandoned. This behavior can be complicated to deal with as it raises the possibility that ending would be premature and possibly harmful. Also possible, however, is that clients choose this means to make known their lack of self-confidence in making their way independently, or their reluctance to leave the relationship. One effective way to address such dynamics is to be transparent about the process and discuss issues in detail with the client. Whether or not you offer to continue to work with a client for a longer time is a matter of your professional judgment, your supervisor's judgment, and all the other constraints in the agency or funding sources, such as managed care.

A second possibility is for clients to threaten to leave the relationship early in anticipation of ending. This often seems like an "I'll fire you before you fire me" response to minimize a sense of abandonment and is sometimes called **flight**. In this case, you will want to make every effort to engage the client in the process for at least one more session in which you can address the issue of ending and strive for closure. Clients who pointedly (and physically) avoid the ending steps in the work, in some cases are the ones to benefit most in personal growth by a positive ending process.

The identification of shortcomings in your own work is another area in which you may get an unexpected challenge. When you ask for ideas about those aspects of the intervention that did not unfold as you or the client had hoped or expected, you must be truly open to receiving a critical answer. An account of your shortcomings or those of the process itself can come as a surprise to you, especially if you have not heard such expressions of dissatisfaction along the way. Although hearing critical comments can be difficult, you can choose to learn from them and remain open to the meanings your client has in making them.

Making and Clarifying Plans   Although there are times when the work is clearly finished and the client is ready to move ahead without your assistance, this does not always happen. You may determine the best course of action is to make a referral to a different type of service, or transfer your client to another social worker in your agency or to a different agency. For example, you have worked with a client named "Sam" throughout the school year in which you had your practicum at the agency where Sam receives services. As the month of May nears, you realize that it is not likely that he will complete the work he wanted to do before you leave your position. In negotiation with him, you will need to reassess, much as in the earlier phases, where he is in the agreed-to work, where he wants to go from here, and through what arrangement it is mostly likely he can continue his work effectively. You can help to clarify his options and assist him in assessing his own needs at the point in which you must terminate with him. Be aware that this stage represents a potential ending to services, which may either set him back toward reaching his goals or promote a continuation in his growth.

When you decide to refer the client to another agency, you will assume the role of broker. As discussed previously, the broker is responsible for establishing a relationship with a network of resources. Regardless of your experience or skill level and the success of your work with the client system, you have the potential to undo any client gains with an inappropriate or ill-conceived referral.

In those cases when the client is ready with some certainty to end professional services, a plan is needed for maintaining the gains and/or continuing further growth in the community. Some clients who no longer have the protective atmosphere of the client–worker relationship may find it difficult to maintain the changes they made without some clear way to reinforce them. You can help by identifying and exploring the situations that are likely to challenge the client's gains and consider strategies for addressing future stresses. You can also help by encouraging the client to identify a natural network of support before ending the work, or identifying other community resources that will be available. Consider again the termination with Sam. You and Sam may identify formal (e.g., agencies, services, organizations) and informal (e.g., individuals) resources that are available to him following the termination of his relationship with you. Most clients will have to return to the context in which their struggles arose, so a strategy to cope with that environment can be critical to maintaining the gains. In Sam's case, a "rehearsal" of his response to potential situations that may arise may be a strategy that he can rely on when you are no longer a resource for him.

Sharing Responses to Endings   Identifying and articulating one's feeling about ending may be the most sensitive of the dimensions of ending the work. You will need to anticipate, to the extent that you can, the way in which your client will respond and those issues that will require attention. Remember that many clients have endured a series of difficult endings in their lives. For example, they may have experienced relationships that abruptly fell apart without their having any control or understanding of them. They also may have been removed from abusive homes or witnessed violence that resulted in death or separation. The devastation of poverty and social exclusion frequently creates the chaotic climate that leads to turbulence and disconnection. If ending well with your client turns out to be the most positive aspect of your work together, that, in and of itself, will be work well done and could provide a model of a healthy ending to a relationship.

Like their clients, social workers themselves may have experienced similarly chaotic, sometimes traumatic, disruptions. It is crucial that social workers know and understand their own history with regard to disengaging from relationships. Many social workers struggle as much as or more than clients in termination, and they need to gain the insights that will allow them to facilitate a professional process that benefits the client. Many new social workers are surprised to realize how attached they become to a client, and find they are not prepared to respond appropriately to their feelings or the client. This understandable reaction is an issue for supervision. To facilitate this process, the social worker can recall that the relationship is for the clients' well-being, and not for her or his own well-being.

In discussing feelings about termination, you can let clients know about your ambivalent feeling about the ending: that you feel sad at ending the relationship; but that you have enjoyed knowing them, and that you have confidence that they will meet their own needs effectively in the future. It may be helpful to offer the possibility of future work together if the client needs assistance. It is generally not appropriate to express acute feelings of loss so that clients feel they must help you cope, and it is not appropriate to continue the relationship beyond whatever follow-up arrangements you might make without a new process. Exhibit 5.4 depicts two termination-related exchanges between Virginia and her social worker as they move toward ending their working relationship.

Over the course of a career, many client situations challenge these guidelines. There may be situations, particularly in rural social work practice, that involve the potential for **dual relationships**. A dual relationship exists when the social worker has both a professional and a personal relationship with the client. For example, a social worker would be in a dual relationship if she or he is working with the client in a social work capacity and purchases real estate from the client. Such situations have less than clear boundaries. In these cases, the social worker can seek dialogue with supervisors and peers to resolve issues for which no simple rule is adequate. The following describes another situation that may challenge these guidelines.

Respecting Cultural Consistency   Just as social workers are ethically bound to honor the cultural dimensions that the client brings to your work together, social workers

EXHIBIT 5.4

The Dialogue of Termination

The two examples of an exchange between Virginia Stone (www.routledgesw.com/cases) and her social worker presented here demonstrate the power of an effectiveness of the termination process.

As you recall, Virginia has been working with a social worker on a number of challenging issues, including housing, caregiving, and grief and loss. Due to the number and intensity of the issues they worked on together, the relationship spanned over a year. The time has come for them to terminate the social work intervention. As you will learn in reviewing the two samples of dialogue presented here, terminations can be handled in different ways. Which of the two examples would you choose?

Termination Option #1	Termination Option #2
Social Worker: "Virginia, as we discussed the last time we met, today will be our final meeting. I want to take this opportunity to review our progress."	Social Worker: "Virginia, I think today should be our final meeting. What do you think of this idea?"
Virginia: "I've been thinking a lot about this since last time and am feeling good about things."	Virginia: "What do you mean? I didn't know we had to stop. Did I do something wrong?"
Social Worker: "Looking at the contract that we developed early in our time together, let's take a look at each of the items on the list." "Before we get started looking over the list, I want to let you know that I have enjoyed working with you and seeing you make such positive changes in your life. I will miss our meetings. I want you to know that you can feel free to contact me if you feel any needs in the future."	Social Worker: "No, you haven't done anything wrong. I just decided that we have accomplished as much as we are probably going to. Let's do a quick re-cap. I think that will help you see what I mean."

must also anticipate and attend to the meanings they make of endings. Clients who identify as ethnically different from the dominant culture may have approaches and reactions to endings that are different from that of the social worker. The social worker is, thus, bound to incorporate cultural diversity into the termination process. Termination processes and rituals need to be culturally appropriate (Fortune, 2009). For example, it is not uncommon in some cultural groups for a child's schoolteacher to be invited to a family birthday party. If the client lives in a culture with tightly woven informal ties, a client may view the formal aspects of ending the work and cutting off the relationship as a reflection of your annoyance or rejection.

On the other hand, some clients may find it difficult to share their emotions verbally about ending because their cultural orientation encourages a restrained and private approach to sentiment. It may be more productive to emphasize the return of the client to her or his ethnic community, whose support and nurturance will help to consolidate the gains. This rejoining of the community is viewed as especially critical to communities of color (Lum, 2004). In some situations a client may bring you a gift, a gesture that represents a more comfortable way to express feelings, reflect celebration, and offer a suitable token of closure. In others you may want to maintain a more formal, businesslike relationship similar to the tone maintained throughout the work. Avoid objectifying or stereotyping any client by focusing solely on cultural difference (Diller, 2011). You will need to be mindful of your client as a whole person who brings idiosyncrasies as well as cultural traditions to the social work relationship. The dynamics of endings probably engender more commonalities than differences, and the person sitting across from you saying good-bye is, after all, the same person you have shared the work with all along.

Finally, your own cultural sensibilities about endings will influence the scenario as well. Anticipating your own patterns is helpful, particularly if they are likely to vary from those of your clients in any significant way. As mentioned, endings can evoke difficult feelings for all people, and some of us have developed more sophisticated ways than others to get around them. Even in the social work literature, there is more attention to beginnings than endings. Endings can represent a metaphorical death, and by recognizing your responses to that, you will be able to say goodbye to clients in an effective, positive, and professional way.

STRAIGHT TALK ABOUT TERMINATION AND ENDINGS

The termination processes discussed thus far have assumed conditions in which ending is planned. However, endings often are not planned and are not under your control and your role becomes to negotiate the unexpected. Earlier we explored scenarios in which the client leaves the relationship before you expect. In addition to life-changing events, clients terminate because they do not feel the relationship has been fully established. For example, when the client is not clear about expectations or does not share the social worker's understanding of the purpose, the meetings may seem unfocused and without direction. Social workers identify outcome goals that the client may not find relevant (even when clients "agree" to them). If there is not sufficient clarity about an ending point in the work, the client may not be committed to remaining engaged in the process. In such cases the work may continue, but the client grows discouraged.

There are countless reasons for the work to end prematurely, all of which present the social worker with dilemmas regarding the appropriate response and its meaning to the client system. Without pressuring the client unduly, the most useful strategy is to make contact, if possible, and encourage the client to return to the work, if only to end it in a more purposeful way. This approach conveys respect for the integrity of the work while leaving the client in control of the future of the work. This contact provides an opportunity to explore the dynamics of the relationship, which may provide important information to inform your future work.

In institutional settings in which the client has been transferred to another unit or service, you may want to petition your supervisor for a single meeting so that you can reconnect with your client, if only briefly, to review the work and acknowledge the shift in care. Although institutions tend to organize themselves in terms that meet the staff's, rather than clients', needs, make an effort to prioritize the latter whenever you can. When you have made every effort, either to continue the work with a client or simply to have one session to end your work together, and your client does not respond, you will need to respect the manner of ending she or he has chosen. It is the client's choice at that point, and you, representing the ideal of self-determination, will humbly understand the limits of your influence. You will most likely hope that your client has made a new plan.

An ending that will occur for most social workers at some point in their career is the termination that results from the worker leaving the organization. The already complex process of termination is made more challenging when the social worker informs the client that she or he is leaving the program or organization. When the social work relationship ending is worker-initiated, the client can feel a loss of control, disappointment, and/or anger, both over the ending and the future of her or his intervention (Siebold, 2007). While the social worker and client are best served by following a traditional termination process to the extent possible, another important task is to openly process feelings about the termination. For example, you may say to the client, "You may not have experienced the ending of a formal helping relationship before. What feelings are you having about our work coming to a close?"

FORMAL EVALUATIONS

The term evaluation raises anxiety in many practitioners, but most social workers can appreciate the importance of evaluating practice. Evaluation can provide feedback regarding goal achievement, the utility of a particular method and about the experience of the client in the work. Evaluation can be globally-focused, behaviorally-directed, and process-oriented. Evaluations can also reflect on individual progress, group development, and changes in power structures as it recognizes success. In short, evaluation is useful for practitioners when viewed as a tool for development rather than a threat.

The following discussion will highlight issues in evaluation as they increasingly occur in everyday practice.

Priorities in Evaluation

A longstanding debate continues regarding the types and relevance of various evaluative strategies that are most appropriate for social work practice. As you recall from Chapter 4, some experts maintain that social workers need empirical, evidenced-based practice to function in our contemporary society. Practice evaluation data can have multiple uses, such as informing and improving your practice assessment and interventions, providing data to incorporate into proposals for funding, and program planning. While considerable attention is devoted to justifying social work practice, social workers are ethically obligated to maintain their professional commitments and values. Bloom, Fischer, and Orme (2009, p. 15) suggest that, in order to be an evaluation-informed practitioner, one must strive to be a **scientific practitioner**. A scientific practitioner combines the use of evidence and evaluation without compromising the "art and creativity of practice," thus scientific practice includes: (1) incorporating research and evaluation to identify interventions that are known to be effective; (2) systematically monitoring and evaluating one's practice through single-system designs (described below); (3) being committed to ongoing learning to improve practice competencies; (4) approaching social work practice with a goal of problem-solving, investigation, and discovery; and (5) remaining committed to the values and ethics of social work practice (p. 15).

Social work ethics mandates that the provision of service obligations take precedence over data collection and evaluation efforts. However, evaluative strategies are an important component of effective practice. Evaluation of practice can provide feedback that is consistent with social work practice requirements, values, commitment to informed practice, and serve to empower both the client and the social worker. Imagine how empowered a client may feel when they realize she or he now has experience in successfully overcoming a challenge that has been plaguing her or him for years.

In the following two sections, two major methods of evaluation will be presented: empirical design processes and reflective assessment. These two evaluation methods serve different purposes, and they can help to balance the overall activity. First, they recognize the contemporary requirement for evidence-based practice, that is, practice guided by empirical, scientific evidence that the intervention has been successful. In addition, they can validate the contemplative, postmodern social worker's inclination to critique the traditional processes of practice and evaluation through focused critical reflection.

Quantitative and Empirical Processes: Evidence-Based Practice

Quantitative and empirical evaluation processes have two tools in common: single-subject design and goal attainment scaling (GAS).

Single-Subject Design Applicable with any theoretically guided intervention, the **single-subject design** (SSD) is a grouping of evaluative procedures based on an intuitive framework for examining changes in one client over time (Fischer & Orme, 2008). Usually, the social worker and client system complete repeated measurements of an action, feeling, or behavior over the course of their work together. For example, consider Virginia's return to her walking program. The two of you could use a single-system design approach to charting and monitoring her progress. The visual depiction of her activity provides you both with an accounting that can serve as the basis for discussion, revising the intervention plan, as well as evaluation of progress. Conversely, a social worker could follow one intervention over a series of clients. Single-system design evaluation plans serve to assess, monitor, and adapt to changes and compare the effectiveness of different interventions (Bloom et al., 2009, pp. 264–265).

In order to administer this design effectively, the client and social worker meet over a period of time to allow for repeated measurements. The social worker and client first agree on the behavior, attitude, or belief to be measured and the way in which this variable will be measured. The behavior(s) selected is one that should reflect(s) the goals of the work. Peripheral concerns, (e.g., if the client arrives on time) are not typically the focus of a single-subject design evaluation. There is no maximum number of attributes that the social worker and client can select, but in general you will want to limit them to a few after considering a wider range (Bloom et al., 2009).

Measurement can be attained by frequency (the number of occurrences) or through a standardized scale that yields a numerical result. The social worker and the client establish a relatively consistent interval for taking measurements throughout the course of the evaluation. For example, if you want to monitor the number of new social contacts your client initiates over time, consider the accumulated frequency over a standard period of time (e.g., every two weeks).

In most cases, the phases of your evaluation begin with a **baseline** (the rate at which or number of times the behavior occurred before the client came to you), intervention, **maintenance** (the period of stabilizing client gains), and follow-up. The measures can then be charted to depict a visual pattern. If a baseline cannot be established because your client needs intervention right away, improvements can still be plotted as they occur during the intervention (for example, after one month, then two months of working together).

If a baseline can be established without withholding the intervention, the differences between no intervention and intervention can be depicted. This provides a bit more evidence that the improvement is a result of your work as it assumes that the baseline measure would continue without your intervention (this is, of course, a big assumption). If the intervention is interrupted (e.g., the client or you go on vacation and no one fills in for you) and the frequency of your client's social initiations is reduced, you can see if restarting your work results in renewed improvement. If it does, the connection between your work and your client's improvement is strengthened, and the possibility that some other event brought on the improvement is reduced. However, such interruptions may not be in the client's best interests, and the course of the work should not be disrupted simply to demonstrate its success. The single-subject design is highly flexible and generally easy to use. Exhibit 5.5 provides an example of an SSD graph.

Goal Attainment Scaling Used in a variety of settings, **goal attainment scaling** (GAS) represents a standardized framework that is customized by inserting individual goals. The first step of the multi-phase process is to identify two to five client goals and develop a scale for each of them based on the quality of the outcome. The following is a useful scale (Bloom et al., 2009):

0   Most unfavorable outcome thought likely.
1   Less than expected success.
2   Expected level of success.
3   More than expected success.
4   Most favorable outcome thought likely.

EXHIBIT 5.5

Simple Single-Subject Design

In this example of the single-subject design model, you can see that during the baseline period, before the work began the client initiated three, then two, then no new social contacts at intervals of two weeks. During the weeks of service, the numbers increased from two to seven, with a setback at week 8. After the work was over, the client initiated seven, then five, then six, and seven new contacts. This indicates improvement from the baseline period and extends over a four-week period following the work.

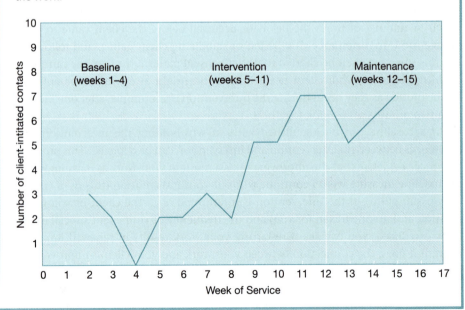

In this model, in a few words, the social worker and client describe the client's condition or status before the intervention on each goal, reflecting position 1 on the scale. The next step is to indicate the way in which deterioration may look at the lowest point (0). Finally, the social worker and client describe the best scenario (4), and they distinguish between levels 2 and 3. For example, if one of your client's goals is to attend parenting classes as part of a plan to regain custody of her children, you may agree on the statements depicted in Quick Guide 15. Consider that you have also agreed on two additional goals: attending GED classes and maintaining a clean apartment.

Following this process, you and your client can add further precision to measuring goal achievement by assigning a relative weight to each goal reflecting its importance in the individual case situation. As you can see in Quick Guide 15, the individual weight is 75 for attending parenting classes, 15 for keeping her apartment clean, and 10 for attending GED classes, for a total weight of 100. Your client's progress is tracked by placing a check mark in the cell that best describes the client's status at the point of entry into the social work relationship (acting as a baseline) and an X indicating the best description at the point of ending. You then calculate the weighted change score by subtracting the beginning score from the ending score and multiplying the difference by the weight.

The next step is to compute the percentage of possible change for each scaled goal. To calculate this percentage, you determine the highest possible mark on the scale and then divide it into the actual weighted change score. Finally, you calculate an overall score by summing all the possible scores for all the goals and dividing that number into the sum of the actual weighted change scores. Although this procedure may seem daunting and overly empirical, it becomes intuitive with practice.

Originally developed for use with individual clients, goal attainment scaling is well-suited to a range of social work interventions, including child and adult mental health, families, and organizations. GAS has also been shown to be an effective strategy for evaluating crisis interventions (Roberts, 2008). With crisis interventions and GAS both having an emphasis on short-term, structured and specific characteristics, the social worker engaged in crisis intervention work can easily and quickly use GAS to evaluate for both the client and her or himself the process and outcomes of their work together.

Other Forms of Evaluation   There are other quantitative measurement scales and other methods of attaining evaluative data that are not always quantitative. The latter includes such instruments as client satisfaction scales or client evaluations of the agency, the social worker, or both. Although these tools are often considered highly subjective and not particularly rigorous, they can frequently provide both the social worker and the agency with valuable information about the client's experience.

QUICK GUIDE 15   QUANTITATIVE AND EMPIRICAL PROCESSES

Client: _Clarissa_

Key: ✓ = Beginning level   × = Ending level

Attainment Grade	Task 1: Attend parenting classes	Task 2: Attend GED classes	Task 3: Keep apartment clean
0 Most unfavorable outcome likely	✓ No attendance at parenting classes	No attendance at GED classes	✓ No satisfactory ratings for cleanliness
1 Less than expected success	Attend less than 50% of the time	✓ Attend less than 40% of the time	Receive satisfactory ratings less than 60% of the time
2 Expected level of success	Attend 50–75% of the time	Attend 40–60% of the time	Receive satisfactory ratings 60–80% of the time
3 More than expected success	× Attend 76–95% of the time	Attend 61–85% of the time	Receive satisfactory ratings 81–95% of the time
4 Best anticipated success	Attend 96–100% of the time	× Attend 86–100% of the time	× Receive satisfactory ratings 96–100% of the time

Summary	Task 1	Task 2	Task 3	Total
Percent of goal	75	10	15	100
Change in score	3	3	4	
Total score	225	30	60	315
Possible total score	300	40	60	400
Percent of goal attained	75%	75%	100%	79%

Postmodern Views of Evaluation   In this world of managed care and increasing calls for evidence-based accountability, effective social workers must be knowledge-able about documenting, evaluating, and accounting for the usefulness of their efforts. To be able to choose the right evaluative method and be informed about your options, you should know the shortcomings and criticisms of each method.

Critics further charge that such models exclude the richer and nuanced contributions of aspects of client situations that are not easily quantified, as well as qualitative research, and overshadow the ethnographic forms of evaluation that question the assumptions of the everyday world.

These approaches have been based on expectation, researcher bias, and a political agenda that most social workers find unhelpful. Even when workers find themselves in a situation in which they must accommodate the system by demonstrating the value of their work through empirical evaluations, they cannot afford to de-emphasize the possibilities of vulnerabilities and opportunities for error in the evaluations themselves. This is a place for a form of bilingualism—that is, you will need to speak the language of contemporary demands, and at the same time keep alert to and keep up with the readings of their critiques.

There are social workers who find these empirical methods mechanical or lacking in substance, and want to examine their work on additional levels. Although the support for evidence-based practice in quantitative terms is strong in the profession, social workers are not restricted to these evaluative strategies. Social workers can also use the processes of reflection about their practice, as discussed below (see Lawler & Bilson, 2004).

Qualitative and Reflective Processes

Now we will look at other ways to evaluate social work practice. We will explore case studies, explorations of compatibility with theoretical perspectives, and quality of relationship. These methods have the power to expand your thinking about social work practice. These are not meant to compete with empirical processes, but to balance the experience of self-evaluation.

With any of these methods, many questions could be asked; we suggest some here. The most useful perspective is to focus your inquiry purposefully on a specific set of outcomes. If you want to take your inquiry further, consider engaging your supervisor as a second reader in a case study or your peers in a conversational group to explore particular issues. Such a focus is also a useful framework for ongoing staff meetings and professional development activities.

Case Studies Like single-system designs, **case studies** involve intensive analysis of one individual, group, or family, and depend on accurate, careful, and detailed record keeping. A case study typically begins with the engagement of the client and social worker and continues throughout the course of the work. Case studies do not generate empirical data from planned comparisons because they are an accounting of the client's situation while working with you. However, case studies, still in use in contemporary practice, have a long history within the social work profession and provided the basis for the evolution of the formal evaluation process (Bloom et al., 2009). While space prohibits the presentation of a case study here, as they can be lengthy, you are encouraged to review the interactive cases found on the book's companion website for the Sanchez and Stone families or Carla Washburn, (www.routledgesw.com/cases). As you review the cases and complete the interactive assignments, you can document your thoughts, reactions, and plans in the online notebook. These notes can provide the foundation for a case study. Upon completion of the full planned change effort, you will have ample information to finalize a case study in which you can evaluate progress and efforts.

A full case study, though certainly not a new method, can provide you with a rich history for postmodern reflection. For example, in reviewing the initial contact, you might wonder if your sensitivity matched the client's need for validation, consider other ways you could have articulated your purpose, or reflect on the course of your work if you had taken another tack. Or perhaps you thought you were clear about the agency requirements, but looking back on the records, you can see where there might have been some confusion in the language. How might the work have gone if those requirements were clear to the client? There are hundreds of ways you can reflect on the work that may be helpful, both in supervision and on your own. A record of your observations, what you thought about it, and what the client said—all of these can provide material for analysis later. Case studies are particularly useful in noting your own growth as you learn from the experiences that your clients have with you and.

Inherent in the process of compiling a case study is the ability of the social worker to communicate clearly, succinctly, and professionally in creating an agency document. Recall from Chapter 4 the discussion related to general uses and components of documentation. Such guidelines continue to be essential during the intervention, termination, and evaluation phases. During these phases of social work practice, a well-organized and articulated social work record is essential for both the client and the social worker. To help you in developing your knowledge and skills regarding professional social work writing, Quick Guide 16 provides guiding principles for clinically-focused practice writing. Quick Guide 17 presents a sample case summary. With the integration of standardized forms and electronic records, case summaries may be abbreviated or encompassed within a "fillable" on-line form, but the data gathered and compiled continues to include key items of information related to the client's situation (identified need for services, assessment and planning, actions taken, and termination and evaluation notes).

Explorations of Compatibility with Theoretical Perspectives   Another strategy to evaluate your work is to explore its consistency with the perspectives you want to guide your work. This approach is especially helpful when those perspectives present challenges to you and stretch your thinking.

Social work practice has been placed with four frameworks thus far: social justice, human rights, the strengths perspective, and critical social construction. These theoretical frameworks introduce multiple perspectives, and therefore can be translated into broad criteria for evaluating the work you want to do. For example, are you consistently recognizing your clients' strengths, or do you tend to be pulled into the pathology orientation that historically dominated much of social work

QUICK GUIDE 16   GUIDING PRINCIPLES FOR CLINICAL WRITING

- Keep the values and ethics of the social work profession at the forefront of your writing. Just as with your practice, your commitment to client self-determination, strengths, empowerment, and cultural competence must be ever present as you write about clients in any form of documentation, including case records, case studies, letters, emails, and court reports.
- In keeping with your commitment to ethical practice, maintain your writing focus on words that do not label, denigrate, depersonalize, or marginalize the clients about whom you are writing (e.g., do not use words like "abusive parent," "handicapped boy," or "welfare mother").
- Extending the strengths perspective into your documentation requires the social worker to use strengths-focused language in order to provide "voice" to the client's narrative story (e.g., "In sharing her experiences of surviving a sexual assault, Mary focused on the coping strategies that she used to regain her self of safety and security.").
- Maintain your person-centered practice standards to emphasize the client's right in the areas of confidentiality and self-determination. Operationally, respectful writing means that you include only information that is relevant to the current situation. If you believe that collateral sources can benefit from additional information, you can consider an alternative form of communication (e.g., case conference, telephone contact, etc.) with a release of information signed by the client.
- Ensure your knowledge of and compliance with agency and state requirements regarding information that can be communicated about a client, including health or disability status and compliance with Health Insurance Portability and Accountability Act (HIPAA).
- Always contemplate individuals and groups who may have access to the writing that you have produced, including clients and their families, co-workers, court systems, or even media outlets and ensure that your writing is fact-based or that opinion-based content is clearly labeled as such.

Source: Sormanti, 2012, pp. 129–131.

Resources to Support Practice-Related Writing:

American Psychological Association. (2010). *Publication Manual of the American Psychological Association (6th ed)*. Washington, D.C.: American Psychological Association.

Green, W. & Simon, B. L. (2012). *The Columbia Guide to Social Work Writing*. NY: Columbia University Press.

Kagle, J. D. & Kopels, S. (2008). *Social work records (3rd ed)*. Long Grove, IL: Waveland Press, Inc.

Purdue Online Writing Lab (OWN).

Szuchman, L.T. & Thomlison, B. (2011). *Writing with style. APA style for social work*. Belmont, CA: Cengage Learning.

practice? Are you alert to social justice concerns when you meet with clients who seem unable to make their way in this culture? Can you truly remain open to the multiple realities that critical social construction emphasizes? Do you rationalize human rights violations because they are so common in our culture?

These considerations can also apply to more specific practice perspectives, such as feminist or narrative lenses. If, for example, you adopt a feminist theory that stresses the importance of power analysis, is your work consistent with that type of

QUICK GUIDE 17   CREATING A CASE SUMMARY

Effective and accurate documentation is essential for social work practice. While formats and content are agency-specific, the following example provides an abbreviated presentation of a typical case summary that you might prepare. For this example, let us return to Jasmine Johnson, a client discussed in Chapters 3 and 4.

Opening summary

Jasmine is a 33-year-old African American woman and a single parent for a 14-year-old son, Devon. Jasmine requested services from the agency to help her improve her relationship with her son and to find better strategies for disciplining him. She admits to having hit him when she believes he is being disrespectful to her but denies any current or past abuse or neglect.

Assessment

Family history: Jasmine was married at age 18 and gave birth to Devon when she was 19 years old. She and Devon's father divorced two years ago when Devon, aged 12, was starting middle school. Jasmine was awarded sole custody of her son and monthly child support, but the payments are sporadic. To save money, Jasmine and Devon moved out of the family home and live in a 1-bedroom apartment across town where Devon sleeps on the fold-out couch in the living room. The move required Devon to attend a new school.

Employment and financial situation: Jasmine has worked in the housekeeping department of a large hospital for the past eleven years. The hospital provides comprehensive benefits (e.g., health insurance, retirement, and educational support) but her salary is low and she often struggles to pay all her bills each month.

Social support and resources: Jasmine and her family did not have any family living in the community where she moved with her then-husband for his job. Her ex-husband remains in the area, but has remarried and is expecting a new child. He seems to have little time for Devon but does see him occasionally, usually when Jasmine contacts him and asks him to see his son.

Jasmine's supports in the community now include a tight-knit group of co-workers, a neighbor, and members of her church. Her co-workers provide emotional support and often invite the Johnsons for holidays. The neighbor frequently "cooks too much food" and brings dishes over for Jasmine and Devon. Her church friends have provided spiritual support which Jasmine finds comforting.

Jasmine and Devon have received support through the church's Christmas adopt-a-family program, the youth programs, and the food and clothing pantry. Devon is eligible for the breakfast and lunch program at his school.

Prioritized concerns: Jasmine's primary concern is her relationship with her son. While she wishes that he did not speak disrespectfully to her and violate the rules she has established, she recognizes that he is a teenage boy whose life was turned upside down by the divorce, the move to a smaller apartment and a new school, and the lack of support from and contact with his father. She wants to improve her relationship with Devon and find alternative ways to establish and maintain acceptable boundaries for his behavior.

Strengths and areas of challenge: Jasmine possesses a number of strengths, including: 1) desire to be a good parent and not use physical discipline; 2) history of consistent employment that provides benefits; 3) while not extensive, an active support system; 4) willingness to seek help for relationship challenges and use community resources; and 5) resilience to overcome adversity.

Areas of challenge for Jasmine include: 1) history of physically striking Devon and lack of knowledge about other parenting possibilities or strategies; 2) low self-esteem—Jasmine assumes her son's disrespect for her is her fault for having divorced his father and taken him away from Devon, moved him to a new area and school, and never having enough money to provide for anything beyond the necessities; and 2) stress related to her income, including sporadic child support payments from her ex-husband.

Intervention plan: With monthly reviews, a three-month contract was jointly developed by Jasmine and social worker, including:

Goal	Client Tasks/Timeline	Social Worker Tasks/Timeline	Follow-Up	Termination
1. *Improve my relationship with my son*	*Begin attending weekly family therapy with my son as soon as an appointment can be made.*	*Refer Jasmine and her son to a family therapist and communicate regularly with the therapist regarding progress (with Jasmine's informed consent).*	*At 3 months, Jasmine and Devon are attending family therapy.*	*At 6 months, social worker recommends case be closed as goals have been met.*
2. *Learn better strategies for disciplining my son, particularly when I am angry*	*Participate in weekly parents of teens class and support group (next group begins the first of next month).*	*Refer Jasmine to parenting class and support group and communicate regularly with the group facilitator regarding progress (with Jasmine's informed consent).*	*At 3 months, Jasmine is a regular member of the class/support group.*	*At 6 months, social worker recommends case be closed as goals have been met.*
3. *Get Devon's father to pay child support more consistently*	*As soon as possible, contact Legal Services Child Support Enforcement office to inquire if they can help.*	*Provide Jasmine with Legal Services contact information and eligibility requirements.*	*At 3 months, Jasmine has made an appointment with Legal Services*	*At 6 months, social work recommends case be closed as goal is in process of being met.*

Intervention (including service options and purpose, goals, and plans of service)
Goal #1: Jasmine and Devon attended eight sessions with the family therapist. They continue to attend, although Devon sometimes refuses to go with his mother. He has attended six of the eight sessions and agrees to "keep trying it for a while." The therapist reports to the social worker that she believes the Johnsons are making small strides toward improving their relationship. As suspected, Devon is extremely angry with his mother and does not understand why things had to change. Jasmine refuses to disclose to Devon that his father's drinking and infidelities are the reason for the divorce. Early on, there was an episode of physical contact in which Jasmine slapped Devon for calling her a name.

QUICK GUIDE 17   CONTINUED

Goal #2: Jasmine has been regularly attending the Single Parents of Teens classes and support group. Not only has she found the information provided very helpful, she has found a new group of friends who share her experiences, empathize with her, and offer helpful suggestions.

Goal #3: Jasmine was slow in contacting Legal Services, but once she got an appointment and completed the application, she was seen by an attorney and social worker. A letter has been sent to her ex-husband regarding his delinquent payments. He has yet to respond. Should he not respond, she will have to return to court and request enforcement.

Closing summary
During the past six months that the social worker and Jasmine have been working together, she has initiated work on each of the three goals outlined in the contract. Positive changes have been slowly occurring in her relationship. There have been no episodes of physical contact in five months. While they still occur, the number of episodes of Devon violating curfew and speaking disrespectfully to his mother have decreased somewhat.

Shortly after the implementation of the intervention, the social worker learned that an allegation of child abuse has been made against Jasmine. Upon further investigation, the social worker learned that the call to the child abuse hotline had been made by Devon months earlier after a particularly emotional confrontation with Jasmine. The report was unsubstantiated.

The social worker is recommending closure of this case as substantial progress is being made on all goals. Jasmine and the social worker will discuss termination and evaluation. Should Jasmine feel she is in need of additional services, she will be invited to request her case be re-opened.

Sample Case/Progress/Interim notes (brief excerpts from the case record):

October 1: Jasmine Johnson came to the agency seeking help with her 14-year-old son. She believes he is "out of control" and she is worried that she will become abusive. She has physically struck him on several occasions when he has violated her rules and or spoken disrespectfully to her. She feels she is at her "wit's end." Intake assessment forms completed. Social worker asked Jasmine to bring Devon to the next meeting so his perspective could be included.

November 28: Jasmine and Devon have attended two family therapy sessions. Devon was a reluctant participant but did agree to attend with his mother. Jasmine reports that he said very little in the first meeting, but opened up more in the second session. Her fears are confirmed—he is very angry with her. Jasmine has attended two Single Parents of Teens classes and support group meetings. She reports that she is getting a lot out of the sessions, particularly in terms of the tips she is getting for ways to interact with Devon. She has not yet contacted the Legal Services office.

analysis? Do you return to a more traditional perspective regarding the issues that your client brings by emphasizing her reluctance to leave an abusive relationship or her lack of self-esteem? Can you keep an analytical structure of gender relations in the forefront rather than falling back into our society's tendency to blame women for occupying a power-down position? Which aspects of feminist theory do you carry out well, and which seem to call for continued growth?

If your framework is narrative, are you completely open to the complexity of the client's story? Do you wish you had been more transparent in your responses to it? Do you recognize your client as expert, or is there a temptation to believe you know better? Which aspects of the perspective are troubling to you? Which seem to come naturally? These considerations, of course, do not yield empirical data; rather, they can help you decide to what degree you can work within the constraints of particular perspectives, and they can help you identify the ways in which you want to grow intellectually and skillfully.

Explorations of Quality of Relationship   The nature of the relationship you develop with your client offers another opportunity for exploration. Is the relationship consistent with your purpose in the work? Was openness a characteristic of the connection early on? Was openness difficult for either you or your client to establish? What can you learn from the client's struggle? What can you learn from your own? What cultural dimensions influenced the development of the relationship, and what was successful in working through those issues (see Maramaldi, Berkman, & Barusch, 2005)?

This might be a situation in which to look at your own idiosyncrasies. For example, do you respond more easily to people most like you? Do you wonder if you encouraged the client's dependence on you? Do you struggle with keeping useful boundaries between you and your client? Are you comfortable with the amount of self-disclosure you engage in? Are there some kinds of clients that are hard for you to be positive about?

Additional questions that can arise out of this kind of self-examination lead to more generic issues: What is the ideal relationship between client and worker? How does it look? Is it different in one setting from another? Is it likely that all your client relationships will fall into this range of ideal? How does the ideal relationship interface with the client's goal attainment?

STRAIGHT TALK ABOUT EVALUATION AND RECLAIMING OUR KNOWLEDGE

As the discussion on intervention, termination, and evaluation comes to a conclusion, consider the distinctiveness of social work as a profession and consider its greater purposes, as social workers are informed by social justice, human rights, strengths, and the value of multiple realities. This is a profession that lives through a combination of practical orientation and a strong sense of caring. As you struggle to account for yourself and your professional knowledge and competencies, remember social work's legacy of context and care. These are always difficult to measure, and as long as you are pressured to assign numerical indicators, some of your most important contributions could be missed. You will recall from Chapter 1, we used the term "practice wisdom." Practice wisdom is the social worker's application of her or his "accumulation of information, assumptions, ideologies, and judgments" (Barker, 2003, p. 334). Identified through reflecting on one's practice experiences, practice wisdom enables the social worker to translate empirical and conceptual knowledge into practice behaviors that are most appropriately suited to the client situation (Chu & Tsui, 2008). Social workers' distinctive knowledge, based on a practice wisdom of person-in-environment, strength and struggle, and heart and grit is the "humble stuff of lived experience and values and flies in the face of most current views about how social workers know what they know" (Weick, 1999, p. 327).

As an empowering practice, then, with real people and real misery as well as real joys, social work will ask other questions about its effectiveness, including:

- Who benefits from this work? If the goals of social work relate to helping clients find empowerment, how are they realized? If a client demonstrates improved capacity to manage a household budget, for example, is there a link to her experience of poverty? Is it identified and challenged? Will she quietly and skillfully manage on close to nothing (and is this progress?), or will the benefit go beyond, to others like her, and to challenge the structure that supports poverty?

- Whose values are most salient? Social work's values are at the heart of the work. Do they dominate the client relationship? How do social workers negotiate differing values with people who do not share theirs? This is one of social work's most challenging dilemmas.

- What changes have occurred in the power structure? Have social workers helped to raise consciousness about oppression and the internalization of it? Have clients joined with others to respond to oppressive imbalances in the structural arrangements of our culture? As work with clients ends, is some move toward empowerment visibly in progress? (Lee, 2001).

These questions lead us back to the beginning of our exploration of social work practice. As a social worker, you will likely find satisfaction in connecting with clients. You will struggle to meet the demands of their preferred realities and document them for those who require an accounting. You will experience frustrations and successes, answer many questions, and come up with many more. The world will change dramatically and will challenge you with its excitement and danger as well as its incredible potential. You will figure out how to respond to it in ways that are consistent with your values, your social work ethics, your sense of social justice and human rights, and your respect for different views and experience.

Your own story as a social work practitioner will be embedded in the hundreds of stories of your individual clients, groups, and families, the organizations and communities you serve, and in the story of global change. Your choices are legion and your opportunities enormous. In the end, these will return to the story of the profession. You as a member of the next generation of citizen/social workers will author the next chapter.

CONCLUSION

In this chapter we have looked into several dimensions of the intervention, termination, and evaluation actions that social workers take. The practice setting, theoretical perspectives, and perception of roles influence the ways in which you work to support clients' strengths and to support their environments. The overall fit of your activities with and your beliefs about people creates a sound backdrop for expanding your work into other system levels. The next chapters will integrate and extend these same processes to groups, families, organizations, and communities. This will serve both to consolidate the principles and skills in this first part of the book and to take them beyond, across system levels.

In the paradoxical way that some things constantly change while they remain the same, so endings and evaluations continue and evolve. All the same, we will all experience new ways to do things in the future of social work practice. Some of you will work in much more complex settings that integrate public and private sectors through partnerships and alliances. Some of you will choose more radical forms of practice in which you will challenge the historical and professional legacies you see as unjust or obsolete. Others will continue to practice with only incremental changes from the models under which you trained. All of these dimensions of practice will have implications for beginning and ending the social work relationship, for executing and evaluating the work, and for grappling with the obstacles that get in the way of the vision. There are no magic formulas for anticipating all of the implications of change for social work. Your flexibility, integrity, and penchant for the experiential context of your work, as well as your caring for people who struggle, will be your own best guides for your future practice.

MAIN POINTS

- The most pressing client issue from the client's perspective is the starting point for the intervention. This issue is defined by the context of the client's situation and by the actions agreed upon in the assessment and planning phase.

- To support clients' strengths, social workers act in context to normalize and capitalize on those strengths. Social workers engage in responding to feelings, determining their meaning, and supporting diversity.

- To support clients' environments, social workers are accountable to the client system; they should follow the demands of the client task; maximize the potential supports in the client's environments; identify, reinforce, and/or increase the client's repertoire of strategic behaviors; and they apply these principles to themselves.

- Examining traditional social work roles and their assumptions within the context of contemporary practice provides another perspective the context of the roles of case manager, counselor, broker, mediator, educator, client advocate, and collaborator.

- Exploring a case situation through the lens of empowerment perspectives demonstrates the work in context and how it fits with the perspectives emphasized in this book.

- The planned ending process with clients consists of several components that can benefit and empower clients by consolidating the gains of the work and the relationship. Social worker and client must have clarity regarding timing, original agreement, successes and failures, and responses to termination.

The same basic process for ending work, when flexibly used with different emphases, can be applied to families, groups, organizations, and communities with additional and specific components to consider with groups (to be discussed in Chapters 7, 9, 11, and 13).

- Unplanned endings pose a special challenge to both social workers and clients. Social workers can attempt to reconnect and end the work, but may have to acknowledge the limits of their influence and honor client self-determination.

- Quantitative and empirical evaluation processes are increasingly required in social work practice. Two options for evaluation are the single-subject design and the goal attainment scaling.

- Qualitative and reflective practices also constitute an important method for evaluation and professional growth as they relate to philosophical commitments, theoretical perspectives, and relationship building.

EXERCISES

a. Case Exercises

1. Go to www.routledgesw.com/cases, review the video vignette with Emilia Sanchez and respond to the following questions:
   a. What strengths does she possess?
   b. What thoughts and/or feelings resulted from watching the video that, if verbalized, would not reflect a strengths-based approach?
   c. As the social worker, what are your next steps with Emilia?
   d. Either with a group in or outside of class, develop a strengths-based intervention plan for Emilia.

2. Go to www.routledgesw.com/cases and click on Carla Washburn. Begin by reviewing the engagement and assessment phases. After your review of the first two phases, click on Phase 3: Intervention. Complete each of the tasks identified in the five steps (introduction, goals and needs, client tasks, social worker tasks, timeline, and coalitions).

3. Go to www.routledgesw.com/cases and click on Brickville (with your focus on Virginia Stone and her family). Begin by reviewing the engagement and assessment phases. After your review of the first two phases, click on Phase 3: Intervention. Complete each of the tasks identified in the five steps (introduction, goals and needs, client tasks, social worker tasks, timeline, and coalitions).

4. Go to www.routledgesw.com/cases and click on Brickville. With your focus on Virginia Stone and her family, review the four components of the social work intervention, including engagement, assessment and planning, intervention, and termination and evaluation. Upon completing the tasks identified in each section, develop a case summary using the guide included in Quick Guide 15.

5. Go to www.routledgesw.com/cases and click on RAINN. After reviewing the information, click on Engage, review the two client scenarios (Sarah and Alan), and respond to the three questions that are listed below the scenarios. In addition, develop a list of skills that you would need to develop in order to competently work with a survivor of sexual assault.

b. Other exercises

6. The admissions unit of a psychiatric care facility issues a daily report to all staff on a single sheet of paper that summarizes all the patient admissions, discharges, visits, legal proceedings, and other activities for the preceding 24-hour period. This summary is meant to convey useful information for all staff and it is viewed as helpful to social workers who needed to monitor client status. One of the categories on the form is entitled "body count" and is a tally of the number of patient/residents actually in the hospital at midnight. A social worker from a local community mental health agency was visiting her client who was in the hospital and she heard reference to this sheet. She was horrified at the language of "body count," to which you were by then accustomed.

a. What do you think is the issue here? Why does it matter? Be as specific as you can.

b. In what way would you address it? Would such an activity be consistent with your view of a social worker's role?

c. Develop a plan that includes at least three steps you might take.
   Compare with other students and be prepared to discuss in class or write brief responses to each question to submit.

7. Tammy is a 35-year-old Caucasian female seeking treatment after her release from a 21-day residential drug/alcohol treatment facility. She is referred to your agency by the public child welfare agency. As a result of continued substance

abuse and an arrest and conviction for driving under the influence with her eight-year-old son, Jared, in the car, physical custody of Jared was granted to Tammy's mother.

Tammy has a 20-year history of drug and alcohol abuse and she has been diagnosed with Bipolar Disorder. She was recently prescribed medication by the staff psychiatrist at the residential treatment facility. It is a new medication and is not covered by her insurance. She has been non-compliant with medication in the past due to the side effects and her drug/alcohol use. She has had brief periods of sobriety but often relapses after a few weeks. This is the longest she has been sober since the birth of her son eight years earlier.

Tammy has never been married and has a difficult relationship with her family of origin. Her mother placed her in foster care at the age of eight due to Tammy's behavior. Tammy reports that her mother was physically and emotionally abusive to her and often would leave her with various relatives when her mother found a new boyfriend. Tammy's father is not involved. Tammy has few friends and little contact with her mother. She is angered that her mother has custody of her son. Tammy has been involved with her son's father sporadically for the past nine years. Currently, she names him as a source of support.

Tammy is not currently employed but receives public assistance in the form of Medicaid, disability assistance, and food stamps. She lives with her boyfriend but would like to have her own apartment. She has her high school diploma and is interested in continuing her education.

Partner with other students and complete the following exercises:
a. Using narrative interventions, reconstruct this case from a strengths-based perspective.
b. What roles would you play in helping Tammy?
c. Construct a strengths-based plan of intervention utilizing solution-focused interventions.
d. Share your findings with the class and compare plans of interventions.

8. Reflect on a time in your life when you contemplated making a change. What did you do? Was it successful? What factors led to the success? If not successful, what was missing?

9. Identify an area or behavior in your life that you would like to change (e.g., texting while driving, exercising, budgeting money, or time management). For one week, chart your journey in a journal, and note those factors that are helping you to maintain the change and those that are a negative influence on your efforts to maintain the change. At the end of the week, reflect on your progress or lack thereof. Consider your feelings before the change, during the change, and the results.

10. Write your own life story from a strengths-based perspective.

CHAPTER 6

Social Work Practice with Families: Engagement, Assessment, and Planning

The social work profession and the family have traveled a long distance together, sometimes in close companionship and sometimes on divergent paths, only to meet once again on the same road. Our profession began in the company of the family and has returned to it once again.

Ann Hartman and Joan Laird, 1983

Key Questions for Chapter 6

(1) What competencies do I need to engage with and assess families? (EPAS 2.1.10(a) & (b))
(2) What are the social work practice behaviors that enable me to effectively engage and assess families? (EPAS 2.1.10(a) & (b))
(3) How can I use evidence to practice research-informed practice and practice-informed research to guide the engagement and assessment with families? (EPAS 1.2.6)
(4) How do the perspectives and experiences from my present family and/or family of origin impact my engagement with and assessment of client families?

FAMILY IS THE EARLIEST, MOST BASIC, AND, SOME SAY, most challenging small group one can experience during a lifetime. It is also probably the most powerful in shaping who we become. For some, family means home, safety, and acceptance. For others, family means violence and danger. Some people may feel important and cherished with family or never quite good enough or even useless. Others may feel swallowed up in their family's dysfunction, or may long for, and bask in, the wholeness of unconditional support. Most of us experience a mix of feelings in between these. Family is a complicated enterprise, and many of us harbor some of its tensions that make us both joyful and troubled. Virtually all members of society have experienced some kind of family, and most have ideas (or dreams) of the qualities that an ideal family could or should possess.

This chapter explores the concept of family—definition, meaning, and place within the contemporary social context—and the process of engagement and assessment with families. We will also look at theoretical perspectives for working with traditional and contemporary family structures as well as dynamics, skills, and tools for working with the range of families. This chapter will also guide you through challenges and strategies for understanding the impact that family issues can have on your clients and you.

FAMILIAR PERSPECTIVES AND SOME ALTERNATIVES

The enormous and rapid changes in social rules in most Western countries have led many to contend that the "traditional" family has been lost. A traditional vision of the ideal U.S. family portrays a nuclear group consisting of two heterosexual adults and two or perhaps three children. The father supports the family economically, and the mother supports it emotionally. There are clear roles, rules, and jobs that each member undertakes. If the mother also works outside the home, she is still free to participate in the kindergarten car pool, do the laundry, entertain friends, and "be there" for her husband and children. A more contemporary version of the father makes him increasingly sensitive to the feelings and needs of his wife and children, but his work still takes priority. In contrast, the National Association of Social Workers (NASW) (2007a, para. 3) provides this definition of the contemporary family: "two or more people who assume obligations and responsibilities generally conducive to family life." This inclusive perspective on the family embraces parents who are divorced, separated, unmarried, grandparents, gay, lesbian, bisexual, transgender, or questioning, adoptive, and fostering, along with couples who have no children, partnered couples, and families caring for older adult members. Social workers must use practice approaches that recognize the diversity of family constellations (Hull & Mather, 2006). For example, to avoid assumptions and confusion, the social worker should ask the client to describe and define her or his family unit (Wood & Tully, 2006) rather than make assumptions, based on household composition. Given the changing nature of the family and the fluidity of membership in some families, it is important to ask each member of the family, "Who do you consider to be part of your family?" A follow-up question may then be, "Of these people, who is biologically and/ or legally related to you?" For instance, a client's "aunt" may not be a legal or biological family member but is considered by the client to be a part of her or his family.

Those with nostalgic older visions of family are appalled at what they see today as a lack of morality in many young families. There is distress about young adults who live together with no permanent commitment. Single women often choose to become parents and do not suffer the social stigma so prevalent only a few generations earlier. Parents who are gay, lesbian, bisexual, transgender and questioning (LGBTQ), who earlier had to conceal their sexual identities, are joyfully parenting children, and many are serving as foster and adoptive parents in conjunction with state child protection agencies. In the past, LGBTQ individuals were not even given the option to foster or adopt children; now they are recruited by these organizations. Although these developments in our U.S. cultural norms are lamented by some, fear of change may overshadow the research about new, more inclusive family and parenting arrangements. We will take a more in-depth look into this issue later in the chapter.

Nonetheless, there are real issues in the surrounding context of the contemporary family that create concerns for social workers. The U.S. divorce rate of 52 percent for men and 44 percent for women (U.S. Census, 2010b) is closely related to the ever-growing number of children who live in a single parent-headed household with incomes below the poverty level. The percentage of children who live in poverty with a single mother has reached 32 percent, while single father-headed households experience poverty rates of only 16 percent (U.S. Census, 2011a). Some believe that commitment to the stability and endurance seems to have vanished. While the number of unmarried teen parents is slowly declining (31.2/1000 teen females in 2010, down from 34.2/1,000 teen females in 2008) (Hamilton, Martin, & Ventura, 2012), the rate of births to teen parents of color continues to be high (36–47 births/1,000 teen mothers) (Hamilton et al., 2012). The associated legacies of perpetuated poverty, increased family violence, and health and mental health issues, and a sense that two generations—the child and the child's child—have sacrificed much of their potential, provide little hope for the future. Clearly, the change in predominant family compositions has required changes in service delivery, and impacts society. The widening of the income equality gap and economic pressures resulting from the recent economic recession has created additional challenges for families that impact their well-being. The result of such change has been serious societal issues with which society and social work must grapple.

There are other ways to look at family. In keeping with this book's focus on multiple realities, we will explore the experiences of an array of family constellations to expose illusions about the family and develop a more balanced perspective. This chapter will discuss the experiences of both traditional and nontraditional families. Consider Exhibit 6.1, which describes the experience of family for countless people who have been marginalized, that is, who have lived in the margins of our culture and others.

HISTORICAL ANTECEDENTS FOR FAMILY SOCIAL WORK

The social work profession has a long history of working with families, shaped by the context of the times. In community mental health centers and youth agencies, hospitals and schools, and welfare and child protection efforts, social workers work to strengthen families. Collins, Jordan, and Coleman (2013) encourage social work students interested in working with families to explore this area of practice using the following list of questions:

- What is the purpose of family social work?

- How does family social work differ from family therapy?

- How can I work effectively with families who are different from my own family?

- What is my role as a family social worker?

- How will I know what factors contribute to the family's difficulties?

- How should I work with an entire family and with all members in the same room at the same time?

- How will I know what questions to ask family members? What do I say to the family?

- How do I engage all the members of the family, particularly if they seem resistant, feeling blamed, uncommunicative, or overpowered by another member?

- What should I do if family members get angry at me or another member of the family?

- What do I need to know to help families change? What knowledge will help the families begin to change?

- What skills will I need when there are young children in the interview? Older children?

- What can I do to protect individual family members when the rest of the family is attacking or blaming?

- How do I help families that are paralyzed by a crisis to rise about it and solve their problems?

- What do I need to know about family social work when working with families of different ethnic, racial, or sexual orientation backgrounds?

- What skills are needed for prioritizing the family's problems and then for each of the phases of work with families (pp. 1–2).

Why is there such a concern for the maintenance of the family? What does our culture expect the family to do, and how do we think the family should work? Although there are many possible responses to these questions, two particular perspectives are examined that seem to have special relevance for social workers today—the family as a functioning unit and the family as a system.

EXHIBIT 6.1

*Family: Views
from the
Margins*

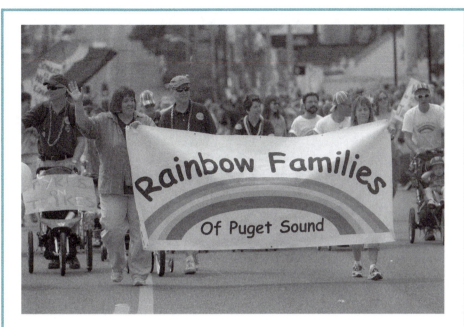

©: Harry Hu, courtesy of Shutterstock® images

- What we may consider now to be the ideal family has never actually flourished in any culture for any length of time: Children have historically been considered commodities that enhanced the economic status of their fathers, who owned them, and their value was often equated to the amount of work they did. Childhood as a time to be nourished and cherished is a relatively new and narrowly prescribed phenomenon of Western culture and some nations in the East. The United Nations instrument "The Rights of the Child" reflects the need for considering children as genuine people and not possessions. In contrast, in parts of the United States, children are prostitutes, drug dealers, and hired thieves. In much of the world they are all these and also soldiers.
- Ideal conceptions of the family have historically served to restrict and diminish the role of women as categorical caretakers. Many women throughout history have been required to abandon their dreams and have also been seen as property to be exploited. Men, too, are assumed to fit into tightly proscribed roles that may not be compatible with their identities or goals.
- In many families of the past, infant and childhood mortality was high and parents may have died by their early 40s. Such circumstances produced a crisis for remaining family members, resulting in placements with distant relatives, community members, or in orphanage care. The idealistic notion of earlier times places blinders on the realities of disease, early death, and other forms of danger that surely shaped the overall experience of family.

EXHIBIT 6.1

Continued

- It is still the family, even in contemporary U.S. society, that is the primary force for socialization and nurturing of children and support of the community. As an example, the families of children experiencing mental illnesses still provide most of the care and nurturing of their adult children, in spite of federal and state programs designed to assist them.
- The definition of family as rigidly restricted to biological and legal ties and heterosexual partners or adoption has always marginalized and scapegoated significant numbers of people who have meaningful and productive relationships and who make significant contributions to the community, the socialization of children, and the general economic and social order.
- More contemporary notions of family have liberated both men and women to develop and carry out the roles of child caretaking, economic provision, management, personal development, and health care in a way that does not deny their individual aspirations and talents; the same principles hold for gay, lesbian, bisexual, and transgender families with biological or adopted children.
- Contemporary families have greater biological control over the number and timing of pregnancies and can plan family composition in a way that is consistent with their financial capacities and other internal demands (for example, one partner is in school or another is committed to the care of a parent). Women are now more able to exercise control over their reproduction, and make decisions about their future.

Family as a Functioning Unit

A concrete way to think about the importance of the family is to explore the societal expectations of the family. The following functions are among those that are typically viewed as critical to the contemporary maintenance of families:

- Provide the material and economic necessities for sustenance and growth.
- Offer members emotional security, respect, safety, and a place for appropriate sexual expression.
- Provide a haven for privacy and rest.
- Assist, protect, and advocate for members who are vulnerable or who have special needs.
- Provide support for members' meaningful connection and contribution to community life.
- Facilitate the transmission of cultural heritage.
- Provide a socially and legally recognized identity.
- Create an environment in which children can be nurtured and socialized.

The responsibilities reflected here emphasize not only the functional roles of individual family members and their needs and identities but also the connection to their communities and the overall societal environment. This compilation is not prescriptive; that is, it does not specify *how* children should be nurtured but allows for individual and cultural interpretation. Rather than seeking individual or family dysfunction, the exploration of these tasks in various areas of family life tends to highlight strengths as well as areas for improvement. In that respect, this set of functions serves as a useful guide for assessing the degree to which societal expectations are met in any particular family.

While families serve a critical function in society, we must recognize they have needs which may not be met, thus requiring the involvement of a helping professional. Needs may be categorized in many different ways, but one strategy is to consider the family as a system with a practical purpose. Building on the work of Kilpatrick and Cleveland (1993), Kilpatrick (2009) presents a strategy for classifying family needs by levels, including:

Level 1—basic survival. Needs are in the areas of food, shelter, medical care.
Level 2—structure and organization. Needs center on setting limits and safety concerns.
Level 3—space. Needs relate to issues of privacy, access, and boundaries.
Level 4—richness and quality. Needs exist in areas of inner conflict, intimacy, and self-actualization (p. 4).

Taking into consideration the type and level of need, the social work assessment and intervention process can be focused within a conceptual framework that encompasses both context of those persons with whom you work (i.e., family/community, couple/dyad, and individual) and orientation of the intervention you choose with the family. Will the intervention have a focus on behavioral/interactional change, experiential aspects of clients' thoughts and feelings, or historical, emphasizing family-of-origin issues (Kilpatrick, 2009, p. 10)? Incorporating these complexities of the family system into your social work intervention can help to gain insight into the way in which the family functions, their needs, and the most effective strategies for helping them to reach their desired goals.

Family as a System

Because social work focuses on interactions among people and between people and the environment, the profession enthusiastically adopted systems theory in the 1970s. **Systems theory** posits that a system involves a series of components that are highly organized and dependent upon each other in an orderly way. In the profession, this conceptualization is applied to the multiple levels of practice (individual, group, family, organization, and community). The systems perspective remains influential in social work theory in spite of a growing number of critiques that suggest it is too rigid and tends to place the social worker outside of the work. Nevertheless, systems theory holds continuing authority in many views of structural arrangements, particularly the family. Three elements of systems theory are particularly important:

- Change in one component

- Subsystems and boundaries

- Family norms

Change in One Component   Possibly the most powerful idea in the systems theory for social workers is that change in one part of the system will affect all other components. Social workers, therefore, seek to learn about aspects of a client's environment, including family functioning. For example, knowing that a child's father has just been sent to prison is useful information when exploring reasons for that child having angry outbursts or sullen withdrawals in school. In another example, a mother being physically abused by her intimate partner is likely to have repercussions on her daughter's fragile health. Social workers often find such connections intuitive and useful. Still, you will want to guard against seeing such a situation as automatically producing one type of response. In systems theory, one set of actions can predict multiple sets of reactions. For example, the child whose father goes to prison may respond by being more attentive to her or his mother or by working harder in school. As another example, consider the family in which the primary wage earner becomes unemployed. This event can create a ripple effect within the family. While one of the adolescent children may seek employment to help the family, another may demonstrate anger that her or his perceived needs will not be met.

Subsystems and Boundaries   Another dimension of systems theory that is relevant to social work is the concept of subsystems. **Subsystems**, or components of a system that also have interacting parts, provide a mechanism for organizing relationships and planning ways to engage with them. In systems theory, the individual is a subsystem of the family, the family is a subsystem of the community and the community is a subsystem of the culture. A family may also be a subsystem of more than one larger system, or of differing systems, so you must be thoughtful about making unqualified judgments regarding the place that an individual or group occupies within the system. For example, in a blended family, there may be members who consider themselves part of the family and community from the previous marriage. Social workers have the opportunity to support and facilitate such healthy transition relationships for client systems. Exhibit 6.2 depicts the components of a family system.

In thinking about the concept of family, social workers often distinguish between the subsystem of the parents and the subsystem of the children. The relationship between these subsystems is reflected in the types of **boundaries**, or limits that separate the systems that the family constructs. If the children are included in all decisions the family makes, the boundaries are **permeable**, meaning that information and interchange goes easily across them. However, permeable boundaries can be taken to the extreme of **diffuse boundaries**, which means that boundaries are too loose and that parents should assume more decision-making authorities to maintain appropriate boundaries between them and their children.

Appropriate boundaries between the subsystems of parents and children may vary considerably depending on culture, the times, background, and/or the boundaries within which the parents themselves were reared. While you may consider a boundary to be inappropriate if a mother who uses her pre-teen daughter as her primary confidante, particularly related to her relationship with the child's father, other families may view this as acceptable. Can you cite examples in your own family in which these boundaries are similar or different from those of your friends or other extended family members? Further, consider the way in which your experience with your own family might relate to families with whom you will be working.

Family Norms   Most families establish **family norms**, or rules of conduct, that are related to boundaries and subsystems. These can be similar to the norms described in Chapter 7, in application to groups, but have an additional complication in

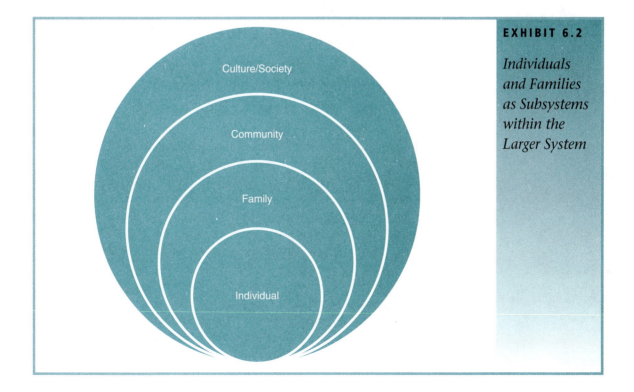

EXHIBIT 6.2

Individuals and Families as Subsystems within the Larger System

Culture/Society

Community

Family

Individual

families in that they are often held as sacrosanct and not negotiable. Family norms may also never be articulated, despite the fact that all members of the family are clear about them. This implicit aspect of norms can make them difficult to address and challenge, so much so that family members may not even realize that there are rules; nevertheless, everyone understands the allowable behavior of family members. For example, all the members of a family may understand that no one will enter into a dispute with Dad at the dinner table, or that everyone will attend religious services, or that all of the children will go out of state to college. Some of these rules apply to everyday boundaries and may simply make some mundane things a lot easier (for example, if a door is closed, one is not to enter without knocking). Other such rules may signal secrets that are taboo or too difficult to talk about or that perpetuate unjust or oppressive situations, such as all the female children know not to find themselves in the same room alone with Grandpa, or no one asks Mom how she got a bruise on her face.

In applying a systems analysis to family norms, a social worker may recognize that interrupting the family's patterns of behavior or relationship by breaking a rule is, in fact, feasible and desirable. For example, a social worker may point out that one of the children spoke out one day about the bruises on Mom's face. This disclosure led to the mother talking about the violence which began the process of empowerment and decreased family violence. Yet, this process might also result in violence directed at the child who raised the issue in the first place; therefore, the social worker would not likely encourage a child to take such an action without support and protection. Family norms in such cases are often very powerful and need to be carefully evaluated before any family member is put at risk.

Implications of Family Systems Theory for Generalist Practice

Along with the notion of function, two specific dimensions reflected in family systems theories have influenced generalist social work practice with families. The first is family structure, and the second is intergenerational patterns. In many respects these represent a classic approach to Western ideology of the family and have influenced the responses of many social service policies and agencies. You may discover that these ideas have shaped your thinking also. As a basis for considering family structure and intergenerational patterns, consider the following practice principles for social work assessment and intervention with families that have evolved from a systemic perspective (Logan, Rasheed, & Rasheed, 2008, pp. 184–185):

1. Family is considered within a "context" that is comprised of multiple systems.
2. Rooted in the basic systemic foundation, the family "is more than the sum of its individual parts," all of which serves to function as a unique system.
3. A change within one part of the family system creates change in the entire system.

4. Viewing the family as a unique system provides the practitioner with the opportunity to focus on the issues that present challenges to the entire system.
5. A systemic-focused assessment and intervention provides a view of the family as a complex system.
6. Behaviors are viewed as a product of the multi-faceted system and not the result of one individual or action.
7. A systems perspective that promotes a strengths-based perspective frames the family assessment within the context of the environment in which they live.
8. Family members, particularly those in minority groups, are viewed within the context of their family system as well as the larger societal system.
9. Family function may be impacted by the legal, social, and economic biases and discrimination that affect families with members who are considered to be in cultural, racial, ethnic, religious, or sexual minority groups.

Family Structure   The relationship among the generations of a family, especially between the subsystems of children and parents, is the **family structure**. One of the early scholars in defining models for family interventions, Minuchin (1974) posits that the boundaries between children and parents should be clear and that parents should be in charge of major decisions as they also carry out appropriate caretaking functions. The difficulties that families experience are usually thought to be a result of blurring the boundaries between these two subsystems.

Some family boundaries may be so diffuse that the result is **enmeshment**, which suggests that family members are too close, have few distinctions in role or authority, and enjoy little autonomy or independence (Nichols, 2011). As an example, consider the family in which the adult children share virtually every life experience with their mother, seldom make decisions without consulting one another and her, and are emotionally dependent on one another. In an enmeshed family, a routine life experience, such as a job change or change in dating relationship by one member of the family creates strong reactions by others in the family.

On the other hand, if the boundaries between family members are too rigid, the family is thought to be **disengaged**. In this situation, the subsystems are so separated that there is little sense of family identity, and parents are apt to relinquish much of their caretaking role as they pursue their own interests and the children pursue their own. In a disengaged family, a significant job change or a divorce in the family may be barely acknowledged by other family members.

When you read about or work with young people who seem to have little or no effective connections with their families, and have experienced school or legal problems, you may wonder about the boundaries (or lack of) established by the parent(s) and the parents' perception of their own roles. In some respects, you are using this theory when you cite the misplacement or laxness of parental boundaries when children go astray. The work in such cases is to restore clear and appropriate boundaries between children and parents that support parent caretaking and authority. This particular position is reflected in court decisions regarding the delinquency of adolescents and a judge's requirement, for example, that parents receive training on managing their children or that they supervise a child's curfew restriction.

Intergenerational Patterns The identification of **intergenerational patterns** has likewise played an important role in social work practice with families. The term refers to the assertion that families transmit their patterns of relationship from one generation to the next (Papero, 2009). For example, if your adult client, Jane, is so closely connected to her mother that she experiences great anxiety when they are separated and therefore cannot work outside the home, Jane is likely to establish that kind of relationship with her daughter as well. The anxiety generated by any effort to be separate from her mother is contagious and makes it difficult for Jane to think clearly because her feelings are so intense. In this way she becomes dysfunctional, tends to be dominated by feelings, and passes that pattern on to the next generation. This emphasis on feeling in a family sometimes results in constant emotional uproar, frequent violence, major feuds, difficulties with the law, and generalized struggle in accomplishing the basic family functions considered earlier.

Although the whole of intergenerational theory is complex, it has influenced attitudes about families. The use of the phrases "welfare families" and "incestuous families" reflects the use of intergenerational theory. These terms reflect the assumption that problematic, emotional patterns and the resulting behavioral consequences (such as violence, inability to focus on work, and substance abuse) appear to be transmitted from generation to generation. Social work then involves breaking such thinking and cycles, bolstering the strengths, and supporting an appropriate level of autonomy in individual family members. These principles are reflected in many social and educational programs that are designed to break patterns of economic dependence, addictions, lack of educational focus, and build up healthy bonds between family members.

Professionals incorporate a systems orientation when considering crime, addiction, or school violence among youth, and assume the causes to be related to the families involved, regardless of evidence. Sometimes children behave illegally or violently even when they have caring, hardworking parents who are doing the best they can. Therefore, the applicability of family systems theory, like any other theory, can be questioned, and does not fit in all situations. The desire to find a rational cause for human behavior sometimes sets in motion the use of methods that have been used before. People are also often eager to blame a child's problems on the family's behavioral shortcomings or background while not addressing the broader (also systems) aspects of poverty, disenfranchisement, challenging school situation (e.g., bullying), or racism.

Systems perspectives can be helpful and support logical approaches in assessment, especially of complex arrangements, like the family. These perspectives have a general cultural appeal, and they do not constitute a magic, one-stop answer for conceptualizing about, assessing, or working with families. While systems views have strong currency in today's analyses of social issues, other ways of thinking about them may be relevant. You must be careful not to blame or scapegoat any particular person simply because it seems logical or fits with a possible systemic interpretation of a family situation. As you continue with your social work education and develop your approach to practicing social work with families, you will be exposed to a wide array of philosophical and theoretical frameworks. Your professional obligation is to consider all the available options and determine the approach(es) that is(are) most appropriate for the families you serve.

THE CONTEMPORARY CONTEXT FOR FAMILY SOCIAL WORK

The real-world, real live family of today is only rarely the idealized outdated television version with a stay-at-home mother, fully employed father, and two bright, talented (and usually white) children. Social workers often work with families who were once seen as "other"; that is, they did not fit dominant fantasies of family life. The following sections briefly identify several types of family constellations that have not traditionally been considered mainstream but are a vital part of the contemporary family landscape—grandparents rearing grandchildren; gay, lesbian, bisexual, transgender, and questioning parents; single-parent families; families of multiple racial and ethnic heritage; families that include persons with disabilities; blended families, international families, and families with multiple problems—and suggest some specific implications for working with them.

Beyond these types of families, other current configurations appearing in the literature (and in practice) include adoptive families, foster families, step families, dual wage earning families, multi-generational families, LGBTQ families, and, of course, many combinations of these types. In the coming generations, the social work profession will need to expect and remain open to ever-evolving forms of the family. This kind of sociocultural change provides social workers with the opportunity to contribute to a sustained and meaningful impact that will benefit clients across all levels of society. Exhibit 6.3 provides additional insights into this growing and changing population with whom social workers are working.

Grandparents Rearing Grandchildren

In many cultures of the past, grandparents had a significant and ongoing role in the nurturing and socialization of children. Some cultural groups today, typically those who are less mobile or those of strong ethnic identification(s), have maintained those patterns, as consistent with their cultural and instrumental needs. The extended family is an age-old pattern of organization that has been obscured by the mainstream societal changes of the industrialized and "informationalized" 20th and 21st centuries. These changes reflect a break with the traditional cultural patterns of their parents and their parents' parents.

EXHIBIT 6.3

LGBTQ Couples as Families

According to the 2010 Census, there were 131,729 same-sex married couple households and 514,735 same-sex unmarried partner households in the United States (U. S. Census Bureau, 2011a). This information does not include LGBTQ couples who do not live in the same households. As of 2013, nine states and Washington, D.C. have passed legislation allowing same-sex marriage, but 31 states continue to constitutionally prohibit same-sex marriage.

Social workers need to stay abreast of public policies that impact LGBTQ couples:

The Defense of Marriage Act (DOMA) "amends the Federal judicial code to provide that no state, territory, or possession of the United States or Indian tribe shall be required to give effect to any marriage between persons of the same sex under the laws of any other such jurisdiction or to any right or claim arising from such relationship" (Library of Congress, 1996). DOMA establishes that the Federal definition of marriage includes legal unions only between one man and one woman. It also defines "spouse" as only a person of the opposite sex (Library of Congress, 1996).

As of the beginning of 2013, there are 37 state laws and/or constitutional provisions, which limited marriages to relationships between a man and a woman. There are nine states, along with the District of Columbia, which issued marriage licenses to same-sex couples. In California, a federal appeals court found that the state constitution's restriction on same-sex marriage was invalid, but has postponed enforcement pending appeal.

Five states allow civil unions, providing state-level spousal rights to same-sex couples. Same-sex marriage has recently replaced civil unions in three other states, Connecticut, Vermont, and New Hampshire. In six states, domestic partnerships are provided by states, which grant nearly all or some state-level spousal rights to unmarried couples (National Conference of State Legislatures (NCSL), 2012).

Upcoming Supreme Court Cases—Two same-sex marriage cases were heard by the U.S. Supreme Court in 2013. The Supreme Court reviewed California's ban on same-sex marriage along with New York's previous ruling eliminating a benefit of DOMA which addresses same-sex couples' access to the same benefits as heterosexual couples.

Sources: Library of Congress, 1996; National Conference of State Legislatures, 2012; U.S. Census Bureau, 2011b; Stempel, 2013.

In contemporary society, there has been a reemergence of grandparents assuming primary (rather than supportive) parenting roles (Hayslip & Kaminski, 2005), many as a result of family violence, drug addiction, and/or incarceration of their adult children. In fact, over 1.8 million children currently reside with a grandparent and have no parent living in the home (Kreider & Ellis, 2008). The growing pressures on many child protection agencies have contributed to the increase in parenting grandparents because child protection workers often see biological relatives as preferable to, and more available than, unrelated foster parents. Many grandparents are healthy, active, and potentially able to take on the responsibility of raising their children's children.

Much more is involved, however, than simply being "able." Many grandparents have reached a point in their lives when they can pursue their own interests and dreams that have been put on hold while they worked and reared families or they may still be engaged in the workforce on a full or part-time basis. Others may find it exhausting to keep up with young children, who have come from dysfunctional situations and have multiple needs, demands, and activities. Some grandparents take on the unexpected role joyfully and fully, and others are enormously burdened, and sometimes guilt ridden because of their own children's inabilities to parent. They may also be struggling with aging, illness, and their own continued need for employment. In any event, many parenting grandparents, even if eager to care for grandchildren, are likely to want and need significant support from social agencies.

Social workers working with grandparents need to use the skills and perspectives of generalist practice. Generalist practitioners are trained to recognize the need for and offer several types of support as they sensitize themselves to the complexities of the emotional and instrumental stresses that grandparents experience. Grandparents may need financial support (Fuller-Thomson & Minkler, 2005), empowerment, self-esteem building communication skills, resource navigation, advocacy, policy development (Cox, 2008), and frequent reassurance that they can and do offer their grandchildren a secure and stable home (Bullock, 2005). In some situations, birth parents recovering from substance abuse or other challenges have visiting privileges or partial child caretaking responsibilities on a preliminary or trial basis. In such cases, there may be considerable tension between grandparents and parents. These and other conflicts may indicate the need for additional ongoing assistance from social workers. Despite the multiple challenges present in such situations, the focus of assessment and intervention should remain on the child(ren) and can include the school system and other involved community resources (Shakya, Usita, Eisenberg, Weston, & Liles, 2012).

Lesbian, Gay, Bisexual, Transgender, and Questioning Couples and Families

Social workers work with LGBTQ clients in a variety of ways, as individuals, as couples, as families, and as groups. Social workers can play an important role when working with same sex couples as families, at all levels of social work practice. One of the most difficult and distinctive issues that LGBTQ couples face, compared to heterosexual couples, is a lack of marriage equality. At the micro level, sexual and gender minority therapy (SGMT), previously referred to as "gay affirmative therapy" or "sexual affirmative therapy", is integrated by practitioners within existing therapy models (Butler, 2009). SGMT is based on the premise that practitioners should first educate themselves, understand and challenge the context of heterosexism, self-reflect, and locate her or his own position and transparency in order to ensure he or she can provide competent services to this population (Butler, 2009; Rostoky & Riggle, 2011).

LGBTQ couples may be considered unique in that they struggle for recognition of their commitment, both culturally and legally. They may have to overtly psychologically support one another (more than a comparable heterosexual couple). They also have unique challenges regarding gender roles; that is, traditional gender roles may not be applicable, and they must negotiate them.

In the context of couples and family interventions, social workers need culturally specific knowledge, skills, and values. Practitioners can convey support and validation of the same-sex relationship in the context of promoting psychological health and wellness by supporting self-determination and human intimacy needs (Rostoky & Riggle, 2011). In working with SGMT couples, social workers should have specific cultural competence in the area of gender roles as they have been found to have a greater impact on the relationship than sexual orientation (Butler, 2009). Using a narrative approach, social workers can work with LGBTQ couples to deconstruct gender role expectations (Butler, 2009).

Social workers can also support same-sex couples by collaborating with the couple to learn strategies for coping with the stress that accompanies discrimination in the form of marriage inequality. Incorporating a strengths-based approach and intervention is also helpful as such an approach can enable the same-sex couples to identify and appreciate the stresses they have faced and overcome together (Rostoky & Riggle, 2011). Taking into consideration the marriage inequality faced by these clients in most states in the U.S., social workers need skills to support and encourage the couple to obtain legal documentation to protect their relationship (Rostoky & Riggle, 2011).

At the group practice level, social workers again have the opportunity to address the discrimination couples face in the form of marriage inequality by providing psychoeducational support and consultation within the community (Rostoky & Riggle, 2011). SGMT promotes connecting LGBTQ couples with wider systems and valuing multiple perspectives (Butler, 2009). Social workers can work with local community organizations, school, religious groups, and other agencies to reduce the prejudice and discrimination directed toward LGBTQ couples and to find support for marriage equality (Rostoky & Riggle, 2011).

In working with organizations and communities, social workers' knowledge and research skills position us well to facilitate marriage equality, thus filling in the gaps in societal awareness of LGBTQ couples (Rostoky & Riggle, 2011). Currently, most of the research that has been conducted with this population has focused on LGBTQ family issues, specifically children or heterosexual family members. Social workers can also engage in political advocacy efforts to show their support for marriage equality among all sexes and genders, as well as educate themselves about local and state laws that affect their clients (Rostoky & Riggle, 2011).

Parenthood may come differently to lesbian, gay, bisexual, transgender, and questioning (LGBTQ) individuals and couples who are married or in civil unions. The person may be the custodial parent of children from an earlier relationship. Some seek artificial insemination and give birth to children, while others become adoptive parents. Also, many informal arrangements for parenting still exist, particularly in some cultural communities.

Recently, states have begun to support the adoption or foster care placement of children in state's custody with LGBTQ parents. The ever-increasing pool of children needing a home and the increasing number and type of adoptions being granted has led, just as with grandparents, to less traditional, more creative efforts in placement planning (Barth, 2008). These types of arrangements have been a highly controversial strategy for dealing with child custody arrangements within the child welfare community because it strikes at the core of the idealized version of the family. Concerns about identity issues for the child, parental adequacy, and the overall mental health of the parents and children have been raised and researched. More than two decades of research on the impact of parental sexual orientation on children's well-being, however, demonstrates no detrimental effect on children's emotional, psychosocial, or behavioral well-being as a result of being reared by LGBTQ parents (Pawelski et al., 2006).

As prospective parents, lesbian, gay, bisexual, transgender, and questioning persons (LGBTQ) still face obstacles in their pursuit of foster care or adoption and experience institutionalized stigma even at the hands of social workers. Lacking any evidence to the contrary, social workers in both the practice and policy components of the profession should support the efforts of all persons seeking parenthood who are deemed eligible through the assessment process (i.e., able to provide a loving, supportive, and stable environment for a child). Social workers can de-emphasize the search for dysfunction and pathology as they give expression to the strengths and resilience of the parents (see Van Den Bergh & Crisp, 2004). Social workers can also recognize the effects of lingering cultural discrimination directed against the LGBTQ community and draw upon a critical awareness of their own biases regarding the strengths and viability of such people as parents.

Issues that the social work practitioner can be aware of to work effectively with gay, lesbian, bisexual, transgender, and questioning parents revolve around sensitivity to the strengths and challenges they face. The strengths perspective may be particularly helpful in working with LGBTQ parents. Helping the parents identify not only their own strengths, but the strengths of the system in which they live, can be an informative, and even transformative, strategy for your work together.

Competent practitioners must also engage in reflection regarding their own attitudes, values, and expectations about LGBTQ parents (Hull & Mather, 2006, p. 218). You must be aware of the challenges they face that are similar to those encountered by all parents (e.g., parental roles, disciplines, etc.) and those that are different (e.g., lack of legal protections, community supports, etc.). Consider the family in which one of the partners of a lesbian couple gave birth to a child conceived through a sperm donation. Given that gay marriage is currently legal in only fourteen states and Washington DC, the two mothers cannot be married in their state. Should the couple end the relationship, the non-biological mother may

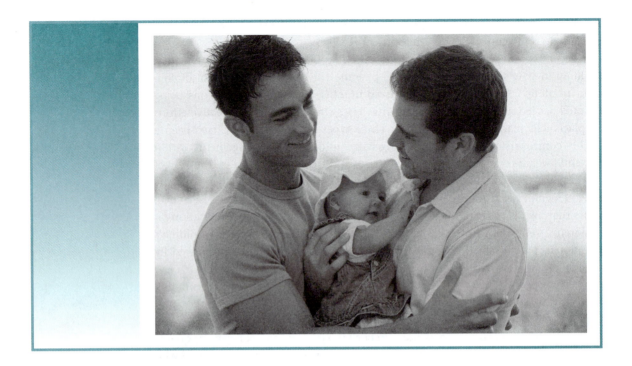

have no legal rights to share custody of the child. These family arrangements are strengthened by strong social worker emotional and logistical support.

Single Parent Families

While competence in the language that you use is critical in all social work encounters, speaking with and about client systems in a linguistically competent manner is particularly important when working with families. Social workers are ethically bound to develop awareness of appropriate language (oral and written) to be used with the diverse communities with whom they work (NASW, 2012–2014a). Single-parent families are a group that is often referred to in ways that are not strengths-based or empowering and can be, in fact, derogatory. A term like "single parent," without the corresponding "double parent," implies that one is normal and does not require description, while the other is "other." As you notice the implications of such terms as "broken family" or "split family," consider how deprecating labels influence initial perceptions and may affect the work that follows. It is easy to lose sight of the strengths and commitment of women or men managing families on their own if the work is prefaced with a sense of deficiency or deviance.

Society and, at times, some social service providers, have historically viewed single parenthood as a blight that necessarily leads to insecure, delinquent, and otherwise unhappy and dysfunctional households. At any point, over one quarter of children live in a household headed by a single parent; particularly if the household head is female, these families report lower levels of income than two-parent families or single male-headed households (Kreider & Ellis, 2011). A review of research on single fathers yields findings that indicate that single fathers, who tend to come to single parenting later than single mothers and often do not experience the financial disadvantages that single mothers do, and may approach parenting differently than their female counterparts, are shown to be caring and effective parents to their children (Biblarz & Stacey, 2010).

While research has shown that children reared in single parent families can face more economic, educational, and well-being challenges than their counterparts in two-parent families, having two parents in the home does not ensure the absence of negative outcomes (Musick & Meier, 2009). Growing up in a family in which conflict is handled in a healthy manner also has a strong correlation to the children's later well-being (Musick & Meier, 2009). On the other hand, there is some support in both the scholarly literature and practice community for recognizing the unique challenges of single parenting, and the way that such parenting impacts both the social work relationship and the parenting functions. Four major issues that frequently arise from divorce or separation are: (1) a lack of resources to cope with stress, finances, or other responsibility; (2) unresolved family-of-origin (family in which you grew up) issues often brought on by the single parent's need for assistance from her or his parents, at least temporarily; (3) unresolved divorce or relationship issues, such as anger, grief, or loneliness; and (4) an overburdened older child. Known as a **parentified child**, an older child who is not yet an adult may be pressed into providing excessive household chores or care for another family member. This, in turn, creates concern that the parentified child's own physical and emotional health and well-being is compromised due to the developmentally inappropriate life experiences (Earley & Cushway, 2002).

With the focus of engagement, assessment, and intervention being on the family itself, social work practice with single parent families can use the family's strengths to create and stabilize coping skills. Drawing from the work of several family scholars, skills for social work practice with single parent families include (Atwood & Genovese, 2006; Jung, 1996):

- *Joining*, similar to engagement, reflects the social worker's effort to show clients that they are cared about and that the social worker understands them and their struggles.

- *Empowering clients* supports their activities and capacity to address their own issues; and values their uniqueness and skills. In particular, the social worker can aid the parent in clarifying and reinforcing the parental role, while serving in a nurturing and supportive role to the other family members.

- While maintaining a focus on the family, the social worker can *aid the individual members in identifying strengths and resources within the family unit* (e.g., the parent is fully employed with a flexible work schedule to allow for involvement at the children's school), the extended family (e.g., grand-parents are committed to helping with childcare), and the community (e.g., the community has active, well-organized after school programming).

- *Involving significant family members* emphasizes collaboration, reduction of stress, and pooled resources.

- *Allocating agency resources* focuses on agency planning, outreach, and networking.

- *Highlighting small changes* emphasizes the strategy of making small shifts that ease overextended schedules and increase energy; such changes can also highlight success and autonomy.

- *Articulating self-efficacy* emphasizes competence, accomplishments, and empowerment for greater control over management of family issues, ideally for all family members.

These knowledge and values are consistent with a strengths-based, empowering approach that recognizes both internal and external factors and supports single parents in their ongoing efforts to provide security and nurturance for their children. Further, these knowledge and values can enhance the social worker's efforts to engage and assess the family system by conveying a sense of care and concern for the individual members, identifying and building on the strengths of each member and the unit as a whole, and emphasizing the self-efficacy of the family system.

Families of Multiple Racial and Ethnic Heritages

The growth of families with multiple racial and ethnic backgrounds is notable in most U.S. cities and towns. Interracial and interethnic marriages, civil unions, and partnerships have been gaining in acceptability since the 1960s and are certainly increasing in real numbers (Amato, Booth, Johnson, & Rogers, 2007; U.S. Census Bureau, 2011a; 2012a). Shifting immigration patterns in the United States, globalization, and the breakdown of ethnic barriers all appear to have an effect on the incidence of racially and ethnically mixed families.

Perhaps few other developments in the everyday life of our communities offer a greater opportunity to view people differently than the growth of families with multiple racial and ethnic heritages. While some members of society will persist in grieving for the purity of "race" (a social and cultural construction by most accounts), others value the contributions of other cultures and challenge the notions associated with racial privilege. It is important, however, not to minimize the negative power of the persistent oppression met by many ethnically diverse families in our culture. In this arena, professionals also need to be educated in this multicultural society regarding our national and cultural history. Gaining awareness of our own cultural and ethnic heritages and values and oppressions we have encountered is a critical step of becoming a culturally competent practitioner (Kohli, Huber, & Faul, 2010). Flexibility, shared goals, and a willingness to explore and address challenges are critical in working across culturally and ethnically diverse communities. As with all other aspects of individual and family assessment and intervention, race and ethnicity should not solely define the family (Logan et al., 2008). The social work assessment should encompass the many and varied facets of the family's life and the environment.

There are a number of models that can guide your intervention with a multiracial family. Two are highlighted briefly here. "**Posture of cultural reciprocity**," proposes an approach for working with diverse families (Kalyanpur & Harry, 1999). This process requires that social workers recognize the cultural aspect of their own personal values as well as those of the social work profession. As depicted in Exhibit 6.4, this posture occurs in four steps. These principles imply a constructionist understanding of cultural difference and value the distinctions without the value of the social worker's orientation. These principles also provide a useful framework for working with people of other cultures and are consistent with social justice and human rights as they enhance inclusion and reflect a basic assumption of cultural strengths.

Cultural attunement embodies self-awareness as a strategy to inform practice. The concept of cultural attunement requires the social worker to go beyond just raising her or his own self-awareness of their own and others' cultural heritages. Being culturally attuned to multiracial families means that you must gain new information about "racial legacies" and the way in which they influence racial self-identity (Jackson & Samuels, 2011, p. 239). Social work skills that can be particularly helpful in assessing and planning with a culturally attuned frame include: asking open-ended questions regarding racial identity; connecting multiracial families to resources for multiracial families; being vigilant about racial/ethnic-focused issues; and developing practice wisdom regarding the unique experiences of the multiracial family (Jackson & Samuels, 2011).

Families Including Persons with Disabilities

Social workers work with families in which one or more members has a physical, cognitive, and/or mental health disability. Grounded in systems theory and currently used in developing health care-supported patient care programs, **family-centered care** is a ". . . philosophy of care that permeates all interactions between families and healthcare providers. This philosophy places a high value on the contributions made by the family members in relation to their healthcare needs" (Bowden & Greenberg, 2010, p. 5). Family-centered care has evolved into a concept of services as "family-driven." This shift expands the notion of family-centered services and is based on the assumption that the family determines what it needs (Seligman & Darling, 2007, p. 14). This strengths-based approach is a promising method for working with families in many arenas, especially with those who have

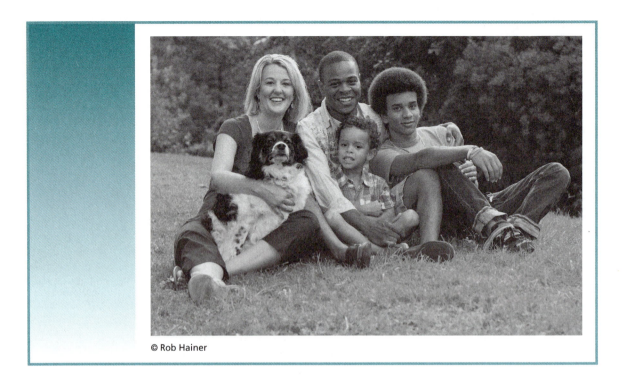

© Rob Hainer

disabilities. When children have comprehensive and severe health challenges, such as neuro-developmental delays, interdisciplinary teaming (group of professionals from different disciplines who work together toward the client's goals) is an appropriate response. Social workers can play an important role on such teams that address many needs of children with disabilities that go beyond medical and educational requirements across the life span. With our commitment to a strengths-based, person-in-environment perspective, we have the opportunity to empower families by recognizing that they are the experts on their lives (Tomasello, Manning, & Dulmus, 2010). As an example of a role for a family-centered social worker, many agencies employ social workers to help higher-functioning adults with developmental disabilities learn job skills. Thus, it is very valuable for social workers to be able to work with adults who have developmental, mental or physical health, or cognitive disabilities and their families and support networks.

As one example, when a child with profound disabilities is born, family members usually have to reorganize their everyday lives as well as their long-term dreams. One parent may have to stop working to facilitate the services and treatments the child needs. The time requirements for involvement with school teams, health care teams, and interprofessional teams, as well as the individual services of a speech therapist, audiologist, occupational therapist, pediatrician, psychologist— the list is sometimes quite long—can turn a family upside down. Siblings are affected, family interactions are affected, and parents often struggle with the

STEP	EXAMPLE	
"Step 1: Identify the cultural values that are embedded in the professional interpretation of a student's [or client's] difficulties or in the recommendation for service."	This would lead to asking why, for example, a culturally different client's behavior is bothersome to you. (Is she late for appointments? Does she interrupt you? Does she respond to you indirectly? How do you interpret her behavior?)	**EXHIBIT 6.4** *Working with Diverse Families: Racial and Ethnic Diversity*
"Step 2: Find out whether the family being served recognizes and values these assumptions and, if not, how their view differs from that of the professional."	For example, you may discover that your client has a different sense of time from yours and that punctuality has little meaning for her. Here you would want to explore how she approaches time, what it means to her, and whether she recognizes your approach to it.	
"Step 3: Acknowledge and give explicit respect to any cultural differences identified, and fully explain the cultural basis of the professional assumptions."	This requires you to enter into a dialogue regarding your assumptions and beliefs and how they are different from those of your client. For example, you might recognize and appreciate the less frantic approach to time and deadlines while you explain the need in your agency to abide by a schedule.	
"Step 4: Through discussion and collaboration, set about determining the most effective way of adapting professional interpretations or recommendations to the value system of this family."	Work out a solution that respects the nature of the family's values. You might settle on a more flexible appointment time at the end of the day, or agree on a time range, or make outreach visits if that is possible.	

Source: Kalyanpur & Harry, 1999, pp. 118–119

emotional ramifications as well as the physical consequences of exhaustion. Social workers can offer support, time management ideas, and help with expanding parents' ability to identify resources. In addition, many families struggle with gaining access to services they are entitled to receive and therefore may need social work advocacy to negotiate a complex system.

When working with families that have members with disabilities, social workers may be challenged by societal views of individuals and families that are not strengths-based, but emphasize the individual's deficits. In response, social workers and disability scholars have proposed the following set of beliefs as a foundation for working with such families (Mackelprang & Salsgiver, 2009):

- Persons with disabilities are capable, have potential, and are important members of society.

- Devaluation and a lack of resources, not individual pathology, are the primary obstacles facing persons with disabilities.

- Disability, like race and gender, is a social construct, and intervention with people with disabilities must be political in nature. There is a Disability culture and history that professionals should be aware of in order to facilitate the empowerment of persons with disabilities. There is a joy and vitality to be found in disability. Persons with disabilities have the right to self-determination and the right to guide professionals' involvement in their lives (pp. xvi–xvii).

Grounded in a strengths-based perspective, each of the previous statements is critical not only for the social worker to adopt, but equally as important for the person with a disability, the family, and the community in which the individual and family live. Social workers have the opportunity and ethical responsibility to empower clients systems to embrace such a belief system. Individuals and organizations within our society may not always embrace a strengths-based perspective. In such situations, the social worker may need to become an advocate for the person with a disability.

Disabilities should be viewed within a diversity (or social) model in which societal attitudes, structures, policies, and institutions are seen as responsible for imposing limitations on persons with disabilities. Person-first language is currently in use but "disability identity language" may more appropriately frame the disability as a characteristic of diversity. These ideas imply a social work presence based on advocacy, structural principles, and the skills to work for social justice.

There is a growing need for social workers who want to work with families in which a member has a disability. Social workers may engage in significant relationships that focus on empowering the family and the person with a disability to engage in self-determination, self-advocacy, and independence negotiating life transitions with family members, organizations, and themselves (Beaulaurier & Taylor, 2007). Working within a framework of promoting client needs and self-determination, the person with a disability and their family members can be empowered to: (1) expand their range of options and choices; (2) prepare them to be more effective in dealings with professionals, bureaucrats, and agencies that often do not understand nor appreciate their heightened need for self-determination; and (3) mobilize and help groups of people with disabilities to consider policy and program alternatives that can improve their situation (Bueaulaurier & Taylor, 2007, p. 65). It is important, however, to clarify the role the family members, including siblings, would like to have in the assessment and intervention process. While family-centered care is built on the notion of the professional partnering with the family members, not all families may want a high-level role (Lotze, Bellin, & Oswald, 2010).

Lastly, consider that the social worker often has a dual responsibility when working with the family that includes a member with a disability (Hull & Mather, 2006). In working with both the person with the disability and the other family members, the social worker may have to balance differing or conflicting needs and goals. For example, a child may resent the attention given to her or his sibling related to the sibling's disability, not understand the reasons the family cannot participate in a certain activity, or be embarrassed to have a sibling with a disability. The social worker's role may be to focus a part of the intervention on the needs of the sibling who does not experience a disability.

Blended Families

Families become blended in different ways. For U.S. Census purposes, a blended family is considered one in which a parent remarries and the children who reside in the home do not share a biological parent (Kreider & Ellis, 2011). Other blended families include domestic partner relationships, civil unions, and nonrelated families who co-reside in the same household. Approximately 16 percent of children are part of a blended family (Kreider & Ellis, 2008).

While most blended families come together without specifically seeking the services of a helping professional, working with families prior to or as they blend into the new family constellation can be a valuable experience for the family. An intervention with the "pre-blended" family can incorporate four stages of work: discovery, education, parental unification, and family unification (Gonzales, 2009). These stages of work entail working through the process of getting to know one another, helping the family anticipate upcoming events through education about child and family development, and aiding the parents and then family member to unify can serve to prevent challenges in the future.

Social workers working with a blended family should be aware of the family history and be sensitive to the dynamics that may occur when two families merge into one. Incorporating information about family blending is a critical component of the assessment and intervention process. Family members may not be aware of or able to articulate challenges they are experiencing regarding the "merger" of the two family units. The social worker who strives to stay attuned to the issues that can occur when families consolidate can identify the reason the family is struggling.

When working with a blended family, the social worker begins by identifying the strengths of the individual members and the family as a unit. Within the assessment process, the social worker can help the family to identify and discuss the roles of individual members along with boundaries between members and the multiple families coming together. It is important to remember that each member of the newly created family unit must be viewed within the context of both of the systems (i.e., original family and new family) in which they exist. There are, however, unique aspects of working with the blended family. Competence in working with blended families requires knowledge of family development and transitions, involvement of noncustodial parents, extended families, and helping families nego-tiate new and different family roles, boundaries, relationships, and traditions. The social worker can also engage with and assess blended families by helping them identify their expectations for the forming of this new family. Adapted from Shalay and Brownlee (2007, p. 24), the following questions for clients may be helpful to this process:

1. What do you perceive others think it means to be a family?
2. How do you think your views of what it means to be family have been shaped by what other people think it means to be a family?
3. How might ideas about families on TV have influenced how you expected things would be as a family?
4. If you were a nuclear family what might be different in how you relate to each other?
5. What do you think expectations about a perfect family encourage you to believe about each other?
6. How might expectations about what a family should be have influenced what you expect from each other?

International Families

Social work practice with families in contemporary society requires global compe-tency. If you are practicing social work with families in the U.S., you will likely encounter families who have arrived in the U.S. as immigrants or refugees. If you are a social work practitioner outside the U.S., you must have extensive knowledge of international issues. While working with families in the U.S. or abroad may require a different knowledge base regarding immigration, legal and governmental issues, cultures, and customs, there is a practice skill set that is common to work to all international family social work practice.

To gain competencies in thinking and working internationally, you can learn as much as possible about the family or families with whom you will be working. As with social work practice with individuals who have relocated to the U.S., it is important to be prepared for working with families who are new to their country. Before you meet the client(s), expose yourself to information about their culture, heritage, relocation history and experience, language, customs and traditions, spiri-tual practices, and community. While reading about your client's country of origin and culture can be helpful, seek out others who can provide you with personal or professional experiences and guidance. Remember also that the client family can ultimately be your best source of information and insight. Allow yourself to learn from them, especially about them as a unique family. While it is important with all client systems to explore their views about working with a helping professional, it is particularly important to understand the perceptions and beliefs about receiving help from the family and those who share their cultural beliefs and traditions.

While there may be common characteristics to groups of people who share a country of origin, culture, or traditions, each person within the family and the family itself should be viewed as individual. You may find as many similarities between a family from the U.S. and a family from Ghana as between two families from Ghana. Learning about the lives of the families that you work with will be an ongoing process that can unfold as you build rapport and trust with the members.

While much of social work practice knowledge and skills you learn is applicable to all families, there are certain competencies that are unique to working with a family that has relocated from their country of origin. First, it is critical to understand the cultural norms of your client family related to the definition of family. Be certain that you have a clear understanding of who is considered to be a member of the family, the relationships of family members to one another, the meaning of those relationships, and any hierarchical traditions that may exist within the family unit. For example, is "family" considered to be the nuclear unit or the larger, extended family? Are persons who are not biologically or legally linked considered to be part of the family? What rules and tasks guide the family members in their daily lives and in making major life decisions such as marriage, parenting, residential arrangements, education, careers, religion/spirituality, and financial priorities?

Regardless of the family's origins, you can use a strengths-based approach in completing your assessment and intervention planning. Using the International Family Strengths Model, DeFrain and Asay (2007a, p. 452) suggest that family strengths can be assessed on the basis of: (1) appreciation and affection; (2) positive communication; (3) commitment to the family; (4) enjoyable time together; (5) sense of spiritual well-being; and (6) ability to manage stress and crisis effectively. While these attributes can be applied to families of any ethnic, cultural, or heritage background, they are particularly helpful when considered within the cultural context of the family with whom you are working, as these family dynamics can have different meanings when viewed within the cultural background of the client system.

Building on family strengths can serve as a particularly helpful strategy as families work to adjust to their new country and environment. Parents, for example, may struggle with their children adopting the customs, language, and dress of their culture or older adults may find it challenging to live in a world that is unfamiliar to them. Using the family's strengths can empower the family members to find their place within their new home while maintaining their connections to their heritage. You can help to make the global connections between the world from which the family has come and the one they have entered by pointing out and affirming a family's ability to enjoy being together despite the challenges of adjusting to life in their new country and home.

While the preceding discussion has focused on family situations and circumstances, the real world of social work practice means that individuals and families may present multiple concerns and dilemmas. Known as **multi-barrier families** or families with multiple problems, the challenges may encompass economic, health, behavioral, social, and psychological issues (Hull & Mather, 2006). For example, a grandparent who is rearing her adolescent grandson may also be faced with a custody battle with his biological parent; a couple with a child born with a disability may, at the same time, be grappling with the grandmother's cognitive impairment; a blended family may be coping with employment layoffs and foreclosure proceedings on their home.

Even with multi-barrier families, the social worker's role is to approach each family as a unique system with strengths and individualized needs. Listening to each member of a family unit enables the social worker to gain insight into the perceptions, relationship dynamics, and possibilities held by the individuals within the collective family system. To be a social worker who is competent in working with families, one needs to develop a repertoire of practice behaviors that encompass family-focused knowledge, skills, and values. Prioritizing problem-solving into short and longer-term goals and promoting a supportive and nurturing environment can be a focus for the social worker. The social worker may find that attention must be given to both the internal and external challenges that are confronting the family (Janzen, Harris, Jordan, & Franklin, 2006). For example, an internal challenge faced by a family may be the substance abuse by one of the members; an external challenge may be the family's inability to qualify for subsidized housing or financial assistance. While different practice behaviors may be required to address internal versus external issues, the social worker may find that she or he serves a number of roles (e.g., broker, advocate, counselor, or educator). The remainder of this chapter will highlight a sampling of those practice behaviors needed to work effectively with families.

CONTEMPORARY TRENDS AND SKILLS FOR ENGAGEMENT AND ASSESSMENT WITH FAMILIES

Theoretical perspectives are a reflection of the sociocultural context and climate. As with social work practice with individuals, there is a wide array of theoretical approaches for assessing and intervening with families. "Most practitioners, educators, and researchers tend to practice, teach, and do research based on multiple and interrelated theories" (Logan et al., 2008, p. 177). While three different theoretical perspectives are presented here, you will, through your career, develop the approach that is most consistent with your philosophical and practice perspectives. Each of the frameworks presented here has some components in common and others born in reaction to each other. All correspond in some ways to traditional perspectives and offer an evolving focus. Regardless of the theoretical approach(es) that you use, social work practice with families should encompass goals that are situational-focused, structured, realistic, concrete, and achievable (Logan et al., 2008).

Narrative Theory in Family Engagement and Assessment

Narrative theory is based on a postmodern, constructionist perspective that enables client systems to make sense of their lives through "stories" or the client system's perception of an individual or a situation. Family interpretations of ongoing events either tend to support the ongoing narrative or refute it. Those stories that are included in the interpretation serve to organize subsequent experience. When there are exceptions, they are often dismissed or forgotten as not representative of the real family. The language used to interpret and describe various family stories is significant and fits into the context of the ongoing experience. Exhibit 6.5 outlines the tenets on which a narrative family assessment and intervention is based. The following examples explore the main ideas of an approach based in narrative theory.

As opposed to seeking a diagnosis, conducting an assessment from the narrative perspective involves helping the family members to tell their stories which then be used to inform the intervention. In essence, this results in the intertwining of the assessment and intervention processes as the stories bring to light the family's strengths and provide direction for the deconstruction of the old stories (Williams, 2009).

The issue that brings the family to the social worker is daughter Liza, who is six years old, the last child, and the only girl in a single parent, male-headed household from an economically affluent neighborhood. Liza has been cast in the role of the family "misfit." Her behavior has been described as oppositional and she is clumsy, speaks disrespectfully, and is disruptive. Any incident involving Liza (e.g., forgetting her pencil or knocking over her milk) becomes just another piece of evidence

1) Language (i.e., word choices) helps to define the meaning given to life events and provides the context for change.
2) Related to language, stories help families give meaning to their life events.
3) The stories created by each family member shape subsequent life events and family members may recall life events differently. It is important to acknowledge all stories as multiple realities can and do exist simultaneously.
4) Social context, specifically culture, influences values, social roles, gender relationships, and concepts of justice which, in turn serve to define the stories family members create.
5) Stories are not necessarily based in facts, but may be the result of family members' perceptions of life experiences, causing strengths and positive alternatives to be lost.
6) Stories can be used to encompass possibilities for growth and healing.
7) Families are not the problem, families experience problems.

EXHIBIT 6.5

Tenets of a Narrative Family Intervention

Source: Adapted from Van Hook, 2008, p. 169–170.

for the family. Her family members often shake their heads at her behavior, and wonder what to do with someone who is (in their view) oppositional, clumsy, disrespectful, and disruptive. When Liza's first-grade teacher reports to her father that Liza is exceptionally well liked by both her peers and teachers and that she is bright and fun, Liza's father is incredulous. He suspects the teacher has her confused with another student. Or Liza must be faking at school. The *real* Liza, as everyone knows, is oppositional, clumsy, disrespectful, and disruptive, as misfits are inclined to be.

The story that Liza tells about herself is different from that which is perceived by her family. Each story carries the power of the context to perpetuate and expand it, which in turn will influence the way Liza, as the major character, plays her role. If her family persists in maintaining the original perception of Liza, she is likely to respond over time by becoming increasingly rude, failing, or developing truly disruptive conduct. On the other hand, if her family at any point re-authors their perceptions by recognizing the exceptions to their ideas about Liza, her story may unfold quite differently. Everyone has multiple stories, but some have more power, relevance, and a wider audience than others. Liza's alternative story (told by her teacher) has the potential to influence her future in positive and significant ways.

Thickening the Story   Although the narrative framework has many components, the exploration in this chapter will include the most relevant concepts for generalist social work practice with families. You may recall, **thickening the story** refers to the social worker's effort to expand "thin" (Morgan, 2000) or **problem-saturated stories** that are one-dimensional perspectives on a truth that client systems created about themselves that may or may not be based in fact (Kelley, 2009). This attempt to create a more complex story may achieve the larger goal of instilling hope that the client system can make positive changes. Liza's first story is a good example of a thin account. She has no redeeming virtues and is simply perceived as an oppositional, clumsy, disrespectful, disruptive misfit. A thickened version of Liza's story reveals her likable personality, talents, and ability to connect with people in spite of, or in addition to, any behaviors that are oppositional, clumsy, disrespectful, and disruptive.

The Smith family provides another example of the value of reframing the story. The Smiths are a family that has experienced considerable challenges in child rearing. One child has been taken into the custody of the state, and now child protection workers are investigating to determine if another child should be removed for reasons of safety. The mother disparagingly claims, in defeat and sarcastic resignation, that her family is "just one of those families." Child welfare workers may likewise view the family as "just one of those families" because various children have been in custody for three generations (as was Ms. Smith).

Rather than assessing the narrowly-defined dysfunction of this family, the narrative social worker would search for the exceptions to this story to enrich it and make it more complex. Rather than maintaining a focus on problem-solving, the narrative social worker collaborates with her or his clients to "enhance their awareness of how cultural forces have lulled them into accepting problem-saturated ways of living (Williams, 2009, p. 205). For example, the social worker can ask about Ms. Smith's ability to keep a family together for ten years in the face of poverty, or to overcome a major childhood health challenge, or survive homelessness. The effort is to expand the narrow failure story so that the family can see itself as having potential, which in turn can support re-authoring the story to reflect the way the family would like it to be. The family then can shape its future to fit the new story. Such an approach can be contrasted with the one taken in the section "Intergenerational Patterns," earlier in the chapter. Through a different lens, it offers the potential for hope through development of the family's resilience and positive attributes.

A family's ability to be resilient can be a powerful aspect of the social work intervention. In keeping with the practice approaches presented here, the social worker should perceive that resilience begins with the beliefs, socially constructed judgment and evaluations that each family member creates (Benard & Truebridge, 2013, p. 205). Some families need help identifying their areas of resiliency. Social workers can help families by incorporating the following resiliency-oriented beliefs about families (Benard & Truebridge, 2013:

- All people have the capacity for resilience.

- Most individuals do survive and even thrive despite exposure to severe risk.

- One person can make a difference in the life of another person.

- Coming from a risk environment does not determine individual or family outcomes.

- Challenging life experience and events can be opportunities for growth, development, and change.

- There is nothing wrong with you that what is right with you cannot fix.

- Bad behavior does not equate with being a bad person.

- As a practitioner, it is how you do what you do that counts.

- To help others you need to help yourself.

- Resilience begins with what one believes (p. 207).

Resiliency can be viewed as the family's ability to "absorb the shock of problems and discover strategies to solve them while finding ways to meet the needs of family members and the family unit" (Van Hook, 2008, p. 11). The social worker's role is to focus on empowering the family to operationalize their capacities for resilience, specifically by:

- Incorporating a sense of hopefulness and purpose into the meaning that families assign to situations (e.g., pointing out ways in which the family can show support for the family member who has just completed a substance abuse treatment program);

- Supporting organizational structures that provide effective leadership and a balance of flexibility and stability;

- Promoting clear, empathic and supportive communication patterns;

- Emphasizing existing positive family members' relationships;

- Promoting family members' problem-solving abilities; and

- To the extent possible, improving and enhancing the social support system and community and economic resources accessible to the family (Van Hook, 2008, p. 23).

Externalizing Problems The notion that problems are external to the family is known as **externalization**. The problem is not the client system itself but is the result of an issue that is separate from the client, thus the focus of the intervention is also then external to the client system (Kelley, 2009). Narrative social workers try to identify and help the family to name the issue that is creating difficulties. By objectifying or personifying it, family members can develop a relationship with the challenge, rather than be consumed by it, and ultimately they may control the challenge.

For example, if a family feels overwhelmed by the demands of a child with disabilities, the resulting "worry" may be externalized. The social worker can then ask about the feelings of being overwhelmed, help family members label their feelings, and support all those times when the family takes control over "the Worry." By separating the issue (or "worry") from the family's identity, the worker and the family can explore ways to defeat their concerns or at least keep them at bay.

Unearthing the Broader Context One of narrative theory's most relevant contributions to generalist social work practice is a consistent emphasis on the political context of the family. The social worker will be highly sensitized to the danger of reinforcing the oppressive dimensions of a dominant pattern (such as racism) in society. For example, consider six-year-old Damion who appears to be having a fearful reaction about going to school. The reaction seems to be extreme for the situation. The social worker will not want to externalize this prematurely as "the school creeps" or "school scares" if in fact Damion is being taunted and bullied because of his ethnicity. Using narrative theory, the social worker seeks to identify any political factors that impact the situation with the client and family, and through a partnership with the client and family, address those factors that are negatively shaping and impacting the challenge at hand. In the case of Damion, it will be important for the social worker to elicit the client and his family's perception of the climate at his school that may promote an environment in which Damion does not feel safe. The social worker can work with Damion and his family to develop an externalized version of the story and incorporate the school into the situation.

Solution-Focused Family Work

Like many contemporary family models, **solution-focused practice** deemphasizes history and underlying pathology by defining the family broadly and not limiting its conception to traditional forms or even requiring all the members to be present in the meeting with the practitioner (Nichols, 2011). With a focus on brief interventions that narrowly define the arena of specific problems within the context of particular environmental variables, solution-focused family work has been used with a range of life situations and groups.

Approaching family social work from a solution-focused perspective is grounded in a set of assumptions, that include (Koop, 2009):

1) The family is the expert.
2) Problems and solutions are not connected.
3) Make unsolvable problems solvable.
4) Change is constant and inevitable.
5) Only a small change is needed to make an impact.
6) Keep it brief.
7) Keep the focus on the future.
8) Focus on the family members' perceptions (pp. 147–148).

Solution-focused social workers usually emphasize a cognitive approach, support a collaborative stance with clients, and tend to reject notions that problems serve any unconscious or ulterior motive. Accordingly, solution-focused social workers believe that individuals want to change, and they believe that any attribution of resistant behavior to families is more about the interpretation of the practitioner than it is about families. The founder of solution-focused therapy, Steve deShazer (1984), early in his work declared resistance "dead" and in turn redefined clients' balking at practitioner directives as their way of educating the social worker about what is needed to help them. As depicted in Exhibit 6.6, solution-focused family interventions are based on seven tenets.

Solution-focused social workers emphasize the future, in which solutions can be used within the specification of clear, concrete, and achievable goals. The simplicity of this approach, along with its time-limited, specific emphasis, has enabled solution-focused work to become an important contemporary model as it generally aspires to short-term, specific, and direct results, thus avoiding costly protracted professional relationships. Long used in community-based programs, solution-focused interventions have shown promise in addressing family and relationship problems, particularly related youth and families (Kim, 2008b; Nowicki & Arbuckle, 2009). The strengths and client perspectives of the approach have made

EXHIBIT 6.6

Tenets of Solution–Focused Family Interventions

1) Emphasis is placed on future and ways in which the future will differ from the past.
2) Solutions may be unrelated to the problem's history; therefore, understanding the past may not be helpful to developing future-focused solutions.
3) Negativity and pessimism can overshadow family members' abilities to see positive alternatives to their ways of relating to one another.
4) People do want to change. Resistance can be a trigger for the social worker to identify different strategies for intervening.
5) Because family members can be influenced by the social worker, the practitioner's focus should remain on empowering the family to understand their problems as well as the possibilities for solutions.
6) Family members can be encouraged by the social worker to change the language they use to discuss their issues from problem-oriented to solution-oriented.
7) Family members determine those areas of focus that are important to them and, as a result, are most appropriate to formulate goals for the intervention.

Source: Adapted from Van Hook, 2008, p. 148–149.

solution-focused practice popular for use in schools settings along with the other components, including portability, adaptability, brief time frame, and the opportunity for small changes to matter and applicability for cultural competence (Kelly, Kim, & Franklin, 2008, p. 8).

In solution-focused work with more than one person, the emphasis is on the relationship, not the individual, and finding and maintaining a common goal (De Jong & Berg, 2013). Solution-oriented social workers need specific skills for working with families as families often have one or more of the following pre-conceived notions about their needs (Sebold, 2011):

- Families see problems stemming from the relationships among the members.

- Families often see one person as needing to change.

- Families often view problems as belonging to the child(ren) (p. 211).

With a focus on developing solutions and de-emphasizing ongoing descriptions of the problem, the solution-oriented social worker enables the family to "know" their problems *and* the solutions and work together as a group to build on one another's ideas and competencies to develop solutions (Sebold, 2011). This strengths-based, future-oriented perspective approach is established from the outset of the social worker-family relationship and continues on throughout the intervention.

The assessment process begins with a series of questions to elicit the perceptions of each of the members. The social worker then uses the family's perceptions to co-construct a plan for intervention (De Jong, 2009). With family groups, questions can focus on the relationships among the members, even the ones who are not present. Questions included in a solution-focused intervention are:

- *Joining:* Initially chatting informally with the family members can serve to build rapport (Koop, 2009).

- *Normalizing:* When possible, helping the family to view the current situation as normal behavior can help them to envision a future in which they do not feel in crisis (Koop, 2009).

- *Goal-formulation:* Questions aimed at goal-formulation prompt the client system to consider the way in which their situation will be different if the problem that brought them to the social worker is no longer a problem (e.g., "What will be different if the problem is resolved?"). The "miracle" questions are aimed at helping the client system envision life if a miracle occurred that eliminated the presenting problem. In the engagement and assessment phases of work, goal-formulation can serve several purposes: enable the members of the family to communicate their individual goals to one another; focus on the members of the family on a common direction for work; and enable the members to identify and build on individual strengths in pursuit of the agreed-upon goals.

- *Exception-finding:* Critical to the assessment process, questions developed to identify exceptions help family systems recall experiences in which they were successful and provide opportunities for identifying strengths and resources available to incorporate into the intervention.

- *Scaling:* Scaling questions invite the family system to quantify the past and the future within the context of the problem or crisis they are experiencing. The clients are asked to use a scale of 1–10 to rate their belief that a solution will be found for the issue that brought them to see you. During the engagement and assessment phases of the intervention process, scaling questions help to establish the point from which the work will begin and identify current and past successes and areas for future growth.

- *Coping:* Aimed at issues of coping, coping questions strive to connect the family members to coping strategies that have or could be used. Such questions can engage and invest the client system in the helping process as well as assess past successes and failures, which can then be used to develop the plan of work for the current intervention.

- *Circular questions:* A family member's perception about what other people (including other family members) think of her or him can influence actions;

therefore, asking questions about what the family members believe others think of them can serve to can deeper understanding of the clients' concerns (e.g., "What do you believe your wife thinks about you when she feels you are not listening to her?") (Koop, 2009).

Like narrative proponents, solution-focused social workers concentrate on identifying and bolstering the attempts made by families that have been successful. The goal for solution-focused social work with families is to increase the discussion about solutions and decrease the focus on problems. Client families are asked to remember when their efforts worked, even when they seem like very small incidents occurring rarely. Solution-focused social workers direct their attention to those exceptions and explore the contextual factors that made the exception possible. In this way social workers give families the message that they have the strengths to cope, that they have in fact done it successfully before, and that they can do it again (De Jong & Berg, 2013).

Solution-focused practitioners have been credited with promoting a greater emphasis on strengths through their "exception" question that encourages the identification of, and focus on, those strengths that are relevant to the current situation (Weick, Kreider, & Chamberlain, 2009). The "exception" questions allow the client to place strengths within the context of times and situations in which the client was successful.

Environmental Focus   With an ecological orientation, solution-based social work looks to the community as a resource and always seeks to understand the problem in terms of the relationship to the surrounding context.

For example, when the social worker views the client within the context of the environment in which the client has grown up and currently lives, the social worker may assume that a woman who abandoned her children is embedded within a culture in which she experiences gender discrimination, poverty, unmet mental health challenges, or perhaps racism. Such assumptions can then help to explain the client's current inability to care for her children. The intervention may then be focused on education, mobilizing resources, and developing a support system to support the client.

All of these considerations are part of the assessment, and a single diagnostic or strictly pathology-oriented label as a unitary explanation is viewed as inadequate. The overall understanding of the family's difficulty is rooted in their everyday, unique living experience to which they bring their own personalities and idiosyncrasies within the larger context, which also shapes that experience.

Constructionist and Social Justice Approaches to Family Social Work

The contemporary approaches described in this chapter are complementary and share some constructionist notions that are represented in the client-defined meanings of family, the lack of rigid ideas of so-called normal family development, and the collaborative partnerships built with client systems. Constructionist theories incorporate a critical perspective that reaffirms the long-standing tradition in social workers working with families. Critical social construction suggests the development of a perspective that focuses more directly on constructionist ideas and social justice principles. Narrative and solution-focused concepts also relate to social justice issues in their concerns for the contextual locations that clients experience on a daily basis. In that respect, the approaches are more alike than they are different, and each has a positive contribution to make to contemporary social work practice.

Approaching social work interventions with families from a constructionist perspective enables the social worker to help families to tell their stories and acknowledge the meaning of those stories. During the assessment and planning phase of the intervention, the social worker can use the family's stories to identify individual and family strengths and those times when the family was able to respond in a way that is different from their current situation, and explore the implications of those stories on their functioning and potential change (i.e., exceptions) (Holland & Kilpatrick, 2009). Principles of constructionist thought that are helpful in working with families include (Holland & Kilpatrick, 2009):

- Family stories transmit meaning, create coherent sequences, shape identity, organize values and explain choices, and involve alternative interpretations.

- To function as a family, the family members must have shared meanings.

- The meanings of stories cannot be changed by outside individuals (p. 26).

Critical Constructionist Emphasis   Critical constructionist social workers explore the meaning of family within a broad contextual framework. Constructionist descriptions of the family present the social worker with multiple perspectives that can be viewed critically; as such models have implications for social work practice. For example, if you assume a theoretical model in which the family is considered basic for human survival and absolutely sacrosanct, you might view the family, as many did for centuries, as immune from external interference in its internal dynamics, including family violence. If, however, you assume that the meanings (or realities) that client systems make of their lives occur within a larger community, you and the client system can view their situation within the context of the groups to which they belong (e.g., racial, ethnic, socioeconomic, religious, etc.) (De Jong & Berg, 2013). Using the critical constructionist emphasis, the solution-focused intervention then becomes a collaboration between the social worker and the family in which the members of the family explore their realities (i.e., problems, miracles, successes, strengths, and solutions) while incorporating the influence of the multiple groups within which they live their lives (e.g., neighborhood, extended family, schools, job settings, and church) (p. 369).

Social Justice Emphasis   Constructionist theorists call for consideration of both external and internal dimensions of social justice. From an external perspective, social workers will direct their attention to ensuring that all families are granted the rights and privileges of society, not just the idealized families of dominant groups. Diverse families, by ethnicity, sexual orientation, socioeconomic class, or any other difference, should be guaranteed the same access to the benefits of the culture. When they are not, the social worker is called upon to intervene in whatever ways are applicable, including legal advocacy, legislative advocacy, public education, or other forms of social action.

The internal focus requires the social worker to look within the family itself for reflection of justice for all family members. Clearly the social worker needs to challenge overt and specific oppressive behaviors, such as intimate partner violence and child abuse, but also is encouraged to look at family structure, gender dynamics, and roles. Critical constructionist social workers will address concerns that are external and have clear internal ramifications through such activities as education and advocacy for more just family practices and policies. Such a perspective reflects the continuous and energetic efforts of the social work profession to develop practice models that both confront and support various dimensions of contemporary society.

Generalist Practice Skills Guidelines for Family Engagement and Assessment

While models may differ somewhat, the following list includes family-oriented engagement and assessment practice behaviors that are common to most models:

- Ensure the family is as physically comfortable as possible.

- Work to facilitate a respectful tone throughout the meeting.

- Transmit positive regard or warmth, support, and respect in verbal and nonverbal practice behaviors.

- Engage with and hear from each member of the family, inviting each to share their perception of the family's strengths, areas for concern, and reason for seeking services.

- Ask each family member her or his perception of the family's purpose and goals in coming to see you.

- Agree upon the expectations and focus of the work.

- Recognize your own biases around family forms and norms.

- Observe the family's communication and interrelationship patterns.

- Inquire about, observe and discuss the role and emotional function that each family member fulfills within the family, particularly within the context of intergenerational relationships.

The engagement and assessment process should be completed expediently and thoroughly. A key aspect of the engagement process is for the social worker to "join" with the client system. The concept of joining entails the development of an alliance between the members of the family and the social worker in order to build trust and rapport (Van Hook, 2008). Having established a trusting relationship is critical for moving forward into the assessment and planning phases of the social work intervention. Family systems are complex and encompass multiple perspectives, thereby creating the need for an assessment process that is unrushed and includes the perspective of each member of the family system (Logan et al., 2008). Family assessment processes are typically determined by the agency. Your agency may or may not use a standardized assessment process. If you are in a setting where you will use a formalized assessment protocol with standardized measures, your role is to clarify for the family the purpose and logistics related to the measures to allay potential anxiety and frustration. Specifically, you can clarify the timing, place, and format of the standardized assessment measure, the meaning of the score or outcomes, and the way in which the information will be shared and used (Corcoran, 2009). While your agency protocol may provide a structure for completing the assessment, content areas that a social worker can address include (Van Hook, 2008, p. 67):

- What are the sources of distress in the lives of family members?

- How do family members view these issues?

- What aspects within the family and their extended world contribute to these sources of distress?

- Are there additional factors that contribute to this distress?

- What are the resources for coping and support possessed by family members, the family as an organization, and their external world?

- How can family members use these resources?

- How can these resources be enhanced?

- What barriers are preventing family members from using these resources?

Family assessment encompasses an array of assessment tools and strategies. The following discussion highlights the use of mapping with families.

Mapping: A Family Assessment and Planning Tool   Competency in assessing and planning for family-focused interventions includes gaining skills in mapping the family situation. Chapter 4 presented genograms and ecomaps as helpful mapping tools for assessment and planning with individuals. Typically included as part of the assessment phase of the social work intervention, these two tools are also widely used with families and offer many uses for social workers. Genograms and ecomaps are compatible with most models of social work practice with families. For example, everyone in the family may be asked to participate in the genogram, or each member could make her or his own map of the family relational patterns (see Exhibit 6.7). Whether it is a genogram or another mapping activity, the process of collecting the information can provide the social worker with insights into the way in which the family members define membership in the family, perceive the current situation, or

EXHIBIT 6.7

Graphic Representation of Different Views of the Family within the Family

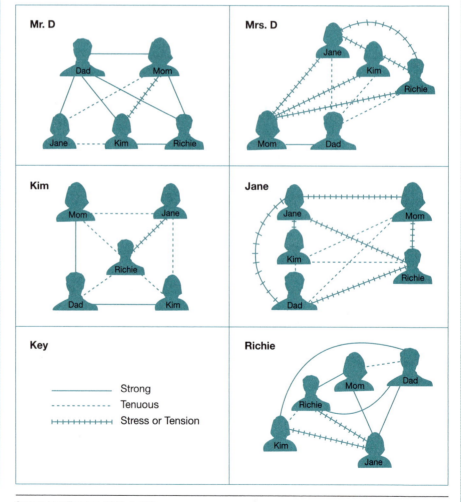

Key

——————— Strong

----------- Tenuous

++++++++ Stress or Tension

Source: Van Treuren, 1993, p. 119

interact with one another within the interview and on paper (Minuchin, Colapinto, & Minuchin, 2007).

Genograms are particularly illuminating assessment tools for family social work because they provide a visual depiction of family structure and patterns. Beyond collecting factual information about multiple generations of family members, the genogram can serve as an "information net" in which data and insights can be all captured within the larger, intergenerational content. For example, the presenting problem may be viewed within the larger context of the family's issues, the immediate household may be seen within the context of the extended family and community, the current family situation is a component of the history of similar patterns, nonthreatening questions are perceived in light of painful inquiries, and facts are compared to judgments regarding family patterns and function (McGoldrick, 2009, p. 411).

The Cultural Genogram is a tool with multiple purposes—building rapport, family assessment, and supporting culturally competent practice (McCullough-Chavis & Waites, 2008). Building on the foundation of the genogram, a cultural genogram incorporates the perspective of the client system in areas of culture that impact the family's experience. Culture can encompass, but is not limited to, race, ethnicity, sexual orientation, social and political influences and oppression, socioeconomic status, and religious and spiritual influences. McCullough-Chavis and Waites (2008) outline the role of the social worker in completing a cultural genogram, which is to identify intergenerational patterns and focus on strengths within the context of the larger socio-cultural-political world in which they live.

First developed by Hardy and Laszloffy (1995) for use with family therapy students, the cultural genogram has been adapted for use with social work practice (Warde, 2012). Students are encouraged to complete their own cultural genogram to gain insight into the way in which the client family might experience this aspect of assessment. Modifying the original list of items to consider when developing a cultural genogram, Warde (2012) presents a list of eleven questions one should consider when completing a cultural genogram. For a list of the questions, see Quick Guide 18.

Ecomaps and other variations that demonstrate relationship patterns can liberate some families from what seems like endless talking, and they usually enjoy developing them and examining the final product. Ecomaps can be used in a visual service evaluation when the goal has been to expand community connections in general or specifically (for example, engaging in more recreational pursuits) or to alter them (such as improving the relationship between the school and the family of a child with disabilities).

Other mapping techniques can prove helpful in social work practice with families. Maps are limited only by imagination. They represent relationship complexities, the passing of time, interacting components, interpersonal interactions and patterns, levels of intimacy, specific types of connection (such as material or emotional support), and spirituality (Hodge, 2005b). One such map is the

QUICK GUIDE 18   QUESTIONS TO CONSIDER WHEN
                 COMPLETING A CULTURAL GENOGRAM

1. If other than Native American, under what conditions did your family come to the United States?
2. What were/are your family's experience with oppression?
3. What significance do race, skin color, and hair play in your family?
4. What role does religion play in your family?
5. How are gender roles defined in your family?
6. How does your family view people who are lesbian, gay, bisexual, transgender, or questioning?
7. What prejudice or stereotypes does your family have about your own racial group and other racial groups?
8. What principles shaped your family's values about education, work, and interaction with people outside the family?
9. What are the pride/shame issues of your family?
10. What impact do you think these pride/shame issues will have on your work with clients who are culturally similar and dissimilar?
11. As you reflect on the answers you gave to the previous questions, how do you think the values you got from your family of origin will influence your ability to work with clients whose values and beliefs are discernible different from yours?

Source: Warde, 2012, pp. 574–575.

culturagram which represents a family's experiences in relocating to a new culture (Congress, 2004; 2009). With the increase and diversity of families coming to this country as immigrant or refugees, social workers need culturally competent assessment skills. Targeted specifically for use in engaging and assessing families who have immigrated to this country, the culturagram enables the social worker and family to empower from the perspective of their culture. The resulting map illustrates content from inquiries relating to the specifics of the family's experience from immigration to their celebration of values in a new land. A culturagram and the areas for discussion are shown in Exhibit 6.8. This visual and interactive tool helps social workers and families understand the family's internal experiences, recognize differences between and within families, see ways in which the family has been successful, and, importantly, pinpoint areas for planning for potential intervention (Congress, 2009).

More literal maps of physical arrangements such as floor plans in housing situations illustrate concretely the challenges in daily living or the disparities in economic circumstances. For example, a map that shows five children's cots in a tiny bedroom or an older adult on the couch demonstrates a person-in-environment reality that may be difficult to comprehend fully through verbal means. A legend on the map that describes the meaning of all symbols and a general heading to orient the reader can be used and are especially helpful in any creative or unconventional mapping.

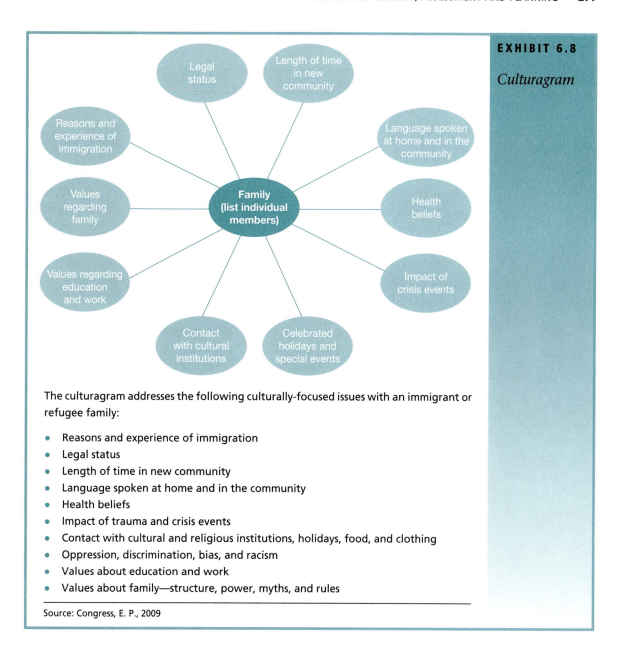

EXHIBIT 6.8

Culturagram

The culturagram addresses the following culturally-focused issues with an immigrant or refugee family:

- Reasons and experience of immigration
- Legal status
- Length of time in new community
- Language spoken at home and in the community
- Health beliefs
- Impact of trauma and crisis events
- Contact with cultural and religious institutions, holidays, food, and clothing
- Oppression, discrimination, bias, and racism
- Values about education and work
- Values about family—structure, power, myths, and rules

Source: Congress, E. P., 2009

STRAIGHT TALK ABOUT FAMILY SOCIAL WORK PRACTICE

Families are a powerful ingredient in our lives. Families have inspired fierce loyalties, lethal conflicts, abject miseries, and quiet pleasures throughout all of history, and continue to do so today. Whether you view your own family as supportive or toxic or any of the many positions in between, reaching a peace with your own feelings can enhance your work with other families. It is difficult to assess and intervene with the family situations of others if they trigger feelings because of their similarity to (or even difference from) your own. Your family concerns need not be perfect or even fully resolved, but your feelings and concerns about your own family situation should not intrude into or influence your work in ways you do not recognize. Such an issue falls into the arena of supervision, and you will benefit from sharing with your supervisor any current struggles you are engaged in with your own family, especially if you are also seeing families in your practice.

Granting that you enjoy a sense of comfort with your own family, you will likely experience situations, at some point, in which your feelings are difficult to manage. Egregious abuse exists in some families, and although contemporary theoretical perspectives can help you temper your responses and recognize that individuals and families do the best they can, the litany of injuries or aggressions emerging in court reports or police accounts or living room conversations can bring on powerful emotions in the most seasoned and balanced social worker. Fortunately, you can use supervision, agency supports, peer connections, and personal strategies for coping with such feelings and reactions. Many social workers see professional therapists to process their family challenges and avoid the influence of their family challenges on their professional practice. The most encouraging dimension for social workers today is that the majority of families inspire the greatest admiration for their resiliency, spirit, resourcefulness, and agency in the midst of potentially demoralizing circumstances.

Another important "straight talk" item for social work practice with families is the need for accurate and comprehensive documentation. Family-related interventions to be documented can include child welfare situations (i.e., child protective services and foster care), adoptions, and early interventions. Such cases may require the creation of documents for: intake assessments, progress/case notes, reports, case referrals or transfers, treatment planning, and evaluations (McGowan & Walsh, 2012). Social workers working with families of adults may have to initiate documents plans for members with addictions, disabilities, health concerns, relationship challenges, or residential placements. In all situations, the social worker's focus should focus on including only relevant information framed in a strengths-framework that represents the perspectives of all members of the family.

As in social work practice with individuals, documentation is a critical, although more complex, practice behavior. You will recall from Chapter 4 the components of basic documentation (see Chapters 4 and 5 for a review of the guidelines). While these guidelines are applicable to documenting the family interventions, there can be the "group" aspect of family work to consider. Recording the assessment and intervention phases of social work practice with families requires the social worker to encompass all members of the family who are participating in the intervention process and to give voice and perspective to the individual contributions. Quick Guides 19 and 20 provide guidelines for family-focused information to be included in the documentation of a family assessment.

QUICK GUIDE 19 DOCUMENTATION OF A FAMILY ASSESSMENT

Demographic Data (include all members participating in the assessment and intervention):
- Names, birthdates, and relationship to others
- Contact Information

Family Information:
- Presenting need(s) or concern(s)
- Living situation (e.g., members of household and level of stability)
- Family (composition—parents, siblings, spouse/significant other(s), children, and others (extended family and friends); level of support; and family history of mental illness, as applicable). A genogram and/or ecomap may be a helpful tool to gather and depict this information
- Timeline—significant life events experienced by the family
- Cultural environment (traditions and cultural view of help-seeking)
- Religion/spirituality (statement of beliefs and levels of activity and satisfaction)
- Family strengths and significant events, including trauma (e.g., physical, sexual, and/or emotional abuse or neglect and experience with perpetrator(s))

Individual Family Member Information:
- Individual family member information, including:
  - Educational history of each member (highest level achieved, performance, goals, and challenges)
  - Substance use/abuse (history of addictive behaviors—alcohol, drugs, gambling, sexual, or other)
  - Emotional/behavioral functioning and treatment history
  - Risk factors
  - Physical health
  - Legal status or concerns
  - Financial/employment circumstances (employment status, satisfaction, financial stability, areas of concern or change)

Social and Environmental Information:
- Strengths and concerns regarding physical environment, as applicable (e.g., structure, neighborhood, and community)
- Safety issues (e.g., risks or concerns of and for individual members and social worker)

Summary
- Current providers (including psychiatrist, primary care physician, therapist, caseworker, etc.)
- Community resources being used (including support groups, religious, spiritual, other)
- Family goal(s) for intervention
- Summary of social worker's observations and impressions

Adapted from St. Anthony's Medical Center, St. Louis, Missouri; Missouri Department of Social Services

QUICK GUIDE 20   DOCUMENTATION OF A FAMILY INTERVENTION PLAN

Intervention Plan:

- Preliminary assessment
- Preliminary plan for intervention and plan for change (to be developed at first visit), including:
  - What will each family member do differently?
  - How does each family member view themselves accomplishing changes?
  - What support and services are needed to accomplish plan for change?
  - Who will provide support and services?
  - Who will arrange for support and services?
- Interventions and plans for emergency/safety needs
- Other interventions needed
- Needs (include date, identified need, status (active, inactive, deferred, or referred), and reason for deferral or referral)
- Strengths
- Facilitating factors for intervention
- Limitations
- Barriers to intervention
- Other care providers/referrals and purpose (including plan for service coordination)
- Plan for involvement of individual family members, extended family members, significant others and friends
- Review and termination criteria/plan
- Planned frequency and duration of intervention

Adapted from St. Anthony's Medical Center, St. Louis, Missouri; Missouri Department of Social Services

CONCLUSION

The contemporary family both supports and challenges the social worker. Social workers engage with the family and its struggles in our culture, thus a goal for the profession is to develop additional and relevant models for working with them that recognize their strengths, agency, and resilience. Education and advocacy for shifts in the structural and political arrangements that exist for families are also required.

As a culture we still value the family, and social workers can be a part of the solution for creating environments in which families of all kinds are validated and supported.

As the structure and meaning of family itself continue to change, you can stay alert for your own capacities to honor those notions of others. As a form of "group," the family has particular resonance and serves as a grounding point for understanding human collectives. With that dimension in mind, this exploration will move to the intervention, termination, and evaluation of your work with families.

MAIN POINTS

- Historical antecedents for involvement with families, including family function and systems theories, shape the way in which social workers engage with and assess families.

- An idealized, or fantasy, notion of the American family still exists today, but social workers recognize and work with many forms, including grandparents raising grandchildren; lesbian, gay, bisexual, transgender, and questioning families; single parent families; families of multiple racial and ethnic heritages; families with members who have disabilities; blended families; and families with multiple challenges.

- Several contemporary theoretical perspectives have emerged that are consistent with critical social construction, the strengths perspective, and social justice orientations, including narrative, solution-focused, and constructionist approaches.

- Your practice setting will guide much of your work with families, but the skills and practice behaviors that you have learned for engaging and assessing individuals and groups will be applicable in working with families. Additionally, family-oriented skills and practice behaviors are needed, including engaging the whole family, reframing, and recognizing your own biases around family forms.

- Mapping tools can be helpful in assessing and evaluating the work with families; they can also help to empower families to change.

EXERCISES

a. Case Exercises

1. Go to www.routledgesw.com/cases and review the case file for Roberto Salazar. As the undocumented nephew of Hector and Celia Sanchez, Roberto has consistently earned an income but has also experienced several health challenges. He is currently living with the Sanchez family due to an injury that prevents him from working. He has a number of skills but his current injury and inability to work has him feeling defeated.

   You are the social worker charged with monitoring the status of Hector and Celia's Section 8 housing voucher. While Hector and Celia generally manage their rent payments, they are having difficulty meeting the schedule due to extra expenditures in support of Roberto. Your agency is responsible for controlling expenses and complying with federal regulations. Your supervisor is especially concerned with this aspect of the program.

   On your visit to the Sanchez home, Hector assures you that—even though he knows the landlord can evict him and his family for violating regulations regarding occupancy—Roberto is family and, of course, he and Celia will house and feed him. He remembers his own loneliness when he came to the U.S. and that his uncle helped him. He has no doubt that he can assist Roberto by providing temporary housing and support. Hector explains to you that it is important for immigrants to stick together and support one another, especially family. You are feeling some pressure from the agency to report and help resolve the issue of Roberto's unacceptable presence in the Sanchez home. You are concerned that your supervisor will look unfavorably on you if you allow Roberto to continue to live in the house.

Respond to the following questions:

a. How might a family focus differ from an individual focus in this situation?

b. How will you respond to Hector? Your supervisor?

c. How might diversity be a factor in this situation? Compare your responses to those of your peers. Identify and team up with another student whose approach seems similar to yours and develop a unified approach. Brainstorm in class regarding different or creative ways to approach this situation.

2. Go to www.routledgesw.com/cases and review the case for Carla Washburn. Create a genogram of her family. Explore the connections between Carla and her family members and the ways in which those connections impact her relationships within the family. Address the following:

- What are the strengths of the family?
- What are the issues that have impacted the family?
- How have those issues impacted the various relationships?
- Who has the "power" in the family?
- If you were a social worker working with this family, what issues would take precedent?

3. Go to www.routledgesw.com/cases and review the case for Brickville, focusing on Virginia Stone and her family. Review the genogram for the Stone family and provide an analysis of the information provided by responding to the following questions:

- What additional information do you believe would be helpful to include in the genogram?
- What are the patterns that emerge as you review the Stone's genogram? In addition to general patterns, comment on potential themes in the areas of:
  - boundaries between family members
  - intergenerational family relationships and patterns
  - single parenting
  - grandparents rearing grandchildren
- What strengths and areas of challenge are evident?
- What information does the genogram yield that suggests priorities for planning a social work intervention?

4. Go to www.routledgesw.com/cases and review the case for Hudson City. The Patel family is one of the many families displaced by Hurricane Diane. The members of the Patel family include:

- Hemant and Sheetal—both in their late 40s, they immigrated to the U.S. from India fifteen years earlier. They own and operate a family restaurant in the neighborhood in which they live.
- Rakesh, Kamal, and Aarti are the Patel's three children. The oldest son, Rakesh, is 18 years old and is his first semester at the University of the Northeast. He lives at home and commutes to school each day. The younger son, Kamal, is a 16-year-old high school junior. The Patel's daughter, Aarti, is age twelve and in the 7th grade.
- Bharat and Asha are Mr. Patel's parents who came to live with their son and his family when the restaurant opened ten years ago. They are both in their early 70s and help part-time in the restaurant. Bharat had cardiac bypass surgery last year. Asha suffers from hypertension. Their medications were left behind when the family fled from the storm.

All the members of the Patel family work full- or part-time in the restaurant. The Patel's restaurant and home sustained major damage as a result of the storm. While the restaurant and house can be rehabilitated, the damage is extensive and repairs will likely take weeks to months to complete. The Patels are staying with friends in a nearby community, but feel they should make other arrangements and not impose on their friends' hospitality. As the entire family income is derived from the restaurant, money is a concern.

You are working as a volunteer mental health disaster responder and have been asked to work with the Patel family who has come to the Emergency Center. Develop a list of culturally competent engagement strategies that will be helpful as you begin your work with the Patel family, including additional information and resources you will need.

5. Go to www.routledgesw.com/cases and click on the case for Hudson City. Returning to the information provided regarding the Patel family, click on Assess the Situation and respond to My Assess Tasks. Using the Patel family information provided here, complete Tasks #1 and #2 as it relates to the Patels. Once you have assessed the issues and needs facing the Patels, develop a preliminary plan for your social work intervention.

b. Other exercises

6. You are a social worker on an interprofessional team that works with children who are on the autism spectrum, and their families. Three-year-old Jenny is referred to your team. She is the light of her father's life—she is lively, energetic, and bright-eyed. In the last year, she has become quiet, preferring to play by herself, and is less interested in the special outings her father loves to share with her.

After a series of anxious appointments with the pediatrician, Jenny was referred to a specialist in developmental pediatrics. Many observations and checklists later, Jenny was diagnosed on the autism spectrum. Her parents, Catherine and Jason, were devastated. Her two-year-old brother, Sammy, was oblivious.

Over a period of a month, Catherine began to adjust to the diagnosis. She connected with a supportive group of parents coping with children on the autism spectrum and read all she could about autism. She also spent considerable time with Jenny, playing and coaxing her to interact with her. Jason, however, was notably uninterested in Catherine's activities. He began to refuse to go to Jenny's doctor's appointments. During one argumentative dinner with Catherine, he stated that he did not believe the diagnosis; he thought Jenny was fine, just going through a stage, and accused Catherine of "selling out" her own daughter. Jenny was referred to the interprofessional team by her pediatrician. Catherine engaged in the process enthusiastically, if painfully. Jason attended the assessment and seemed sullen, participating very little. The team concurs that the family would benefit from your "support work" around the diagnosis. Catherine and Jason agree to meet with you and you speculate this might be your only chance to engage Jason.

Respond to the following questions to compare with your peers.

a. What is your assessment of this family? Identify a theoretical perspective that is most applicable to working with this family. How does your choice of perspective influence your approach to this family? Be specific.

b. Generate a list of three questions or issues that you think are important to address in your first meeting.

c. How might you attempt to engage the family, especially Jason? As you compare responses with your peers, what different (from your own) perspective was most useful to you?

7. In working with Jenny's family (from exercise #6), develop a solution-focused plan for the assessment and planning phase of the social work intervention.

8. In an alternative approach to working with Jenny's family (from exercise #6), develop a plan for assessment and planning using a narrative approach.

9. This chapter includes a range of contemporary family structures about which social workers must have knowledge and skills for competent practice. Select one of the groups discussed in this chapter and conduct a search of the evidence-based practice approaches currently utilized with the group you have selected. Prepare a brief summary of the knowledge and skills needed for effective practice.

10. Create a genogram of your family. Explore the connections within the family and the ways in which those connections impact the relationships within the family, particularly your relationships. Address the following:

- What are the strengths of your family?
- What are the issues that your family has faced?
- How have those issues impacted the various relationships?
- Who has the "power" in the family?
- If you were the social worker working with your family, what issues would take precedence?
- What have you learned about your family from this exercise?

CHAPTER 7

Social Work Practice with Families: Intervention, Termination, and Evaluation

. . . to think larger than one to think larger than two or three or four this is me this is my partner these are my children if we say, these are my people who do we mean? how to declare our bond how to keep each of us warm we are in danger how to face it and not crack

Melanie Kaye/Kantrowitz, in *We Speak in Code: Poems & Other Writings*, 1980

Key Questions for Chapter 7

(1) What competencies do I need to intervene with families? (EPAS 2.1.10(c))

(2) What are the social work practice behaviors that enable me to effectively intervene with families? (EPAS 2.1.10(c))

(3) How can I engage in research-informed practice and practice-informed research to guide the processes of intervention, termination, and evaluation with families? (EPAS 1.2.6)

(4) What potential ethical dilemmas might I expect to occur in intervening with families? (EPAS 2.1.2)

SOCIAL WORKERS HAVE A LONGSTANDING HISTORY OF intervening in family situations and crises. Dating to the era of Mary Richmond and the Charity Organization Society, and Jane Addams and the Settlement House movements, social workers have focused on intervening with families (Logan et al., 2008). Just as social work practitioners respond to societal changes, social workers have also adapted their practice behaviors, including knowledge, skills, and values, to the developmental stages of families or changing structure of families. While families are generally self-sufficient in meeting their ongoing financial, emotional, and caregiving needs, when they seek help outside the family, they require a response that is developed for that family's needs (Briar-Lawson & Naccarato, 2008). Family social work interventions require competencies to address the complexities of the contemporary family, which may include culture, racial and ethnic diversity, financial and legal challenges, and intergenerational relationships and dynamics. Different from family therapy, family social work is an approach based on generalist social work skills for intervening with families who are at-risk. Family social work assumes the intervention is family-centered, and support can be provided in the family's home or in the social worker's office and in times of crisis (Collins, Jordan, & Coleman, 2013). Family social work practice interventions may be focused on: (1) reinforcing family strengths to prepare families for long-term change, such as a member arriving, leaving, needing care, or dying; (2) creating concrete changes in family functioning to sustain effective and satisfying daily routines independent of formal helpers; (3) providing additional support to family therapy so families will maintain effective family functioning; and/or (4) addressing crises in a timely way to enable the family to focus on longer-term concerns (Collins et al., 2013, p. 3).

Essential to an effective intervention with families is the engagement and assessment. Building on the assessment that focused on the family's strengths and self-determined needs, the intervention process is an opportunity to collaborate with the family to facilitate growth and change. With its emphasis on brief, efficacious interventions, managed care has influenced contemporary social work practice with families by focusing the social worker clearly, systematically, and succinctly on identifying and assessing the problem or concerns, developing and implementing an intervention plan, and terminating the working relationship (Jordan & Franklin, 2009, p. 429). This chapter will highlight theoretical frameworks and practice behaviors that will be helpful to your work with families.

THEORETICAL APPROACHES TO INTERVENING WITH FAMILIES

Just as with individuals, family intervention is a planned change process in which the social worker and client system work together to implement the steps to reach the goals established in the assessment and planning process. Research has shown that families, even those who endure intense or chronic stressors, can be resilient (Benard & Truebridge, 2013). An array of theories provide the underpinning for the approaches to social work practice with families, including systems, ecosystems, family life cycle, cultural and social diversity, strengths-based, and empowerment (Logan et al., 2008, p. 184). The social worker who is well grounded in theoretical approaches to working with families can select the approach(es) and techniques that is (are) best suited for the social worker's practice philosophy and the needs of the client family. In an effort to best serve the families with whom they work, practitioners "often use a combination of family techniques from different models rather than adhering to one particular approach. Integrationism [i.e., blending models and techniques], technical eclecticism [i.e., using different techniques] and the use of common factors are the preferred ways that most practitioners work" (Franklin, Jordan, & Hopson, 2009, p. 434). As a practitioner, you will recognize that theories each have their own limitations within the context of the client family's ethnic, cultural, familial traditions and your scope of practice as a social worker (Hull & Mather, 2006). However, the family intervention models that are most effective typically share certain elements, including education, opportunities to practice and model new behaviors and skills, and multi-faceted intervention plans (Franklin et al., 2009). As an ethical and culturally competent social work practitioner, you are responsible for gaining the training necessary to use the evidence on available family models and select the approach or combination of approaches that you believe will be most effective for your client.

Created by Hull and Mather (2006), Exhibit 7.1 depicts a framework for approaching family intervention from a multidimensional perspective. As shown in the exhibit, the process of developing a family intervention begins with viewing the family within their environment, followed by the selection of a relevant theoretical approach, and concludes with the creation of an intervention that uses appropriate techniques.

Following is a discussion that explores theoretical approaches using the strengths and empowerment, narrative, and solution-focused perspectives. In keeping with the overall approach of this book, the theoretical perspectives presented here will be within the postmodern grouping of frameworks. We will also learn to help families grow and change by aiding them in identifying and building on strengths, reconstructing their life experiences, and developing new realities. While postmodern approaches may be perceived as counter to traditional systemic approaches, Logan and colleagues (2008) posit that, in fact, the two complement one another. Systems theories help the practitioner to view and frame the family within the context of environment, while the postmodern constructs help the social worker to view the family within the context of the meaning of the presenting issues that are provided by the family.

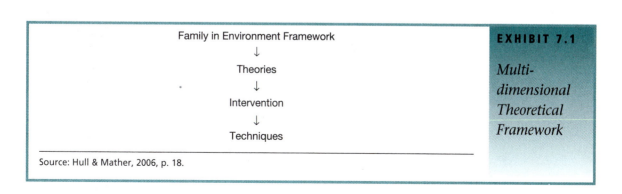

Family in Environment Framework
↓
Theories
↓
Intervention
↓
Techniques

EXHIBIT 7.1

Multi-dimensional Theoretical Framework

Source: Hull & Mather, 2006, p. 18.

Strengths and Empowerment Perspectives and Family Interventions

Having completed an assessment and planning process that identifies the strengths on which the family can build, an intervention in the strengths tradition strives to not only enhance the family's assets but to empower the family to develop new coping and resiliency strategies. From a strengths perspective, challenges are viewed as opportunities and possibilities (Saleebey, 2009). An intervention that is grounded in a strengths perspective is one that builds capacity and assets and focuses on solutions (Briar-Lawson & Naccarato, 2008). For example, an intervention that emanates from the traditional deficit-based perspective will view the family as the source of its problems (e.g., poor parenting, dysfunctional relationships, or irreparable problems). A strengths-based intervention identifies the family's assets (e.g., the parents are committed to placing value on being together as a family, productive children and the family has remained together in the face of adversity) and capacities and focus on solutions (e.g., the family is willing to work on the challenges that brought them to a social worker).

In the face of the complexities of "being" a family in contemporary society, practitioners may find it easier (although not ultimately as effective) when developing an intervention plan with a family to focus on the problems that exist within the family, rather than the strengths. Instead, a strengths-based approach could entail asking the family members, for instance, to describe the characteristics of a healthy, strong family can lead to a discussion of those characteristics that are shared by their own family. To address the family's current situation, it is important to understand their views on strengths and to incorporate those strengths into the planning and intervention process (DeFrain & Asay, 2007b). Engaging in an exploration of those actions that the family members can take individually and collectively can result in an altered perspective for the family (and possibly the social worker, as well). Gaining insight into interacting in a new way with one another and the environment can be an empowering experience for the family. For example, consider the case of the resident of Brickville (www.routledgesw.com/cases), Virginia Stone. You will recall from previous chapters that Virginia is currently struggling with an array of challenges. In your initial intervention, you might lean toward focusing on the most compelling issues (e.g., her caregiving stressors or home ownership dilemma). It may be most helpful to Virginia in the longer term to help her to identify the strengths and previous coping experiences that her family and she possess so that she may use those strengths-based experiences to help resolve her current challenges. For example, strengths possessed by this family include their commitment to caring for older members and remaining connected to one another even through times of adversity.

Grounded in a commitment to build on family strengths, empowerment-oriented practice is applicable to family interventions. Having been developed over the past several decades from a concept to practice principles and methods, empowerment-oriented interventions extend beyond intentions to encapsulate the principles and actions (Parsons, 2008, p. 124). As an example, Dunst and Trivette (2009), leading scholars in this arena, have continued to evolve their family-systems model for early childhood and family support interventions. Moving away from the traditional paradigm that emphasizes an intervention based on the family's deficits and the professional's expertise to a contemporary capacity-building paradigm, Dunst and Trivette propose that effective interventions should focus on models that embrace: promotion, empowerment, strengths- and resource-based, family-centered models (2009, p. 128). This paradigm shift is intended to aid professionals in developing help-giving practices that encompass a capacity-oriented approach to identifying and mobilizing family concerns and priorities, abilities and interests, and supports and resources. In a capacity-building approach, the role of the social worker in providing services becomes more relational and participatory. In addition to demonstrating traditional social work practice skills of active listening, compassion, empathy, and respect, the capacity-focused family social worker emphasizes possibilities for change in an individualized, flexible, and responsive manner (Dunst & Trivette, 2009, p. 131).

Empowerment-driven interventions are helpful for families in crisis—especially those who have experienced a history of crises—and can aid the social worker in helping the family to create solutions. An empowerment perspective is grounded in a belief that the stressors and trauma a family experiences can be buffered by a repertoire of protective factors available in their environment (i.e., family provides caring relationships, maintains high expectations, and provides opportunities for meaningful participation and contributions) (Benard & Truebridge, 2013, p. 208). In essence, the family has the skills and resources they need to be resilient and adaptive in the face of adversity. For example, consider the family who has survived 2012 Hurricane Sandy but lost their home. They are a large family and could not find temporary housing in one place. As a result, they are staying in different locations with family, friends, and in shelters, but they come together once each week to work on rehabilitating their home so they can return there as a family.

An empowerment approach uses seven principles of practice (Wise, 2005):

1. Build on strengths and resources and diminish oppressive factors. As noted, the strengths that can be used in addressing the challenges must first be identified by the family. The family then reviews existing and potential resources and begins the mobilization of those resources. Oppressive factors or barriers to growth and change may lessen as family members perceive options and possibilities. Strategizing with the family about ways in which oppressive factors may be confronted, ameliorated, or minimized can also be empowering. A first step, however, may be for family members to confront the oppressive factors that may be perceived to exist *within* the family. For example, family members may be stifling anger at another member for having a disability. Until this anger is acknowledged and addressed by all the members of the family, the family is

unlikely to be able to collaboratively work toward resolution of the presenting concern.

2. Multicultural respect. Multicultural respect requires attention to a wide and growing array of phenomena, including race, ethnicity, gender, age, socio-economic status, religious/spiritual beliefs, sexual orientation, differing ability, language, and developmental phases. The family may be impacted in multiple areas. The role of the social worker in helping the family create an intervention is to ensure awareness by all members of their perceptions and experiences in these areas and to help the family understand the meaning and impact and confront stereotypes and barriers.

3. Recognize needs at the personal, interpersonal, and community levels of empowerment. While family members may well know their needs, they may have difficulty, particularly during a crisis, articulating those needs to one another or the social worker. A successful empowerment-focused intervention relies on the social worker to help the family create solutions that are directly linked to their needs. Regular individual and group check-ins are necessary to ensure that the needs have been accurately and thoroughly voiced and are being addressed through the plan that was developed for the intervention. Needs can and do change and the social worker can help the family to recognize that and maintain a realistic approach to success.

4. With sufficient resources, family can empower themselves. Upon identifying and mobilizing resources, the social worker can facilitate an intervention plan. The social worker does not have the ability to complete the work for the family, but can, however, monitor and interpret the family's use (or lack) of the resources. For example, consider the value of helping the family to mobilize resources from their religious or spiritual community. The religious community can not only provide tangible and emotional resources but can serve as a recognized authority that may be of help in engaging and intervening with family members (Nakhaima & Dicks, 2012).

5. Support is needed from each other, from other families, and from the community. Receiving support from within the family and outside the family can be the impetus that the family needs to reach their agreed-upon goals and solutions. The role of the social worker may be to normalize experiences, provide information, and connect the family to one another and others.

6. Establish and maintain a "power WITH" relationship. Power can serve as an asset and a barrier in a family intervention. Being able to convey to the family that each member has power, the family as a group has power and the social worker has power. Most importantly, the social worker and the family can share the power for the purposes of achieving the goals of the intervention. Interventions should not rely on the "power" of any one or sub-group of the family-social worker partnership, but should be shared in a collaboration using the strengths, assets, and resources that each person or sub-group brings to the intervention.

7. Use cooperative roles that support and assist family members. Implementing the intervention requires that each member assume a variety of roles over the course of the relationship. Such roles may include co-consultant, co-collaborator, guide, co-teachers/learner, co-investigator, and co-creator (pp. 86–88). The social worker is in a position to point out ways in which the family members can use their knowledge and skills.

To bring these principles to life, consider the situation being faced by the Murray family, a three generation family living together in the same house. William (55-year-old high school teacher) and Genevieve (50-year-old occupational therapist) Murray have been married 27 years and have three children: Elle, a 25-year-old unemployed licensed practical nurse, recently returned to her parents' home with her two children ages four and two years, following a divorce; Stephen, 21, who lives at home, works part time, and attends a local university; and Samantha, 16, who is a high school junior. Recently, William's mother, Edna, 76, moved into the house. Edna suffers from Alzheimer's disease. After a recent car accident, the family determined that Edna is no longer able to safely live in an independent living situation. The arrival of Elle and her children and Edna resulted in Stephen and Samantha having to give up their bedrooms. A makeshift bedroom has been created for Samantha in the basement and Stephen is sleeping on the fold-out couch in the den. While the crisis that brings the Murray family to your agency is Samantha's arrest for driving under the influence of alcohol and subsequent suspension from school, it is immediately evident that this is a family in crisis in several additional areas: Edna's illness and increasing need for care; Elle's adjustment to divorce and single parenting; displacement and lack of privacy for Stephen and Samantha; and the stress experienced by William and Genevieve in supporting the family.

Using strengths and empowerment-based perspectives, how can this family be supported through this challenging period in their lives? Consider first the strengths and resources that exist. William and Genevieve have a longstanding marriage; are employed; have opened their home to their daughter, her children, and William's mother; and are willing to provide care for these family members. The family can be a resource for itself but an important intervention strategy is to ascertain from each member their perception of the issues and any factors that are barriers to resolution of the issues. Samantha, for example, may view her grandmother as the problem as Edna has taken her room and her parents' time and resources, leading her to argue constantly with her parents and spend as much time away from home as possible. Helping the family to articulate their needs within a multiculturally respectful way is the next step in creating alternatives with the family. For example, providing information about Alzheimer's disease and its course may help the family better understand and accept Edna's behavior and needs. The social worker can enlist ideas from each family member about ways in which each member of the family can help and offer suggestions for accessing resources outside the family.

Collaborating with the family to access and mobilize resources can not only provide a model for them, but can also engage them in an alternative to their present incapacitation. Examples of collaborating with the family include: (1) Capitalizing on Elle's professional expertise as an LPN, the family can apply for a family caregiver program in which a family member can be paid to care for an older adult. Elle can contribute financially to the family, care for her grandmother and her children, and work toward rebuilding her life; (2) Co-investigating with Stephen options for using his experience as a camp counselor to apply for a live-in resident assistant position on campus can provide him with space and privacy; and (3) Samantha's substance use and arrest has effectively gotten her parents' attention. Guiding the family to consider the various responses and treatment options can enable them to make choices together and learn from one another to co-create a new way of being a family. While the social worker may guide the family members toward resources, the members would be encouraged to handle as many of the logistics of accessing resources as possible.

Narrative Theory and Family Interventions

Like strengths and empowerment approaches, a narrative approach to intervening with families also incorporates strengths, viewing the family as experts on the family unit, and collaboration between the social worker and the family. In hearing each family member's perceptions of the family and the problems that brought them to a social worker, the family members are able to identify the meaning of the problem and discover alternatives to those meanings that will aid in changing the family's interactions (Kelley, 2009). As with the narrative approach to working with individuals, the problems confronting the family are assessed through respectful listening. The family's perceptions are reflected upon and deconstructed, then reconstructed by challenging perceived truths. Through the reconstruction process, the family members in collaboration with the social worker are able to create an intervention plan that enables them to arrive at unique outcomes that have meaning and viability within their family unit.

Implementation of an intervention based in a narrative approach is the culmination of the family-social worker partnership. The family members' story is the intervention and the social worker's role is to empower the clients by supporting their strengths (Williams, 2009). A narrative approach provides the social worker with a variety of strategies that will optimize the family's strengths to expand their perceptions of themselves and their problems and to create a new vision. Within the discovery process, the family has the opportunity to envision a future in which the current problem persists or a future in which the problem is altered or resolved through their actions. Through collaboration with the social worker, clients can become empowered when their stories are heard, resulting in their capacity to construct new stories (and realities) (Williams, 2009).

Narrative social workers find that a variety of strategies and questioning formats are needed to empower clients for change. Interventive techniques can include (Van Hook, 2008, pp. 171–175; Williams, 2009):

- *Listen to the family tell their problem.* Ask each member of the family to share their concerns.

- *Normalizing.* Listening and empathizing can serve to build rapport and trust between the family and the social worker.

- *Externalizing the problem.* Collaborating with the family, the social worker can help them to separate the problem from the person. The partners can then create a team to tackle the problem and not the individuals who make up the family.

- *Mapping the problem.* Looking for patterns from the past can help the family to understand the ways in which the problems were sustained and the impact the problems had on the family. Mapping strategies can include:

  ○ Searching for a unique outcome—identify a time when the family experienced success in overcoming a problem.

  ○ Asking spectator questions can help the family to consider how others view them.

  ○ Reauthorizing the family's story to emphasize a perception in which the members have been able to overcome adversity (also known as significance questions).

  ○ Identifying cultural messages that support problem-saturated stories—examining the influences of previously received cultural messages on the family's ability to interact with one another and handle life's responsibilities.

- *Findings news of a difference:* Identifying evidence of change, no matter how small, can serve to move the family beyond the problem behaviors and into a new, alternative reality.

- *Asking therapeutic questions:* Ongoing use of questions can help the family to continue to tell their stories and re-author new stories that create a healthier environment. Therapeutically-focused questions can focus on: opening space for possibilities; effecting change to amplify news of differences; preference questions (i.e., comparing past and the present times); developing stories that highlight differences; meaning questions (e.g., getting to the perceived meaning of family's actions); and future-oriented questions.

- *Scaffolding:* Once the old story begins to be deconstructed, a new story (i.e., competence) can be constructed to replace it. Scaffold questions can help to move the story focus from exceptions (e.g., a time when the family was happy) to significance questions (e.g., acknowledging the importance of an action/event) to spectator questions (e.g., understanding ways in which family members experience one another).

- *Collapsing time and raising dilemmas:* The past and present are both important aspects of evolving the problem to a newly constructed story.

- *Enhancing change:* The social worker may challenge the story to motivate clients to examine the old stories to abandon their reliance on their problem-saturated stories.

- *Predicting setbacks:* The social worker can help the family to accept that they will find it difficult to give up on problem-saturated stories and setbacks are likely to occur. Anticipating such an eventuality may disempower the potential impact of the setback.

- *Creating ways to reinforce the new narrative:* Encourage the family members to identify strategies and individuals who can help them maintain the changes they have made.

Returning to the Murray family, their crisis could be framed using a narrative approach by the social worker listening to each member sharing her or his views on the family situation. As you can imagine, the perceptions of the Murray family are likely to be quite different. William and Genevieve may share that they are doing their best to provide for all the members of the family and they feel betrayed by Samantha's arrest and suspension. Samantha (as noted earlier) may believe her parents have given more to other members than they have to her, particularly her grandmother. Struggling with cognitive impairment, Edna may feel she is a burden to her family but feels powerless to change the situation. Elle likely also feels guilt for being unable to support her children and herself. Stephen is feeling pressured to hold down a job and maintain his grades and scholarship so that he can move out of the house. After reaching a consensus with the family regarding the desired outcomes, the social worker can begin deconstructing and reconstructing the family's perceptions by externalizing the problems (i.e., focusing the family on the issue not the person). Should the family, for example, choose to focus on stabilizing the situation with Edna's care; the social worker can externalize Edna's behaviors as, because of her cognitive impairment, outside her control. The social worker can then help the family to envision life if they take no steps to improve their perceptions of Edna's situation, as well as a life in which they understand the disease, coping strategies, care and respite options, and ways to enjoy their remaining time with Edna. While reconstruction of Alzheimer's disease will not alter the course of the disease, the quality of life for Edna and her family can be enhanced through challenging the family's problem-saturated perceptions. Edna will be viewed as an honored member of the family, not as a burden.

Solution-Focused Family Interventions

Like other postmodern family-focused interventions, solution-focused family interventions also emphasize strengths and empowerment, client self-determination, and collaborating with the social workers to construct new realities by mobilizing assets and resources. Solution-focused interventions differ from other similar approaches in the use of questions that move the client from crisis to solution through the co-construction of solutions (De Jong, 2009).

With an emphasis on the relationships and competence, family solution-focused interventions incorporate explorations of the skills, strengths, and competence of clients in a way that is consistent with many postmodern approaches. This focal point solidifies the social worker-client relationship as a collaboration focused on building on past successes (De Jong & Berg, 2013). The assumptions inherent in their ecological orientation encourage social workers to look to environmental, structural supports for solutions rather than to internal dynamics for pathology. Social workers do not disregard individual responsibility for behaviors such as those that occur in child abuse or intimate partner violence, but these are viewed as evidence that the client's external resources and skills are underused (Christiensen, Todahl, & Barrett, 1999). For instance, family violence may occur when a family is experiencing stress but not using resources outside the family (e.g., social, health, mental health, or financial aid services).

Employing a solution-focused intervention with a family shifts the family's focus to a hopeful, future-oriented view of their lives. The social worker's role in creating interventions is to help the family mobilize their energies to achieve solutions using existing and expanded coping strategies in a concrete behavioral approach (Van Hook, 2008).

You will recall from Chapter 6 that a series of questions are used for assessment and planning of the solution-focused intervention. Upon completion of the assessment, the social worker and the client develop a plan for change. While the intervention process should be driven by the family's identified needs, goals, strengths, and resources, the social worker can be most helpful by developing a repertoire of skills and strategies for aiding the family in achieving their mutually-determined goals. Exhibit 7.2 provides a listing of six tasks for implementing a solution-focused approach.

Once the plan is underway, the social worker checks in with the members to monitor progress through the use of "what's better?" questions. The scaling questions that were included in the assessment phase can become a part of the intervention as well. Scaling questions can help review previously discussed solutions and exceptions, and highlight changes as they are made (Nichols, 2011). For example, the social worker might ask the family members to rate on a scale from 1–10 their feeling when they first came to see the social worker and compare those responses with a current rating of feelings on the same issue. Scaling questions can also be used to anticipate future feelings and behaviors (e.g., "on a scale from 1–10, how confident are you that you will be able to sustain this change?").

EXHIBIT 7.2

Solution-Focused Social Worker Tasks

- Create interactional balance and balance between the problem and solution-focused talk. Maintaining a balance between the persons who speak ensure that each voice is heard. Maintaining a balance of content ensures that the emphasis remains on talk about solutions and not about the problems.
- Use effective listening and summarizing skills. Staying tuned in to the contributions of each member of the family and regularly summarizing their input can serve to re-energize the clients and the social worker to remain focused on the goal and ensure that each person's voice is heard.
- Introduce transitions that will move the conversation from problem-focused to solution-focused. To maintain the focus on solutions, the social worker can regularly infuse affirmations or the family's strengths that include statements that convey support of the family's efforts.
- In order to sustain the solution emphasis, the social worker must focus on the family's current realities, that is, key in on those issues being raised by the members. When issues are not addressed, there is a tendency for them to be forgotten. The social worker can help to redefine such issues from problem- to solution-focused, but can promote the process by staying focused.
- Facilitate a "family reflecting pool." As issues are discussed and solutions initiated, each member must be given the opportunity to reflect on the issue or change from her or his vantage point, as each is likely to view the item or issue in a different way from other family members.
- Establish goals and negotiate tasks. While "homework" is typical in any social work intervention, solution-focused tasks should emphasize the desired goals and solutions versus the problems. For example, one of the stated goals is for the family to spend more time together. Before the next session, the family agrees to have dinner together three times in the upcoming week.

Source: Sebold, 2011, p. 217–228.

Additional techniques for completing the solution-focused intervention include (Koop, 2009, pp. 158–160; Nichols, 2011, pp. 257–258; Van Hook, 2008, p. 155):

1) Providing compliments as often as possible to emphasize strategies that have been successful. Compliments may be direct, indirect, or self-compliments.
2) Focusing attention on the family members' relationships with one another. Questions such as "how is your relationship different when you actively listen to her when she speaks?" can help the family keep the emphasis on changing their relationships.
3) Maintaining throughout the intervention phase a positive, future-oriented emphasis on "who, what, when, where, and how" questions.

4) Once the family has identified goals, the social worker can shift the focus to a range of behavioral tasks in which the family can engage, including:

  - Doing more of what works—if the family has identified interactions and strategies that work, encourage them to continue them.

  - Doing something different—introducing the idea of trying new strategies for relating to one another.

  - Going slowly—promoting a slow, incremental approach to change.

  - Doing the opposite—encouraging the family members to engage in behaviors and interactions that are the opposite of what they are currently doing.

  - Predicting tasks—helping the family to predict outcomes and to identify patterns that occur when changes are experienced.

5) Finding, amplifying, and measuring progress for the purposes of monitoring signs of positive movement toward desired goals.

6) Taking a break within an interaction for the social worker and family to provide feedback to one another.

7) Recapping at the end of the meeting the work of the family and social worker and providing suggestions for future work (i.e., "homework" that focuses on observing successes, engaging in new tasks, and predicting desired changes). Tasks can be considered as three different types: formula—general tasks in which family is asked what they might do differently; perception tasks—observational tasks in which family is asked to pay attention to and note differences in one another's behaviors; and behavioral tasks—tasks in which the family members take action and interact different with one another.

Returning to the Murray family once again, consider the intervention from a solution-focused perspective. During the assessment and planning phase, you questioned each of the members regarding their perceptions of life in their household. Imagine William and Genevieve responses to goal-formulation or miracle questions. They will likely talk about having imagined a near "empty-nest" household with their two older children living on their own and Samantha about to head off to college. Samantha's response to the "miracle" question might likely involve her grandmother not living with the family, and not facing legal issues related to her driving under the influence arrest and her school suspension. Elle's "miracle" might include employment, a supportive partner and a home of her own. Stephen's miracle may involve a room of his own. Edna may wish desperately to have her memories back and to return to independent living.

Given the diverse array of goals that may be expressed by each of the family members, helping the Murray family to connect with a realistic set of goals can be a complicated process. Highlighting the fact that the family members care for one another is a technique to foster goodwill and find common ground on which the members can agree (De Jong & Berg, 2013). In working with the Murray family, reminding them of their commitment to and concern for one another can be a regular part of the intervention. Imagine that the agreed-upon goal is to find a solution to the overcrowded housing situation. Your role can be to work with the family to develop concrete and achievable short- and long-term solutions, check in regularly with "what's better?" questions, and terminate when you and the family agree the goals have been achieved.

Regardless of the theoretical approach that guides your work with families, your social work values and ethical standards will provide the foundation on which you will develop interventions to be implemented with families. Ensuring that the client system's rights to self-determination, strengths, and diversity are honored is the priority for your intervention with families. Emphasizing the practice behaviors to enable you to become a practitioner who is competent in social work practice with families will be the focus of the following discussion.

CONTEMPORARY TRENDS AND SKILLS FOR INTERVENING WITH FAMILIES

Families are made up of individuals and are a form of a group, and as such, benefit from the careful use of the same practice behaviors that assist individuals and groups. Interventions with families are likely to vary according to your practice setting and the constraints of your agency. For example, if you are a member of the intake unit of a child protection team, your intervention with the family will probably differ from that of your colleague who works in a community mental health agency. The theoretical lens through which you are working will also influence the way you intervene with family members. You may develop an intervention plan from a systems focus, or you may work with family members to build an intervention plan based on their perceptions of ways in which you might help them, as in solution-focused work. In any situation, your intervention begins with an invitation to the family to tell their story, but your agency mission and purpose and your own theoretical biases will influence the intervention approaches you take.

Social work practice interventions with families shares many similarities with individually-focused interventions. Recall from Chapter 5 the discussion on roles that a social worker may have in working with individuals (e.g., case manager, counselor, broker, mediator, educator, client advocate, and collaborator). Each of these roles is applicable for working with families, particularly in light of the setting in which the intervention may occur. Family-focused social work practice can take place in an array of settings, including child welfare, mental health centers, schools, health care facilities, and community centers, to name a few. For example, the social worker working with a family in a child welfare setting may engage in all the roles, but emphasize case management and brokering activities in particular in order to reunify the family. In a health care setting, the social worker's emphasis may be on education and advocacy, for instance. With families, it is important to consider all the members' perspectives, recognize relationship dynamics, and the strengths-based intervention goals that will optimize family functioning.

As with individuals, the setting in which you practice and your philosophical and theoretical approach will frame your intervention activities. While model-specific practice behaviors have been previously discussed, there are additional general practice skills and behaviors that transcend the continuum of practice approaches. Building on the practice behaviors used in the phases of family engagement and assessment, the following strengths-based skills for intervening with families can be helpful (Benard & Truebridge, 2013, p. 207; Hull & Mather, 2006):

- Identify the issues and concerns, use active listening to enable the family members to tell their story and reflect on the information shared by the family members.

- Acknowledge the pain.

- Look for and point out strengths.

- Ask questions about survival, support, periods of time that were positive for the family, interests, dreams, goals, and pride.

- Resilience begins with what one believes and all people have the capacity for resilience.

- Link strengths to the goals and dreams of the family members (both group and individual).

- Find opportunities for family/members to contribute to the intervention by helping to educate other members and serve as helping agents in achieving the family's agreed-upon goals.

- Use brainstorming for solutions as a strategy to help the family to view the situation and themselves differently.

Written homework assignments, task designation, and teaching are strategies that can be helpful but must be appropriate to the family's situation, their investment in the process, and the framework you are using in the intervention. Return for a moment to the Murray family scenario and consider the above list of practice behaviors. In order to mobilize the family into working toward crisis resolution, you can begin by asking each member her or his priorities for change. From those verbal-izations, it is likely that you will glean the pain, strengths, goals, and dreams felt by each of the family members. You may choose to engage the family in brainstorming strategies they can use to address each of the areas of concern or assign the family homework in which they develop ideas to address their concerns. An alternative may be to ask the family to have a family conference and bring their ideas back to the next meeting with you. Once the family has developed a range of ways to address their prioritized concerns, consider asking them to have a discussion in which specific tasks are identified and assigned. Be sure to explore the possibility that the expertise for problem-solving resides within the family, and individual members can function as teachers and guides.

In addition to the individual and group skills, reframing, perspectival (or circular) questions, family group conferencing, motivational interviewing, and reenactments (i.e., role-playing or rehearsals) are a sampling of practice strategies with good applicability in many family situations when carefully used. Discussed in Chapter 6 as an assessment tool, mapping is an important strategy for the intervention process.

Reframing

An approach used frequently in social work with families, as well as with individuals, groups, communities, and organizations, reframing is a practice skill in which the social worker conceives of and describes a situation in different terms. Reframing can be particularly helpful in family conversations in which one member makes an incendiary statement to or about another family member. Carefully used, reframing can assist both recipient and "sender" to view the situation with diminished uproar so they can begin to listen to each other. Focused on strengths and positive alternatives, reframing must be appropriately timed to have a meaningful impact. To have a significant effect, the social worker must stay carefully attuned to the family members' dialogues to identify opportunities for reframing as they occur (Minuchin et al., 2007).

For example, a 15-year-old boy, who sees his mother as an autocratic barrier to his enjoyment because she will not allow him to go out with friends who drive, says, "There is no person on the face of this earth who is more controlling and overprotective than my mother. She is just like Hitler! She keeps me locked up in the prisoners' camp." You may suggest that the teen's mother cares so much for him that she fears he will be hurt in an automobile accident or in some other way if he goes out with his friends.

When reframing, offer a plausible alternative that does not resonate as a "gimmick" or "Pollyanna" type of effort to diffuse strong feelings and, accordingly, will be heard by the parties involved. The danger lies in interpreting the thoughts or feelings of another person without directly having been told. In the example of the 15-year-old teen and his mother, it is quite likely that the mother is not intentionally attempting to torture her son (and that she truly worries about his going out with friends who drive), but he may or may not be able to "hear" her sentiment as reframed. Another reframing effort may be more effective depending on the nature of the relationship and the people involved. Developing the content of such interpretations requires judgment and skill; use reframing cautiously and only when conditions are relatively straightforward. How can reframing be used with the Murray family? Instead of focusing on the upheaval created by Edna, Elle, and Elle's children moving into the house, consider emphasizing the strong family commitments and caring environment for members who are in need of support.

Perspectival Questions

Mentioned in connection with individuals in Chapter 5 and with group work practice in Chapter 9, perspectival questions can be effective in family social work. By seeking the perspective of another family member, you can help clarify the feelings and meanings of one member's view of another. If the family is experiencing stress because the eldest son is leaving home, you may ask the teenage daughter, "What do you think your mother will do to prepare for Johnny's leaving?" Or you may ask the mother, "What will your daughter miss most about Johnny?"

The responses to these questions can communicate ideas and feelings that no one in the family has openly or previously recognized. Such assistance in communication is relevant when family members assume they know all they need to about the responses of other family members as a result of long-term, "stuck" patterns of argument or difference or "saving face." As in the use of reframing, perspectival questioning is a strategy to be used carefully and only when you are confident that you can respond appropriately to any statement. The daughter in the example just provided may respond with, "Mother will sew name tags in Johnny's underwear so he won't lose it in the dorm laundry room at college," or, alternatively, she may say, "Mother will no doubt start to drink again." The same element of the unexpected that can create new ways of thinking for families can also throw a curve ball to the unwary or unprepared social worker. Utilizing perspectival questions with the Murray family could potentially yield some illuminating insights. Consider, for example, the new perspective that could be uncovered if Edna were asked about the support that her son and daughter-in-law have provided to Elle and her children and her response was that they should not have invited Elle and the children to move into their house. By expecting the unexpected and maintaining flexibility, the social worker who incorporates perspectival questions can be prepared for the unexpected.

Family Group Conferencing

A strategy for use with families, family group conferencing (FGC) is an empowerment-focused intervention aimed at creating or strengthening a network of support for families as they are experiencing a crisis or transition. Originally developed for work with families in which children were at risk for abuse or neglect, this practice strategy has been extended to other family situations, including families with older adults experiencing life changes. The family conference usually occurs after the assessment and planning phases, and is a collaborative effort that includes the social worker, family (including extended family members), and members of the family's community who are existing or potential resources for the family (Wise, 2005).

The conference goal is to gather the family members with people who are connected to the family in order to make decisions regarding a response to the presenting challenge. The social worker confers individually with each potential participant prior to the conference to ensure that each agrees to be actively involved in decision-making and action steps. During the conference itself, the desired outcomes are determined by the participants themselves with the strengths and areas for concern being included in the planning process (Brody & Gadling-Cole, 2008). Once a plan is established, the group adjourns and may reconvene after a period of time has elapsed in which the plan is implemented to discuss progress or re-negotiate the plan.

Return for a moment to the Murray family. If you were to convene a family group conference with the Murrays, consider those people you would invite to participate and the reasons for inviting them. What goals could provide the Murrays

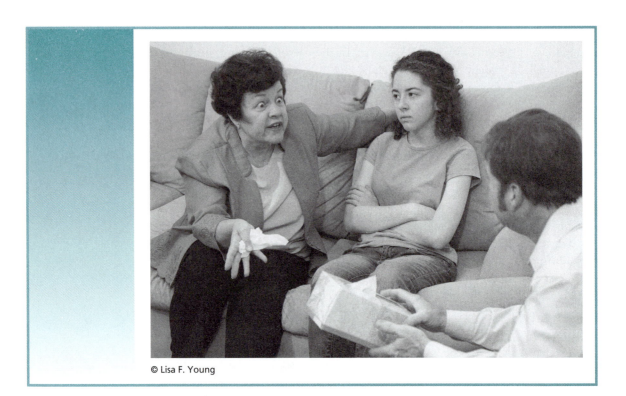

© Lisa F. Young

with a much-needed support network and stronger coping skills? What are their strengths? How might they benefit individually and collectively from participation in a family group conference? What is your role? While answers to these questions can only be speculative, you can use this exercise to begin to see yourself in the role of a family social work practitioner.

Motivational Interviewing

As you recall from Chapter 5, motivational interviewing (MI) has been introduced for use with a variety of clients, including those who are non-voluntary, experiencing substance abuse, or intimate partner violence (Wahab, 2005). Using the four processes of MI—engaging, focusing, evoking, and planning—to promote behavior change, MI is well-suited for situations in which the client is uncertain about making the change and/or the time is limited (Miller & Rollnick, 2013; Wagner, 2008).

Motivational interviewing is also applicable to social work with families. Miller and Rollnick (2013) offer strategies for engaging in motivational interviewing with families with adolescents. Using the FRAMES strategy, the social worker can conduct a Family Check-up that provides the social worker and the family with the opportunity to: (1) **F**eedback of personal status relative to norms; (2) **R**esponsibility for personal change; (3) **A**dvise to change; (4) **M**enu of change options from which to choose pursuing change; (5) **E**mpathetic counselor style; and (6) support for **S**elf-efficacy (Miller & Rollnick, 2013, p. 375). For example, using the FRAMES strategy in the case of the Murray family, the social worker may opt to check in with the family in this way:

1) Provide Feedback to each family member regarding their proposed solutions for the identified stressors currently affecting the family.
2) Designating Responsibility for change—clarifying roles and tasks for each member of the family.
3) Advise on change—provide information to the family on the impact of ongoing stress, Alzheimer's Disease, and potential positive outcomes of collaborative change.
4) Provide a Menu of options—presenting family members with an array of options for behavior change, healthier interactions, services and resources that may be mobilized within and outside the family.
5) Empathetically validate the concerns expressed by each member of the family and acknowledge the pain they are experiencing.
6) Self-efficacy of each member of the family can be regularly reinforced by the social worker identifying their strengths, commitment to change, and progress toward goals.

Motivational interviewing provides another opportunity for you, as a social worker, to engage in a collaborative partnership with the client family aimed at providing the opportunity for change. If you opted to employ motivational interviewing with the Murray family, you may begin by providing feedback to them based on the perceptions they have shared with you regarding the various crises that are occurring within the family. They also have the opportunity to provide feedback to one another. After they share feedback, you can empathetically reiterate that the family members are the experts about themselves and it is within their power and responsibility to implement change. Try to create an environment in which the family is empowered to view themselves as having the capacity to respond to their crises with resilience and efficacy.

Incorporating motivational interviewing into social work practice with families can present challenges that do not exist in working with individuals. Given that families come to social workers often times as the result of their inability to resolve relationship challenges on their own, ensuring that each member of the family is given adequate opportunity to speak is critical (Miller & Rollnick, 2013). Moreover, the social worker will need to be able to balance the interactions to maintain a focus on positive change as opposed to continuing with arguments and negative discussions.

Re-enactments

Participation in experiential activities can provide insights and alternatives for families who are experiencing a crisis or challenging transition. Re-enactments can be completed in the form of role-plays or rehearsals. Re-enacting a particularly challenging interaction and then role-playing or rehearsing the scenario with alternative behaviors can be a powerful experience mechanism for the family to "try on" new ways of being a family. Viewed as a safe way to share feelings and rehearse, role-plays can be carried out in a variety of settings, for a range of situations, and revisited as the work progresses. Considerations for developing role-played activities include (Hull & Mather, 2006, pp. 163–164): (1) purpose and parameters are to be discussed; (2) members can play themselves or other members of the family; (3) members should play the roles accurately and consider their feelings as they move through the rehearsal; (4) the role-play can be stopped so members can discuss, reflect, and change interactions; and (5) the role-play should be de-briefed so alternatives can be explored. A re-enactment may be an ideal activity in which to engage the Murray family. Once the family has identified the issues that are their highest priority to address, you can help them to "rehearse" the change strategies they have brainstormed through an experiential exercise. With the multiple generations, issues, and priorities that exist within the Murray family, role-playing can enable the family to work on individual issues and relationships. Imagine a role-play in which William and Genevieve share with Samantha their feelings and concerns regarding her life choices and decision-making. More importantly, envision a dialogue between Samantha and her parents that any one of the three may stop so they may regroup, change course, or ask for input. Such a rehearsal may enable the family to change a pattern of interactions.

Mapping as an Intervention

Mapping strategies have been examined primarily within the context of assessment. They do, however, have a place within the intervention process itself. If not completed during the assessment phase, mapping can be incorporated into the intervention phase of work. During the intervention, mapping in the form of genograms, in particular, can be used for clarifying family patterns, framing and detoxifying family issues, and in developing the intervention plans (McGoldrick, Gerson, & Petry, 2008). Using the patterns and unhealthy family issues to identify and facilitate change plans can be a liberating experience for the family members. McGoldrick and colleagues (2008) promote the use of genograms as an intervention strategy to empower clients through changing existing relationships. Being able to see the historical patterns of loss, relationships (healthy and unhealthy), physical and mental health issues, substance use, responses to stress and crisis, and cultural traditions can illuminate for family members the options they have for change. Creating and discussing genograms can also provide family members with an opportunity to engage in intergenerational dialogue. Consider the Murray family, for instance. Providing the family members with the opportunity to engage in dialogue with Edna could provide them with family history they had not previously known, as well as have meaningful time with her before her memory fades away. The social worker can incorporate the genogram into the development of the intervention by asking members to identify strengths on which they can build in relationships and cultural traditions (McCullough-Chavis & Waites, 2008). They may also be able to identify patterns of substance abuse, trouble with the law, or other troubling patterns that can inform their present collective and individual work.

Ecomaps and culturagrams are also assessment tools that can be integrated into the intervention. Using the baseline ecomap or culturagram as a strategy for monitoring change throughout the intervention provides the family and the social worker with a visual depiction of their work. Updating the ecomap or culturagram can indicate those areas in which progress is being made or not made and the barriers preventing success. New maps can be constructed as a means for ritualizing a successful outcome. As with social work practice with individuals, documentation is a critical component of the family intervention. Along with maintaining copies of the assessment tools mentioned here, the client portfolio also includes a record of the intervention plans. Exhibit 7.3 offers a sample family intervention plan template followed by Exhibit 7.4 which provides an example of documenting the intervention plan developed with the Murray family.

As with social work practice with individuals, intervening with families requires the social worker to complete comprehensive and ongoing assessments from which flexible, individualized interventions can be created through collaboration with the family. The outcome of a successful intervention is, of course, the termination.

EXHIBIT 7.3
 	
Documentation of a Family Intervention Plan
	Intervention Plan:
	• Preliminary assessment
	• Preliminary plan for intervention and plan for change (to be developed at first visit), including:
	   ○ What will each family member do differently?
	   ○ How does each family member view themselves accomplishing changes?
	   ○ What support and services are needed to accomplish plan for change?
	   ○ Who will provide support and services?
	   ○ Who will arrange for support and services?
	• Interventions and plans for emergency/safety needs
	• Other interventions needed
	• Needs (include date, identified need, status (active, inactive, deferred, or referred), and reason for deferral or referral)
	• Strengths
	• Facilitating factors for intervention
	• Limitations
	• Barriers to intervention
	• Other care providers/referrals and purpose (including plan for service coordination)
	• Plan for involvement of individual family members, extended family members, significant others and friends
	• Review and termination criteria/plan
	• Planned frequency and duration of intervention
	
	Adapted from St. Anthony's Medical Center, St. Louis, Missouri; Missouri Department of Social Services

Our focus will now turn to the phases of terminating and evaluating the family intervention.

ENDING WORK WITH FAMILY CONSTELLATIONS

The general principles for ending interventions apply to all levels of practice. The need for culturally sensitive practice plays out in individuals, families, groups, communities, and organizations. Just as you need to explore the meaning of endings with individual client systems, so you do for families. This discussion assumes a cumulative recognition of the important areas for ending the work, based on considerations covered so far, and a flexible application with greater emphasis on some principles than others according to context. With those principles in mind, we will look to some specific variations as additional perspectives.

In voluntary family work, endings tend to occur when the family is satisfied that they achieved their goals. In some circumstances , the restrictions of third party

EXHIBIT 7.4

Documenting the Intervention Plan: The Murray Family

Preliminary assessment

The Murray family has requested services from this agency in order to address a number of crises and concerns within the family. The family is comprised of William (55 year-old-high school teacher) and Genevieve (50-year-old occupational therapist) and their three children (Elle, 25-year-old divorced single mother of two- and four-year-old children; Stephen, 21-year-old college student; and Samantha, 16-year-old high school junior). Along with William's mother, 76-year-old Edna, all members of the family reside in the couple's now overcrowded home. Stephen and Samantha were displaced when their bedrooms were given to Edna and Elle and her children. Edna can no longer live alone as she is experiencing cognitive impairment (Alzheimer's Disease) and presents safety concerns at her assisted living facility.

The Murrays sought help because Samantha was recently arrested for driving under the influence and suspended from school. During the assessment, information was shared that suggests the family has been in crisis for some time and that Samantha's arrest and suspension brought the crisis to a climax.

Preliminary plan for intervention and plan for change

During the first meeting of the entire family, each member was asked to share their concerns, needs, and potential solutions. After each person had the opportunity to artic-ulate each of these areas, the social worker provided a summary of the information shared and the family and social worker collaborated on a list of highest priorities, resulting in the development of the following preliminary plan:

1) Genevieve agreed to contact the local chapter of the Alzheimer's Association to obtain information on services available for families experiencing dementia. She will specifically inquire about programs that provide information on Alzheimer's Disease and provide financial support for care needs (e.g., Family Caregiver Support Program).
2) All family members agreed they would attend a presentation for families on Alzheimer's Disease provided by the Alzheimer's Association.
3) Stephen will contact the campus housing department at his university to learn about applying for a resident advisor position which would provide him with tuition support and free housing in exchange for living in one of the student residential facilities. In the interim until this goal may be achieved, William and Genevieve agreed to work with Stephen to fix up the basement so he may have a private bedroom and workspace.
4) Genevieve, William, and Samantha all agreed to attend the court-mandated program for teens arrested for driving under the influence.
5) Samantha agreed to attend the alternative school program for the duration of her school suspension.

Interventions and plans for emergency/safety needs

Two areas of immediate concern were raised regarding safety needs. The following plan was agreed on by all members of the family:

EXHIBIT 7.4

Continued

1) Elle agreed to provide care for Edna during the day when Genevieve and William are at work. This will allow Genevieve and William to feel that Edna is safe and that Elle can provide supervision and transportation. Elle will be able to remain home with her children and not bear the expense of child care.
2) Samantha agreed not to drink and to be subject to a periodic alcohol test if her parents are uncertain about her sobriety.

Other interventions needed
Longer term interventions may include:

1) Exploration of all family members' feelings regarding the overcrowded living conditions in the home and stressful relationships.
2) Discussion regarding Stephen's living arrangement if he is not accepted for a resident advisor position.
3) Decision-making regarding Edna's ongoing care needs as her disease progresses.
4) Discussions regarding Elle's permanent employment and living situations.
5) Reestablishing a trusting and healthy relationship between Samantha and her parents.

Needs
At this preliminary phase, the primary needs are:

1) Establish a safe environment for Edna
2) Address Samantha's legal, school, and alcohol issues
3) Provide adequate space for Stephen and Samantha
4) Address family stressors

Strengths
The Murray family has several important strengths on which to build, including:

1) Couples' longstanding marital and employment history and commitment to each other and their family members as evidenced by their willingness to open their home to Edna and Elle and her children.
2) Families' commitment to care for one another

Facilitating factors for intervention
The family members' willingness to care for one another is the primary facilitating factor in the intervention. Additionally, having resources within the family (e.g., Elle's availability to care for Edna and her expertise in nursing care) and outside the family (e.g., Alzheimer's Association, alternative school, etc.) enable the family to access needed services.

Limitations and barriers to intervention

1) While plans are underway to address the overcrowding situation, change may take some time. Coping with the stress of the cramped living quarters in the interim presents a particular challenge.

2) While she agreed to attend the alternative school and participate in family therapy, Samantha appears angry and may become reluctant to actively engage, particularly if the home continues to be a stressful environment and she feels she has no attention or privacy.

3) The family may be feeling so overwhelmed by the multitude of issues and tasks to be addressed, they may be unable to mobilize for change.

Other care providers/referrals

1) School personnel at the alternative school and Samantha's regular school
2) Alzheimer's Association
3) Family Caregiver Support Program
4) Substance Abuse Treatment Program

Plan for involvement of individual family members, extended family members, significant others and friends

At this time, there is no plan to include other family members. However, the family mentioned that William has two sisters that live out of town and may be willing to help with Edna's care at some point.

Review and termination criteria/plan

All agreed that the goals will be achieved when the family members feel they are in better control of their lives, specifically:

1) Overcrowded housing issue has been resolved
2) Plans for Edna's long term care needs are determined
3) Elle's employment and housing plans are clarified
4) Samantha has successfully completed the court-mandated program and has returned to a student in good standing at her school (one-year minimum of no school violations)
5) Stephen has a permanent solution for housing.

Planned frequency and duration of intervention

Initially, the plan is for the social worker and family members to meet weekly. Social workers will be available by telephone in the interim. After the first four meetings, social worker and family will discuss the plan for ongoing contact. As issues resolve, meeting frequency will decrease with the plan being for termination to occur within three months of the intake.

Adapted from St. Anthony's Medical Center, St. Louis, Missouri; Missouri Department of Social Services

insurers or managed care companies may mandate an earlier end point. With a lessened focus on the relationship with the social worker than exists in individual work, the emphasis often falls on examining the ways the family wanted the dynamics of their relationship or their relationship with outside entities to be different, and the extent to which they have been successful. There is also likely to be some focus on translating the gains into future situations that the family can anticipate so that responses can be predicted. For example, if a family is struggling with the decision to allow an adolescent son freedom to develop a unique identity when he has a history of legal altercations, it will be useful for the family to consider ways in which they will manage that issue when he leaves home for college or when the next sibling reaches an age to declare herself or himself a separate person. These positions are all consistent with the principles of review and exploration highlighted earlier in Chapter 5 regarding terminating with individuals.

To take a different perspective, the following discussion will identify brief responses to ending work with families from the perspectives of the previously discussed theoretical frameworks, strengths and empowerment, narrative, and solution-focused approaches. These approaches strive to minimize the difficulty of endings. In general, they propose a naturalized and comfortable process that is flexible and controlled by clients whenever possible.

Endings with Strength and Empowerment

Viewing each family as individuals and as a whole means that the social worker's role is to help each person articulate her or his feelings about the ending (Wise, 2005). The family members, individually and as a group, can benefit from the opportunity to talk about feelings and insights about the strengths that each individual and the group brought to the intervention. These insights can reinforce the successes that have been accomplished through the intervention and enable the members to acknowledge the ending. Keeping in mind the original goal, the social worker and the family can focus on the future and the ways in which the changes can be sustained. If the goals they hoped for were not achieved, but the relationship is terminating nonetheless, the termination phase can focus on lessons learned that the family can use in the future.

Just as assessment and intervention with families is approached from a strengths perspective, so too is the termination process. Building on the strengths that were identified in the assessment process and those identified or created during the intervention phase, the strengths- and empowerment-oriented social worker can focus the termination process on strengths as well. The existing and new strengths can become the basis for the family to sustain the changes they have made. Together, the social worker and the family can review the family's strengths. The social worker can then ask the family to consider the way in which they can apply these strengths to future situations. The family can also use these strengths as coping skills when and if they encounter new challenges. For example, the social worker may ask the family members, "How can ending our work together help you to achieve your goals?" (Wise, 2005, p. 215). To further probe, you can ask the family members to speculate on their motivation and ability to continue working on their goals even after the formal intervention has ended.

Endings in Narrative-Focused Work

In narrative work, as with other approaches, there is an emphasis on normalizing the point at which the family decides to end. Narrative social workers often punctuate the ending of their work by working with families to develop rituals or ceremonies in which the family invites an audience to witness the changes they have made and to rejoice in their achievements. For example, asking siblings, other professional who have worked with the family, and/or extended family to attend a meeting can be a validating experience for all. Public acknowledgment of the family's successes not only celebrates them but also provides a structure for their supportive maintenance when the work is over (Morgan, 2000). This focus, like solution-focused work, represents a departure from traditional views of endings while acknowledging the same concerns about maintaining gains. The reduced emphasis on stages with specific boundaries in both these approaches emphasizes the view of the client as the expert.

Endings in Solution-Focused Work

Solution-focused work emphasizes ending almost from the beginning. As a short-term intervention approach, a solution-focused approach stresses that the clients have abilities to manage their lives competently. Because this approach is built on the premise that change can occur within a brief, time-limited period, using scaling,

© Lisa F. Young

an early question the social worker might ask is, "What [number] do you need to be in order not to come and talk to me anymore?" (De Jong, 2009). This question refers to the number from 1 to 10 that reflects the degree of well-being that the client reports. In this approach, a family's concerns about needing further work are honored, and they determine the number and content of further sessions. There is very little emphasis on the relationship between the social worker and the family because "not coming to talk to me anymore" is seen as the preferred reality and a natural and comfortable conclusion to a problem for which the family is already likely to have a solution (which the social worker helped to bring to light). In this sense, then, ending is seen as success almost by definition. Termination, as well as follow-up (e.g., checking in with the family, inviting the family for a return of follow-up session, or making referrals) when possible, is as equally important to the planned change process as any other stage of the relationship. Bringing the intervention to a close can serve as an opportunity for the social worker and family to engage in: (1) a recital (i.e., a review of the work); (2) creating an awareness of the changes made; (3) consolidating gains (i.e., celebrating changes and successes), and; (4) providing feedback to the social worker; and (5) preparing the family for handling challenges that arise in the future (Collins et al., 2013, p. 447).

Evaluation of Social Work Practice with Families

Evaluation of family interventions helps you as a practitioner and your organization determine if the intervention has been complete and is effective. By gathering information from the family members at the beginning of the working relationship, evaluation of family interventions also enables the social worker to identify the changes that were or were not made and the reasons that the intervention was or was not effective (Hull & Mather, 2006). If you have used evidence-based practice approaches, your evaluation can provide insights and contributions to your practice or your agency's practice. While evaluation of your interventions with individuals can yield similar information about your practice, it is critical that you do not assume that evaluation of family interventions can be completed with the same evaluative strategies. Just as families are unique, so, too, are evaluations of family interventions.

The ongoing evaluation of the family work that social workers do is often largely contingent on, and defined by, the context and goals of the original contact. For example, if you are working with a family in child or adult protective services, the first goal may be the continued safety of a child(ren) or adult. There may be other goals, such as the parents' improved skills in managing a family, meeting the health needs of a particular child or adult, or providing appropriate care for an older adult. Goals in cases such as these, in most cases, are documented in written goals, and you will want to pay attention to them along the way.

QUICK GUIDE 21   STRENGTHS-BASED MEASURES FOR FAMILIES

Caregiver Well-Being Scale

I. ACTIVITIES

Below are listed a number of activities that each of us do or someone does for us. Thinking over the past three months, indicate to what extent you think each activity has been met by circling the appropriate number on the scale provided below. You do not have to be the one doing the activity. You are being asked to rate the extent to which each activity has been taken care of in a timely way.

1. Rarely	2. Occasionally	3. Sometimes	4. Frequently	5. Usually

	1	2	3	4	5
1. Buying food	1	2	3	4	5
2. Taking care of personal daily activities (meals, hygiene, laundry)	1	2	3	4	5
3. Attending to medical needs	1	2	3	4	5
4. Keeping up with home maintenance activities (lawn, cleaning, house repairs, etc.)	1	2	3	4	5
5. Participating in events at church and/or in the community	1	2	3	4	5
6. Taking time to have fun with friends and/or family	1	2	3	4	5
7. Treating or reward yourself	1	2	3	4	5
8. Making plans for your financial future	1	2	3	4	5

II. NEEDS

Below are listed a number of needs we all have. For each need listed, think about your life over the past three months. During this period of time, indicate to what extent you think each need has been met by circling the appropriate number on the scale provided below.

1. Rarely	2. Occasionally	3. Sometimes	4. Frequently	5. Usually

	1	2	3	4	5
1. Eating a well-balanced diet	1	2	3	4	5
2. Getting enough sleep	1	2	3	4	5
3. Receiving appropriate health care	1	2	3	4	5
4. Having adequate shelter	1	2	3	4	5
5. Expressing love	1	2	3	4	5
6. Expressing anger	1	2	3	4	5
7. Feeling good about yourself	1	2	3	4	5
8. Feeling secure about your financial future	1	2	3	4	5

Source: Berg-Weger, Rubio, & Tebb, 2000; Tebb, Berg-Weger, & Rubio, 2013.

QUICK GUIDE 22   STRENGTHS-BASED MEASURES FOR FAMILIES

Family Support Scale

Name _____   Date _____

Listed below are people and groups that oftentimes are helpful to members of a family raising a young child. This questionnaire asks you to indicate how helpful each source is to your family.

Please circle the response that best describes how helpful the sources have been to your family during the past three to six months. If a source of help has not been available to your family during this period of time, circle the NA (Not Available)

How helpful has each of the following been to you in terms of raising your child(ren):	Not Available	Not at All Helpful	Sometimes Helpful	Generally Helpful	Very Helpful	Extremely Helpful
1. My parents	NA	1	2	3	4	5
2. My spouse or partner's parents	NA	1	2	3	4	5
3. My relatives/kin	NA	1	2	3	4	5
4. My spouse or partner's relatives/kin	NA	1	2	3	4	5
5. Spouse or partner	NA	1	2	3	4	5
6. My friends	NA	1	2	3	4	5
7. My spouse or partner's friends	NA	1	2	3	4	5
8. My own children	NA	1	2	3	4	5
9. Other parents	NA	1	2	3	4	5
10. Co-workers	NA	1	2	3	4	5
11. Parent groups	NA	1	2	3	4	5
12. Social groups/clubs	NA	1	2	3	4	5
13. Church members/minister	NA	1	2	3	4	5
14. My family or child's physician	NA	1	2	3	4	5
15. Early childhood intervention program	NA	1	2	3	4	5
16. School/day-care center	NA	1	2	3	4	5
17. Professional helpers (social workers, therapists, teachers, etc.)	NA	1	2	3	4	5
18. Professional agencies (public health, social services, mental health, etc.)	NA	1	2	3	4	5
19. _____	NA	1	2	3	4	5
20. _____	NA	1	2	3	4	5

Source: Dunst, Trivette, & Deal, 2003, pp. 155–157

QUICK GUIDE 23   FAMILY STRENGTHS PROFILE

Recording Form

Family Name _____   Interviewer _____

INSTRUCTIONS

The Family Strengths Profile provides a way of recording family behaviors and noting the particular strengths and resources that the behaviors reflect. Space is provided down the left-hand column of the recording form for listing behavior exemplars. For each behavior listed, the interviewer simply checks which particular qualities are characterized by the family behavior. (Space is also provided to record other qualities not listed.) The interviewer also notes whether the behavior is viewed as a way of mobilizing intrafamily or extrafamily resources, or both. A completed matrix provides a graphic display of a family's unique functioning style.

FAMILY MEMBER	DATE OF BIRTH	AGE	RELATIONSHIP

FAMILY BEHAVIOR	Commitment	Appreciation	Time	Sense of Purpose	Congruence	Communication	Role Expectations	Coping Strategies	Problem Solving	Positivism	Flexibility	Balance			TYPE OF RESOURCE	
															Intrafamily	Extrafamily

NOTES

Source: Dunst, Trivette, & Deal, 1988

The focus of evaluation in interventions with families is on the family unit itself and not the individuals within the family. An examination of the family's ability to have new behaviors and coping skills, realistic attitudes, and new information and learning will promote enhanced well-being for the entire family (Wise, 2005). For example, if you and the family are able to determine that the power has shifted among and between the family members, this could be indicative of an effective family intervention. Alternatively, if family members agree that the stress level within the family has decreased or the quality of the interactions has improved, the intervention may be deemed successful. Family evaluations may focus not only on the outcomes of the goals established during the assessment and planning phases, but on the relationship with the social worker and the agency as well.

Strengths-Based Measures for Families   While family-focused intervention evaluations differ from evaluations of individual and group practice, the evaluative strategies described in Chapter 5 provide a basis for developing plans for evaluation of family interventions. Ensuring that the focus of the evaluation is on the family and not the individual members, strategies such as single-system design, goal attainment scaling, and case studies, can be effective evaluation tools. There has been an array of evaluation measurements developed specifically for use with families. While the scope of this book cannot address the vast number of selections that are available for evaluating your practice with families, the following discussion will briefly explore the selection of measures that are grounded in a strengths-based perspective.

Several instruments are designed to be used in strengths-based practice with families and also to allow social workers to document their service effectiveness (see Early & Newsome (2005) for detailed review of strengths-based family assessment tools). Standardized evaluative tools are increasingly important as agencies and practitioners are held accountable for measurement of outcomes by funders, boards of directors, client advocacy organizations, and the social work profession itself. Additionally, practice evaluation instruments can be helpful in maintaining the social worker's focus. Some of the instruments emerged as strengths-based emphases were introduced in the 1980s and remain useful tools today because they measure family perceptions and assets. With the advent of evidence-based practice, there has been an increase in the number of standardized family assessment measures from which to select. Early and Newsome (2005, pp. 390–391) offer the following guidelines to consider when incorporating standardized assessment measures in family-focused social work practice:

1) Select a measure with an emphasis on consistency and appropriateness to client situation.
2) Explain to the family the reasons for using the measure (e.g., method for efficiently collecting information to guide the helping process) and specific details about the measure's contents and outcomes.

3) Allow for adequate and appropriate time, space, and materials for completing the measures.

4) Ensure that the family members understand the items and feel comfortable asking questions about the assessment tool.

5) When at all possible, score the measure in the family's presence.

6) Share the scores and interpretations with the family.

7) Maintain the assessment in agency records for review/comparison in the future.

8) Repeat the measure over time to assess progress toward goals.

While your agency or you will select the evaluative strategy that is most appropriate to your setting and the families that you serve, the following is a small representative list of reliable strengths and empowerment-focused evaluation measures that may be of help to you as you consider evaluating your practice:

- *The Caregiver Well-Being Scale* (Berg-Weger, Rubio, & Tebb, 2000; Tebb, 1995; Tebb, Berg-Weger, & Rubio, 2013): A strengths-based clinical measure to help family caregivers or adults or children identify the strengths and areas for change in their caregiving experience, this scale is applicable for families caring for adults and/or children. See Quick Guide 21 for an example.

- *The Parent Empowerment Survey* (see Dunst, Trivette, & Deal, 2003): Designed to measure parental perceptions of control over life event (see Herbert, Gagnon, Rennick, & O'Loughlin, 2009 for review of empowerment measures).

- *The Family Support Scale* (see Dunst et al., 2003): Measures what is helpful to families. See Quick Guide 22 for an example.

- *The Family Strengths Profile* (see Dunst et al., 2003): Designed to chronicle family functioning, the profile provides a qualitative format for identifying and assessing family strengths and type of resources needed. Quick Guide 23 provides an example of this measure.

- *The Family Resource Scale* (see Dunst et al., 2003): Measures the adequacy of resources in households with young children and emphasizes success in meeting needs, while it also identifies needs.

- *The Family Functioning Style Scale* (see Dunst et al., 2003): Measures family values, coping strategies, family commitments, and resource mobilization. Families indicate to what degree various statements are "like my family."

- *The Family Empowerment Scale* (Koren, DeChillo, & Friesen, 1992): Measures family empowerment on three levels: family, service system, and community/ political.

• *The Behavioral and Emotional Rating Scale: A Strengths-Based Approach to Assessment* (Epstein, 2004) and *The Behavioral and Emotional Rating Scale (2nd edition): Youth Rating Scale* (Epstein, Mooney, Ryser, & Pierce, 2004). These scales focus on children and youth to determine the presence of behavioral or emotional conditions.

In strengths- and empowerment-oriented measurements, self-reporting is seen as an asset. Self-reporting can complement the traditionally-oriented, scientific measurements in which the goal of objectivity is thought to conflict with the biases in self-reporting. Bias is inherent within self-reported information because it is difficult to be objective about yourself. The strengths perspective supports the expertise of individuals and families about their own lives, experience, and aspiration, thereby making self-report a natural and theoretically consistent method of data collection.

The empirical procedures in these scales are just a few among many. Some of these are flexible and, with creativity, they can apply to a variety of situations. Using both quantitative and qualitative evaluative strategies can provide the social worker and the profession with a comprehensive picture of the intervention. Remember, as well, that all evaluative measures have their limitations. Drawing conclusions regarding the impact of the change may not be possible because change may have occurred separately from the intervention (Hull & Mather, 2006). Further, just because the goals of the intervention were not achieved does not mean that positive or meaningful change did not occur. In those situations in which the identified goals are not met by the time the intervention must end (i.e., as in the case of managed care, court- or school-mandated treatment, etc.) or the family terminates prior to the agreed upon ending point, the social worker must process this experience. Talking with a supervisor or colleagues regarding the possible reasons for this unanticipated outcome can be an opportunity to professional development for the social worker. While practice evaluations can be immensely helpful tools, they must be viewed within a context for family, yourself as a practitioner, and your agency.

Consider also your own role with the family and reflect on the viability of your relationship with them. Reflection is typically a more introspective and interactive process. Some questions you can ask yourself and members of the family are: Does each member feel valued as if she or he can contribute to the work? Are there issues regarding the family's culture? Does the family still agree with the direction of the work? How is the work changing their experience? Checking in with families, through a dialogic process, to make sure they feel heard, understood, and are invested in the work you are doing with them is just as important as it is with other levels of practice. Be certain as well to remain attuned to non-articulated feedback from the family members. Lack of follow through with assignments or commitments and nonverbal gestures can be indicators of the family members' feelings about the intervention (Hull & Mather, 2006).

STRAIGHT TALK ABOUT FAMILY INTERVENTION, TERMINATION, AND EVALUATION

Practice with families is a complex enterprise, and the intervention, termination and evaluation processes can include the unexpected. Family members have individual relationships, networks, and influences outside the family; therefore, the work that is accomplished within the intervention may be positively or negatively impacted by those external persons or groups. Within the family unit, the members may establish alliances that can also serve to strengthen or, in some cases, undermine the work within the intervention. Staying attuned to the family members' descriptions of their activities, relationships, and pressures may aid you in identifying those potential unanticipated occurrences within the intervention.

Just as with terminations with individuals, ending work with families can be emotional, particularly if the family members have developed a positive relationship with the social worker. The social worker may even be viewed as a member of the family; therefore, termination can elicit powerful reactions from the family. Sensitivity to the family's cultural norms and feelings is important for the social worker (Logan et al., 2008). Terminations can also elicit negative responses from some family members. As a result, members may refuse to participate or may display anger, denial, anxiety, or even regression as the termination approaches (Fortune, 2009). As the social worker, you may find yourself juggling a variety of different responses from family members to the ending of the family intervention. Addressing the individual and collective reactions to termination, while building on the strengths and gains of the intervention, can serve as an intervention in and of itself. Empowering the family to handle a change (perceived possibly as another loss) can be a meaningful new experience for the family as they can provide support to one another, model new behaviors, and mobilize strengths and resources developed during the intervention.

Evaluations of family interventions may also yield unexpected results. As you complete the evaluative process, you may have anticipated a particular outcome. If, for instance, you completed a pre- and post-intervention evaluation and the members of the family provide responses different from those you expected, you may be surprised at the family members' perceptions. Such occurrences can provide you with the opportunity to explore with the family their responses so you may gain insight into differing interpretations.

CONCLUSION

Facilitating an intervention with a family from engagement through termination and evaluation can be an immensely rewarding professional accomplishment for you and transformative for the family. Working with families requires the social worker to develop a repertoire of practice behaviors that include theoretical frameworks and skills to optimize family strengths and create and mobilize needed resources. This chapter further explored the integration of several theoretical approaches into social work practice with families and provided examples of ways in which the approaches can be applied to family situations. While refining your theoretically-driven social work practice is a lifelong process, identifying the theoretical approaches that are most consistent with your professional and personal value systems is an important early commitment for your social work development. Clarifying your own views on families and your role as a family social worker are exploratory exercises that can be helpful along your journey. Along with the provision of theoretical underpinnings for developing family interventions, this chapter highlights strategies for working with families that can be used in a range of settings and with diverse types of families.

MAIN POINTS

- Social workers have an array of theoretical perspectives to choose from to guide interventions with families. The social worker's training, philosophical and value system, and agency orientation will provide the primary influence for selection.

- Approaches for developing intervention plans with family groups highlighted in this chapter include strengths, empowerment, solution-focused, and narrative perspectives. While each shares similarities with the others, each has characteristics that make it unique.

- While specific practice behaviors are included within the various models of family intervention, there are basic skills for working with families that are found in most of the models: collaboration, using strengths, and supporting each member of the family's voice.

- Both your own and your clients' families can impact your work with families. Ongoing evaluation includes not only documenting achievement of externally imposed goals (e.g., school or court system) but also determining if your role and relationship with the family are working.

- Because the social work intervention with a family is multi-faceted and vulnerable to influences in and outside of the relationships, the evaluation process should incorporate candid discussion of those potentially influential factors. When ending work with families, the social worker must consider the potential impact of the professional-client relationships that formed during the work, the theoretical perspectives they used, and the practical, contextual dimensions of the work.

● The evaluation of families may emphasize an empirical process and/or a qualitative one. Standardized tools may be helpful in the evaluation process of family social work. In some family models, the emphasis is on the family's qualitative satisfaction with the outcome of the work; postmodern views of evaluation question the emphasis on standardized, scientific, and quantitative measures and remind social workers of their susceptibility to bias even when their work is supported by numbers.

EXERCISES

a. Case Exercises

1. Go to www.routledgesw.com/cases and review the case files for each member of the Sanchez family. A number of potential ethical issues may emerge as you work with this family. Using the NASW *Code of Ethics* (available at naswdc.org), identify the ethical issues or dilemmas that you anticipate could arise, citing the core social work and ethical principle that is relevant to the issue you identify. Upon completing this task, write a brief reflection on your findings.

2. Go to www.routledgesw.com/cases and review the case file for Carmen Sanchez. Address Critical Thinking Questions 1, 2, and 3. For Critical Thinking Question 2, identify at least one article in each of the two areas that concern Carmen: the impact on families of children with special health needs and outcomes of children in different types of families.

   Gather into groups with four to five of your classmates and develop a potential work plan for the family, based on your answers to the Critical Thinking Questions, focusing on the following areas:
   a. Identify the areas of potential challenge.
   b. Develop strategies for working with the entire Sanchez family around these challenges.
   c. Develop a plan to insure Carmen's maximum participation in the process.

3. Go to www.routledgesw.com/cases and review the case file for Carla Washburn. While Carla does not have the traditional family network, she does have a support system of persons to whom she is connected. Strategize about ways in which you might integrate each of the members of her support network into your intervention with Carla, identifying the strengths and potential contributions each can make. You may wish to review the case files and ecomap to develop your plan.

4. Go to wwww.routledgesw.com/cases and review the case file for Riverton. While the Riverton case initially appears to be a case focused on a neighborhood and a community, each community is comprised of individuals and families. In your role as the social worker who has just moved into the Riverton community, consider the Williams family (not described in the case file). Joyce

is a 48-year-old single mother who lives with her two children, 18-year-old Amanda and 17-year-old Jason, and her mother, 77-year-old Nina. Joyce divorced her husband as a result of his chronic alcoholism and she is worried about Jason as she knows he regularly drinks and uses marijuana. She has come to your agency and asked for your help with Jason. In light of the alcohol and drug issues that are occurring in the neighborhood, she feels powerless to handle the situation alone. She cannot afford to move out of the neighborhood as the house is owned by her mother and Joyce is unable to work full-time due to the caregiving responsibilities she has for her mother. Utilizing your knowledge of the Riverton community, its resources and current culture, develop a strategy for engaging, assessing, and intervening with the Williams family.

5. Go to www.routledgesw.com/cases and review the case for Brickville, focusing on Virginia Stone and her family. Based on the initial assessment and planning process you conducted in collaboration with Virginia (you may want to review Exercise #3 in Chapter 6), you and she have determined that a family conference will help to address the multiple concerns related to her mother's care, home ownership, and response to the proposed plans for neighborhood development. Using the information available to you (including the eco-map and genogram), develop two separate written plans for a family conference from two perspectives (narrative and solution-focused), including your responses to the following questions:

   • Who should be invited to participate in the family conference?
   • What is an optimal location for holding the conference?
   • Based on discussions with Virginia, develop a list of:
       ○ Potential agenda items
       ○ Individual and family strengths and areas of concern
       ○ Available and needed resources (within the family and community)
   • What is your anticipated role?
   • How might the family genogram and/or eco-map be incorporated into the family conference to develop a collaborative intervention, particularly as it relates to providing care for family members.

   Upon completing your plans for a family conference, reflect in writing on three areas:

   • Differences and similarities of a narrative or solution-focused approach;
   • Ways in which strengths-based perspective can be integrated into the conference;
   • Possible motivational interviewing strategies you can employ during the family conference.

6. Go to www.routledgesw.com/cases and review the case for Hudson City and the information provided in Exercise #4 in Chapter 6 regarding the Patel family. Using a strengths-based, solution-focused approach, develop a summary of the four-phase planned change model intervention (engagement, assessment/planning, intervention, termination/evaluation) you would facilitate with the

family. Be sure to include your theoretical approach(es) and incorporate the available resources in Hudson City.

b. Other exercises

7. As a social work practitioner at a community mental health center, you serve primarily individual and family client systems. You have recently been called by the James family and will conduct an intake appointment later on today. You have the following information about the family:
   - The father, self-identified as African American, made the appointment.
   - The family includes the mother, father, their two adolescent sons, and the father's parents who share the home with the family.
   - The elder son, age 18, is of most concern to the family, having expressed suicidal thoughts and recent but increasing withdrawal from school, family, and community life. Last year this son was a well-known school athlete and this year is not active in any school or athletic activities.
   - The parents suspect that alcohol or other drug use is involved in the family.
   - Both sons are reluctant to attend the appointment but will because their father has indicated they will.
   - Mother will "go along."

   In your preparation for this appointment, you consider several dimensions of the work that appear below. In small groups, discuss these and explore the questions. Report back to the entire class.
   a. You are not African American but are of Jewish heritage, which is relatively rare in the town. You know there are cultural differences between this family and you but believe you can bridge those to some extent because you consider yourself different culturally as well. What might you need to consider in your own assumptions?
   b. What model of family social work (of those in the chapter) do you believe will provide the most useful base? Discuss the reasons for this selection.
   c. What specific information will be important to first clarify?
   d. What specific approaches will be most important here with this particular family?
   e. How would you begin your intervention with this family? What practice behaviors will you use? What might you actually say? (Give an example)

7. Using the strengths-based strategies highlighted in this chapter, review the following list and describe in detail the way in which you would incorporate each into an intervention with the James family (from exercise #6):
   - Identify the issues and concerns, use active listening to enable the family members to tell their story and reflect on the information shared by the family members.
   - Acknowledge the pain.
   - Look for and point out strengths.

- Ask questions about survival, support, periods of time that were positive for the family, interests, dreams, goals, and pride.
- Resilience begins with what one believes and all people have the capacity for resilience
- Link strengths to the goals and dreams of the family members (both group and individual).
- Find opportunities for family/members to contribute to the intervention by helping to educate other members and serve as helping agents in achieving the family's agreed-upon goals.
- Use brainstorming for solutions as a strategy to help the family to view the situation and themselves differently.

8. Using a solution-focused approach, identify the techniques reviewed in this chapter that you believe will be appropriate for use with the James family described in exercise #6. Be specific in describing the way in which you would implement the strategies.

9. Termination and evaluation are critical aspects of the social work intervention. Conduct a review of the research to identify evidence-based practice skills and practices that are applicable for facilitating an effective termination and evaluation with a family. Share your findings in class and compare the results of your review.

CHAPTER 8

Social Work Practice with Groups: Engagement, Assessment, and Planning

Alone we can do so little. Together we can do so much.

Helen Keller

Key Questions for Chapter 8

(1) What competencies do I need to engage with and assess client systems at the group level of social work practice? (EPAS 2.1.10(a & b))

(2) How can I use evidence to practice research-informed practice and practice-informed research to guide the engagement and assessment practice behaviors with groups? (EPAS 2.1.6)

(3) What are the potential ethical issues that may occur in social work practice with groups, particularly in the early phases of the group's development? (EPAS 2.1.2)

(4) What knowledge and skills do I need for culturally competent group-level engagement and assessment practice? (EPAS 2.1.4)

NONE OF US LIVES WITHOUT SOCIAL CONNECTIONS. Many of us spend much of our lives negotiating our closeness to family, neighbors, friends, associates, and colleagues. Regardless of the ways in which the connections are experienced, virtually everyone has relationships to small collectives of other people or groups. In this context, group refers to the natural or planned associations that evolve through common interest (e.g., supporting the local Little League), state of being (e.g., having a child with a disability), or task (e.g., working together at a place of employment). Connectedness to groups depends not only on an individual's needs for affiliation but also on cultural norms, social arrangements, and social location (e.g., faith traditions, children's school, or neighborhood of residence). Within social work, **group work** is a "goal-directed activity that brings together people for a common purpose or goal" (Toseland & Horton, 2008, p. 298).

This chapter addresses the nature of groups, briefly reviews the history of group work in social work practice, and explores the dimensions of group work that relate to types and purposes of groups. Along with Chapter 9, in this chapter you will explore the purpose of groups and the relationship of groups to other areas of social work practice and practice behaviors for approaching the various aspects of the process of group work from engagement and assessment through intervention, termination, and evaluation.

GROUPS: THE SOURCE OF COMMUNITY

The social dimension of social work implies that people need and want to relate to others within the context of a "community." Yet the ways to meet this need are not always clear to social work professionals or the clients they serve. In contemporary U.S. culture, there is a pervasive emphasis on independence, mobility, and pursuit of success. Employment opportunities far away, upward mobility, and pressures to achieve professionally, socially, and economically influence most people and have developed new definitions and parameters for community. Such influences are not necessarily negative, but they can take a heavy toll on one's sense of connection and linkages (i.e., community) to stable, consistent groups on which they can depend over time.

A brief on-line search using the term "support groups" or a review of the advertisement section of any major newspaper provides evidence for the need we have to be connected with others. The number of announcements for therapy groups, support groups, community groups, and educational groups suggests that, as a culture, people are looking for a way to relate to others that is outside of themselves. In other words, people seek out groups in order to form a community. What do artificially created group experiences (i.e., those group experiences developed as a service) offer to people? Such groups provide a sense of belonging or community, a chance for reality testing, a source of mutual aid, and a means of empowerment (Reid, 2009, p. 433). By implication, social group work affords people the means to participate in significant experiences that may be lacking in the natural contexts of their everyday lives. While family, friends, and co-workers may be empathetic and supportive of our challenges, we may find a stronger connection with others who share our lived experiences.

Group as a Natural Orientation

Beyond individual idiosyncrasy, culture has an important impact on the amount and type of connections people seek. "People relations" (Diller, 2011, p. 73) is one of the cultural paradigms that distinguish one cultural group from another. For example, European-Americans are more apt to be individual in their social relationships in contrast with the collateral focus of many other cultures, Latino/a Americans, in particular. The degree to which a culture embraces individualism over collective demands varies greatly. Cultural paradigms within some groups that place more emphasis on group or familial connection than on independence can create conflicts among group members and between members and the group leader or facilitator (Ringel, 2005). The social worker facilitating the group must be culturally astute and aware of the cultural backgrounds of the group participants, and the cultural influences that affect group dynamics. Brown (2013) offers strategies for culturally competent group facilitation:

- Be open to learning about cultures different from your own.

- Do not overwhelm group members with too much information at one time.

- Regularly check-in with group members to ensure clarity of understanding.

- Attend to your communication skills, including the use of open-ended questions and avoidance of technical words and jargon.

- Ask group members to share traditions related to respectful interactions, culturally sensitive issues, and taboos (p. 52).

Exhibit 8.1 provides additional suggestions for developing culturally competent group practice skills.

Implications of Cultural and Global Connections for Social Work Practice   Because our society focuses more on self-determination than on cooperation, the social work professional may observe and perhaps question the impact of social connections through group interventions. As a social worker, you can make a commitment to self-determination (a hallmark of social work practice) and still know that it is not understood the same way in all cultures. The postmodern, reflective thinker will notice that in some circumstances, these concepts are empowering but they can also be oppressive due, in part, to the fact that the primary focus is on the individual as opposed to the larger, more inclusive group.

An increasingly global perspective on social work practice adds support for increasing sensitivity in this area. In 1996, the NASW *Code of Ethics* was amended to include an international perspective in the statement "social workers should promote conditions that encourage respect for cultural and social diversity within the United States and globally" (Standard 6.04). This addition to the *Code of Ethics* indicated an increasing global consciousness, a perspective that has become well integrated into social work practice in the 21st century.

Most practicing helping professionals benefit from exploring the degree to which their own orientation to achievement, independence, and competition as

EXHIBIT 8.1

Cultural Competence in Group Work

Building on cultural competence practice with individuals and families, social workers practicing with groups can benefit from incorporating culture-specific strategies as outlined here. While these practice guidelines are intended to enhance your cultural competence in social work with groups, they are not intended to suggest that these strategies apply to all members of these populations or to detract from the need for you to gain person-centered skills that focus on the individual members.

Latino/a Americans—With a commitment to collectivism, family traditions, harmonious interpersonal relationships, and respect, consider the following as you develop a group:

- Ensure that written materials are available in Spanish.
- Assess level of acculturation within various contexts, including physical and mental health, school, family, and work.
- Make no assumptions about group members and be open to learning about individual members' language, origins, and history.
- Be flexible and fluid with the timing and flow of the group meeting.
- Allow adequate time for engagement and trust and relationship building, including facilitators sharing personal information about themselves and their family.
- Use story circles/storytelling to enhance relationship building, collaborations, and social action.
- Integrate use of activities to encourage artistic expression (e.g., painting, acting, theater).
- For curriculum-oriented groups, ensure content and materials are culturally specific and appropriate.

African Americans—Consider the use of an Afrocentric approach which brings together experiences of Western and African cultures by:

- Emphasizing the interconnections among the individual, family, and community to enable the individual to see her or himself within those contexts.
- Maintaining a focus on African American culture and use of its strengths.
- Presenting yourself as respectful and genuine.
- Upon gaining acceptance by the group, maintaining a consistent and active role in the group process.

Asian-Americans—Understanding that Asian-American cultures differ from that of Western culture in a number of different areas can be helpful in incorporating such strategies as:

- Recognizing the importance that the family (versus the individual), harmony, independence, privacy, expression of feelings, and respect for authority plays can make a group intervention complex.
- Given the diverse groups within the Asian culture, gaining insight into your own assumptions, biases, and lack of information and the implications of each of these for the intervention.

- Understanding potential differences in communication styles (i.e., emphasis on non-verbal communication) can enable you to be comfortable with silence, for instance.
- Acknowledging group members' strengths, particularly in terms of bicultural skills.
- Considering impact of similarities and differences in areas of: length of time in the U.S., cultural origins, migration and loss issues, acculturation to Western culture, intergenerational and gender roles/conflicts, and experiences in the U.S. (particularly related to discrimination and oppression).
- Consider such techniques as: normalizing feelings and experiences, psychoeducational activities, non-confrontational approaches, and self-disclosure.

Native Americans—While few group work approaches have been developed with specific emphasis on the Native American culture, strategies to consider including are:

- Strive for each member's voice to be heard, specifically in terms of sharing individual stories and making decisions for the group.
- Acknowledge and gather information on tribal-specific traditions, ceremonies, spiritual implications, and context.
- Incorporate positive and honest humor.
- Maintain consistency in being "present" and genuine with group members.

Undocumented Immigrants—With a diverse array of personal and family histories and a potentially high level of anxiety regarding legal status and possible deportation, group work with immigrants who are undocumented can benefit from a specialized skill set, including:

- Acknowledge and celebrate the members' resilience to face challenges and the strengths they have developed as a result of their lived experiences.
- Be knowledgeable about the legal issues associated with having an undocumented status.
- Ensure support of agency administration to provide services to this population.
- Active outreach may be needed to enable this population to feel comfortable in joining a group.
- Clarify for yourself the information that you need to know and that which you do not need to know—group members may be reluctant to share specific information regarding their living situations.
- Promote relationship building and trust by inviting members to share their stories and later, addressing such issues as marginalization, isolation, and discrimination.

Sources: Chen, Budianto, & Wong, 2011, pp. 90–93; Furman, Rowan, & Bender, 2009; Greif & Morris-Compton, 2011; Harvey, 2011, p. 268; López and Vargas, 2011, pp. 144–145; McWhirter et al., 2011, pp. 79–80; and Ringel, 2005.

cultural variants is not compatible with the cooperation and collaboration that clients from other cultures may value more highly. Regardless of your own cultural heritage, take care not to privilege your position as normal just because it is the one with which you are most familiar. You may be well served in some instances, but impeded in your effectiveness in others. For instance, independence, as an ideal, can create obstacles in working cross-culturally with clients who do not share an understanding or enthusiasm for its relevance in their lives. As an example, if you encounter a child, Jared, in a school setting, who appears to lack an eager, competitive spirit, who seldom raises his hand when a teacher asks a question, and who always defers to others, you may attribute a deficit of one kind or another to him. You may find him slow, shy, or lethargic, and you may see him as dependent, or even as depressed or developmentally delayed. Jared may simply be reflecting the cultural imperative to cooperate, to prioritize the communications of others, and to behave demurely in the company of people who are older and who have authority.

The nature of "groupness" is complex and variable according to social location. While all people need and seek social connections, this phenomenon is tempered and shaped by cultural expectations related to family and community, customs, propriety, loyalty, authority, individualism, and the way in which these factors fit together. Although Western values of competitiveness and individualism have been responsible for much of the accomplishments and power of U.S. culture, these values have the potential to create disconnection, isolation, and detachment as well as a fertile environment for the design of constructed groups, particularly in the human services. The social work profession has responded to and continues to be vigilant about this need throughout a long history of social work group practice.

Historical and Contemporary Contexts for Group Work

Like other legacies in social work, social work practice with groups has roots in England and the Industrial Revolution. The political and economic context of this time period resulted in disrupted lives and broken social connections of countless children and families. Such a sense of isolation led groups to come together around common interests and needs. With a sense of mission, volunteers of this era brought groups together for social, recreational, advocacy, and social action. The time was ripe for the development of group social work (Alissi, 2009; Furman, Rowan, & Bender, 2009; Reid, 1997).

Group work developed in the United States in the 19th century in the midst of professional and political tensions regarding the perceived need (or lack thereof) for public, religious, or philanthropic organizations to involve themselves in the lives of U.S. citizens. Inspired by religious and philanthropic organizations, the concept of bringing people together in small groups became a popular strategy for helping clients within community-based settings (e.g., YMCA/ YWCA, Boy/Girl Scouts, and faith-based community centers). The early approach focused on individuals and their need for change. In contrast, another group of helping professionals of the time used group efforts focused instead on social reform with a humanitarian impulse, and believed that social change was the critical ingredient in making a positive difference in people's lives. These reformers were more likely to see the group (rather than the individual) as the medium for that form of intervention. You will notice here some reverberations from the social control/social change tension discussed in Chapter 1. In addition, group work was not yet firmly a part of social work practice. This segment of the group movement were often partisan Socialists, concerned with political action and identified with not just social work, but also elected officials, clergy, and public health officials, to name a few.

By the end of the 19th century, the Progressive Era added fuel to the growth of group work. Settlement houses, community organizations, and self-help groups sprang up in response to the influx of immigrants and the dramatic needs of the teeming urban environment. These organizations stressed group methods (e.g., language classes, cooking groups, recreation, the arts, and youth services) and were aimed at the social justice issues of inclusion and acculturation. They were designed to maximize the ability of newly arrived residents to achieve their desired quality of life through access to society's assets. Still, group work was not clearly identified with social work.

Throughout the 1930s, group work continued to have less status than social casework in the minds of many professionals. This perception was due, in part, to the fact that recently-developed curricula in schools of social work were aimed at individual casework, a result of the pervasiveness of Freud's influence. Group work had by then a strong association with recreational activities (e.g., sponsoring dances or creating arts and crafts with children). Such activities were not held in as great esteem as the more clinically focused casework. When group work had developed a greater affinity to social work, practitioners proposed their own association, which emphatically declared itself a part of social work, but as a discrete unit, using distinctive methods within the practice of social work with groups.

In the 1950s, group work expanded from the community into hospitals and psychiatric facilities and introduced **therapeutic group work** or **treatment groups**. These therapeutically focused groups were designed to heal or help people change. This shift altered the nature of the formerly community-based model by adopting a more professional stance. Through the process, group work began to impede on the boundaries of casework, and the distinctions between the two started to blur.

Three classic models for group practice—the **social goals model**, the **reciprocal model**, and the **remedial model**—emerged between the late 1950s and the 1970s. They reflect much of the work that came before them, as well as after, because theory is often embedded in earlier theory. Social workers still use these perspectives in contemporary social work practice with groups in various current contexts and will be discussed in detail later in this chapter and in Chapter 9. See Exhibit 8.2 for a brief description of the origin and aim of these three classic models.

By the 1970s, the **Council on Social Work Education (CSWE)** the accrediting body for social work education in the United States, required all schools of social work to adopt a generalist focus throughout undergraduate programs and for the

EXHIBIT 8.2	MODEL TYPE	MAJOR FOCUS	SOCIAL WORKER ROLE	EXAMPLE	ORIGINAL AUTHORS
Classic Models for Social Group Work, 1950s to 1970s	Social Goals	Democratic values, social conscience, responsibility, and action; uses strengths of members.	Fosters social consciousness and serves as model for democratic values.	School groups that promote student affiliation and contributions to student governance.	Pappel and Rothman, 1962
	Reciprocal	Interaction in an attempt to fulfill mutual affiliation goals; mutual aid.	Serves as mediator between each member and the group as a whole; finds common ground.	Adolescent children of incarcerated parents developing coping skills.	Schwartz, 1961
	Remedial	Prevention and rehabilitation aimed at behavior change and reinforcing individual behaviors.	Works both in the group and outside of it to ameliorate conditions in environments; acts as motivator.	Discharge group in mental health settings to increase patient capacity to negotiate community.	Vinter, 1974

first half of master's programs. With an aim toward integrating all practice methods across levels, the generalist focus requirement served to de-emphasize the distinctive role of group work as a method and, many believe, to forsake its soul. Most school curricula already emphasized casework, and with the CSWE mandate, there was little incentive to develop more group work courses. The result was that many social work students did not complete coursework that focused on social work practice with groups. Nevertheless, a strong core of social workers committed to the power of social work with groups remained, and the International Association for Social Work with Groups (IASWG) was founded in 1979. First issued in 1999 and revised in 2006, the IASWG provides *Standards for Social Work Practice with Groups*, a guide for effective practice with groups that is widely used in contemporary social work practice. The second edition of the *Standards* provides practitioners with guidelines and practice perspectives for gaining knowledge, tasks, and skills for use in group work that include: core values and knowledge; phases of the group process (pre-group planning, beginning, middle, and ending); and ethical considerations.

The climate of social work practice today offers practitioners a unique opportunity to work with groups in ways that will help to meet the needs individuals have for genuine connection and social action. A group-focused orientation is one of the characteristics that distinguish social work group practice from psychology or mental health counseling groups. In group work, the social worker's effort is on the development of the group, and while individual well-being is one goal, it is achieved through the interactions and structures of the group.

DIMENSIONS OF SOCIAL WORK PRACTICE WITH GROUPS

For this discussion, a social work group intervention refers to a small, face-to-face gathering of people who come together for a particular purpose. The major dimension of a group experience is the interdependence among person, group, and social environment. Like many aspects of social work practice, the concept of group work can be delineated in several ways to represent distinctions. As we begin this exploration into social work practice with groups, the first issue to consider is the purpose that a group intervention can serve. To place the following discussion into a practice and organizational context, consider that groups provide avenues for socialization or re-socialization while occurring within an agency or community environment— which can, at times, result in a peace co-existence or conflict (Ephross, 2011).

Types, Forms, and Functions of Groups

The major division at the most basic level in social work groups is between formed or constructed groups and unconstituted, **natural groups.** Natural groups occur in the context of socialization and are not organized from the outside. These may be based on spontaneous friendships, common interests, or common social location, such as living in the sophomore wing of a college dormitory. Families are the original natural group. Natural groups usually do not have formal sponsorship or agency affiliation, but social workers may have occasion to work with them (particularly families). Social workers and their agencies can also provide support to these naturally formed groups in a variety of ways (e.g., offer meeting space, access to office equipment, or staff consultation).

Social action (empowerment)

Social workers are more likely to facilitate **formed groups**, which are organized by an institution or organization, such as a school or hospital, agency, or community center. Formed groups can be divided between three models: **task groups,** designed to accomplish a specific purpose; **social action** or **goals groups** (previously described), focused on advocating for social justice; and **client groups,** geared toward personal change. These models can be further delineated as follows:

committees working toward a goal.

1. Task groups include task forces, committees and commissions, legislative bodies, staff meetings, interprofessional teams, case conferences and staffing, and social action groups. The task group is aimed at facilitating a change that is external to the group with a focus on a specified purpose, policy development, completing a product or a plan, or creating a mechanism for collaborative

decision-making (Strand et al., 2009, p. 42). The social worker can function as a convener, member, chair/leader, facilitator, or a combination of these roles. The social worker in the leadership role is responsible for initiating and monitoring the meeting and progress toward the stated goals and objectives, managing the group interactions and maintaining focus (Furman et al., 2009). Task groups are explored in more detail in Chapter 10. You may also visit http://www.routledgesw.com/ to learn about a task group that functions in the community of Riverton to oversee the activities and growth of the community.

2. Social action or goals groups are a form of a task group created to address a social issue to empower individuals or a community (Toseland & Horton, 2008). The social action approach has a number of strengths, including (a) the collective effort of a group of people can be more powerful than that of the individual; (b) the social worker is not the expert leader, but a facilitator for the group; (c) groups can help to harness the individual capacity to create social change; (d) professionals and group members work in partnership; (e) the agenda is determined by the group members; and (f) groups can create a safe environment for the individual and collective exploration of issues of oppression, discrimination, and disadvantage (Fleming, 2009, pp. 275–276). As with task groups overall, the social worker can function in a variety of roles. As an example, the parents of the Riverton community come together to address their growing concerns about alcohol abuse among the youth in their neighborhoods.

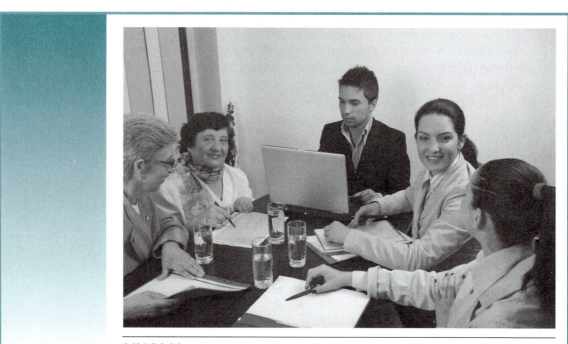

© Blaj Gabriel

3. Client treatment groups may be aimed at support, education, growth, therapy, socialization, empowerment, and remediation. Client groups can be formed for two purposes:

    (a) **Reciprocal groups**, also referred to as support, mutual aid and mutual sharing groups, form to enable members who share a common experience to provide support and mutual aid to one another. With an emphasis on self-help and not specifically on therapeutic intervention, reciprocal groups can range from informal to highly structured to psychoeducational (blending of mutual support and educational focus). Reciprocal groups provide members with an opportunity to experience "shared empathy," which is the experience that brings members together and provides the potential for cohesion and mutual problem-solving (Furman et al., 2009, p. 63). Finding others who share similar life experiences can be validating and affirming for group members as well as provide opportunities to share valuable insights and coping strategies.

    This model for group work intervention has wide applicability, particularly among adults who face a new or unanticipated struggle and can benefit from education as well as group support. **Psychoeducational groups** focus on the education of group members regarding a psychological condition. One approach has been especially helpful to parents of young adult children experiencing mental illness. Frequently, the individual develops new symptoms in their early 20s; their parents may not have been touched by mental illness before. Local community mental health agencies often offer group sessions to the families to help them learn more about mental illnesses, what to expect in terms of their children's behavior and symptoms, how they can best provide support, and how they can cope with their own grief. These groups, which were started in the mental health arena by the National Alliance for the Mentally Ill (NAMI), have been particularly effective. Psychoeducational groups usually incorporate considerable factual information, but also rely on a supportive and accepting attitude both by worker/facilitators and other group members. Groups can be structured, with a curriculum and lessons in sequence, or freer in form. In some locations, parents who originally attended these groups have become group facilitators themselves, generally with training and technical support from the local agency.

    Social work involvement in reciprocal groups can range from initiator to facilitator to "silent" support person. The social worker role will be related primarily to the origins of the group (i.e., a larger role if social worker-initiated and a lesser role if member-initiated). In the case of a psychoeducationally focused group, the social worker may have a more formalized role based on possessing a particular knowledge or skill expertise. An example of a psychoeducational group is a grief support group for children living in the Riverton community who have lost a family member to alcohol or drug abuse.

An example of a **support group** in contemporary life is the support group for persons who are in the early stages of dementia, most often of the Alzheimer's disease type. Social workers are frequently in the position of working with persons who either have dementia, live with someone who has dementia, or love someone who has dementia. The associated stigma and isolation for some of the men and women living with dementia can be as devastating as the disease. This makes support a critical component, and the support group can offer a chance to share feelings, combat loneliness, gain information, exchange resources, and normalize the overall experience. Similar issues arise for families and other loved ones of someone with dementia and social workers may facilitate groups for them as well. Social workers need to understand the effects, symptoms, and issues that people with or touched by dementia experience. Alzheimer's disease and other dementia can invoke volatile emotions, therefore it is particularly important for facilitators to acknowledge and understand their own reactions and biases regarding the disease and those living with it.

(b) **Remedial groups** are for changing behavior, restoring functioning, or promoting coping strategies of the individual members who join the group voluntarily or involuntarily (Toseland & Horton, 2008). The social worker's role is typically that of facilitator or leader, because clinical knowledge and skills are necessary for direction. Returning to the Riverton community as an example, a remedial group may be formed at a mental health center or hospital to provide psychotherapy for substance-abusing clients.

In most cases, the group's major purpose and form is evident in its title. Many groups have multiple purposes. Groups may also be distinguished by the role of the social worker. In treatment or psychotherapy groups, the social worker may use methods consistent with counseling and interpretation, while in educational groups the focus may be on teaching and processing. Task groups are likely to direct the social worker's focus on facilitation, as she or he assists the group in taking action to address an undertaking. See Exhibits 8.3–8.5 which depict phases of group interventions, including social worker and member roles. Utilizing the descriptions of groups developed by and with residents of Riverton, these exhibits contain examples of the beginning phases—pre-group planning, engagement, and assessment—of group processes implementing the social goals/action, reciprocal, and remedial models.

The first decision that you must make is to determine if a group experience will meet the needs you have identified. While group interventions can be powerful and have the potential to address a number of individual, community, or societal needs, you must assess the situation at hand to discern if a group approach will be most

---

PHASE I: BEGINNING

EXHIBIT 8.3

Riverton Against Youth Drinking ("RAYD"): An Example of Social Goals/Action Group

Background: Concerned about the use and abuse of alcohol among their adolescent children, a group of parents in the Riverton community approach a local community service agency to ask for help in addressing this problem. Later phases of the group's work will be highlighted in Chapter 9.

Note: While the stages of group interventions are not linear and may, in fact, overlap, the following depicts a possible approach to responding to the identified need.

PRE-GROUP PLANNING AND ENGAGEMENT	ASSESSMENT
Meet with parent groups to gather information	Determine individual and group members' "agendas"
Identify current and potential stakeholders who are/may be invested in the issue	Conduct community assessment, including needs, assets, and resources (see Chapter 10 for further information on community assessment)
Identify interests of group members	
Research evidence for approaches for facilitating social goals group on this topic	Gather and analyze data from assessment; identify and prioritize options for intervention
Determine general focus/goal of launching an intervention	Re-determine/confirm focus of Intervention
Identify role for agency and social worker	Finalize plan for intervention, including objectives, tasks, activities, persons/groups responsible, time frame, and plans for evaluation and sustainability
Arrange first meeting and logistics, including time, location, refreshments, etc.	Re-clarify agency and social worker roles and responsibilities
Develop agenda for first meeting	Revisit needs
	Make plans for continued assessment

---

effective. In addition to bringing people together who have a common life experience, concern, or need, a group effort can promote an environment for creativity and problem-solving, influence individual thoughts and behaviors, and provide a convenient strategy for delivery of services to a large group of clients with similar issues (Garvin & Galinsky, 2008). While all of these can be valid reasons for launching a group intervention, consider if the potential gains to be achieved for the group as individuals and a collective are optimally efficacious and efficient.

EXHIBIT 8.4

Riverton Children's Grief Support Group: An Example of Reciprocal Group

PHASE I: BEGINNING

Background: A social worker in a local community service agency has become aware of a number of children of Riverton who have lost a parent to alcohol and substance-related deaths. The social worker takes steps toward offering a support group to the community that includes to an educational focus. Later phases of the group's work will be highlighted in Chapter 9.

Note: While the stages of group interventions are not linear and may, in fact, overlap, the following depicts a possible approach to responding to the identified need.

PRE-GROUP PLANNING AND ENGAGEMENT

Gather information to support the need and appropriateness of this group intervention

Analyze data and confirm plans to move forward with forming group

Research evidence for approaches for facilitating reciprocal group with children

Determine group components:

- Composition of group (number, age, range, and gender)
- Recruitment strategies
- Format (open or closed)
- Time frame (time-limited or ongoing)

Determine and implement appropriate recruitment strategies

Conduct screening interview with potential members (see note in Assessment regarding group membership)

Invite group members (including obtaining written permission from legal guardians)

Determine roles of agency, social work facilitator, children, and legal guardians

ENGAGEMENT AND ASSESSMENT

Pre-Group

Prior to first meeting, meet individually with parents/guardians and separately with children to assess interest in and appropriateness (i.e., "fit") for psychoeducational support group

First Session

Introduce self and ask members to introduce themselves

Orient members to group, including review of purpose, goals, rules, norms, format, time frame, intervention plan, termination, evaluation, and confidentiality

Assess individual member goals, function, and interaction with other members

Assess group cohesiveness

Continue to assess individual and group needs (for support and education), interests, strengths, and "agendas"

Monitor and assess social worker role

Administer pre-group measurements to be utilized in the evaluation process

EXHIBIT 8.5

*Riverton
Mental Health
Center Group
for Persons
with Dual
Diagnosis: An
Example of
Remedial
Group*

PHASE I: BEGINNING

Background: A new social worker at the Riverton Mental Health Center has recently assumed leadership for a clinical intervention group for persons with dual diagnoses (i.e., substance abuse and mental illness) who receive outpatient services at the agency. The group is diverse in membership, including mixed genders, range of ages, and mandated and voluntary members. Membership turnover is dependent on members' "graduation" from the treatment program; therefore, the group often has entering and exiting members. Two new members have been referred to the group. This will be the first time new members have been referred since the social worker took over responsibility for the group. Later phases of the group's work will be highlighted in Chapter 9.

Note: While the stages of group interventions are not linear and may, in fact, overlap, the following depicts a possible approach to responding to the identified need.

PRE-GROUP PLANNING AND ENGAGEMENT	ENGAGEMENT AND ASSESSMENT
Obtain information on potential new members from referral sources and agency records, as appropriate	First Session
	Facilitate introduction of new members to group and review group expectations, norms, and rules
Research evidence on incorporating new members into an existing group	
Determine structure for admission, including criteria and process	Assess individual member goals, interests, and "fit" with group
	Assess member reactions to new group members
Meet with potential new members to screen for potential "fit" with group purpose, goals, and other members	
	Assess group cohesion
Invite new members to first session, introduce self, and provide orientation (e.g., composition, goals, expectations, norms, and rules)	Monitor/assess progress of other members

Recognizing that the individual's work is completed within the context of the group's fluid and interactive (and sometimes conflictual) dynamic, ask yourself if your desire to establish a group is meeting the client system's needs or your needs to efficiently serve a larger group of clients, meet your agency's revenue goals, mount an advocacy effort, or a combination of reasons. Quick Guide 24 provides a set of questions to consider as you are weighing the pros and cons of forming a group.

QUICK GUIDE 24   THE PROS AND CONS OF CREATING A
GROUP: QUESTIONS TO CONSIDER

As you weigh options for intervening with client, organization, and community systems, your first task is to determine if a group intervention is the most effective approach. To clarify your goals, consider the following questions:

- What are my reasons for choosing a group intervention over an individual or family intervention? Specifically, what are the needs that I have identified within my clients, my agency, or the community?
- What type of group intervention am I considering—social action, task, reciprocal, or remedial? What are my reasons for selecting this format for the intervention?
- What would the goal(s) of the group be? For the group? For me? For the agency or community?
- Will the group be an open or closed group (i.e., continuous group of members or open to members entering and leaving as needed)?
- Will the needs of the group members be best met by the group's duration being time-limited or open-ended?
- What will be the eligibility criteria for membership in the group and who will determine that?
- Do I have the requisite competence to facilitate a group intervention?
- Is the best approach to be the sole facilitator or would have a co-facilitator better serve the group?
- Do I have the support of my supervisor and agency administration? If not, am I aware of the process for gaining approval?
- What resources do I need to offer the group—possibilities include: meeting space, supplies, and funds for recruitment, refreshments, transportation, and child or adult care.
- What options exist for gaining the resources needed for the group?
- If this is a client group, will there be a charge for participation?
- What is the optimal number of members needed to participate in the group?
- Is there an adequate pool of potential group members within my agency or community?
- If I am uncertain about the pool of candidates for the group, how would I recruit members? What marketing strategies would be appropriate?
- What are the appropriate meeting dates, times, frequency, and longevity for the group?
- When *will* the group meetings begin?
- How much time do I need to prepare for leading the group?
- How will the group activities be recorded and evaluated?

Group Work Logistics

Social work groups may occur in community agencies, schools, community mental health centers, medical practices, public assistance offices, job training centers, residential care settings, church or faith facilities, or any other setting in which participants come together. The physical location may be a setting that group members already use (such as a school), or it may be a local community facility that makes itself available to such activities (a community hospital housing a grief and loss group, for example). Many residential settings such as prisons or mental health facilities also host social work groups, and these may be restricted to residents, their significant others, or may include a mix, such as a group for about-to-be-released prisoners and their partners.

Social work groups may differ on other variables such as the number of group meetings or the way in which they are organized. A group may meet for a fixed number of sessions or it may be ongoing, with changing membership over time. Some groups are structured as **closed groups** in which the membership and number of sessions are fixed. Many others are **open groups**, which allow new members to join at any time (or occasionally only at fixed times, such as after the third and sixth sessions). In developing plans for a group intervention, consider which of these formats will best meet the needs of the target population for the group. Open groups may offer flexibility for the facilitator and group members and economic advantages for the organization, but this format may lack the cohesiveness and continuity which prevail in a closed group format. Consider also the similarities and differences in the skill set required for facilitating each type of group. To effectively lead an open group, the social worker must be able to quickly develop an empathetic connection to the group members, promote cohesion in each meeting, and know the appropriate times to use more active and less active facilitative skills (Turner, 2011).

Being a voluntary or mandated group is another important distinction. In mandated situations, the social worker may have different expectations (not always realized) of member investment, and the influence of the mandating institution (such as the court) is likely to be greater relative to voluntary groups. Many scenarios in involuntary treatment employ groups as the method of choice. For example, recall the innovative practice in the family group decision-making model in Chapter 7, which involved a child protection violation and used a large group of community and extended family members. More traditional models also use groups for working with clients challenged by intimate partner violence, parenting issues, and substance abuse. Group work focuses particularly on interrelatedness and extension to the "outside" world, thus creating opportunities to engage involuntary clients in a process from which they can benefit long after the treatment period.

Three important areas for social work group practice include process (how people do what they do), linking (making connections with other people and situations), and inclusion (involving everyone present) (Thomas & Caplan, 1999). These areas are especially applicable for mandated groups as they focus on connecting members through the group process. Some of the skills necessary for successful group work are validating experience, clarifying, paraphrasing, linking one member's response to another's, collaborating, developing group rituals, roleplaying, setting tasks, and processing body language (Thomas & Caplan, 1999). These skills draw upon a combination of individual and extended group work skills that can facilitate the work of connection.

THEORETICAL APPROACHES TO ENGAGEMENT AND ASSESSMENT WITH GROUPS

Just as with social work practice with individuals and families, developing competencies for engaging and assessing in group practice begins with identifying a theoretical stance from which you will work. In keeping with the commitment of this text to the strengths-based perspective, the following discussion will be grounded in the premise that social work practice with groups is approached from the concept that all members have strengths on which the goals and objectives can be built. As Kurland (2007) notes, "the very act of forming a group is a statement of our belief that every member of the group has something to offer the others, something to give to others, not just to get from them" (p. 12).

Since all groups create and function as a system, most theoretical frameworks for group practice derive from the systemic perspective (Garvin & Galinsky, 2008). Thus, you can apply the knowledge you have gained about systems theory with individuals and families to your work with groups. You may begin by viewing groups as fluid, dynamic interactions between a set of individuals who develop interdependence on one another. When the group composition is altered (e.g., a member joins or exits), the dynamics and interpersonal interactions of the group subsequently change as well. A systemic perspective suggests that the work of each phase of the group process "coalesces into a meaningful whole" (Manor, 2008, p. 101). Group work can be highly effective when approached from a strengths-based perspective. For example, consider the powerful impact to be made when you focus on the group members' strengths and abilities as opposed to their limitations (Ephross, 2011). Building on the conceptualization that social work group practice is guided by both systemic and strengths-based frame works, the following discussion will look at narrative and solution-focused perspectives and group work.

Narrative Approach in Group Engagement and Assessment

Incorporating a narrative approach with groups begins with viewing the client system as a collaborator. With a group, the number of potential collaborations is significantly increased. Having a group of individuals who share common experiences can further aid in the process of engaging the client to elicit her or his story, then challenging the client's perspective, and partnering to reconstruct a new story/reality. Members can benefit from not only sharing and reconstructing their own narrative, but listening and contributing to other group members as they reconstruct their own, individual stories.

The narrative framework places an emphasis on the client as the expert on her or his life (Kelley, 2008). Within the context of assessment in group practice, group members can work together with one another and the social worker to identify members' strengths. The assessment process can also help members externalize or separate themselves from their problems for the purpose of planning for change. As with social work practice with individuals and families, narrative theory has been integrated with other theoretical and practice approaches; next we will explore using a narrative approach blended with a solution-focused approach.

Solution-Focused Approach in Group Engagement and Assessment

The solution-focused approach is becoming increasingly relevant to group practice. You will recall from earlier discussions of using solution-focused approach with individuals and families that this approach emphasizes brief, targeted interventions. A solution-focused approach "encourages more purposeful interaction among group members" (De Jong & Berg, 2013, p. 286). With its grounding in strengths-based perspective and emphasis on solutions, this approach can quickly focus the members on the issues that brought them to the group, aid them in collaborating on the development of a plan for change, and activate the planned change—all with the input and support of other group members and the social work facilitator.

Group interventions are often intentionally time-limited because of the nature of the work (e.g., mandated groups or psycho-educationally focused groups), financial or agency resources, or characteristics of the group members (e.g., children or adolescents). In engaging potential group members, the social worker can emphasize the time-limited, targeted, future-oriented nature of a solution-focused group. This orientation clearly sets the stage from the engagement phase that your work together will be purposeful, occur within a specified time period (ideally 6 to 12 meetings), and emphasize concrete, achievable outcomes. Such an approach is likely to appeal to many potential group members who may be reticent about joining a group. Solution-focused strategies have been shown to be particularly helpful with children and youth in addressing bullying behaviors (Young, 2013) and clients mandated for intervention (e.g., prison inmates and offenders of intimate partner violence) (Uken, Lee, & Sebold, 2013; Walker, 2013).

Because of the pragmatic, outcomes-oriented nature of the solution-focused approach, the assessment phase of solution-focused group work promotes a range of helpful techniques, such as creating individualized therapeutic goals, the use of scaling questions gauge the initial concerns expressed by the members of the group and will enable the group members to monitor their progress throughout the intervention. Introducing assessment through the use of the standard series of solution-focused questions highlights previous successes, strengths, and resources while focusing the client (and the group) on viable solutions. For example, returning to the group of Riverton residents who have lost someone to substance abuse, the social worker can begin the assessment phase by asking individual members the "miracle" question: "How would your life be if you were no longer acutely grieving the loss of your loved one?" The worker can then ask the group member to recall a time when they were successfully coped with a challenge or crisis. While the social worker recognizes that grief is not easily resolved, she or he can guide the group members to consider alternative strategies for coping with their loss. The benefit of using such an approach in the group setting is that group members can share ideas and strategies, help to identify strengths in themselves and others, and support and nurture one another.

Solution-focused approaches can be effectively integrated with other intervention approaches. For example, incorporating strategies from the strengths- and narrative-based schools of thought can serve to enhance the impact of the intervention (Kelley, 2008). All three approaches emphasize engagements and assessments focused on the resources of each person with the goal to empower and change. Narrative-focused techniques can elicit the stories of the group members and help develop alternative and unique change outcomes for the individual and the group.

There is an array of effective theoretical or philosophical frameworks available for your work with groups. Regardless of the orientation(s) to which you subscribe, remember that your client in group work is, in fact, the group itself, and the group experience can be a powerful one for both you and the group members.

CONTEMPORARY TRENDS AND SKILLS FOR THE BEGINNING PHASES OF GROUP WORK: ENGAGEMENT AND ASSESSMENT

As with social work practice with individuals and families, pre-planning, engagement and assessment, and planning are critical to an effective social work intervention with a group. These areas coincide with the phases of the group intervention—planning, beginning, middle, and ending phases. Group practice skills build on the skills and knowledge that you have gained for working with individuals and families; here we will discuss new skills for pre-group formation planning, engaging and assessment, group logistics, and process (Ephross & Greif, 2009, p. 681).

Pre-group Planning

A successful social work group intervention requires planning prior to the first meeting. There are many considerations that you should address before developing a group in social work practice. As the practitioner, there are nine areas you need to consider before organizing a group. These nine areas (adapted from Kurland & Salmon, 1998, p. 24) provide a useful guide:

- Need

- Purpose

- Composition, eligibility, and appropriateness

- Structure

- Content

- Agency context

- Social context

- Pre-group contact

- Contacting prospective group members

You should think about each of these areas within the context of the agency, your supervisor's input or direction, and the larger social environment. These areas are interrelated, and decisions in one category may influence decisions in another. While there is room for multiple approaches in group work practice, the considerations here do not presuppose certain answers. They are simply areas to which you can give thought, as they are likely to be the source of unexpected obstruction later if ignored in the beginning. See Exhibit 8.6 for schematic drawings relating to pre-planning models, while Exhibit. 8.7 presents an example of the operationalization of the pre-planning process. Let us return to Jasmine Johnson's situation in which she requests your help with learning alternative strategies for interacting with her teen son. A component of her contract with you was to participate in a Parents of Teens Support Group. Exhibit 8.7 may be viewed from your perspective as the social worker who will create and lead that group.

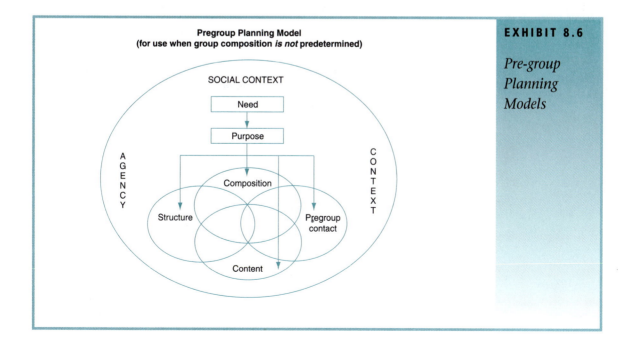

Pregroup Planning Model
(for use when group composition *is not* predetermined)

SOCIAL CONTEXT

Need → Purpose → Composition

AGENCY — CONTEXT

Structure — Pregroup contact

Content

EXHIBIT 8.6

Pre-group Planning Models

EXHIBIT 8.6

Continued

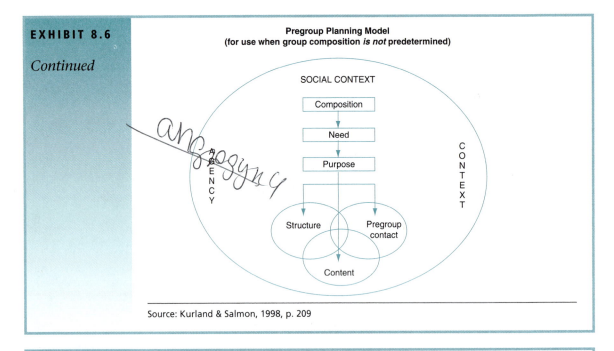

Source: Kurland & Salmon, 1998, p. 209

EXHIBIT 8.7

Pre-Planning for a Group Intervention: Parents of Teens Support Group

Your agency has experienced an increase in the number of parents of teens seeking services due to their concerns about their relationships with their adolescent children. In consultation with your supervisor and colleagues, a decision is reached to form a support group for this population. You have been asked to lead this effort. Using Kurland & Salmon's (1998) list of pre-planning tasks, you consider the following:

Pre-Planning Issue/Task	Consideration for Parents of Teens Support Group
Need	62% increase in the past six months of parents of teens seeking services due to concerns about their relationships with their teenage children.
Purpose	After discussion at staff meeting, family service staff agree that the parents can benefit from a reciprocal, psychoeducationally-focused group intervention
Composition, eligibility, and appropriateness	*Composition*: The group will be targeted to parents of adolescents aged 12–19 years and will not have a minimum or maximum number of participants required. *Eligibility*: Based on the changing needs of the target population, the group will be open to any interested parents of teens. The participants are not required to be currently receiving services from the agency. *Appropriateness*: Due to the psychoeducational/support orientation of the group, any parent feeling they are in need of support will be appropriate for the group. This type of group is consistent with other services offered by your agency.

Pre-Planning Issue/Task	Consideration for Parents of Teens Support Group
Structure	The group will meet monthly for 90 minutes in the agency's multi-purpose room. You will serve as the primary facilitator with the social work student completing practicum with you this year serving as the co-facilitator. The agency will provide refreshments. Child care will be offered for any parents with young children. Service learning students from a nearby university will oversee the childcare area.
Content	As the aim of the group intervention is focused on provision of mutual aid and education, each session will begin with a brief presentation by one of the facilitators or another professional. The parents will collaborate with the co-facilitators to determine topics of interest. Following the presentation and discussion, the members will be given the opportunity to "check-in" with one another, raise issues, and ask for input from the group regarding concerns they are experiencing.
Agency context	With support from your supervisor, agency administration, and your co-workers, this group intervention helps to promote the agency mission of providing services to families and children.
Social context	A psychoeducational, reciprocal support group meets a need within the community that no other agency or institution is currently meeting. Should members need additional support, your agency provides individual and family services.
Pre-group contact	Your social work student and you will develop a program flyer that will be circulated among agency staff and posted on agency bulletin boards and website. The program will also be promoted to other social service agencies serving this population, school social workers, a community service website, and in the organization section of the local newspaper.
Contacting prospective group members	Prospective group members may be referred by social service professional or contact the agency directly. You and your social work practicum student will conduct a brief intake interview with each potential member to determine her or his appropriateness for the group. If the group is appropriate for the group, she or he will be invited to the first meeting.

Need To determine if there is a need for a group experience, you may begin by identifying the major and relevant issues that confront the population you would work with. You want to know your clients well and be aware of the needs as perceived by potential members. Establishing a vital, functioning group is dependent on having an understanding of members' lives and struggles and being able to focus on some aspect of their lives that is important to them. In-depth knowledge of your target group can influence your recruitment and retention strategies, meeting location, group agendas and activities, and the impetus for potential members to participate (Finlayson & Cho, 2011, p. 491). For example, if you work with several young mothers who live in poverty, consider the decisions you will make regarding the scheduling and location of meetings and the need to offer transportation and child care. You will need to consider the direct dimension of the battle of living on a limited income (e.g., managing a meager household budget, taking an assertive stand with landlords, or meeting children's needs) rather than offering a group whose activity is based on an issue that is not relevant for the members (e.g., needlework skills). On the other hand, needlework skills may be very appealing to women who have little outlet for creativity or companionship and seldom feel as if they accomplish much through the day. The point is to know your clients' needs and respond to them in a way that is consistent with your agency's purpose. Sources of data that may prove helpful include a community needs assessment, agency service statistics, and interviews with staff and clients.

Purpose Consider both collective and individual objectives: What hopes will the group as a whole have? What expectations will individuals have? Ask yourself, what is the function of the group and what will your role be? The focus may be on, for example, counseling, teaching, or facilitating social action. Consider ways in which member interaction will contribute to the purpose of the group. The primary focus of participation in a structured group intervention should always be maintained on meeting the goals of gaining knowledge and growth that can be applied to the members' lives (Ephross, 2011).

Composition, Eligibility, and Appropriateness The number of members and their characteristics, such as gender, age, experience, skill, beliefs, and values, serve as the group's composition. The major concern in determining the composition of a group is the degree of homogeneity or heterogeneity that will be preferable and conducive to the group achieving the desired outcomes. In general, scholars agree that some common characteristic or situation optimally provides a unifying focus, but there should also be some difference to sustain interest and the potential for growth through exposure to different ideas. Frequently a particular condition, such as living with cancer, can bridge many differences on other dimensions, such as age or ethnic background, but these aspects should be evaluated carefully in each situation.

In addition to individual descriptive variables, behavioral characteristics are also important. The group has the potential to be more successful if members have a compatible (among each other) interpersonal style, level of verbal development, and understanding of the potential for groups. This does not mean the same level, but ideally the variation should not be so great as to present overwhelming obstacles. Different types of groups will vary on the balance of these components—for example, similar ages in children's groups would probably be more important than in most adult groups.

The need and purpose of the group intervention will help to determine the eligibility criteria and type of members that are appropriate for the group. As you are exploring the potential for forming a group, take into consideration the impact of the focus of the group and the ability of members to connect to one another. For example, consider these questions. Will caregivers of spouses with Alzheimer's disease have issues that are similar or different from caregivers of adult children with a developmental disability? Will people in recovery from an addiction be eligible to remain in the group if they are found to have relapsed? Staying focused on the intended goals of the group intervention will help you answer these questions and create a group of people who will be able to help each other.

Structure   Determine if a group will be open or closed and if there will be any "trade-offs" for your particular group. What is the agency's position on this question? What are the challenges to you with either form? What type of group will best address the short- and long-term needs of the members?

Group leadership is an area to be addressed as you begin developing a group intervention. Will the group have a sole facilitator or will co-facilitators better meet the needs of the group. While a single facilitator may be more economic in terms of time and financial resources, there may be compelling reasons for co-facilitation, including: physical safety for members and facilitators, opportunity for a student to gain group experience; and the benefits of role modeling by the facilitators (Ephross, 2011).

Structure also refers to the logistical arrangements of the group: location, frequency of sessions, time of meetings, and duration. Other practical questions include: What type or size of room will be optimal? Will members require transportation or child care? Will there be a fee? How will members maintain confidentiality? What level of agency coordination will be required?

Content   You should arrive at the content of group through analyzing the purpose of the group, the members' needs, and agency and personnel resources. The activities or other means used to accomplish the group's purpose may require special equipment or educational or art materials. Consider the agenda and content of the meetings. Who will be responsible for making arrangements for the group, establishing timelines, creating an agenda, and developing a group purpose? If the group will use discussion, will the content facilitate interaction among members?

Agency Context   Consider how the agency will affect the group and how the group will affect the agency. Specifically, do the agency administration and personnel endorse group work for the population served, and is group work consistent with the agency's mission and emphasis? Do not assume support without confirming it. Your group is likely to have repercussions for others. For example, a children's group is often noisy and may be disruptive to other staff and clients. The support staff may inherit increased administrative responsibilities with the addition of group work to the agency's repertoire of service. Individual social workers may feel possessive of their clients and may be reticent to refer current clients to a group experience. It is to your advantage to address these and other concerns as directly as possible prior to creating the group.

Social Context   Finally, consider social and cultural influences that may influence the group's bonding and functioning. Will the group compete with other community services? Are there appropriate resources for members after the group? Do the cultural contexts of the members support group participation? For example, if you want to facilitate a group for adolescent girls, you will want to consider whether their families will approve of that kind of activity.

Pre-group Contact   Prior to a first meeting, consider these issues related to contact with potential group members: How will members be recruited or referred? What will you use to promote the group and how will you promote it? Will you conduct individual pre-group screening interviews to determine if someone is appropriate for the group? How will members prepare themselves for the group experience? How will you facilitate the members' orientation to the group process so they can experience maximum participation and benefit? While each group and each potential member is unique, developing a plan to address these questions can enable you to assemble a group composed of members with whom you are familiar and who are already oriented to the purpose, structure, and format of the group they may be joining.

Contacting Prospective Group Members   There are many ways to build up the membership of a prospective group and to connect with potential group work clients, including outreach and on-site service referral. **Outreach** is a method for contacting people in their homes and communities to inform them of services and information about which they may not have been aware (Barker, 2003). Reaching out to potential group members may be accomplished through connections with other professionals in the community (e.g., school guidance counselor). Other times, outreach may require a more concerted coordination campaign (e.g., advertising and individual contacts), particularly if potential clients fear discrimination or barriers to eligibility.

Contacting prospective group members directly through **on-site service** referral is a frequently useful way to connect with potential members. You may, for example, recruit members from your caseload of individual clients, or you might ask your colleagues for referrals after they give you their support. Postings and announcements are helpful, but they must be paired with personal contact, such as another staff member's enthusiastic recommendation, to be effective.

In nearly all scenarios, a pre-group interview is ideal. First, it allows you to get an in-depth sense of the potential member and her or his "fit" with the goals and purpose of the group and if she or he is an appropriate member. A pre-group meeting also provides an opportunity to assess the potential dynamic components in relation to other members of the group. At least as important, it provides the opportunity for the prospective group member to air any anxieties and develop a sense of this new experience, to ask questions, and to make a more empowered choice about joining the group. A pre-group meeting also is a time to raise questions or concerns regarding fees or associated costs of joining the group. Finally, you can recognize this contact with group members as a form of engagement, assessment, and planning that carries with it all of the requirements in the way of knowledge and skills that engagement and assessment and planning with individuals entails.

Providing the potential or new group member with printed information regarding the group experience can be an important aspect of the individual's entry into the group. Such a document may contain information on (Brown, 2013):

- Group purpose and goals;

- Techniques, activities, procedures, and format that will be included in the group experience;

- The individual's right to refuse participation;

- Limitations of the group intervention;

- Potential risks and benefits;

- Leader's credentials and group experience;

- Leadership of the group if leader is not available;

- Implications of any diagnoses that may have been made and the role of testing, if it occurred;

- Documentation, including recordkeeping, reports, and client access to records;

- Payment process, if applicable (pp. 19–20).

Engagement

Overlapping with the important pre-group planning phase, engagement is the beginning phase of the group intervention. The *Standards for Social Work Practice with Groups* (IASWG, 2006, pp. 10–17) provides practice behavior guidelines for the practitioner working in the engagement or beginning phase of the group work intervention, including such pre-group activities as:

- Identify member aspirations and needs as perceived by the member, agency, and yourself.

- Clarify member goals and expectations along with the person's feelings about joining the group.

Following the pre-group phase of work, practice behaviors needed for continuing the engagement and assessment of group members include:

S.W
toolbox

- Develop contracts for explication of individual and group goals, tasks, and activities for the duration of the group and beyond.

- Following your own introduction and clarification of your role in the group, invite each member to introduce themselves and share their reasons and hopes for joining the group.

- In collaboration with the group members, develop a clear statement of purpose, rules and norms, and roles that incorporates the individual and group member and agency goals, needs, and perceptions.

- Develop, as appropriate, content, activities, and resources that are relevant for the group purpose.

- Promote group cohesion among members and between the members and you by establishing rapport with each member and the group as a whole by high-lighting common interests and goals, direct interactions, and potential link-ages to one another and you.

- In cooperation with the group members, establish the work plan for the group for the rest of the beginning phase as well as the remainder of the group planned time together (or for the individual's time in the group if the group is open-ended and not time-limited).

- Awareness and overt recognition of the unique characteristics of each group member, including but not limited to cultural and ethnic heritage, age, gender, sexual orientation, presenting concerns, and noting that each person brings strengths to the group process.

A first session ideally begins with you and members sharing their expectations for the group. Be transparent about what you (you alone or with a co-facilitator) hope to accomplish. Likewise, members are encouraged to talk about their perceptions of their roles. Confidentiality is often one of the first dimensions discussed, and, as you can imagine, unless all members feel safe in revealing their struggles and feelings, it is not likely that many will participate fully.

Establishing **norms**, or expected rules of conduct, creates a productive group climate and requires active participation from members so the social worker is not in the position of dictating regulations for the group. The actual norms for the group will depend on the type of group. For example, a socialization group for seven-year-old boys in residential treatment may include "no hitting" as the major expectation. "No shouting" might be applicable to an anger management group, or "celebrating holidays" to a single parents' group. Some groups also discourage contact between members outside of the group, because it may dilute the group process, and others encourage it, because it fosters translation of group benefits into the "real world." The primary emphasis here is to facilitate group members' involvement through a relatively clear set of behavioral expectations that in turn will increase their comfort in being in the group and will encourage their maximum participation. If, for example, group members have differing cultural heritages, and some members interpret lateness as disrespectful while others view it as culturally appropriate or simply flexible, the social worker may opt to explore timeliness as an area for negotiation. Knowing the membership can help you anticipate particular issues that may affect group process. All of these early negotiations with group members serve, like the interview, as important opportunities for both engagement and ongoing assessment.

The engagement phase can be challenging for both the social worker and the group members. The social worker is trying to engage with each individual member and the group as a whole as well as promoting cohesion among the members themselves *and* establishing the group structure and format *and* keeping the group on task and target for the previously stated goals. Creating an environment that is safe, comfortable, and supportive is essential to the members' ability to establish rapport and engagement with the process and you as the facilitator (Furman et al., 2009). Achieving the desired level of engagement with and among group members can then empower the members to begin sharing with and supporting one another, thus alleviating the full responsibility for leadership from the social worker. Also challenging is the engagement of new members or facilitators who join an established group. The social work facilitator is responsible for engaging the new member and encouraging the group to do the same or if she or he is the new member, reaching out to the members. Attrition is a particular concern if members do not feel engaged in the first meeting. Members who are in a group voluntarily but who do not feel connected to the group or the facilitator may feel reticence about returning to the group.

The beginning phases of group work can present challenges for group members as well. Despite your best efforts to orient members to the purpose, structure, and format of the group, members may still be uncertain or even resistant about participating in the group, their role in the group, perceptions of others about them (as well as their perceptions of others), and concern that the group will not meet their individual needs (Yalom & Leszcz, 2005). Being attentive to individual reactions and responses will ensure that individuals are not "lost" or deterred from investing in the group experience.

Assessment and Planning

As with social work practice with individuals and families, the transition from one phase of work to another is rarely linear or clearly delineated. Just as engagement can be an ongoing process, assessment and planning may also be revisited throughout the duration of the group experience. Assessment and planning both logically and naturally occur as potential members are recruited and screened for membership and again as the group is forming and collaborating on the development of individual and group contracts. The need for assessment and planning can recur throughout the life of the group as individual and group goals change and evolve, as members arrive and depart, and unanticipated events influence group interactions (e.g., conflict, change of facilitator, or termination).

Within the context of group practice, assessment is a strategy for determining if the issues and characteristics presented by the group member are consistent with those of other members as well as a tool for monitoring individual and group progress toward goals. Recall the earlier example of the group for Riverton children who had lost a family member to substance abuse. As the facilitator of this group, you may have to determine if an individual who has lost a close friend is an appropriate candidate for membership in this group.

Assessment can also be employed to measure such group-related issues as cohesiveness or group facilitator skills (Macgowan, 2009b). Upon determining the area of assessment that you want to measure, you can opt for assessment by using standardized measures, observation, group member self-reports, or feedback from an external source (e.g., person or video-/audio-recording).

As with any area of social work practice, group leaders must be cognizant of the ethical obligations associated with engaging and assessing members of a new group. Such ethical considerations include (Brown, 2013):

- All assessment techniques and instruments must have sufficient and appropriate validity and reliability.

- Group leaders must have formal training and supervised practice for assessing group members.

- Group leaders must always practice within their areas of competence.

- Group members must provide informed consent for participation in the group experience and be informed of any information resulting from the assessment that will be shared with others (p. 23).

Planning within the assessment phase of group work often requires attentiveness and flexibility. While most group facilitators spend considerable time and effort in the pre-group planning phase and in developing an agenda or plan for each group session, the experienced group practitioner can attest to the need to be able and willing to adjust quickly and creatively to a need to shift plans. Regardless of the type of group you are facilitating, it is likely that at any meeting a member(s) will have an issue, crisis, request, or behavior that will need to take precedence over your plans for that session. While you will want to be responsive to the needs of the individual(s), you must try to balance the needs of the group. You may be able to set aside your plans for that session to devote time to the individual, but use caution to ensure that the other members or agenda items are not sacrificed in the process.

As noted, flexibility is an essential aspect of the social work practice with groups, particularly the beginning stages of group work. Despite the need for adaptability, the social worker may find that the engagement and assessment processes of most group experiences will include comparable and expected areas of emphasis.

STRAIGHT TALK ABOUT GROUP ENGAGEMENT AND ASSESSMENT

For many students and new workers, learning to trust the group process and to maintain a stance of **facilitator** (not necessarily "leader" and certainly not "runner of") can be challenging. Learning to share the control of the relationship(s), to share the helping role with group members, and to allow the group its own path will help you develop important practice skills. Such a position, however, can create challenges for the social worker. A tolerance for relinquishing control will place you in good stead. Despite your best efforts to refrain from controlling the group, it is important to recognize that you will, in fact, influence and shape the norms of the group simply due to your role as a facilitator/convener (Yalom & Leszcz, 2005). Fortunately, early anxieties regarding control and its management abate substantially with experience.

When embarking on an experience in which you will serve as a group leader or facilitator, it is particularly important to think about the experience within the context of the members' participation. With that in mind, consider the following assumptions one can make about group members and their roles (Brown, 2013):

- Each group member has a unique personality and history and can make a unique contribution to the group.

- Members are not always aware of the fantasies and fears that may be influencing their lives.

- Some group members may be at a crossroads in their lives that prompt fears and anxieties about group participation. Such dilemmas may present in the form of defensiveness within the group.

- Group members use different strategies to make sense of their experiences (p. 59).

Surprisingly, many workers fail to attend thoroughly to the logistics, or the detailed mechanics, of group preparation and implementation. While you consider the philosophical dimensions of launching a group intervention, also make sure there are enough chairs, the meeting is not scheduled on a religious holiday, all members have transportation to the group, and child/adult care is provided as needed. Ensure, for example, that the group for male perpetrators of violence does not meet at the same time and place as the group for their survivors. Consider competition with other known schedules, so that the parenting group does not conflict with the mothers' and children's group. While it is not possible to avoid all conflicts or awkwardness, giving thought to as many of these aspects as you can is worth the effort.

Particularly important to the engagement and assessment phases of group work is actively listening to the messages and communication being conveyed to you by group members (Shulman, 2009b). This requires you to have awareness of and empathy for the thoughts, feelings, and reactions that are held by you, group members, and others (e.g., family, staff, or referral sources). For example, if you are facilitating a group for Riverton residents concerned about the use of alcohol and drugs by local teens, it is crucial that you "tune in" to your own experiences and feelings related to substance use and abuse and the origins and meanings of the statements being made by the Riverton residents. Listening is important for your ability to work with any population as it will enable you to determine if you have biases, unresolved personal concerns, or conflicted values that may prevent you from objectively and empathetically serve a client system. In keeping with being in tune with the needs of your group members, be mindful of such additional facilitative strategies as (Ephross, 2011):

- Ability to say less (as opposed to more) to avoid interfering with the group's process—your role may need to be more active in the beginning, but should decrease as the group process unfolds (i.e., group members should be doing approximately eighty percent of the talking);

- Recognition that the power of the intervention comes from the group interaction, not the social worker;

- Summarizing group members' discussions and providing a bridge to the next topic or area of work;

- Limit-setting through the clear and transparent expectations and policies, negotiating individual and group contracts for work, and transitioning the group through the various phases of the group process.

An issue related to attending to logistical details and "tuning in" is documentation of the group experience. While documenting the process of the group experience

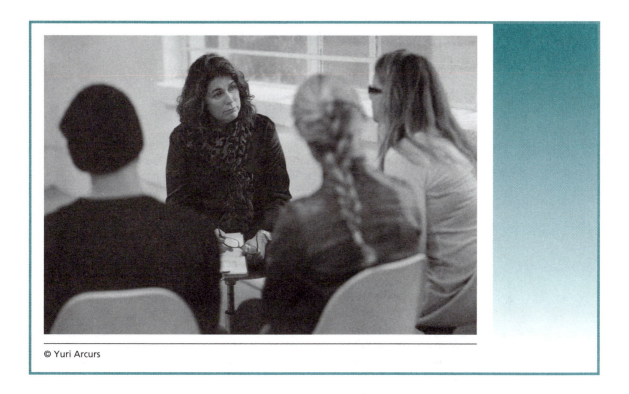

© Yuri Arcurs

presents a unique set of challenges, it need not be an overwhelming or complex task. Documentation of any group experience serves a range of purposes, including: (1) insights into the positive and challenging events that occurred during the group session; (2) recording gains and potential future challenges; (3) negative interactions among group members; (4) interpretation of behaviors and interactions (including cohesion, process, norms, new directions, and gaps); (5) the termination and evaluation process; and (6) accountability for billing, planning, and referral sources (Yalom & Leszcz, 2005). Typically, the facilitator maintains two separate records of the group experiences. The group's record includes information on attendance, general themes, cohesion, interactions, and plans, while documentation in the individual group members' record includes only information regarding that client and her or his goals, needs, etc. In order to protect individual client confidentiality, the names of other group members should not be included in the individual client document. Documentation should reflect the tenor and flow of the session itself. For example, if you are using a solution-focused approach, your assessment documentation can replicate the focus on solutions versus a focus on problems (De Jong & Berg, 2013). Exhibit 8.8 provides sample items of documentation that may be included for a client-oriented group session and Exhibit 8.9 includes a list of questions the social worker can ask the client to assess and document if she or he is appropriate for membership in the group.

EXHIBIT 8.8

Information to Include in a Group Assessment/ Intervention Plan

Demographic Data:

- Name
- Contact information
- Legal status and needs
- Group participation needs (e.g., child or adult care needs, transportation, etc.)
- Presenting concerns as they relate to the group purpose or focus
- Current living situation (level of stability, support, and safety)
- Social environment (level of activity, satisfaction, and relationships with others)
- Cultural environment (client satisfaction and view on helping-seeking; and cultural view of help-seeking, particularly in the group environment)
- Religion/spirituality (statement of beliefs and levels of activity and satisfaction)
- Military experience (branch, time in service, discharge status, coping with experience, and view of experience)
- Childhood (supportive, strengths, and significant events, including trauma)
- Family (composition—parents, siblings, spouse/significant other(s), children, and others; level of support; and family history of mental illness)
- Sexual history (activity level, orientation, satisfaction, and concerns)
- Trauma history (physical, sexual, and/or emotional abuse or neglect and experience with perpetrator(s))
- Financial/employment circumstances (employment status, satisfaction, financial stability, areas of concern or change)
- Educational history (highest level achieved, performance, goals, and challenges)
- Substance use/abuse (history of addictive behaviors—alcohol, drugs, gambling, sexual, or other)

History of Emotional/Behavioral Functioning:

For each of the following areas, gather information regarding: current status (current, previous, or denies history); description of behavior; onset and duration; and frequency

- Self-mutilation
- Hallucinations
- Delusions or paranoia
- Mood swings
- Recurrent or intrusive recollections of past events
- Lack of interest or pleasure
- Feelings of sadness, hopelessness, isolation, or withdrawal
- Decreased concentration, energy, or motivation
- Anxiety
- Crying spells
- Appetite changes
- Sleep changes
- Inability to function at school or work

- Inability to control thoughts or behaviors (impulses)
- Irritability or agitation
- Reckless behavior, fighting, or fire setting
- Stealing, shoplifting, or lying
- Cruelty to animals
- Aggression

Past and Current Behavioral Health Treatment History (i.e., individual, family, and/or other group experiences):

- Date(s)
- Program or facility
- Provider
- Response to treatment

Mental Status Exam:

- Attention (rate on scale of: good, fair, easily distracted, or highly distractible; and describe behavior)
- Affect (rate on scale of: appropriate, labile, expansive, constrictive, or blunted; and describe behavior)
- Mood (rate on scale of: normal, depressed, anxious, or euphoric; and describe behavior)
- Appearance (rate on scale of: well groomed, disheveled, bizarre, or inappropriate; and describe behavior)
- Motor activity (rate on scale of: calm, hyperactive, agitated, tremors, tics, or muscle spasms; and describe behavior)
- Thought process (rate on scale of: intact, circumstantial, tangential, flight of ideas, or loose associations; and describe behavior)
- Thought content (note: normal, grandiose, phobic, reality, organization, worthless, obsessive, compulsion, guilt, delusional, paranoid, ideas of reference, and hallucinations; and describe behavior)
- Memory (note: normal, recent (good or impaired), past (good or impaired); and describe behavior)
- Intellect (note: normal, above, below, or poor abstraction; and describe behavior)
- Orientation (note: person, place, situation, and time; and describe behavior)
- Judgment and insight (rate on scale of: good, fair, or poor; and describe behavior)
- Current providers (including psychiatrist, primary care physician, therapist, caseworker, etc.)
- Community resources being used (including support groups, religious, spiritual, other)
- Client goal(s) for treatment
- Summary—including social worker's assessment of client "fit" with the group (see Exhibit 8.9 for assessment questions).

Adapted from St. Anthony's Medical Center, St. Louis, Missouri; Women's Support and Community Services, St. Louis, Missouri

EXHIBIT 8.9

Screening Questions for Group Assessment

A component of the assessment process for a group intervention is to determine a client's appropriateness for membership in a group. This phase of assessment can also help to ensure emotional and physical safety for all group members. The following list of general questions can aid in evaluating client appropriateness and safety:

- How does the client respond to opinions, thoughts, and insights that differ from her or his own?
- When the client becomes angry or upset, what is her or his reaction and thought process?
- Is the client able to express her or his emotions in an appropriate way and to assume responsibility for the emotion?
- How are the client's emotional responses triggered?
- What is the developmental age of the client? Is the client able to cope with negative emotions and thoughts at an appropriate developmental level with other group members?
- Does the client demonstrate:
  o Impulse control challenges?
  o Appropriate boundaries?
  o Self-awareness?
  o Self-destructive behaviors?
  o Potential to monopolize or disrupt the group?
  o Ability to respond to social cues?
  o Sensitivity toward others?
  o Potential for personal growth?
  o Appropriate group interaction behaviors?
  o Difficulty making decisions?
- Is the client's behavior potentially going to limit group participation or benefit?
- If the client is currently experiencing a crisis, will the benefits of the group outweigh risks?

Adapted from Women's Support and Community Services, St. Louis, Missouri

While documenting the work of non-client groups—social goals/action and task groups—may include some of the information found in a client group (e.g., attendance, themes, and plans), the focus is more typically directed toward creating a record of actions, decisions, and plans. Often compiled in the form of minutes or notes, documenting group process and outcomes for social action/goals or task groups emphasizes the work being completed as opposed to the interactions among the group members. See Quick Guides 25 and 26 for templates that you can use to record the work of a non-client group. Quick Guide 25 provides a template for a matrix-style record, while Quick Guide 26 provides an outline for a narrative-style document.

The early phases of a group experience can bring unique and possibly unexpected challenges for the social worker. In fact, your group experience may serve to dispel some of the myths associated with creating and facilitating a group regarding potentially conflicting agendas and roles and the perception that all members will be committed to supporting other members (Zandee-Adams, 2013). Specifically, you may encounter situations in which your goals in establishing the group differ from that of group members, your role as a provider of individual and family services creates a conflict with your role as a group facilitator, or you find that some members of the group are not able or interested in productively engaging with other group members. Four examples of challenges specific to a group experience include: (1) perceived goal incompatibility; (2) member turnover; (3) delayed results; and (4) sub-groupings (Yalom & Leszcz, 2005, pp. 298–299). Somewhat interrelated, each of these situations relates to group member expectations and dynamics. Group members may struggle to view the group process as being helpful to them, particularly when compared to an individual helping relationship or in an immediate time frame, thus they may then leave the group. Group members often find that the common experiences they share extend beyond the group and lead to alliances within the group session and/or socializing outside the group. While not necessarily negative, such relationships can be disruptive to the group process.

QUICK GUIDE 25   TASK GROUP DOCUMENTATION TEMPLATE

AGENCY / ORGANIZATION NAME
GROUP NAME

Date
Present:
Absent:
Minutes submitted by:

ISSUE	DISCUSSION	FOLLOW-UP / RECOMMENDATIONS	PERSON(S) RESPONSIBLE
Call to Order			
Minutes			
Announcements			
Old Business			
New Business			
Adjournment			
Future Meetings			

QUICK GUIDE 26   TASK GROUP DOCUMENTATION TEMPLATE

Agency / Organization Name
Group Name
Date

In attendance:
Absent:

1. Call meeting to order
2. Review meeting agenda
3. Review minutes from previous meeting
4. Announcements
5. Old business
6. New business
7. Adjournment and next steps

Respectfully submitted,
Note taker's name and title

Regardless of the challenge that may present itself to you as a group facilitator or leader, maintaining a transparent, open, and equitable style will best serve both the group and your own sense of competence. Remember, the "basic reason for doing group work is the power of the group, *not the worker*" (Ephross, 2011, p. 13). Gaining as much group experience as possible, particularly facilitator or leadership experience, throughout your social work education can also prepare you for being a contributing member and capable leader in your social work career. As we continue the exploration into social work practice with groups, consider the valuable learning that you can gain by experiencing different roles within a group, including member, facilitator, and observer.

CONCLUSION

This chapter advocates for practitioners to mediate the culturally imposed isolation of many individuals through groups. There are many exciting adventures into group work in the service of contemporary theoretical perspectives, social justice, and diversity that we could not delve into depth here. Scenarios relating to cultural inclusion, gender and disability, collaboration, and spirituality in models all point to the empowering direction that social group work is taking. Group work has renewed a significant potential for the future and particular relevance for the social justice, diversity, and human rights connections that give social work its meaning.

The focus will now turn to the next phases of social work practice with groups. Building on the pre-planning, engagement, and assessment work that has been completed, the social worker–facilitated group moves into the intervention or middle phase of work followed by the termination and evaluation (or ending) phases of the group experience.

MAIN POINTS

- All people are members of groups that provide meaning and critical human connections. Western philosophy tends to underemphasize the gifts and power of group connection.

- Group work in the social work profession has been a controversial topic but remains a vital part of practice that lends itself especially to social justice, diversity, and human rights perspectives.

- Organizing a group requires careful planning and continuous consideration for the value of the group as a whole.

- Traditional theoretical models for group work include the task group, social action or goals model, the reciprocal model, and the remedial model.

- Social work group practice employs a variety of theoretical frameworks. The approaches highlighted in this chapter include: strengths and empowerment, narrative-focused, and solution-focused perspectives.

- Engaging and assessing group members individually and collectively is the beginning phase of group formation.

- While primarily completed during the beginning phases of group work, engagement and assessment can be ongoing aspects of the group experience. The fluid and evolving nature of group work can result in changing membership and leadership, new and unexpected issues, and interpersonal dynamics and conflicts that can all influence the course of the early (and later) stages of the group intervention.

EXERCISES

a. Case Exercises

1. Go to www.routledgesw.com/cases and review Carla Washburn's video vignette and complete the following:
   a. Summarize the group's activities as they are depicted in the vignettes.

   b. Document the group practice behaviors that the social worker, Shannon, is utilizing.
   c. Identify any challenges you anticipate that may occur in completing a group level intervention with the members of this group.
   d. Brainstorm about the next steps that you would initiate as the social worker facilitating this group.
2. Review the Carla Washburn video vignette and explore options for facilitating this group using a range of different approaches, including:
   a. Psychoeducational group
   b. Reciprocal group
   c. Remedial group
   After you have considered strategies for facilitating the group using the three different models, respond to the following questions:
   a. How does each group differ in its focus?
   b. How does the social work role differ in each group?
   c. What engagement skills did the social worker utilize?
   d. Utilizing the case vignette as an example, role-play the group as a one of each of the following: (1) psychoeducational, (2) reciprocal, (3) remedial
3. Go to www.routledgesw.com/cases and review the case for Brickville, focusing on Virginia Stone and her family. In the Intervention section, review Vignette #3 which describes the use of a social action group intervention focused on Virginia's efforts to save the park that was created in memory of her family members who were lost in the apartment fire twenty years earlier. Using the information that you have available to you, develop a written plan for:
   a. Determining the need for this group
   b. Identifying the purpose a task group would serve in this situation
   c. Propose appropriate group composition and their potential contributions
   d. Develop your thoughts regarding group structure and content
   e. Reflect on the meaning of such a group forming within the context of the agency and community context
   f. Describe your plans for initiating pre-group contact, engaging group members, and assessing members' potential commitment and contributions
   g. Assess available and needed resources and potential barriers to success
4. Go to www.routledgesw.com/cases and review the case for Hudson City. Recall from Chapters 6 and 7 that the Patel family experienced significant impact from Hurricane Diane. Several weeks after the hurricane, Sheetal (wife of Hemant and mother of Rakesh, Kamal, and Aarti) confides in you that she is concerned that her 12-year-old daughter, Aarti, is not coping well with life following the hurricane and their displacement from their home and restaurant. They have been able to return to their home and are working on getting the restaurant re-opened. Aarti has returned to her school, but continues to have nightmares about the storm, is uncomfortable being away from her parents, and her appetite seems to have lessened. Both your co-workers and you

are hearing similar concerns being expressed by parents whose families were affected by the storm. Describe in writing your plan for developing a group intervention to address the needs of children who survived the hurricane, including:

- Type of group approach (include format and structure)
- Plans for member eligibility, recruitment, and parent involvement
- Strategies for engaging group members in a culturally competent manner, keeping in mind that the community is comprised of a diverse and large immigrant population
- Strategies for assessing group members' appropriateness for the group.

5. Go to www.routledgesw.com/cases and review the case for Riverton, then, referring back to Exhibits 8.3, 8.4, and 8.5 in this chapter, conduct a search of the literature on group-level practice in order to determine the following:

   a. Riverton Against Youth Drinking (RAYD): evidence-based practices for facilitating social goals groups on teen drinking.

   b. Riverton Children's Grief Support Group: evidence-based practices for facilitating reciprocal groups with children.

   c. Riverton Mental Health Center Groups for Persons with Co-Occurring Diagnoses: evidence-based practices for facilitating a treatment group for this population and for incorporating new members into an existing group.

b. Other Exercises

6. As a skilled individual and group practice social worker at a local community health center, you have several young clients who have been diagnosed with attention deficit hyperactivity disorder (ADHD). The clients are Hispanic children who range in age from six to eight years of age. Although you usually meet with the children individually, you notice that when their parents pick them up from appointments, some of the parents appear sad about their children, while others appear anxious, frustrated, or angry. The children themselves seem somewhat isolated and all are experiencing social, academic, and behavioral problems in school.

   Assume that you have the time, interest, and agency support to offer a group. Choose one of the following interventions from the list below that you think will be the most helpful:

   a. A play/social skills group for the children.

   b. A support group for the parents.

   c. A psychoeducational group for the parents.

   d. An empowerment group for the children.

   Be prepared to provide a rationale for your choice to your classmates. How might one choice intersect with another? Compare with peers.

7. You work for a child welfare organization and are facilitating a support group for adolescent females who have recently given birth and are preparing to

return to their high schools. Some of the babies are being partially cared for by their grandparents, and some have been adopted through the agency. Some of the group members have concerns about returning to school and others are eager to get back into a "normal" social life again. Most members are participating well, although one member, Janine, has said almost nothing in the three meetings that have already occurred. All the members of the group are African American. You are a white, female social work practicum student, 23 years old.

At the beginning of the fourth meeting, the mood of the entire group seems contentious. After brief preliminary pleasantries and a restatement of the agenda for this session (hoping that would bring everyone on board), you realize that Janine is quietly crying in the corner. At the same time, two of the other members start calling your name angrily, competing for your attention. They tell you they are annoyed at the group, at the plan for today, at the agency, and at Janine who is sitting there acting like a "baby."

Respond to the following:
a. Identify two skills from the chapter that you would use and provide an example of the way in which you would perform the skills.
b. Provide a rationale for your selection of these particular skills. What are the expected results from the use of the skills?
c. Which of the models described in this chapter offers the best explanation for the group dynamics?

8. Attend a mutual aid group in the community and write a reflection about your experience, including:
a. Describe the group type, purpose, and structure.
b. Identify group leader and member roles.
c. Reflect on your previous experiences as a group member. What role do you often play? Why? Do you want to do things differently?

9. In small groups of three or four, create your own social action group.
a. Identify an issue that is of mutual interest to group members.
b. Determine the roles for each member.
c. Develop a plan of action for the group. Prepare as a presentation for the class.

10. Your field instructor at your practicum has invited you to join her in co-facilitating a psychoeducational support group for persons who serve as caregivers for a family member experiencing Parkinson's Disease. In addition to co-leading the group each session, your field instructor has suggested that you assume responsibility for leading one session on a topic of your choice that will be relevant for this group of primarily wives and adult daughters. This is your first group work experience and you are unfamiliar with this medical condition. To accomplish your task:
a. Review the literature to learn about Parkinson's Disease.
b. Develop a plan for the session that you will lead, including identifying a relevant topic.

CHAPTER 9

Social Work Practice with Groups: Intervention, Termination, and Evaluation

I found myself slipping into that self trashing thing, man, you know, putting myself down, thinking and saying I'm a dumb broad, ugly and worthless, just like J. used to tell me. But they got on me, those awesome women! They told me I was breaking the friggin' rules! Me! Breaking the rules, and then I remembered what they meant. We're not doing that stuff in this group. The end. Not okay. They are really the most awesome! What would I be without them?

Marcy (of the Debbie, Joan, Marcy, and Kate Group for Survivors of Intimate Partner Violence.)

Key Questions for Chapter 9

(1) What competencies do I need to intervene, terminate, and evaluate with client systems at the group level of social work practice? (EPAS 2.1.10(c & d))

(2) How can I use evidence to practice research-informed practice and practice-informed research to guide the evaluation of a group I am facilitating? (EPAS 2.1.6)

(3) What is the appropriate response for a social worker leading a group if one group member violates the confidentiality of another member of the group? (EPAS 2.1.2)

(4) What is distinction between the appropriate social worker role in facilitating an intervention with a self-help support group and a therapy group? (EPAS 2.1.3)

THE EFFICACY OF SOCIAL WORK PRACTICE INTERVENTIONS, terminations, and evaluations with groups stems from the engagement and assessment phases. The middle and ending phases of work, interventions, are the period of the group experience in which the "majority of the work of the groups gets accomplished" and endings are "the time to consolidate the work of the group" (Toseland & Horton, 2008, p. 302). Terminations and evaluations are complex because the dual focus is on both the individual as well as the group.

To complete our exploration of work with groups, this chapter continues the group experience from the development of the intervention process through the termination and evaluation phases. We will also focus on theoretical frameworks for group interventions and models of group intervention and look at the social work practice behaviors needed for groups. The chapter will continue with a look at the final phase of the group intervention: termination and evaluation. To set the stage for delving into the middle and ending stages of group work practice, let us first consider the key issues of social justice, diversity, and human rights.

INTERFACE: SOCIAL JUSTICE, DIVERSITY, AND HUMAN RIGHTS

Social work with groups is a natural setting for practitioners who are committed to social justice, diversity, and/or human rights concerns. As discussed elsewhere in this book, much of social injustice is rooted in exclusion—from resources, opportunities, respect, supports, and so on. This kind of exclusion is especially evident in the experiences of those considered "other" or different. Even in our current culture, that can mean people with disabilities, people of color, groups living in poverty, older adults, persons who are gay, lesbian, bisexual, transgender, or questioning; unfortunately the list is very long (see Greif & Ephross, 2011). An ongoing debate within group work practice is the social worker's response to issues of diversity within the group intervention. Are group interventions more effective if the group is heterogeneous or homogenous? Most scholars agree that evidence-based practice is critical for group work, particularly the need to identify evidence to support the intervention(s) and inform the decision to offer a heterogeneous or a homogenous group structure (Toseland & Horton, 2008). Diverse groups are reflections of the world in which most people live, but not all individuals may feel comfortable or safe taking personal risks with others whose reasons for joining the group are different from their own. In addition to consulting research on group diversity, social workers can also benefit by examining their own views (including their own "isms") on the groups they will be bringing together for a group intervention (Toseland & Horton, 2008).

Group work practice brings people together in meaningful ways that can serve as a forum for increasing understanding, appreciation, and respect for others. In short, group membership can reduce the effects of exclusion and the injustices associated with those feelings of marginalization. When working with groups, you can identify, establish, articulate, and mediate the rights, as well as needs, of group members within the microcosm of the group. This can be an important and empowering experience for many people who may have rarely (or never) understood their own social contexts in terms that affirmed their rights as human beings (Kurland et al., 2004). This arena—human rights and social work with groups— holds great promise for the further integration of human rights practice into the profession.

Approaching group work with an orientation to social justice requires a commitment to learning about and embracing a number of conceptual foundations. Singh and Salazar (2011) suggest the social justice-oriented group work is based on the following foundations:

- The centrality of multicultural competence—integral to competence for group facilitation and social justice, multicultural competence is essential, but recognizably a skill set that the social worker will strive to achieve throughout her or his entire social work career. The diversity of our contemporary society means that, as a social worker, you will routinely interact with and serve a wide range of individuals who are members of groups, thus, the need for not just cultural competence, but *multi*cultural competence becomes paramount to your practice.

- The interplay between content and process—the commitment to a social justice orientation enables the social worker conducting groups to address social inequities and oppression within any group setting and among group members.

- The influence of privilege and oppression—delving into the impact of group leader and members' experiences with privilege and oppression is critical for social justice-oriented group work. Questions to consider may include: "What are group members' needs, perceptions, experiences, and wants with regard to the injustices they face and their efforts toward empowerment and freedom from self-blame? How are these injustices experienced in the community? How is empowerment defined and perceived individually and collectively by community members?" (p. 218).

- Effects on power dynamics within and outside groups—emphasizing issues of power within the group can and should have the added benefit of empowering group members to engage in advocacy and change in other areas of their lives.

THEORETICAL APPROACHES TO INTERVENING WITH GROUPS

Just as there are many theoretical models for social work intervention with individuals and families, there is also a full legacy of theory related to group interventions, processes, skills, and ending points. Subscribing to a specific theoretical

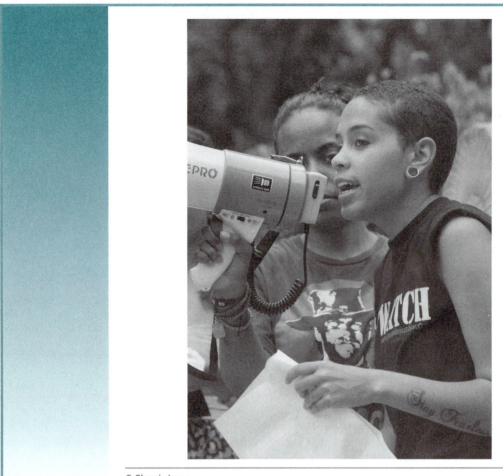

© Glynnis Jones

perspective can influence the group intervention in terms of guiding the formation of the group, defining roles, and impacting group dynamics (Macgowan, 2008).

In this section, we will continue our examination of theory-driven approaches to group practice. Following an overview of theoretical applications, we will explore several classic, contemporary and developmental models. Later, we will look at intervention skills, examples of current groups, and finally, contemporary innovations in group work.

Strengths and Empowerment Perspectives on Group Intervention

As you recall from Chapter 8, this book is grounded in the premise that social work practice with groups should be approached from the position that all group members bring strengths to the group. A strengths-based perspective integrates easily with other theoretically driven intervention approaches. Within the intervention itself, the social worker can use the strengths for a range of purposes, including developing individual and group goals and sharing resources. Strengths can affirm and motivate the individual's change process through the focus of "possibilities versus problems," enable the individual strengths to serve as models for other group members through the sharing of ideas and resources, and help identify and integrate the individual members' strengths into strengths for the group. Approaching the group intervention from a strengths-based perspective requires the social worker to help create an environment in which the following three norms are accepted by all the group members (Benard & Truebridge, 2013):

- Participation—all group members are recognized as being equal participants with each having the right to the same opportunities for voice.

- Communication—interactions among group members and the facilitator must be respectful (e.g., allowing everyone to speak without interruption or side conversations).

- Interactions—in order for all members of the group to contribute equally, members and the leader should be committed to arriving on time and staying for the duration of the group (p. 215).

One of the theoretical models that can help incorporate a strengths perspective into a group intervention is empowerment. With origins in an ecological perspective and aimed at addressing social injustices, an empowerment-focused group intervention emphasizes reciprocal connections with members' environments (Hudson, 2009, p. 48). Within this context, empowerment as a principle generally incorporates three major areas of concern: (1) the personal, including attitudes, values, and beliefs; (2) the interpersonal, including knowledge, skills, and networks; and (3) the sociopolitical, including individual and collective action (East, Manning, & Parsons, 2002). These components are well-suited to **empowerment groups** because membership itself can support the personal and interpersonal dimensions of empowerment. The critical analysis of the political environment and individuals' participation in change efforts is also an important component of the empowerment process. This means that group members are empowered from the earliest planning and participate in such processes as the identification of needs, as discussed earlier (Breton, 2004).

In helping to negotiate a change between the group members and their environment, the role of the social worker is to collaborate with the members to mediate between the members and the entities or issues within their environment that creates oppression or injustice (Hudson, 2009). For example, the social worker is thus viewed as a "co-activist" working along with the group to achieve their goals. Such an approach works with many types of group interventions, including social goals/action and reciprocal mutual aid groups.

Recall Georgia's situation from Chapter 1; Georgia experienced intimate partner violence and after working with a social worker individually, she joined an empowerment group with other women who had been in violent relationships. This group supported Georgia's personal needs for esteem and dignity, offered her the opportunity to expand her interpersonal skills and connections, and opened the door to analyze and take action in the wider context of societal institutions that both sustain and challenge the status quo (see Donaldson, 2004). The quote from another survivor of intimate partner violence, Marcy, which appears at the beginning of this chapter, shows us just how powerful the group process can be.

Narrative Theory and Group Interventions

Building on a strengths- and empowerment-focused engagement and assessment process, a narrative approach in intervening with groups continues to emphasize not only the collaboration between the client and social worker, but the collaboration among group members as well. A narrative-oriented group intervention requires the social worker and members to listen to the voices of each member and aid in the deconstruction and reconstruction of the individual or group story. In the case of a mutual aid or therapy group, the stories will be individual, but in a social goals/ action group, the "story" may be the group's story. Reshaping individual or group perceptions sets in motion a plan for members to achieve the unique outcome desired by the individual group member(s). The group members can then contribute to individual or group change process by brainstorming and processing the members' motivations, options, and behaviors.

One of the hallmarks of the narrative approach is the use of witness groups and community supports. **Witness groups** are people called together by the social worker to serve as "witnesses" to discussions between the social worker and the client and/or among the group members. In the case of a group intervention, the witness group is already in place to serve in this capacity. Known as the outside-witness group, these people provide feedback to the social worker and individual group member based on the dialogue they have just heard (Morgan, 2000). Such feedback can include questions, observations, and interpretations. The individual receiving the feedback then has the opportunity to ask questions and respond. This process aids in the development of an alternative approach to the client's current dilemma or concern.

The strategy of using "insider" knowledge (i.e., hearing from others with similar life experiences) is a staple of the narrative approach. This practice strategy is well suited for use with a group intervention, particularly if the group members share similar life experiences and are at different phases of their experiences. For example, Hall (2011) describes a narrative approach in use with a group of males who have battered their partners. Using narrative strategies, the group leader was able to work with the group members to address issues of male power, privilege, and entitlement by externalizing the violence outside of the individual. Using this technique, the males in the group were able to gain insight into the origins of their belief systems (also known as principle of least contest), thus freeing them to determine if they wished to continue their behavior or change (Hall, 2011, p. 180). Such understanding promotes responsibility for choice and, ultimately, assuming responsibility for one's choices. As noted in Chapter 8, narrative approaches are also well suited for application with other theoretical frameworks.

Solution-Focused Group Interventions

Solution-focused interventions with groups are similar to family interventions. While a group of family members and a group of unrelated people may be of similar size, have a common area of concern, and identify similar goals, the dynamics of interpersonal interactions will likely differ. Family members have a history together, while the members of a group intervention do not typically have an existing relationship that shares the intensity, commitment, or future orientation of a family group. Nonetheless, much of the knowledge and skills that you can attain for working with families can be applied to a solution-focused group intervention with a formed group.

To set the stage for implementing a group intervention from the solution-focused perspective, think about the work accomplished during the individual client engagement and assessment phases of group work. During the beginning phases of group work, you collaborated with the clients through a series of questions to identify desired new realities and available strengths and resources that can be mobilized to achieve the clients' goals for change (De Jong, 2009). For the intervention plan, you can continue to build on the questions from the assessment phase by asking the clients to consider again the "miracle," "exceptions," and "scaling" questions to solidify the plan for change. While the questions are posed to individual group members, the entire group is a resource for development of a plan for change. Not only can the members contribute to the development, implementation, and evaluation of individual change plans, they can continue to be a resource throughout the change process through their own questions, observations, and experiences. Once the plan is developed and underway, you can incorporate questions to monitor the members' progress by asking group members to describe changes they are experiencing (i.e., "what's better?").

As noted throughout the discussions of solution-focused interventions with individuals, families, and groups, this approach is used in conjunction with other approaches (e.g., narrative therapy and cognitive behavioral approaches) to enhance the effectiveness and accountability of interventions. De Jong and Berg (2013) suggest that social workers implement a solution-focused intervention with a group after becoming competent with solution-focused work with individuals and families. In practice, it may be easier and more effective to start by using this approach with individual or small family client systems before attempting to manage a larger scale group intervention with which you are not yet comfortable or proficient.

The solution-focused group intervention is particularly well-suited for a variety of client populations and settings. With an emphasis on highlighting positive changes in the client's life and individualized treatment plans developed by the client, this intervention has shown promising outcomes with adults, adolescents, and children and with clients who are not voluntarily participating in the group (Greene & Lee, 2011). Used with adults who are incarcerated, in mental health settings (in- and out-patient), and substance abuse treatment programs, solution-focused interventions "can often be like doing individual therapy in front of a group" (Greene & Lee, 2011, p. 203).

Equally as promising is the integration of solution-focused group interventions with adolescents and children. Attributes of the solution-focused intervention that make it a desirable choice for teens and children are the brief time-limited format, its flexibility, future-oriented focus, de-emphasis on problem "talk," and the ability to build the intervention around a specific topic or theme (Greene & Lee, 2011).

Developmental Models

One of the classic theoretical perspectives on group work, the **developmental model**, is defined by the assumption that the group members (individually and collectively) grow and change as the group process unfolds. Developmental models assume that the group changes and grows in semi-predictable ways. This assumption does not mean the group goes through a rigid progression but rather a series of ripening relationships in which members are perhaps ambivalent about joining at the beginning, then jockey for position within the membership, grow closer together through the work of the group, establish differences from one another, and finally separate at the group's ending. This perspective reflects the idea of stages (also referred to as phases) and has been extremely influential in contemporary group work. Developmental models are still the norm in many practice contexts and are frequently very useful in alerting the worker to possible dynamics, gauging what is happening, and thinking about how to intervene. Two different models—the Boston Model and the relational model—are examined here.

Boston Model   First developed at Boston University's School of Social Work, the **Boston Model** (Garland, Jones, & Kolodny, 1965) has remained a prominent feature in social work education and particularly in practice. The Boston Model outlines five stages of group development: preaffiliation, power and control, intimacy, differentiation, and separation.

- During **preaffiliations** members may feel some ambivalence or reservations about joining the group as well as excitement and eagerness. For example, someone joining a support group for people diagnosed with an illness may be eager to connect with others who have a similar experience, while wondering if she or he will find others who share experiences, fears, and needs.

- In the **power and control stage**, members vie with each other and with the social worker for influence and status within the group. Continuing with the support group for the newly diagnosed person, members who are further along in their illness, treatment, or recovery may perceive themselves as having more status and influence within the group than those members who are recently diagnosed.

- **Intimacy** occurs when the members, having worked through their power issues, become closely connected; they may seem more homogeneous than at any other time in the group. Having processed the issues of power and control, the support can begin to bond around their common life experiences. Members will often share coping strategies and develop relationships outside of the group sessions to help each other through crises.

- During **differentiation** members feel they are safe enough to express and value the differences among each other and the worker; the homogeneity of the former phase matures into a respect for difference. Returning to the illness support group, members may gain enough comfort with one another that they can confront one another on such issues as difference of opinion, coping behaviors, or lack of compliance. Such confrontation can occur successfully only when members have reached a point of mutual respect for one another.

- In the final stage, **separation**, members begin to withdraw from the group in anticipation of its ending. Members of an illness support group may separate as they finish treatment, recover, or learn the illness is terminal.

Although the creators of the Boston Model propose a general progression through these stages, they do not assume that progress will occur as a rigidly linear sequence. There are likely to be points in the life of a group in which one or more members seem to loop back to the behavior common to a previous stage or tend to jump ahead to another one. See Quick Guide 27 to learn how the developmental stages have been applied to three different group populations. While these phases of group process are not typically associated with task groups, one could argue they are in fact, relevant for working with tasks groups as task groups form, bond, and progress through similar relationship-building stages as client groups.

Other authors have created models of group development in which the stages divide slightly differently, and some have additional substages. The group population also influences the degree to which members progress through the phases and the way in which they progress. For example, in an adaptation applied to older institutionalized residents in a group, Kelly and Berman-Rossi (1999) found that

	BOSTON PROTOTYPE	FEMINIST	FEMALE ADOLESCENT FOSTER CARE GROUP	OLDER INSTITUTIONALIZED PERSONS: FLOOR GROUP
	Garland, Jones & Kolodny, 1965	*Schiller, 1995, 1997*	*Lee & Berman-Rossi, 1999*	*Berman-Rossi & Kelly, 1997*
Stage 1	Preaffiliation	Preaffiliation	Preaffiliation: • Approach-Avoidance • Power and Control	Approach-Avoidance
Stage 2	Power and Control	Establishment of a Relational Base	Intimacy and Flight	Intimacy
Stage 3	Intimacy	Mutuality and Interpersonal Empathy	Differentiation	Power and Control 1: Challenging the Institution
Stage 4	Differentiation	Challenge and Change	Termination	Power and Control 2: Challenging theWorker
Stage 5	Termination	Termination		Differentiation & Empowerment

QUICK GUIDE 27 — THREE MODELS FOR STAGES OF GROUP DEVELOPMENT BASED ON THE BOSTON MODEL PROTOTYPE

Adapted from Berman-Rossi & Kelly, 2003

separate stages emerged in which the members first challenged the institution and then challenged the worker. In an empowerment-oriented group (Lee & Berman-Rossi, 1999), adolescent girls in foster care demonstrated an impulse to take flight rather then enter the intimacy stage which may be a result of their family history of chaos and separation).

As with the selection of any intervention approach, professionals must consider the needs of the group and the model or approach that will best serve those needs. With its emphasis on power and control, the Boston Model may be most appropriately used with group members that are more comfortable with competition, power, and conflict (e.g., younger groups) and groups that can move quickly and with independence (Schiller, 2007).

Relational Model This model derives from feminist theorists and practitioners who have objected to the exclusion of women in developmental theory-building. For example, many feminists challenge Erik Erikson's famous male-normed psychosocial sequence of life stages on grounds that he has stereotyped girls as being concerned with "inner space" and boys with "outer space." Some feminists believe the intimacy stage, a clearly relational dimension, actually precedes the identity stage in girls, which reverses Erikson's order. Over two decades ago, Carol Gilligan (1993) suggested that the identity and intimacy stages are intertwined in girls.

The feminist orientation to the importance of relational aspects of development offers a different emphasis for women and girls and appears in group work models as well. Although the **relational model** incorporates stage development, the model also proposes that women go through stages that are different from those of the Boston Model. The second and third stages reflect the emphasis on relationships that are established before the conflict, or challenge, stage. The original model is posed as follows (Schiller 1995; 1997; 2003):

- *Preaffiliation:* Members experience ambivalence about joining.

- *Establishment of a relational base:* Members build strong, affective connections with others.

- *Mutuality and interpersonal empathy:* The connections deepen into a commitment to mutual aid.

- *Challenge and change:* Differences are recognized, and the connections may change in nature.

- *Termination:* Members conclude their work and separate.

This model is useful in feminist groups or in groups composed mainly of women because it supports one of the more accepted gender constructions relating to women's development and theory (Lesser et al., 2004): the importance of established relationship and relational patterns as a precursor to engagement in challenge, such as self-advocacy, or taking risks previously not attempted. Specifically, women benefit in a group environment when they are able to develop relationships with other women who share life experiences and/or are similar to one another. Creating connections can enable women to feel secure and safe within the group, leading to a comfort in sharing with others (Lesser et al., 2004). A relational approach may also be applicable for other groups who may have experienced oppression or displacement, and for which confrontation is not motivating (e.g., immigrants and refugees) (Schiller, 2007).

Relationships and connections are clearly at the heart of this model of group intervention. Thus, a key role for the social worker leading a relational group is to help empower group members to feel safe so they may then move into the phases of the group process in which they take risks and address areas of concern (Schiller, 2007).

There are many valid theories and perspectives that can be used to guide group interventions. Each social worker must determine the theoretical perspective that is

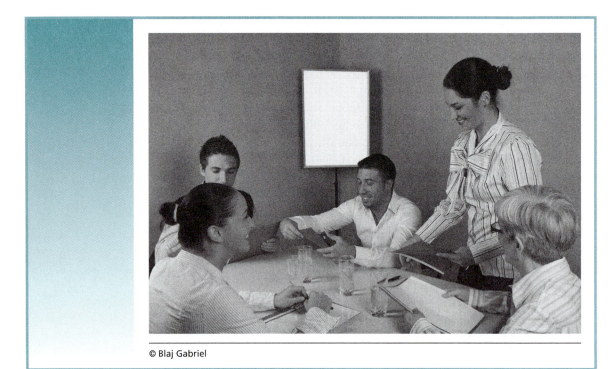

© Blaj Gabriel

most compatible with her or his philosophy and professional and personal value systems, given the agency structures and guidelines and funding sources. Along with comfort level, the practitioner must develop competency in the approach(es) they choose. Regardless of which theory you choose, demonstrating competency through practice behaviors is essential.

CONTEMPORARY TRENDS AND SKILLS FOR THE MIDDLE PHASE OF GROUP WORK: INTERVENTION

The middle phase of the group experience is when the social worker, the client, and the entire group implement the plan to work toward their goals. The social worker and group move into a pattern of interaction in which cohesion, unity, integration, trust, and communication are all enhanced (Macgowan, 2008, p. 284). The primary function of the middle, or intervention, phase of group work is to carry out goals. The *Standards for Social Work Practice with Groups* (IASWG, 2006) provides guidelines for organizing this phase of work and identifying skills needed:

1. Support progress toward individual and group goals—having established both individual and group goals in the assessment phase, the members can

plan and implement the steps needed to accomplish the goals. The social worker must be attentive to the need for goals to be re-negotiated during this phase of work.

2. Attend to group dynamics and processes—the social worker must be vigilant in her or his ongoing observations of group dynamics and processes. As group members become familiar with one another, they may feel more confident confronting one another, which can create conflict within the group. Moreover, the social worker must be mindful of alliances that form within the group and outside the group and the impact of those relationships on individual and group functioning.

3. Identify and access resources within and outside the group—as the work phase progresses, the social worker should know of and have access to resources that may be helpful to the members of the group or the entire group.

4. Have knowledge, skills, and other resources of group work, group members, and sources outside the group—the social worker may encounter situations, dynamics, and needs (e.g., group member conflicts, non-compliance with rules, or needs unable to be met by a group experience) within the intervention phase that require additional knowledge, skills, or resources that can be gained through researching, consulting with colleagues, and even conferring with the group members themselves.

5. Use evidence-based practice techniques in facilitating the group—the social worker is responsible for familiarizing herself or himself with the research available for the type of the group intervention with which they are working.

Examining the literature for evidence-based group interventions can help your group practice. Having both quantitative and qualitative evidence to support the "best available" practices is known as **evidence-based group work** (EBGW) (Macgowan, 2009a, pp. 132–133). Using rigor, impact, and applicability as the criteria for determining the strength of the evidence, EBGW enhances practice and policy accountability, enables social workers to improve practice competencies using empirically validated tools and research outcomes, and ultimately bolsters the efficacy of the group intervention. Crafting an evidence-based approach to implementing and evaluating a group intervention includes seven principles outlined in Exhibit 9.1. While the group format and the social worker's role can vary during this phase of work, a set of practice behaviors exist to facilitate the "work" phase of group practice.

Social Work Group Interventions

As we discussed in Chapter 8, there are four types of groups within which practitioners often work: task groups; social action/goals groups; reciprocal groups (including psychoeducational groups and support groups); and remedial groups. These groups often have overlapping outcomes. For example, the support group educates, the psychoeducational group empowers, the social goals group supports, and all deal with some aspect of social justice, diversity, or human rights, as each issue and

EXHIBIT 9.1	When reviewing the research on approaches to group interventions, consider the following principles:
Principles for Evidence-based Group Work	(1) The way in which client needs and strengths were assessed; (2) Identification of desired outcomes; (3) Risks involved in various approaches; (4) Compliance with the intervention plan; (5) Client responses to intervention; (6) Assessment of outcomes; and (7) Distinction between individual and group outcomes.

Source: Comer & Meier, 2011, pp. 464–470

population represents some dimension of exclusion, which in turn leads to unmet needs and violation of rights (see Goodman, 2004).

At the same time that group work has many traditional approaches in full use today, it also reflects, as does the profession as a whole, the sociocultural context of the times. Accordingly, several innovations in working with groups reflect current theoretical, political, and social issues. Two contemporary issues that the profession has addressed through group work models are intimate partner violence, with constructionist groups, and new approaches to corrections or crime restitution, through restorative justice groups. Each of these will be discussed as an example of a constructivist approach to group intervention.

Each of the efforts described here represents a vital, responsive attempt to counter the negative effects of a contemporary social issue, and each demonstrates creativity and courage. Note that these are living works in progress and as such may not be proven effective, and many conclude with recommendations to improve the experience. Although they are based on recognized social work perspectives and guided by research inquiries, they will no doubt evolve and be fine-tuned as they undergo evaluation procedures to gauge effectiveness and pinpoint the need for change. They take risks in forging new territory and reflect group work's potential.

Constructionist Groups for Women Experiencing Intimate Partner Violence
A **constructionist group** is a group intervention that is facilitated from a social constructionist perspective. This approach requires the facilitator to recognize that reality is created through shared meanings, and offers members the opportunity to develop new understandings of themselves through the group process. A constructionist group intervention embodies feminist and narrative theories as well as the postmodern notion of the way in which a person develops a new and preferred **representation of the self**, or a new view of her or his own worth and identity. In this feminist group, the members accomplish their new representations of the self

by resisting and protesting the male violence they have experienced. The work of the group includes three processes: (1) revealing and undermining the oppressive discourse relating to women experiencing violence, which is a *political* process; (2) identifying and detailing the protest that women actually use in response to violence, the recognition of which reflects *change*; and (3) reconstructing the identities of participants based on the protest. These activities work together to promote first the seeking of resistance (i.e., confronting difficult issues) then an anchoring of resistance (i.e., identifying potential change), culminating in the telling of a new story that elaborates a new identity (Roche & Wood, 2005). This last process is celebrated in an empowering "**definitional ceremony**" (Wood & Roche, 2001a, p. 17), which allows the women to present to an audience of people important to them their new understandings of self. The definitional ceremony includes a first telling of the story by the group member with a response from a witness, followed by the witness re-telling the story, and finalized by the original speaker re-telling the story incorporating the new insights provided by the witness (Leahy, O'Dwyer, & Ryan, 2012).

To illustrate, the social worker in this group points out the common themes of the women's conversation relating to their reactions to violence. For example, some women adopt a socially imposed understanding, which incorporates shame and guilt when male partners are violent toward them. They believe that their own shortcomings cause violence against them and that they are responsible for changing their behaviors in exchange for safety. After a period of time in which the social worker expresses support for the woman, the worker can then help to counter the woman's feelings of shame and guilt by asking perspectival questions that help to break the logic of self-deprecation (for example, "What would your sister say about the way Mike treats you?" "What did the court say about this?"). Such questioning over time encourages a focus on multiple realities by helping women see that others would not think they "deserved" violence or "had it coming," or should "just put up with it."

At this point the social worker seeks descriptions from the women in the group regarding their actual responses, that is, the ways they have resisted and protested. Protest may be in the form of simply not accepting the negative statements made by the batterer, or it may be considerably more confrontational, such as obtaining a restraining order. Some protests may be viewed as passive (giving older bread and milk to an abusive partner while saving fresher food for a child). These incidences of protest, however they are expressed, begin to form the basis for a new understanding of the self as a person of agency who can make real and meaningful life changes.

Group members ask where a woman got her ideas for the protest or the courage to carry it out, and they also consider what the protest says about her. These explorations challenge the woman's identity as helpless and worthless as they lead to a new view. The social worker and other group members then anchor this new more positive representation through reinforcement. The members do this by seeking to enrich the story through the woman's further detailed description, and finally they celebrate her new identity as she sees it through a definitional ceremony to be created collectively by the woman, the group members, and the social worker.

Through an emphasis on process rather than group stages, this group is committed to helping the women in its membership discover the other side of their survivorship and become who they want to be.

New models like this one, based on narrative ideas of the story and constructionist ideas of self, are highly useful in political contexts that highlight contemporary views on gender and power relationships. They are especially applicable with groups addressing sexual assault, intimate partner violence, relationship issues, and in community mental health centers.

Restorative Justice Groups for Combating Crime In another response to a contemporary phenomenon, in this case the climate of punishment and stricter approaches to criminal offenders, social workers have been among those advocating for a different strategy. Seeing the criminal justice system as bogged down in practices that neither heal nor rehabilitate, scholars and practitioners have developed an approach thought to be both more relevant and responsive to the issues of offenders as well as survivors, particularly in cases involving gendered violence against women (see van Wormer, 2009). A loosely associated collection of strategies called **restorative justice groups** focus on crime as an interpersonal conflict that has repercussions on the victim, offender, and community at large. The emphasis is more on the harm done to the relationships of those hurt, and their restoration (see, for example, Boyes-Watson, 2005), than on the violation of the law (Lovell, Helfgott, & Lawrence, 2002) or on the impact on women (van Wormer, 2009). The involvement of the community as an invested party in the occurrence of crime is an important focus: the community suffers when its members are engaged in crime through damage to property and relationships, and the community benefits when relationships are restored.

Based on an actual series of groups conducted at the Washington State Reformatory, the purpose of the groups was to address: (1) offender accountability, (2) the rights of victims, and (3) citizen involvement in the justice process in a way that balanced all three. The major work of the three groups was accomplished through the story of each participant's personal crime experience. Each week one victim, one offender, and one community member shared their personal accounts. Such storytelling increases understanding, validates experience, reduces isolation, and increases the vision for change. Group participants then determined how offenders could respond to the needs of individual victims and what needed to be done to repair the harm done.

The group progress and process variables of these groups were seen as largely consistent with classic models of developmental group work theory (that is, there was initial anxiety and a stage of conflict, followed by greater connectedness) but were also influenced by individual members so that each of the three group meetings reflected different stages of development. A number of additional obstacles to the development of group unity were noted, such as the emphasis on crime, the large number of participants, emotional fragility of participants, problematic group dynamics at times, safety concerns, confidentiality issues, and the implications of diversity, among others. This emphasis on an alternative strategy to respond to crime that heals and helps people reconnect with each other holds encouraging promise in a society struggling with the alienation of both victims and perpetrators. A recent addition to this concept is the enactment of Neighborhood Activity Boards. In many communities, groups of volunteers come together to meet with first-time, non-violent offenders and those people victimized by the criminal activity to discuss the impact of the crime. The offender is typically required to complete community service along with participating in the impact panel.

Motivational Interviewing As discussed in Chapters 5 and 7 in the context of working with individuals and families, motivational interviewing (MI) is an approach that can be introduced into the group setting as well. Known as GMI (group motivational interviewing), implementing an MI-focused group is built on the same premise of engagement, focus, evoking and planning. GMI, in particular, requires the facilitator to emphasize collaboration, autonomy, support, and empathy through the use of reflective listening and change talk (Hohman, 2012). MI scholars, Miller and Rollnick (2013), support the use of MI with a range of group interventions but offer two cautionary notes: 1) the group leader should be competent in the facilitation of MI with individuals before attempting to incorporate it into a group experience; and 2) due to the larger number of participants, there will be fewer opportunities for change talk which may result in less predictable outcomes.

Social Work Skills for Group Interventions

While all theoretical models require skills, and group work interventions may seem different from one-to-one models in social work settings, many of the same generalist practice roles and skills of individual and family interventions are not only applicable but vital to group work interventions. When working to maintain a group-centered focus during the intervention, you will find that listening, supporting, and empathizing all have as important a place in group work as they do in work with individuals. While the following section provides a more in-depth discussion of specific skill areas needed for group interventions, Exhibit 9.2 provides a comprehensive list of general skills that are important to remember when intervening at the group level.

Here are some additional skills critical to group practice, adapted from the authors' practice experience as well as Brown, (2013), IASWG (2006) and Middleman and Wood (1990, pp. 96–102):

Leadership

- Maintaining a "**thinking group**" posture assumes an orientation in which you, as the social worker, consider the group-as-a-whole first and individual members second. This concentration on the whole can require a paradigm shift from thinking of the individual exclusively. For example, you may avoid

EXHIBIT 9.2 *Skills for Group-level Interventions*	When working with groups of any type, a diverse array of skills are needed, including: 1) Understand your relationship to your agency and the way in which you both fit within the context of the larger community. 2) Understand the flow of group work from beginnings through endings. 3) Interact with group members with cultural awareness and sensitivity. 4) Be prepared to advocate for individual clients, the group, and your agency. 5) Practice within the ethical guidelines of the profession. 6) Help the group to establish adaptive norms. 7) Ensure that self-disclosure is consistent with agency policy and meets the needs of the group (as opposed to you). 8) Use of self can help reflection and role modeling for the group. 9) In working with group members to establish goals, ensure they are consistent with the purpose of the group. 10) Regularly seek feedback from the group regarding members' feelings about the group and the process. 11) Collaborate with group members to identify short- and long-term goals. 12) Clarify members' perceptions of time, particularly in terms of change. 13) Provide information to group members that is relevant to the purpose of the group (e.g., medical/health information or legal processes). 14) Be able and willing to say you lack information when that is the case. 15) Incorporate a variety of strategies and techniques into the group process (e.g., art projects, role-playing, relaxation exercises, or videos, speakers, or exercises). 16) Promote expression of feelings within the group. 17) Demonstrate your respect for the group when feelings are shared—active listening, reflecting, and tracking are strategies for showing your interest. 18) Normalize group members' feelings. 19) Engage members on a cognitive level (i.e., thoughts and feelings). 20) Be willing to incorporate past experiences and family history to help group members connect with emotions. 21) Partialize the presenting issues to enable group members to avoid feelings of being overwhelmed. 22) Use confrontation with individuals and the group when needed for issues related to compliance or engagement, for example. 23) Maintain the focus on the present, including use of events in the media to emphasize human nature and social justice. 24) Offer strategies for resolving interpersonal conflicts. 25) Model empathy and use of "I" statements and contracts. 26) Promote member self-esteem and competence. Source: Adapted Greif & Ephross, 2011, pp. 489–493

a prolonged exchange with a single group member because that focus hinders the group's communication.

- **Balanced leadership** can challenge social workers who believe they must have control of the group and its agenda or it will explode or become chaotic. In actuality, if the social worker allows the group to evolve without close attention to process, it *can* become chaotic, members may be emotionally hurt, or the group fragments and loses its meaning for the members. The social worker's ability to effectively facilitate depends on many factors: group connection, functioning, and the presence of internal or **indigenous leadership**; that is, leadership that evolves within the membership.

Generally, the social worker is more directive in the early stages of groups, in groups with lower-functioning members, in groups with little indigenous leadership, in open-ended groups, and in task-oriented groups. As the group progresses, the social worker role is to retreat and encourage growth in group ownership of the activity. The key here for any social worker is to recognize group needs and to be flexible with respect to the degree of direct leadership used. The overall goal for group workers is typically to reduce their activity to as little as possible while maintaining self-awareness and a safe environment and encouraging members to be in charge of their own group.

- **Scanning** is a strategy for maintaining visual observation of all members—the "group version of the attending skill."

- Maintaining **cohesiveness**, or connectedness, means sustaining a sense of "we" through language, encouragement of rituals (for example, marking the beginning and end of each meeting in a specific way), and recording the group's progress. When groups have too much or too little cohesiveness, the leader can address the issue in an effort to uncover the causes (e.g., group member anxiety) (Berg, Landreth, & Fall, 2013). These skills contribute to group members' spirit and facilitate a sense of belonging to something significant. Development and recording (through a chart on the wall, for example) of group agreed-upon norms or customs contributes to a sense of connection, as well.

- Assisting group members in making progress toward goals through support, programmatic activities, addressing obstacles, assessing progress, and re-contracting for goal achievement, as needed.

- Promoting development of mutual aid; may involve re-review of group norms and values and conflict resolution.

- Reviewing and reiterating definitions and rules related to confidentiality with the group, particularly related to sharing information about other group members outside of the group meetings.

Communication

- You must carefully choose the patterns of communication used in your group. If you respond only to the members who speak up, there is likely to be a subset of members who are marginalized and excluded. On the other hand, if you always go around the group, member by member, some members will feel pressed to contribute, and all will feel a certain amount of routinization. A more effective approach is to encourage a respectful balance so that all members can have their opportunity to speak without any one member dominating. Alternatively, you may choose to invite participation by all members (especially those members who remain quiet) and ask if others in the group think or feel the way this (currently speaking) member does. Remind members periodically of the group's commitment by verbalizing the norms that the membership agreed upon, and emphasize the group's accomplishments and history when appropriate.

- Responding empathetically is a critical skill in the context of the group intervention that requires the group leader to: focus on the person speaking, restricting questioning to only those areas that need clarification, allow the group member to finish speaking, and resisting the temptation to provide your own answers to client situations.

- A challenging group work intervention skill is **redirection,** or redirecting questions and concerns away from you back to the group or to individual members. For example, some members will continue to address you over time as the source of authority for the group. Given the power dynamic that many group members may have experienced as clients in other services, such behaviors are not unexpected. By the same token, some members may complain about other members through a third party (often you). In both these situations, the social worker can redirect the message. The goal is to facilitate direct, constructive, communication within the group and the environment that supports it. Exhibit 9.3 provides an example of a redirection within a group using the two scenarios mentioned here.

- Establishing both consensus and difference occurs when you invite agreement and disagreement on issues (e.g., the visitor issue). Registering dissent in a group that approves something heartily, particularly for a person who has not been highly vocal, can be challenging. Early and strong feelings of connectedness and strong group bonds can make that dissent even harder. Later, as the group matures, expressions of difference should be less troublesome to members, but continue to support difference and encourage others' capacities to respond.

- **Exercising silence** can be challenging. If the facilitator is talking, members cannot. The group should engage in most of the interchange and frequently

Following is an example that you, as the group facilitator, can use to redirect a group session in which one member of the group appears to be leading the group in a different direction:

A member asks if visitors can attend a group meeting. That issue has not been previously addressed, so you submit the question to the full membership. In this instance, you turn the question back to the group:

"How do others see this question?" or "How do you as a group want to handle this?"

Within this response you may also want to invite quieter members to participate while softening the messages of the louder voices.

A second scenario involves one member of the group complaining about another member. In this scenario, you may simply say,

"Why don't you tell Bernice that?" or "I don't think you need my help in talking to Kate about that."

EXHIBIT 9.3

When Redirection is Needed in Group Work

can be supported in achieving that by the social worker's well-placed silence, which allows the communication patterns of members to develop.

Problem Solving

- **Connecting progress to goals** Summarizing progress, identifying options, prioritizing decisions, mediating conflicts, confronting lack of progress and group interactions, and weighing potential outcomes are skills and activities that a social worker employs in problem-solving during the intervention phase of group work. On occasion, the social worker may have to negotiate an amended contract with the individual members or the entire group. The social worker may also identify the next discussion areas for future group meetings.

- **Locating resources to benefit group members** involves the mutual identification of resources for group members and accentuating inclusion of natural assets (e.g., friends, family, or neighbors) into the helping network that may also include services, and emphasizing the connections between the group and the community. Engaging in a joint discussion with and among members early in the process conveys the expectation that the group has both the ability and the responsibility to deal constructively with its own issues. As resources outside the group are identified, the potential network expands for all members and supports the interdependence between members, groups, and the environment.

- **Making use of group process and problem solving** The tension between the needs of individual group members and those of the group as a whole is the substance of social work practice with groups. Negotiating differences and the creative enrichment that is possible from the process are the greatest values of the effort. The goal then becomes the reconciliation of difference through a genuine compromise that benefits both the individual and the group. One of the group's clearest responsibilities is to establish an acceptable expression and appreciation for difference. Consider an example, described in a social worker's notes of the eighth meeting of a socialization group of 12-year-old girls, who were referred by their school as having a "rocky time" both at home and in adjusting to middle school life.

The girls were bustling around preparing crepe paper streamers and searching for birthday candles, giggling, joking about how old Lila was really going to be. Some said she was probably going to be 60 or so, judging by how glum she had seemed last week about the party they were planning. Lila was late, and when she finally showed up, she looked more miserable than ever. Finally, she blurted out, "I HATE BIRTHDAYS!!" in a voice very unlike her usual somber tones. The other girls were horrified and silent for a moment—almost unheard of in this group. Lila started to cry. Finally, she choked out the story: Her mother had died the night before her birthday two years ago, and she didn't know how to tell anybody in the group that before. The very word "birthday" was a terrible reminder. She didn't want to celebrate.

The girls seemed to feel sorry, they liked Lila, but they also really wanted to celebrate birthdays in this group. It was an important ritual for them. I confess I didn't have a clue what to do, as their facilitator. After a moment, Betsy, whose grandmother came from France, cheerfully volunteered, "Well, let's be trés français in this group and say we're celebrating our anniversaries! That's what the French call them, the anniversary of birth!" The others responded loudly, hoping their ritual was rescued from certain demise. Lila was silent. She looked up. Finally she almost smiled and said, "I think that would work." And that was that. The group took on a "French theme" ever after and was the only group of 12-year-olds I ever knew that celebrated their anniversaries!

Management of Group Function and Process Inherent in all effective social work interventions is the social worker's ability to interact competently with the client systems. Encompassed within those interactions is an awareness of the spectrum of potential roles that are represented by both the social worker and the group members. Social worker roles with groups have been highlighted throughout this and the previous chapter, but will be summarized here followed by an overview of the roles displayed by group members that social workers in group practice may encounter.

Social Worker Roles While the social worker's primary role is to provide leadership for the group intervention, this role often encompasses a range of roles and skills in order to be effective. The type, format, and goals of the group may determine the role that the social worker will play. The social work group practitioner may find her or himself needing to function in one or more of the following roles (Berg et al., 2013; Furman et al., 2009; Collins & Lazzari, 2009, pp. 299–302; Reid, 2002, pp. 435–436):

- Serving as a **facilitator** requires the social worker to invite sharing and participation, reframe and link issues, and maintaining group boundaries and rules to promote appropriate interactions. The facilitative role requires the social worker to be a skilled listener as well. In a task group, the role of the facilitator may include setting the agenda, maintaining the group's focus on the tasks, and providing documentation of the meeting. Regardless of the group setting, the social worker should strive to maintain an ongoing awareness of the "unconscious group process" (i.e., understanding issues that permeate the group's functioning) (Levy, 2011, p. 155).

- The social worker in the **synthesizer** role summarizes the group members' discussions, identifies themes and patterns, and connects content from one session to the next to promote continuity and substantive discussion.

- **Norm setting** is demonstrated when the social worker provides information regarding appropriate group member behavior through role modeling and direct feedback. For example, the social worker establishes appropriate group interaction by encouraging the use of direct interactions, use of "I" statements, appropriate challenges, and concrete examples, and helping to set the rules at the beginning of the group. Part of norm setting includes the issue of self-disclosure, which can be challenging for many, including the group facilitator. As the leader, you can appropriately share information about yourself as well as suggest group activities that focus on attitudes, values, and beliefs as opposed to more threatening exercises that emphasize sensitive content areas.

- Social workers functioning as **educators** or teachers within a group setting find themselves providing factual information and content specific to the goals of the group.

- As group leaders, social workers can empower group members through promoting **self-advocacy** that can be applied both inside and outside of the group setting. In fact, the group can serve as a place for members to rehearse their newly learned self-advocacy skills.

- As with social work practice with individuals and families, social workers may **collaborate** with another professional. In group work, co-leadership is often an effective strategy in group intervention that involves equal commitment, motivation, and vision and builds on the strengths that each of the leaders brings to the intervention.

Group Member Roles Group members bring their unique characteristics and traits to the group experience regardless of the type of group or its purpose. These qualities can be experienced by the social worker as both strengths and challenges. Ideally, group members will be open to new information, growth, and change, and will be willing and able to actively participate in the group process (Furman et al., 2009). While such characteristics and qualities as these are obvious strengths, even challenging behaviors can be reframed and used for positive individual and group outcomes. If you observe behaviors that suggest that the individual is being resistant (e.g., unwillingness to engage or exhibiting disruptive behaviors), you may be encountering a lack of trust or sense of insecurity (Berg et al., 2013). See Quick Guide 28 for a list of questions that may be helpful in managing resistance.

The social worker can set the stage for appropriate group member interactions by incorporating expectations for appropriate group interactions and responses into the beginning phases of the group intervention, but may still have to work with challenging interactions that result from personality characteristics that are likely to emerge within the group process.

There are some group member roles that commonly emerge within a group intervention. As individual personalities emerge, they will influence and interact with the dynamics of the group itself (much like the dynamics of the family interaction). The competent group practitioner can thus begin to anticipate these roles and behaviors and, having previously considered these possibilities, be prepared with an appropriate response. You must exercise caution, however, to ensure that you do not generalize or stereotype the group member behaviors, but respond to each person as unique. Four of the potentially challenging group member roles and possible social worker responses that you can expect include the following (adapted from Berg et al., 2013; Furman et al., 2009; Yalom & Leszcz, 2005, pp. 391–405):

- The "silent" group member is challenging because it is difficult to determine if the individual is not speaking because she or he is not engaged or is uncomfortable or intimidated, and thus not able to benefit from the group experience. Silence does not necessarily mean that the person is not engaged. While it is possible to experience vicarious gains without active engagement, the social worker typically strives to turn the reticent group member into an active participant. Inviting the individual to participate, noting non-verbal gestures, and speaking with the member outside of the group about her or his silence are all strategies for promoting participation. Should these strategies result in continued lack of participation, the social worker has the option to allow the individual to continue as silent in the group or to develop an alternative intervention outside the group for the individual. As you consider the way in which you are going to address the silence, take into account the responses from the other group members.

QUICK GUIDE 28   LIST OF QUESTIONS THAT MAY BE HELPFUL IN MANAGING RESISTANCE

If you encounter a group member or members who you feel are being resistant to engaging in the group process, consider the following questions:

1. What is the nature (e.g., behavior and attitudes) of the resistance?
2. Are such behaviors as monopolizing or joking disrupting group function and process?
3. How does resistance impact other areas of the individual's life?
4. How are other group members responding to the group member displaying resistance?
5. How are you responding to the group member displaying resistance?

After reflecting on these items, your role as the group facilitator is to share your observations with the group and, collectively, brainstorm possible causation and responses.

Source: Berg, Landreth, & Fall, 2013, p. 125.

- Equally as challenging for a group leader is the "monopolizer" who is perceived as talking too much. In this role, the group member may attempt to offer her or his opinion on virtually every statement made by others or may spend an inordinate amount of time describing her or his own situation or needs. Monopolizing can present itself in different forms, including the "compulsive talker," "intellectualizer," "special interest pleader," or "manipulator," all of whom may be operating out of fear or a need to control the situation. While understanding the reasons for this person's behavior is important for changing the behavior, the impact on the group process and members can be negative. As with the "silent" group member, the social worker can address the monopolizing behavior within the group her or himself or encourage the group to address the behavior, work with the monopolizer outside the group to address the reasons she or he feels compelled to speak so frequently, or develop an alternative intervention strategy.

  Groups of individuals within the group can form sub-groups or cliques which can also monopolize the group's time and energy as well as isolate or create divisions or conflicts. Allowing the group itself to manage sub-groups when they form is ideal; the social worker can ensure that the process is fair and respectful.

- The group member who appears to reject help/ideas can be viewed as both a challenge and a resource. Such avoidant behavior can signal depression or lack of problem-solving skills. As a challenge, the "help-rejecting" or complaining group member is likely to have a negative influence on the group dynamics and be unable to experience actual change or growth. As a resource, the negative perspective can be used by the other group members to see the potential possibilities (if only as a reaction to the negativity). The social worker can respond, not to encourage the individual, but to maintain a focus on concrete feedback and the group process and can encourage the group to respond to this member as well. The leader may also seek to build trust with the member displaying avoidant behaviors.

- The "caregiver" (also known as the coordinator or rescuer) is the group member who strives to take care of others, including the group facilitator. Not surprisingly, the caregiver often neglects to attend to her or his own needs, but uses others as a way to avoid addressing individual challenges. The social worker can respond to the caregiver by acknowledging her or his history of altruistic caregiving, praising the caregiver for her or his willingness to now take care of her or his own needs, and incorporating gentle confrontation when the caregiver attempts to care for others as a way to impede personal progress.

- The "attacker" can stimulate the group by her or his assaults on other members or the facilitator, but can be disruptive as well. Acknowledging the attacker's behavior is a first step toward exploring the underlying reasons for the aggressive behaviors. Confrontation is required if the attacks become personally targeted.

- Certain "dependent" behaviors can be challenging to manage in the group setting. For example, the "harmonizer" strives to maintain peace within the group; the "clown" uses humor (often to mask depression or fear); and the "poor me" member seeks constant affirmation. As a facilitator, you can initiate a discussion focused on the styles that the members possess and the function those styles serve in their lives.

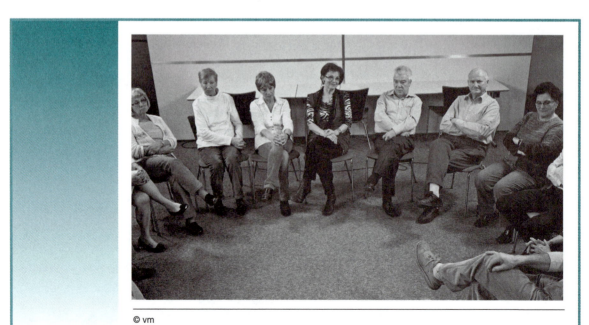

© vm

QUICK GUIDE 29   SUMMARY OF INTERVENTION SKILLS FOR
SOCIAL WORK GROUP PRACTICE

The social worker engaged in the intervention phase of social work practice with groups should be:
- knowledgeable and skilled in group leadership (e.g., logistics and time management);
- facilitating group communication and group dynamics;
- competent with individual and problem-solving;
- focused on promoting progress toward group and individual goals;
- able to manage of group functions.

As the discussion of the intervention or middle phase of the group work process comes to a close and the exploration shifts to the termination and evaluation phases of group work, a review of the skills needed for competently intervening with groups may be helpful. See Quick Guide 29 for a re-cap of the skills presented.

CONTEMPORARY TRENDS AND SKILLS FOR THE ENDING PHASE OF GROUP WORK: TERMINATION AND EVALUATION

Although all of the concepts explored in terminating (i.e., ending) and evaluating social work with individuals and families can be applied to most clients in any constellation, there are some additional considerations and dynamics that often occur in social work practice with groups. As in social work terminations and evaluations with individuals and families, the intensity of the phases of ending a group and evaluating the work depends on the type and function of its purpose.

Social Work Group Endings

Social work practice with groups ends in many ways and evokes a range of member responses and interactions. Terminations may occur when a member opts to leave the group, when the group reaches a pre-determined time limit, or when the leader leaves the group (Furman et al., 2009). Regardless of the reason for the group's termination, endings have the potential to evoke emotional responses from the members; therefore, the social worker's role in termination is to "help members examine their accomplishments, review their experience together, and prepare for the future . . . and express and integrate positive and negative emotion" (Garvin & Galinsky, 2008, pp. 291–292). Group members may experience such positive emotions as success and elation and/or such negative emotions as loss, threat, rejection, abandonment, or anger—all of which may relate both to experiences from the group and their own lives (Furman et al., 2009). The group leader may notice that group members regress back to previous behaviors, withdraw from the group, panic, or begin to devalue the group experience (Brown, 2013). For example, members of an educational group are likely to experience fewer highly emotional responses than those of a treatment group. A group that has met only six times will probably not have the level of investment in the group process as a group that has met for three years. Addressing members' responses is a part of the social worker's responsibility in helping the group to arrive at its endings. In any event, ending with groups is often a complex endeavor as you deal with endings on three different levels:

- The relationship between group members and the social worker.

- The relationships among the group members.

- The structure of the group itself.

A practitioner needs to consider the termination phase of group work from the theoretical framework they are using. We will now look at endings from the theoretical perspectives discussed earlier

Endings in Group Work with Strengths and Empowerment   Continuing with the integration of strengths and empowerment concepts into the termination phase can enable the individual members and the group to review the progress made toward their goals and develop strategies for sustaining the changes. In the case of social work groups with clients, the social worker can invite each member to review and reflect on her or his individual experience in the group, including strengths brought to the group process, status in the beginning, middle, and endings phases of work, change experienced, and plans for maintaining the change(s) while using the group's strengths. Having individual members engaged in this process provides an opportunity for the social worker and other group members to contribute to this process. Other group members can also take advantage of their fellow group members' reflections for their own review and sustainability processes.

A strengths-based perspective can further enable the social worker and the group members to reflect on the group strengths that have evolved as the group moved through various phases. The social worker can use the group ending as an opportunity to provide feedback on the changes observed in the group's engagement, cohesion, and work. Additionally, the group members can reflect on their experience being part of a strengths-focused group experience. Such a reflection can serve to empower the group members and the social worker to integrate the power of the group process.

In situations in which the individual or group goals are not realized, the formal ending of a task, social action, or client-oriented group can still be oriented toward a strengths perspective. One strategy is to engage in an exercise in which the members review the strengths that existed at the outset of the group, those strengths gained or mobilized during the group, and those strengths that can be carried on by the members after the group is terminated. While the members (and the social worker) may be dismayed by the perceived failure of not achieving their goals, planning ways in which the members can continue to work toward achieving the goals can be empowering.

Endings in Narrative-Focused Group Work With an emphasis on strengths, termination of a narrative-focused group lends itself well to the use of a ritual or ceremonial activity as well as the public acknowledgement of growth and change. Group members can continue as collaborators with one another and the social worker to plan a celebration to recognize the ending of the group's formal phase of work together. This "definitional" ceremony can acknowledge the achievement of goals and the next phase of the individual and group members' growth experience as well as help individuals to reclaim or redefine themselves (Morgan, 2000, p. 121).

As with individual and family work endings, public testimonials are a part of the termination process (Morgan, 2000). Using the group members to listen to individual testimonials and provide feedback can serve to empower the members' changes and to solidify plans for maintaining change beyond the formal group experience. A process similar to that used with individuals can be employed with groups, with the group members serving as the outsider-witnesses. The definitional ceremony begins with the social worker and group members listening as the individual group member re-authors her or his work in the group. The witnesses then reflect back to the individual re-authored story, the individual member responds to the feedback, and the entire group engages in discussion about the process. This process can be helpful both as a tool for recognizing individual and group strengths and goal attainment and to evaluate the process of change.

Endings in Solution-Focused Group Work Termination of the solution-focused group intervention can be viewed as the achievement of the initial and overall goal for the work of the group. Solution-focused group interventions identify issues and plan and begin a planned change effort. In the case of a group intervention, the other group members provide a structure for vetting the issues as well as the solutions. You will recall that solution-focused interventions are grounded in the ongoing use of a series of questions to elicit strengths, thoughts and feelings regarding change, and developing plans for change. You can bring this technique into the termination phase as well; you can ask members about the progress they've made via scaling questions (e.g., "On a scale of 1 to 10, where were you when you began this group? Where are you now? Where do you need to be in order to leave this group and maintain the change?") (De Jong, 2009). The group members can involve themselves in the individual member's response by providing their own observations of her or his change process. Shifting the emphasis from the present to the future can also empower the individual and group members to perceive themselves as separate from the group and the social worker leading the group, thus enabling them to view themselves as empowered to implement and maintain the desired changes.

Regardless of the theoretical perspective employed for the group intervention, a number of competencies are needed for effectively bringing an intervention to an end. As with all aspects of the social work intervention, groups are made of unique individuals and situations, and the social worker must be attuned to those aspects. However, there is also a set of termination-related skills specific to group practice.

Skills for Social Work Group Terminations

Just as the other phases of the group intervention have a primary function and requisite skill set, so too does the termination phase. With an emphasis on consolidating the work, the social worker focuses on bringing closure for the individual group member, the group itself, and for her or himself (IASWG, 2006; Toseland & Horton, 2008). As a result of the complexity and intensity of group endings, even those that are planned, social workers need a skill set that is reflective of the unique features of the group intervention. The social worker should recognize and attend to all the meanings that evolve (Kurland & Salmon, 1998). A particularly powerful aspect of the termination comes in the form of individual and group reflection. Group members and the facilitator have the opportunity to reflect on commonalities, differences, accomplishments, and the development of relationships, all of which can promote individual and group self-awareness (Drumm, 2006). Let's now look at each of the multiple areas related to group endings.

Ending the Relationship between Group Members and Social Worker   A more extensive examination of the ending of the relationship between group members and the social worker is warranted, as this ending, more than the other two, has implications for the social worker. In this final phase of any type of group (i.e., task or client group), the social worker has several responsibilities with respect to the entire group, including (Brown, 2013; IASWG, 2006; Furman et al., 2009; Kurland & Salmon, 1998; Toseland & Horton, 2008):

- Prepare members for ending (from the mid-point of the group intervention).

- Assess progress toward achievement of group goals.

- Help stabilize member and group gains.

- Anticipate and elicit individual and group responses to ending.

- Plan timing and content to maximize the sessions/meetings left.

- Help group members express their ambivalence about the group's ending and address individual and group reactions and behaviors to individual or group accomplishments, including affirmations and confidence building regarding achievements.

- Share observations of progress and confidence in members' abilities to function successfully without the group or in the case of a task group, continue working toward identified goals (it may be helpful to identify any obstacles to success and needed connections to resources outside the group).

- Support members' efforts to begin the process of separating from the group and identify strategies for implementing change and applying new knowledge.

- Develop awareness of ways in which individual and group change will impact systems external to the group.

- Help members connect their experiences in the group to life experiences in the future.

- Develop awareness of your own feelings regarding ending and reflect on and share feelings with the group.

- Elicit feedback from the group members about the group process.

The social worker's task is to help the group end positively and help members' achievements translate into the "real world" outside the group. The social worker also has to monitor her or his own responses; after all, she or he has invested a great deal of effort in facilitating an effective experience, and more successful groups may experience more difficult endings. Recalling the overall purpose of the group and focusing on the specifics of the process can help balance the response between task and emotion.

There are also a number of typical group behaviors at ending that may be directed either at the social worker or the group as a whole. These include: (1) denial (or simply "forgetting" that the group is ending); (2) **clustering**, moving toward more connection rather than less; (3) **regression**—either claiming verbally, or acting out in behavioral terms, that the group is not ready to end; (4) withdrawal or passivity related to active participation, (5) rebellion; or (6) flight—leaving the group before it ends (Furman et al., 2009; Reid, 1997).

The responses to ending are similar to those that occur in intervening with individuals and families. The fact that they may be multiplied by the number of people in the group can make them feel quite momentous to you as the social worker. For example, when an entire collective of 13-year-old girls makes it clear, through sudden and orchestrated hostility to you, that they do not want the experience to end, you can certainly feel the power of the group. In this case, just as in individual or family work, you can view the group's reaction as a function of the process (and perhaps of the success of the group), rather than focused personal assault.

Social worker skills that are particularly useful in ending work with groups include (Middleman & Wood, 1990):

- *Focusing on group:* As always, in group work, this skill keeps the social worker focused on the processes of the entire group and the priority of its development as an entity rather than on individual members.

- *Summarizing:* Completing a review of group decisions and actions is a useful strategy for ending group work because the group can discuss their achievements.

- *Voicing group achievements:* The social worker and group members can acknowledge the group's successes and validate the members' hard work.

- *Preserving group history and continuity:* This skill involves emphasizing the entity of the group in its social location and linking its history to the members' futures. In the process of ending, the social worker can focus on the group's continuity as translation to the world outside of the group.

Ending the Relationships among Group Members In this aspect of ending, members may exhibit individualized versions of denial or flight as well as variations of these. Some members may not attend meetings that are specifically dedicated to ending activities. Others may attend but refuse to enter any group interactivity about endings, or they may simply resign themselves to rejection. Individuals may become increasingly short-tempered and impatient with other members, as if to negate the importance of their relationship and to render ending insignificant or even a relief. This behavior can occur among members who have worked the hardest at making connections with one other.

In other situations, individual members will question their ability to maintain the changes they have made without the assistance of the group and the social worker. These members will sometimes lobby for individual sessions with the worker or a reconstituted "mini group" in which only a few members of the original group would attend. In addition, some individuals may initiate more intense relationships with other group members outside the confines of the group meetings, as if to negate the need for the group. The most helpful thing you can do is articulate your observations regarding group dynamics. Staying focused on the group, rather than on the individuals, can be challenging, but it is part of negotiating a successful ending.

Ending the Group Itself This ending is at once philosophical and technical. On the philosophical level, reflect on your own feelings about ending this unit of work and this group of unique characters. How will it contribute to your professional growth? What could you have done differently? How will members benefit from it? If the group has been difficult, you may struggle with feelings of inadequacy or a sense of

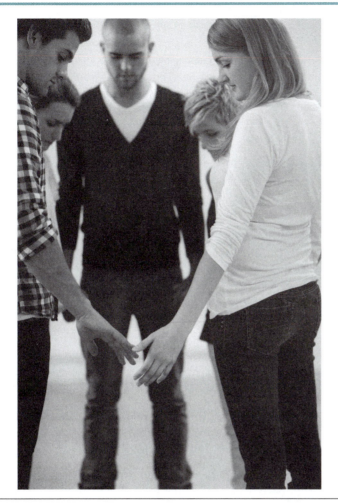

© Yuri Arcurs

work left undone. When there is an overall sense of the group's having gone well, you may feel exhilarated by a sense of accomplishment, of having crossed a particular hurdle, or of entering into the realm of the skilled. When you consider a metaphor for your experience, would it be death? Divorce? Disengagement? A required course? Graduation?

On a much more practical side, you will need to close out the records of participation, complete the evaluation process (addressed shortly), and terminate the logistical arrangements such as space and place. Finally, you will need to honor follow-up commitments and successfully make any referrals or transfers.

As an example of the issues that can arise when terminating with a group, consider the following group scenario:

A community-based agency that serves new immigrants offers a group for high school-aged students focused on the students' transitions from their country of origin to their newly adopted country. The group has a secondary purpose: providing an opportunity for the students to practice their English skills in a safe environment. The group composition is mixed gender and ethnicity. The social worker who is charged with facilitating this group has developed her cultural competency through her commitment to learn as much as she can about the students' heritage and traditions, language, the rules and norms for gender interactions, and faith traditions. She personally conducts an interview with each student who is referred to the group and her or his parents/family/guardians so she can be familiar with the individual student's needs and goals for joining the group.

The current group of students has developed into a cohesive group, particularly around the issues of being "Americanized" as they are enthusiastically adopting the customs of teens in their new country. The group members also share similar struggles with their parents who are distressed that their children are abandoning their heritages. The social worker has become aware of a potential dilemma. The time-limited group is scheduled to come to an end but the social worker has been approached by a number of the parents who have asked her to continue the group for the purpose of reconnecting the teens to their ethnic and cultural roots. While the teens enjoy the group, they have already planned their "graduation" celebration and appear ready to move on with life outside the group. The social worker is conflicted— she empathizes with the parents' concerns but believes the group should terminate as planned. What options or alternatives might the social worker consider in order to meet the needs of both groups?

In sum, endings can and should be a time for reflection and celebration. Equally important for all social workers in group practice, but particularly critical for those in the early stages of their career, is reviewing the group process as it has impacted your personal and professional growth. This exploration will now come to its own ending with a discussion of the process of evaluating the group intervention as experienced by the group members and the social worker.

Evaluation of Social Work Practice with Groups

Evaluation of practice with groups serves the same purpose as evaluating practice with individuals and families: to examine the work, the process, and the social worker's skills. Specifically, an evaluation of a social work group intervention reviews the progress and reflects on the process (Furman et al., 2009). While there are similarities in the evaluations of individual, family, and group interventions, there are also differences. Unlike family interventions that focus exclusively on the unit and individual intervention evaluations that focus solely on the individual, the evaluation of a group intervention encompasses both the individual and the group, thus moving evaluation to a level of complexity not typically found with individual and family evaluations.

As noted previously, groups include individuals who arrive at the group with individual goals, personalities, needs, and expectations. Oftentimes, the social worker must consider evaluative strategies within the context of a large, diverse group of individuals who perceive their experience differently from one another. You must frame an evaluation of any group intervention within the context of the purpose, type, structure, and format of the group. To further heighten the complexity of group evaluation, the social worker must work within the agency or organizational structure in which the group is conducted. Having to address multiple needs with a group of individuals thus requires the social work group practitioner to have a clear and thoughtful approach to evaluation of the group intervention *prior* to the first meeting of the group.

Regardless of the method(s) used to evaluate the group intervention, it is important for everyone involved in the intervention to participate in the evaluative process (Garvin & Galinsky, 2008). There are many strategies available for accomplishing the goals for this phase of the group intervention (Bloom, Fischer, & Orme, 2009; Furman et al., 2009; Garvin & Galinsky, 2008):

- Review individual and group member accomplishments with an emphasis on preparing for the future, sustaining change, and ensuring the inclusion of support systems to reduce risk for failure.

- Gather group members' impressions of the group experience and the activities/programming. Data can be collected publically as part of the group process (within the group or written evaluations) or anonymously (in writing), using caution to avoid "satisfaction-only" surveys as they typically do not accurately reflect growth and change, but members' feelings about the facilitator, setting, etc.

- Administer pre- and post-group measures of behaviors, attitudes, and function. Consider the use of previously validated and standardized measures that have been administered on groups comparable to the group intervention you are evaluating. Such measures will provide you with evidence-supported data from which to interpret your findings. While standardized measures of the individual are appropriate for use in group interventions, consider also the use of standardized measurements developed specifically for group interventions (e.g., see Group Engagement Measure (originally developed by Macgowan, 1997; further psychometric testing: 2000, 2003 (with Levenson), and 2005)).

- Through direct observation by the social worker, document behaviors and changes in individual group members and the group. Data can be gathered quantitatively and/or qualitatively.

- Complete a self-evaluation, including exploration into such areas as: meeting group member needs, development of appropriate structure and interventions, and assessment of own performance as a social work practitioner. As part of reflecting on your role within the group, you may want to conduct a self-evaluation so that you can grow and evolve as a group facilitator. Quick Guide 30 provides a strategy to help you engage in a self-evaluation.

- Solicit direct observation and feedback by other professionals.

In the practice of social work intervention, termination, and evaluation services with groups, the social worker will find that each group will develop its own personality, thus making each group experience unique. There are, however, aspects of each phase of the process that you will find are often replicated when you are providing leadership to a group. Recall from Chapter 8 the examination of the engagement and assessment phases of three group models (social goals/action, reciprocal, and remedial models) used within groups consisting of parents from the Riverton community. Returning to the Riverton example, Exhibits 9.4, 9.5, and 9.6 depict the intervention, termination, and evaluation phases from the perspectives of the three models.

In addition to the type(s) of evaluative strategies for examining group interventions that we have discussed, consider using the data that you gather and analyze to develop evaluation tools that can be used for future groups (Garvin & Galinsky, 2008). For example, you and other group facilitators may find it helpful to have a menu of strategies for monitoring group progress or a manual for conducting a group intervention. Exhibit 9.7 offers a sample of a facilitator evaluation that can be completed by group members.

QUICK GUIDE 30   GROUP FACILITATOR SELF-EVALUATION

When reflecting on your experience leading a group, ask yourself the following questions:

1. How did the group experience me?
2. What feelings did I experience in this session? Did I express those feelings? Did I have some feelings with which I did not feel comfortable?
3. What were my reactions to various group members? Did I feel "turned off" to some members, rejecting? Do all members know I care about them? Do they feel accepted by me?
4. What did I communicate to each member? Did I say what I really wanted to say? Was my message clearly stated?
5. How much time did I spend focused on the content of the discussion rather than on the interaction taking place or feelings and needs subtly expressed?
6. What do I wish I had said or done? What would I do differently next time?
7. Did I dominate? How willing was I for someone else to assume the leadership role?

This reflection can be completed following each session as well as when the group comes to a close. Upon finishing this reflection, consider ways in which you may strengthen your group skills.

Source: Berg, Landreth, & Fall, 2013, p. 138.

PHASES II and III: MIDDLE AND ENDING WORK

Background: Concerned about the use and abuse of alcohol among their adolescent children, a group of parents in the Riverton community approach a local community service agency to ask for help in addressing this problem.

Work thus far: Stakeholders and their interests and goals have been identified. The social worker's role has been agreed upon. A community needs assessment has been conducted, including strengths, resources, needs, and priorities. A plan for intervention, termination, and evaluation has been established and will focus on developing and mounting a public education campaign to raise awareness about the issue of teen drinking.

Note: While the stages of group interventions are not linear and may, in fact, overlap, the following depicts a possible approach to responding to the identified need.

INTERVENTION	TERMINATION	EVALUATION
Identify community partners who will support the education campaign and help with dissemination	Terminate intervention	Conduct evaluation
		Analyze data gathered from evaluation effort
Confirm the plan, time frame, and resources for intervention, termination, and evaluation continue to be viable		Implement plan for sustainability
		Document findings
Launch the intervention Monitor progress, particularly dissemination and relationships with community partners		
Adapt the intervention, as needed		
Revisit plan for evaluation and sustainability		

EXHIBIT 9.5	
Riverton Children's Grief Support Group: An Example of Reciprocal Group	**PHASES II and III: MIDDLE AND ENDING WORK** Background: A social worker in a local community service agency has become aware of a number of children of Riverton who have lost a parent to alcohol and substance-related deaths. The social worker takes steps toward offering to the community a support group that includes to an educational focus. Work thus far: Based on the social worker's assessment of community need and interest, group members were recruited, screened, and invited to join the group. A first session was planned and has been held, at which time group rules and norms were determined collaboratively by the social worker and the group members. Individual group goals and needs were shared. The social worker's role as a facilitator/educator was established. Note: While the stages of group interventions are not linear and may, in fact, overlap, the following depicts a possible approach to responding to the identified need.

INTERVENTION	TERMINATION	EVALUATION
Social worker begins each session by reviewing group rules and norms and conducting member check-in	Begin termination as planned	*Individual*
	Check in with each group member regarding feelings regarding the termination of the group and the process	Determine if goals were met (informal or formal)
Social worker engages in ongoing assessment of individual member needs, group interactions, and group cohesiveness		Administer post-group collection of data
Social worker has developed a repertoire of agency and community resources available to suggest as needed	Invite each member to talk about individual gains and continuing needs	*Group*
		Determine if group goals were met (informal or formal)
Revisit group needs and adapt intervention and educational programming plans as appropriate	Discuss plans for sustaining change and any perceived obstacles to maintenance	Ask members to provide feedback regarding satisfaction with the group process
Share information, as agreed upon prior to group initiation, with legal guardians	Provide resources as needed to help members sustain change	Document findings
Monitor individual and group progress and adapt as needed		
Regularly revisit time frame and plans for termination and evaluation	Conduct termination ritual or celebration	
Invite suggestions from group members regarding plans for recognizing group termination		

PHASES II and III: MIDDLE AND ENDING WORK

EXHIBIT 9.6

Riverton Mental Health Center Group for Persons with Dual Diagnosis: An Example of Remedial Group

Background: A new social worker at the Riverton Mental Health Center has recently assumed leadership for a clinical intervention group for persons with dual diagnoses (i.e., substance abuse and mental illness) who receive outpatient services at the agency. The group is diverse in membership, including mixed genders, range of ages, and mandated and voluntary members. Membership turnover is dependent on members' "graduation" from the treatment program; therefore, the group often has entering and exiting members. Two new members have been referred to the group. This will be the first time new members have been referred since the social worker took over responsibility for the group.

Work thus far: The social worker has gathered information on eligibility criteria for group membership and integrating new members into an ongoing group. The social worker has met with the two persons who have been referred and determined they would be appropriate for inclusion. The two members have been oriented and attended their first meeting. During this session, the social worker introduced the new members to the group, revisited group rules and norms, and assessed the individual goals and needs and group cohesion.

Note: While the stages of group interventions are not linear and may, in fact, overlap, the following depicts a possible approach to responding to the identified need.

INTERVENTION	TERMINATION	EVALUATION
At the beginning of each session, social worker reminds members of group rules and norms	Ongoing as membership is open	Complete formal evaluation as required by agency
Social worker conducts check in by asking members to share with the group the events/actions since the last session	Determine termination ritual appropriate to an open-ended group	Obtain information from existing members regarding achievement of goals and experiences with group format and process (e.g., open vs. closed and time-limited format) and social worker leadership
Social worker assesses individual member needs and goals, and monitors progress towards goals (critical as each person may potentially be at a different point in their progress)	Prepare existing and remaining members for termination	
	Check in with members regarding their feelings about termination	Document findings
Social worker assesses group cohesion		
Members with longer membership serve as guides/mentors for newer members		

EXHIBIT 9.7

Group Counselor Rating Scale

Instructions: Rate your group counselor as you see her/him functioning in your group.

Respect: Shows a real respect for the group members by attentiveness, warmth, efforts, to understand and freedom of personal expression.

	5.0	4.5	4.0	3.5	3.0	2.5	2.0	1.5	1.0
Very high			high		moderate		low		very low

Empathy: Communicates an accurate understanding of the group members' feelings and experiences. The group members know the counselor understands how they feel.

	5.0	4.5	4.0	3.5	3.0	2.5	2.0	1.5	1.0
Very high			high		moderate		low		very low

Genuiness: Realness. Everything she/he does seems to be real. That's the way she/he really is. This person doesn't put up a front.

	5.0	4.5	4.0	3.5	3.0	2.5	2.0	1.5	1.0
Very high			high		moderate		low		very low

Concreteness: "Tunes in" and responds to specific feelings of experiences of group members. Avoids responding in generalities.

	5.0	4.5	4.0	3.5	3.0	2.5	2.0	1.5	1.0
Very high			high		moderate		low		very low

Self-Disclosure: Lets group know about relevant immediate personal feelings. Open, rather than guarded.

	5.0	4.5	4.0	3.5	3.0	2.5	2.0	1.5	1.0
Very high			high		moderate		low		very low

Spontaneity: Can respond without having to "stop and think." Words and actions seem to flow easily.

	5.0	4.5	4.0	3.5	3.0	2.5	2.0	1.5	1.0
Very high			high		moderate		low		very low

Flexibility: Adapts to a wide range of conditions without losing her/his composure. Can adapt to meet the needs of the moment.

	5.0	4.5	4.0	3.5	3.0	2.5	2.0	1.5	1.0
Very high			high		moderate		low		very low

Confidence: Trusts her/his abilities. Acts with directness and self-assurance.

	5.0	4.5	4.0	3.5	3.0	2.5	2.0	1.5	1.0
Very high			high		moderate		low		very low

Open-ended questions may also yield insightful group perceptions about the facilitator:

1. Of what changes have you become aware in your attitudes, feelings about yourself, and relationships with other people?
2. How did the group experience help these changes to come about?
3. What did the group leader do that was most helpful and least helpful to you?
4. Was the group experience hurtful to you in any way, or did it have any negative effect on you?
5. Briefly identify any group exercises you especially like or disliked.
6. In what ways do you wish you had been different in the group?
7. How are you most different as a result of the group experience?

Source: Berg, Landreth, & Fall, 2013, p. 143–144.

STRAIGHT TALK ABOUT GROUP INTERVENTION, TERMINATION, AND EVALUATION

The social worker's overall role and purpose is to encourage and mobilize the strengths of the group. The concern for individual well-being and growth is augmented by the social factors of the group, one member to another. Consistent with trusting the group process, the social worker should strive to avoid overinvestment in the centrality or power that may attribute to her or his role. The goal, after all, is for the group to gain its voice and develop its strength, even as individual members continue to grow. You will not be able to take credit, even in your own mind, for all of the potential successes in your group. In exchange, you will have the privilege of experiencing the power of group connection and the autonomy it ultimately can exercise as it liberates the power of its members. The emphasis on the group does not mean that your own role is any less important. You are responsible for the safety of each member in the group and for ensuring the group processes its own activity. Accordingly, your role is to evaluate group process and functioning on an ongoing basis, just as you do in other forms of social work practice interventions. This will vary according to the nature of your group purpose, goals, and format. For example, if you are working in a task group, monitoring progress in completing the group's project will be the focus of the intervention and evaluation processes. If you facilitate a group for school-aged children, you must make sure to use an appropriate developmental level. Other forms of evaluation that are especially useful come from members: Is the group meeting their social and affiliation needs? Do they continue to feel safe in it? Is it a helpful forum to address the issues they want to deal with? As always, consider the work of evaluation as an ongoing process.

CONCLUSION

In emphasizing the importance of relational components in our lives, first as people and then as social work practitioners, this chapter has presented social work practice with groups in the role of mediating a range of social and emotional issues, including isolation, oppression, and life crises. Currently there are many exciting adventures into social work practice with groups that build upon contemporary theoretical perspectives, social justice, and diversity. Scenarios relating to cultural inclusion, gender and disability, collaboration, and spirituality in models that emphasize process over stages and story over problem all point to the empowering direction that social group work is taking in the history of the profession. Social work practice with groups offers significant potential for the future and is particularly relevant for the social justice, diversity, and human rights connections that give social work its meaning.

MAIN POINTS

- Effective social work practice interventions with groups provide an interface for social justice, diversity, and human rights.

- Middle-phase (intervention) and ending phase (termination) strategies were approached from the perspectives of strengths and empowerment, narrative and solution-focused approaches.

- Developmental models, such as the Boston Model and others based on it are widely used theoretical perspectives on group development. Many applications of, and departures from, this model can be found in the contemporary practice environment.

- Social workers working with groups hone their skills for intervening with individuals and must develop additional skills for group intervention in the areas of group leadership, community, problem-solving, and management of group functioning.

- Contemporary examples of innovative, evidence-based group practice models, such as constructionist groups and restorative justice groups, help to provide vision and possibility for responding to current cultural and social issues as they unfold.

- Termination occurs in three distinct areas of group practice interventions: between the group members and the social worker, among the group members, and the group itself.

- While evaluation of group practice shares some commonalities with evaluation of individual and family interventions, evaluating group interventions is more complex as examination of the individual members of the group and the group itself is both required.

EXERCISES

a. Case Exercises

1. Go to www.routledgesw.com/cases and review Carla Washburn's video vignette and consider the roles each member plays for the following activities and questions:
   a. Gather into groups. Starting the group session from the conclusion of the video vignette, role-play the next session. What happens next? Process the group session with the class.
   b. Round robin: Each student takes the opportunity to role-play the social worker. Change roles when the "social worker" is not sure how to proceed with the group. Debrief about the experiences and practice behaviors demonstrated for each role-play. What were strengths and areas for growth for each student as a facilitator?
   c. Select a member of the group and discuss her or his role in the group process.
   d. Identify the social worker's strengths as a group facilitator along with those practice behaviors that may be improved.
2. Termination of a group intervention can be challenging. Returning to the grief support group depicted in the Carla Washburn video vignette, role-play the final session. Consider the following:
   a. What is the most important role the social worker plays at this stage of the group process?
   b. What practice behaviors are critical for the termination phase of a group intervention?
   c. Brainstorm strategies for responding to the array of possible member reactions to the ending of the group experience.
3. At the conclusion of a group intervention, the evaluation of the effectiveness of your interventions is critical. Research various evaluation tools and complete the following for the grief support group in which Carla Washburn is a member:
   a. Create a satisfaction survey.
   b. Create a pre-test/post-test.
   c. Create a six-month evaluation tool.
4. Go to www.routledgesw.com/cases and view the Riverton video vignette that depicts a group meeting of the Riverton Neighborhood Association. Upon viewing the video, respond to the following:
   a. What model of group intervention is being conducted in this vignette?
   b. Identify practice behaviors and skills covered in this chapter that the group facilitator is demonstrating in the meeting.
   c. Compare and contrast group facilitation skills needed for a group such as the Riverton Neighborhood Association and a client-focused group.
5. Go to www.routledgesw.com/cases and view the Riverton video vignette that depicts a group meeting of the Riverton Neighborhood Association or the Carla Washburn video vignette that depicts a grief support group. Using the Group

Counselor Rating Scale (Exhibit 9.7), complete an evaluation of the group leader. Upon completion of the evaluation, write a reflection identifying the group leader's strengths and areas for growth and change.

6. Go to www.routledgesw.com/cases and review the case for Brickville, particularly Virginia Stone and her family. In Chapter 8 (Vignette #3), Virginia was involved in the creation of a social action group targeted at saving the park that was built in memory of her family members who were lost in the apartment fire twenty years earlier. The exercise in Chapter 8 focused on determining the need, purpose, composition, structure, and content for such a group. Using the information that you have available to you, develop a written plan that includes:

    a. Development of the social action plan.

    b. Strategies for implementing the plan.

    c. Resources needed to implement the plan, including individuals, groups, organizations, and funding, as appropriate.

    c. Plan for determining the success or failure of the social action effort.

    d. Your reflection on the process of implementing a social action plan at the community level.

7. Go to www.routledgesw.com/cases and review the case for Hudson City. Recall from Chapters 6, 7, 8 that the Patel family experienced significant impact from Hurricane Diane. As a result of her response to the experience, the 12-year-old daughter, Aarti, was referred to a group to help her develop her coping skills. While Aarti was a regular and active participant in the support group to which you referred her, there is mounting concern that she continues to struggle with the same challenges that resulted in the referral to the group (e.g., nightmares, discomfort when required to be away from her parents for activities other than school and group, and decreased appetite). Describe in writing your thoughts about the concerns being expressed by her parents and the leader of the support group and a plan for addressing the ongoing challenges that Aarti and her family are experiencing, including:

    • Continuation in the support group

    • Alternative intervention strategies

    • Resources needed for a revised intervention plan

b. Other Exercises

8. To relate the information covered in this chapter to your own group experience, reflect on a specific experience you have had as a member of a group by responding to the following items:

    a. Describe in detail a group to which you belonged (may be a current group). Include:

        • type of group (may use one of the types described in Chapter 8)

        • purpose of the group

- structure of the group (e.g., open or closed membership, time-limited or open-ended, number of members, eligibility for membership)
  - your role within the group
  b. Consider the quality of your involvement by reflecting on:
  - How did you feel about being a member of the group? Your role? Your contributions?
  - Did the group fulfill stated expectations? Your expectations? If not, explain the reasons.
  - What were the strengths of the group?
  - What are areas for the group's growth or change?
  - Group leadership of the group—was it formally determined or evolved naturally? What was the style of the leader(s)?
  c. Based on your experience and your new knowledge of the group process, reflect on the following:
  - Would you engage with the group differently? If yes, how would your involvement change? Explain your reasons.
  - Was the group formally or informally evaluated? What were the outcomes?

9. Develop a plan for the way in which you, as a group leader, will respond to each of the following behaviors that may emerge during the course of your experience in group work:
   a. "Silent" group member
   b. "Monopolizer"
   c. "Help-rejecter/avoider"
   d. "Caregiver/coordinator"
   e. "Attacker"
   f. "Harmonizer"
   g. "Clown"
   h. "Poor me" group member
   After developing your response plan for each behavior, reflect in writing on the challenges you anticipate facing and strategies for learning and growing as a group facilitator.

10. Recall from Chapter 8 that you, as a practicum student, were invited to serve as a co-facilitator for a psychoeducational support for family caregivers of persons experiencing Parkinson's disease. In the previous exercise, your focus was on familiarizing yourself with Parkinson's disease and develop a plan for the session that you would lead. In preparing for the intervention, terminations, and evaluation phases of group work, respond to the following items:
    a. Identify potential ongoing needs that caregivers of persons with Parkinson's disease will have for pyschoeducational support.
    b. Develop a plan for evaluating the support group with a specific emphasis on strategies you will use to gather feedback from the group members.

CHAPTER 10

Social Work Practice with Communities: Engagement, Assessment, and Planning

Change will not come if we wait for some other person or some other time. We are the ones we've been waiting for. We are the change that we seek.

Barack Obama, Feb. 5, 2008

Key Questions for Chapter 10

(1) What competencies do I need to engage and assess communities? (EPAS 2.1.10(a & b))

(2) What are the social work practice behaviors that enable me to effectively engage and assess communities? (EPAS 2.1.10(a & b))

(3) How can I utilize evidence to practice research-informed practice and practice-informed research to guide the engagement and assessment with communities? (EPAS 2.1.6)

(4) How can I apply critical thinking to engagement and assessment with communities? (EPAS 2.1.3)

(5) How can I apply social work values and ethics to community engagement and assessment? (EPAS 2.1.2)

COMMUNITY PROVIDES THE PLACE IN WHICH PEOPLE FIND identity and meaning for their lives in their various roles as individuals, parents, children, partners, friends, and professionals. **Community** is the structure, both tangible and metaphoric, that supports interaction and connectedness among people over time. The characteristics of the community in which people grow, live, and develop can have important implications for the resources and opportunities available to those who inhabit the community. Communities are the central context of social work practice with all types of client systems; therefore, community practice is an important aspect of generalist social work practice.

This chapter examines the concept of community and your relationship to it as a practitioner. This chapter will explore the types of community and functions through which community is given meaning, and consider methods of inquiry into its study, including community analysis, community needs assessment, and community asset mapping. Finally, the need for and avenues to a global perspective is considered.

FAMILIAR PERSPECTIVES AND SOME ALTERNATIVES

Much of contemporary research and literature about community focuses on an increasingly impersonal and complex U.S. society as influences that work against community work (Brueggemann, 2013). The forces working against connections within communities include technology that allows people to share interests and build bonds with people all over the globe, and the individualistic character of U.S. culture, which provides less social reinforcement for community involvement than in other cultures. Globalization is a force that may also work against developing strong place-based community connections, as corporations and financial capital shift quickly from place to place to find the most profitable locations for business, and workers move to places to find optimal employment opportunities. The human service system reflects society's focus on individualism in its emphasis on the individual and family and the perpetual pursuit of self-fulfillment. Encouraging individuals, families, and groups to work to improve their communities is part of social work practice.

Community sectors, such as education, housing, health, recreational opportunities, local businesses, and employment opportunities are important to the quality of life for community residents. Local relationships, experiences, resources, and opportunities continue to play an important role in the daily lives of people, and local residents invest time, energy, and resources into creating community resources and opportunities that will positively impact their quality of life. For example, local residents and business owners work hard to maintain and increase property values and decrease crime in their neighborhood. Similarly, residents will strive to prevent the location of hazardous environmental materials in their neighborhood, and to garner resources to increase the quality of public education in their community. Compelling challenges, issues, and incentives for residents to take action on behalf of a community still exist. The idea of **interdependence**—the idea that individuals are dependent on one another—resonates in practice models with individuals, families, and groups that emphasize health and recovery based on both professional and peer support.

Community Practice and Generalist Practice

Promoting community involvement is important for social workers who primarily work at the community level, as well as for those who work at the individual, family, and group level. Communities play a critical role in clients' lives because communities comprise the environment within which individuals live their lives, and are the formal conduit through which resources, formal and informal systems, and political, social, and economic forces shape individuals, families, and neighborhoods. Communities therefore shape experiences and influence the ability of social workers to affect the outcomes of their work with client systems. Even when social workers never go outside of the traditional one-to-one social work relationship, the success of their efforts depends in large part on the nature and responsiveness of the clients' communities. For example, a client who is young and low-income with two children seeking shelter is impacted by the community's overall capacity to provide decent, affordable housing for single people who receive public assistance. If this client seeks your assistance to locate housing, you need to know about the resources for shelter, transitional housing, and low-income housing available in her community, as well as resources to combat discrimination if the client suspects that she is denied housing illegally (such as rental housing that is not available to her because the landlord will not rent to single mothers with children who receive public assistance). Other considerations about her housing choices may include employment, schools, child care, the quality and quantity of afterschool programs, and the existence of a community center. She may be very interested in information about the overall safety of the community, to include the rate of crime, presence of former partners that pose safety concerns and presence of specific gangs in the area. To practice competently, social workers need knowledge of community resources, as well as skills to address challenges related to such resources, the entity(ies) that make(s) decisions about resources, the individuals or bodies that possess decision-making power about resources and ways to advocate for resources for clients. Social workers also need knowledge about the various dimensions of a community to be an effective catalyst to change communities. Skills working with individuals, groups, families, and organizations are vital to community practice, and skills working with communities are important to every other type of client system.

Working with communities includes mastery of many social work competencies and practice behaviors (CSWE, 2012). For example, social workers must be able to respond to the contexts that shape practice (EPAS 2.1.9) by being proactive and engaging in community work that will seek to prevent problems and unnecessary challenges from occurring. As in work with other client systems, social workers also employ ethical principles (EPAS 2.1.2), critical thinking (EPAS 2.1.3), and practice culturally competent practice (EPAS 2.1.4) in community practice. A major outcome of community practice is the advancement of human rights and economic justice (EPAS 2.1.5), the use of research-informed practice (EPAS 2.1.6) and the use of evidence-based practice. Lastly, the use of the change process (i.e., engagement, assessment, intervention, termination, and evaluation) is utilized in practice with all types of clients, including community. This chapter will explore many of these competencies, and discuss the practice behaviors associated with them. Discussed are types of communities, the nature of community functions and ways to understand a community. These topics assist with mastery of the competencies related to responding to contexts that shape practice (EPAS 2.1.9), and critical thinking (EPAS 2.1.3).

DEFINITIONS AND TYPES OF COMMUNITY

Several types of community are discussed in the social work literature. This section describes three types that are often described: spatial, social, and political communities (Chaskin, 2013). Personal communities are also discussed.

Spatial Community

Communities can be understood as geographic entities, such as a town, city, small neighborhood, or college dormitory. **Spatial Communities** are structures of connectedness based on a physical location. These communities may have clear, physical boundaries, such as a river, mountain, gate, or wall, or a legally defined boundary, while other communities of locality may only have boundaries that are agreed upon by **stakeholders**, or those who have an interest in community affairs, such as county or city officials, or neighborhood leaders. People also construct "cognitive maps" of their communities that inform their relationship to their physical space, movement within their spatial community, and their social interaction. These boundaries may provide safety and security for community members, but may also be a means of exclusivity for others. The degree to which community residents perceive themselves as community members will depend on many dimensions, but access to the community's benefits is among the most influential. Those residents of a community who do not access community benefits, such as a community center, the public library, and other resources, may not feel personally affiliated with their community of residence. Large communities of locality, such as New York, are likely to have many communities within the larger community. Communities of locality of all sizes can be diverse: For example, Jackson Heights, New York, with 175,000 residents in the borough of Queens, is one of the most diverse communities in the U.S. and world, with over 1 million immigrants and 138 spoken languages (Colangelo, 2009).

Social Communities

Groups that share a common interest, concern, norms, identity, or interactions, and share a similar sense of belonging are also communities. One type of **social**

community, a community of identity, relates more to affiliations than a location, such as a student community, an Asian community, a lesbian community, a veterans' community, or a skateboard community. As in communities of locality, people will differ on the meaning of and extent of affiliation with a community of identity and their affiliation with a particular type of community of identity may change over time. For example, the Jewish community may play a significant role for a lifetime for some, and have less significance for others throughout their lives. In another example, the community of those who skateboard may be very important for several years, and fade in importance after adolescence. Some social workers have a particular interest in specific communities of identity for their entire careers, such as women who experience intimate partner violence, or those who have lost their partner to Alzheimer's Disease. Social workers may develop interest in a particular community of identity based on their personal experiences, or early professional experiences. While social communities have the potential to function as exclusionary associations, people can find a powerful sense of connection and commitment in their social community.

- People are often part of more than one type of community. For example, a person may have affiliation with the community in which they live, a worship community, an online community of gamers, a community of yoga teachers, his/her dorm, and a community of undergraduate students. A social community consists of a collection of both locality and identity communities, and often serves to provide meaning to one's identity. These unique arrangements of place and non-place communities are networks within which one interacts, and serve to integrate personal and professional lives. Social workers may be interested in the personal community of the clients they serve because personal communities provide socialization and resources, such as helping networks (formal and informal), that may be helpful for clients facing a crisis or challenges. Personal communities can also provide cross-cultural dimensions that aid in a wider world view.

Political Communities

Community as a political unit—a basis for representation, collective deliberation, mobilization and action—is another type of community. **Political communities** serve as both a venue through which people participate in democratic governance and promote social change through community organizing and political mobilization. The spatial community, as a formal political unit, and the social community, through which people interact, are both incorporated in this type of community. Efforts to promote democracy using political communities focuses on increasing the abilities of both geographic and social communities to increase their capacity to be involved in governing, toward increasing their self-determination. Social workers may utilize the political community of clients to encourage civic engagement

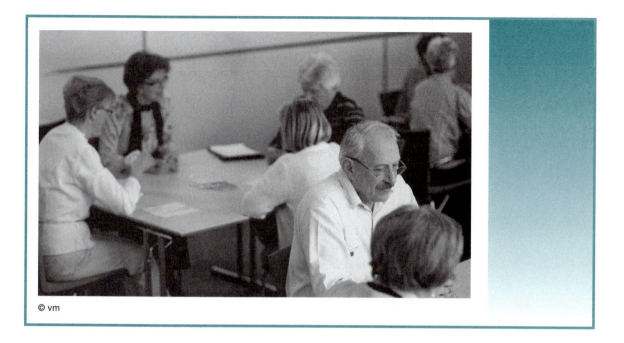

© vm

through activities, such as attending neighborhood meetings, supporting candidates for office, meeting with elected officials to share ideas about local needs,
voting, and being involved in grassroots community organizing efforts.

COMMUNITY FUNCTIONS

A traditional view of community includes the idea that community performs certain
necessary functions for its residents or members, including the following (Streeter,
2008; Warren, 1978):

- Production, distribution, and consumption of goods and services. This may
  include the basic needs of food, clothing, shelter, medical care, and employment. People must also have adequate wages to access goods and services.

- Transmission of knowledge, social values, customs, and behavior patterns of
  residents or members. This socialization process guides the perceptions and
  attitudes of residents about their view of themselves, others, and their rights
  and responsibilities. Both formal institutions, such as schools and faith
  communities, as well as informal institutions, such as friends and peer groups,
  can be involved in this function.

- Social control to maintain conformity to community norms. Laws, rules, and
  regulations, enforced by formal governmental entities such as police and

court systems, as well as informal systems of enforcement, such as schools, families, peers, and organized neighborhood watch, serve to reinforce community standards. Patterns of service provision that regulate access to resources, (e.g., eligibility guidelines for local food pantries), also serve as a mechanism of social control.

- Social participation through formal and informal groups. Interaction with others through groups, associations, and organizations provides social outlets, and the way to build natural helping and support networks. People are engaged in social participation when they are involved in sports leagues, volunteer, vote, attend Parent Teacher Association (PTA) meetings and attend local music festivals.

- Mutual support. Families, friends, neighbors, and volunteers provide aid and support one another, and assist individuals and families to solve problems independent of professionals. Due to the complexity of modern society, this function is often supplemented by the work of human service professionals, such as social workers.

UNDERSTANDING A COMMUNITY

Given the complex nature of communities, possessing an understanding of the many ways that a community can be understood and examined is imperative for moving into the change process of engagement, assessment, intervention, and termination and evaluation. We will examine communities as a social system, an ecological system, as a center for power and conflict, and from two contemporary perspectives: strengths, empowerment and resiliency, and post-modern.

Community as a Social System

Communities can be viewed as a social system through the lens of general systems theory. General systems theory offers a helpful framework with which to analyze and understand communities. General systems theory posits that a system, such as a community, is composed of multiple intersecting components that relate to one other, and are also part of larger systems, such as a larger community. Communities are part of subsystems that perform specialized functions for the larger system, or community as a whole. Through community assessments (discussed below), social workers can critically assess the extent to which subsystems, such as the function of mutual support, or the business subsystem within a community, meet the needs of the community, and advocate for a higher level of functioning of a subsystem, if needed (Netting, Kettner, McMurtry, & Thomas, 2011; Streeter, 2008).

Community as an Ecological System

The ecosystems perspective emphasizes the interdependence of people and their environment in our understanding of communities. The spatial organization of community resources, the relationship of these resources to one another and to groups of people, and the corresponding social and economic consequences is a meaningful view of community. For example, the physical feature of a major road or highway bisecting a community can have implications for the social organization and economics of the community. The physical aspect of a major road bisecting a community can result in some businesses with many customers, and some businesses closing. The social organization implications of the road can include the ways in which individuals and groups interact (or do not interact) with one other. Other concepts related to the ecosystems perspective that may be helpful include the topic of competition, which may occur between communities for resources, or within a community between groups. For example, competition for land is common in many communities, as some groups want to develop land for residences and businesses, others would like to keep land available for the public uses of parks, community centers and hiking trails, while others may advocate for keeping land devoted to family-based agriculture. The dominance of communities (i.e., political or economic) over one another or of one group over another within a community often results in differential access to resources, and has consequences for the dynamics of social interaction within a community. Dominance of a group can translate to access to better schools, employment, health care facilities, and public services such as police and fire protection. The ecological system perspective can help in understanding a hierarchical, uneven power structure of a community. Other related concepts of segregation (i.e., the isolation of groups within a community), centralization (i.e., concentration of resources in one part of a community), and succession (i.e., the movement of groups of people into and out of areas of a community) also aid in analyzing communities (Netting et al., 2011; Streeter, 2008). These concepts help to analyze and explain the ways in which populations move and settle in various areas of communities, and resource availability in areas of communities.

Center for Power and Conflict

Communities are settings in which political and social dynamics and conflict are powerful forces. Opportunities and constraints for community members are often significantly impacted by power. Often, the interests of one segment of a community clash with the interests of another segment, and a struggle can emerge. Conflict and power theories can create conditions that promote change (Weil & Ohmer, 2013).

Three distinct theories assist in our understanding of the community as a setting for power and conflict. They are described here (Hardina, 2002):

Power Dependency Theory This theory focuses on the dynamics associated with dependent relationships of communities to their sources of resources. Communities may be dependent on external forces that provide needed resources, which can dramatically affect the dynamics of the communities. For example, community dependency on a funder with close ties to a large retail chain may influence their decisions about promoting small, locally-owned businesses.

Conflict Theory Using this theory, social workers view the community as divided into influential and non-influential groups that compete for limited resources. Other important assumptions of this theory include the assumption that the influential group has power over the non-influential group, and that dimensions of diversity play a central role in oppression.

Resource Mobilization Theory The focus of this theory is the conditions needed to promote change in community practice. Large scale community change can more easily occur when groups that are excluded from a decision-making process create a collective identity and protest their exclusion as a group. Groups also need to create an appealing message to attract people to join them, and create an inclusive structure.

Taken together, these theories inform the social work profession's thinking about the community as a setting in which power and control are forces to be recognized. Groups within a community vie for power and control to implement change that will benefit their interests, even if the change may oppress others within the community. This perspective can aid social workers in understanding that change can occur within communities from rational planning and collaborative efforts, as well as from confrontation, efforts to build power, and negotiation. Dimensions of diversity, such as race, socio-economic status, and ethnicity, as well as the factor of interests, such as area of the community, residential or business, can be driving factors in community conflicts. Viewing the community as a center for power and conflict can help social workers assess the community power structure, understand the reasons and the process for community decision-making, and their roles in community processes. Social workers may also use this lens to learn more about ways in which marginalized groups are oppressed in communities, as well as the ways in which power is maintained by powerful forces in communities (Netting et al., 2011; Streeter, 2008).

Contemporary Perspectives for Community Practice

This section discusses two contemporary perspectives that help in understanding and assessing communities. The strengths, empowerment and resiliency perspectives will be examined, as will the postmodern perspectives.

Strengths, Empowerment, and Resiliency Perspectives As previously mentioned, the strengths perspective, originally presented by Dennis Saleebey (2013) focuses on identifying possibilities and assets of individuals and communities, rather than deficits and problems. The application of the strengths perspective to communities that have few resources can be challenging. Identifying strengths in such communities can lead to empowerment, or assisting communities to recognize the resources they possess and help to develop power to effect change. The recognition of resources can lead to resiliency, or the potential of problem-solving. For example, community leaders in communities with large plots of vacant land and boarded-up homes may be challenged to think about the land and homes as valuable, rather than as problems. However, using a strengths perspective, leaders may be able to view vacant land as a resource with many possible uses, including for community gardens, greenhouses for small businesses, or other uses. Community strengths also include the skills and talents of the residents. Later in this chapter, community asset mapping, a tool to use in community assessment, will be discussed as a means to implement the strengths, empowerment and resiliency perspectives (Netting et al., 2011; Hillier & Culhane, 2013; Ohmer & DeMasi, 2009).

Community in a Postmodern Perspective The postmodern perspective assumes that knowledge is socially constructed, and multiple "truths" exist, depending on the perspective taken. Postmodern approaches, including social construction and critical social construction approaches, invite examination of the cultural assumptions that underlie many of the arrangements of power and politics, and these approaches tend to be critical of assumptions or theories that claim absolute or authoritative truth. Social workers using this perspective are interested in the assumptions and explanations about the current state of affairs and causes of perceived problems in the community, as well as examining situations from multiple perspectives. For example, social workers using the postmodern perspective would be interested in learning about different perspectives and assumptions surrounding the presence of undocumented immigrants in a community to learn about the various viewpoints. They would also be interested in the cultural symbols and norms that are being used in a community, such as the ways in which the social structures of specific populations are organized, and the cultural symbols used to signify the structure (Weil & Ohmer, 2013).

This section will discuss traditional and contemporary perspectives on community work and the ways in which these perspectives can inform engagement, assessment, intervention, and termination with communities. The traditional and contemporary perspectives on community aid in understanding communities as setting in which different lenses can be used to understand the dynamics and decision-making processes in communities. The perspectives also help to explain the sources of and barriers to change in ways that inform the change process (i.e., engagement, assessment, intervention, and termination and evaluation with communities).

ENGAGEMENT AND ASSESSMENT OF COMMUNITIES

Engagement of Communities

Engagement, the first step in the change process, can be approached in many different ways. When working with individuals, families, groups, and organizations in communities, many of the skills of engagement and assessment discussed in previous chapters are helpful. The active listening skills, among others, are as useful in working in community practice as they are with individuals, families, and groups and organizations. Engagement with community work involves working with all other client systems on behalf of entire communities.

Social workers begin to work with communities through involvement in challenges and opportunities as the primary focus. For example, social workers may work for such community-based services as an education program attached to a local public school, and discover the lack of employment for community residents. Alternatively, social workers employed by a local or state correctional system may learn about a grant opportunity to prevent juvenile crime, and engage the local community to plan and write a grant to benefit the local community. Social workers may also engage in community practice through their work with a population. A social worker in a care facility for older adults may learn about the lack of respite services available for family care providers. The social worker may help the care providers organize themselves to approach a potential funder, such as local, state, or federal legislators, or local foundation, to advocate for funding for respite care. Lastly, social workers also engage with communities based primarily on setting. For example, a social worker who is employed by an elementary school may learn about hazardous waste materials being dumped into a neighborhood, endangering the health of the children of the community. The social worker may work to engage local leaders of the community to conduct community-wide meetings and/or communicate with the appropriate decision-makers and work toward a resolution to protect the health of the children. There are many ways that social workers become engaged with communities, either formally through employment or a volunteer role at the community level, or by involvement through a challenge/opportunity, population or setting about which they learned through their primary professional roles with micro or mezzo client systems (Netting et al., 2011).

Assessment Process

The assessment process often occurs simultaneously to the engagement process, and can consist of several different types of techniques. The following discussion will explore comprehensive community-based analysis and a community needs assessment as two community assessment techniques. Community asset mapping will also be discussed as a strengths-based technique of community assessment.

Comprehensive Community-Based Analysis   *Exam*

Social workers in different settings and jobs need an understanding of the overall community in which they serve client systems, as well as an understanding of the population of a community and the primary challenges faced by a community. Understanding communities involves learning about the structures and functioning of a community. Developing an accurate knowledge base about a community can lead to more effective assessments and interventions with individuals, groups, families, organizations, and communities. An overall understanding of a community includes learning about the following major community domains (Chaskin, Brown, Venkatsh, & Vidal, 2009; Sherraden, 1993):

Physical Setting   The physical setting of a community includes the geography (e.g., presence of water or flat or hilly land), main geographical boundaries and natural barriers, and the degree to which communities are integrated or isolated from surrounding neighborhoods. For example, is the community near a downtown area, a vital entertainment or shopping district, or a medical complex? Do the streets dead-end or go through to other communities?

History   The history of a community includes the identity of the population(s) that originally settled the community, time period of settlement and the major historical events that shaped the community. Additionally, you might also consider the ways in which the architecture and layout of the community reflects early inhabitants, and whether the community history impacts the current dynamics of community functioning. Questions that can be asked include: What is the history of different populations settling in the community? Have transitions occurred? If so, have these transitions been marked with conflict?

Demographics of the Population   Knowledge about the current population of the community, as well as the well-defined and informal subpopulations with distinct cultures within the community, is very important. Questions to be considered include: What are the largest population groups in the community? Can the community be characterized generally as homogeneous or heterogeneous, considering different variables?

Economic System   The economic system includes employment for community residents, types, number and industry of community large businesses, the presence of small, locally owned businesses, the presence of stores that residents can utilize for their basic needs, such as grocery stores and co-ops, farmer's markets, clothing stores, and hardware stores, the rate of employment in the community and type of transportation available to community residents. Questions to be asked could include: Who are the major employers of the community? What is their relationship to the community? What are the needs of the employers?

Political System   An awareness of the political system provides helpful information about key decision-makers within and for the community. Learning about all types of elected officials with decision-making authority about the community will help to obtain a more complete understanding of the community. Also seek information about the level of political activity (for example, by looking for bumper stickers and yard signs). Additionally, information about the degree to which the business community is organized into a business association and involved in politics is also helpful information. You might inquire about the degree to which human service systems are involved in the local political system, the degree to which the political system is organized and connected to community residents, and the level of activity of local politicians.

Social Characteristics   Questions to consider regarding the social characteristics include: What are the characteristics of residents in terms of social class, race, ethnicity, age, and other dimensions of diversity? Is the community known as friendly or unfriendly to new residents and visitors? Are there many places of worship? What size are the congregations and which denominations are present? Are there formal or informal meeting places besides places of worship (i.e., coffee shops, meeting halls, clubs, associations, etc.?) What is the condition of the parks or recreational areas? What are the housing conditions of the neighborhood in terms of upkeep, quality, and the proportion of rental versus family owned? Does it vary by section? Is housing for sale? Is the for-sale housing dispersed or clustered? Is there evidence of construction and home repair? Are there strong institutions in the community related to social needs?

Human Service System   The human service system includes education and human services of all types. Questions to consider include the following: What kinds of public and private schools are located in the community? What is their educational quality, physical condition, and funding sources? What kinds of voluntary agencies are located in the community? How available are services to residents? How well organized are the organizations within the community? Are there strong or weak networks among the professionals in the community? Are external resources brought into the community and distributed to residents?

Values, Beliefs, Traditions   While observing and building relationships to learn about values, beliefs, and traditions, consider the following questions: What do community residents value? Are there differences based on race, ethnicity, and sections of the community or another dimension of diversity? Do members of the community celebrate specific traditions that may be unique to that community, or to a sub-population of the community?

Evidence of Oppression and Discrimination   Using a social justice perspective to learn about communities requires a concern with oppression and discrimination within the community, and/or from other communities. Questions to consider include: Is there a history of oppression and discrimination in the community (such as separate recreational facilities, housing patterns that suggest discrimination, and/or school enrollment and quality patterns that suggest discrimination)? Are there current patterns of discrimination and oppression?

Learning about these aspects of a particular community will assist you to discover its unique characteristics, including strengths, challenges, history, and concerns of the residents. The answers to these questions could be used by creating a formal document for an organization or community, or could be utilized informally.

One tool useful for understanding the connections among aspects of a community is the **sociogram**. A sociogram (similar to an eco-map) is a visual tool for assessing community connections and dynamics. It is important to note which subsystems interact and the nature of the interaction. It is also important to note which subsystems do not yet have any interactions so that potential linkages can be considered. The use of a sociogram can lead to understanding about isolated aspects, as well as well-connected aspects, as well as the nature of those connections. The focal system is considered the "client system," that is, the system that is the focus of intervention, as displayed in Exhibit 10.1.

The methods by which you can learn about the overall functioning of a community are similar to the methods of a needs assessment. Another way to study a community is to narrow the focus to a particular community of identity or population and to assess the degree to which the social services system meets their needs. This process, called a needs assessment, is sharply focused to consider the gap between needs and resources. The findings inform the planning process for specific social work community interventions, and can be considered more practical than comprehensive studies. Ideally, gaining overall knowledge about a community through a community analysis and gaining more focused knowledge through a needs assessment are integrated processes, rather than constituting an either/or choice.

Community Needs Assessment

Many social workers begin to learn about a community through the focus of the predominant population they are serving, or because of a specific community challenge faced in social work service delivery, such as poor quality housing, gangs, or truancy. A needs assessment is a formal process for identifying unmet community needs, placing needs in order of priorities and planning to target resources to solve problems. The overall process of a community needs assessment can be compared to a research project. As with a research project, the purpose of a needs assessment may be shaped by the goals of the sponsor of the study. For example, a social service organization may want more information about the needs of the older adult population in a community, but may not be as interested as you are, as a researcher, in

EXHIBIT 10.1

Lakeshore Sociogram

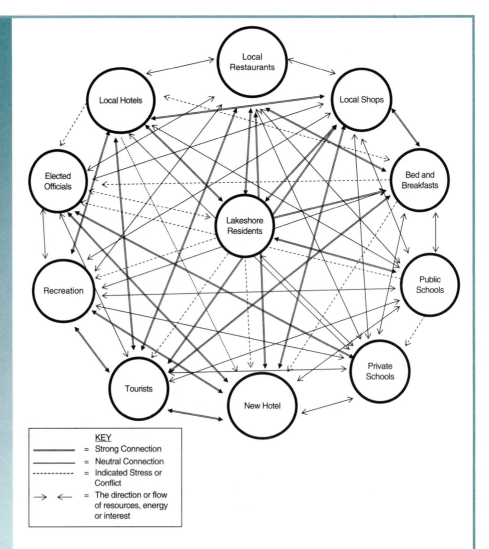

KEY

───────	=	Strong Connection
─────	=	Neutral Connection
- - - - - -	=	Indicated Stress or Conflict
→ ←	=	The direction or flow of resources, energy or interest

Lakeshore is a town in the northern part of the United States, and it is a popular tourist destination in the warmer months because of the beautiful lake and beaches surrounding it. The many restaurants and shopping districts economically prosper in those warm months. As evident from the sociogram, there are varied relationships between the various entities in the town. A few are described below.

1. The restaurant owners have a strong positive relationship with the local shops because they recommend the restaurants to shopping tourists. The residents also are supportive of local shops, and enjoy a strong positive relationship.

2. There are many thriving small bed and breakfasts and locally owned hotels, but this year a large, high rise hotel is scheduled to be built in the town. This will be the first hotel of this kind in Lakeshore, and there are mixed feelings about what this hotel

will bring the town. Therefore, the relationship between the hotel, and the bed and breakfasts and local hotels is stressed/conflicted.

3. Due to the tourism industry and lake, there are many recreational opportunities in the town, such as mini golf courses and lake/water activities, but the residents get upset in the tourist months when they are very crowded and increase their prices. Therefore, the relationship between the residents and the tourists, and between the residents and recreation, is stressed/conflicted.

4. There are both public and private schools in Lakeshore. The public school leadership feels that the private schools drain resources from the public schools, because the parents of the private school children are not as supportive of the campaigns for additional public funds for schools, and fewer students in the public schools means fewer state funds for the schools. Therefore, the relationship between the two is stressed/conflicted, with a one-way energy flow.

5. Elected officials voted and passed the plans for the addition of the new, high-rise hotel in town. The owners of the new hotel therefore have a positive relationship with the elected officials, while the owners of the local hotels, bed and breakfasts, and residents have a conflicted relationship with the elected officials. While some residents believe the hotel will benefit the town's small businesses and overall economy, most prefer to support locally owned, smaller hotels and bed and breakfasts.

examining the growing lesbian-gay-bisexual-transgender (LGBT) older adult population. This difference of interest may require a negotiation about the needs assessment process, tools, data sources, and reporting. Regardless of the sponsor, the needs assessment should be conducted using six recommended steps, which are to: (1) review the evidence; (2) assess local knowledge; (3) select study methods; (4) conduct the study; (5) process and study the data; and (6) report the findings (Mulroy, 2008, p. 386). The research process should be guided by the principles of evidence-based practice, as discussed here.

Using Evidence-Based Practice in Community Practice Using the steps of evidence-based practice, social workers begin with a review of the relevant research literature about similar communities and theories of change to guide the development of the design of the needs assessment. The next step is to clarify the unit of analysis for the study, whether that is a specific population, a geographic area or a particular challenge, such as homelessness, or a combination of units. Consultation with community members and other interested parties, and the sponsor, about the current evidence, local knowledge, research design, study methods, analysis, and the structure of the report can help to achieve the highest quality needs assessment (Mulroy, 2008).

Research methods used for a comprehensive community analysis can also be used for a comprehensive needs assessment or a needs assessment that is focused on a particular population or challenge. An understanding of each of these approaches can inform the determination of the most appropriate method(s) for a particular situation through engaging in evidence-based practice. Methods of gathering data about a community discussed below include observation, use of census and administrative data, interviews with key informants, focus groups, community forums, and survey data (Royse, Staton-Tindall, Badger & Webster, 2009; Ohmer, Sobek, Teixeira, Wallace & Shapiro, 2013). The use of maps to visually display data and community asset mapping are also discussed.

Community Needs Assessment Process   Social workers are involved in community needs assessments for many reasons, including seeking new resources and support for a program, targeting a program to best meet community needs, or simply getting to know the community to better serve individuals, families, and groups. Funders considering a request for program funding will often require justification for the proposed program or services, which may include demonstration of community need. The findings of a community assessment can be used as the basis to modify policy, such as in a situation where an organization, due to increased demand, was considering changing their eligibility policy for their food pantry to the population with the highest unmet need, be that women with children, runaway youth, or women who have experienced intimate partner violence. Organizations may wish to improve services to a particular group of clients, and undertake a needs assessment to learn about, for example, the unmet needs for single men in the community. Finally, social workers may also be involved in a needs assessment to establish or strengthen partnerships. For instance, a homeless shelter may be encountering children on an increasing basis who are medically fragile. The staff of an organization may conduct a community needs assessment to collect the data about the health needs of homeless and near-homeless children, to have the information needed to approach local health providers to develop a service partnership.

There are many potential sources of data, either primary or secondary, or quantitative or qualitative, for a community needs assessment. Discussed next are the following kinds of data: observation, service statistics and previous studies, census data, administrative data, other data, interview, focus groups community forums, and survey data. Several of them, as well as guidelines for making decisions about methods, are discussed below (Mulroy, 2008; Netting et al., 2011; North Central Regional Center for Rural Development, Iowa State University, n.d.; Ohmer et al., 2013).

Sources of Data

Observation   The purpose of observation is to collect information about the community processes and events as they occur. Communities can be observed as a nonparticipant, where the observer simply witnesses, but does not engage in events, and as a participant in activities. Observation can be achieved through physically walking around and/or attending events within the community, to include the city hall, coffee shops, community centers, busy parks, commercial strips, fairs and markets, and schools. Data gathered through this method includes notes about observations, items in local newspapers, pamphlets that describe community resources, local maps, local directories, and historical markers. Observers also attend popular community events, such as free concerts, plays and/or political rallies, to notice aspects of community life, such as ethnic composition, geographical divisions, and apparent patterns of community life. For example, an observer may detect the presence or absence of late-night street activity, the number of older adults visible in a community, the number of children playing outside during school hours, and the number of young people hanging out on the streets during the day.

Participant Observation   occurs when an observer joins in community events and interacts with local residents. For example, a participant observer could eat at local establishments and interact with patrons and staff, while remaining in a learning mode by asking questions. During the interaction, a participant observer takes the perspective of a respectful learner and avoids taking the stance of an expert or a change agent. Other aspects to notice include interpersonal relationships, patterns and styles of residents relating to one another, and relationship of residents to the space in the community.

Service Statistics and Previous Studies   Data from local human service organizations may be helpful for the needs assessment. Such data can include rate of utilization of services, types of services provided, waiting list information, and caseload data, as well as data from other types of organizations (such as businesses, faith communities, neighborhood groups, youth organizations, and others). This information may be available through a variety of sources, such as annual reports issued by organizations, public data available on the internet from organizations or community collaborations, through a contact person at an organization, or from an elected official who represents the community or an appointed official. Similarly, previous studies about the origins of community problems may be helpful, such as studies from the public health department or community organizations.

Use of Census Data   The U.S. Census Bureau conducts a national census every 10 years, and gathers extensive demographic information about people living throughout the nation. The Census Bureau also collects some data annually through the American Community Survey from a sample of residents. Census data can be accessed through a variety of databases and websites, some of which are very user friendly, and can be accessed at small geographic levels within broader communities.

Administrative Data   is data publically available through school districts, public assistance offices, child welfare offices, public health agencies, and police departments. Administrative data can be helpful in understanding community issues concerning a wide variety of issues, to include local academic performance, truancy, child abuse, rate and prevalence of sexually transmitted disease, teen pregnancy, crime, and other issues. These data are typically available at the zip code level, and may be social indicator data, or serve as a proxy for other kinds of information, such as the number of young people who drop out of high school because of the demands of parenting, that is not directly collected by any institution or organization.

Other Data   may include data available from human service organizations about their clients served, and/or community-level data on populations or issues. These data may be publically available, or could be made available on request to social workers. These organizations may collect data to ensure that their services are meeting the community needs that are the highest priority, or due to funder requirements. The data may be collected community-wide, or may just be a sample. See Exhibit 10.2 for ideas for sources of census and administrative data.

Mapping of Data   The use of geographic information systems (GIS) technologies is enhancing the usefulness of data that is attached to a specific geographic location. Using GIS, census, and other types of data may be visually mapped to combine relevant data onto one map. GIS is computer technology that utilizes geocoding of data that are mapped spatially, and allows researchers to identify spatial patterns among challenges and resources (Hillier & Culhane 2013). For example, as Exhibit 10.3 demonstrates, mapping both probable subprime loans and foreclosures on the same map can add to the depth and complexity of a needs analysis, and provide even more useful data. This map can inform a discussion of a local task force working on foreclosure prevention about the possible relationship of subprime home mortgage loans and the rate of foreclosure in St. Louis City, Missouri. GIS also offers the possibility of adding more layers of data, such as race and ethnicity to this map, so that a possible relationship of race, subprime home mortgage loan, and foreclosure could also be studied.

Interviews with Key Informants   Although any person with some level of knowledge can be an informant, cultivating relationships with key informants who can act as guides to the inner workings of community life is useful. **Key informants** are individuals who have expertise in a given area, such as history of business sector of a community, or have formal or informal influence in an issue or with a population of interest. These may be formal leaders, (e.g., mayors, business association chairs, executive directors of organizations, clergy members, or alderman/city council people), or informal leaders, (e.g., longtime citizens' advocates, volunteers for the community association, or gang leaders).

National Center for Health Statistics	This site's links lead to information such as descriptions of recent health surveys and data collections on vital statistics. This link was developed and managed by the Centers for Disease Control and Prevention.	**EXHIBIT 10.2** *Sample of Sources for Census and Administrative Data*
Bureau of Labor Statistics	The Bureau of Labor Statistics, updated by the Department of Labor, provides FTP links for downloading raw data on Local Area Unemployment statistics and Geographical Profiles.	
County and City Data Books	County and City Book, from the U.S. Census Bureau, provides information about individual cities and counties in the U.S.	
FedStats	This site includes a listing for approximately 100 federal agencies (e.g., National Center for Health Statistics) with links to information on statistics, and other resources.	
U.S. Census Bureau	The most up-to-date information from the Census Bureau is available from this site. To gather information about a site, you can use "QuickFacts," and select your state.	
Bureau of Justice Statistics	This site contains information on crime, criminal offenders, victims of crime, and the operation of justice systems at all levels of government.	
Statistical Abstract	This site provides a summary of statistics on the social, political, and economic organization of the United States	
National Neighborhood Indicators Partnership	This network of the Urban Institute and 36 cities supports development and use of neighborhood indicators across many domains. Each partner city maintains neighborhood-level indicators across topic areas.	
DataPlace	DataPlace is a free resource for housing, economic and demographic data, and has guides and analysis to help users understand data sources and interpret the indicators.	
The Census Bureau's Data Ferret	The Data Ferret allows users to map census data for specific geographic locations.	
The Centers for Disease Control and Prevention	The Center for Disease Control and Prevention has data related to health, such as mortality, births, sexually transmitted morbidity available for specific locations.	
Annie E Casey Foundation Data Center: Kids Count	Access hundreds of measures of child well-being on a national and state level.	

Sources: St Louis University Pius Library (n.d.); Ohmer et al., 2013

EXHIBIT 10.3

GIS Map of St Louis City Foreclosures and Probable Subprime Loans

St. Louis City Foreclosures and Probable Sub-Prime Loans

Foreclosed Properties
— 7 Foreclosures
— 3 Foreclosures
— 1 Foreclosure

Probable Sub-Prime Loans by Census Tract
- More than 40%
- 30% to 40%
- 20% to 30%
- 10% to 20%
- Less than 10%
- No loans made

Sources: St. Louis City Assessor's Database and Home Mortgage Disclosure Act Data

If you are seeking information about systemic and political barriers to solving community problems, carefully select key informants who have extensive history with the community, population, or issue studied. Choosing key informants who are well informed about the institutions involved in shaping the community, population and/or challenge, both past and present, is also helpful. This person can provide information about both the day-to-day dynamics and the past and present forces that impact the dynamics. If you are just seeking key informants to learn the

*Key Informant
Interview*

© CREATISTA

lived reality of community life, you may want to consider someone who does not necessarily have the qualities mentioned here, but who has a helpful perspective to provide to the data collection, such as a longtime resident or matriarch of a family who has been in the community for several generations. This type of key informant may be able to provide information about residents' lived community experience, values and beliefs, and/or oppression, and discrimination. To locate key informants, begin by approaching leaders of community meetings, leaders of community organizations, and those quoted in local news sources, to include websites and newspapers. Your first key informants may direct you to other people you might contact for an interview. Quick Guide 31 provides a structure for a key informant interview and examples of questions to ask key informants. The questions relate to informants personal views and their sense of significant community facts, relationships, and dynamics.

Focus Groups A moderated discussion among a group of people who share a common characteristic, or a focus group, is another method of collecting data about a community. The common characteristic could be participants in the same program, living in the same community, or caregiving for an older adult. Questions asked in focus groups can include questions about the most important issues, the

QUICK GUIDE 31   GUIDE TO KEY INFORMANT INTERVIEWS

General Guidelines

Prepare a few general questions prior to conducting the interview, based on your previous research about the community.

The format should be flexible to allow for more depth on some questions, depending on the answers.

Prepare for a 30–40 minute interview, with the flexibility for a longer interview if allowed by the key informant.

Prepare for the interview ahead of time by educating yourself with available data from census and administrative data, prior needs assessments, observation, and/or other available data.

Interview Format

Display the interview skills discussed in Chapter 3, such as empathy, genuineness, warmth, and others.

At the beginning of the interview, develop rapport by engaging the key informant, define the purpose of the interview, agree on the time allotted for the interview, and provide the format to the key informant (such as the number and topics of the questions, the issue of confidentiality, etc.) and information about what will be done with the data. If taping, obtain consent for taping the interview.

At the end, consider offering an open-ended question for the key informant to share any other pertinent information about which you might not have asked, or they might not have remembered to tell you.

Questions

Consider funneling the questions (i.e., moving from general questions to specific).

Avoid using jargon, and double-barreled, leading, long, and negative questions.

Ask about strengths of the community, as well as challenges.

Ask about internal structure of the community (i.e., organizations, decision-makers), as well as the external structure

Sample Questions for Key Informants

Tell me a little bit about your history with the community. Why have you chosen this community in which to live/work/volunteer?

What are the advantages to living/working/volunteering in this community? What are the main challenges?

What are the organized groups in this community? How do these groups relate to one another?

Who is significantly involved in community affairs in this community? Which groups, if any, do they belong to? Are they elected or appointed to any official positions? Who are key decision-makers in this community? Who influences them?

Who has been involved in efforts to make changes to or advocate for the community?

What were those efforts? What were the results of those efforts?

What groups or types of individuals are not served by the community? In what ways?

What groups or individuals are not involved in community affairs? What might explain the lack of engagement?

reasons that something is a challenge, how a challenge exists in a community, and questions about attitudes, beliefs, and opinions. Due to the ease of facilitation, focus groups are an inexpensive, flexible, and efficient way to collect data. The open discussion among participants provides a venue for people to build their thoughts and ideas off the comments from others.

Community Forum Public meetings in which information is exchanged and debated, and strategies considered and critiqued are community forums. In these forums, community residents can be educated about an issue, and state their preferences and/or present their demands. Forums can be organized to introduce an idea for solving a problem or debating an issue. Participants can range from all community residents to a select number of persons, based on specific criteria. The format usually consists of a formal presentation and a general session or breakout sessions to facilitate a higher level of interaction. Careful facilitation is needed to ensure that everyone feels welcome to participate, and that a small minority of participants do not dominate the discussion.

Survey Data Surveys are a common method of collecting data for community practice. Survey data is often used to gauge attitudes, beliefs, and opinions about an issue, or a proposal. Surveys should be widely disseminated, be clear, easy to complete and consist mostly of closed-ended questions so the survey can be given quickly to a large number of people via door-to-door, face-to-face in public spaces, or over the web, telephone, or through the use of other technology. Surveys can deliver information about specific needs within a community or population that even census data and administrative data cannot provide. Surveys can provide information about the availability and accessibility of services, and can identify unmet needs or gaps in services. Depending on the amount of resources available, the survey can be created or one could be purchased that has been tested in the past. Small targeted surveys involve collecting data from a small group within a larger group or community without trying to generalize the finding to the larger population. Small surveys may be given to certain types or groups of residents, business owners, organizations, and service providers. For example, data on the impacts of use of methamphetamine in a community could be obtained by surveying those involved with this issue (e.g., treatment providers, physicians, social workers, clergy, health providers, lawyers and judges, and others directly involved).

Determining Your Assessment Approach

There are several important considerations for designing a community needs assessment. Key principles to guide the design of a community needs assessment include (Mulroy, 2008; Ohmer et al., 2013):

1. *Value participation from diverse constituencies*—Seek multiple perspectives on the community and experiences in the community, particularly those that may be

QUICK GUIDE 32   SAMPLE NEEDS ASSESSMENT SURVEY QUESTIONS

Circle if the following are needs for you or your family.

Medical Healthcare	Job Transportation	Childcare
Dental Healthcare	Medical Transportation	Elder Care
Vision Healthcare	Housing	Legal Services
Prescriptions	Disability Assistance	Utilities
Mental Healthcare	Housing Loans	Counseling
Hospice	Housing Repairs	Domestic Violence Services
Clothing	Employment	Income Tax Preparation
Food	Education	Senior Services

What are your barriers to childcare services, if any? (Circle All That Apply)

None Needed		
No Barriers	Location of Childcare Providers	Not Enough Childcare Providers
Cost		
Hours Not Sufficient	No Transportation	Quality of Childcare Providers
Children Have Special Needs		

How many household members do NOT currently have health insurance? (Including Medicare, Medicaid, CHIP, Private Insurance) _____

Of those with NO health insurance, how many are: Under 18: _____ Over 65:_____

What are your barriers to health care? (Circle All That Apply)

No Barriers	No Doctor in My Area	No Childcare During
Cost	No Doctor will take my	Appointment
No Insurance	Insurance	
No Transportation to Doctor		
Fear		

What are your barriers to employment? (Circle All That Apply)

No Barriers	Pay Too Low To Support	Lack of Training or
No Jobs For My Field	Family	Experience
No Transportation	No Childcare During Work	Mental Disability
	Physical Disability	

What are your barriers to reliable transportation? (Circle All That Apply)

No Barriers	Price of Gas	No Routes Near Work
No Car/Can't Afford Car	No Private Transportation	
No Public Transportation	No Routes Near Home	

What are your major housing concerns? (Circle All That Apply)

Rent too high	Utilities too high	Can't find house in price range
House needs major repairs	Can't afford house payments	
		No Concerns

Circle if you HAVE a:

Phone	Computer	Internet Access

What do you feel is the primary cause of unemployment in this community? (Check only one)
- ☐ Lack of child care
- ☐ Not enough jobs
- ☐ Wages are too low
- ☐ Lack of encouragement to work
- ☐ Lack of education
- ☐ Not enough on-the-job training
- ☐ Lack of transportation
- ☐ Not enough help available to find a good paying job
- ☐ Other
  _____

What do you feel is the primary cause of transportation barriers in this community (Check only one)
- ☐ Suspended driver's license
- ☐ Lack of reliable/affordable vehicle
- ☐ Insurance prices
- ☐ Gasoline prices
- ☐ Bus service not available/reliable
- ☐ Other
  _____

What do you feel are the biggest problems facing youth (ages 5 to 17) **in the community? (Check up to three)**
- ☐ Not much to do away from school
- ☐ Lack of adult role models
- ☐ Adults not in touch with needs of youth
- ☐ Stress
- ☐ Depression
- ☐ Alcohol/drug abuse by youth
- ☐ Alcohol/drug abuse in family
- ☐ Lack of opportunities to develop skills needed as an adult
- ☐ Violence

What do you feel are the biggest problems facing adults in the community? (Check up to three)
- ☐ Inability to pay all bills and on time
- ☐ Stress
- ☐ Bad credit
- ☐ Lack of education
- ☐ Lack of assets
- ☐ High rent/mortgage costs
- ☐ Alcohol/drug abuse
- ☐ Low wages
- ☐ Nowhere to turn for help in crises
- ☐ Unemployment
- ☐ Other
  _____

Do you have a bank account (checking or savings)? Yes No

Do you presently use check cashing or cash advance services instead of banking services? Yes No

Sources: Wayne-Metropolitan Community Action Agency (2007), CHANGE, Inc. Community Action Agency, (n.d.).

previously overlooked and undervalued, such as disadvantaged and oppressed populations. While gathering data from diverse constituencies may be challenging, you will need to carefully consider the way in which you can fairly report on dissenting opinions in your final report.

2. *Use multiple methods*—Both quantitative and qualitative methods offer unique types of data for the project. Quantitative data, such as service statistics, Census and administrative data, mapping, and survey data, offers reliability, replicability, and transferability. Qualitative data, including observations, participant observations, interviews, focus groups, and community forums, offers a richer, holistic picture of communities and their inhabitants. Using both types provides the most informative community needs assessment.

3. *Encourage civic participation and technical elements*—Encourage participation by key stakeholders and/or members of the community in the design and selection

of technical elements, such as formulating the research questions, selecting data collection methods, the selection of survey questions, focus group partici-pants and key stakeholders, as well as for the collection and analysis of data and formulating recommendations, if appropriate. Full participation by stake-holders and/or community residents will help to ensure that the data gathered is relevant, and may be useful for efforts to improve the community, as well as build capacity in the community.

4. *Keep the assessment realistic*—Community stakeholders and agency staff want usable knowledge as evidence for local community and agency decision-making and community improvement. Lengthy assessments and overly long docu-ments may not be helpful.

5. *Value strengths and asset-building*—Along with needs, note strengths and assets of the community. Institutional resources, such as churches, locally owned businesses, nonprofit organizations, schools, financial institutions, networks of organizations, and individuals can all be considered strengths. Asset building programs, such as those that encourage savings, employment, small businesses, local investment of resources, and other types of assets are intended to increase the individual and collective assets of a community. Local control of resources serves to empower residents and strengthen the community.

The purpose, desired impact, and potential uses of the assessment and resources must be major considerations about your methods (North Central Regional Center for Rural Development, n.d.; Ohmer et al., 2013). Questions to consider include:

- What do you/your sponsor hope to learn?

- How will the information be used?

- Can existing data provide the needed information?

- Can you combine existing data with newly gathered data?

- What resources do you have for the project?

- What might be some of the other potential benefits choosing particular methods?

The purpose of the assessment will help to shape the specific data you collect. For example, if you are conducting a needs assessment about financial services for low-income residents in a community, you might ask a key stakeholder, "When you think about the residents using financial institutions in this community, what services do they need that currently do not exist locally?" or "What type of institu-tions, if any, would be more beneficial to local residents?"

If your project is viewed as controversial, or you anticipate a skeptical or even a hostile response to the findings, plan the most rigorous data collection you can afford on the budget you have been given. Political issues surface in a needs assessment, because the data may be used to convince decision-makers to approve and/or fund a program or service, modify or end a program or service, or to recognize a previously unrecognized challenge in the community. Assessments can challenge the status quo in communities, and therefore be contentious. Including specific influential individuals and organizations in the assessment may help the findings to be seen as more credible. Other individuals and organizations have less credibility in a community, and data from them may cast doubt on your findings.

Major considerations for an assessment will be financial resources and time. For example, social workers interested in creating a new financial education program for local youth may have few resources to conduct a needs assessment, and little time before a proposal is due. However, a new city council member may ask their social work staff member to provide a more comprehensive community assessment, and provide adequate resources and time to carry out a longer, more involved assessment. If you have little of both funds and time, consider using data that is publically available, including those data available from government sources, United Way in the local area, nonprofit organizations, and perhaps including a focus group and/or a community forum. If you have more time and/or resources, you may add small targeted surveys, key informant interviews, and/or larger surveys. Exhibit 10.4 provides information about the way in which the time frame, budget, expertise, and possible designs are interrelated factors in designing a community needs assessment.

In sum, key considerations about needs assessments, the scope of the type of information you need, intended use of the data, political considerations, and funding and time resources available for either type of assessment will shape the methods used for the assessment. For examples of community needs assessments, and a sample assessment conclusion, see Exhibit 10.5.

Assessing Specific Population Needs and Social Problems

Social workers often work with community members who are vulnerable, at risk, or otherwise in need of particular services; this includes runaway youth, older adults, people with HIV/AIDS and their families, people with disabilities, families who are working poor, and formerly hospitalized psychiatric patients. Likewise, social workers often work to alleviate issues in the community. Creating or continually modifying services to effectively and efficiently meet the needs of specific populations or targeted at a specific issue is critically important, and can help ensure the success of long-term funding sources. Needs assessments are often focused on a particular population or about a particular social problem. Both a general needs assessment and one targeted to a specific population or community challenge uses the same process and data collection methods as a general needs assessment.

	TIME FRAME	FINANCES	EXPERTISE	POSSIBLE DESIGN
EXHIBIT 10.4 *Considerations for Needs Assessment Designs*	6 months to 1 year (or even longer) to complete a needs assessment	Financial support-grants or other significant funding in excess of $1500 to complete the needs assessment*	Expertise-needs assessment researchers are primarily research and/or evaluation staff with some experience in needs assessment*	• Probability surveys; personal interviews
	3–6 months to complete a needs assessment	Some financial support—small grants or funding ($500–1500) to complete the needs assessment	Some expertise-needs assessment researchers are primarily staff with some experience in research of evaluation	• Small targeted surveys
	Less than 3 months to complete a needs assessment	Limited financial support—small grants or funding ($500 or less) to complete the needs assessment	Limited expertise-needs assessment researchers are primarily agency staff or students who have other commitments and limited research or statistical expertise	• Focus group • Community forum • Unobtrusive measures including secondary data collection from agency files

(left axis: Resources; right axis: Scientific Rigor)

* Note: In needs assessment projects that are funded by larger grants, a professional organization may be used
Reference: Royse, Staton-Tindall, Badger, & Webster 2009

Understanding the needs of a particular population or about a particular challenge can be achieved through a community needs assessment focused on a specific population or challenge. The goal of this type of needs assessment is to learn about the community from the perspective of a specific population or about the particular challenge. In the process of a community needs assessment, social workers work toward understanding the history and characteristics of a population or challenge and profile the specific challenges associated with the population or challenge. For the needs assessment focused on a population, the perspective of the population about the community and patterns of resource availability, among other things, is important to identify in the process. When learning about community characteristics, information about community strengths, issues and problems from the perspective of a specific population is important. Learning about differences between groups in the community is important, such as the dominant values of each and methods of oppression and

- East Missouri Action Agency, Inc. conducted a comprehensive community needs assessment for 2011 that provides an overview of the community conditions in several rural Missouri counties.
- The Social Development Commission in Milwaukee Wisconsin completed a community assessment for Head Start Programming in 2012 that provides a comprehensive examination of multi-systemic factors that impact child care in their area.
- The Office of Housing and Human Services Department of Seattle Washington developed a community assessment of need for housing and services for homeless individuals and families In the Lake City Neighborhood in Seattle in 2012.
- The Healthy York County Coalition and Healthy Adams Coalition conducted a health needs assessment for York and Adams Communities, Pennsylvania in 2012.

Need Assessment Summary Example

Conclusions based on analysis of quantitative and qualitative data:

The data gathered through the Needs Assessment demonstrates that:

- The need for affordable housing throughout Seattle is significant;
- In recent years, the Office of Housing has invested in affordable housing in Lake City for chronic homeless single adults;
- The City's investment in affordable housing appropriate for families has been less emphasized in Lake City, although the wait list for the Seattle Housing Authority Lake City Court project would indicate that demand for affordable housing for families is robust; the level of demand is corroborated by the qualitative data generated from the Human Services Department Survey of food bank clients;
- Given the constraints in operating and services funding, Office of Housing is unlikely to fund more than one permanent supportive housing high-needs project through the 2014 Notice of Funding Availability; and
- A vast majority of the comments received directly by the City from concerned community members requests that the City consider activating the Fire Station 39 property for civic amenities, especially for youth and seniors.

Source: City of Seattle, 2012.

EXHIBIT 10.5

Examples of Needs Assessments

---

discrimination by dominant group(s) in communities towards other populations. For needs assessments focused both on populations and community challenges, learning about the power structure of the community, while learning about other aspects of the structure of the community, is helpful. Questions about resource distribution and decision-making processes can help uncover these dynamics (Netting et al., 2011). For example, if a social worker is learning about the needs of a Filipino population within a city, asking key informants about the relationship of Filipino leaders to leaders of the wider community may be helpful in learning about power, dominance, and oppression. If the needs assessment is focused on a particular community challenge, such as homelessness, key informants can be asked about the history of the location of the shelters in the community, the history behind the funding patterns for homeless services, and/or the relationship of key providers to political decision-makers in the community. Exhibit 10.6 provides an example of a needs assessment focused on the human social impact of a proposed change. Exhibit 10.7 provides an example of a needs assessment focused around a particular community challenge.

Mapping Community Assets

Social workers using a strengths-based approach to working with communities seek to learn about and identify the people, institutions, and organizations in the community, as well as those who work on behalf of a community, in the assessment process. Social workers must possess knowledge of the resources available to work on local issues to using a strengths-based approach to effectively address the challenges that face communities. The key to this approach is the idea that collectively, the resources available within the community offer the capacity to address local issues. Asset mapping prepares the way for an intervention that focuses on effectiveness, interdependencies within a community, and seeks to empower people through identifying ways that people can contribute to a community change effort (Hiller & Culhane, 2013). Like individual, family, and group assessments, the information gathered in the process can be useful in planning a community intervention.

The community mapping process is the first stage of an asset-based community intervention, generally called the asset-based community development approach. This approach was first developed by McKnight and Kretzmann (1996), and is spearheaded by the Asset-Based Community Development Institute at Northwestern University. Using a strengths-based approach, the first activity of community practice is to inventory, "map," the assets of a community, which includes members of the community, both those that currently participate in community affairs and those who do not, as well as institutions, and formal and informal organizations. Conducting an inventory of the assets of individual people includes the identification of abilities, talents, gifts, and capacities of community members. For example, community members may have home repair, child/older adult care, craft, music, and other types of skills that are underutilized. Exhibit 10.8 provides an example of the topics included in an individual capacity inventory. After asking people questions on these topics, individuals would then be asked to prioritize their skills, about their involvement in community activities, their interests in starting a small business, and their current business activities. Formal and informal organizations and associations that exist within the community are also mapped, to include economic, education, political, religious, and kinship. Associations can include many types of formal and informal organizations and groups, such as self-help groups that assist with addictions, youth groups, environmental groups, and charitable groups. Institutions can include parks, libraries, schools of all types, law enforcement, hospitals, and other health care resources (Beaulieu, n.d; McKnight & Block, 2010).

In addition to creating or modifying services, or learning more about a community, a needs assessment can also be conducted to assess the impact of a potential change in a community on the human social fabric of the community. This type of assessment can be done to analyze the potential social impacts of any policy, plan, program, project or proposed facility, such as a new development project or change to an existing facility. This type of assessment will discern the potential consequences of a change, such as a new housing, commercial property, or transportation development, on the ways in which people live, work, recreate, relate to one another, organize as a community, or their norms, values and beliefs. All types of impacts, including social, cultural, demographic, economic, social–psychological, and political are options to be assessed (IOCPG, 2003).

The potential sources of data are identical to other types of community assessments, such as use of census data, surveys, key informant interviews, focus groups, public meetings, and historical documents. Key to the process is the opportunity for the affected populations to be heard through the assessment, and therefore have input into the decision-making process about a proposal. The variables measured can include population characteristics, community structures, resources, and potential individual and family changes (IOCPG, 2003).

Social Work: Practice in Action – Social Impact Assessment

A semirural community near an urban area in New Mexico was under threat of significant disruption from a proposed 14-acre development. This proposed development could have significantly changed the social fabric and quality of life of neighborhood residents. The Rio Grande Educational Collaborative proposed a 35,000 square foot learning facility on land that had been planned for a storm water drainage pond. Students and faculty affiliated with The Resource Center for Raza Planning engaged in data collection through use of census data, historical documents, previous studies about the site, survey interview data, key informant interviews, and focus group data. Data collected related to the programmatic and facility characteristics. At the end, they produced an 82-page report, and presented findings to the public and decision-makers. These findings included community concerns about traffic and parking, property values and potential displacement of residents. The finding also included recommended criteria for site selection for the facility, and alternative activities for the site that reflected community preferences. While the residents were supportive of the programming, the impact of the facility would be ultimately negative on the community. County officials ultimately rejected the proposed development; instead, a water detention pond with walking trails and a working community farm were built on the site.

Source: Cordova, 2011

EXHIBIT 10.6

Social Impact Assessment

EXHIBIT 10.7

Case Study—
Community
Practice and
Child Welfare

A social worker working in child welfare services in a smaller community can engage in community practice in a variety of ways. One social worker in child welfare was working in a community within a county characterized by a higher-than-average rate of poverty, substance abuse, and criminal justice violations. A substantial number of children in the county endure prolonged childhood sexual abuse. These children are first placed in foster care, but many are removed shortly thereafter and placed in residential facilities because their acute emotional disruptions are reflected in dangerous or out-of-control behaviors. However, residential care is more costly than placement in a foster home, and has implications for both the current quality of life and for the future community integration of the children.

Due to the behaviors displayed by the children who have been abused in her caseload and those of her peers, the social worker forms a working group, composed of caseworkers, supervisors, foster parents, former foster children, and allies in other organizations, to complete a needs assessment. The group reviews previous needs assessments of foster children in that community, as well as U.S. Census data, public health data, juvenile court data, educational data and other administrative data, and decides to complete a needs assessment with a survey. The survey is given to all foster parents, and those providing any services to foster children, including teachers. The survey is designed to elicit strengths, resources, and stressors.

The plan is, as a group, to analyze the data, and integrate the survey data with previous data and studies, and issue a report to the child welfare supervisor for the county. Additionally, the group will ask that the needs assessment, which will include recommendations, be shared with other local decision-makers, to include politicians, in an effort to change policy and possibly raise funds for additional services, if needed.

Exhibits 10.8 and 10.9 provide examples of community asset mapping tools for associations/ organizations and institutions. There are several helpful tools available from the internet, including one available from the U.S. Department of Housing and Urban Development (HUD) entitled "Connecting to Success: Neighborhood Networks Asset Mapping Guide."

The process of mapping assets will vary, depending on your needs, sponsor, and resources. While some circumstances may lend themselves to a thorough mapping process in a relatively short period of time, in other circumstances, the mapping process may take a year or longer. Like a community needs assessment, the process of asset mapping is an assessment process that provides a foundation for a community intervention, yet is also a process that may continue while an intervention is underway as well. Chapter 11 will discuss the next steps for using the community mapping data for an intervention. Discussed next are skills for community-based participatory research.

CATEGORY	EXAMPLE OF SKILLS	
Health	Caring for older adult or person with a mental illness	**EXHIBIT 10.8**
Office	Typing, writing letters, telephone skills	
Construction and Repair	Painting, roof repair, tuckpointing, demolition	*Capacity*
Maintenance	Washing windows, mowing lawns, gardening	*Inventory for*
Food	Catering, bartending, baking, washing dishes	*Individuals*
Child Care	Caring for children, assisting with field trips	
Transportation	Driving a taxi, truck, or ambulance, hauling	
Operating Equipment and Repairing Machinery	Repairing electronics, using a forklift	
Supervision	Completing forms, planning work for others	
Sales	Operating a cash register, selling services	
Music	Singing, playing an instrument	
Security	Guarding property, installing security systems	
Other	Sewing, upholstering, managing property	

Adapted from Kretzmann & McKnight, 1993

Types	Examples of Types	
Artistic	Artists Coalition	**EXHIBIT 10.9**
Business	Business Association	
Charitable Groups and Drives	Red Cross, United Way	*Capacity*
Church Groups	Service, Prayer, Youth, Women's and Men's, Choir	*Inventory for*
Civic	Lions, Rotary	*Associations/*
Collectors Groups	Stamps, Antiques	*Organiza-*
Community Centers	Senior Centers	*tions—*
Ethnic Associations	League of Americans of Ukrainian Descent	*Abbreviated*
Health and Fitness	Basketball League	*List*
Interest	Antique car owners, Book clubs	
Local Media	Local cable TV, local community radio	
Mutual Support	Le Leche League, Alcoholics Anonymous	
Neighborhood	Block Group, Community Development Corporation	
Outdoor	Biking, Hiking, Rollerblading	
Political	Ward Democratic Party	
School	Parent-Teacher Association	
Service/Nonprofits	Habitat for Humanity	

Adapted from: McKnight & Block, 2010

EXHIBIT 10.10	TYPES	EXAMPLES OF CAPACITIES WITHIN TYPES
Capacity Inventory for Local Institutions— Sample	Historic/Arts Council Groups	Training, Personnel, Space/Facilities, Materials/Equipment
	Hospitals/Health Care Facilities	Expertise, Financial
	Libraries	Expertise, Materials, Fundraising Resources
	Local Government	Expertise, Space/Facilities, Financial
	Military facilities	Expertise, Speakers
	Older Adult Facilities	Expertise, Speakers, Space/Facilities
	Parks	Personnel, Space/Facilities, Materials/Equipment
	Police	Personnel, Authority, Financial
	Public Transportation	Expertise, Financial, Authority
	Schools	Personnel, Space/Facilities, Students, Financial

Source: McKnight & Block, 2010.

SKILLS FOR COMMUNITY-BASED PARTICIPATORY RESEARCH

The community analysis and needs assessment process offers valuable opportunities to engage in community-based participatory research. This research methodology involves the engagement of a wide group of people with interest in the community and/or the research, or stakeholders. Involving community members, representatives of organizations, elected officials, and/or other researchers in the research process makes the research more informed by and responsive to the community's needs.

The participatory research method is guided by the following key principles (Sohng, 2008):

- Seek to identify and work with communities as a whole as well as to strengthen the social bonds of community through the engaging community members.

- Use a strengths-based approach by identifying, building on and promoting strengths and assets, as well as social structures and processes that promote community involvement in community decision-making.

- Seek collaborative involvement with partners in all phases of the research with particular attention to community members' knowledge, sharing information and resources among all involved, and an equitable decision-making process among the partners.

- Structure the process so the members of the community and community groups have the power and ability to act on the research findings.

- Seek to promote and develop the capacity of local people and organizations to create and sustain any change that may occur as a result of the research process and outcomes.

Participatory research can be used when employing a variety of research tools and techniques. The research process itself is a mechanism through which the well-being of communities can be enhanced through the inclusion of community members and organizations in all phases of the research, including the research question. Promoting the community and community process through the research method increases the likelihood that the data and analysis will accurately reflect needs, and that community residents will engage in action on the identified needs of the community.

It is important to recognize and respect the centrality of the community experience to community experts. In this way it is consistent with critical social construction, acknowledging the multiple realities that are brought to bear in any community context. Participatory action-research offers community members an opportunity to take their power back and use their needs to transform their lives.

CONTEMPORARY TRENDS IMPACTING COMMUNITY PRACTICE

Twenty-first century community social work practice work comes with many opportunities and challenges. Social workers often work within low income communities, and these communities face unique challenges in optimizing recent political, economic, and social trends. Here are some of the major trends and the corresponding challenges to social workers (Mondros & Staples, 2008; Ohmer & DeMasi, 2009; Putnam & Feldstein, 2003: Weil, Reisch, & Ohmer, 2013):

- *The devolution, or decentralization, of control of many federally funded programs and policies, including those that support community practice.* States have increasingly relied on nonprofit and for-profit organizations to deliver social services. This decentralization and cuts in funding has increased the importance of communities and neighborhoods in designing, providing input to, and delivering and raising local funds to pay for services. For example, some federal block grants for child welfare have placed the allocation of funds under state or local control, which offers opportunities for community participation. Social workers are frequently in a position to contribute to these discussions through their work with state and local agencies, public hearings on regulations, and legislative testimony. Social workers have also been involved in raising private and local public funds to pay for resources in their communities.

- *The increasingly multicultural composition of society.* The foreign-born population in the U.S. has grown tremendously, and is now the source of the majority of births. The fastest growing minority group is Hispanics, and there are five states or equivalents that are majority-minority (Texas, California, Hawaii, New Mexico, and Washington DC) (U.S. Census Bureau, 2012b). This increase in minority populations in communities offers the opportunity for social workers to advocate for greater inclusion, reduced conflict between races and ethnicities, participation, decreases in disparities in income and wealth, and social justice through increased attention to community issues that impact these populations, such as immigration, bilingual education, health care, and related topics.

- *The increasing poverty and inequality in the fabric of our economic, social, racial, and ethnic relations.* Poverty has increased in recent years, and is projected to continue to increase into the near future (Brookings, 2011). The widening gap in income and wealth are the most unequal since prior to the Great Depression due to such factors as the decline in unions, outsourcing of employment, stagnation of wages, high unemployment, changes in tax policy, and other factors (New York Times, 2012). Social workers will continue to play a central role in working with and advocating for a more inclusive and responsive community for all citizens. For example, the differential access to technology and the internet is a significant barrier for many individuals and communities, particularly those that are low income.

- *The widening venues and locations for community practice.* Social workers have increased opportunities to work with different types of communities, including those that organize around identity (or shared experiences), geography, and faith. For example, social workers may work with an online community of people with a similar medical diagnosis, a planning group for HIV/AIDS prevention funding, a specific neighborhood, or with people of various faiths. Social workers may also work in communities that are newly experiencing poverty, such as inner-ring and outer suburbs.

- *The increasing integration of community practice ideas and strategies into other models of practice.* For example, elements of community practice are increasingly viewed as a part of work with individuals, families, and groups. Newer practices in services for children and families and older adults increasingly use community-based service practice models. For example, the use of Assertive Community Treatment, a community-based, intensive wrap-around case management program, is an intervention gaining increased usage for individuals with severe mental illness (Slade, McCarthy, Valenstein, Visnic & Dixon, 2012).

- *Distrust of political institutions.* Hyper-partisanship among political candidates and in national and state legislatures has created an atmosphere of estrangement and distrust among the American public at very high levels. Social workers can engage with politicians and political groups to encourage respectful dialogue, and bi-partisanship collaboration on social issues.

- *The decline of democratic participation and civic engagement.* The decline of social capital, including networks, norms, and trust that facilitates collective action, is a growing concern among community practitioners. The degree to which citizens engage in public life affects community practice, including identity and shared values in a community. While not all participation and engagement has positive effects, social workers can work to energize and mobilize a diverse array of individuals and groups to be engaged in public life within their communities.

Having discussed several important trends impacting community practice in the U.S., the next section will focus on the world as a community. This discussion will broaden the topic of community practice, and set the stage for Chapter 11, in which community intervention, termination, and evaluation will be explored.

THE WORLD AS A COMMUNITY

Ease of travel, communication, and economic interdependence impact social work practice in the U.S. and will certainly grow in influence in coming decades. In this section, global interdependence is discussed (the connectedness of all nations), and the implications for domestic community social work practice are explored.

Global Interdependence: Implications for U.S. Practice

Global interdependence influences social work practice in the U.S. in many areas. Most of these have to do with political, social, and technological events. Four influences are described here (Healy, 2008; Reisch, 2013):

- Due to the increased migration in all parts of the world, *culturally competent skills and an understanding of the social problems* associated with refugee status and transborder issues are important for social workers in most U.S. communities. Migration occurs as a result of international events and political forces. For example, increased internal political tensions in Syria resulting from the recent widespread political upheaval in the Middle East, caused over 700,000 people to seek safety and aid in neighboring countries by 2012 (Cumming-Bruce, 2012).

- Social workers *seek information from multiple sources*, rather than from just Western sources, about meeting common social challenges, such as homelessness, poverty, violence, street children, HIV/AIDS, unemployment, increasing longevity, runaway contagious disease, and growing divisions between the "haves" and "have-nots." Mutual inquiries and information sharing are increasingly relevant as these conditions are addressed on a worldwide basis.

- Social workers recognize the need to *build global organizations and coalitions* to work on issues that are interlinked. The actions of and activity in one country influence the social and economic well-being of others, as well as the world's overall social health. For example, social work is involved in international groups engaged in public health initiatives that respond to 1) natural disasters that cross country borders; 2) activities of financial institutions that impact the world economy; and 3) nuclear accidents world-wide.

- Social workers seek *new ways of using technology* to advance universal human rights. The potential for using social media and other technology to share agendas and materials, and to collaborate toward meeting basic human needs, is vast.

Approaches for a Global Community

A global perspective is gaining importance in community social work practice. The following points will be helpful in developing a global perspective and expanding your thinking as a global citizen (adapted from Ramanathan & Link, 2004, pp. 225–230).

1. *Making a personal review of global awareness:* Developing a global awareness first requires an awareness of your present orientation. For example, how often do you keep up with news about other countries, or about international organizations, such as the World Trade Organization (WTO)? How often do you think about economic and/or social conditions in other countries? Do you know where your clothing and shoes are made, or your food is grown, and under what conditions?

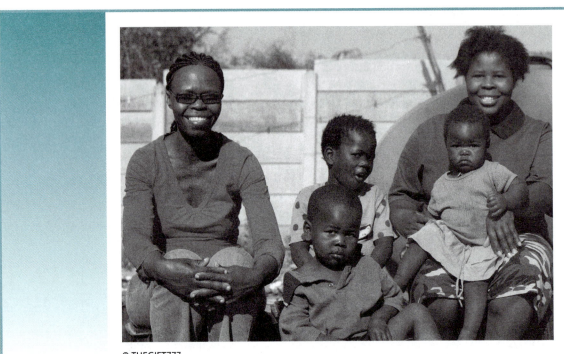

© THEGIFT777

2. *Expanding knowledge of social work practice in a range of countries:* Another factor in expanding your awareness is learning about and gaining an appreciation of social work practices in other countries. Practices in other countries can inform your practice in your location. Using cultural exchanges with social services in other countries, or reading about practices in other countries, can assist you in gaining knowledge. Do you, either consciously or unconsciously, consider yourself the expert and other countries' approaches as secondary or inferior? Awareness of this issue is vitally important to your approach.

3. *Understanding "cultural competence" and respect for language:* Understanding the dynamics of culture and its implications for access to power and resources can lead to highly effective relationships. For example, think about the degree to which you understand the ideas of cultures other than your own, the degree to which your language is respectful about other cultures, and if you avoid assuming your culture is the worldwide norm.

4. *Analyzing global policy instruments built upon consensus:* An understanding of global policy statements that apply to issues of concern to social workers provides an understanding of the foundation upon which social work practice is built. Relevant documents include the UN Convention on the Rights of Persons with Disabilities, the UN Convention on the Rights of the Child, and the UN Convention Against Torture (Scherrer, 2012; Stevenson, 2010).

5. *Becoming historically aware:* Understanding the historical context of U.S. policies is essential for the development of a global perspective. For example, an understanding of the contribution of U.S. policies to the economic situations of other countries can assist in a broader understanding of immigration patterns in the U.S. Regularly accessing reputable domestic and international media sources that provide historical context for current news is one way to further your understanding.

6. *Becoming aware of privilege:* An appreciation of the privilege associated with economic power can assist in the development of a global perspective. For example, awareness of your technological privilege, and issues of distributive justice, energy resources, and other dimensions related to the distribution of resources and the ethics associated with it can be illuminating. In-person exposure to domestic and international populations without the same level of access to resources as you have had can assist in raising awareness.

7. *Reviewing values and ethics:* The ability to understand the global application of the NASW *Code of Ethics* is key to a global perspective. For instance, do you respect the dignity of all the peoples of the earth, or just the dignity of people in the U.S.? Do you reflect a preoccupation with material goods? How do you reconcile this focus with the fact that global resources are finite and inequitably distributed?

8. *Evaluating local variations and uniqueness:* As a social worker, you are obliged to balance the tension between upholding universal principles that will strengthen the profession and valuing individual and local expressions of differences. The

goal of social work practice is not to make everything the same, but to promote a "unified purpose" (Ramanathan & Link, 2004, p. 230).

STRAIGHT TALK ABOUT COMMUNITY PRACTICE

In addition to these forces and trends, globalization has led to deindustrialization and the outsourcing of traditional "blue collar" as well as "white collar" jobs. In particular, the loss of well-paying manufacturing jobs to lower-wage markets has increased the difficulty with which low-income populations can access well-paying jobs with little formal education and training. The corresponding economic insecurity has resulted in weaker local institutions, such as churches, schools, and businesses. Areas of concentrated poverty have left increasing numbers of poor communities isolated, making it difficult for families in those communities to take advantage of mainstream social and economic opportunities. For example, it may be more difficult for people in low-income communities to access available living-wage job opportunities if the jobs are located far from the community and if transportation options are limited.

A related trend is the gentrification of metropolitan areas with rapidly growing populations. Gentrification occurs when low-income communities experience a physical renovation that results in increased property values, and decreasing affordability. Property owners wishing to take advantage of increasing property values may convert their properties into high-cost housing, which can force low-income families to seek housing elsewhere and change the social fabric of the community (Ohmer & DeMasi, 2009). These issues reflect many of the major dimensions of contemporary society that challenge all human service professions, and they also present unique and exciting opportunities for the renewal of vibrant community practice.

CONCLUSION

This chapter has introduced community as a concept that provides the place in which individuals and groups find identity and meaning in their various roles. Most important for social workers, community is a practice arena that impacts all areas of practice, and social workers in many settings will benefit from a working knowledge of community practice. Community is the structure that supports interaction and connectedness among people over time, and can be understood using various theories and perspectives. The characteristic of the community in which people grow, live, and develop has important implications for the resources and opportunities available to community residents. Communities are the central context of social work practice with all types of client systems; therefore, community practice is an important aspect of generalist social work practice. Having considered community engagement, assessment, and the global community, in the next chapter we will examine community intervention strategies, termination, and evaluation processes.

MAIN POINTS

- Communities play a critical role in the lives of workers and clients, even in traditional individual, family, and group practice.

- There are multiple definitions, types, and functions of community, including the use of tradition and postmodern approaches to the community.

- Community engagement and assessment involves many skills and practice behaviors, including community analysis, needs assessment, community asset mapping, and community-based participatory research.

- Various factors, including the population and/or problem focus, aid in the determination of the assessment approach.

- Contemporary trends and globalization are changing community social work practice.

- A global perspective is imperative to contemporary community engagement and assessment.

- Understanding the traditional and contemporary perspectives helps to view community through many different lenses.

- Skills of engagement, assessment, and intervention in community social work build on those relevant for social work practice with individuals, families, and groups. In addition, you will find the skills of participatory action-research useful as an ethnographic approach to your work.

EXERCISES

a. Case Exercises

1. Go to www.routledgesw.com/cases, and click on the Riverton case (click on "Start This Case"). Familiarize yourself with the Riverton Town Map (under "Explore This Town" case study tool), the Sociogram (case study tool) and the Interaction Matrix (case study tool). Answer the critical thinking questions on the Riverton case. Additionally, what other players would you add to the interaction matrix?

2. After completing Exercise #1, consider the following case. In your position as social worker at the Alvadora Community Mental Health Center, you have observed that there are some strained connections between the center's staff and the Hispanic community served. You would like to learn more about the Hispanic community to both become more culturally competent, and learn more about the needs of the community. You decide to explore the idea of a community analysis.

a. Define the type of community you would be studying.

b. Discuss the approach that you might take to conduct a community analysis. What type of information would you seek? Who would you involve? With whom might you talk?

3. After completing Exercises #1 and #2, you decide to conduct a community needs assessment. Using the material in Chapter 10, create a plan for a community needs assessment of the Hispanic population in Riverton, to include the sources of data and assessment approach that you plan to use.

4. Go to www.routledgesw.com/cases and become familiar with the Sanchez family.

   Review the material in the chapter that discusses the world as a global community. Using the Sanchez family as a focal point, identify and describe the ways in which the Sanchez family context in particular is shaped by each of the four dimensions of global interdependence. Add any other ways you think would make an impact.

5. The Chapter 10 section "Approaches for a Global Community" discusses points that could be helpful in creating a global perspective for social work practice. Focusing again on the Sanchez family, apply four of the eight points in the chapter to work with the Sanchez family. In your application, focus your discussion on the ways in which you can accomplish each of the tasks to create a global perspective toward the larger goal of being a culturally competent social worker.

6. Go to www.routledgesw.com/cases and become familiar with the Brickville case. Using the Brickville community redevelopment scenario, create a 10-question survey that could be used for a community needs assessment.

b. Other exercises

7. Select a community of which you are a member. Reflect on an issue that your community faces. What is the issue? How might you conduct a community analysis of your community? How might you conduct a needs assessment of your community? Create a thorough plan for each in a one-two page paper.

8. Select a community within which you are a member. Using the "Create Your Own Ecomap" template, create a sociogram of your community.

9. Using Exhibit 10.6 as an example, create a scenario that begins with an individual case(s), and the need for a community needs assessment becomes apparent. Discuss the methods you would use to conduct the needs assessment in a one-two page paper.

10. Using Exhibit 10.5 as an example, search media sources for another real-life situation in which a community is threatened by development, and an impact assessment could be useful in the decision-making process. In a one-two page paper, describe the situation, and discuss how a social impact assessment could be conducted.

C H A P T E R   1 1

Social Work Practice with Communities: Intervention, Termination, and Evaluation

Passion begins with a burden and a split-second moment when you understand something like never before. That burden is on those who know. Those who don't know are at peace. Those of us who do know get disturbed and are forced to take action.

Wangari Maathai

Key Questions for Chapter 11

(1) How can I prepare for action with all client systems? (EPAS 2.1.10(a))
(2) What are the key interpersonal skills and techniques that I need to know to work with communities? (EPAS 2.1.10(a))
(3) How can I utilize evidence to practice research-informed practice and practice-informed research to guide the intervention, termination, and evaluation with communities? (EPAS 2.1.6)
(4) How can I apply critical thinking to intervention, termination, and evaluation with communities? (EPAS 2.1.3)
(5) How can I apply social work values and ethics to community intervention, termination, and evaluation? (EPAS 2.1.2)

L IKE PRACTICE WITH INDIVIDUALS, FAMILIES, AND GROUPS, the second phase of social work practice with communities is engagement and assessment. Intervention, termination, and evaluation are the middle and ending phases of work with all client system levels. Community practice is a broad term that includes grassroots community organizing, community development, human service program development, planning and coordination, and advocacy (Weil, Gamble, & Ohmer, 2013). There are many types of community interventions, all of which are based on the data gathered and process used for community assessment. The aim of community practice is to shape and create institutions and communities that respond to community needs. Community-level interventions, terminations, and evaluations are focused on the community level, but also impact individual, family, and group change. Focusing on the community as well as individuals, families and groups means that the social worker needs many skills to begin the intervention and facilitate the termination and evaluation processes.

This chapter explores the community practice from the intervention plan through the termination and evaluation phases. Discussed are practice models for community interventions that are based on theoretical perspectives, and this chapter will also provide an overview of social work interventions for communities. The chapter will continue with a look at the final phase of community practice—the termination and evaluation processes. You will learn about the most recognized models for community intervention: planning/policy, community capacity development, and social advocacy, as well as the ways in which they are mixed in practice (Rothman, 2008).

SOCIAL WORK THEORY AND MODELS FOR COMMUNITY INTERVENTION

As discussed in Chapter 10, theory provides a lens through which communities can be understood and analyzed. For example, the strengths approach can be applied to communities, in general, through the identification of assets and possibilities within a community, including individuals. The empowerment approach can be achieved through the realization that a community has the capacity to build on strengths (Netting, Kettner, McMurtry, & Thomas, 2012).

Community intervention is guided by community practice models, which are primarily based in the concepts and language of systems, ecological and power, and change and politics theories (Netting et al., 2012). As seen in Exhibit 11.1, systems theory helps to demonstrate that planned community change reverberates throughout a community, and affects units within and outside of a community. The community intervention chosen, therefore, must account for the possibility that any community change may affect more people than intended. Ecological theory informs community interventions through its focus on competition for limited resources, which can affect the relationship among units within a community or between communities. Community intervention can then account for competition and limited resources. Power, change, and politics theories emphasize the influence of external forces on local communities. Using these theories, community intervention can use the influence of external forces to grow the power and control that a community possesses over internal affairs and in relationships with other persons and institutions that possess power.

THEORIES	CONTRIBUTIONS TO COMMUNITY PRACTICE	
Social Systems	Reveals that changes in one community unit will impact other units Indicates that changes in subunits also influence the larger community	**EXHIBIT 11.1** *Summary of Contributions of Theories to Community Practice*
	Allows comparisons between the functioning of different communities	
Ecology	Sheds light on relationship among community units	
	Recognizes that community groups are competing for limited resources, with survival of those in power	
	Recognizes that groups without power must adapt to community norms	
	Acknowledges the influences of the interconnections and mutual shaping of physical and social structures	
Power, Change, and Politics	Reveals the influence of external sources of resources on local communities	
	Views the community as divided into "haves" and "have-nots"	
	Focuses heavily on the "isms"	
	Acknowledges the role of power in all interpersonal transactions	

Source: Netting, et al., 2011

As discussed in Chapter 10, the data from the community assessment process is the basis for community change efforts, which are often a blend of approaches. The models most commonly used in the literature are Rothman's (2008) three models of community practice: planning/policy, community capacity development, and social advocacy. These three models, explained here, have a common goal to improve social, economic, and/or environmental well-being, and several common elements (Rothman, 2008; Weil & Gamble, 2009; Weil, Gamble, & Ohmer, 2013):

- The formulation of a change goal;
- Roles for staff;
- Leaders and members;
- A process of selecting issues to work on;
- A target of the change effort;
- Assessment of resources needed to produce change;
- An understanding of the role of organizations in the change process.

Planning/Policy

The planning/policy model of community intervention focuses on data and logic to achieve community change by using experts to assist in the process of studying problems and applying rational planning techniques. Social workers using social planning also consider political considerations and advocacy in the process of the intervention, but the primary emphasis is on rational planning.

The planning/policy model is implemented in a range of practice situations. Social workers engage in social planning efforts by participating in efforts to envision, develop, coordinate, deliver, and improve human services. Planning occurs for all types of human services (i.e., child welfare, health, aging) and topics (i.e., gang violence, neighborhood development), and by myriad of hosts, such as local, state, or federal governments, faith-based organizations, and community councils (Sager & Weil, 2013). As one example, social workers use of data is prioritized when social workers are involved in comprehensive planning, such as working with city officials to create a plan for homeless shelters, or prison facilities for the community. In these situations, data, such as U.S. Census data, local government data, or data generated by local nonprofits, is the primary consideration for making decisions. Statistics, computer modeling, and forecasting techniques are often utilized with this model (Rothman, 2008; Weil & Gamble, 2009).

Community Capacity Development

The focus of community capacity development is to foster the local community collective's ability to accomplish change by building relationships and skills that help solve local problems in a cooperative manner. Consensus by the participants is thus the optimal decision-making process for this model. Community capacity development is consistent with the strengths-based approaches of community asset mapping (discussed later in this chapter).

The community capacity development model emphasizes building competency of community members and the community as a whole through self-help and local problem solving. Common themes to this approach include empowerment, solidarity (e.g., achieving harmonious interrelationships among diverse persons), participation in civic action within a democratic process, and the development of leadership among local leaders. For example, neighborhood associations and clubs may work to educate themselves on ways to address a trash dumping problem, or settlement houses may attempt to prevent violence and crime by assisting local citizens and leaders in organizing summer activities for youth. The work of the U.S. Peace Corps, in which international volunteers work with local communities to create a project or increase capacity in an ongoing community effort, is another example of the community capacity development model. For example, a Peace Corps volunteer may work with the local schools to develop their capacity to improve the schools' hygiene facilities, and lower the rate of illness and disease. To do this, a volunteer could work with a local committee involved with the school and help them to raise money, prioritize needs, make plans, contact experts within or outside of the community, and carry out other tasks needed for the project (Rothman, 2008; Weil & Gamble, 2009).

Social Advocacy

The social advocacy model is based in conflict, power dependency, and resource mobilization theories of power and politics (discussed in Chapter 10). This model is both process- and task-oriented. It focuses on shifting power relationships and resources to affect institutional change by applying pressure to a target (e.g., persons and/or institutions) that has created or exacerbated a problem. Through this model, beneficiaries achieve empowerment when they feel a sense of mastery in influencing community decision-making.

A helpful example of the social advocacy model is the work of Greenpeace. To seek solutions to environmental dilemmas, Greenpeace nonviolently confronts decision-makers and those who may influence decision-makers. The goal of their nonviolent actions is to promote public dialogue about environmental issues and to pressure decision-makers (Greenpeace, n.d.). Other social advocacy activities include testifying, protesting, striking, the use of picket lines, and other pressure tactics (Rothman, 2008; Weil & Gamble, 2009). Exhibit 11.2 provides a case example and applies each type of model to the example.

CASE #1	**EXHIBIT 11.2**
The south side of a large Midwestern city is a low-income community populated mostly by Latino and African-American populations. The other parts of the city are mainly populated with White, non-Latino middle and high income families. The south side of the city has a history of oppression, including poorer quality schools and less public funding for roads and other infrastructure. In addition, there is a past history of discrimination against minority families in mortgage lending, which led to a very high rate of rental housing rather than home ownership. There have been several efforts over the past half-century by real estate developers to redevelop the residential and commercial parts of the community, with little success.	*Case Examples and Applications of Community Practice Models*
In the past two years, a real estate developer has been buying up abandoned property in the area, and is now requesting public funding (in addition to bank loans) to redevelop a large area of the community. Community groups and local political leaders have not been asked for their input or feedback on the redevelopment plans.	
Using the **Planning/Policy** model, the community group or local political leader would request that the city planners generate data or utilize previously existing data to create a redevelopment plan for the community.	

EXHIBIT 11.2

Continued

Using the **Community Capacity Development** model, one or more of the community groups from the affected area would begin a process of developing their ability to create a community redevelopment plan that they could present to real estate developers and/ or city officials.

Using the **Social Advocacy** model, one or more of the community groups from the affected area would utilize pressure tactics on a targeted decision-maker to affect the outcome of a decision about public funding for the project, such as specific city elected or appointed officials.

CASE #2

In May, 2011, Joplin Missouri experienced an EF-5 tornado—the highest-strength rating—that destroyed one-third of the city and killed 161 people, including one teen who had received his high school diploma that day. Homes, businesses, a hospital, and the local high school were destroyed (Shelton, 2012). Organizations and religious groups provided tremendous resources, including basic needs (i.e., shelter, food), health services, crisis mental health services, and debris cleanup (Red Cross, n.d.).

The community was faced with the challenging task of rebuilding a large part of their community, including public institutions. To carry out this task and gain consensus among citizens into planning efforts, a Citizen Advisory Recovery Team (CART) was created to provide a citizen voice for Joplin residents in the decisions involved in rebuilding. CART is focused on economic development, school and community facilities development, housing and neighborhood development, and infrastructure and environment. CART membership consists of a diverse set of Joplin citizens. To gain community input into planning, a series of community meetings and open houses have been held for comments regarding a master plan for redevelopment of their community, and the selection of a master developer. Citizens have expressed interest in developing walkable communities that includes diverse, affordable and sustainable housing (Joplin Area CART, n.d.).

The Joplin community is most clearly using the **Community Capacity Development** model because community members are utilizing their abilities to create a community redevelopment plan with extensive community input. Involved community members are also exercising and building their leadership skills by facilitating a process whereby other citizens can participate in a democratic process.

The **Planning/Policy** model is also utilized due to the use of professional planners and other experts who are contributing their technical knowledge and expertise in the planning effort.

The **Social Advocacy** model may be utilized, under certain circumstances. For example, if the decisions made by CART would not be seriously considered by the authorities in their decision-making process, CART may organize activities to apply pressure to targeted decision-makers.

References: American Red Cross, n.d.; Joplin Area CART. n.d.; Shelton, 2012

QUICK GUIDE 33   PROVIDING TESTIMONY

Testimony is often provided to legislative and planning committees. The main purpose of testimony is to gather information and ascertain public opinion. It is helpful to prepare for providing testimony by taking the following steps:

1. Learn about how legislative proposals (bills) works their way through the process in the legislature. Who has sponsored or co-sponsored the bill? What committee(s) has your bill been assigned to? What are the possible outcomes of committee work on the bill? Where would the bill go next if the committee approves the bill? Has a similar bill been introduced in the other chamber?
2. Learn about the history of the topic and bill. Has this bill been proposed before? Who sponsored it? What happened to the bill? Was the topic voted on already by the general public through referendum? Has this bill already been amended?
3. Engage in research about the topic. Research existing statutes that the bill seeks to amend, revise, supplement or delete. If possible, research the cost of the bill, if enacted.
4. Engage in research about the politics of the bill. Which individuals or what groups are working for the bill? Against the bill? What are their perspectives?
5. Research the committee membership. Who is the chair? What is his/her perspective on the topic of your bill? Who else is on the committee? What is their interests, and those of their constituents? How have they voted on this topic before?
6. Determine how long your testimony should be, and depending on time, draft a written statement that: (1) provides factual data needed to support or refute key points of the opposition, including cost estimates (2) analyzes the changes/additions to present law proposed (3) discusses any new problems that may be created by attempts to solve already existing ones, and/or (4) provides any suggestions for needed amendments.

When delivering your testimony, consider the following:

7. Use effective nonverbal communication. You will want to wear professional dress, make eye contact, and have a calm and confident demeanor.
8. Start your testimony with introducing yourself and the organization you are representing. Use full titles to address committee members. Thank the committee chair for allowing you to speak at the beginning and end of your testimony. State your name and background information related to the topic at hand (such as where you live, your credentials, or your connection to the topic). Thank the decision-makers for the opportunity to speak, and clearly state your request for the outcome of the decision-making process.
9. Describe your involvement with the topic, including any context or background that is helpful. If the testimony is related to your employment, provide your employer's name and interest in the topic.
10. Describe how the topic affects you or your clients. Provide both factual and general information, as well as anecdotes. Describe how the pending decision will positively or negatively affect you or your clients, including a description of who will benefit and who will be hurt by the decision.
11. Connect the topic to evaluation of the policy change outcomes. For example, would the proposal provide benefits for the affected? The community? What is most important in this decision?
12. End by thanking the committee again, and offer to be of further assistance. If possible, leave a copy of your written statement with the committee.
13. Convey passion for the topic you are addressing, balanced with professionalism.

14. If you are asked questions, maintain your professionalism. Do not take questions personally, but rather state facts and your position on the bill. Offer to get facts or call on someone else to help, if needed.

Remember that a vote can be the result of a particular amendment to the bill, budget projections, position of party leadership, or complex interrelationships between procedural and substantive issues — not necessarily the subject of the bill.

References: Kleinkauf, 1981; Oregon Legislature, n.d.; Work Group for Community Health and Development at the University of Kansas, 2012.

QUICK GUIDE 34   ACTIVITIES TO PROMOTE SOCIAL CHANGE

Conducting petition drives
Conducting public hearings
Developing relationships with decision-makers
Filing complaints
Lobbying decision-makers
Organizing boycotts
Organizing public demonstrations
Organizing strikes
Providing testimony
Recruiting and developing leaders
Registering voters
Using legal action
Using media
Writing letters to legislators and/or the media

References: Bobo, Kendall, & Max, 2010; Work Group for Community Health and Development at the University of Kansas, 2012.

Blending Models

While the models were presented in a "pure" form, in practice they are often blended in a variety of ways, as described here (Rothman, 2008; Weil & Gamble, 2009). While the same blend occurs more than once, the first model mentioned emphasizes the blended approach:

Planning/Policy Can Be Utilized with Community Capacity Development   with the use of citizen input into a data-driven planning process. For example, the St. Louis, Missouri Mental Health Board (hereafter referred to as "Board") periodically completes a needs assessment on the mental health services of St. Louis, in order to identify the largest unmet needs. The Board then creates a several year plan to allocate funding to best meet those needs. Throughout the process, the Board receives feedback from mental health providers and consumers. In this way, the two models are mixed through the strong reliance on data (Planning/Policy) and the use of citizen and provider input into the planning process (Community Capacity Development) (Rothman, 2008). In another example, data about the increase of rape on college campuses (Planning/Policy) spurred the creation of an on-campus group whose participants were taught how to identify activity that could result in sexual violence, and to intervene as bystanders (Community Capacity Development) (Banyard, Plante & Moynihan, 2007).

Planning/Policy Can Be Utilized with Social Advocacy by emphasizing the use of data and logic in policy advocacy efforts. For instance, the Board can use the needs assessment and funding allocation plans to advocate for policy changes at the local, state, and/or national levels via intensive education and lobby efforts. These changes work to improve services for those with mental health challenges. In this manner, the Board is using data (Planning/Policy) and advocacy efforts (Social Advocacy) to implement community change (Rothman, 2008).

Community Capacity Development Can Be Combined with Planning/Policy (with an emphasis on the Capacity Development) by utilizing institutions that primarily assist communities to increase their development. For example, based on the results of a needs assessment, the Mental Health Board could work with neighborhood providers to strengthen local communities' response to mental health needs, emphasizing a local problem-solving process for working with individuals with chronic mental illness. In a second example, Community Development Corporations (CDCs) are resident-driven organizations that exist to provide assistance to the community. This assistance can include facilitating housing stock improvements, or supporting businesses and commercial real estate efforts, and involvement in child care, community centers, and other components in the community. The CDCs are governed by a board of residents, business owners, and/or local government officials. The CDCs can use data-informed approaches to improve communities, such as create small business assistance programs, create cooperatives, or rehabilitate affordable housing in the community (Garkovich, 2011). In both examples, developing the capacity of local communities (Capacity Development) using data and logic (Planning/Policy) is emphasized to make decisions about the focus of community change efforts (Rothman, 2008).

Community Capacity Development Can Be Combined with Social Advocacy to encourage networks of community stakeholders to put pressure on decision-makers to better the community. This mixed approach can be used by all types of communities, on a wide variety of targets, for policy and practice decisions. For example, a neighborhood group may learn about the plans for a casino to be built in their community, and decide to fight against it by lobbying key decision-makers, delivering petitions, and/or picketing the local government. A group of parents of children who are LGBTQ may decide to engage in an online advocacy effort to advocate for civil rights for lesbian, gay, bisexual, transgender, and questioning (LGBTQ) people in their community. Their efforts may include a sit-in at the office of a local elected official to ask for their support. This mixed approach emphasizes using community capacity (Community Capacity Development) with social advocacy techniques in situations where this mix will maximize the possibility for community change (Rothman, 2008).

Social Advocacy Can Be Mixed with Planning/Policy to use data and logic to support advocacy efforts. This blend can best describe the efforts of many of the prominent social workers in history, such as Jane Addams, John Dewey, Margaret Sanger, and others. These pioneers based their arguments about child labor, housing codes, food and drug safety, and other issues in data and logical arguments. Today, "think-tanks" such as the New America Foundation and others provide well-researched factual reports used by social advocacy groups to press for change. Therefore, the mix of tactics that bring pressure to bear on decision-makers (Social Advocacy) and data and logic (Planning/Policy) is most closely aligned with the roots of the profession (Rothman, 2008).

Social Advocacy Can Be Combined with Community Capacity Development to create strong networks of people engaged in advocacy, which can also focus on developing leadership, empowering participants, and building solidarity. This mixture is most apparent in long-term social advocacy efforts, such as the gay rights movement, the environmental movement, and the women's rights movement. In this combination, pressure tactics and techniques (Social Advocacy) and developing the skills and knowledge of community members (Community Capacity Development) create long-term aptitude for community intervention (Rothman, 2008).

These models, both in pure and mixed forms, offer ways to analyze and describe community interventions. While the framework is helpful to point out the similarities and differences among the models, they provide only a starting point for community intervention. The possibilities for interventions when mixing the models are endless. The mixtures described above can be altered by having a smaller or larger degree of the secondary model in the mix. For example, many faith-based organizations focus on Community Capacity Development through an emphasis on programming for empowerment, leadership development, and solidarity through self-help group work, and engage in only a small amount of Social Advocacy (Rothman, 2008). While there are several other conceptual frameworks for community interventions that provide helpful practice models (see for example Weil, Gamble, & Ohmer, 2013), these models provide a starting point for many types of community intervention. Next discussed are intervention strategies and skills needed for intervention.

EXHIBIT 11.3

Blending Models

The majority of the world's leading scientists agree that global warming is a serious challenge to the long-term viability and sustainability of the planet. Therefore, global warming is the focus of community practice efforts worldwide. 350.org, an organization founded in 2008 by Bill McKibben, a professor at Middlebury College, is working to build political pressure to promote action that lessens global warming and climate change. Specifically, the goal of 350.org is to lower the amount of carbon dioxide in the atmosphere below 350 parts per million, the limit that scientists promote as the maximum amount that the atmosphere can absorb without leading to climate change. 350.org uses the latest scientific data about global warming from the world's leading scientists, which provides a solid evidence base for their work. 350.org encourages localities around the world – nations, cities, towns, villages – and groups of individuals to **build their community capacity** by organizing individuals and groups to collaborate with them on campaigns. The local activist groups sponsor events locally in coordination with local activist groups around the globe. For example, after the November 2012 election, 350.org began a "Do the Math Tour" in which Bill McKibben and 350.org traveled the county to coordinate with the local groups to build a movement through events that featured actors, artists, and musicians. 350.org also engages in **social advocacy** to both educate policy leaders by testifying to legislative committees, and to bring pressure on them to make policy decisions that would lessen global warming. For example, the Keystone Pipeline is a proposed oil pipeline that would run from the tar fields in Canada to the Gulf of Mexico. Scientists maintain that mining the tar fields would release large amounts of carbon in the air, which would contribute to the problem of global warming. In fall 2011, 350.org organized protests in front of the White House to raise concern among the public about the pipeline, and to put pressure on President Obama to halt plans to build the pipeline. Their work was at least partially successful: On January 18, 2012, President Obama suspended work on the pipeline for further study. 350.org provides an example of an effort that blends two models, with their emphasis on building community capacity and social advocacy.

Adapted from: 350.org

CONTEMPORARY TRENDS AND SKILLS FOR THE MIDDLE PHASE OF COMMUNITY WORK: INTERVENTION

Community intervention is action to improve community conditions and quality of life for residents or members. This discussion will focus on the intervention strategies of community social and economic development, community organizing, and community asset mapping. We will also cover conducting meetings and participating in decision-making.

© 350.org

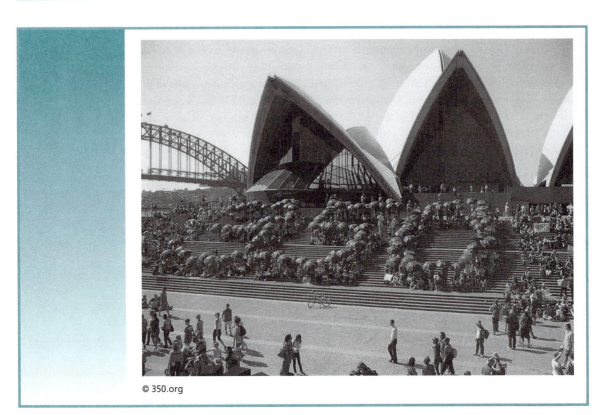

© 350.org

Community Social and Economic Development

Community social and economic development (hereafter referred to as "community development") is a community intervention method that seeks to maximize human potential by improving the physical and social fabric of communities by focusing on social relationships and the environment (Rubin & Rubin, 2008). Community development focused on social development prioritizes relationship-building, education, motivation for self-help, and leadership development, toward the goal of strengthening democracy at the local community level by encouraging local participation in community efforts, and can include efforts to revitalize institutions. Community development focused on economics includes economic development, affordable housing, employment services, and other activities. Often community social development and community economic development efforts are simultaneous and interdependent, and can be viewed as a continuum.

Community development, also called "locality development" and "community building," is an often ambiguous term with a variety of definitions, and can include professions from many fields, including business, sociology, anthropology, psychology, and others (Gamble & Hoff, 2013). Community development work most closely aligns with the Community Capacity Development model discussed earlier, because the goal is to mobilize communities to solve problems and effectively work with institutions, rather than engage in Social Advocacy or Planning/Policy work. However, community development work also can use a mix of models, depending on the needs at the time.

The assumptions that drive community development include (Cnaan & Rothman, 2008, pp. 247–248):

- People may need to become aware of a common problem and create a desire to act to solve problems.

- A diverse group of people across various dimensions of diversity (i.e., race, ethnicity, socio-economic status, etc.) adds value and authenticity to the efforts, and ensures that the interests of more than one group of people are served.

- Local self-determination is valued and fostered by democratic decision-making and participatory democracy.

- Empowerment, or the capacity to solve problems by working with the authorities and institutions that affect their lives, is a central goal of community development.

- The primary constituents of the community development social worker are the community members and community organizations, rather than those with more power.

- Planned change is preferred to inaction that allows current conditions to continue.

Community Development Skills   The most commonly used practice skills are analyzing community issues, facilitating the increase of communication among community members, educating, forming groups, seeking consensus, encouraging group discussion, and focusing to solve concerns and problems common to the group (Cnaan & Rothman, 2008).

Group work, covered extensively in Chapters 8 and 9, is a major part of community development work. To ensure success, community development social workers must employ task group work skills, to include leadership, communication, problem-solving, and management of group function and processes. As discussed in Chapter 9, promoting indigenous leadership in group work directed at community development involves the ability to distribute leadership as widely as possible. An example of a leadership skill that social workers may use, or teach to indigenous leaders, is the facilitation of effective task meeting. Quick Guide 35 provides an overview of the tasks involved in effective meetings. These tasks can be disseminated among individuals during meetings or handled by a small group, as a way to learn and exercise leadership skills.

In task groups, using decision-making processes that promote full participation is an important skill. Decision-making for groups can be handled in many ways, including the **parliamentary procedure**, or **Robert's Rules of Order**, and **consensus decision-making**. Quick Guide 36 provides an overview of Robert's Rules of Order, and Quick Guide 37 provides an overview of consensus decision-making. Both types of decision-making processes are commonly used in task groups, depending on the context of the work. Social workers need familiarity with decision-making processes to fully participate as an individual, and to assist others to participate.

Recruitment of new participants is an ongoing and important community development skill. Participants involved in community development work are often volunteers, and recruitment of new volunteers is important to the success of the long-term goals. The most effective ways to recruit participants include focusing on people who are most likely to join, using a well-formed recruiting message, using multiple recruitment methods, providing orientation for new participants, and making it easy to join activities (Cnaan & Rothman, 2008).

Community Development Programs   Community economic development (CESD) approaches use economic approaches to develop the capacities of low-income people and neighborhoods (Robinson & Green, 2011). Programs that fall into this approach include (Robinson & Green, 2011; Rubin & Rubin, 2008):

- Individual Development Accounts (IDAs). IDAs are matched saving accounts for low-income employed persons who meet income guidelines. IDA programs involve financial education and case management. IDA funds can be spent on approved assets, such as a home, home repair, starting or expanding a small business, or secondary education;

- employment training and placement. Job training programs provide training for employment opportunities, and assist participants in securing and maintaining their employment;

- support of small and home-based businesses. Programs are available to assist people to start and expand small business, including training, technical assistance, support, and linkages to small business loans;

- financial education and credit building. Nonprofit and for-profit organizations provide financial education to build client financial knowledge, and also assist people to build their credit score;

- services to help low-income families purchase a home. Homeownership services are available to assist families to build their credit, locate and secure a home, obtain affordable financing, avoid foreclosure, and maintain their homeownership;

- assistance for families to file their federal and state taxes and receive the Earned Income Tax Credit (EITC), which is a refundable tax credit for working, low income families; and

- human-rights work (i.e., Fair Housing, civil rights, environmental justice, disability, and sexual orientation discrimination).

There are many examples of community social and economic development work. Youth development work often involves leadership development and relationship skills, as well as job training and employment placement services (Chaskin, 2010; Wheeler & Thomas, 2011). Domestic violence services can include education, financial education, credit building, IDAs services, and economic advocacy (Redevelopment Opportunities for Women, n.d.). Building community partnerships for school-based services, such as physical and mental health services, counseling, mentoring, and other programs, provides an example of community development work focused primarily on social development (Poole, 2009). Work with immigrants and refugees can include community development work, including financial literacy; assistance for small business owners to start, expand, and strengthen their business; lending for small businesses; micro business loans through a peer lending program; as well as case management, translation, education and other services (International Institute St. Louis, 2013). Some community development efforts are focused solely on the physical environments of communities, such as the production of affordable housing, commercial space development in low income communities, and/or the redevelopment of entire streets.

QUICK GUIDE 35   ELEMENTS OF EFFECTIVE MEETINGS

STAGE	ELEMENT	NOTES
Preparation	Goals	Develop goal(s) for each meeting.
	Site	Establish a meeting site that is familiar, accessible, perceived as safe, and has parking.
	Date/Timing	Set a date and time that is convenient for the majority of (would-be) participants.
	Facilitator	The facilitator is involved in setting the agenda.
	Agenda	Include the speaker's name in each agenda item, information about the item, and a time limit. Discuss easy items first, followed by hard, followed by moderate decisions.
	Food	Offer food at various times, unless disruptive.
	Recruitment/Turnout	Provide oral and written meeting announcements, and remind people a few days prior to the meeting.
	Meeting Roles	Assign roles ahead of time, including facilitator, note taker, timekeeper, presenters, and greeter.
	Room Arrangements and Logistics	Set up chairs, AV equipment, flipchart, sign-in table, food/drink, and microphone.
	Background Materials	Prepare background materials about pending decisions and preliminary proposals to discuss.
Meeting	Timeliness	Begin and end the meeting on time.
	Welcome, Introductions	Begin with a warm welcome and introductions to set a positive tone, regardless of the turnout.
	Agenda	Review the agenda with the group, and make changes as needed.
	Meeting Rules	Explain any rules utilized, including decision-making rules.
	Discussion	Encourage discussion of various viewpoints; encourage all to speak by drawing out quieter people, limiting those who dominate, and encouraging respect for viewpoints; summarize; and bring closure to discussion.
	Focus	Bring the group back to the agenda if discussion wanders.
	Ending	Summarize meeting results, decisions, and follow-up needed. Thank people for attending.
Follow-up	Notes	Prepare and disseminate meeting notes quickly.
	Thank People	Contact people, especially new people, to thank them for their contribution to the meeting, to encourage follow-up on commitments for action, and to encourage them to attend the next meeting.

Adapted from Bobo, Kendall, & Max, 2010, and Minieri & Getsos, 2007

QUICK GUIDE 36   UTILIZING ROBERT'S RULES OF ORDER

Many formal groups, such as Boards of Directors, committees, and policy-making groups, use some form of a formal decision-making process. The use of *parliamentary procedure*, or *Robert's Rules of Order*, is often used because it is well known, helps to maintain order and allows actions to be taken in an expedient and consistent manner. Although the process can be quite complex, some groups utilize the general rules without learning the minutia. Understanding the major concepts of parliamentary procedure is a critical skill for facilitating and participating in a meeting.

Robert's Rules of Order provide a structured, democratic (majority rules) mechanism whereby formal groups can engage in efficient and fair decision-making. The following are major elements of the process:

- The use of a *motion* to introduce a proposal. Any idea for consideration of a group must be introduced as a motion (i.e., "I move that . . ."). Only one motion can be considered at a time.
- The *seconding* of a motion to move a proposal forward for discussion. A motion cannot move forward in the process unless someone other than the person who made the motion "seconds" the motion (i.e., "I second the motion"). Without a second, a motion dies, and is not discussed.
- The use of *debate/discussion* to enable participants to present perspectives and ask questions about a motion. After a motion is made and seconded, the facilitator can open discussion about the motion, and questions can be asked of the author of the motion.
- *Amendments* to reflect revisions to an original motion based on the debate/discussion. During the discussion, one or more participants may offer an amendment to clarify or narrow the motion. This amendment must be voted on before the original motion is voted on. A majority vote is required to pass an amendment.
- *Majority rules* (i.e., a minimum of 51 percent of members agreeing) to establish a motion as a decision.

Adapted from Rozakis, 1996

QUICK GUIDE 37   UTILIZING CONSENSUS FOR DECISION-MAKING

Real change, at the individual, family, group, community, or organizational level, comes from persons who are personally committed to a decision or direction in which they fully participated. Consensus decision-making, or a cooperative process in which all members develop and agree to support a decision that is in the best interests of the whole group, can be effective in situations in which the following conditions are present:

- Participants feel a genuine stake in the decision.
- Participants share a common purpose and values.
- Participants trust each other.
- Participants are willing to put the best interests of the group over personal preferences.
- Participants can share their ideas and opinions freely, without fear of ridicule.
- Enough time is available for the process.
- Participants can engage in active listening and consider different points of view.

QUICK GUIDE 37   CONTINUED

After meeting preparation work, the process includes:

- Exploring the issue toward the goal of developing an informed, shared understanding of the facts and the issue.
- Establishing decision criteria, including such factors as interests/needs that must be met, resource constraints, and possible ramifications of decisions.
- Developing and discussing a written preliminary proposal.
- Testing for consensus by asking participants whether they can live with the proposal (original or amended), whether it meets the decision criteria, and whether it is the best decision possible.
- Reaching agreement by restating the proposed decision and ensuring that participants can support the implementation of the proposal.

Adapted from Dressler, 2006

EXHIBIT 11.4

Detroit Michigan Promotes Community Social and Economic Development

The economic changes of the past few decades have brought empty boulevards, an abandoned train station, empty high-rises, shuttered storefronts, and semi-deserted neighborhoods to Detroit Michigan. The community is striving to re-make their local economy, with a particular attention to self-reliance. One example is the re-imagining of the growing amount of vacant land in the downtown area toward a new, sustainable, local food system. Community and commercial gardens are springing up on land leased from the city, providing employment and volunteer opportunities. In addition to selling produce at local farmers markets during the summer, some gardens are also installing hoop houses, in which food can be grown year-round. Also planned are indoor tilapia and shrimp farms, tree farms, and other uses of the land that will facilitate employment and sustainability (Bittman, 2011). The emergence of a local food system has been spurred by the Detroit Food Policy Council, which works to create the local policy conditions to facilitate the expansion of the "healthy, sustainable, and just food system" (Detroit Area Food Council, n.d.)

References: Bittman, 2011; Detroit Area Food Council. n.d.

Asset-Based Community Development

Community asset mapping as an assessment process was discussed in Chapter 10. The community data gathered as part of the assessment process can be used for community intervention. After collecting the data, the next step is to group all of the data into categories, such as capabilities of individuals, including those marginalized within the community; associations; local institutions; physical assets of the communities; and (potential) leaders. Exhibit 11.5 provides examples of the types

EXHIBIT 11.5

Community Assets

Associations

Animal Care Groups
Anti-Crime Groups
Block Clubs
Business Organizations
Charitable Groups
Civic Events Groups
Cultural Groups
Disability/Special Needs Groups
Education Groups
Elderly Groups
Environmental Groups
Family Support Groups
Health Advocacy and Fitness
Heritage Groups
Hobby and Collectors Groups
Men's Groups
Mentoring Groups
Mutual Support Groups
Neighborhood Groups
Political Organizations
Recreation Groups
Religious Groups
Service Clubs
Social Groups
Union Groups
Veteran's Groups
Women's Groups
Youth Groups

Local Economy

Banks
Barter & Exchange
Business Associations
CDCs
Chamber of Commerce
Consumer Expenditures
Corporations & Branches
Credit Unions
For-Profit Businesses
Foundations
Institutional-Purchasing Power
and Personnel
Merchants

Physical Space

Bike Paths
Bird Watching Sites
Campsites
Duck Ponds
Fishing Spots
Forests/Forest Preserves
Gardens
Housing
Natural Habitats – Coastal,
Marine, Amphibian
Parking lots
Parks
Picnic Areas
Playgrounds
Star Gazing Sites
Streets
Transit Stops and Facilities
Vacant Land & Buildings
Walking Paths
Wildlife Center
Zoos

Individuals

Gifts, Skills, Capacities,
Knowledge and Traits of:
Activists
Artists
Entrepreneurs
Ex-Offenders
Older Adults
Parents
People with Disabilities
Students
Veterans
Welfare Recipients
Youth

Institutions

Community Colleges
Fire Departments
Foundations
Hospitals
Libraries
Media
Museums
Nonprofits
Police Departments
Schools
Social Service Agencies
Universities

Reference: Kretzmann & McKnight, 2005.

of information grouped under each category. As a social worker, building your relationship with all of these types of assets, as well as relationships between these types
of assets, is a key ingredient in a community change effort. Building strong networks
among these assets will serve to strengthen the social fabric of the community, and
build capacity as a whole community. For example, a social worker may be involved
in establishing a network of social service providers, representatives of educational
institutions, and business leaders in communities to work on local community challenges. Social workers may need to identify the self-interest of the various groups
when recruiting them to become involved, such as mentioning to local businesses
that strengthening their ties to organizations serving local youth also involves the
possibility of expanding their pool of future labor. These efforts can result in a more
self-reliant community.

As relationships are built, the ability of the community to solve problems
locally increases. Social workers prompt associations and institutions to increase
their contributions to community efforts. For example, social workers can facilitate
and support organizations in their work to develop web sites, and provide
information to local newspapers and radio stations to aid the flow of useful
information. Additionally, the process of community asset development may
involve community meetings to develop a local vision as well as strategies to
implement this vision. Community planning processes can be sponsored by
faith communities (such as churches or synagogues), faith networks (such as a
ministerial alliance), associations (such as clubs or groups), or institutions (such
as a local school district or large employer). After a planning process, the planning
group can seek outside resources, if needed, to carry out a community plan. Bringing
in outside resources, such as foundations, government actors and others, *after* a
plan is created ensures that community plans are truly resident-driven. If the
outside resources are brought in during the planning process, careful participatory
planning must occur to ensure that citizens' knowledge and views about what
is good for the community is clearly heard and considered. The outcomes of a
participatory community-driven planning process reflect the desires of the residents
(Weil, 2013).

In addition to community development work, community social work
practice interventions also include community organizing. Having considered
community development, the discussion now turns to community organizing
as a stand-alone community intervention and one that can be integrated with
community development.

Community Organizing

Community organizing is a practice skill that entails using a process to mobilize
people and resources to identify problems and advocate for change to improve the
quality of life in marginalized communities (Ohmer & Brooks, 2013). Community
organizing skills can be used within any of the three models of community practice

mentioned earlier (planning/policy, community capacity development, and social advocacy). The target of community organizing efforts varies widely, and can include local, state, and federal government officials, legislators, private landlords, corporate CEOs, and officials of the World Trade Organization.

While community organizing efforts typically focus on a particular change effort, such as passing a local ballot issue about sales tax, the form that community organizing takes can vary widely. Community organization can include accepting and working with the existing power relationships, or "**consensus organizing**," and challenging the existing power relationship, or "**direct action organizing**." Exhibit 11.6 describes the continuum of services as framed by the degree to which the existing power relationships within a community are accepted.

The left side of the exhibit depicts *consensus organizing*. Consensus organizing involves developing strong relationships and partnerships among and between community members and stakeholders, and with people and institutions that are external to the community and hold power that can facilitate community change.

External powers can include government officials, landlords who own rental property in the community, and/or private business owners. Engaging in consensus community organizing brings together community participants and uses the power structure as a partner in the change effort. Exhibit 11.7 shows the assumptions of the consensus organizing approach.

The right side of Exhibit 11.6 represents direct action community organizing, or *conflict organizing*. This form of community organizing assumes that a disadvantaged population must be organized to make demands on a target for equal treatment/resources, with the larger goal of gaining power and changing the structure of power. With conflict organizing, the power structure is not seen as a partner, but more as a target of action (Ohmer & DeMasi, 2009). The targets of conflict organizing are those with power in the community to make change, such as landlords

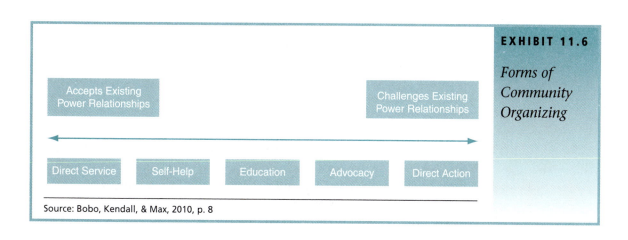

EXHIBIT 11.6

Forms of Community Organizing

Accepts Existing Power Relationships

Challenges Existing Power Relationships

Direct Service   Self-Help   Education   Advocacy   Direct Action

Source: Bobo, Kendall, & Max, 2010, p. 8

EXHIBIT 11.7

Assumptions of the Consensus Organizing Approach

- Ordinary people can and should be involved with creating sustainable community change.
- Identify and build on community strengths and assets, rather than deficits.
- Potential leaders are everywhere, and often need recognition and support to thrive.
- The organizer must be a selfless promoter of others.
- The organizer must seek to achieve self-interest for residents and external partners.
- Powerful people and institutions want to assist with community change.

Adapted from Ohmer & DeMasi, 2009

and government officials—the same people and institutions with which consensus organizers seek to create partnerships.

Community Organizing Skills   For community organizing along the continuum, the three essential elements for community organizing are empowering individuals, building and strengthening community bonds, and building progressive organizations (Rubin & Rubin, 2008). Empowering individuals occurs in a number of ways, including: (1) encouraging participation; (2) arranging tasks so individuals experience success and build their confidence to engage in public affairs; (3) organizing tasks so individuals' involvement is meaningful and builds leadership skills; and (4) recognizing and supporting their efforts (Minieri & Getsos, 2007). Building progressive organizations involves a mission to promote social equity and participatory democracy process (Rubin & Rubin, 2008), such as Robert's Rules of Order or consensus.

People build bonds through developing a shared sense of community. When individuals work together on a common goal through such processes as determining common community issues, analyzing the issues, selecting issues on which to work, developing and implementing strategies, and engaging in evaluation, social networks and bonds are created (Rubin & Rubin, 2008). The process of community organizing across the continuum begins with building relationships, followed by identifying common challenges with a core group. While recruitment occurs continually, the core group works to enact change, even of a small magnitude (Ohmer & DeMasi, 2009).

The ultimate desired outcomes of community organizing efforts frame many aspects of community practice. For example, for conflict organizing, altering the balance of power so that resources are more equitably distributed is the final desired outcome, while at the other end of the continuum in Exhibit 11.6, strong partnerships between community residents and external power sources that result in tangible resources is the desired outcome (Ohmer & DeMasi, 2009). This difference

EXHIBIT 11.8

Community Organizing to Support and Oppose Religious Minorities

In several communities, houses of worship of religious minorities, including Muslims and Sikhs, have experience increasing scrutiny and challenges in their efforts to worship in their communities. Recent examples include: a) a Joplin, Missouri mosque that was set on fire twice in one month, and burned to the ground in the second fire (CNN Wire Staff, 2012); b) a protracted community struggle for the Islamic community to build a mosque in Murfreesboro, Tennessee in which federal authorities were involved (Brown & Hauser, 2012); and c) a mass shooting at a Sikh temple in Oak Creek, Wisconsin (Goode & Kovalski, 2012).

Examples of community organizing can be seen both in support of, and in opposition to, the rights of religious minorities. For example, in the midst of the controversy, supporters of the Murfreesboro mosque created "Middle Tennesseans for Religious Freedom," a local organization to express their opinions and galvanize support. Those opposed to the rights of religious minorities were also organized. Both sides held marches to and an ending rally at the county courthouse. Supporters promoted slogans such as "Freedom of religion means freedom for all religions," while opponents circulated a petition to deny the Islamic community the right to build and open the mosque, expressing concerns that the mosque's members wanted to overthrow the U.S. government and impose Islamic law. The mosque's opponents conducted Christian group prayer services aimed at stopping the construction (AP Worldstream, 2010). Although both sides sought to influence first the County Planning Commission, and ultimately the courts, the mosque finally opened in August, 2012 (Brown & Hauser, 2012).

References: AP Worldstream, 2010; Brown & Hauser, 2012; CNN Wire Staff, 2012; Goode & Kovalski, 2012.

affects the importance of specific skills, such as analyzing the power of a target or prioritizing issues on which to work (conflict organizing) or building relationships with external resources and brokering relationships between community groups and institutions (consensus organizing) (Bobo, Kendall, & Max, 2010; Ohmer & DeMasis, 2009).

A Generalist Approach to Community Intervention

Depending on the context of the community intervention, generalist social work practitioners often integrate aspects of community organizing and community development activities in their practice. For example, in many communities, a shared identity, bonds between residents, the skills for public discourse, the ability to determine priorities among many challenges, the skills to work together on common challenges, and leadership skills are elements that must be developed for community change efforts to be possible. Social workers can play an important role in helping develop these prerequisites. Social workers who work primarily with individuals, families, and groups have opportunities to support the development of these skills, and to encourage people to participate in community efforts. These skills are the foundation for collective action at the community level.

There are many ways that social workers can help build the capacity of individuals to engage in community interventions. At the interpersonal level, social workers emphasize collaboration with their clients to optimize individuals' rights, strengths, and capabilities. Social workers discuss power and control with their clients, to increase client awareness of these dynamics in their everyday life, as well as in community activities. Social workers can regard clients as citizens, consumers, and partners in change efforts, and use dialogue to raise client awareness about the sociopolitical realities. As first suggested by educator Paulo Freire (1973), social workers educate clients about the social conditions, patterns of resource distribution, oppression, and other social and environmental factors that contribute to their situation using respectful discussion and questioning. Social workers help people to become prepared and supported while engaging in collective action.

Social workers strive to provide evidence-based interventions in community practice. Creating a body of research to inform evidence-based practice (first introduced in Chapter 4) has proven challenging, due to the complexity of community interventions, the difficulties of community research, and the lack of capacity of many organizations engaging in community practice to engage in research. Yet, social workers must search for research about interventions prior to beginning. Quick Guide 38 provides resources for locating evidence on community practice interventions. Exhibit 11.9 provides research findings about the most effective community intervention activities that social workers undertake (Ohmer & Korr, 2006).

QUICK GUIDE 38 EXAMPLES OF PUBLIC AND PRIVATE EFFORTS TO PROMOTE EVIDENCE-BASED COMMUNITY PRACTICE

Children, Families and Communities

1. Harvard Family Research Project, Harvard Graduate School of Education
   The Evaluation Exchange is a periodical that contains new lessons and emerging strategies for evaluating programs and policies, particularly those focused on children, families, and communities.

Community Change

2. The Aspen Institute
   Their report, *Building Knowledge about Community Change*, summarizes key learning over the past 15 years about how to evaluate community change initiatives, and to identify strategies for enhancing the evidence base improving conditions in poor communities. The conclusions in the report are based primarily on the experiences of a group of comprehensive community initiatives (CCIs) in the United States and the United Kingdom.

Health

3. King's Fund
   The policy paper, *Finding Out What Works*, provides information about the effectiveness of health initiatives in Britain.

Early Childhood, Health Care, and Housing

4. Centers for Disease Controls and Prevention: Community Preventative Services Task Force
   The community guide includes systemic reviews of interventions in early childhood development programs, culturally competent health care, and housing.

Housing

5. U.S. Department of Housing and Urban Development (HUD)
   The Program Evaluation Division of HUD has done much research on housing issues, including projects such as costs of homelessness, fair housing accessibility, and comprehensive initiatives, such as "Moving to Opportunity".

Mental Health in Communities

6. National Registry of Evidence-based Programs and Practices (NREPP), sponsored by the Substance Abuse and Mental Health Services Administration
   NREPP is an online, searchable registry of mental health and substance abuse interventions.

Neighborhood Research, Policy, and Practices

7. Economic and Social Research Council
   The Centre for Neighbourhood Research (CNR) identifies, evaluates, and synthesizes existing social science research on social, economic and political processes relevant to neighbourhood policies and practices in the UK.

Violence Prevention

8. The Center for the Study and Prevention of Violence (CSPV), University of Colorado, Boulder
   Blueprints for Violence Prevention is a project of CSPV that identifies outstanding violence and drug prevention programs that meet a high scientific standard of effectiveness.

Miscellaneous

9. The Campbell Collaboration
   This international research network prepares, maintains, and disseminates systematic reviews on a wide variety of topics related to social welfare and community practice.
10. Coalition for Evidence-Based Policy
    This nonprofit, nonpartisan organization provides evidence about social programs.
11. Social Care Institute for Excellence
    This charity organization provides evidence about programs, as well as practice tools based in evidence.
12. Society for Community Research and Action, Division 27 of the American Psychological Association (APA).
    The Society provides access to research on community interventions.
13. Society for Child and Family Policy and Practice, Division 37 of the American Psychological Association (APA)
    The Society provides information about services and service structures for children and youth.

Sources: Ohmer, 2008; Thyer, 2008

EXHIBIT 11.9

Effectiveness of Community Practice

Community practice interventions are often complex, with multiple community locations, goals, and activities that make them difficult to specify and evaluate for compliance and fidelity. Community practice interventions:

1. Can have a positive impact on facilitating citizen participation, including increasing collective action and community involvement.

2. Can facilitate personal and collective competencies among participants and increase their connections to their communities, including increasing self-esteem, personal empowerment, and community empowerment, leadership and political skills, and community pride and belonging.

3. Can have a positive impact on improving the physical, social, and economic conditions of communities (i.e., creating and improving affordable housing, increasing homeownership, improving infrastructure and physical appearance, increasing income, investment, and employment, improving high school education, and reducing the sale of alcohol to and use among young people).

4. Also have the potential for no effect. Many studies indicate that interventions do not affect the physical and economic attributes of the communities.

5. Are more likely to involve older female residents, African Americans, and Hispanics in community organizing. Other factors that help to explain and predict citizen participation include interest in the problems the program was attempting to solve, neighborhood perceptions and relationships, and length of residency.

Community practice interventions more easily improve citizen participation and associated benefits (i.e., improving collective action, and personal and political skills of participants) than improve complex physical, social, and economic problems in poor communities. Therefore, social work strategies should simultaneously focus on developing ways to strengthen citizen participation, while at the same time building the capacity of individuals.

Source: Ohmer & Korr, 2006.

Social workers also engage in social planning efforts by participating in proposals for action by elected officials or human service planning councils. They engage through such actions as writing letters, testifying to committees, becoming a member of planning committees, and/or organizing others to lobby planning councils. As part of that process, social workers can carefully create opportunities for participation by community members, so their participation is meaningful and effective, rather than a token effort to involve "residents." For example, social workers invite community residents to testify at public hearings about proposals to close schools in their neighborhood, and help prepare them for the testimony. Social workers also seek resident involvement in neighborhood committees, and work to ensure that residents can voice their opinions, participate fully in decision-making and assist to implement decisions. Social workers also make connections between disparate situations, so that the needs of individuals are connected to broader efforts and wider structures. For example, if a social worker encounters a resident whose child has lead poisoning, the social worker may be able to link this "case" to a broader "cause" of a community problem with lead poisoning due to the old housing stock in the neighborhood and the reluctance of landlords to remediate the lead in their units. Social workers also invite residents to participate in community-wide efforts to alleviate and prevent the problem, such as lead paint screenings in schools, and programs to assist tenants to test for lead paint in their apartments.

GLOBAL APPROACHES FOR COMMUNITY SOCIAL WORK PRACTICE

While all types of social work practice methods, including casework, group work, and family work, are used around the world, community social work practice offers unique contributions as an intervention method. Social workers are concerned about poverty and social issues that they encounter in every country, yet large differences in the scope and severity of social issues exist. While poverty and social issues encountered on a small scale can be addressed through individual, family, and group social work interventions, and a social welfare approach through offering governmental income and/or health assistance, widespread poverty and disasters in countries without a social safety net often requires a community practice approach (Healy, 2008). Exhibit 11.10 provides an overview of strategies to link local social work practice with global social work practice, particularly focused on community practice. While any of the models described in this chapter may be appropriate, given a specific community context, described next will be specific application of community development and community organizing using global approaches and in other countries.

International Social Work Community Development

As with domestic social work community development practice, the spectrum of social and economic development activities is broad, and has many actors. Some large international organizations (e.g., the United Nations Development Programme, World Health Organization, World Bank, International Monetary Fund), as well as national players, such as U.S. Agency for International Development (U.S.-AID) and the U.S. Peace Corps, play important roles in community development work in developed and developing countries through funding, facilitation, oversight, and management of community development projects and programs.

These organizations facilitate and plan the creation of large-scale physical projects, such as the building of dams, small business loans, credit guarantees, and the provision of primary health care, among other activities. Non-governmental organizations, such as the International Red Cross, CARE, Catholic Relief Services, and Save the Children, also focus on development projects that are self-sustaining and have long-reaching positive effects on communities. Examples include forming

EXHIBIT 11.10

Priorities for Social Work Practice Linking the Global and the Local

- Concentrating on community development as a focus for practice, and the incorporation of community development approaches in all social work practice.
- Extending the practice of policy advocacy to international forums.
- Developing techniques to enable the disadvantaged and oppressed to find a voice not merely in national forums but also globally, in international solidarity.
- Making effective use of the new technologies to link both workers and community groups globally.
- Including global forces as a critical component of problem analysis and consciousness raising.
- Social work roles and positions in international nongovernmental organizations (NGOs) and United Nations (UN) agencies.
- Incorporating a strong human rights analysis alongside more traditional social work needs-based practice.
- Seeking opportunities for social workers to develop internationalist understandings through such things as exchange programs and international courses in schools of social work.
- Developing further analysis and research about the link between the global and the local across social work knowledge, values, and skills.

The global local web

References: Ife, 2000, pp. 62–63; Reisch, 2013

local cooperatives, introducing farming techniques, and facilitating preventive health care projects and local sanitation projects (e.g., digging wells and building latrines) (Healy, 2008).

The goal of community development projects is to become self-sustaining by the community. Local-level development, in which the responsibility for the work is at the local community level, is most often used. Local-level development requires that strategies are planned and implemented with and by the persons experiencing the problem or need. The local-level approach requires social workers to focus on the development of relationships with community members, groups and institutions, so that development projects are truly locally determined and directed (Healy, 2008). Exhibit 11.11 provides an overview of key strategies and programs for local-level community development. Exhibits 11.12 and 11.13 provide case

- *Basic literacy courses.* Teachers can be recruited from local communities and trained to provide basic literacy instruction that conforms to local culture, socioeconomic realities and response to the desires of the local population.
- *Primary school education.* Primary school education is a key element to further development. Social workers can provide support to children seeking an education, and can work with the local community to provide resources needed.
- *Basic health care.* Staff can be recruited from local communities and trained to provide basic health care. Social workers can be involved in education about basic hygiene, immunizations, and disease prevention efforts.
- *Adult education, basic training, and people's capacity building.* If desired by the community, social workers can facilitate adult basic education or training in such fields as agriculture, forestry, or marketing for small businesses.
- *Awareness-raising and empowerment.* Through informal or formal dialogue, social workers can assist individuals, families, groups, and communities to understand their life situation of oppression, exclusion, poverty, drug addiction, and others. This realization includes an understanding of the forces that have led to and reinforce the present situation. This realization can lead to change efforts.
- *Local income-generation programs.* Social workers can be involved in education or facilitation of programs that lead to higher income generation at the individual, family or community level. Such programs can lead to better farming methods, increased number of or profitability of small businesses, or large community-wide industries, such as a food processing plant.
- *Credit schemes and people's banks.* To overcome the inability of community members to access financial credit through formal institutions, social workers can be involved in local level, small lending programs (for example, see Exhibit 11.12).
- *Community-based self-help programs.* Social workers can assist to facilitate a planned response by the community to a community need, such as developing a local program to assist the disabled, mentally ill, or AIDS orphans.
- *Leadership development.* Social workers can support existing leaders, as well as train new leaders.
- *Local organization and institution promotion and capacity building.* Social workers may be involved in assisting to create or promote local institutions, such as those that oversee education or community recreation.
- *Linking local organizations to government agencies and international structures.* Social workers can provide the information, support, and connections between local organizations and external resources.
- *Comprehensive community development programs.* Social workers can assist to facilitate the integration of development efforts to create a holistic effort.

EXHIBIT 11.11

Key Strategies and Programs for Local Level Development

Source: Cox & Pawar, 2013, pp. 199–220

EXHIBIT 11.12

International Community Development Case Example— Grameen Bank

An effort to assist one Bangladesh woman by loaning her 27 U.S. dollars has evolved into a world-wide movement to assist the poor to escape dire poverty by providing micro-credit. Many poor small business owners lack the money to purchase needed raw goods or supplies for their business, and they are dependent on high-cost credit from money-lenders. The Grameen (which means "village") Bank was founded on the idea that small loans with reasonable terms would make a large difference in the lives of the poor. The bank began as a very small effort in 1983, and now has over 2,500 branches in 81,000 villages in Bangladesh, with a loan repayment rate of 96 percent.

The bank offers loans without collateral requirements, a credit history, or any legal instruments. The bank makes loans to a self-made group of five friends, rather than an individual. When one wants to take out a loan, the other group members must approve. Members of the group provide encouragement, support, and practical assistance to one another. The groups from each village attend weekly meetings in their village, in which loan repayments are collected, loan applications are accepted, and activities are undertaken to foster community bonds and provide education about important topics. Positive social pressure by the group structure has facilitated high repayment rate of the small loans. The Grameen Bank borrowers also commit to "The Sixteen Decisions," a list of values and activities that foster healthy living, communal action, and education for children.

For his efforts, Muhammad Yunus and the Grameen Bank won the 2006 Nobel Peace Prize.

EXHIBIT 11.13

International Community Development Case Example— Project Restore

Project Restore (PR) is a humanitarian development and relief agency that supports, rehabilitates, and enhances the quality of life and well-being of individuals and communities across the world. By focusing on four key issues, Project Restore promotes self-sustainable, prosperous communities in the U.S. and around the world. The four areas of focus are clean water, education, hunger, and healthcare.

Specifically, PR is currently engaged in community development in a village in Uganda, Africa. The first step in the development process was the identification of the development priorities of the village by the village council (i.e., village leaders). The village council identified the needs, the plan for meeting those needs, their contribution to the development plan, and their request for PR. Projects that have been completed or that are still ongoing include the preparation, purchase, and placement of several water harvesting tanks, the repair of several wells, the distribution of mosquito nets, the purchase and distribution of livestock to produce milk and offspring to sell for food for school lunches, and a matched savings account program for the children in secondary school to help pay for their supplies and tuition. Medical supplies are also furnished to the local clinic.

examples of international community development work that implements several of the strategies and programs.

Globalization and Community Organizing in Social Work Practice

Similarities exist between community organizing efforts at the international level and efforts in the U.S. For example, regardless of the setting or context, empowering individuals, building and strengthening community bonds, and building progressive organizations, are appropriate community organizing goals. Community organizing skills are similar, as the focus is on a particular change effort.

Community organizing efforts, both in the U.S and abroad, are closely related to global issues; therefore, local issues must be viewed within globally interconnected systems (Reisch, 2013). For example, international migration of workers from the Global South to the Global North has created large numbers of workers, some who are not documented, vulnerable to abuses and exploitation by their employers due to a tenuous legal status, and desperate to generate income to support themselves and their families in their home countries. A worldwide effort has ensued to combine the efforts of labor organizing and community organizing to build the power of immigrant workers to raise wages and improve working conditions. These efforts mostly use direct action, or conflict, organizing strategies, and activities to gain changes in public policy (Hanley & Shragge, 2009). Other global community organizing efforts are focused on domestic violence experienced by immigrants (Kasvin & Tashayeva, 2004), workers' rights (UAW Global Organizing Institute, 2012), child welfare issues related to deportation of immigrants, global warming (350.org, n.d.), and a host of other issues that are interrelated in the global interconnections of systems. Due to the transnational nature of local issues, such as unemployment, environmental problems, and public health challenges, local development work must be accomplished within the framework of globalization of human challenges. For example, community development work that intends to impact the local economy must consider the global economic climate, rather than just the local market.

Community social work practice, just like social work practice with other systems levels, ends with the termination and evaluation phase. The next section will consider trends that impact this phase, as well as the skills needed to professionally master the ending phase of social work community practice.

CONTEMPORARY TRENDS AND SKILLS FOR THE ENDING PHASE OF COMMUNITY SOCIAL WORK: TERMINATION AND EVALUATION

Community social work practitioners join with the community in change efforts, and facilitate the leadership of the efforts by the community members. Often, community practice efforts are the result of months and even years (or decades) of work, and consist of many smaller change efforts. For example, social workers may engage in community development and community efforts with the community to rid the community of child lead poisoning. This overarching change effort can involve efforts to change policy at the local level about rental housing, work with landlords to remediate lead paint, the promotion of local school screening for child lead poisoning, and work with the local public health clinic to create an outreach program to prevent lead poisoning and reach persons potentially affected. Each of these may have involved lengthy efforts.

Achieving goals of community change efforts, whether smaller efforts within larger goals, or the larger goal itself, is the catalyst for turning to the next phase of the change effort, termination and evaluation.

Community Social Work Practice Endings

Termination in community social work practice can be more complex than termination with other client systems, due to the potential involvement of many players and institutions in the process. The termination phase in community practice is often termination of the social worker from the community (if moving on to other responsibilities), of the social worker's sponsoring organization from a community change effort (if the organization can no longer participate for some reason), termination of people or institutions from community change efforts, which may continue without them. Termination of one change effort can also occur when the community has prioritized other needs, such as a situation where the community is grappling with a natural disaster. For example, a social worker may terminate with a community lead prevention and remediation effort if lead poisoning levels drop dramatically, and/or if local leadership is effectively working on the issue and the assistance of the social worker is no longer needed.

As in terminations with other client systems, endings can be emotional. Building relationships is a key element to all types of community practice; therefore, the social worker's role in termination is to "help [participants] examine their accomplishments, review their experience together, and prepare for the future" (Garvin & Galinsky, 2008, pp. 291–292). Social workers may also facilitate the expression and integration of positive and negative emotion, which can include such feelings as elation and joy about successes achieved and/or such negative emotions as disappointment, rejection, abandonment, or anger, depending on the circumstances of the termination. While participants in community practice efforts are likely to experience fewer highly emotional responses than those of individual, family or group work, social workers must be attuned to the possibility of emotional reactions to the termination (of all types mentioned above).

Endings in Community Practice Utilizing Strengths and Empowerment   The use of the strengths and empowerment approaches leads the social worker to facilitate the community process of reviewing the progress made toward the previously identified goals and developing strategies for sustainability of the changes. In the case of social work community practice, the social worker can invite each participant to review and reflect on her or his individual experience in the change effort, including strengths brought to the process, any change that they personally experienced, and plans for contributing to the maintenance of the change(s). Having individual members engaged in this process can provide closure for all involved. Like group work practice, participants can also use other participants' reflections to examine their own growth processes.

As community social work practice often involves the use of task groups, many elements of and skills needed for the group work termination process can apply. For example, using a strengths-based perspective, the social worker can assist the group in reflecting on the group strengths that have evolved as the group engaged in community change efforts. The social worker can use the group ending as an opportunity to provide feedback on the individual, group, and community changes observed.

In situations in which the community goals are not realized, the termination process can still employ a strengths perspective. The participants can review the community and group strengths that existed at the outset of their efforts, those strengths gained or mobilized during the process, and those strengths that can be carried on by the participants after the formal change effort has ended. While the members (and the social worker) may be dismayed by the perceived failure of not achieving the desired goals, strategizing about ways in which the participants can continue to work toward achieving the goals can, in fact, be empowering.

Like termination with individuals, families, and groups, a key element of the termination process is a focus on sustaining the gains achieved, such as community bonding, leadership skills, civic engagement, and/or the continuation and growth of community networks and community programs. Regardless of the circumstances of the termination, a focus on community strengths and positive outcomes of the intervention can serve to sustain efforts by energizing community members and institutions to continue their efforts. If the termination occurs because the goal of the community intervention was achieved, the community can build on their successes, and begin the assessment, intervention, and evaluation process anew. However, sustaining the gains from the intervention may involve many people and institutions, particularly if the social worker (and his/her sponsoring organization) supplied many resources for the intervention. New actors, such as new community participants or institutions, may need to become involved to continue with the community change efforts if professional social work resources will not be available. For example, using the lead paint story in the previous section, if the social worker involved in the change efforts related to lead paint worked for the school district and the social worker was transferred to a different school and needed to terminate from the efforts, the social worker would transfer responsibilities to another leader in the effort, such as a co-worker, parent, local development organization staff member, other community resident, or a group of professionals involved in the effort, so that the change effort could continue. If the local leadership was not sufficiently developed to maintain the community change effort, the effort would discontinue. Exhibit 11.14 provides an example of a termination of a community organizing effort.

EXHIBIT 11.14 *Termination and Evaluation*	Communities Facilitating Opportunity (CFO) is an organization that conducts community organizing through a federation of 25 local faith-based institutions. One area of their work focused on the lack of affordable housing production in their community for over a decade. The work of the CFO leaders and members, with the support of staff members, included years of conducting research with both effected individuals, public officials, and others involved in the affordable housing production and maintenance system, holding numerous meetings with relevant public officials to demand answers to questions about the lack of quality affordable housing in their community, and drawing media attention to the problem. The housing department failed time and time again to deliver on promises, despite the availability of federal funding dedicated to the production of affordable housing for the city. CFO also called attention to official audits by the city and federal government that demonstrated a significant level of dysfunction and corruption within the city housing department. One project that captured the most public attention centered on the renovation of two small houses in a working class neighborhood at a cost that exceeded 20 times the assessed value of those properties. The housing agency used many tactics to disempower citizen input, such as verbally promising to take action and not following through, and yelling and saying demeaning things to CFO leaders and members. CFO finally decided to hold a large public meeting to directly address public officials in front of a large number of their constituents. The Mayor and other local public officials were specifically invited to attend the public meeting to directly engage the public, and the leadership of their local government. The overall goals of members for this campaign of CFO were: (1) an accountable city government, (2) a working program for the repair of homes, (3) a way to hold absentee landlords accountable, (4) protection from predatory mortgage lenders, and (5) a focus on building communities—not just homes. In the meeting, the group pointed out that $18 million in funds flowed annually through the city housing agency in a haphazard, yet nontransparent way. They offered specific policy proposals, such as establishing a $5 million fund for minor home repair to add to existing monies, targeting neighborhoods where the existing housing stock was strained. Two weeks after the public meeting, the City Manager moved all personnel out of the city housing agency to other city agencies, saying that he had concluded that the city housing agency was often controlled by outside special interests, that housing services were fragmented and that there was no comprehensive approach for building and selling houses. Completely new staff were needed to correct these deep problems. CFO members would be involved in elements of restructuring and re-staffing the organization. **Termination:** Termination of the campaign occurred when the CFO leadership and membership recognized that at least one of the intervention goals was met; the city was

now more accountable for decisions about affordable housing production. The restructuring of the housing agency was a fundamental shift in the power structure for decisions made about affordable housing in the city. In the end, CFO, along with their partners, succeeded in dismantling and rebuilding a branch of local government that implements housing and community development. CFO action helped to provide the necessary pressure to create change in the structure of the local government. CFO decided to end the previous tactics designed to put pressure on the city, and work with the City Manager to create a new agency that would be transparent and accountable, with the hopes that their other goals could be met through new personnel.

Using the strengths perspective, CFO engaged in reflection to discern group and community strengths present at the beginning, and those gained through the intervention. CFO leadership and membership also engaged in a group process to review their accomplishments, and to discern future movements. The CFO focused on the building of their strength as an organization, their bonding, gained leadership skills, their knowledge of and engagement with civic affairs and city personnel, and the continuation and growth of their network of organizations in the community.

Evaluation: Evaluation of this community practice intervention occurred both in the short-term and the long-term. Throughout the long campaign, the social worker assisted leaders to facilitate their own reflection, reflection of the members about the degree to which they met short-term goals, and documentation of the process. Short-term goals in this case include obtaining: meetings with involved parties and public officials; information; commitments of action; actions taken; and media coverage. Long-term efforts were evaluated over many years, and required documentation of media coverage, turnout at public meetings, and the amount and type of responsiveness of public officials and decision-makers. CFO also collected data on the housing problems over the years from the housing agency, federal agencies, and others. Evaluation also included the extent to which members realized increasing confidence, leadership skills, personal speaking skills, organizing skills, and feelings of efficacy. Methods included review of meeting minutes and other organization (i.e., internal reports), interviews with staff, CFO leadership, and members, and public documents.

Source: Speer & Christens, 2011

EXHIBIT 11.14

Continued

Evaluation of Social Work Practice with Communities

Similar to evaluation with individuals, families, and groups, evaluation of social work community practice interventions can assess the process along the way, the extent to which the goals were achieved, and the social worker's skills in the intervention phase. Just as the community change effort was a collaborative process with the community, so too is the evaluation process a collaborative effort. Community participation is important throughout the change effort for empowerment of participants, and during the evaluation process, collaboration as an equal partner in this process leads to a feeling of ownership of the information. The evaluation process seeks to determine the value of something, and differs from monitoring the intervention (Netting et al., 2012).

The evaluation process begins as an element of the intervention design, and requires social workers and community members first to determine: (1) if both the process and outcomes will be evaluated; (2) the ways in which the process and outcomes will be evaluated; and (3) the means by which data will be collected as the basis for the evaluation. Evaluation of community change efforts may include both an examination of the personal and interpersonal levels, as well as the community level. Evaluation of the community effort may include an evaluation of the group work involved, which is covered extensively in Chapter 9.

Preferably, the evaluation process will include both qualitative and quantitative data to provide information about the process of community change, as well as progress on the desired outcomes at the personal, interpersonal, and community levels. Methods may include pre- and post-measures of community functioning, to include the use of validated and standardized measures, direct observation by the social worker to document change, use of publically available data (i.e., U.S. Census data and others), administrative data from **Management Information Systems (MIS)** from public departments such as policy, public health, child welfare, police and others, GIS mapping (discussed in Chapter 10), and feedback from other professionals (Ohmer, 2008).

An example of a community evaluation process is an evaluation of a community development effort in Perth, Western Australia. The aim of the evaluation was to assess the quality of life in a community that had experienced community development initiatives as compared to a nearby community that had not experienced the initiatives. The residents rated the quality of their lives and communities using the Australian Unity Wellbeing Index to measure individual and neighborhood well-being. Additionally, the well-being of the residents was compared to national averages (Blunsdon & Davern, 2007). In another example, semi-structured interviews and observations were used to evaluate the extent to which an initiative to involve parents in the planning and decisions about delivery methods of a community child development program was successful (MacNeill, 2009).

STRAIGHT TALK ABOUT COMMUNITY INTERVENTION, TERMINATION, AND EVALUATION

Community social work practice, including the intervention, termination, and evaluation phases, offers many rewards and challenges. One challenging aspect of some types of community social work practice is long hours at salaries less than those in individual, family, and group practice. Further, community social work practice can involve working during the day with professionals in organizations and institutions, and in the evenings and on weekends with community participants.

Efforts to change institutions, policies, and practices can take a long time, and there may be many setbacks along the way. Tangible rewards and successes for the work may be few and far between, which can lead to burnout (Rubin & Rubin, 2008).

The rewards include the personal satisfaction of working to change environments to better meet the needs of people, and provide opportunities for the empowerment of individuals and communities. Many community practitioners appreciate the ability to partner with individuals, families, and groups to better their lives, while avoiding the view of persons as "clients," which can include the use of diagnostic labels, treatment plans, and a primarily individualistic perspective. Through community practice, people are involved in decision-making about aspects that affect their lives, sometimes for the first time. Helping people gain their voices and work toward large-scale social change is work toward social justice. The variety of tasks completed, the joy of successes, and the wide autonomy and flexibility of the tasks involved are other factors that draw and keep social workers in community practice (Rubin & Rubin, 2008).

Community practitioners must have energy for long-term work, and be able to see value in the process and effort involved, rather than just the outcomes. The occasional victories, even short-term or small, must provide the drive to sustain community practitioners. The community practitioner must often work diligently on short-term or immediate goals, while keeping the larger, systemic, institutional change in focus, and celebrate small gains.

CONCLUSION

This chapter has presented the range of social work community practice as an important client system level for generalist practitioners. Engaging in community practice offers social workers the opportunity to influence their environments to create communities that are truly responsive to the needs of all members. Community interventions, terminations, and evaluations are complex, with a primary focus on the community, and a secondary focus on individual change. Community practice includes developing leaders, facilitating bonding among residents, and other personal and interpersonal work that is important as a foundation for community change. Such complexity requires the social worker to possess skills with various client systems to implement the community intervention and facilitate the termination and evaluation processes.

MAIN POINTS

- Community intervention uses guided community practice models, which are primarily based in the concepts and language of systems, ecological and power, change, and politics theories.

- The three models most commonly used are Rothman's (2008) three models of community practice: planning/policy; community capacity development; and social advocacy. These models can be blended to best match the context of the community change effort.

- The intervention strategies of community social and economic development, community organizing, and community asset mapping are aimed at improving community conditions and the quality of life for the community residents or members.

- Community social work practice, including community development and community organizing, offers unique contributions as an intervention method both domestically and around the globe.

- Termination in community practice can be more complex than termination with other client systems, due to the potential involvement of many players and institutions in the process.

- Evaluation of social work community practice functions to assess the process along the way, the extent to which the goals were achieved, and the social worker's skills in the intervention phase.

EXERCISES

a. Case Exercises

1. Go to www.routledgesw.com/cases and review the video of the Alverez neighborhood association meeting within the Riverton case. In groups, begin a role-play where the video ends and continue the discussion. Did the Chair of the committee vote? If not, what may have occurred? If the committee delays their vote, what additional information might be helpful to the decision-making process? Summarize the points of view. Which arguments are most persuasive? How might you vote if you were on the committee? How would you like to see this end? Compare your preferences with classmates.

2. After completing Exercise #1, discuss the following questions with your classmates. What other information would you need to make a decision? If you were the facilitator, what might you have done differently as the Chair? What elements of Robert's Rules of Order were used in the Alverez video? What elements were not used? How might other elements have been used? How might that have changed the course of actions in the video?

3. Go to www.routledgesw.com/cases, and become familiar with the Riverton case file, especially the "Your History" section. Choose either the planning/policy, community capacity development, or social advocacy models of community intervention described in Chapter 11 and describe a possible community

intervention for Riverton to address the concerns about the coal-fired power plant. Describe a community intervention using a second model, and compare and contrast the intervention with the first intervention. What are some key differences?

4. Go to www.routledgesw.com/cases and become familiar with the Riverton case file. You would like to begin to address community concerns and issues using a community social and economic development approach. What issues could you address? How would you address the issues using a community social and economic development approach?

5. Go to www.routledgesw.com/cases and become familiar with the Riverton case file. With many types of community interventions, recruiting allies from a diversity of groups adds to the strength of the intervention. Describe how you would recruit from various populations within Riverton to participate in a community intervention.

6. Go to www.routledgesw.com/cases and become familiar with the Brickville case. An evaluation of the youth group community empowerment effort could entail many different types of activities. Create a 5-7 question key informant interview guide that the youth could use for evaluation purposes to gather feedback about the level of involvement and empowerment of neighborhood residents. Included in the interviews would be faith leaders, neighborhood leaders, politicians, and professionals who serve the community through the area nonprofits.

b. Other exercises

7. Choose a social issue that is important to you. Assume the role of a community developer. How would you address the issue using community development skills and techniques?

8. Choose a social issue that is important to you. Assume the role of a community organizer. How would you address the issue using community organizing skills and techniques?

9. Review the categories and examples of assets in Exhibit 11.5. List all of the types of assets present in your community (i.e., campus or neighborhood) within each of the categories.

CHAPTER 12

Social Work Practice with Organizations: Engagement, Assessment, and Planning

"Why study organizations?" There are two answers to this question. The first answer is that we have become a society of organization. Our lives are shaped by organizations, from birth to death. . . . The second is that if we want to change key aspects of our lives and/or society, we almost inevitably must change organizations.

Tolbert & Hall, 2009, pp.1–2

Key Questions for Chapter 12

(1) What competencies do I need to engage and assess organizations? (EPAS 2.1.10(a & b))

(2) What are the social work practice behaviors that enable me to effectively engage and assess organizations? (EPAS 2.1.10(a & b))

(3) How can I utilize evidence to practice research-informed practice and practice-informed research to guide the engagement and assessment with organizations? (EPAS 2.1.6)

(4) How can I apply critical thinking to engagement and assessment with organizations? (EPAS 2.1.3)

(5) How can I apply social work values and ethics to engagement with and assessment of organizations? (EPAS 2.1.2)

INFLUENCING ORGANIZATIONS CAN RESULT IN IMPROVED services for clients. You may think of organizations as small, supportive structures that help to organize the maze of work, or as large bureaucracies that are unresponsive to client needs or individual efforts to improve them. Organizations are "formally structured arrangements of people, tools, and resources brought together to achieve predetermined objectives through institutionalized strategies" (Barker, 2003, p. 308). Social workers work in many types and sizes of organizations, and use their knowledge of organizations to promote the best interest of their client systems. Knowledge of organizations is imperative to professional practice, because most social workers practice within organizations. Although there has been considerable growth in the number of social workers choosing independent practice settings, the majority today work in agency settings (Whitaker & Wilson, 2010).

This chapter focuses on the nature of organizations and social work agencies, particularly as experienced by social work practitioners. Theoretical perspectives on and dimensions of organizations will be explored. We will also discuss the engagement and assessment processes with organizations. The discussion emphasizes the social worker's interface with organizations, and the ways in which organization functions shape professional practice. The chapter will also look at the skills needed for organizational engagement and assessment, and will close with a discussion about types of organizations.

UNDERSTANDING ORGANIZATIONS

Organizations address individual, family, group, and community needs. Organizations, like other client systems, can be understood through theories, models, and perspectives. Prior to moving into the change process, a theoretical understanding of organizations can assist social workers in the process of engagement, assessment, intervention, and termination and evaluation. In this next section, organizations will be described social systems, as well as from the integration of contemporary theories of organizations.

Organization as a Social System

As mentioned in earlier chapters, general systems theory posits that a system, such as an organization, is composed of intersecting components that are part of larger systems, such as the community at large and society. Organizations, therefore, acquire resources from their environments and return products or services to their environment. Understanding organizations requires understanding that organizations exchange resources with their environments (Brueggemann, 2005). In the assessment process, which is described later in this chapter, social workers can examine the extent to which subsystems, such as funders, other organizations, or networks of organizations, meet the needs of the organization. They can use this information to advocate for a higher level of functioning of a subsystem, which will ultimately benefit the organization.

Contemporary Theories and Organizations

Organizational and management theory has a history that dates back to the late 1800s. Like earlier theories, contemporary theories about organizations, such as power and politics, organizational culture, quality-oriented management, and evidence-based management, help to analyze organizations and understand their structure and operations. In understanding organizations, theories of today emphasize the following: (1) the role of culture in helping to understand the ways in which groups of persons affiliated with organizations define and pursue collective organizational goals; (2) the idea of quality has become the benchmark in the design of organizational structures (such as administrative relationships), processes (such as decision-making processes), and the evaluation of success as an organization. In this respect, the process of the work of the organization is as important as the outcomes of the programs and services that are delivered to clients; and (3) there is no one correct approach to structuring organizations. Many aspects of an organization, including size, mission, clients, and staff qualifications, are important to consider when structuring an organization and developing a management style (Netting, Kettner, McMurtry, & Thomas, 2011).

Dimensions of Organizations

Social and human service organizations differ widely along a number of dimensions. These differences affect service delivery to clients, as well as the employee

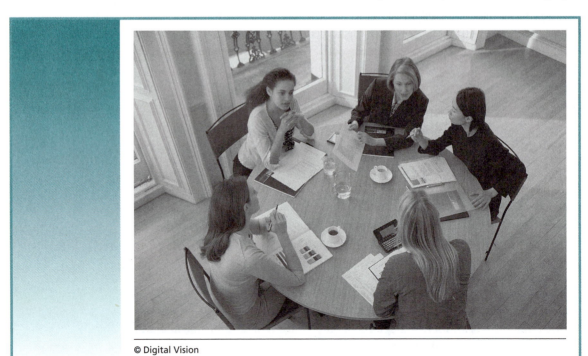

© Digital Vision

experience. The three most important dimensions of difference between organizations are: (1) purpose of the organization; (2) structure of governance; and (3) the internal power relations.

Purpose

The stated purpose of an organization is the rationale for the organization's existence, as well as the agency's goals and activities. While organizational objectives state the ways in which organizations work toward their goals, the purpose describes the concerns of the organization in broad terms. The three types of purposes are: (1) to fill a public mandate; (2) to provide a particular service; and (3) to foster social change in regard to an ideological concern.

Organizations Sanctioned by Law   The law sanctions organizations in several ways. First, organizations sanctioned by federal and state law ("public organizations") provide mandated social services that are widely recognized by the public. For example, adult protection services, available in all 50 states, are usually housed within a large and visible state organization. Social workers representing these organizations are expected to act in the best interests of older adults who cannot protect themselves against abuse, neglect, or exploitation, carry out the activities of daily living, or manage their own affairs. Public organizations are directly accountable to the community, as they derive the vast majority of their funding through tax revenue (i.e., federal, state, county, or local government funds). Second, most social services are offered through nonprofit organizations designated as **501(c)3** organizations by the U.S. Internal Revenue Service (IRS). Nonprofit organizations are sanctioned by the law to meet specified public needs. Designated nonprofit organizations are exempt from paying taxes on organizational income, and donors are allowed to deduct contributions from their taxes (Holland, 2008).

Organizations with Service Goals   Organizations with service goals develop as a result of an agreed upon need or concern. For example, youth at risk of dropping out of school are often seen loitering in blighted areas. Adolescent high school drop-outs are a high-risk population for poverty, health concerns, and criminal activity. Organizations providing youth services offer prevention services to help youth avoid dropping out, assist adolescent drop-outs in acquiring tangible resources, and provide legal assistance and referrals to substance abuse treatment. Service goals are an important type of purpose, as they define the work of the organization and the social need or concern addressed by the organization.

Organizations Arising from Social Movements   Some **grassroots organizations**, which are organizations started by ordinary citizens rather than professionals, arise in response to ideological positions on particular social problems. The early development of shelters for women experiencing intimate partner violence is an example of

EXHIBIT 12.1

Example of Public and Non-Profit Organizations

The Area Agencies on Aging (AAA) is a network of *public* agencies across the country that provides a comprehensible and coordinated system of community-based services for older adults in localities across the U.S. Services can include nutrition programs, case management, abuse prevention programs, legal assistance, personal assistance, and other programs. The AAAs are public organizations because they are directly funded through tax dollars, and overseen by the U.S. Department of Health and Human Services.

NATIONAL AGING SERVICES NETWORK

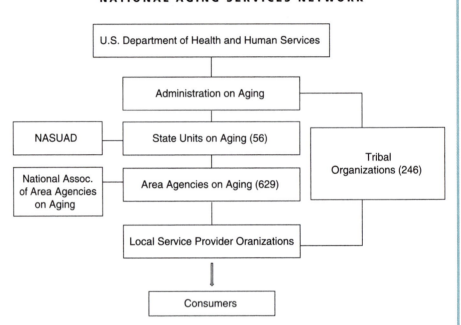

Source: National Association of Area Agencies on Aging, 2012

The Alzheimer's Association (AA) is the leading, global voluntary health organization in Alzheimer's care and support, and the largest private, nonprofit funder of Alzheimer's research. Through over 70 agencies across the country, AAs provide services such as referrals for resources, family education, support, respite care, and other services to families impacted by Alzheimer's Disease. The AAs are *private* organizations because they are not directly supported through tax dollars, but rather through private funds, and are overseen by a Board of Directors.

a **social movement**, a political effort designed to change some aspect of society. A social movement is led by citizens whose commitments and energies are channeled into a political movement, and organizations were created to implement the long-term work of the social movement. As the organizations are created, professionals,

Casa de Esperanza was started to meet the need for a culturally competent domestic violence shelter in St. Paul MN. While there were well-established domestic violence shelters in Minnesota, there was a lack of culturally appropriate services for Latina women. However, not long after it started, the vast majority of those assisted were Anglo and African-American, despite the pervasive problem of family violence for Latina women. However, the board and staff knew that within the Latino community, there was a real need for education, prevention and safe haven. In response, new programs were developed to serve the community and attract Latinas, including a Women's Empowerment program, support groups, advocacy, supportive listening, a 24-hour crisis line, a children's therapeutic program, children's advocacy, and structured daily activities, such as therapeutic dance and Spanish lessons.

Strong resistance within the Latino community to speaking openly about the problem of domestic violence existed, and the message of Casa's leaders was met with hostility and animosity. Exposing women's experience of family violence challenged the image of a happy family, and brought a private matter out into the open, potentially embarrassing family members.

The organization struggled to sort through these cultural forces, and answer important questions. While the mission statement stated that the agency existed to "eliminate oppression and its violence against women and children," many board and staff members felt a unique responsibility to work within the Latino community. This responsibility had further implications regarding expectations for bilingual and bicultural staff and publications, definitions of eligibility for services. Most significantly, should women in crisis be turned away from the shelter because they were not Latina? Receipt of public funding for the shelter required that clients be served on a "first-come, first-served basis," so no shelter or service slots could be reserved for Latinas.

In response, the organization created new programs and services to educate the community about Latino family violence, and conduct outreach to Latinas. Staff and volunteers also began to network with other Hispanic organizations to increase awareness about the problem of family violence. As the organization grew, questions about identity persisted. Were they an organization serving primarily Latinos, or a multicultural organization? The contradictions woven into the fabric of the operations needed to be addressed.

In early 1997, the Board went through a strategic planning process to grapple with their identity. Ultimately, the organization moved from being primarily a shelter to a Latina organization. This affirmation created a need for a new approach to program development and operations, community relations, and an overhaul of the agency systems. Shelter services changed in duration, and were de-linked from community-wide referral system, resulting in more Latina women being served. The emphasis of the organization moved away from shelter to prevention, community education and support, and policy advocacy for Latinos. For example, staff (1) offered expanded case management and referral networks to support women who live with their abusers or other family members; (2) worked to build the cultural competence of other nonprofits; (3) engaged in advocating for public policies that better protected woman;

EXHIBIT 12.2

Change the Mission?

EXHIBIT 12.2 *Continued*	and (4) formed strategic alliances with other organizations to influence policy makers, judges, and law enforcement officials. To correspond with the new emphasis on the community as an agent of change, the mission was changed to "Mobilize Latinas and Latino communities to end domestic violence." References: Casa De Esperanza, n.d.; Sandfort, 2005.

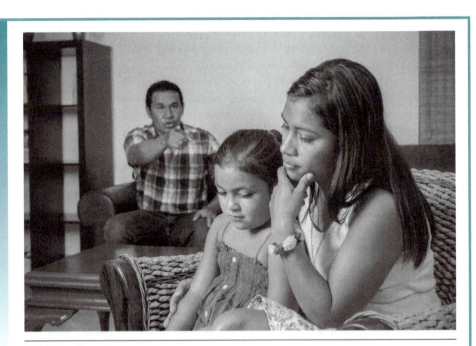

© Chris Fertnig

such as social workers, are employed by the organizations. Frequently, the founders, professionals, and volunteers of such organizations are indigenous to the movement, which means they have personally experienced the oppression that is the focus of the organization. Professionals and volunteers often have extraordinary commitment to the mission of the organization (Hardina, 2012).

Structures of Governance

An organization's leadership is another variable in structure. Organizational structure, much like family structure, refers to the way in which members, tasks, and units relate to one another. The structure shapes the rules, or norms, of the organization. Some of the rules are explicit, such as personnel policies, and others are implicit, such as the best ways to influence the decision of an administrator. These rules, governed by organizational culture (discussed later) may be communicated openly to employees and volunteers, while others may be communicated nonverbally or through interpretation of decisions. In the next section, three kinds of organizational structures will be explored as representative of those found in many contemporary agencies: bureaucracies, project teams, and functional structures.

Bureaucracies Many human service organizations, including state and local government organizations and nonprofits, are structured as a bureaucracy; therefore, social workers benefit from knowledge about the structure of their employing organization.

German sociologist Max Weber invented the term **bureaucracy** as a conceptual type, rather than a reality, of structure. The following 10 points describe the characteristics of a bureaucracy (Weber, 1947, as cited in Netting et al., 2011):

- Each position in the organization has a limited area of authority and responsibility.

- Control and responsibility are concentrated at the top of a clear hierarchy.

- The activities of the organization are documented in a central system of records.

- The organization employs highly specialized workers based on expert training.

- Staff demands require full-time commitment, and each position represents a career.

- Activities are coordinated through clearly outlined rules.

- The relationships among workers are characterized by impersonality.

- Recruitment is based on ability and relevant, technical knowledge.

- The private and public lives of the organization's members are distinct.

- Promotions in the organization are made by seniority and/or achievement.

Several aspects of bureaucracy have been incorporated into the organizational experiences of many professionals, even those in smaller organizations. For example, the notion that recruitment is based on ability, rather than a relationship with other staff members, is a widely accepted idea of fairness in employment practices. On the other hand, the top-down, hierarchical authority or the impersonality of relationships among members is often an aspect of bureaucracies that challenges employees. The organizations that most often display the characteristics of bureaucracies are those embedded in large systems, such as local, state, or federal government; therefore, older adult/child protection, public health and mental health, and corrections, are fields in which bureaucratic approaches are most common.

Project Teams   In a sharp contract with bureaucracy, **project teams** consist of a group of people who collectively work on organizational challenges or opportunities through committee or task force structures (Brueggemann, 2005). Project teams are a flexible way to accomplish work tasks, because the committees may exercise their best collective judgment in decision-making, and the group has minimal hierarchy. Often, such groups find maintaining this structure challenging for many reasons, such as the growth of the group and limitations imposed by a higher authority.

For example, a group of women and men concerned about intimate partner violence may use a project team approach to develop and operate an organization that provides services to survivors of intimate partner violence. The intended services include a domestic violence shelter, therapy, and violence prevention programming. Team members may structure the organization of the shelter staff so that everyone shares the tasks of managing the agency's physical space, and identical salaries are paid to everyone. The project team structure has many positive aspects; however, the structure may be challenged by those with concerns relating to the appropriateness of some duties for those staff with higher degrees (e.g., the appropriateness of a person with a master's degree answering phones or vacuuming the shelter office). The project team approach can be challenged as organizations hire new workers who demand a competitive salary, or as their budget grows from sources that require a hierarchal structure.

Functional Structures   When an agency becomes too large for a single person to administer, a layer of personnel will be added. These administrative additions are usually divided by function or area of responsibility; thus the name **functional structures**. In a community development agency, for example, the executive director may appoint an experienced social worker as the program director of the youth services department, and another as the program director of the affordable housing development unit. In this situation, the two midlevel administrative leaders would be equals, and may form a management team that works directly with the executive director in larger administrative functions and decisions. Frequently, these administrative roles are added to already existing direct service roles. For example, the program director of the youth services programs would retain responsibility for actually implementing one of the programs. As the agency grows larger, the program directors may not provide the direct services due to the heavy demands of the supervisory and administrative activities.

Internal Power Relations

Organizations have overt arrangements of power, such as hierarchical arrangements of personnel. Organizations also have power arrangements that are subtle and are unique to the organization. Chapter 3 discusses several sources of power for social workers, including agency, expert knowledge, interpersonal, and legitimate power. The following discussion considers the view of authority as "**consensual power**," or

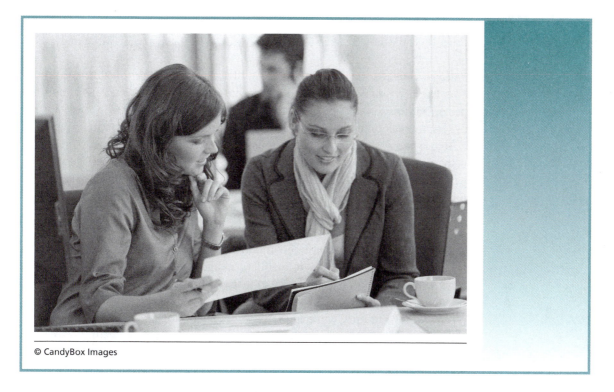

© CandyBox Images

power that is non-coercive and derives from content. In the next section, we discuss authority based on tradition, charisma, and rational/legal principles. Rather than being imposed on people, these sources of power are derived from authority given by people to someone (Rogers, 1975).

Traditional Authority   Authority attributed by title or ancestry, such as a king or a pope might claim, is **traditional authority**. This type of authority is most often seen in the U.S. as based on family relationships and history or inheritance. For example, CEOs of large corporations are often related to other powerful people, such as former presidents or other CEOs, and are frequently members of the original family who started the business. Such authority is seen only occasionally in human service agencies.

Charismatic Authority   This type of authority is considered an unstable but present dynamic in U.S. organizations. As contrasted to traditional authority, the **charismatic authority** model suggests that a captivating personality (rather than heritage, ideas, skills, or commitments) is the variable required to gain power by consensus. This form of authority is often displayed in state and national elections when, for example, entertainers and celebrities run for and win public office without previous political experience. Such authority is often present with founders of human service agencies who are successful at the necessary start-up tasks of garnering supporters, raising funds, recruiting an initial board of directors, and other tasks that involve persuasion.

Rational/Legal Authority   This authority is based on ability to achieve outcomes and, like charismatic authority, is persuasive rather than coercive. An example of a person with **rational/legal authority** is an agency staff member who is an expert in program development and program evaluation. A staff member with a particular expertise and a track record of accomplishments in the area of expertise is likely to be persuasive in an appeal to initiate new programs. Large human service agencies, particularly bureaucracies, often contain staff members with rational/legal authority because the staff is able to specialize and develop expertise. Staff in smaller organizations can also develop rational/legal authority, depending on their backgrounds, interests, opportunities, and agency needs.

In social work practice, these forms of authority can exist on a continuum (i.e., from non-influential to very influential) and/or co-mingle. For example, human service organizations may have an executive director who was the founder and began the position with a great deal of charismatic authority, and developed rational/legal authority while in the position by developing expertise as an administrator. Another executive director may have initially had mainly traditional authority due to a connection with a powerful family member in human services and/or also has or developed charismatic authority due to strong persuasion skills.

Intersections among Dimensions of Organizations

Thus far, the discussion has focused on dimensions of organizations that influence practice and the social worker's experience. These dimensions, purpose, structures of governance, and internal power relations, often intersect in practice, and some dimensions are likely to be intertwined. For example, a domestic violence shelter, whose purpose reflects a social movement and ideological position, is more likely to adopt a project team rather than a bureaucratic structure. With feminist organizational roots, a domestic violence shelter is also more likely to be subject to charismatic or rational/legal authority, as social workers with strong interpersonal skills may tend to take on leadership roles even without the authority that comes with a formal position of authority.

Understanding interconnections among these dimensions aid to understand the nature of organizations and develop a framework for examining their distinctions and impact on social workers. Ultimately, understanding possible interconnections can assist in discerning the combination of dimensions that best fit the talents and work styles of workers. For example, some social workers learn that an organization structure characterized by project team approach and rational/legal authority is the best fit for them. Gaining knowledge about agency dimensions also helps to recognize the ways in which agencies in various environments can most effectively and efficiently help client systems reach their goals.

Social Work Practice in Host Settings

Many social workers practice in **host settings**, such as hospitals, residential care facilities, public and private schools, and correctional facilities. Host settings are organizations in which social workers provide social services as a secondary activity. The following are examples: (1) the primary service in a school is education, yet social workers provide services to augment and support the educational goals; (2) various programs maintained by the court system, aimed at diversion or advocacy, often include social workers; and (3) housing programs and many disability projects employ social workers to support the main goal of the organization. A number of organizational aspects to this arrangement may provide unique opportunities, as well as challenges for the social worker. Next, we will discuss two situations with both opportunities and challenges: being a guest in a host setting, and being a member of an interprofessional team.

Guest Status   Expectations and privilege accompany a **guest status** for a social worker practicing within a host setting. Professionals of other disciplines in the setting may not understand the scope of the social work role, and have inaccurate expectations—too high or too low—of the social worker. At the same time, social workers may experience the privilege of working with other professionals on a team that is able to accomplish more than a social worker could independently. The experience of social worker Diane can illustrate the point.

Diane is a recent BSW graduate hired to facilitate discharges in a residential psychiatric treatment center that has a positive reputation in the community. A staff psychiatrist serves as medical director, and the executive director has a degree in public health. Diane is the first social worker ever employed by the center. The nurses and nurse aids had responsibility for discharge work until the number and pace of discharges outgrew their capacity to conduct discharge planning along with their other nursing duties.

Diane is warmly welcomed by staff, who hopes that she will fill an acute organizational need. Diane is hopeful that she will gain new competencies and practice behaviors because she will be exposed to different perspectives and practices for treatment strategies, medication, and ethics. She knows that she will have the opportunity to observe firsthand the work of the psychiatrist, the public health administrator, nurses, and others, and learn about the ways in which different professional perspectives can assist clients.

While many of the above hopes were realized, Diane also discovers that she does not have a role in decision-making about discharges; rather, the other staff expect her to simply carry out the instructions she is given. The exclusion from the decision-making process occurs because she is viewed as extraneous to the discharge (medical) decisions, rather than for any personal reason. Further, Diane has noticed a lack of professional, dignified treatment of some staff toward patients, but is ambivalent about notifying officials about it. Because she is excluded from decision-making, Diane feels undervalued, and more as a guest than a valued team member.

While she understands that the center is primarily a medical facility and medical issues take priority over other concerns, she also understands the potential value of her involvement in decision-making about discharge. She knows she has much more to contribute than she is currently allowed, and wishes to create the possibility of articulating her possible contributions in a way that will facilitate the staff's appreciation and growth, rather than engendering their resistance and resentment. Specifically, she knows that she needs to educate the staff about the complexities of discharge planning (for example, the need for day programming, employment, training, housing, emotional support, family support, and income support), and the possible contributions that she could make to addressing these complexities within the decision-making process about the timing of discharge, and the appropriate placement for patients. In the future, she may also want to address several practices that are inconsistent with socially just and respectful treatment.

Clearly, a guest status within an organization brings unique challenges for social workers. Social workers who have a guest status must exhibit effective practice behaviors concerning the education of other professions about the roles and responsibilities of social workers. Building credibility and networks of support within host organizations, a keen sense of timing, and displaying diplomacy are key skills in this process. On the other hand, social workers in host settings must also advocate for themselves and their professional obligations for client services.

Interprofessional Teams Projects and programs that include members of several professions (e.g., medicine, public health, public administration, and social work) create **interprofessional teams**. These teams can provide an enriching and exciting atmosphere in which to practice social work. Although the social work profession emphasizes a holistic view of client systems, social workers join many helping professionals in delivering services in a fragmented fashion. Many families seeking the assistance of social workers are also involved with other helping professionals, such as vocational counselors, non-social work therapists, psychologists, income maintenance specialists, physicians—including psychiatrists—and community support workers.

In an interprofessional setting, all professions carry equal power and share decision-making responsibilities—the value is in the total contribution of an integrated approach. In order to be effective, each profession must value the contribution of others. Social workers need competent collaborative practice behaviors when working with other professionals, including conflict mediation skills. A truly interprofessional setting is challenging to implement in practice. For example, in many medically oriented interprofessional teams, physicians are dominant and appear to have a privileged standpoint. Additionally, the socialization of many professions can encourage narrow views to bias the perspective of the chosen profession over other perspectives. Nevertheless, even with such challenges, interprofessional settings offer vast opportunities to wrestle with the challenges of providing an integrated, highly skilled approach in the best interests of clients, as well as to explore the internal dynamics of teaming through the lens of multiple realities.

ENGAGEMENT AND ASSESSMENT OF ORGANIZATIONS

The previous discussion focused on understanding organizations through the use of theory and general organizational dimensions, and made several applications to human service agencies. The next section spotlights the process of engagement and assessment of organizations, including the sources of data and information for the assessment. Engagement and assessment set the stage for the organizational change process of intervention, termination, and evaluation. The section closes with a discussion about integrating the information gleaned in the assessment.

Engagement of Organizations

Engagement of an organization first involves the perception of the organization as a client system. An organization is comprised of many individuals and systems, yet the social worker must view the entire organization as a client system in order to participate in the change process with an organization. This first step in the change process utilizes many of the skills needed for engagement with individuals, families, groups, and communities; namely, the active listening skills and research, evaluation, and analyzing skills discussed in previous chapters. Engagement with organizations involves working directly with all client system levels, within the perspective of the organization.

Social workers can engage organizations for the change process as an employee, volunteer, interested citizen, or as a consultant, although most often the change process occurs with employing organizations. Social workers often see the need for organizational change, so the organization can operate more efficiently and effectively, provide a higher quality of services, and better address human needs. For example, social workers who work for a school system may identify the need to make a change in the schools, and begin to engage other social workers, teachers, principals, administrators, committees, and task groups across the school district and even across districts to address a specific organizational need. Social workers may also engage organizations as part of advocacy efforts. For example, social workers can engage with public agencies that serve older adults to help make organizational changes to better address their clients' needs. Social workers engage with a community of organizations, such as a network of homeless shelters, to work for changes across many organizations, such as to coordinate data management systems to better meet the needs of clients who are homeless, are struggling with substance abuse, and have a chronic mental illness. In all these cases, engagement skills used with other client systems are necessary.

Assessment of Organizations

The overall assessment of organizations involves both a review of the internal environment of the organization, or the internal mechanisms within organizations, and the external environment with which the organization receives and provides resources, such as funders, accreditation organizations, suppliers of goods and services, clients, other organizations, and others. The following assessment framework, which is based on and is an integration of previous frameworks, may be helpful in the assessment task (Gitterman & Germain, 2008b; Miley, O'Melia, & DeBois, 2013; Netting et. al., 2011), and are more fully described here:

Internal Assessment

- Legal basis, mission, by-laws, and history;

- Administrative structure and management style;

- Program structure, programs, and services;

- Organizational culture (i.e., physical surroundings, public relations, language, procedures, social justice/diversity);

- Personnel policies and procedures;

- Resources (i.e., financial, technological, personnel).

  External Assessment

- Relationship with funders and potential funders;

- Relationship with clients;

- Relationship with organizations in network (i.e., referrals and coalitions);

- Relationships with political figures.

Assessment of an organization, similar to assessment with all client systems, involves gathering data. Like community assessment, data can be gathered through observation, written documents, key informant interviews, publically available data, service statistics, previous organizational assessment (partial or full), administrative data, other data, and focus groups. Depending on the size of the organization to be assessed, a public forum and survey data may also be appropriate ways to gather data (Gitterman & Germain, 2008b; Netting et al., 2011; O'Conner & Netting, 2009).

Organizations often create documents that may be helpful in the assessment process. These include organizational charts, policy and personnel manuals, procedure manuals, job descriptions, meeting minutes, and annual reports. Information from media sources and reports from other organizations can also be useful.

Elements of an Internal Assessment

The internal structures and dynamics of an organization affect many aspects of service delivery of the organization, as well as the employee experience (Grace, McClellan, & Yankey, 2009). The following section discusses those elements of an organization that can be considered as part of an organizational assessment.

Legal Basis   Organizations must be recognized by the law to legitimately operate. The **legal basis** for public organizations is a statute or executive order, while a private organization has a legal basis in the articles of incorporation. These documents authorize an organization to officially exist, and define the parameters for their operations.

Mission Statement   Most nonprofit organizations create a **mission statement**, which is a concise, broad statement of the purpose of the organization that describes a shared vision. While the statement is too broad for details, the statement identifies the client system needs the organization meets, the population served, and the intended client system outcomes. The details about programs, services, organizational structure, and other specifics are outlined in other documents, such as annual reports, an organizational chart (discussed below), and program descriptions. The mission statement states why the organization exists and is less changeable than programs and services. Revising a mission statement is needed if an organization perceives a mismatch between the mission statement and current client system needs and organization activities. For example, many child welfare agencies were founded in the early 20th century as orphanages, and needed to revisit their mission statements in light of the focus in child welfare on home-based placements. Exhibit 12.3 provides an example of a mission statement.

Our mission is to enhance the quality of life of older adults, children, and families in the regional area by serving their basic needs by providing: (1) Access to education, counseling and health services; (2) Recreation and social program; (3) Daily nutritional meals.

EXHIBIT 12.3

Mission Statement, Longview Community Center

By-laws   The way in which a nonprofit organization governs itself is described in the **by-laws**. By-laws are legal documents that describe the basic structure and abilities of the board of directors, such as the composition of the board, terms of the members, permanent committees, voting rights, and other matters that concern governance. The by-laws are typically brief, and the rules about them vary from state to state.

History   Like other client systems, organizations create history that defines and impacts the future of the organization. Important aspects of history include the founding of the organization, major funders, influential staff members and administrators, accomplishments, and challenging periods.

Administrative Structure and Management Style   Organizations often depict their administrative structure on an organizational chart that shows the units of the organization, and their relationship to one another. The management style of the organization can be seen in the way work is allocated, decisions are made, the nature of the supervision of employees, and how conflict is handled. Some elements of the management style will be included in written documents, while others can be learned from staff members.

Structure of Programs, Services, and Activities   Human service organizations provide programs and services and/or carry out activities to meet overall organizational goals and objectives. An assessment process would include a review of official documents where these are described, and review the extent to which the programs, services, and activities are consistent with the overall mission, goals, and objectives of the organization, as well as are based on evidence-based practice.

Organizational Culture   Organizational culture consists of many factors, including history, philosophy, styles of communication, patterns of decision-making, expectations, collective preferred personal styles of social workers, myths, behaviors, and formal and informal rules. Culture is also shaped by the purpose, structure of governance and internal power relations. While not reflected in the mission statement or any one official document, the organizational culture is, nevertheless, an important element that shapes aspects of the agency's work and employees' experiences. For example, the extent to which social workers are expected to work overtime without financial compensation or earned time off, or if practicum students take shifts of being "on call," both represent the types of issues that are shaped by organizational culture. Exhibit 12.4 discusses the dimensions of organizational culture. Exhibit 12.5 helps you review your own organizational style.

While the concept of organizational culture is intangible and imprecise, culture is an important dynamic of any organization. In the next section, additional dimensions that shape services will be discussed, including the legal basis, mission statement, by-laws, physical surroundings, public relations, procedures, and social justice/diversity factors.

"Observed behavioral regularities when people interact," including their language, customs, traditions, and rituals

"Group norms," that evolve as standards and values for working together

"Espoused values" that the organization is trying to achieve

"Formal philosophy," the board policies and ideologies that direct the work

"Rules of the game," often known as "the ropes"

"Climate," the physical layout and how it feels

"Embedded skills," the ability to pass along competencies to the next generation

"Habits of thinking, mental models, and/or linguistic paradigms" as things taught to new members as they are socialized to the organization

"Shared meanings," group understandings that develop as they work together

"Root metaphors or integrating symbols," the ideas, feelings, images, and even physical layout that represent the group's artifacts

References: Schein, 1992, pp. 8–10, and O'Connor & Netting (2009)

EXHIBIT 12.4

Dimensions of Organizational Culture

Physical Surroundings   The interior and location of an organization can provide some information about its culture. An organization with dark, messy physical surroundings and/or little privacy for client interactions could be an organization with a culture that places a lower priority on the potential impact of physical surroundings on client outcomes than a clean organization with bright lighting and plenty of space for private interviews. To best serve their clients, many human service agencies are located near their clients' homes, often in low- and middle-income communities. While few social workers are employed by organizations that are housed in luxurious surroundings and/or in expensive neighborhoods, the physical atmosphere and location of an organization reflects and impacts aspects of organizational culture, and impacts employee well-being (Shier, 2012). While the meaning of physical surroundings can be over-interpreted, the organizational environment is an important area to learn about the organization's culture.

Public Relations   Organizations reflect their culture in their **public relations** activities and products (Brueggemann, 2005). Public relations is the practice of managing communication between an organization and the public. Organizations seek to gain support from a positive communication both from the public at large, as well as from specific groups, such as funders, politicians, client populations, and even employees. Organizations can use a variety of mediums to manage their public information and image, such as websites, social media, blogs, printed materials, print newspaper articles and commentaries, and face-to-face encounters. An organization's public image gives clues about the organization's culture.

Language   The **language** used in agency settings includes the tone, range of sentiment, and degree of empathy and respect expressed. In previous chapters, we

EXHIBIT 12.5

Rate Your Organizational Style

Using the key below, rate yourself on the items listed here to review your organizational style. Add other items you think are important. Be prepared to discuss this survey in class and to apply it to your field placement. What obstacles do you encounter in fulfilling these points?

☐ I offer positive feedback to my colleagues for behaviors that contribute to effective services.

☐ I involve my colleagues in seeking changes in policies and programs to improve the quality of services.

☐ I value learning about my colleagues' points of view. For example, I seek feedback that will help me to enhance my competencies and practice behaviors. When I have a complaint, I discuss it with the person directly involved.

☐ I involve others in arranging opportunities to discuss practice/policy issues/topics.

☐ I communicate congratulations to others regarding professional or personal events/accomplishments.

☐ I come prepared for all types of meetings.

☐ I make positive contributions at meetings.

☐ I refrain from idle gossip at work.

☐ I make more positive than negative comments at work.

☐ _____

☐ _____

Key: **0** (not at all) **1** (a little) **2** (a fair amount) **3** (a great deal) **4** (best that could be)

Adapted from: Gambrill, 2013.

discussed postmodern ideas about the role of language and the way people create and sustain meanings based on language. Using postmodernism concepts, language both reflects and shapes the thoughts and feelings expressed. Therefore, the language used in organizations reflects and shapes the self-perceptions of the social workers, their work, and their clients. Social workers' use of disrespectful language toward and about client systems violates the *Code of Ethics* (NASW, 2008), displays a violation of the core commitment to respect people and treat them with dignity, and can affect other social workers through a culture of disrespect. While some organizations may attempt to justify pejorative language patterns by stating that staff members need to "blow off steam," the lack of respectful, strengths-based language can have a powerful, detrimental impact on organizational culture.

Procedures   A simple **procedure**, such as greeting a new client, asking them to sit down, inviting them to an office from the waiting room, or giving them paperwork, strongly impacts the quality of the experience of becoming a client and maintaining that status. Social workers must be respectful and sensitive about the explanation of the procedures concerning such matters as confidentiality, fees, appointment times, and negotiations in scheduling appointments. These aspects of working with clients are relevant as a social worker's expression of respect for individual, couple, family, and group clients, but also as clearly understood agency policy. Quick Guide 39 provides an opportunity to assess client and employee treatment regarding procedures at an organization familiar to you.

Social Justice/Diversity Factors   Aspects of social work practice that affirm social justice and support diversity can be nurtured and sustained across all client system levels, including organizations. Unless organizations promote social justice through policies and practices, clients may find their social workers to be "nice people" but feel victimized by unjust organizational practices. To fully promote social justice, organizations may arrange the internal administrative practices of the agency to reflect diversity and social justice concerns. For example, posters, magazines, and signs in the waiting area can reflect multiple languages and cultures to convey a welcoming atmosphere for clients from diverse backgrounds. Activities and services that clearly take into account cultural values, such as food at events that reflect ethnic food traditions and restrictions send a message. Activities and services can also honor history of groups, and/or reflect histories of oppression for specific populations. Just as ethnically dominant white middle-class social workers struggle to become competent in working with other cultures, so must organizations assess their culture competency and the extent to which the organization works toward social justice goals. Exhibit 12.6 addresses some of the assumptions that underlie organizational practices and approaches that are critical to address in the process toward culture competency.

QUICK GUIDE 39   DIGNITY ASSESSMENT AND HUMAN SERVICES GUIDE

Complete the following assessment utilizing an organization with which you are familiar.

1. Persons seeking services from my agency are more likely to experience:

____a poorly maintained waiting room

____a warm and well-furnished waiting room

____a place to sign in and be told to take a seat

____a courteous and personal greeting

____having their name called out and being told to "follow me" to the office

____being personally met and invited to "follow me" to the office

____nonverbal cues from the staff that they are a bother

____nonverbal cues that suggest we are glad they are here

____treatment that says "you are another case"

____treatment that says "you are a person"

2. Persons seeking services in my agency are more likely to be:

____treated as problems that need to be solved

____treated as partners in a mutual process of deciding how to proceed

____given treatment based on the medical model

____provided treatment based on a competency model

____seen as problems

____seen as people with issues and needs

____seen as needing an expert

____seen as the expert

3. Employees within my setting are more likely to experience:

____getting written memos about new changes

____being asked for input about new changes

____an expectation of independent work without much support

____being supported in their roles

____wishing for another job

____joy in coming to work

____feeling like their consumers are not important to the agency

____feeling their consumers are important to the agency

____feeling like they are a drain to the community

____feeling like they are a resource to the community

____feeling unimportant to the agency

____feeling important to the agency

____lack of respect for other employees

____respect for other employees

4. My experience with the organizational culture is that:

____respect for human diversity is ignored

____respect for human diversity is valued

____membership in the community is blocked to those who are different

____membership in the community is open to all

____social services are at best tolerated

____social services are willingly supported

Adapted from Locke, Garrison, & Winship, 1998, pp. 278–279

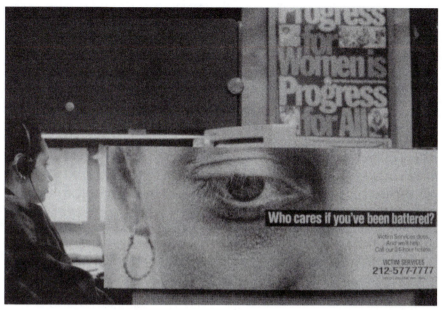

Validating client experience

Organizations that are culturally competent display the following characteristics:

- Respect the unique, culturally defined needs of various client populations.
- Acknowledge culture as a predominant force in shaping behaviors, values, and institutions.
- View natural systems (i.e., family, community, faith communities, healers) as the primary mechanism of support for minority populations.
- Start with the "family" as defined by each culture, as the primary and preferred point of intervention.
- Acknowledge that minority people are served in varying degrees by the natural system.
- Recognize that the concepts of "family," "community," etc., are different from various cultures and even for subgroups within cultures.
- Believe that diversity within cultures is as important as diversity between cultures.
- Function with the awareness that the dignity of the person is not guaranteed unless the dignity of his/her people is preserved.
- Display understanding that minority clients are usually best served by persons who are part of or have knowledge about their culture.
- Acknowledge and accept that cultural differences exist and have an impact on service delivery.
- Treat clients in the context of their minority status, which creates unique mental health issues for minority individuals, including issues related to self-esteem, identity formation, isolation, and role assumptions.

EXHIBIT 12.6

Continued

- Advocate for effective services on the basis that the absence of cultural competence in any part of the organization compromises the cultural competency of the entire organization.
- Respect the family as indispensable to understanding the individual, because the family provides the context within which the person functions and is the primary support network of its members.
- Recognize that the thought patterns of non-Western peoples, though different, are equally valid and influence the ways in which clients view problems and solutions.
- Respect cultural preferences that value process rather than product, and harmony or balance within one's life rather than achievement.
- Acknowledge that when working with minority clients, process is as important as product.
- Recognize that taking the best of the Western and non-Western worlds enhances the capacity of all.
- Recognize that minority people have to at least be bicultural, which in turn creates its own set of mental health issues such as identity conflicts resulting from assimilation.
- Function with the knowledge that some behaviors are the expression of adjustments to being different.
- Understand when values of minority groups are in conflict with dominant society values.

Adapted from: Cross, Bazron, Dennia, & Isaacs, 1989; Lum 2011.

Personnel Policies and Procedures   Staff members are important resources for organizational operations. The size and legal basis of an organization are important factors in the creation of policies and procedures; small, newly created nonprofit organizations have relatively simple and concise policies and procedures, while larger, public organizations often have highly formal, complex policies and procedures. Nevertheless, the development of written policies and procedures, including a plan for recruitment, selection, development, evaluation, and termination, is important. Some organizations also develop plans to enhance staff diversity.

Resources (i.e., Financial, Technical, and Personnel)   Other types of resources are also important to organizations. For example, the adequacy of the financial resources of organizations can be assessed through annual and monthly budgets, where income and liabilities are documented. **Technical resources** include the facilities and equipment of the organization, such as the office space, computers, software, and cell phones. **Personnel resources** include the capacity of current staff. All of these types of resources are important to assess as part of an overall organizational assessment.

Elements of an External Assessment

The external environment of organizations consists of many players. The assessment process focused on the external environment reviews the individuals, groups, organizations, and policies that impact operations. The external environment can offer opportunities and challenges for organizations, and maintaining a focus on relationships with external players is important. The following section discusses those elements external to an organization that can be considered as part of an organizational assessment.

Relationship with Funders and Potential Funders An assessment process should uncover the sources of agency funding, as well as the nature of the relationship between the organization and each funding source. For example, the assessment process would uncover the amount and percentage of the overall budget received from each funding source. The funding sources could include government appropriations and contracts, donations, investment income, fees, fundraising events and activities, and profit-making activities. A source of funding that constitutes nearly half or more of the organization's overall budget indicates a strong relationship. Organizations that rely on a diverse source of funds have increased program and staff flexibility compared to those that rely on fewer sources.

Relationship with Clients Human service organizations rarely have the resources to serve all people who live in their area; therefore, organizations create client eligibility requirements for programs and services. An assessment in this area may include examining how clients are recruited and deemed eligible, the manner in which clients are treated who are not eligible for services, the degree to which clients are mandated to receive services, and which organizations are sources of referrals.

Relationship with Organizations in Network (i.e., Referrals and Coalitions) Constructive, professional relationships with other organizations are imperative to a positive community perception. Organizations that deliver similar services often have motivation to work together to meet community needs, yet often compete for funding from similar sources. Therefore, strong relationships between similar organizations benefit the community through stronger service delivery, collective advocacy efforts, and in other ways, yet can be challenging because of competition for resources. An assessment of this aspect would uncover the nature of the relationship with similar and referring organizations, and those with whom the organization networks. Quick Guide 40 provides guidance on the types of organizational partnerships.

Relationships with Political Figures Elected and appointed officials often carry a great deal of influence over public opinion about and resources for organizations. An assessment would investigate the key political figures for an organization and describe the organization's relationship with them.

QUICK GUIDE 40 GUIDE TO NONPROFIT ORGANIZATIONAL PARTNERSHIPS

A local nonprofit organization, Citizens Against Climate Change (CACC), would like to expand their influence without necessarily expanding their organization. They are exploring the idea of partnering with other organizations either locally, statewide, regionally, nationally or internationally. The forms of partnership from which they could choose are:

Task Force – Task forces are temporary, flexible structures to address a community challenge to be resolved in a relatively short period of time. Membership includes representatives of all types of organizations focused on similar challenges. While the advantages include pooling of resources, ease of short-term commitment, and flexibility in structure, disadvantages include lack of organizational engagement and commitment, resources, and general trust due to the short-term nature of the arrangement.

For example, CACC could decide to create a task force with organizations to promote the creation of bike lanes on local roads.

Collaborative – Collaborative partnerships can be relatively long-term, and involve sharing of resources, such as staff and funds, to engage in sustained service delivery among member organizations. Each member organization provides a unique contribution to combined work. Collaborative organizations can work closely over time and are often motivated to reduce costs, receive funding that otherwise would not be available, or fulfill unmet, complex needs. Advantages include resource sharing, expansion and improvement of services, while challenges include potential competition for similar funding opportunities and creating consensus among diverse partners.

For example, CACC could decide to create a collaborative partnership to deliver ongoing cycle safety courses and bike clubs for community members.

Coalition – Coalitions are groups formed of organizations to take joint action, such as lobbying elected officials, through collective action. While most coalitions have informal structures and fluid membership, some are formal organizations. Member organizations pool resources and devote staff and members to take action. The loose structure and fluid membership is both a strength (i.e., fairly easy to recruit like-minded organizations), and a challenge (i.e., challenge to create consensus with organizations that are diverse and do not work together regularly).

For example, CACC could decide to form or join a coalition to advocate for additional state transportation dollars to be devoted to walkable-bikable community projects, such as sideways, bike lanes, bike corridors, and traffic-calming infrastructure improvements on side roads.

Interfaith Alliance – While faith communities are the lead organizations in Interfaith Alliances (IA), these organizational partnerships also involve other nonprofits, local groups and institutions (e.g., public health departments, or child welfare departments). Advantages of IA include (1) faith communities offer a place of recruitment of active individuals who are motivated by their faith to take action on issues; (2) faith communities can add credibility to efforts to address societal needs; and (3) faith communities can also offer many types of resources. As with other partnerships, challenges include developing consensus among diverse groups and individuals.

For example, CACC could join an Interfaith Alliance at the local or national level to engage in advocacy about emissions standards for autos, or funding for complete composting systems for food waste at schools.

Affiliation with National/International Organizations – National and international organizations sponsor local chapters to work at a smaller level (e.g., state) to carry out their agenda. Local chapters benefit from affiliation by increased political influence, access to funding, and networks with similar-sized organizations across the country or world. Challenges include reaching agreement among diverse

QUICK GUIDE 40   CONTINUED

groups with varying agendas, and/or forfeiting some decision-making powers at the local level to the national/international organization.

For example, CACC could join with other, similar groups to create a chapter of Greenpeace, an international organization focused on climate change.

Social Movement – Organizations can participate in social movements by joining with broad-based coalitions and national organizations dedicated to the same cause. Social movements are often the mechanism for marginalized and oppressed groups to obtain access to resources and political rights, as well as for allies to support them in their advocacy through organizational resources. Rather than a single organization, the work of a movement is carried out through partnerships of multiple organizations and coalitions to generate public support and links to decision-makers and funders.

For example, CACC could join with organizations such as the Global Campaign for Climate Action, 350.org, and other networks that are working with organizations and groups around the world to create political pressure worldwide for action on climate change.

Adapted from: Hardina 2013; Netting et al., 2012

QUICK GUIDE 41   NONPROFIT ORGANIZATIONAL ASSESSMENT

Using an organization with which you are familiar, complete the following assessment:

Internal assessment:

* *Legal basis, mission, by-laws, and history*

___The legal basis is clearly stated in appropriate documents.

___The mission statement is current, accurate, specifies reason for existence, and expected outcomes.

___The by-laws are relevant, current, and accurately portray the needs of the organization.

* *Administrative structure and management style*

___Fit the mission and services of the organization.

___Transparent and structured lines/systems for decision-making exist.

___Decision-making involves broad participation as practical and appropriate.

___Clear communication lines exist for dissemination of decisions.

___Roles are clearly defined.

___Comprehensive, integrated system used for measuring organization's performance and progress on continual basis.

* *Program structure, programs, and services*

___Continual monitoring and assessment of the structure, processes, and programs occurs

___Program evaluation data is collected, used, and is linked to systematic improvements

___Programs and services reflect evidence-based practice.

___Programs and services are efficient, effective, and high quality.

___Programs and services are well-defined and fully aligned with mission.

___A system is in place to collect data about gaps in ability of existing programs to meet recipient and community-wide needs.

QUICK GUIDE 41   CONTINUED

___The need for programs and services is well-documented.

• *Organizational culture i.e., physical surroundings, public relations, language, procedures, social justice/diversity)*

___Physical infrastructure is well-suited to current and anticipated needs.

___Physical infrastructure enhances effectiveness.

___Informal expectations are clearly articulated and supported by staff.

___Communications plan and strategy in place and updated on a frequent basis.

• *Personnel policies and procedures*

___Recruitment, selection, orientation, supervision, training and development, performance appraisal, termination, and grievance processes identified.

___Relationships between and among positions, and position qualifications identified.

• *Resources (i.e., financial, technological, personnel)*

___Funding is sufficient, comes from diverse sources, fits mission, and provides insulation from market instabilities.

___Board members embrace fundraising as a core role.

___Board fundraising plans in place.

___Electronic data systems sufficiently gather and report appropriate data regarding clients, staff, volunteers, program outcomes, and financial information.

External Assessment

• *Relationship with funders and potential funders*

___Fundraising skills and expertise is adequate for funding needs.

___Sustainable revenue-generating activities used.

___System for regular communication and reporting with current funders used.

• *Relationship with clients*

___System to actively recruit and involve clients in offering feedback is used.

___System to actively involve clients in making decisions is used.

___New ideas are continually offered to meet service gaps.

___Communications carry a consistent and powerful message.

___Marketing materials are professional, used consistently, and are current.

___Materials are provided in multiple languages as needed, and reflect diversity.

___Policies and procedures reflect systems that are culturally competent.

___Characterize diversity as an asset.

___Technology needs (e.g. computers, phones, etc.) are adequately met.

___Website is sophisticated, comprehensive, interactive, and regularly maintained.

___Positions adequately and appropriately staffed, vacancies quickly filled.

___Staff are capable, committed, and bring complementary skills and momentum for improvement.

___Feedback from current funders sought and considered.

___System to cultivate potential funders used and continually updated.

___Ideas for revenue diversification continually considered.

___When possible, clients work collaboratively with staff in important roles, such as volunteer positions of leadership.

- *Relationship with organizations in network (i.e., referrals and partnerships)*

___Strong, positive relationships with similar and related organizations exist.

___Reciprocity sought with relevant organizations.

___Presence on relevant partnerships evident, and leadership roles appropriately taken.

- *Relationships with political figures*

___Strong, high-impact, relationships using regular communication with a variety of political entities (i.e., local, state, and federal government) and community leaders exists.

___Proactively and effectively influences policy-making at the local, state, and/or national level.

___Participate in substantive policy discussions with opinion and political leaders.

Adapted from: Netting et al., 2012; Marguerite Casey Foundation, 2012.

ORGANIZATIONAL ENGAGEMENT AND ASSESSMENT AND GENERALIST PRACTICE

While administrators have official roles and responsibilities, and therefore are naturally involved in the organizational change process, social workers in direct practice with individuals, families, groups, and communities, including generalist practitioners, must also be involved with the organizational change process. Both generalist practitioners and administrators are bound by the NASW *Code of Ethics* (NASW, 2008) Section 3.09 to work to improve services, carry out their ethical obligations even if employer structures are challenging, and act to eliminate discrimination in organizations.

What does the ethical obligation to participate in organizational change mean for social workers who are not administrators? Social workers must always learn about as many aspects of their affiliated organization as possible. Many organizational problems emerge through the experiences of clients or members of the community, and defining and documenting client or community member problems is a powerful way to make a strong case for organizational change. Social workers can engage others in identifying and documenting client problems to which the organization contributes (Gitterman & Germain, 2008b). As discussed in Chapter 13, successful organizational change efforts often involve many individuals and groups.

Organizational engagement and assessment involve many of the same competencies and practice behaviors used with other client systems. Discussed in the next section are those skills needed to effectively begin the organizational change process.

SKILLS FOR ENGAGEMENT AND ASSESSMENT WITH ORGANIZATIONS

In addition to the skills previously mentioned in this chapter, (i.e., active listening, research and analysis, group facilitation, and documentation skills), integration of the data gathered in the assessment process must occur to provide direction to the next phases of the change process. One method is the SWOT (i.e., strengths, weaknesses, opportunities, and threats) analysis. In a SWOT analysis, organizational staff identify and assess both internal and external forces that impact the organization (Hardina, 2012).

| **EXHIBIT 12.7**

SWOT analysis | The Hispanic Community Development Center (HCDC), a Hispanic-serving, three-year old nonprofit, wanted to increase their capacity to provide additional services to a growing Hispanic population in the community. While HCDC has been providing food, rent, and utility assistance, and ESL classes for three years with one paid staff member, the Board wants to increase their capacity to provide health services to the population in response to high rates of teen pregnancy, HIV-AIDS, and poor oral health. |

In their planning process, they used a Strengths, Weaknesses, Opportunities, and Threats (SWOT) analysis to analyze the factors affecting change in the organizations, and the strengths and weaknesses both inside and outside of the organization. The SWOT analysis was conducted to help decide between two options: either attempting to raise funds to deliver health services themselves, or partner with an organization(s), such as the public health department, for service delivery at HCDC.

	Strengths	**Weaknesses**
Internal	• Reputation among Hispanics • History in community • Reputation among non-Hispanics • Only Hispanic-serving nonprofit • Evidence of need of health services • Diverse board with community connections	• Lack capacity to deliver health services • Lack of paid enough staff • Little experience in raising money • Little experience in partnering
	Opportunities	**Threats**
External	• Potential partnership with local institutions (i.e., public health department, university) • Potential coalition building with other human service organizations • Create HCDC capacity to meet growing needs	• Other institutions may deliver services without HCDC • If deliver services, increase financial and liability risk • Partner institutions may require proof of documentation status of clients • If fail, damage reputation

Ultimately, the organization decided to attempt to raise money and deliver the health services themselves, rather than partner with another organization. The primary reasons for this decision was to avoid the requirement that HCDC clients show proof of documentation status, and to preserve their reputation among Hispanics in the community. The Board decided to attempt to raise funds, and to request training from other health organizations.

Adapted from: Larson & McGuiston, 2012.

Another method of organizational assessment is a **force-field analysis** (FFA) (Hardina, 2012; Pippard & Bjorklund, 2004), first proposed by Kurt Lewin (1951). The FFA is a mechanism to gather and sort all of the information and data gathered in the assessment process, and provide the basis for a plan for an intervention, as will be discussed in Chapter 13.

An FFA is a method of identifying and assessing the forces that impact a decision about an issue by organizing the assessment data. To begin, a social worker would identify the forces that could impact the outcomes of change efforts, meaning constraints that work to prevent a change and advantages that will help overcome resistance to change. The forces could include influential individuals who could shape the opinion of others or who are decision-makers; organizations, committees and task forces; groups; and political parties. The technique enables a social worker to make a decision about whether to move forward with a change process, and if so, to create a plan based on an evaluation of the forces working for and against a proposed change (Hardina, 2012).

For example, the school social worker mentioned earlier has documented that lesbian, gay, bisexual, transgendered, and questioning (LGBTQ) students experience a higher number of social and academic problems in middle and high school than other students. The social worker has completed an organizational assessment, and would like to synthesize the information to determine whether and how to move forward. Working with a group of students that self-identify as LGBTQ, the social worker would like to engage in a change process to provide more comprehensive services to this population across the school district. After engaging and assessing the organization, the LGBTQ work group conducted an FFA to determine whether to proceed in the change process, and to assist in developing an intervention plan.

As seen in Exhibit 12.8, there are many forces that support an initiative to provide more comprehensive support services to LGBTQ teens, including student leaders, student government, and high school principals. Neutral forces, including the association of principals and school counselors, could support or oppose a change process, and do not yet have an opinion about the possibility. Through lobbying and education, these neutral forces could become supporters, and therefore, may become the focus of such efforts in the intervention phase. The forces that are opposed to providing support services, including several influential teachers, the

EXHIBIT 12.8

Force Field Analysis, Assessment of Forces Impacting LGBTQ Initiative

SUPPORTING FORCES	NEUTRAL FORCES	OPPOSING FORCES
Student leaders	Principal Association	Four influential teachers
Student government	School counselors	Parent Association
All high school principals	Local TV and radio station	Two student groups/clubs
American Civil Liberties Union	Chair of the School Board	Three School Board members
Three School Board members		All middle school principals
Local activists		

parent association and others, would work against a change process. As other forces are discovered, they could be added to the analysis. The FFA is one tool to assist the LGBTQ work group in making a decision whether to proceed with their efforts, and in making an intervention plan.

The advantage of an FFA are numerous—the individuals, groups, and coalitions relevant to the issue are identified, as well as the driving and restraining forces most likely to effect the change effort. The strength of each force is assessed and ranked, and the amenability to change of each force is ranked as high, low, or uncertain. A plan for change is then created based on the information contained in the FFA. The FFA is a simple technique that can be used with groups of all sizes as a group decision-making tool that fosters creativity and critical thinking. The social worker must demonstrate keen group facilitation skills to avoid a focus on forces against change at expense of forces for change, to avoid the domination of a minority of the group, and to encourage the group to be specific (Pippard & Bjorklund, 2004).

STRAIGHT TALK ABOUT PRACTICE WITHIN ORGANIZATIONS

Different types of organizations offer distinct professional rewards, opportunities, and challenges. Expectations and experiences differ from organizational setting to setting, and work style preferences that fit one type of organization may not be a match at another organization or type of organization. The following discussion will highlight several of the different types of social service organizations.

Although working for public organizations brings challenges, there are advantages unique to employment with public agencies. Compared to working within the private (i.e., nonprofit and for-profit) sector, needed services can be offered to clients with less consideration given to cost effectiveness, because there are fewer demands for demonstrated outcomes than in nonprofit and for-profit organizations. In stable economic times, social workers within public agencies enjoy relative predictability and job security, with highly structured job levels and raise structures, especially in the military and federal government. Some social workers in public organizations earn higher salaries than in the nonprofit sector (Whitaker & Wilson, 2010). Many clients served in public organizations are those without many alternatives; therefore, social workers within these agencies are implementing the historical preference of social work for working on behalf of the poor. Lastly, social workers in public organizations gain invaluable experience with a wide range of client issues and with clients with complex problems.

The number of social workers at for-profit social service agencies, such as private practices and for-profit health care systems, has grown in recent years (Whitaker & Arrington, 2008). In contrast to public and nonprofit organizations, for-profit (or proprietary) agencies seek to produce a financial profit for their owners or shareholders. Social workers in residential care facilities, medical and psychiatric hospitals, long-term care for persons with disabilities, home health services, health maintenance organizations, substance abuse treatment centers, correctional settings, and child welfare services may be in for-profit settings.

Depending on the type of services provided, social workers in for-profit organizations may enjoy a more comfortable physical setting, more resources, use of cutting-edge interventions and treatment modalities, and higher expectations of efficiency and effectiveness than in other settings. Salaries, however, are generally similar for for-profits and nonprofits (Whitaker & Wilson, 2010). In some for-profit settings, a wide socioeconomic diversity of clients may seek services. Social workers may also enjoy the opportunities to advocate for the primary goal of client-centered human services to meet community needs, rather than a profit (Kong, 2007).

Most social service organizations are nonprofit (Holland, 2008). Advantages to working for a nonprofit organization are numerous, and include the following: (1) social workers generally have little need to advocate internally to maintain the historical commitment to serving the poor; (2) the funding base is often a diverse mixture of sources, including grants, contracts, memberships, fee for service, investment, donations, and events (Netting et al., 2012). Social work employees may enjoy more autonomy, flexibility, and creativity in service delivery due to the multitude of funding sources; and (3) social workers in faith-based nonprofit organization can implement their religious traditions and beliefs in their employment setting.

While there are other types of organizations beyond public, for-profit, and 501(c)3 nonprofit organizations (i.e., hybrid nonprofit and social enterprises, whereby nonprofit organizations engage in commercial activity (Cooney, 2006), other classifications of 501(c)), these three are the central types of organizations that employ social workers. While generalities may be helpful, each setting offers a unique working environment. Prestige, an important element to social worker commitment and job satisfaction (Carmeli & Freund, 2009), can be found in many different settings. Social workers who explore types of organizations may gain more insight about the best fit for their preferred work style and career aspirations. Both for-profit and nonprofit organizations can engage in advocacy. Quick Guide 42 provides more details on the types of advocacy activities in which organizations engage.

QUICK GUIDE 42   ORGANIZATIONAL POLICY ADVOCACY ACTIVITIES

Complete the following tool about organizational policy advocacy activities using an organization with which you are familiar.

In the past, our agency has:

(Organizational Activities)

___Testified at public hearings held by the city council, state legislature, or other decision-making body.

___Participated in legislative or policy working groups with government officials.

___Engaged in nonviolent civil disobedience (i.e., deliberately broke a law to draw attention to unjust government policies, programs, or actions).

___Sent unique letters, e-mails, faxes, or texts to the city council, the mayor, local government agency directors, or senior staff members regarding legislation, government policies, government programs, or other issues that affect our clients.

___Participated in rallies, protests, vigils, and/or demonstrations to draw attention to an issue that affects our clients.

___Attempted to engage television, radio, print, or web-based media reporters to give attention to legislation, government policies, government programs, or other issues that affect our clients.

___Submitted letters to the editor or op-ed pieces to the local media regarding legislation, government policies, government programs, or other issues related to our client population.

___Helped draft legislation.

___Sponsored or cosponsored forums or other community events to educate the general public about legislation, government policies, government programs, or a social issue.

___Submitted formal comments on rules, regulations, strategic plans, or other administrative governmental documents.

___Met with the city council members, the mayor, and/or local government agency directors or senior staff to discuss legislation, government policies, government programs, or other issues that affect our clients.

___Contacted city council members, the mayor, and/or local government agency directors or senior staff to discuss legislation, government policies, government programs, or other issues that affect our client populations.

___Participated in letter-writing campaigns, "sign-on" letters, "call-in days," postcard drives, petition drives, or e-mail drives to contact public officials about legislation, government policies, government programs, or other issues that affect our clients.

___Submitted articles in our newsletter about legislation, government policies, government programs, or other issues that affect our clients.

___Posted fact sheets, issue briefs, articles, and/or testimony about legislation, government policies, government programs, or other issues that affect our client population on our Web site.

___Invited council members and/or the mayor to visit our program(s) to educate them about the issues that affect our clients.

___Actively participated in coalitions related to our area of service or issue of concern. (*Actively participated means attended and gave input at coalition meetings, joined and actively participated in coalition committees, attended coalition events, etc.*)

(Direct Client Activities)

___Met with and/or distributed written information to clients to educate/inform them about legislation, government policies, government programs, or upcoming public policy activities, (e.g., meetings, public hearings).

QUICK GUIDE 42   CONTINUED

___Solicited input from clients to inform our agency's advocacy priorities.

___Included clients when making visits to the city council, state representatives, or other decision-makers.

___Provided skill-building workshops to clients to encourage their public policy participation. *Skill building may include writing and giving testimony, writing letters, making phone calls, meeting with decision-makers, and other tactics.*

___Met with clients to help them formulate direct action strategies around issues of their choice.

___Conducted voter registration drives.

___Facilitated transportation for clients to encourage their participation in public policy activities and/or to vote at the polls.

Adapted from: Plitt & Shields, 2009

CONCLUSION

This chapter has introduced organizations as an important arena for the social work change process. Social workers in direct practice and their supervisors are uniquely informed about the impact of organizational operations on client systems. Social workers may best be able to identify unmet client system needs, and initiate a change process designed to meet the best interests of the client system—whether that be an individual, family, group, or community. Social workers, therefore, have a mandate to engage people in the organization and external to the organization, and learn about both the internal and external environments of organizations to competently lead and participate in organizational change processes. In addition to engagement, this chapter focused on the assessment process to provide the foundation needed to initiate the change process. Organizations are an important context of generalist social work practice with all types of client systems. Chapter 13 will focus on organization intervention strategies, termination, and evaluation processes.

MAIN POINTS

- Social workers work in many types of and sizes of organizations, and use their knowledge to promote the best interests of their client systems.

- Organizations, like other client systems, can be understood using various theories, models, and perspectives, including systems theories and contemporary organizational and management theories.

- Three main dimensions of difference between organizations are: (1) purpose of the organization; (2) structure of governance; and (3) internal power relations.

- Social workers also practice in host settings, which are organizations in which social workers provide social services as a secondary activity.

- Social workers in a variety of roles can change organizations to provide a higher quality of services.

- The overall assessment of organizations involves both a review of the internal environment of the organization, and the external environment.

- The NASW *Code of Ethics* provides direction to both generalist and specialist social workers to work to improve services, carry out their ethical obligations in the work place, and to act to eliminate discrimination in organizations.

- A helpful skill in the assessment process is a force-field analysis (FFA), a tool to sort information and data gathered in the assessment process and aid in decision-making about the change process.

- The type of organization in which a social worker is employed offers different professional rewards, opportunities, and challenges.

EXERCISES

a. Case Exercises

1. Log onto www.routledgesw.com/cases and review the Sanchez family case. Imagine you were hired as a social worker approximately three months ago at a community center that serves the Sanchez family. As you have settled into your job responsibilities, you notice some tensions within the agency. Several social workers are grumbling at "the way things are around here."

   As you consider the reasons for your feelings of being unsettled, you decide to gather information about the organization to gain a better understanding of the dynamics. Referring back to the chapter, discuss ways in which you might obtain knowledge about each factor, and how each factor could influence the experience of staff members (one paragraph for each): purpose, structure of governance, and internal power relations.

2. After you have completed #1 (above), you still are not sure about the dynamics that have led you to feel unsettled, and co-workers to grumble. You decide to learn more about the agency, but are not quite ready to undertake a full organizational assessment. You decide to start your mini-assessment by focusing on culture. Using the concepts described in the chapter, describe the elements of culture that exist in the center, and how you would go about learning them, to include the types of individuals you might interview, the documents you would seek, the groups you would access, and any other source of information you might utilize. Justify your choices.

3. Log onto www.routledgesw.com/cases. Review the Riverton case file (i.e., Your History and Your Concerns). View the community sociogram, and note all of the organizations and their relationships to one another. Develop a sociogram for an organization with which you are familiar.

4. Using the Riverton case (at www.routledgesw.com/cases), answer the Critical Thinking Question #2.

5. Using the Riverton case (at www.routledgesw.com/cases), answer the Critical Thinking Question #3 by assuming that the organization is the client. What would be your next steps after deciding that an organization in the community is the client? Which organization (use the sociogram and/or town map to review the possibilities)?

6. Go to www.routledgesw.com/cases and become familiar with the Brickville case. Several events have occurred that prompt the Brickville CDC to conduct an organizational assessment. First, the Brickville CDC has been asked to join the coalition that is working for the redevelopment plan. Second, as part of the needs assessment outcomes, the youth development organization encouraged the Brickville CDC to become more politically engaged for the benefit of the neighborhood. The CDC director has stated that the organization has never taken a stance on an issue before. Olivia and her colleagues have decided to work toward organizational change and create a process whereby the Brickville CDC can take a stance on neighborhood issues. In a brief, one-page paper, discuss the elements of an internal assessment that would need to be included to assess for political engagement. Explain the rationale for your choices.

b. Other exercises

For all exercises below, write a one-two page paper with your findings.

7. Choose an organization with which you are familiar. Familiarize yourself with the elements of an organizational assessment, as discussed in Chapter 12. Interview a person familiar with the organization to gather as much information as possible related to the internal and external elements of an organizational assessment. As part of the interview, ask whether the organization has completed an organizational assessment in the past, and whether there are any written documents that describe the assessment that you could review.

8. Using the SWOT diagram in Exhibit 12.7 as an example, complete a SWOT diagram for an organization with which you are familiar. Briefly explain and justify the contents of your SWOT analysis.

9. Using the examples of forms of partnership in Quick Guide 40, describe the forms of partnerships that a nonprofit, "Men Against Sexual Assault" could take if they wanted to expand their influence without expanding their organization.

10. Using Exhibit 12.2 as the case (Casa De Esperanza), describe how three of the 10 "Dimensions of Organizational Culture", as described in Exhibit 12.4, could be implemented. That is, if Casa De Esperanza wanted to implement a culture that was friendly and welcoming to the Latino community, what would three of the 10 'look like'?

Social Work Practice with Organizations: Intervention, Termination, and Evaluation

The time when you need to do something is when no one else is willing to do it, when people are saying it can't be done.

Mary Frances Berry

Key Questions for Chapter 13

(1) How can I prepare for action with all client systems? (EPAS 2.1.10(a))

(2) What are the key interpersonal skills and techniques that I need to know to work with organizations? (EPAS 2.1.10(a))

(3) How can I utilize evidence to practice research-informed practice and practice-informed research to guide the intervention, termination, and evaluation with organizations? (EPAS 2.1.6)

(4) How can I apply critical thinking to intervention, termination, and evaluation with organizations? (EPAS 2.1.3)

(5) How can I apply social work values and ethics to intervention, termination, and evaluation with organizations? (EPAS 2.1.2)

CONSIDER THE FOLLOWING SITUATIONS:

Toby, a tenth-grader, left Dan (the social worker)'s office commenting that he wished that other kids would just "leave him alone," and that he wished he "knew other kids like him." Toby, who shared with Dan that he thinks he is gay, was the third student that week to say similar things to Dan, who is struggling with a response to the needs of lesbian, gay, bisexual, transgendered, and questioning (LGBTQ) students. Dan has seen these students struggle with bullying, less social integration, and poor school performance, which they often say is due to a lack of acceptance by teachers, administrators, and peers.

Carrie, a social work case manager at a mental health service organization, is at the end at her rope. Four of the clients on her caseload, who are dual diagnosed with a chronic mental illness and a substance abuse issue, have become homeless this month due to the lack of affordable rental housing in the community. The few units that are available are owned by landlords who will not rent to clients of the organization.

These are situations that may prompt organizational change that is a result of client needs not adequately being met by the agency, the institution, or community. Organizational change can range in size from large (e.g., changing the decision-making process within the organization), to small (e.g., changing eligibility for one program, or the working hours for staff members), and from short-term (e.g., creating a short-term project) to long-term (e.g., creating new programs). Large-scale change, such as a legal merger with another organization, can change the nature and mission of organizations. However, small-scale change can also make an important difference to the client systems and community, such as offering a new program that allows homeless individuals who have a chronic mental illness and substance abuse problems to live in supportive housing while the clients work to reduce and eliminate substances from their lives. Both types of changes involve utilizing the change process of engagement, assessment, intervention, termination, and evaluation.

As discussed in Chapter 12, the impetus for organizational change can emerge from many sources, including administrators, direct practice staff, stakeholders, and people outside an organization. Social workers' concerns for an aspect of service, whether ineffective, wasteful, or in some other way troubling, may be the most accessible route to effect change. As front line staff, social workers are often the first to notice that clients experience difficulty with organizational practices, and they can voice their concerns as part of the engagement and assessment process, and participate in the next parts of the change process. This chapter will focus on the change process from the perspective of direct service social work staff members.

After completing the engagement and assessment process outlined in Chapter 12, the social worker, with allies who have formed a "change work group," must consider possible solutions, develop a change proposal (i.e., intervention) to pursue, select an intervention strategy, and if successful, possibly be involved in the implementation of the intervention, as well as its termination and evaluation. Organizations change in much the same way as individuals. Organizations structured as bureaucracies, like people with rigid personalities, tend to change slowly;

and organizations with a long history can resist change because staff feel that "we have always done things this way," and change may be a great deal of effort. Organizations with a more open, flexible structure, like people who are flexible, tend to make purposeful changes easily. Based on assessments, social workers collaborating with a change work group must choose the intervention strategy to best match the organization and the context of the change.

This chapter will examine ideas social workers in change work groups can use to change policies, programs, projects, and practices of organizations. Based on the engagement and assessment phase of the change process, the next three steps—intervention, termination, and evaluation—can help organizations to become more responsive to the individuals, families, groups, and communities they serve. First discussed are approaches, perspectives, and models for interventions with organizations. In the next section, a framework for organizational change is provided. The challenges and methods for implementing the organizational change are explored, followed by a discussion of termination and evaluation of change in organizations. The chapter ends with an overview of the challenge of maintaining a hopeful stance with clients regarding organizational change.

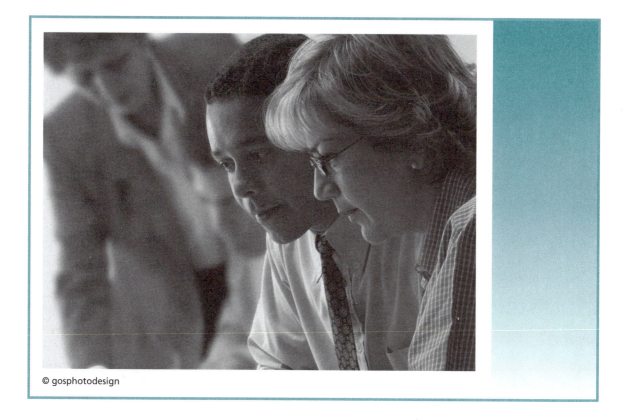

© gosphotodesign

APPROACHES, PERSPECTIVES, AND MODELS FOR INTERVENTIONS WITH ORGANIZATIONS

Approaches, perspectives, and models that are grounded in theory can be used to describe organizations and inform the change process for organizations. In the following section, the organization is described as a self-learner, relative to a systems approach, a social ecology approach, the power and politics model, postmodernist approaches, and a social constructionist approach. We will discuss each approach as well as the implications for the social worker.

Self-Learning Model

Gambrill (2013) describes the **self-learning model** as a contemporary organizational climate that emphasizes the ability of organizations to self-correct when needed. The increasing emphasis on accountability and accessibility to clients, increasing use of information technology, and a limited resource pool, lead to the ability of the organization to improve the quality of its decisions and develop new knowledge. This model maintains that organizations seek and use corrective feedback from internal and external sources by ongoing monitoring and continuously soliciting feedback from client systems about their experiences with services, as well as from other stakeholders who provide information about the external environment of the organization. This model also assumes a rational process in which all members of an organization agree on the mission, goals, and objectives of the organization, and will work collaboratively to achieve them. Although no organization perfectly implements its mission, goals, and objectives, the self-learning model has widespread applicability in small, well-focused organizations with clear goals and values. Smaller organizations rely on common ground, the wisdom and creativity of staff, and the capacity of groups to develop positive directions.

This model is closely related to the ecosystems perspective, described fully in Chapter 1 as a perspective focused on the fit between the environment and a human system. As mentioned in Chapter 1, the ecosystems perspective can relate to all client systems, including work within organizations to create more responsive policies and programs (Gitterman & Germain, 2008a). The model is also related to the **social ecology approach**, which assumes that the organization is continually interacting with and adapting to its environment. An organization must continue to adjust and adapt to environmental changes in order to survive and prosper. With the social ecology approach, change efforts may emanate from changes that occur externally, which has created a need for change in some part of the organization. For example, when economic conditions force many families to seek services, different policies and procedures may be needed to adequately serve the larger number of clients with a higher level of needs. Social workers need to pay attention to changes in the organization's environment (e.g., new funding sources, a change in an area of social policy, new political support for an idea about human services), and help the organization strategize to make needed changes (Cummings & Worley, 2009).

Social workers within organizations that are using the self-learning model contribute to an organizational culture focused on receiving feedback from the internal and external environment, learning, and seeking knowledge about ways to improve their functioning and programs/services. This model is well-recognized in organizations that are involved in networks of organizations, have close relationships with their funders, and/or have a highly developed internal evaluation and feedback systems.

Systems Model

The **systems model** recognizes an organization as a system composed of individuals, subsystems, rules, roles, and processes operating within the wider environment. Using a systems approach, change in one part of the organization can create changes in other parts of the organization. This model asserts that efforts involved in organizational maintenance and survival need to be balanced with achieving organizational goals. For example, job stress, staff disagreements, and social and emotional needs of employees need to be addressed because, unaddressed, these issues have potential to divert workers from their commitments. Change efforts in this model are more likely to include such maintenance functions as clarification of goals, improving morale, and emphasizing better communication among employees.

The systems model is represented in such activities as agency retreats, training sessions, and requests for staff feedback on redefining agency direction (Campbell, 2000). In an important respect, this approach recognizes the impact of human service work by acknowledging the stresses that accompany working within organizations, and recognizing the necessity to attend to the human side of the professionals who constitute the organization and engage in the work.

Power and Politics Model

Assuming that the organization is essentially a political body, the **power and politics model** emphasizes competition for resources, personal advancement, and inter- and intra-power struggles. The model asserts that the primary path to change requires strategic access to decision-makers and/or the people who have the greatest power and primary influence over decision-makers. A common tactic is to work to convince influential people that the proposed change is both in the organization's and the individual's personal best interest. Pressure from outside sources, such as the media, is also a potential strategy to gain the support of influential people (Pfeffer, 1992). This model is related to the **critical social construction** approach, first introduced in Chapter 1, as a postmodern approach. The approach is based in a contemporary analysis of power, which recognizes that any social group can shape its beliefs to its own benefit at the expense of other groups (Hartman, 1994). The analysis of power includes questioning the power relationships between decision makers and others, which can lead to using the power and politics model of organizational change.

The power and politics model can most easily be adapted to large bureaucratic organizations, where change can be more difficult. However, the ideas in this model are adaptable to any size organization. The model reflects the reality of conflict over resources and power that can emerge in change efforts, and the necessity of consideration of the role that politics and power play in change efforts.

Postmodern Approaches

As discussed in Chapter 1, in a postmodern view of change, actions, interactions, and patterns of relationships play an important role in the change process. Interaction patterns between people and between units become stable, dominate, and occur repeatedly in a dynamic process, and the language used in organizations can serve to reinforce the patterns and processes (Hasenfeld, 2000).

Recognizing the power of language, the process of social meaning–making, and the potential for taking part in reshaping their world, social workers can engage with people, groups, and committees within bureaucratic organizations to influence the development of individual and organizational approaches. There is nothing inevitable about the structures and processes that shape and guide institutions or practice—people have created them and have the ability to change them. Changes to improve the organization's functioning can occur through understanding the language, symbols, relationships, and dialogues that structure the organization, and using dialogue to explore the perceptions, values, ideologies, ideas of reality, and assumptions held by staff members, stakeholders, and decision-makers for the organization (Hasenfeld, 2000). While not an easy or quick process for change, the importance of dialogue and language cannot be overstated.

Social Constructionist Approach

A social constructionist approach to organizational change emphasizes the impact that social processes, such as dialogue, have on the perception of social reality, which impacts the prospects for change. Therefore, dialogue about an organization's problem has an impact on the perception of problems, and can be one of the most effective tools in building support for a change proposal. Dialogue that is continuous, patient, and respectful can positively impact the view of staff about the change proposal, which can serve to break down structural barriers to organizational change.

Organizations rarely use only one approach or model in change efforts; they usually use a mixture. These approaches and models offer perspectives on change efforts, offer a lens through which change efforts can be viewed, and offer ideas to social workers involved in organizational change efforts. In the next section, we will explore a framework for intervention with organizations. We will discuss recruiting allies into a "change work group," choosing feasible solution(s), selecting a change strategy, implementing the change strategy (i.e. intervention), terminating the change effort, and evaluating the change effort and resulting program or project.

FRAMEWORK FOR ORGANIZATIONAL CHANGE

Gathering Allies and Creating a Change Work Group

Promoting change within organizations can be challenging, and often require the efforts of more than one person. A group, informal or formal, adds credibility and power to a change effort, and also allows members to share work. Even if the engagement and assessment process began with one person, social workers will want to identify supporters and allies while assisting with the change process. Volunteers will vary from mildly supportive to highly active. Those who are supportive may change their involvement level throughout the process, with some people beginning as mildly supportive, and at some periods, actively joining the work, while others that may begin as active members of a change work group may lessen their work responsibilities at certain times. The key is to continually recruit allies and change work group members throughout the change process, so that even if membership of the group changes, a change work group is always in place to support the effort. While some change processes are short-term, many are long-term and require a great deal of energy and allies (Packard, 2009).

In the ally recruitment process, social workers must raise the concerns discovered in the assessment process in staff and committee meetings, and in discussions with their colleagues. When trying to garner support for a change proposal from other colleagues, social workers will want to be as explicit as possible, and use client examples when applicable. Statements about problems that are in clear, behavioral, and values-oriented terms are the most effective. In these discussions, the client problems must be translated into potential solutions in which the organization can participate. For example, if you think the problem is that LGBTQ adolescents in a school district need additional social and administrative support, the social worker must first consider solutions in which the organization can participate. Can each school in the district partner with the local mental health center to provide education about sexuality and gender to all students? Should the partnership provide in-school or in-home family therapy related to sexuality and adolescents? Should the partnership provide individual therapy? Should the school district provide services without organizational partners, either in-school or in-home? Should the school district engage the parent-teacher association in their efforts? Rather than provide therapy, should the school refer LGBTQ students to private therapists? Or should the school provide services more quietly, so as not to arouse opposition, by

EXHIBIT 13.1 *Origins of Organizational Change*	The origins for organizational change can occur internally from staff members, administration, or members of the Board of Directors, or externally from other organizations, funders, or others. Consider the following examples:

Annie works for the Santa Clara County Social Service Agency (SSA). Years ago, she noticed that the client population was increasingly diverse, with growing numbers of Asians, Hispanics, Hawaiian/Pacific Islander, Black, and multi-racial clients. At a staff meeting, she initiated a discussion about culturally competent practice, and most of the staff agreed that they did not know enough about it, and needed to know more. Her supervisor agreed that this issue needed to be studied, with the possibility of educating staff, and making changes to the organization. He authorized a committee, chaired by Annie, and asked her to recruit other staff for the committee. Over many years, major organizational changes occurred as a result of committee efforts. Three separate committees composed of staff at various levels now meet on a regular basis to discuss cultural issues and promote agency-wide change. One committee consisted of representatives from separate employee committees that are organized primarily by race or ethnicity. They collaboratively discuss and make policy recommendations to the SSA director. The second committee includes the agency director and various managers, and makes decisions about policies. The third committee consists of representatives of department cultural committees (i.e., one each in adult and aging, families and children, etc.). This committee monitors the progress being made regarding culturally responsive policies, procedures, and training programs related to improving client services in each department, and solicits staff feedback. All three committees contribute to increased intergroup collaboration, the direct involvement of the agency director, increased capacity for employees on all levels to be heard, and increased focus on shaping policy for cultural competency.

Adapted from: Chun-Chow & Austin, 2008

Ethan works for The Island, an agency that does exemplary work with disadvantaged adolescents and their families. Even though Ethan loved the direct services and clinical work, he felt that he was working solely toward the goal of teens and their families adjusting to challenging community situations, rather than also encouraging them to try to improve community conditions. The surrounding community struggled with high unemployment, poor housing, underperforming public schools, and needed more responsive local politicians. In talking with his co-workers, he realized that many felt that way. He invited his co-workers to join him informally at lunch to discuss possibilities, including evidence-based programs that sought to involve clients directly with community systems. Eventually, committee members engaged in work – one team located a recent community assessment about youth and family involvement in their community, another team engaged in an organizational assessment, including speaking informally to other staff, administrators, and community leaders about the issue, while a third team researched evidence-based community programming for youth. The Island administrators eventually agreed to appoint a formal committee to work on the idea. Out of these efforts came new programming. Youth civic action teams now work out of local community centers, in partnership with The Island staff, to address community issues of concern to teen members and their peers. The goal is to assist youth to be key agents of change in activities with the potential to transform the community conditions that create problems in their lives.

Adapted from: Evans, Hanlin, & Prillehensky, 2007.

providing, but not widely marketing, support services through the counseling department? Translating the problem into potential solutions will help others understand, propose other solutions, and have input into decisions. After recruiting allies into a change work group and establishing the group dynamics—leadership, decision-making, and other aspects (see Chapter 9)—the group must generate possible solutions and select one solution to address the problem.

Considerations for the Development of Feasible Solutions for Organizational Change

The change work group, including the social worker, must ultimately develop a potential solution to the identified problem(s) that is acceptable to the decision-maker(s) and that addresses the identified client system problem to the best of the organization's ability, based on the information gathered and analyzed in the engagement and assessment process. The proposed solution is a "**change proposal**," which varies in shape, such as a formal, written document for more in-depth change proposals, or an oral presentation for smaller change proposals. Decision-makers for change proposals within organizations can be colleagues (who may be able to make decisions about small changes related to organizational practices, such as changing the way the telephone is answered or email is sent), administrators, the executive director or director, members of the board of directors, legislative bodies, or funders of the organization. Additionally, the change work group must also select a feasible solution that is based in evidence-based practice (as first defined and discussed in Chapter 4). There are several important *considerations* for selecting feasible solutions, including the following:

1. Depending on the scope of the problem, potential solutions, and size of the organization, the change work group must account for *resistance to change*, as discussed in Chapter 12 (Tolbert & Hall, 2009). According to systems theory, all organizations seek to maintain the status quo, or stability. **Inertia** can impede change by preserving a stable state that actively works against change. Change work groups must expect some opposition to change, regardless of the specifics, because change takes energy away from other pursuits (Gambrill, 2013) and individuals have preferences for stability (Tolbert & Hall, 2009).
2. Employee attitudes and behaviors impact the success of change efforts (Shin, Taylor, Seo, 2012). Therefore, the amount of organizational *effort* and *risk* involved is an important consideration (Shin, Taylor & Seo, 2012). Those change processes that will require considerable time, energy, and/or risk to the organization involve in-depth change, and will involve a high level of challenge to the change work group. If, for example, an organization has spent significant resources on a program, the process for ending that program may take a long time. In another example, a change proposal that involves implementing activities that are new to the organization may be perceived as highly risky to the financial stability and reputation of the organization. A high level

of effort and risk inherent in a change proposal typically translates to a high level of challenge for the change proposal.

3. The change process may encounter *competition* for resources and attention from other change processes. The assessment process should have uncovered any other change process occurring within the organization, as well as any plans that will structure future change efforts. For example, organizations often create **strategic plans**, which are comprehensive, formal plans for the organization's future. These plans often involve incremental, highly-focused modifications to current operations that are projected to contribute to a preferred result for the organization (Austin & Solomon, 2009). A change process occurring in another part of the organization can impact a change proposal if the organization does not have enough resources to consider or implement more than one change proposal at a time.

4. The organization must possess the *ability* to implement the change, experience a *need* for change, and the change proposal must *match with the mission and values* of the organization (Frey, 1990). The engagement and assessment process, depending on the methods used, may have made administrators and staff aware of a possible problem, potential solutions, and the possibility of an organizational change effort. If not, staff members and administrators must become aware of the problem, become dissatisfied with the current situation, and perceive that a proposed solution will alleviate the problem. In sum, the organizational system that supports the current structure that creates or exacerbates the problem must become weakened.

5. You must consider *perceived advantages and disadvantages* to the organization and staff (Shin, Taylor & Seo, 2012). For example, if potential solutions will result in more work for a particular staff member or group of staff, the person(s) or unit(s) involved should be consulted before choosing a solution. Others' input may shape the change proposal itself or strengthen the support for the proposed solution; their suggestions and concerns can be considered and possibly addressed in the solution and change strategy (discussed later in this chapter). Consulting with person(s) or unit(s) may garner their support. If possible, implementing a solution should be shared widely.

6. Gathering *history* on the organization's policy-making efforts or program changes will provide helpful context to future change efforts. For example, did prior change efforts induce staff disgruntlement or staff support? Were changes perceived as coming from the top down (i.e., imposed from administrators) or from the bottom up (i.e., suggested by staff)? Long-term staff members may be helpful sources of historical information.

7. In discussions with other staff members about potential solutions, the change work group should also gather an initial impression about change ideas, and the degree to which they are *understandable*, and likely be met with apathy, resistance, or support. The change work group must learn about formal and informal groupings of staff members and charismatic leaders within the organ-

ization, and account for the sentiment of such "subgroups" and leaders in the change proposal.

8. Prior to developing a change proposal, the change work group must engage in *evidence-based practice* by researching the identified problem and potential solutions using evidence-based literature (Johnson & Austin, 2006). This information must be integrated with the expertise of the change work group, and the values, experiences, and expressed wishes of the client system.

9. The *timing* of a proposed solution can significantly impact the proposal's reception. For example, the time in which one administrator is leaving an organization and a new administrator is arriving is a window of opportunity for some change proposals. The change work group may take advantage of this vacuum of administrative power by proposing changes to organizational practices (possibly including a change that was not acceptable to the outgoing administrator), such as a policy that allows staff and/or clients to be part of the committee that screens and interviews candidates for administrative positions.

These considerations speak to the need for a comprehensive process to determine a solution. Some considerations may be more important than others, and there may be special considerations for certain organizations. Developing a change proposal involves thinking through such considerations. Your proposal may also be impacted by your chosen change strategy (discussed later in this chapter). Additionally, the proposal may evolve as you garner more information.

Change Proposal Form   The change proposal may be in the form of a policy, program, project, personnel, or practice, or some combination (Kettner, 2002; Netting et al., 2012). The **policy** approach involves a formal statement regarding the direction for a course of action. A policy change often involves the decision of people with high decision-making authority, such as administrators, elected officials, or a board of directors, that involves large-scale change to create new or amend existing policy. For example, a change work group in a school system that is striving to create improved services to LGBTQ students in the school district may determine that the most effective change strategy is to work toward a harassment policy that would include harassment based on sexual orientation.

A **program** solution involves the creation of or change to ". . . structured activities, [which are] designed to achieve a set of goals and objectives" (Netting et al., 2012, p. 325). Programs are designed to provide services to a client system, and are long-term activities. These are often high-profile aspects of an organization, because client systems interact with, and know organizations for, their programs. For example, a program approach to the perceived unmet needs of LGBTQ adolescents in the school system would be to create an education program about sexual orientation for all students. **Projects** are similar to programs, but are typically smaller, more flexible, can be adapted to changing needs relatively easily, and are not permanent.

A demonstration project, a short-term test of an idea, can be a less controversial way of implementing change. For example, the education program described above could be implemented for a specific time period, such as a semester, with the possibility of extension of the program in the spring semester, and the possibility of changing the program in the first semester, as needed. A change in **personnel** can address different types of problems in programs and projects. Staff members within organizations may lack the specific competencies or practice behaviors to effectively work within programs or projects, and a personnel approach is needed. A personnel approach can include additional education, internships, change in responsibilities for staff, or complete change of staff. Changes that involve personnel must be undertaken carefully, with a thorough examination to determine if such a change will better serve the client system (rather than simply change office dynamics). Using the example of the unmet needs of the LGBTQ adolescents, the proposed solution may be to educate teachers to become more supportive of LGBTQ adolescents in the school. Lastly, a change for an organization can involve a **practice**, or the way in which organizations implement basic functions, which may or may not be formally described in written documents. For example, a sub-set of counselors or teachers may become the unofficial resource and support persons for LGBTQ adolescents in each school, so LGBTQ adolescents have supportive adults in each school (Netting et al., 2012). Exhibit 13.2 provides a summary of these approaches. Exhibit 13.3 provides a case example of an organization that implemented these approaches to change.

Selecting an Organizational Change Strategy

Thus far, the social worker has completed the engagement and assessment process, gathered allies, and created a change work group. Together with the change work group, the social worker has taken many factors into consideration when developing a proposed solution, including evidence-based practice, and made a decision about a specific change proposal, or intervention, to pursue that entails a change in the organization. The next step in the process is to determine the strategy for making a change. A **strategy** is an overall approach to a change effort. In contrast, a **tactic** refers to specific actions, or skills, taken to implement a strategy (Hardina, 2012). This section will include discussion of strategies, while the next section focuses on tactics, or specific skills, needed to implement strategies.

Change Strategies There are three basic strategies for organizational change: collaborative, campaign, or conflict (Brager, Specht, & Torczyner, 1987). A **collaborative** change is one in which the change work group and the decision-maker(s) *agree that some type of change in the organization is required*, and co-operation is needed to create a joint effort to create change in the organization. The change work group and the decision-maker(s) need to create a partnership to communicate, plan, and coordinate and share tasks to implement a change. All parties involved agree that a change is needed, therefore, the group's decisions will determine the approach (i.e.,

APPROACH	DEFINITION
Policy	A formally adopted statement that reflects goals and strategies or agreements on a settled course of action.
Program	Prearranged sets of activities designed to achieve a set of goals and objectives.
Project	Similar to programs, but have a time-limited existence and are more flexible so that they can be adapted to the needs of a changing environment.
Personnel	Persons who are in interaction within the change arena.
Practice	The way in which organizations or individuals go about doing business. Practices are less formalized than policies and may be specific to persons or groups.

Source: Netting, Kettner, McMurtry, & Thomas, 2012, p. 327

EXHIBIT 13.2

Approaches to Organizational Change

The local mental health organization has a long-standing program for the chronically mentally ill who also have a substance abuse problem, or "dual diagnosed" clients. In recent years, the social work case managers have noticed increasing difficulty locating affordable, decent rental housing for clients in the dual diagnosed program. The social work case managers have convened a change work group, and they are considering a variety of change approaches, including the following:

A **policy** change—The change work group may approach the administration and the board of directors to change organizational policy, so the organization can move from only providing social services to an organization that also owns and manages affordable, supportive housing for clients.

A **program** change—The change work group may propose to the administration that the organization seek to partner with local private landlords to provide the intensive, on-site case management and supportive services needed to maintain a stable living environment through a live-in care provider. The organization will guarantee that the rent and utilities will be paid on time, and that the apartment will be kept clean. The live-in care provider will be the first-responder for any problems in the building that involve the client.

A **project** change—This change would be the same as the program change (described earlier), but would involve a six-month trial period. During the trial period, the social worker who is overseeing the project reports weekly to the administrator, who then reports on the project monthly to the board of directors. Ongoing adjustments will be made to the project as needed. If the project is deemed successful, the board of directors may consider creating a long-term program.

A **personnel** change—Using this approach, social workers will be trained to become trainers to the family members of clients about being live-in case providers to their

EXHIBIT 13.3

A Dearth of Affordable Rental Housing: A Case Example of Approaches to Change

EXHIBIT 13.3

Continued

family member with chronic mental health challenges. The trained live-in family members will allow clients to live with their families, and alleviate the need for rental housing.

A **practice** change—Using a practice approach, social workers will learn different approaches for assisting clients to live together in their current rental housing, so that at least two clients can live in each apartment. This will have the effect of housing more clients with the same number of rental units.

whether a policy, program, project, personnel, or practice), the ways in which the resources needed can be obtained, and other details of implementation. Choosing this strategy means that there is little opposition to a change, and the change can best be carried out collaboratively. For example, if the change work group and the school principal and administrators agree that LGBTQ adolescents need additional support and that the school should and can assume a supportive role, the change work group and administrators could partner in a change effort to determine the form that the support would take (e.g., further education of teachers, support groups, and/or education of the students), and to implement the change.

A **campaign** strategy is used when *communication can occur* between the decision-makers and the change work group, but there is *no agreement that a change is needed*. The key to this strategy is the willingness of the decision-makers to listen to arguments on behalf of a change proposal. The decision-makers may need additional information or persuasion. For example, if the change work group and the school principal and administrators do not agree that LGBTQ adolescents need additional support from the school, the change work group could choose a campaign strategy of providing additional information, developing persuasive arguments, and arranging regular communication about this topic with the principal and administrators.

The third strategy, **conflict**, can be used when *the decision-makers are opposed to a change, and are unwilling to communicate with the change work group*. Due to the lack of communication, the change work group is unable to educate or persuade the decision-makers through organizational processes, and is only able to influence the decision-makers through a public conversation. This change strategy involves efforts to draw support from a wider group of supporters, and often involves public conflict. The conflict strategy often involves heated and/or passionate discussion that includes negative reactions, and is therefore not typically used as a first change option. For example, if the school principal and administrators do not agree that the school can take a role in providing additional support for the LGBTQ adolescents, and are unwilling to communicate with the change work group about the topic, the change work group could choose to take a conflict strategy. The group may decide to organize a march or rally to apply additional pressure to the decision-makers to begin communicating with the group. Exhibit 13.4 provides an overview of Change Strategies and Tactics.

RELATIONSHIP OF DECISION-MAKERS AND CHANGE WORK GROUP	TACTICS	EXHIBIT 13.4
Collaboration	1. Implementation	*Strategies and Tactical Behaviors*

Decision-makers and change work group agree (or are easily convinced to agree) that change is needed, and resources must be allocated for a change.	2. Capacity Building
	   a. Participation
	   b. Empowerment	

Campaign	1. Education	

Decision-makers are willing to communicate with the change work group, but do not agree that a change is needed or that resources are needed for a change.	2. Persuasion
	   a. Co-optation
	   b. Lobbying
	3. Mass Media Appeal	

Contest	1. Bargaining and Negotiation	
Decision-makers oppose change and/or allocation of resources and are unwilling to communicate with the change work group.	2. Group Actions	

Adapted from Netting, Kettner, McMurtry, & Thomas, 2012, p. 345

Contemporary Tactics and Skills for Interventions with Organizations

The skills needed for interventions with organizations are built on the skills for intervention covered in previous chapters (i.e., relationship skills in Chapter 3, intervention skills with individuals, families, groups, and communities in Chapters 3–12). In addition to basic intervention skills, social workers need specific skills for working with change processes in organizations. The following tactics, or skills, are organized by the strategy with which they are most commonly associated. The terms tactics and skills are used interchangeably in the following section.

For collaborative change strategies:

Implementation Skills   Implementation skills are those that involve solving problems and making decisions about logistics. Examples include engaging in research about an issue, developing written materials relating to the change proposal (e.g., written proposals, fact sheets), creating and facilitating task groups and workshops, and communicating with interested parties and decision-makers (Schneider & Lester, 2001).

Capacity Building   Building the capacity of client systems has two components: (1) participation, or involving members of the client system in the change process; and (2) empowerment of clients through participation in the effort. These efforts, both a process and an outcome, can improve the ability of client systems to remove real or perceived barriers to participation in change processes, and increase the likelihood of client systems participating in future change processes.

To elaborate on the earlier example of the principal and administrators agreeing that LGBTQ adolescents in the school needed additional support and that the school could take a role in providing additional support, these collaborative change skills could be used to create a new program. The change work group can use supporters and friends of LGBTQ students and LGBTQ students themselves to provide assistance with every aspect of the program, including researching, analyzing, and creating program ideas, facilitating groups, educating other students and education personnel about their unmet needs, and other tasks. Involving the LGBTQ students and student supporters in this effort can increase their competence in these skills, and potentially enable them to teach them to others in a manner appropriate to their stage of life development.

For campaign change strategy:

Education   Education involves communication skills, which may include in-person meetings with individuals and groups, formal and informal presentations, written materials, and education materials designed for persons and groups influential with decision-makers. The goal of such efforts is to present different types of information to impact the perception, knowledge, attitude, and/or opinions of decision-makers through information.

Persuasion   Convincing others to accept and support a particular view of an issue is the goal of persuasion. Skillful communication that appeals to the reasoning of the decision-makers is an essential part of persuasion. The change work group must discern the information or incentives that would be important to the decision-maker, and make every effort to appeal to these. Additionally, choosing people with credibility with the decision-makers to communicate with the decision-makers also helps make persuasive argument. One form of persuasion is **co-optation**, defined as ". . . minimizing anticipated opposition by including those who would be opposed to a change effort in the change effort" (Netting et al., 2012, p. 349). Including the opposition in the change effort can neutralize the opposition because the opposition was part of designing the change effort, and may be able to advance an interest through it. Lobbying is the use of persuasion with targeted decision-makers who are neutral or opposed to the change effort (Schneider & Lester, 2001).

Mass Media Appeals   This skill refers to the use of all types of media to influence public opinion, as well as the opinion of decision-makers, either directly or indirectly. Involved in this skill is the development and shaping of news-worthy stories that will affect viewer opinion in the hoped-for direction.

In the example of the unmet needs of LGBTQ adolescents in the school setting, these campaign skills can be applied if the change work group and school principals

QUICK GUIDE 43   PERSUASION SKILLS

Persuasion means to convince someone to do something that they might not otherwise do through use of reason. Eight skills of persuasion are:

1. *Target your case on the other person*. Find out as much as you can about the person you wish to persuade, including their roles in organizations as well as individual characteristics. Learning about their values, priorities, goals, motivations, personality, and habits will assist to shape a reasoned argument that appeals to them.

2. *Be clear about "who", "what" and "why."* Create a reasoned argument that includes the essentials and that appeals *to the other person* (not necessarily yourself). The reasoned argument should not be constructed as a debate – there are no winners/losers.

3. *Highlight common ground*. Build your reasoned argument on interests that both sides can agree on, even if lofty (such as "freedom" or "justice")

4. *Keep it simple*. People tend to make decisions by generalizing from a limited amount of evidence. Using a few, but powerful arguments that provide evidence of a unifying theme, presented in simple and relevant terms is the most effective.

5. *Appeal to "head" and "heart."* Persuasive arguments include both rational and emotional elements. Pairing case stories or anecdotes told with vivid language with compelling "hard" evidence is particularly effective.

6. *Delivery matters*. Effective verbal delivery includes the use of "I" statements, taking responsibility for your statements, projecting a positive image and adopting an active tone, showing respect to others and giving them credit, telling the truth and showing a willingness to learn from experience. Effective nonverbal behaviors includes using a clear and concise tone of voice, being calm, relaxed and confident (but not macho), using statements that are carefully articulated, and being attentive to the nonverbal behaviors of the other person.

7. *Use dialogue, rather than monologue*. Use active listening by asking for information, summarizing, and testing for understanding. Respond in a constructive way to comments made by the other party. Dissent and disagreement are natural and functional, in that they acknowledge differences of roles, goals, values and personal qualities out of the open.

8. *Work with challenges*. When differences arise in the conversation, one response is to ask more questions. After learning where the other party stands on the matter, ask questions to learn the basis for their position, whether they are interested in re-assessing their position, and if they have any ideas for resolving the differences. If confronting the other party, it is helpful to first summarize the other party's concerns and priorities, and discuss any areas of your proposal that would address any of their concerns (i.e., common ground). It can also be helpful to offer your ideas as suggestions, rather than proposals. Above all, avoid hostile or aggressive responses.

Adapted from: Manning, 2012.

are able to communicate about the need for additional support, but the principals did not agree that additional support was needed and/or that the school could take a role in providing additional support. The change work group can be involved in education efforts with the principal through such efforts as holding meetings, presenting factual information about LGBTQ adolescents and the challenges they face, providing statistics on the number of LGBTQ adolescents in the community, and submitting op-ed articles and letters to the editor to the local newspaper. The change work group can also engage in persuasive efforts; the group can appeal to the interests of decision-makers by describing potentially increased academic performance and decreased fighting by LGBTQ adolescents, and increased tolerance for diversity throughout the school that would result from the new program. The change work group can also use cooptation by inviting the principal or another administrator to be part of the change work group (or an advisory committee to the change work group), or lobby the principal and other administrators who are neutral or opposed. As part of the lobbying effort, the change work group can also use websites, blogs, and social media, as well as print media, to influence the opinion of other students, staff, parents, and district administrators about the unmet needs of LGBTQ adolescents in the hope that these populations will be persuaded to attempt to influence the principal's opinion.

For contest change strategy:

Bargaining and Negotiation Discussing a change proposal, with the possibility of both the decision-maker and the change work group making compromises to their preferred change proposal, involves bargaining and negotiation skills. Bargaining and negotiation skills are used when both the decision-maker and the change work group understand the position of one another, understand the change proposal, and there is a sense of urgency on both sides about settling the matter. Rather than confrontation, at the core of this skill is the assumption that both sides use persuasive arguments about their position on a change proposal, and that both give and receive accommodation to their preferences in the final decision. This process may involve a third party acting in the role of a mediator (Schneider & Lester, 2001).

Group Actions Group actions include many activities designed to increase political pressure on decision-makers. These confrontational tactics cover a wide range of legal and illegal activities, including rallies, demonstrations, marches, picketing, sit-ins, vigils, blockages, strikes, slow-downs, boycotts, class action lawsuits, and civil disobedience. Several of these actions require the involvement of attorneys and other professionals, while others are possible with a skilled social worker, change work group, and/or a large group of supporters (Schneider & Lester, 2001).

Ethic and Change Tactics The choice of tactics utilized for a change effort is influenced by a number of factors, to include the type of relationship between the decision-maker(s) and the change work group, the degree to which the sides agree on the goal, the extent of the communication, as well as social work ethics. Actions taken, particularly group actions that can involve confrontation, should be undertaken after careful thought and consideration, as well as preparation of the client systems involved for any possible negative consequences, such as negative publicity, fines, lost wages, or physical injury. As mentioned, when there is a moderate amount of agreement and communication between the parties, more co-operative tactics should first be attempted prior to campaign tactics, and conflict-oriented tactics are often the last set of tactics used (Netting et al., 2012). The *Code of Ethics* (NASW, 2008) should always be used as a guide for ethical decision-making.

Returning to the example of the unmet needs of LGBTQ adolescents in a school setting, if the change work group attempts tactics associated with collaborative and campaign strategies without any success, the next set of tactics utilized may be those of the contest strategy. Ultimately, the change work group wants the principal to implement a new program, and the principal has rejected the idea and is unwilling to formally communicate further about the change proposal.

In response, the change work group may consider several different actions in terms of perceived effectiveness, best estimate of any negative consequences of each, and their comfort level with each. The change work group may decide to organize a march to raise awareness of this unmet need. The march can be on public property in front of the school, and can occur before or after school hours, so no school or district rules will be violated. This choice of a tactic involves several skills needed by the social worker, including using the research-based evidence about social action in general, and marches in particular, and empowerment work with LGBTQ adolescents in academic settings, and integrating the research findings with the professional and client experience and preferences. The social worker may also seek to involve external organizations that specialize in advocacy and diversity issues. If this, or any subsequent actions, successfully persuades the principal and administrators to begin formally communicating again with the change work group, bargaining and negotiation between the principal and the change work group may produce a satisfactory outcome, such as a modified version of a program to be used for one year, as a project, with evaluation occurring throughout and at the end of the year. Exhibit 13.5 provides a case example of the use of strategies and tactics.

Similar to change efforts with other client systems and levels of practice, not all change efforts are successful. Change work groups may need to change strategies or tactics, and the end result of the change process may differ from the original proposals. A proposed program may be a short-term, small project, a policy change may differ from the original intention, and an attempt to create a project may require a policy change. Some change efforts are not successful at all, and the status quo is maintained. At this point, the social worker, along with the change work group, must reassess the situation to determine next steps. The change effort may benefit from starting over at the engagement and assessment phase to determine if the identified unmet need may still be as urgent, or other data needs to be collected. Alternatively, the change effort may need to begin anew at the intervention stage, where the decision to pursue an intervention, the type of intervention, and/or the change strategy may need revisiting. An evaluation of the process so far will help determine if different directions may yield more successful results, toward the goal of better meeting the needs of the client system. Overall, advocates for change at all client system levels benefit from persistence because many factors may be impacting

EXHIBIT 13.5

A Dearth of Affordable Housing: Strategies and Tactics

The social work case managers of a local mental health organization who work with clients who have dual diagnoses and are experiencing challenges in locating affordable rental housing have convened a change work group. The goal of the change work group is to pursue a policy change, so the organization can develop and manage affordable rental housing. The decision-makers in this situation are the board of directors, which includes the Executive Director. The work change group is considering a variety of change approaches, including the following:

The change work group may first attempt **collaborative change strategies** with the decision-makers. If all agree that a policy change is needed so the organization can develop and manage affordable rental housing for clients, the work will involve implementation skills. The social worker and change work group may be involved in such activities as locating and presenting data regarding affordable housing development and management, creating written materials relating the policy change, creating and facilitating a task group (which includes clients), and communicating with other housing developers and managers, interested parties and decision-makers. Another tactic used is capacity building. The social worker, with the change work group, would ensure that clients would be involved in the change process, to possibly include participating in the change work group itself or selected activities. This involvement can be considered empowerment work with the clients, in that the social workers involved with each participating client can work to build client skills related to organizational change tasks (e.g., participating in task groups and public speaking), and client self-image.

The change work group may decide to begin with **campaign change strategies**, if collaborative change strategies are unsuccessful, or if decision-makers will communicate with the change work group, but do not agree that a policy change is needed. The work change group can utilize education skills, to include conducting in-person meetings with individuals on the board of directors and others who can influence board members, such as long-term employees. The group can also provide formal presentations at the board meetings, as well as create educational materials for these meetings. In addition to education efforts using facts, the work change group must also utilize persuasion to convince the board of directors to accept and support a policy change. The work group attempts to appeal to the interests of board members, to include better meeting the needs of clients, as well as potentially raising new revenue for the organization, and increasing the status of the organization among peer organizations. The change work group carefully chooses persons with credibility to communicate with the board members, to include clients, former clients, and long-time employees. The change work group may also utilize cooptation if they invited a member of the board of directors to join the change work group in determining the exact direction and wording of the policy change proposal. Change work group members may also lobby board members about the policy change.

The change work group may decide, after unsuccessfully attempting a campaign change strategy, to utilize a **contest change strategy**. After careful thought and deliberation, the change work group may utilize a group action to raise the pressure on the members of the board of directors. For example, the change work group may decide to organize a rally, march, or a vigil, along with other similar service providers who are experiencing the same challenges with affordable rental housing. The publicity materials specifically request that organizations respond to the need for affordable rental housing for the chronically mentally ill. If board members feel there is some urgency in settling the situation, the change work group may engage in **bargaining and negotiation** with the board of directors. In this process, the two sides may agree on a policy change for the organization that looks similar to, but is the same as, the original policy change sought by the change work group.

the possibility of change, including external factors, such as a poor economy. Many change efforts take a long time, even years (Schenider & Lester, 2001). If the change process has been successful thus far, the next step is to implement the change process within the organization, as discussed in the next section.

IMPLEMENTING ORGANIZATIONAL CHANGE

If the change work group has been successful in its work to create an organizational change, the next step is to implement the organizational change. At this point, the change effort converts to administrative functions, such as a new or modified policy, program, project, personnel, or practice change. A change in one element of the organization, such as a new policy, can often impact change in another area, such as a new program, project, or even another policy change. For example, a policy change that affects the members of a committee that screens and interviews candidates for administrative positions will result in practice changes: clients will now be recruited for the committee and educated about organizational personnel procedures, interviewing techniques, and written evaluation process for interviews. Those changes that involve policy, program, or project most significantly impact organizations, and those that impact personnel and practices, while important, may not represent an in-depth change to the organization. The following discussion applies to implementing a new or modified program or project, including developing goals, objectives, and evaluation criteria, and the possible use of a Gantt chart to guide the time frame of activities. Implementing a new or modified program or project involves similar components.

Implementation Structure

Successful programs and projects need structure to guide implementation, and for evaluation purposes, although the elements for a project may be less elaborate than those for a program due to the short-term nature of a project. The elements of a program include goals and objectives, timelines, eligibility criteria, rules and procedures, an evaluation plan, and a management information system (Hardina, Middleton, Montana, & Simpson, 2007). **Goals** are broad statements related to an ideal state for a target, such as population or community, while **objectives** are steps toward reaching the goals. Objectives can relate to an outcome, a specific task, a process, or the means to completing a task. A **timeline** spells out in detail the activities that will carry out the goal and objectives, with specific deadlines in place. The **eligibility criteria** define the group of clients who can participate in the program, while the rules and procedures provide the structure for the day-to-day functioning of the program, such as the roles that individuals will play, the decision-making process, the responsibilities for each person involved, and the process for delivering the program. The **evaluation plan** provides the details about the instruments and/ or data to be collected on a timetable, and the identity of those that will collect, analyze, and report on the program data. The **management information system** is the process for collecting program data, and is often a type of software or internet-based application.

For example, if the change work group focused on the unmet needs of LGBTQ adolescents is successful in promoting a new program within the school to better educate, support, and nurture LGBTQ students, the next step is to create the elements of a program. The change work group, the school social worker, and/or administrators can create program goals and objectives, and corresponding evaluation criteria, such as the following (Hardina et al., 2007):

Program Goal: To enhance the academic and social functioning of LGBTQ students and their supporters in Jefferson High School.

Outcome Objective: By December 2012, at least one support group and three sexual orientation educational sessions will be offered to students.

Evaluation Criteria: Number of support groups and educational sessions offered.

Process Objective: By November 30, 2012, recruit at least 10 students for an LGBTQ support group through one-to-one contact and advertising in the school.

Evaluation Criteria: Number of students recruited, number of in-person recruiting contacts made, amount of school newspaper coverage.

Process Objective: By October 2012, create outlines of two different curricula related to sexual orientation education for consideration by the administration.

Evaluation Criteria: Number of existing curricula reviewed, number of curricular outlines created.

Gantt Chart

An important component of planning program implementation is specifying activities that will implement objectives and a time frame for each of them so that actions can be undertaken in a logical, sequential order. The specification of activities and a corresponding time frame can be viewed in a **Gantt chart**, as displayed

ACTIVITY	SEPT	OCT	NOV	DEC	
Produce recruitment materials and begin recruiting for support group	X				**EXHIBIT 13.6**
Locate and review at least three sexual orientation education curricular materials	X				*Gantt Chart, LGBTQ Support Group and Sexual Orientation Education*
Create at least two outlines of a sexual orientation education curricular		X			
Recruit five students		X			
Recruit five additional students			X		
Facilitate one weekly support group.			X	X	
Conduct one education session			X		
Conduct two education sessions				X	

Adapted from O'Connor & Netting, 2009

in Exhibit 13.6 (O'Connor & Netting, 2009). A Gantt chart provides a visual display of the activities that must be undertaken and the time frame for the completion of each activity, which can be helpful in both implementing a program, and evaluating the success of the implementation (discussed later in this chapter). The Gantt chart depicts a sample of the activities to be completed for implementation of an LGBTQ support group and sexual orientation education sessions.

For the implementation process, in addition to the activities in the Gantt chart, client eligibility criteria, program rules and procedures, and a management information system will be created to track the program participants, as well as overall evaluation criteria for the program.

Challenges to Implementation

Due to the complexity of organizations, implementation of a change effort can be fraught with difficulty. The organization may be facing challenges imposed by external constraints, such as a scarcity of available funding for the change proposal. Exhibit 13.7 provides an example of the organizational challenges of implementing change.

The challenges faced by social workers who are attempting to implement a change can include the following (Winship & Lee, 2012):

Change Participant Affects   Although the change process has been successfully approved and authorized, the staff members involved in actually implementing the change may have a significant impact. Change proposals often encounter resistance from staff members with a different perspective or philosophy, or who simply have a personal conflict with a member of the change work group. Staff members may oppose the change for many reasons, including a different worldview about the potential for change in people and organization, a distrust of non-experts (or experts), or a fear of conflict, among other reasons. If the staff member was opposed to the change initially, the staff member may covertly express her or his opposition through inaction or subversion, may simply incorrectly implement the change due to a lack of understanding or skill, or may decide to implement the change with her or his unique style such that the original intent is not realized.

Generality of the Change Changes that are major in scope, such as policy changes, tend to be worded too generally; therefore, the implementation of the change may suffer from distortion because the staff member making the change may not understand or be suited to make the intended change.

Organizational Supports Change proposals may be adopted with low levels of commitment by the decision-makers, and the implementation consequently may suffer from inadequate financial, planning, implementation, and other types of resources. A partial implementation of a change proposal may mean that the change is unsuccessful, when a complete implementation may have resulted in a highly successful implementation. A decision-maker's perspective on change may be affected by relationships with other organizations because a change could potentially create or exacerbate competition with other organizations or unnecessarily duplicate another organization's program. This could happen while the administrator is trying to create a stronger relationship with another organization. In short, support for the implementation by the organization's decision-makers can be affected by many factors other than the merits of the change proposal. Exhibit 13.7 provides an example of the ways in which staff resources impact change efforts.

TERMINATION AND EVALUATION OF CHANGE IN ORGANIZATIONS

The next phase in the change process, termination, can apply to the change process and/or termination from the client system of the organization. Most social workers engaged in a change effort from within an organization will continue to participate in the work of the organization as an employee or a volunteer. In a sense, many organizations experience continual change processes, as the organization seeks to maintain programs and services that are relevant to client system needs.

If the change process has been unsuccessful, the change work group may decide to begin anew at the assessment phase to gather more information and consider different possible unmet needs as the basis for a new intervention effort. The group may also decide to pursue a change effort based on the same unmet need, but with a different change proposal and/or a different strategy for change. Alternatively, the change work group may decide to abandon intervention efforts for now and

EXHIBIT 13.7

Organizational Challenges of Implementing Change

The death of an infant under the supervision of the San Mateo County Human Services Agency (HAS) ultimately led to a decision to seek accreditation in all eligible agency services by the Council on Accreditation (COA). Accreditation by an outside body, such as the COA, provides an external, unbiased "stamp of approval" on an organization, and is a confirmation of the highest level of professionalism of an organization. The process of seeking accreditation is a challenging, arduous, resource-laden process of organizational self-assessment toward meeting specific standards supported by documented evidence. Ultimately, the goal is to build capacity of the organization toward better organization and client outcomes.

A "change work group," the Quality Assurance and Accreditation Committee, consisted mostly of administrators, while smaller sub-committees were established of staff members. As the two-year process got underway, it was clear that some staff on the subcommittees were passive and/or resistant to the work. In general, staff were not highly motivated to respond to communication or meet deadlines for deliverables. Staff lacked clarity about the importance of the work, and questioned how the work involved in seeking accreditation would help clients. They were also frustrated that they were asked to work overtime to meet their regular job requirements as well as accomplish tasks needed for accreditation efforts. Some staff felt that the process de-valued their many years of practice experience, and reflected judgment on the quality of service they had been providing.

In response to early problems, the value of the accreditation process to client services and service outcomes was clarified. Additionally, communication systems were clarified, administrators provided more encouragement to accomplish tasks and assistance in balancing work priorities, and "tip sheets" on relevant topics were delivered to each subcommittee. Yet, even after staff better understood the importance of the work to their clients, staff were resistant to solve the problems unearthed in the process, such as a lack of formal written procedures, documentation, and evaluation in all areas required by COA. Administrators repeatedly reminded staff of the importance of the work to client outcomes, and encouraged them to take some ownership of the process as a legacy of their work at the agency. Finally, a mock site visit by COA volunteers (prior to the "real" site visit by COA evaluators) led to clarification for the staff of the inadequacies of the products produced thus far and an increased focus to complete the work as required by the COA. While challenged to finish the work within deadlines, staff then felt a higher level of camaraderie with one another and administrators, who also worked overtime during this period. Ultimately, HSA received accreditation by COA.

Source: Winship & Lee, 2012

disband. In this case, termination by the change work group from the change process may occur until the next unmet need is identified, when the change process can begin anew (possibly with a different change work group).

If the change process has been successful, the end of the change effort may occur when the change proposal has been approved by the decision-makers, or after the policy, program or project change has occurred, and an evaluation has determined that the change has positively impacted the organization. The change work group may be disbanded either after the approval or implementation and evaluation (or may stay together and begin the next organizational change effort).

When the change work group is disbanded, as with other client systems, the termination may evoke an emotional response from participants, and group termination processes may be helpful (see Chapter 9). Change work groups are one type of task group, and members may have built relationships with one another. Just as in other groups, the role of the social worker in termination is to help the group members examine and celebrate their experiences and accomplishments, and discuss the ways in which their shared experiences and skills may be useful to the participants in the future (Garvin & Galinsky, 2008). Social workers may also facilitate the expression and integration of positive and negative emotion, depending on the circumstances of the termination. While change work group members are likely to experience fewer emotional responses than those of other client systems, social workers must always be attuned to the possibility of emotional reactions.

Evaluation of Social Work Practice with Organizations

Similar to evaluation with social work practice with individuals, families, groups, and communities, evaluation of social work practice with organizations is an important part of the change process. The evaluation process can focus on the change process itself, as well as the result of the change process (i.e., the new or changed policy, program, or project that resulted from the change process). The evaluation of both the change efforts and evaluation of policies, programs, and projects have similar components.

Evaluation of an advocacy effort or of a program or project begins with a decision about the measurable objectives, usually made at the beginning of a change effort. The evaluation process begins as an element of the change effort, and requires a decision: (1) if both the process and outcomes will be evaluated; (2) the ways in which the process and outcomes will be evaluated; and (3) the means by which data will be collected as the basis for the evaluation. The goal of the evaluation process is to determine the *value* of something, which differs from simply monitoring an intervention (Netting et al., 2012).

Types of Evaluation   For both the change process and the implementation of programs and projects, there are three types of evaluation that can be used to assess the objectives: (1) process, (2) outcome, or (3) impact evaluation. A **process evaluation** focuses on the *degree to which the effort operated well*. For example, did the change work group have a sufficient number of persons for the work involved? What methods were used to recruit persons to the change work group? If evaluating a program, a process evaluation could focus on whether sufficient resources were available for the program, the ways in which decisions were made as a group, or whether there was sufficient and timely communication between staff members implementing a program. An **outcome evaluation** focuses on *information about specific results* that the effort achieved. Questions to be answered may include, did the work group successfully arrange meetings with decision-makers? Create educational materials? Were there any policy changes? Were new programs or projects created as a result of policy changes?

An outcome evaluation for a program focuses on the results of program efforts. For example, did support groups meet? Were educational trainings held? The objectives for the program should be reviewed, and success in their achievement should be noted. An **impact evaluation** reviews the *impact of the efforts*, such as individual or community-level behavioral changes (Edwards & Yankey, 2006). For example, in relation to advocacy efforts, is there a new decision-making process in the organization that is more participatory? In relation to a new program, are LGBTQ adolescents achieving at higher academic levels as a result? Have clients experienced behavioral changes as a result of a new policy, program, or project? Have specific changes occurred in the community, such as decreased suicides or increased involvement in community programs?

Structure of Evaluation   The structure of evaluation involves four specific concepts: inputs, activities, outputs, and outcomes. **Inputs** are those resources necessary to implement a change effort or a program. Inputs can include funding, equipment, staff, time, expertise, and other resources needed for the effort or program. **Activities** are those actions that organizations take to produce change. Activities can include attending meetings, creating flyers, interviewing clients, and conducting assessments. **Outputs** are products that emerge from the activities. Outputs are often measured by a number (e.g., number of clients served by a program, flyers produced, or hours worked). **Outcomes** are the benefits gained or changes that have occurred as a result of the activities. Outcomes may relate to behavior, skill, knowledge, attitudes, values, condition, or other attribute. In essence, the outcomes are the impact made by the change effort or program (Dudley, 2009).

Logic Model   A **logic model** is a graphic depiction of the relationship of inputs, activities, outputs, and outcomes. Logic models provide a way to demonstrate the links between resources, efforts, accomplishments, and the impacts of change efforts and programs (Hardina, 2012). Exhibit 13.8 provides an example of a logic model used for a program of rental housing for dual-diagnosed clients.

In this example, funding is needed to purchase and/or renovate an apartment building (*input*), so that clients can be housed with a trained, supportive roommate and provided with intensive case management (*activities*). These activities may result in clients being housed in a decent, affordable unit, leading a more stable life, and being compliant with their medication (*output*), so that fewer clients would be homeless and/or incarcerated (*outcome*). This logic model can be useful in making a

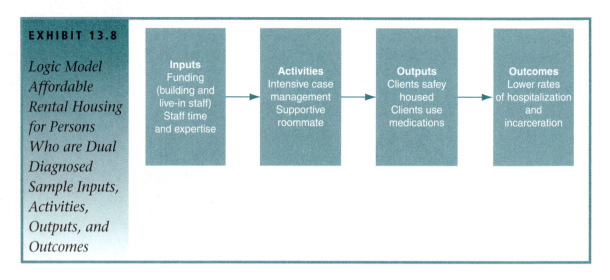

EXHIBIT 13.8

Logic Model Affordable Rental Housing for Persons Who are Dual Diagnosed Sample Inputs, Activities, Outputs, and Outcomes

Inputs
Funding (building and live-in staff)
Staff time and expertise

Activities
Intensive case management
Supportive roommate

Outputs
Clients safey housed
Clients use medications

Outcomes
Lower rates of hospitalization and incarceration

persuasive argument to a decision-maker who is interested in decreasing the number of dual diagnosed clients who are hospitalized or incarcerated. Other decision-makers may be interested in other outcomes, such as lowering levels of homelessness among persons who are dual diagnosed in the community to improve the relationship between the police force and the organization. Logic models provide a rational connection between inputs, activities, outputs, and outcomes, and are often used in evaluating change efforts, programs, and projects (Hardina, 2012).

Information and Data Sources   Developing and maintaining an adequate system for tracking information and data about change efforts, as well as programs and projects, is the backbone to the evaluation process. Information (hard copy and/or electronic) that may be helpful includes the following (Schneider & Lester, 2001):

- Minutes of meetings, logs of activities, sign-in sheets
- Information noting time spent on activities, appointments, assessments, client progress, activities in need of completing, and accomplishments
- Client system evaluation materials, to include standardized measures
- Organization strategic plans, mission, value statements, goals, objectives, and timelines
- Media coverage
- Funding sources, amounts, responsibilities, and required communications
- Information about key individuals to change efforts or programs/projects
- Government organizations related to the change effort and/or programs/projects

- Previous internal and external evaluations of advocacy efforts and programs/ projects

- Records about previous internal and external advocacy efforts.

As with evaluations of community change efforts, the evaluation process ideally includes qualitative and quantitative data to provide information about the process and outcomes of organizational change. Methods may include pre- and post-measures of organizational and/or community functioning, such as validated and standardized measures, direct observation, use of publically available data (i.e., U.S. Census data and others), and feedback from other professionals.

Roles in Evaluation   Generalist social work practitioners commonly contribute in several ways to the evaluation efforts. Social workers can lead and/or assist with evaluation efforts by helping maintain organizational records, submitting data for an analysis, participating in interviews and/or focus groups, or creating questions to be used in the evaluation process. Participation on evaluation teams and committees provides a way for social workers to learn about and direct the evaluation efforts, and some social workers function in the role of researchers to collect, analyze, and report on quantitative and qualitative data. Organizations benefit from well-designed and executed evaluation efforts.

STRAIGHT TALK ABOUT ORGANIZATIONAL LIFE

This chapter has highlighted both the challenging and the exhilarating aspects of social work practice in an organizational setting. Social workers can be tempted to view the organization as a source of challenges in practice. Sometimes organizations can be perceived as posing confounding or complex barriers to the helping process due to policies, procedures, and practice requirements.

In much the same way that some people blame their families for their challenges, some social workers point to the organization as the source of the problem when work becomes challenging or proves more difficult than expected. Shifting responsibility for challenges to organizations relieves the burden of responsibility from the social worker for a role in those organizational challenges. Social workers may not always fully understand the practice constraints inherent in organizations (such as constraints on practice by funders or regulators), and may find it easier to adopt a cynicism that eases their sense of responsibility. A related problem can occur if the social worker joins with the clients to collude about the problems of the organization as the source of the clients' challenges. In doing so, the social worker may feel temporarily relieved by engaging the client in her or his desperation with the organizational system. However, such collusion can convey a sense of hopelessness to the client, when the social worker's goal may be to convey a sense of hopefulness about the client's situation. In its most extreme implication, a hopeless stance may promote a generalized, scornful distrust of all helping efforts. The client may generalize that all helping efforts are ineptly carried out by social workers who are helpless and caught in troubled organizational structures that fail to implement their mission statements. Social workers, at times, must identify problematic agency policies or obstacles to clients. An element of empowerment practice is creating an alliance with clients, or a joint effort designed to promote more effective responses to clients. However, social workers must be able to convey an overall hopeful message to clients about their interaction with an organization.

At the same time, social workers must invest in a thorough engagement and assessment process prior to engaging in change efforts within and for an organization. For example, social workers need to understand the dynamics of bureaucracies and the slow nature of change within bureaucracies before engaging in a change effort. Social workers can be discouraged to enact change by their senior colleagues who believe that change efforts will create no effect, or afraid of being sanctioned or fired if they attempt to create change without first building credibility.

Social workers who facilitate organizational change efforts must be well-informed, and have completed the earlier phases of the change process, knowing that every change effort will encounter resistance. In addition to understanding the organization, social workers must also understand their own strengths and weaknesses, and enlist allies to assist with the effort. However, a social worker who does not address any problematic organizational policy or practice due to fear of criticism or loss of employment is likely to have a difficult time in a social work career. Social work practice requires principled, thoughtful, and respectful risks across all settings to fully implement the work of the profession.

CONCLUSION

Organizations are structures that shape and facilitate social work practice. The change process in organizations provides an opportunity to offer improved services to client systems. While the change process can be lengthy and complex, the process is an opportunity to make changes that positively impact a large number of people, including entire communities. Most organizations undergo at least modest change on a regular basis due to changes in many factors, such as funding, relationships, personnel, accreditation requirements, or accountability requirements, and staff members are in a unique position to implement the change process based on feedback and critical thinking about client system needs as experienced by staff working directly with clients. While organizations can seem vague and too complex to change, understanding and impacting organizations is important to social work practitioners on all levels because of the significant impact on clients and practitioners. Taking an active role in shaping the organization is a significant aspect to generalist social work practice.

MAIN POINTS

- The approach of an organizational change effort will be impacted by the results of the engagement and assessment process, as well as the approach, perspective, or model utilized.

- The organizational change effort is facilitated by using a framework.

- Gathering supporters and allies into a change work group, considering important factors when choosing a change proposal, and selecting an organizational change strategy are vital steps in the intervention.

- Social workers consider social work ethics when choosing specific tactics to utilize for the change process.

- The implementation of an organizational change is facilitated by a structure, as well as consideration of challenges to implementation that can impede the implementation.

- Termination of a change effort can occur after a change proposal has been successful or after the implementation of the change.

- The evaluation phase can include evaluation of the change effort as well as evaluation of the change, such as a program or a project.

- Social workers should exercise caution about identifying organizational challenges with client systems, and only do so while maintaining a hopeful stance about the ability of the organization to assist the client system.

EXERCISES

a. Case Exercises

1. Go to "http://www.routledgesw.com/cases" and become familiar with the Carla Washburn case, to include reviewing her client history, concerns, and goals. Explore the town map, and determine those organizations that may be able to assist Carla with her concerns and goals. Choose one of the organizations and consider the way(s) in which the organization may be able to assist Carla with one or more of her concerns and/or goals. Imagine that you are employed by the organization, and the assistance needed for Carla is currently not offered by the organization. Using the material from Chapter 13, describe:
   - The type of approach, perspective, or model with which you most closely identify.
   - The way in which you would go about creating a change work group.

- Two to three possible solutions to Carla's concern or goal with which the organization could assist.
- Two to three considerations that are important to consider in deciding on the change proposal.

2. Go to "http://www.routledgesw.com/cases" and become familiar with the Riverton case, to include the history, concerns, and goals, as well as the town map and the interaction matrix. Imagine that you decide to work to find a solution to the problem of public intoxication by working with the organizations in the community as a "non-employee."

   Which organizations would you approach to develop a community-wide response to this problem? What kind of changes might be needed in those organizations to better meet the unmet needs of the clients in the community? What steps might you take to facilitate the development of a change work group in these organizations? What might be some feasible solutions that organizations could implement through a partnership?

3. Go to www.routledgesw.com/cases and become familiar with the Brickville case. After an organizational assessment related to organizational engagement in political affairs, the Brickville CDC decided to move forward with a change proposal to engage more fully in local politics. The social worker, Olivia, and colleagues formed a committee to work on the organizational change effort. For this change effort, create a goal, outcome objective, and evaluation criteria. In addition, create two-three process objectives and corresponding evaluation criteria for the change effort.

4. Using the Brickville case scenario described in #3, describe a policy, program, project, personnel, and practice approach to more fully engaging in local politics as an organization.

5. Go to www.routledgesw.com/cases and become familiar with the RAINN case by reviewing the RAINN Components and Eco-map. Discuss the approaches, perspectives, and models discussed in this chapter (i.e., self-learning model, social ecology approach, systems model, power and politics model, post modern approaches, and social constructionist approach) related to RAINN. If you were to describe RAINN using each one of these, what would you notice in particular? How would you be able to tell whether the approach, perspective, or model was relevant to RAINN?

b. Other Exercises

6. Review Exhibit 13.3. Create a different policy, program, project, personnel, or practice approach to the case provided.

7. Review Exhibit 13.3. Create an approach to change that mixes these approaches.

8. You are a social worker at an organization that provides treatment for adolescents who have alcohol and drug addiction issues. Yesterday, you suggested that the organization extend the service hours of the organization into the

evenings and weekends so that the families of the clients would have greater access to meet with the staff, participate in treatment planning, and provide additional face-to-face support for their children. The staff was enthusiastic about the idea, and you agreed to the director's request that you compose a written proposal to be discussed at the next staff meeting.

In your weekly meeting with your supervisor, you learn that she is upset with you. In your discussion, she is curt and states that you may not have taken into account the increased amount of work that extended service hours would entail. She states that increased service hours will have a negative impact on her life in terms of her social life and time with family members, and cost the agency additional funds. Considering the material discussed in Chapter 13, discuss the factors that may have led to this encounter in terms of creating a change proposal. Discuss possible next steps for this change process.

9. Using the two scenarios in Exhibit 13.1, create a problem statement that could be used in a change effort. The problem statement should be explicit, clear, and behavioral, and includes values-oriented terms and client examples.

10. Using the case scenario in Exhibit 13.7, apply the key points in Quick Guide 43. What steps could have been taken to be more persuasive to those opposed?

REFERENCES

350.org. (n.d.). *Homepage.* Retrieved form 350.org

Abramowitz, M. (2005). The largely untold story of welfare reform and the human services. *Social Work, 50*(2), 175–186.

Abramson, J. (2009). Interdisciplinary team practice. In A.R. Roberts, *Social workers' desk reference* (2nd ed.) (pp. 44–50). New York: Oxford Press.

Alissi, A. S. (2009). United States. In A. Gitterman & R. Salmon, *Encyclopedia of social work with groups* (pp. 6–12). New York: Routledge.

American Red Cross. (n.d.). *Red Cross continues to help Joplin recovery from 2011 tornado.* Retrieved from http://www.redcross.org/news/article/Red-Cross-Continues-to-Help-Joplin-Recover-from–2011-Tornado

Amato, P. R., Booth, A., Johnson, D. R., & Rogers, S. J. (2009). *Alone together: How marriage in America is changing.* Cambridge, MA: Harvard University Press.

Anderson, K. M. (2013). Assessing strengths. Identifying acts of resistance to violence and oppression. In D. Saleebey (Ed.), *The strengths perspective in social work practice* (6th ed.) (pp. 182–202). Boston: Pearson.

AP Worldstream. (2010, July 15). *Planned US mosque draws opponents, supporters.* Retrieved from high-beam.com/doc/1A1-D9GV6I8G0.html

Arrington, P. (2008). *Stress at work: How do social workers cope? NASW Membership Workforce Study.* Washington, DC: National Association of Social Workers.

Atwood, J. D. & Genovese, F. (2006). *Therapy with single parents. A social constructionist approach.* New York: The Haworth Press.

Austin, M. J. & Solomon, J. R. (2009). Managing the planning process. In R. J. Patti (Ed.), *The handbook of human services management* (pp. 321–337). Thousand Oaks, CA: Sage Publications.

Banyard, V. L., Plante, E. G., & Moynihan, M. M. (2007). Bystander education: Bringing a broader community perspective to sexual violence prevention. *Journal of Community Psychology, 32*(1), 61–79.

Barker, R. L. (2003). *The social work dictionary* (5th ed.). Washington, DC: NASW Press.

Barsky, A. E. (2010). *Ethics and values in social work.* New York: Oxford University Press.

Barth, R. P. (2008). Adoption. In T. Mizrahi & L. E. Davis, *Encyclopedia of social work* (20th ed.) (pp. 1:33–44). Washington, DC and New York: NASW Press and Oxford University Press.

Beaulaurier, R. L. & Taylor, S. H. (2007). Social work practice with people with disabilities in the era of disability rights. In A. E. Dell Orto & P. W. Power, (Eds.), *The psychological and social impact of illness and disability* (5th ed.) (pp. 53–74). New York: Springer Publishing.

Beck, J. S. (2011). *Cognitive therapy for challenging problems: What to do when the basics don't work.* New York: Guilford Press

Benard, B. & Truebridge, S. (2013). A shift in thinking. Influencing social workers' beliefs about individual and family resilience in an effort to enhance well-being and success for all. In D. Saleebey, *The strengths perspective in social work practice* (6th ed.) (pp. 203–220). Boston: Allyn & Bacon.

Berg, R. D., Landreth, G. L., & Fall, K. A. (2013). *Group counseling concepts and procedures* (5th ed.). New York: Routledge.

Berg-Weger, M., Rubio, D. M., & Tebb, S. (2000). The caregiver well-being scale revisited. *Health and Social Work, 25*(4), 255–263.

Berg-Weger, M. (2013). *Social work and social welfare. An invitation*. New York: Routledge.

Berman-Rossi, T. & Kelly, T.B. (2003). *Group composition, diversity, the skills of the social worker, and group development*. Presented at the Council for Social Work Education, Annual Meeting, Atlanta, February.

Biblarz, T. J. & Stacey, J. (2010). How does the gender of parents matter? *Journal of Marriage and Family 72*, 3–22.

Bittman, M. (2011, May 17). Imaging Detroit. *New York Times*. Retrieved from http://opinionator.blogs.nytimes.com/2011/05/17/imagining-detroit/

Bloom, M., Fischer, J., & Orme, J. G. (2009). *Evaluating practice: Guidelines for the accountable professional* (6th ed.). Boston: Allyn & Bacon.

Blunsdon, B. & Davern, M. (2007). Measuring wellness through interdisciplinary community development: Linking the physical, economic and social environment. *Journal of Community Practice, 15* (1/2), 217–238.

Bobo, K., Kendall, J., & Max, S. (2010). *Organizing for social change*. Santa Ana, CA: The Forum Press.

Boland-Prom, K. W. (2009). Results of a national study of social workers sanctioned by state licensing boards. *Social Work, 54*(4): 351–360.

Bowden, V. R. & Greenberg, C. S. (2010). *Children and their families: The continuum of care*. Philadelphia: Wolters Kluwer/Lippincott Williams and Wilkins.

Bowlby, J. (1969). *Attachment and loss: Vol. 1, Attachment*. New York: Basic Books.

Bowlby, J. (1982). *Attachment and loss: Vol. 1, Attachment* (2nd ed.). New York: Basic Books.

Boyes-Watson, C. (2005). Seeds of change: Using peacemaking circles to build a village for every child. *Child Welfare, 84*(2), 191–208.

Briar-Lawson, K. & Naccarato, T. (2008). Family Services. In T. Mizrahi & L. E. Davis, *Encyclopedia of social work* (20th ed.) (pp. 2:206–212). Washington, DC and New York: NASW Press and Oxford University Press.

Brager, G., Specht, H., & Torczyner, J. (1987). *Community organizing*. New York: Columbia University Press.

Breton, M. (2004). An empowerment perspective. In C. D. Garvin, L. M. Gutierrez, & M. J. Galinsky (Eds.), *Handbook of social work with groups* (pp. 58–75). New York: Guilford Press.

Brill, C. (1998). The new NASW code of ethics can be your ally: Part I. *Focus Newsletter*. Retrieved from http://www.naswma.org/displaycommon.cfm?an=1&subarticlenbr=96

Briskman, L. & Noble, C. (1999). Social work ethics: Embracing diversity? In J. Fook & B. Pease (Eds.), *Transforming social work practice: Postmodern critical perspectives* (pp. 57–69). London: Routledge.

Brody, K. & Gadling-Cole, C. (2008). Family group conferencing with African-American families. In C. Waites (Ed.), *Social work practice with African American families: An intergenerational perspective*. New York: Routledge.

Brookings Institution. (2011, September). *An update to "Simulating the effect of the 'Great Recession' on poverty"*. Retrieved from http://www.brookings.edu/research/reports/2011/09/13-recession-poverty-monea-sawhill

Broussard, C. A., Joseph, A. L., & Thompson, M. (2012). Stressors and coping strategies used by single mothers living in poverty. *Affilia, 27*, 190–204.

Brown, N. W. (2013). *Creative activities for group therapy*. New York: Routledge.

Brown, R., & Hauser, C. (2012, August 10). After a struggle, Mosque opens in Tennessee. *New York Times*. Retrieved from http://www.nytimes.com/2012/08/11/us/islamic-center-of-murfreesboro-opens-in-tennessee.html

Brueggemann, W. G. (2005). *The practice of macro social work*. Belmont, CA: Thomson Higher Education.

Brueggemann, W. G. (2013). History and context for community practice in North America. In M. Weil's (Ed.), *The handbook of community practice* (pp. 27–46). Thousand Oaks, CA: Sage.

Buck, H. G., Overcash, J. & McMillan, S. C. (2009). The geriatric cancer experience at the end of life: Testing an adapted model. *Oncology Nursing Forum, 36*(6), 664–673.

Bullock, K. (2005). Grandfathers and the impact of raising grandchildren. *Journal of Sociology & Social Welfare, 32*(1), 43–59.

Burry, C. (2002). Working with potentially violent clients in their homes: What child welfare professionals need to know. *Clinical Supervisor, 21*(1), 145–153.

Butler, C. (2009). Sexual and gender minority therapy and systemic practice. *Journal of Family Therapy, 31*(4), 338–358.

Butler, A. C., Chapman, J. E., Forman, E. M., & Beck, A. T. (2006). The empirical status of cognitive-behavioral therapy: A review of meta-analyses. *Clinical Psychology Review, 26*, 17–31.

Campbell, D. (2000). *The socially constructed organization.* London: Karnac Books.

Carmeli, A. & Freund, A. (2009). Linking perceived external prestige and intentions to leave the organization: The mediating role of job satisfaction. *Journal of Social Service Research, 35*(3), 236–250.

Carter, L. & Matthieu, M. (2010). *Developing skills in the evidence based practice process.* St. Louis, MO: Washington University in St. Louis. Presented March 12, 2010.

Casa de Esperanza. (n.d.). *History.* Retrieved from https://www.casadeesperanza.org

CHANGE, Inc. Community Action Agency. (n.d.). *County needs assessment.* Retrieved from http://www.virtualcap.org/downloads/VC/US_NA_Examples_CHANGE_Inc_Community_Needs_Survey.pdf

Chaskin, R., Brown, P., Venkatsh, S., & Vidal, A. (2009). *Building community capacity.* New York: Aldine de Gruyter.

Chaskin, R. J. (2010). The Chicago School: A context for youth intervention, research and development. In R. J. Chaskin (Ed.), *Youth gangs and community intervention: Research, practice, and evidence* (pp. 3–23). New York: Columbia University Press.

Chaskin, R. J. (2013). Theories of community. In M. Weil's (Ed.), *The handbook of community practice* (pp. 105–121). Thousand Oaks, CA: Sage.

Chen, E. C., Budianto, L., & Wong, K. (2011). Professional school counselors as social justice advocates for undocumented immigrant students in group work. In A. A. Singh & C. F. Salazar, *Social justice in group work. Practical interventions for change* (pp. 88–94). New York: Routledge.

Christiensen, D. N., Todahl, J., & Barrett, W. C. (1999). *Solution-based casework: An introduction to clinical and case management skills in casework practice.* New York: De Gruyter.

Chu, W. C. K. & Tsui, M. (2008). The nature of practice wisdom in social work revisited. *International Social Work, 51*(1), 47–54.

Chun-Chow, J. & Austin, M. J. (2008). The culturally responsive social service agency: The application of an evolving definition to a case study. *Administration in Social Work, 32*(4), 39–64.

City of Seattle, Washington. (2012). *A community assessment of need for housing and services for homeless individuals and families in the Lake City neighborhood.* Retrieved from http://seattle.gov/realestate/pdfs/Needs_Assessment_data_report.pdf

Clowes, L. (2005). *Crossing cultures in systems of care.* Presented at the 1st New England LEND Conference, Burlington, VT.

Cnaan, R. A. & Rothman, J. (2008). Capacity development and the building of community. In J. Rothman, J. Erlich, & J. Tropman (Eds.), *Strategies of community intervention* (7th ed.) (pp. 243–262). Peosta, Iowa: Eddie Bowers Publishing Co., Inc.

CNN Wire Staff. (2012, August 6). *Missouri mosque destroyed in second fire in a month.* Retrieved from http://articles.cnn.com/2012–08–06/us/us_missouri-mosque-burned_1_vandalism-and-anti-muslim-sentiment-mosque-islamic-center

Colangelo, L. L. (2009, July 12). Queens one of the most diverse places on earth, new figures show. *New York Daily News.* Retrieved from http://articles.nydailynews.com/2009–07–12/local/17929058_1_dominicans-hispanic-queens

Collins, D., Jordan, C., & Coleman, H. (2013). *An introduction to family social work* (4th ed.). Belmont, CA: Brooks/Cole.

Collins, K. S. & Lazzari, M. M. (2009). Co-leadership. In A. Gitterman & R. Salmon, *Encyclopedia of social work with groups* (pp. 299–302). New York: Routledge.

Comer, E. & Meier, A. (2011). Using evidence-based practice and intervention research with treatment groups for populations at risk. In G. L. Greif & P. H. Ephross (Eds.), *Group work with populations*

Conan, N. (2012, February 15). Providing therapy across different cultures. *Talk of the Nation, NPR.* Retrieved from http://www.npr.org/2012/02/15/146936181/providing-therapy-across-different-cultures

Congress, E. P. (2004). Cultural and ethical issues in working with culturally diverse patients and their families: The use of the culturagram to promote cultural competent practice in health care settings. In A. Metteri, T. Krôger, A. Pohjola, & P. Rauhala (Eds.), *Social work visions from around the globe* (pp. 249–262). Binghampton, NY: Haworth.

Congress, E. P. (2009). The culturagram. In A. R. Roberts, *Social workers' desk reference* (2nd ed.) (pp. 969–975). New York: Oxford Press.

Cooney, K. (2006). The institutional and technical structuring of nonprofit ventures: Case study of a U.S. hybrid organization caught between two fields. *Voluntas: International Journal of Voluntary and Nonprofit Organizations, 17*(2), 143–161.

Corcoran, J. (2009). Using standardized tests and instruments in family assessments. In A. R. Roberts, *Social workers' desk reference* (2nd ed.) (pp. 390–394). New York: Oxford Press.

Cordova, T. L. (2011). Community-based research and participatory change: A strategic multi method community impact assessment. *Journal of Community Practice, 19*(1), 29–47.

Council on Social Work Education (CSWE). (2012). *Educational policy and accreditation standards.* Washington, DC: Author.

Cox, C. (2008). Empowerment as an intervention with grandparent caregivers. *Journal of Intergenerational Relationships, 6*(4), 465–477.

Cox, D. & Pawar, M. (2013). *International social work: Issues, strategies, and programs.* Thousand Oaks, CA: Sage Publications, Inc.

Cross, T. L., Bazron, B. J., Dennis, K. W., & Isaacs, M. R. (1989). *Toward a culturally competent system of care.* Washington, DC: Georgetown University Development Center.

Cumming-Bruce, N. (2012, September 12). U.N. says Syrian refugee numbers are surging. *New York Times.* Retrieved from http://www.nytimes.com/2012/09/28/world/middleeast/un-says-syrian-refugee-numbers-are-surging.html?_r=0

Cummings, T. G. & Worley, C. G. (2009). *Organizational development and change.* Mason, OH: South-Western Cengage Learning.

DeFrain, J. & Asay, S. M. (2007a). Epilogue: A strengths-based conceptual framework for understanding families worldwide. In J. DeFrain & S. M. Asay, *Strong families around the world: Strengths-based research and perspectives* (pp. 447–466). New York: Haworth Press, Inc.

DeFrain, J. & Asay, S. M. (2007b). Family strengths and challenges in the USA. In J. DeFrain & S. M. Asay, *Strong families around the world: Strengths-based research and perspectives* (pp. 281–307). New York: Haworth Press, Inc.

De Jong, P. (2008). Interviewing. In T. Mizrahi & L. E. Davis (Eds.), *Encyclopedia of social work* (20th ed.) (pp. 2:539–542). Washington, DC and New York: NASW Press and Oxford University Press.

DeJong, P. (2009). Solution-focused therapy. In A. R. Roberts, *Social workers' desk reference* (2nd ed.) (pp. 253–258). New York: Oxford Press.

De Jong, P. & Cronkright, A. (2011). Learning solution-focused interviewing skills: BSW student voices. *Journal of Teaching in Social work, 31,* 21–37.

De Jong, P., & Berg, I. K. (2013). *Interviewing for solutions* (4th ed.). Belmont, CA: Brooks/Cole.

deShazer, S. (1984). The death of resistance. *Family Process, 23,* 11–21.

Detroit Area Food Council. (n.d.). *Homepage.* Retrieved from http://www.detroitfoodpolicycouncil.net/

Diller, J. (2011). *Cultural diversity: A primer for the human services.* Belmont, CA: Thompson/Brooks/Cole.

Dolgoff, R., Loewenberg, F. M., & Harrington, D. (2012). *Ethical decisions for social work practice.* Itasca, IL: F. E. Peacock.

Dombo, E. A. (2011). Rape: When professional values place vulnerable clients at risk. In J. C. Rothman (Ed.), *From the front lines: Student cases in social work ethics* (3nd ed.) (pp. 185–188). Boston: Allyn & Bacon.

Donaldson, L.P. (2004). Toward validating the therapeutic benefits of empowerment-oriented social action groups. *Social Work with Groups, 27*(2), 159–175.

Dressler, L. (2006). *Consensus through conversation.* San Francisco, CA: Berrett-Koehler Publishers, Inc.

Drumm, K. (2006). The essential power of group work. *Social Work with Groups, 29*(2/3), 17–31.

Dudley, J. R. (2009). *Social work evaluation: Enhancing what we do.* Chicago, IL: Lyceum Books, Inc.

Dunst, C. J., Trivette, C. M., & Deal, A. G. (2003). *Enabling and empowering families: Principles and guidelines for practice.* Newton: MA: Brookline Books.

Dunst, C. J. & Trivette, C. M. (2009). Capacity-building family-systems intervention practices. *Journal of Family Social Work, 12,* 119–143.

Dybicz, P. (2012). The hero(ine) on a journey: A post-modern conceptual framework for social work practice. *Journal of Social Work Education, 48*(2), 267–283.

Earley, L. & Cushway, D. (2002). The parentified child. *Clinical Child Psychology & Psychiatry, 7*(2), 163–178.

Early, T. J. (2001). Measures for practice with families from a strengths perspective. *Families in Society, 82*(3), 225–232.

East, J. F., Manning, S. F., & Parsons, R. J. (2002). Social work empowerment agenda and group work: A workshop. In S. Henry, J. East, & C. Schmitz (Eds.), *Social work with groups: Mining the gold* (pp. 41–53). New York: Haworth Press.

Eaton, Y. M. & Roberts, A. R. (2009). Frontline crisis intervention. Step-by-step practice guidelines with case applications. In A. R. Roberts, *Social workers' desk reference* (2nd ed.) (pp.207–215). New York: Oxford Press.

Edwards, R. L. & Yankey, J. A. (2006). *Effectively managing nonprofit organizations.* Washington DC: NASW Press.

Ephross, P. H. (2011). Social work with groups: Practice principles. In G. L. Grief & P. H. Ephross, *Group work with populations at risk* (3rd ed.) (pp. 3–14). New York: Oxford University Press.

Ephross, P. H. & Greif, G. L. (2009). Group process and group work techniques. In A. R. Roberts, *Social workers' desk reference* (2nd ed.) (pp. 679–685). New York: Oxford Press.

Epstein, M. H. (2004). *Behavioral and emotional rating scale: A strengths-based approach to assessment* (2nd ed.). Austin, TX: PRO-ED.

Epstein, M. H., Mooney, P., Ryser, G., & Pierce, C. D. (2004). Validity and reliability of the Behavioral and Emotional Rating Scale (2nd ed.): Youth Rating Scale. *Research on Social Work Practice, 14*(50), 358–367.

Evans, S. D., Hanlin, C. E., & Prillehensky, I. (2007). Blending Ameliorative and transformative approaches in human service organizations: A case study. *Journal of Community Psychology, 35*(3), 329–346.

Finlayson, M. L. & Cho, C. C. (2011). A profile of support group use and need among middle-aged and older adults with multiple sclerosis. *Journal of Gerontological Social Work, 54,* 475–493.

Fischer, J. & Orme, J. G. (2008). Single-System Designs. In T. Mizrahi & L. E. Davis, *Encyclopedia of social work* (20th ed.) (pp. 4:32–34). Washington, DC and New York: NASW Press and Oxford University Press.

Fleming, J. (2009). Social action. In A. Gitterman & R. Salmon, *Encyclopedia of social work with groups* (pp. 275–277). New York: Routledge.

Freedenthal, S. (2008). Suicide. In T. Mizrahi & L. E. Davis, *Encyclopedia of social work* (20th ed.) (pp. 4:181–186). Washington, DC and New York: NASW Press and Oxford University Press.

Frey, B. A. (1990). A framework for promoting organizational change. *Families in Society, 71*(3), 142–147.

Fortune, A. E. (2009). Terminating with clients. In A. R. Roberts, *Social workers' desk reference* (2nd ed.) (pp. 627–631). New York: Oxford Press.

Franklin, C., Jordan, C., & Hopson, L. M. (2009). Effective couple and family treatment. In A. R. Roberts, *Social workers' desk reference* (2nd ed.) (pp. 433–442). New York: Oxford Press.

Freire, P. (1973). *Education for critical consciousness.* New York: Seabury Press.

Fuller-Thomson, E. & Minkler, M. (2005). American Indian/Alaskan Native grandparents raising grandchildren: Findings from the Census 2000 Supplementary Survey. *Social Work, 50*(2), 131–139.

Furman, R., Rowan, D., & Bender, K. (2009). *An experiential approach to group work*. Chicago, IL: Lyceum Books, Inc.

Gamble, D. N. & Hoff, M. D. (2013). Sustainable community development. In M. Weil (Ed.), *The handbook of community practice* (pp. 215–232). Thousand Oaks, CA: Sage Publications.

Gambrill, E. (2013). *Social work practice: A critical thinkers guide*. New York: Oxford University Press.

Garkovich, L. E. (2011). A historical view of community development. In J. W. Robinson, Jr. & G. P. Green (Eds.), *Introduction to community development* (pp. 11–34). Los Angeles, CA: Sage Publications, Inc.

Garland, J., Jones, H., & Kolodny, R. (1965). A model for stages of development in social work groups. In S. Bernstein (Ed.), *Explorations in group work: Essays in theory and practice* (pp. 12–53). Boston: Boston University School of Social Work.

Garvin, C. D. & Galinsky, M. J. (2008). Groups. In T. Mizrahi & L. E. Davis, *Encyclopedia of social work* (20th ed.) (pp. 2:287–298). Washington, DC and New York: NASW Press and Oxford University Press.

Garvin, C. (2009). Developing goals. In A. R. Roberts, *Social workers' desk reference* (2nd ed.) (pp. 521–526). New York: Oxford Press.

Gilligan, C. (1993). *In a different voice*. Cambridge, MA: Harvard University Press.

Gitterman, A. & Germain, C. B. (2008a). Ecological framework. In T. Mizrahi & L. E. Davis (Eds.), *Encyclopedia of social work* (20th ed.) (pp. 2:97–102). Washington, D.C. and New York: NASW Press and Oxford University Press.

Gitterman, A. & Germain, C. B. (2008b). *The life model of social work practice: Advances in theory and practice* (3rd ed). New York: Columbia Press.

Gonzales, J. (2009). Prefamily counseling: Working with blended families. *Journal of Divorce & Remarriage, 50*, 148–157.

Goode, E., & Kovalski, S. F. (2012, August 12). Wisconsin killer fed and was fueled by hate-driven music. *New York Times*. Retrieved from http://www.nytimes.com/2012/08/07/us/army-veteran-identified-as-suspect-in-wisconsin-shooting.html?pagewanted=allhttp://www.nytimes.com/2012/08/07/us/army-veteran-identified-as-suspect-in-wisconsin-shooting.html?_r=1&pagewanted=all

Goodman, H. (2004). Elderly parents of adults with severe mental illness: Group work interventions. *Journal of Gerontological Social Work, 44*(1/2), 173–188.

Grace, K. S., McClellan, A., & Yankey, J. A. (2009). *The nonprofit board's role in mission, planning and evaluation*. Washington DC: BoardSource.

Grant, D. (2008). Clinical social work. In R. Mizrahi & L. E. Davis (Eds.), *Encyclopedia of Social Work. National Association of Social Workers and Oxford University Press, Inc. Encyclopedia of Social Work: (e-reference edition)*. Oxford University Press. Retrieved April 1, 2010 from http://www.oxford-naswsocialwork.com/entry?entry=t203.e63

Gray, M. (2011). Back to basics: A critique of the strengths perspective in social work. *Families in Society: The Journal of Contemporary Social Services, 92*(1), 5–11.

Gray, M., Coates, J., & Hetherington, T. (2012). *Environmental social work*. New York: Routledge.

Greene, G. J. & Lee, M. Y. (2011). *Solution-oriented social work practice*. New York: Oxford University Press.

Greenpeace. (n.d.). *About us*. Retrieved from http://www.greenpeace.org/usa/en/campaigns/

Gregg, B. (2012). *Human rights as a social construction*. New York: Oxford University Press.

Grieco E. M., Acosta, Y. D., de la Cruz, P., Gambino, C., Gryn, T., Larsen, L. J., Trevelyan, E. N., & Walters, N. P. (2012). *The foreign-born population in the United States: 2010*. Washington, D.C.: U.S. Census Bureau.

Grief, G. L. & Morris-Compton, D. (2011). Group work with urban African American parents in their neighborhood schools. In G. L. Grief & P. H. Ephross, *Group work with populations at risk* (3rd ed.) (pp. 385–398). New York: Oxford University Press.

Grief, G. & Ephross, P. H. (Eds.). (2011). *Group work with populations at risk* (3rd ed.). New York: Oxford University Press.

Hall, J. C. (2011). A narrative approach to group work with men who batter. *Social Work with Groups, 34,* 175–189.

Hamilton, B. E., Martin, J. A., & Ventura, S. J. (2012). Births: Preliminary data for 2011. *National vital statistics reports, 61*(5). Hyattsville, MD: National Center for Health Statistics.

Hanley, J. & Shragge, E. (2009). Organizing for immigrant rights. *Journal of Community Practice, 17*(1), 184–206.

Hardina, D. (2002). *Analytical skills for community organization practice.* New York: Columbia University Press.

Hardina, D., Middleton, J., Montana, S., & Simpson, R. A. (2007). *An empowering approach to managing social service organizations.* New York: Springer Publishing Company.

Hardina, D. (2012). *Interpersonal social work skills for community practice.* New York: Springer.

Hardy, K. V. & Laszloffy, T. A. (1995). The Cultural genogram: Key to training culturally competent family therapists. *Journal of Marital and Family Therapy, 21,* 227–237.

Hartman, A. & Laird, J. (1983). *Family-centered social work practice.* New York: Free Press.

Harrington, D. & Dolgoff, R. (2008). Hierarchies of ethical principles for ethical decision making in social work. *Ethics and Social Welfare, 2*(2), 183–196.

Hartman, A. (1994). *Reflection & controversy: Essays on social work.* Washington, DC: NASW Press.

Harvey, A. R. (2011). Group work with African American youth in the criminal justice system: A culturally competent model. In G. L. Grief & P. H. Ephross, *Group work with populations at risk* (3rd ed.) (pp. 264–282). New York: Oxford University Press.

Hasenfeld, Y. (2000). Social welfare administration and organizational theory. In R. J. Patti (Ed.) *The handbook of social welfare management* (pp. 89–112). Thousand Oaks, CA: Sage Publications.

Haynes, K. S. (1998). The one-hundred year debate: Social reform versus individual treatment. *Social Work, 43*(6), 501–511.

Haynes, K. S. & Mickelson, J. S. (2010). *Affecting change* (7th ed.). Boston: Pearson.

Hayslip, Jr., B. & Kaminski, P. L. (2005). Grandparents raising their grandchildren. A review of the literature and suggestions for practice. *The Gerontologist, 45*(2), 262–269.

Head, J. W. (2008). *Losing the global development war.* Leiden, The Netherlands: Martinus Nijhoff Publishers.

Healy, L. (2008). *International social work: Professional practice in an interdependent world.* New York: Oxford University Press.

Healy, L. M. & Hokenstad, T. M. C. (2008). International social work. In T. Mizrahi & L. E. Davis, *Encyclopedia of social work* (20th ed.) (pp. 2:482–488). Washington, DC and New York: NASW Press and Oxford University Press.

Healy, L. M. & Link, R. J. (2012). *Handbook of international social work: Human rights, development, and the global profession.* New York: Oxford.

Herbert, R. J., Gagnon, A. J., Rennick, J. E., & O'Loughlin, J. L. (2009). A systematic review of questionnaires measuring health-related empowerment. *Research and Theory for Nursing Practice: An International Journal, 23*(2), 107–132.

Hillier, A. & Culhane, D. (2013). GIS applications and administrative data to support community change. In M. Weil's (Ed.) *The handbook of community practice* (pp. 827–844). Thousand Oaks, CA: Sage.

Hodge, D. R. (2005a). Social work and the House of Islam: Orienting practitioners to the beliefs and values of Muslims in the United States. *Social Work, 50*(2), 162–173.

Hodge, D. R. (2005b). Spiritual life maps: A client centered pictorial instrument for spiritual assessment,planning, and intervention. *Social Work, 50*(1), 77–87.

Hohman, M. (2012). *Motivational interviewing in social work practice.* New York: The Guilford Press.

Holland, T. (2008). Organizations and governance. In T. Mizrahi & L. E. Davis (Eds.) *Encyclopedia of Social*

Work (pp. 3:329–333). Washington DC: NASW Press and Oxford University Press.

Holland, T. P. & Kilpatrick, A. C. (2009). An ecological system—social constructionism approach to family practice. In A. C. Kilpatrick & T. P. Holland, *Working with families. An integrative model by level of need* (5th ed.) (pp. 15–31). Boston: Pearson.

Hong, P. Y. & Song, I. H. (2010). Glocalization of social work practice: Global and local responses to globalization. *International Social Work, 53,* 656–670.

Hopson, L. M. & Wodarski, J. S. (2009). Guidelines and uses of rapid assessment instruments in managed care settings. In A. R. Roberts, *Social workers' desk reference* (2nd ed.) (pp. 400–405). New York: Oxford Press.

Hudson, R. E. (2009). Empowerment model. In A. Gitterman & R. Salmon (Eds.), *Encyclopedia of social work with groups* (pp. 47–50). New York: Routledge.

Hull, G. H. & Mather, J. (2006). *Understanding generalist practice with families.* Belmont, CA: Thomson Brooks/Cole.

Human Rights Education Association. (n.d.). *Simplified version of the University Declaration of Human Rights.* Retrieved from http://www.hrea.org/index.php?base_id=104&language_id=1&erc_doc_id=5211&category_id=24&category_type=q3&group=

Ife, J. (2000). Localized needs and a globalized economy. *Social Work and Globalization (Special Issue), Canadian Social Work, 2*(1), 50–64.

"Indicators for the Achievement of the NASW Standards for Cultural Competence in Social Work Practice." (2008). In T. Mizrahi & L. E. Davis (Eds.), *Encyclopedia of social work. National Association of Social Workers and Oxford University Press, Inc. (e-reference edition).* Retrieved from http://www.oxford-naswsocialwork.com/entry?entry=t203.e427

International Association for the Advancement of Social Work with Groups, Inc. (IASWG) (2006). *Standards for social work practice with groups* (2nd ed.). Alexandria, VA: AASWG, Inc.

International Federation of Social Workers (IFSW). (2012). *Ethics in social work: Statement of principles.* Retrieved from http://ifsw.org/policies/statement-of-ethical-principles/

International Institute St. Louis. (2013). *Economic development.* Retrieved from http://www.iistl.org/edintro.html

Interorganizational Committee on Guidelines and Principles for Social Impact Assessment (IOCPG). (2003). Principles and guidelines for social impact assessment in the United States. *Impact Assessment and Project Appraisal, 21*(3), 231–250.

Jackson, K. F. & Samuels, G. M. (2011). Multiracial competence in social work: Recommendation for culturally attuned work with multiracial people. *Social Work, 56*(3), 235–245.

Janzen, C., Harris, O., Jordan, C., & Franklin, C. (2006). *Family treatment: Evidence-based practice with populations at risk.* Belmont, CA: Thomson Brooks/Cole.

Jayartne, S., Croxton, T. A., & Mattison, D. (2004). A national survey of violence in the practice of social work. *Families in Society, 85*(4), 445–453.

Jenson, J. M. & Howard, M. O. (2008). Evidence-based practice. In T. Mizrahi & L. E. Davis (Eds.), *Encyclopedia of social work* (20th ed.) (pp.2:158–165). Washington, DC and New York: NASW Press and Oxford University Press.

Johnson, M. & Austin, M. J. (2006). Evidence-based practice in the social services: Implications for organizational change. *Journal of Evidence-Based Social Work, 5*(1/2), 239–269.

Joplin Area CART. (n.d.). Homepage. Retrieved from http://joplinareacart.com/

Jordan, C. (2008). Assessment. In T. Mizrahi & L. E. Davis, *Encyclopedia of social work* (20th ed.) (pp 1:178–180). Washington, DC and New York: NASW Press and Oxford University Press.

Jordan, C. & Franklin, C. (2009). Treatment planning with families: An evidence-based approach. In A. R. Roberts, *Social workers' desk reference* (2nd ed.) (pp. 429–432). New York: Oxford Press.

Jung, M. (1996). Family-centered practice with single parent families. *Families in Society, 77*(9), 583–590.

Kagle, J. D. (2008). Recording. In T Mizrahi & L. E. Davis, *Encyclopedia of social work* (20th ed.) (pp. 3:497–498). Washington, DC and New York: NASW Press and Oxford University Press.

Kagle, J. D. & Kopels, S. (2008). *Social work records* (3rd ed.). Long Grove, IL: Waveland Press, Inc.

Kalyanpur, M. & Harry, B. (1999). *Culture in special education*. Baltimore: Paul H. Brookes.

Kasvin, N. & Tashayeva, A. (2004). Community organizing to address domestic violence in immigrant populations in the U.S.A. *Journal of Religion and Abuse, 6*(3/4), 109–112.

Kelley, P. (2008). Narratives. In T. Mizrahi & L. E. Davis (Eds.), *Encyclopedia of social work* (20th ed.) (pp. 3:291–292). Washington, DC and New York: NASW Press and Oxford University Press.

Kelley, P. (2009). Narrative therapy. In A. R. Roberts (Ed.), *Social workers' desk reference* (2nd ed.) (pp. 273–277). New York: Oxford Press.

Kelly, T. B. & Berman-Rossi, T. (1999). Advancing stages of group development theory: The case of institutionalized older persons. *Social Work with Groups, 22*(2/3), 119–138.

Kelly, M. S., Kim, J. S., & Franklin, C. (2008). *Solution-focused brief therapy in schools. A 360-degree view of research and practice*. New York: Oxford University Press.

Kettner, P. M. (2002). *Achieving excellence in the management of human service organizations*. Boston: Allyn & Bacon.

Kilpatrick, A. & Cleveland, P. (1993). *Unpublished course materials*. University of Georgia School of Social Work.

Kilpatrick, A. C. (2009). Levels of family need. In A. C. Kilpatrick & T. P. Holland, *Working with families. An integrative model by level of need* (5th ed.) (pp. 2–14). Boston: Pearson.

Kim, J. S. (2008a). Strengths perspective. In T. Mizrahi & L. E. Davis (Eds.), *Encyclopedia of social work* (20th ed.) (pp. 4:177–181). Washington, DC and New York: NASW Press and Oxford University Press.

Kim, J. S. (2008b). Examining the effectiveness of solution-focused brief therapy: A meta-analysis. *Research on Social Work Practice, 18*, 107–116.

Kim, H., Ji, J, & Kao, D. (2011). Burnout and physical health among social workers: A three-year longitudinal study. *Social Work, 56*(3), 258–268.

Kisthardt, W. E. (2013). Integrating the core competencies in strengths-based, person-centered practice. In D. Saleebey (Ed.), *The strengths perspective in social work practice* (6th ed.), pp. 53–78. Boston: Allyn & Bacon.

Kleinkauf, C. (1981, July). A guide to giving legislative testimony. *Social Work*, 297–303.

Kohli, H. K., Huber, R., & Faul, A. C. (2010). Historical and theoretical development of culturally competent social work practice. *Journal of Teaching in Social Work, 30*, 252–271.

Kong, E. (2007). The development of strategic management in the non-profit context: Intellectual capital in the social service non-profit organization. *International Journal of Management Reviews, 10*(3), 281–299.

Koop, J. J. (2009). Solution-focused family interventions. In A. C. Kilpatrick & T. P. Holland, *Working with families. An integrative model by level of need* (5th ed.) (pp. 147–169). Boston: Pearson.

Koren, P. E., DeChillo, N., & Friesen, B. J. (1992). Measuring empowerment in families whose children have emotional disabilities: A brief questionnaire. *Rehabilitation Psychology, 37*, 305–310.

Kreider, R. M. & Ellis, R. (2011). Living arrangements of children: 2009. *Household Economic Studies. Current Population Reports*, P70–126. Washington, DC: U.S. Census Bureau.

Kretzmann, J. P. & McKnight, J. L. (1993). *Building communities from the inside out: A path toward finding and mobilizing a community's assets*. Evanston, IL: Center for Urban Affairs and Policy Research.

Kretzmann, J. P. & McKnight, J. L. (2005). *Discovering community power: A guide to mobilizing local assets and your organization's capacity*. Evanston, IL: Asset-Based Community Development (ABCD) Institute.

Kurland, R. & Salmon, R. (1998). *Teaching a methods course in social work with groups*. Alexandria, VA: Council on Social Work Education.

Kurland, R., Salmon, R., Bitel, M., Goodman, H., Ludwig, K., Newmann, E.W., & Sullivan, N. (2004). The survival of social group work: *A call to action*. *Social Work with Groups, 27*(1), 3–16.

Kurland, R. (2007). Debunking the "blood theory" of social work with groups: Groups workers are made and not born. *Social Work with Groups, 31*(1), 11–24.

Larson, K. & McGuiston, C. (2012). Building capacity to improve Latino health in rural North Carolina: A case study in community-University engagement. *Journal of Community Engagement and Scholarship, 5*(1), 14–23.

Lawler, J. & Bilson, A. (2004). Towards a more reflexive research aware practice: The influence and potential of professional and team culture. *Social Work & Social Sciences Review, 11*(1), 52–69.

Leahy, M. M., O'Dwyer, M., & Ryan, F. (2012). Witnessing stories: Definitional ceremonies in narrative therapy with adults who stutter. *Journal of Fluency Disorders, 37*, 234–241.

Lee, J. A. B. & Berman-Rossi, T. (1999). Empowering adolescent girls in foster care: A short-term group record. In C. W. LeCroy (Ed.), *Case studies in social work practice* (2nd ed.). Pacific Grove, CA: Brooks/Cole.

Lee, J. A. B. (2001). *The empowerment approach to social work practice* (2nd ed.). New York: Columbia University Press.

Lee, M. Y. (2009). Using the miracle question and scaling technique in clinical practice. In A. R. Roberts, *Social workers' desk reference* (2nd ed.) (pp. 594–600). New York: Oxford Press.

Lee, M. Y. & Greene, G. J. (2009). Using social constructivism in social work practice. In A. R. Roberts (Ed.), *Social workers' desk reference* (2nd ed.) (pp. 294–299). New York: Oxford Press.

Lesser, J. G., O'Neill, M. R., Burke, K. W., Scanlon, P., Hollis, K., & Miller, R. (2004). Women supporting women: A mutual aid group fosters new connections among women in midlife. *Social Work with Groups, 27*(1), 75–88.

Levy, R. (2011). Core themes in a support group for spouses of breast cancer patients. *Social work with groups, 34*, 141–157.

Lewin, K. (1951). *Field theory in social science.* New York: Harper and Row.

Library of Congress. (1996). *Defense of Marriage Act.* Retrieved from: http://www.govtrack.us/congress/bills/104/hr3396#summary/libraryofcongress

Locke, B., Garrison, R., & Winship, J. (1998). *Generalist social work practice: Context, story, and partnerships.* Pacific Grove, CA: Brooks/Cole.

Logan, S. L. M., Rasheed, M. N., & Rasheed, J. M. (2008). Family. In T. Mizrahi & L. E. Davis (Eds.), *Encyclopedia of social work* (20th ed.) (pp. 2:175–182). Washington, DC and New York: NASW Press and Oxford University Press.

López, L. M. & Vargas, E. M. (2011). En dos culturas: Group work with Latino Immigrants and Refugees. In G. L. Greif & P. H. Ephross, *Group work with populations at risk* (3rd ed.) (pp. 144–145). New York: Oxford University Press.

Lotze, G. M., Bellin, M. H., & Oswald, D. P. (2010). Family-centered care for children with special health care needs: Are we moving forward? *Journal of Family Social Work, 13*, 100–113.

Lovell, M. L., Helfgott, J. B., & Lawrence, C. (2002). Citizens, victims, and offenders restoring justice: A prison-based group work program bridging the divide. In S. Henry, J. East, & C. Schmitz (Eds.) *Social work with groups: Mining the gold* (pp. 75–88). New York: Haworth Press.

Lowery, C. T. & Mattaini, M. (2001). Shared power in social work: A Native American perspective of change. In H. E. Briggs and K. Corcoran (Eds.), *Social work practice: Treating common client problems* (pp. 109–124). Chicago: Lyceum Books.

Lum, D. (2004). *Social work practice and people of color: A process stage approach* (5th ed.). Belmont, CA: Thomson Brooks/Cole.

Lum, D. (2008). Culturally competent practice. In T. Mizrahi & L. E. Davis, *Encyclopedia of social work* (20th ed.) (pp. 2:497–502). Washington, DC and New York: NASW Press and Oxford University Press.

Lum, D. (2011). *Culturally competent practice: A framework for understanding diverse groups and justice issues.* Belmont, CA: Brooks/Cole Cengage Learning.

Lundahl, B. W., Kunz, C., Brownell, C., Tollefson, D., & Burke, B. L. (2010). A meta-analysis of motivational interviewing: Twenty-five years of empirical studies. *Research on Social Work Practice, 20*(2), 137–160.

Lundy, C. (2011). *Social work, social justice, and human rights: A structural approach to practice*. North York, Ont.: University of Toronto Press.

Macgowan, M. J. (1997). A measure of engagement for social group work: The Groupwork engagement measure (GEM). *Journal of Social Service Research*, *23*, 17–37.

Macgowan, M. J. (2000). Evaluation of a measure of engagement for group work. *Research on Social Work Practice*, *10*, 348–361.

Macgowan, M. J. & Levenson, J. S. (2003). Psychometrics of the Group Engagement Measure with male sex offenders. *Small Group Research*, *34*(2), 155–169.

Macgowan, M. J. & Newman, F. L. (2005). Factor structure of the Group Engagement Measure. *Social Work Research*, *29*(2), 107–118.

Macgowan, M. J. (2008). Group dynamics. In T. Mizrahi & L.E. Davis, *Encyclopedia of social work* (20th ed.) (pp. 2:279–287). Washington, DC and New York: NASW Press and Oxford University Press.

Macgowan, M. J. (2009a). Evidence-based group work. In A. Gitterman & R. Salmon (Eds.), *Encyclopedia of social work with groups* (pp. 131–136). New York: Routledge.

Macgowan, M. J. (2009b). Measurement. In A. Gitterman & R. Salmon (Eds.), *Encyclopedia of social work with groups* (pp. 142–147). New York: Routledge.

Mackelprang, R. W. & Salsgiver, R. O. (2009). *Disability: A diversity model approach in human service practice*. Chicago, IL: Lyceum Books, Inc.

MacNeill, V. (2009). Forming partnerships with parents from a community development perspective: Lessons learnt from Sure Start. *Health and Social Care in the Community*, *17*(6), 659–665.

Madigan, S. (2011). *Narrative therapy*. Washington DC: The American Psychological Association.

Manning, T. (2012). The art of successful persuasion: Seven skills you need to get your point across effectively. *Industrial and Commercial Training*, *44*(3), 150–158.

Manor, O. (2008). Systemic approach. In A. Gitterman & R. Salmon (Eds.) *Encyclopedia of social work with groups* (pp. 99–101). New York: Routledge.

Maramaldi, P., Berkman, B., & Barusch, A. (2005). Assessment and the ubiquity of culture: Threats to validity in measures of health-related quality of life. *Health & Social Work*, *30*(1), 27–36.

Marguerite Casey Foundation. (2012). *Organizational capacity assessment tool*. Retrieved from http://caseygrants.org/resources/org-capacity-assessment/

Mason, J. L. (1995). *Cultural competence self-assessment questionnaire: A manual for users*. Portland, OR: Portland State University, Research and Training Center on Family Support and Children's Mental Health. Retrieved from http://www.racialequity-tools.org/resourcefiles/mason.pdf

McCullough-Chavis, A. & Waites, C. (2008). Genograms with African American families: Considering cultural context. In C. Waites (Ed.), *Social work practice with African-American families: An intergenerational perspective* (pp. 35–54). New York: Routledge.

McGoldrick, M., Gerson, R., & Petry, S. (2008). *Genograms assessment and intervention* (3rd ed.). New York: W.W. Norton & Company.

McGoldrick, M. (2009). Using genograms to map family patterns. In A. R. Roberts, *Social workers' desk reference* (2nd ed.) (pp. 409–423). New York: Oxford Press.

McGowan, B. G. & Walsh, E. M. (2012). Writing in family and child welfare. In W. Green and B. L. Simon, *The Columbia guide to social work writing* (pp. 215–231). NY: Columbia University Press.

McKnight, J. L., & Block, P. (2010). *The abundant community: Awakening the power of families and neighborhoods*. San Francisco, CA: Berrett-Koehler Publishers.

McKnight, J. L. & Kretzmann, J. P. (1996). *Mapping community capacity*. Evanston, IL: Institute for Policy Research. Retrieved from http://www.racialequitytools.org/resourcefiles/mcknight.pdf

McNutt, J. & Floersch, J. (2008). Social work practice. In T. Mizrahi & L. E. Davis (Eds.), *Encyclopedia of social work. National Association of Social Workers and the Oxford University Press, Inc.(e-reference edition)*. Retrieved from http://www.oxford-naswsocialwork.com/entry?entry=t203.e375-s2

McWhirter, P. T., Robbins, R., Vaughn, K., Youngbull, N., Burks, D., Willmon-Haque, S., Schuetz, S., Brandes, J. A., & Nael, A. Z. O. (2011). Honoring the ways of American Indian women: A group therapy intervention. In A. A. Singh & C. F. Salazar, *Social justice in group work. Practical interventions for change* (pp. 73–81). New York: Routledge.

Meyer, C. (1993). *Assessment in social work practice*. New York: Columbia University Press.

Middleman, R. R. & Wood, G. G. (1990). *Skills for direct practice in social work*. New York: Columbia University Press.

Miley, K. K., O'Melia, M. W., & DuBois, B. L. (2013). *Generalist social work practice: An empowering approach*. Boston: Pearson Allyn & Bacon.

Miller, L. (2011). *Counselling skills for social work*. London, Thousand Oaks, CA: Sage.

Miller, W. R. & Rollnick, S. (2013). *Motivational interviewing: Helping people change* (3rd ed.). New York: The Guilford Press.

Minieri, J. & Getsos, P. (2007). *Tools for radical democracy*. San Francisco, CA: Jossey Bass.

Minuchin, S. (1974). *Families & family therapy*. Cambridge, MA: Harvard University Press.

Minuchin, P., Colapinto, J., & Minuchin, S. (2007). *Working with families of the poor* (2nd ed.). New York: The Guilford Press.

Mondros, J. & Staples, L. (2008). Community organization. In T. Mizrahi & L. E. Davis (Eds.), *Encyclopedia of social work* (pp.1:387–398). Washington DC and New York: NASW Press and Oxford University Press.

Morgan, A. (2000). *What is narrative therapy?* Adelaide, South Australia: Dulwich Centre Publications.

Moxley, D. (2008). Interdisciplinarity. In T. Mizrahi & L. E. Davis, *Encyclopedia of social work* (20th ed.) Washington, DC and New York: NASW Press and Oxford University Press. (e-reference edition). Accessed August 17, 2010 from: http:// www.oxford-naswsocialwork.com/entry?entry?t203.e200

Mulroy, E. (2008). Community needs assessment. In T. Mizrahi & L. E. Davis (Eds.), *Encyclopedia of social work* (pp. 1:385–387). Washington DC and New York: NASW Press and Oxford University Press.

Musick, K. & Meier, A. (2009). Are both parents always better than one? Parental conflict and young adult well-being. *Rural New York Minute, 28*, 1.

Nakhaima, J. M. & Dicks, B. H. (2012). A role for the religious community in family counseling. *Families in Society Practice and Policy Focus*.

National Association of Area Agencies on Aging. (2012). *National aging services network*. Retrieved from http://www.n4a.org/about-n4a/join/

National Association of Cognitive-Behavioral Therapists. (2013). *Cognitive behavioral therapy*. Retrieved from: http://www.nacbt.org/whatiscbt.aspx

National Alliance on Mental Illness (NAMI). (2013). *Cognitive behavioral therapy (CBT)?* Retrieved from http://www.nami.org/

National Association of Social Workers (NASW). (1996). *Code of ethics*. Washington, DC: NASW.

National Association of Social Workers (NASW). (2001). *NASW standards for cultural competence in social work practice*. Washington D.C.: NASW. Retrieved from http://www.naswdc.org/practice/standards/NAswculturalstandards.pdf

National Association of Social Workers. (2007b). *Indicators for the achievement of the NASW Standards for Cultural Competence in Social Work Practice*. Washington, DC: NASW.

National Association of Social Workers. (2007a). *Children and families*. Retrieved January 18, 2013 from: http://www.socialworkers.org/pressroom/features/issue/children.asp

National Association of Social Workers (NASW). (2008). *Code of ethics*. Washington, DC: NASW.

National Association of Social Workers (NASW). (2012). *Practice*. Retrieved from http://www.social-workers.org/practice/

National Association of Social Workers-California Chapter. (2012). *Online continuing education*. Retrieved from http://www.socialworkweb.com/nasw/

National Association of Social Workers. (2012–2014a). *Cultural and linguistic competence in the social work profession. Social work speaks: National Association of Social Workers policy statements 2012–2014.* Washington, DC: NASW Press.

National Association of Social Workers. (2012–2014b). *Professional self-care and social work. Social work speaks: National Association of Social Workers policy statements 2009–2012.* Washington, DC: NASW Press.

National Association of Social Workers. (2013a). *Draft NASW Guidelines for Social Worker Safety in the Workplace.* Washington, D.C.: NASW.

National Association of Social Workers. (2013b). *Standards for social work case management.* Washington, D.C.: NASW.

National Association of Social Workers (NASW). (n.d.) *NASW WebEd.* Retrieved from http://www.naswwebed.org/

National Conference of State Legislatures (NCSL). (2012). *Defining marriage: Defense of marriage acts and same-sex marriage laws.* Retrieved from: http://www.ncsl.org/issues-research/human-services/same-sex-marriage-overview.aspx

Netting, F. E., Kettner, P. M., & McMurtry, S. L., & Thomas, L. (2011). *Social work macro practice.* Boston: Pearson Allyn & Bacon.

Newhill, C. E. (1995). Client violence toward social workers: A practice and policy concern. *Social Work, 40,* 631–636.

New York Times. (2012, October 16). *Income inequality.* Retrieved from http://topics.nytimes.com/top/reference/timestopics/subjects/i/income/income_inequality/index.html

New Zealand Association of Social Workers (NZASW). (1993). *Code of ethics.* Aoteora, NZ: NZASW.

Nichols, M. P. (2011). *The essentials of family therapy* (5th ed.). Boston: Pearson.

Nissly, J. A., Barak, M. E. M., & Levin, A. (2005). Stress, social support, and worker's intentions to leave their jobs in public child welfare. *Administration in Social Work, 29*(1), 79–100.

North Central Regional Center for Rural Development, Iowa State University. (n.d.). *Community assessment.* Des Moines, IA: Author

Nowicki, J. & Arbuckle, L. (2009). The social worker as family counselor in a nonprofit community-based agency. In A. R. Roberts, *Social workers' desk reference* (2nd ed.) (pp. 45–53). New York: Oxford Press.

O'Connor, M. K. & Netting, F. E. (2009). *Organization practice: A guide to understanding human service organizations.* Hoboken, NJ: Wiley.

Ohmer, M. L. & Korr, W. S. (2006). The effectiveness of community practice interventions: A review of the literature. *Research on Social Work Practice, 16*(2), 132–145.

Ohmer, M. L. (2008). Assessing and developing the evidence base of macro practice: Interventions with a community and neighborhood focus. *Journal of Evidence-based Social Work, 5*(3/4), 519–547.

Ohmer, M. L. & DeMasi, K. (2009). *Consensus organizing: A community development workbook.* Thousand Oaks, CA: Sage Publications, Inc.

Ohmer, M. L., Sobek, J. L., Teixeira, S. N., Wallace, J. M. & Shapiro, V. B. (2013). Community-based research: Rationale, methods, roles, and considerations for community practice. In M. Weil's (Ed.), *The handbook of community practice* (pp. 791–807). Thousand Oaks, CA: Sage.

Ohmer, M. L. & Brooks, F. (2013). The practice of community organizing. In M. Weil (Ed.), *The handbook of community practice* (pp. 233–248). Thousand Oaks, CA: Sage Publications

Oregon Legislature. (n.d.). *How to testify before a legislative committee.* Retrieved from http://www.leg.state.or.us/comm/testify.html

Packard, T. (2009). Leadership and performance in human services organizations. In R. J. Patti (Ed.), *The handbook of social welfare management* (pp. 143–164). Thousand Oaks, CA: Sage Publications.

Papell, C. P. & Rothman, B. (1962). Social group work models: Possession and heritage. *Journal of Education for Social Work, 2*(2), pp. 66–77.

Papero, D. V. (2009). Bowen family systems theory. In A.R. Roberts, *Social workers' desk reference* (2nd ed.) (pp. 447–452). New York: Oxford Press.

Parsons, R. J. (2008). Empowerment practice. In T. Mizrahi and L. E. Davis (Eds.), *Encyclopedia of social work* (20th ed.) (pp. 2:123–126). Washington, DC and New York: NASW Press and Oxford University Press.

Pawelski, J. G., Perrin, E. C., Foy, J. M., Allen, C. E., Crawford, J. E., Del Monte, M. Kaufman, M., Klein, J. D., Smith, K., Springer, S. Tanner, J. L., & Vickers, D. L. (2006). The effects of marriage, civil union, and domestic partnership laws on health and well-being of children. *Pediatrics*, *118*, 349–364.

Payne, M. & Askeland, G. A. (2008). *Globalizaiton and international social work: Postmodern change and challenge.* Burlington, VT: Ashgate Publishing Company.

Pfeffer, J. (1992). *Managing with power and politics: Influence in organizations.* Boston, MA: Harvard Business School Press.

Pippard, J. L. & Bjorklund, R. W. (2004). Identifying essential techniques for social work community practice. *Journal of Community Practice*, *11*(4), 101–116.

Plitt, D. L. & Shields, J. (2009). Development of the policy advocacy behavior scale: Initial reliability and validity. *Research on Social Work Practice*, *19*(1), 83–92.

Poole, D. L. (2009). Community partnerships for school-based services. In A. Roberts (Ed.), *Social workers desk reference* (pp. 907–912). New York: Oxford University Press.

Pope, N. D., Rollins, L., Chaumba, J., & Risler, E. (2011). Evidence-based practice knowledge and utilization among social workers. *Journal of Evidence-Based Social Work*, *8*, 349–368.

Potocky, M. (2008). Immigrants and refugees. In T. Mizrahi & L. E. Davis, *Encyclopedia of social work* (20th ed.) (pp. 3:441–445). Washington, DC and New York: NASW Press and Oxford University Press.

Putnam, R. D. & Feldstein, L. M. (2003). *Better together: Restoring the American community.* York: Simon & Schuster.

Ramanathan, C. S. & Link, R. J. (2004). *All our futures: Principles and resources for social work practice in a global era.* Belmont, CA: Brooks/Cole.

Randall, A. C. & DeAngelis, D. (2008). Licensing. In T. Mizrahi & L. E. Davis (Eds.), *Encyclopedia of social work* (20th ed.) (pp. 3:87–91). Washington, DC and New York: NASW Press and Oxford University Press.

Rapp, C. A. & Goscha, R. J. (2006). *The strengths model: Case management with people with psychiatric disabilities.* New York: Oxford University Press.

Rawls, J. (1971). *A theory of justice.* Cambridge, MA: Harvard University Press.

Reamer, F. G. (2003). Boundary issues in social work: Managing dual relationships. *Social Work*, *48*(1), 121–133.

Reamer, F. G. (2006). *Social work values and ethics* (3rd ed.) New York: Columbia University Press.

Reamer, F. G. (2008). Ethics and values. In T. Mizrahi & L. E. Davis (Eds.) *Encyclopedia of social work* (pp. 2:143–151). Washington DC: NASW Press.

Reamer, F. G. (2009). Ethical codes of practice in the US and UK: One profession, two standards. *Journal of Social Work Values & Ethics*, *6*(2), 4.

Redevelopment Opportunities for Women. (n.d.). *Economic programs.* Retrieved from http://www.row-stl.org/content/REAP.aspx

Reid, K. E. (1997). *Social work practice with groups: A clinical perspective* (2nd ed.). Pacific Grove, CA: Brooks/Cole.

Reid, K. E. (2009). Clinical social work with groups. In A. R. Roberts, *Social workers' desk reference* (2nd ed.) (pp. 432–436). New York: Oxford Press.

Reichert, E. (2011). *Social work and human rights: A foundation for policy and practice.* New York Columbia Press.

Reisch, M. (2013). Community practice challenges in the global economy. In M. Weil's (Ed.), *The handbook of community practice* (pp. 47–71). Thousand Oaks, CA: Sage.

Ringel, S. (2005). Group work with Asian-American immigrants: A cross-cultural perspective. In G. L. Greif & P. H. Ephross, *Group work with populations at risk* (2nd ed.) (pp. 181–194). New York: Oxford University Press.

Roberts, A. R. (2005). Bridging the past and present to the future of crisis intervention and crisis management. In *Crisis intervention handbook: Assessment, treatment and research* (3rd ed.) (pp. 3–34). New York: Oxford University Press.

Roberts, A. R. (2008). Crisis interventions. In T. Mizrahi & L. E. Davis, *Encyclopedia of social work* (20th ed.)

(pp. 1:484–491). Washington, DC and New York: NASW Press and Oxford University Press.

Roberts-DeGennaro, M. (2008). Case management. In T. Mizrahi & L. E. Davis, *Encyclopedia of social work* (20th ed.) (pp. 1:222–227). Washington, DC and New York: NASW Press and Oxford University Press.

Robinson, J. W. & Green, G. P. (2011) *Introduction to community Development: Theory, practice, and service-learning.* Thousand Oaks, CA: Sage.

Roche, S. E. & Wood, G. G. (2005). A narrative principle for feminist social work with survivors of male violence. *AFFILIA, 20*(4), 465–475.

Rogers, C. (1957). The necessary and sufficient conditions of therapeutic personality change. *Journal of Consulting Psychology, 22*, 95–103.

Rogers, E. E. (1975). *Organizational theory.* Boston, MA: Allyn & Bacon.

Roosevelt, E. (1958). Presentation of *In your hands: A guide for community action for the tenth anniversary of the Universal Declaration of Human Rights* [online]. Available: www.udhr.org/history/inyour.htm

Roscoe, K. D., Carson, A. M., & Madoc-Jones, L. (2011). Narrative social work: Conversations between theory and practice. *Journal of Social work Practice, 25*(1), 47–61.

Roscoe, K. D. & Madoc-Jones, L. (2009). Critical social work practice: A narrative approach. *International Journal of Narrative Practice, 1*, 9–18.

Rostoky, S. S. & Riggle, E. D. B. (2011). Marriage equality for same-sex couples: Counseling psychologists as social change agents. *The Counseling Psychologist, 39*(7), 956–972.

Rothman, J. (2008). Multi modes of community intervention. In J. Rothman, J. Erlich, & J. Tropman (Eds.), *Strategies of community intervention* (7th ed.) (pp.141–170). Peosta, Iowa: Eddie Bowers Publishing Co., Inc.

Rothman, J. C. (2009a). An overview of case management. In A. R. Roberts, *Social workers' desk reference* (2nd ed.) (pp. 751–755). New York: Oxford Press.

Rothman, J. C. (2009b). Developing therapeutic contracts with clients. In A. R. Roberts, *Social workers' desk reference* (2nd ed.) (pp. 514–520). New York: Oxford Press.

Royse, D., Staton-Tindall, M., Badger, K., & Webster, J. M. (2009). *Needs assessment.* New York: Oxford University Press.

Rozakis, L. (1996). *New Roberts Rules of Order.* New York: Smithmark Reference.

Rubin, H. J. & Rubin, I. S. (2008). *Community organizing and development.* Boston: Pearson Allyn & Bacon.

Rutgers School of Social Work. (2007). *Continuing education.* Retrieved from http://socialwork.rutgers.edu/ContinuingEducation/ce.aspx

Sager, J. S. & Weil, M. (2013). Larger-scale social planning: Planning for services and communities. In M. Weil (Ed.), *The handbook of community practice* (pp. 299–325). Thousand Oaks, CA: Sage Publications

Sandfort, J. (2005). Casa de Esperanza. *Nonprofit Management & Leadership, 15*(3), 371–382.

Saint Louis University Pius Library (n.d.). *Research guides.* Retrieved from http://libguides.slu.edu/index.php

Saleebey, D. (2013). *The strengths perspective in social work practice.* Boston: Allyn & Bacon.

Scherrer, J. L. (2012). The United Nations Convention on the Rights of the Child as policy and strategy for social work action in child welfare in the United States. *Social Work, 57*(1), 11–22.

Schein, E. H. (1992). *Organizational culture and leadership.* San Francisco: Jossey-Bass.

Schiller, L. Y. (1995). Stages of development in women's groups: A relational model. In R. Kurland & R. Salmon (Eds.), *Group work practice in a troubled society: Problems and opportunities* (pp. 117–138). New York: The Haworth Press.

Schiller, L. Y. (1997). Rethinking stages of group development in women's groups: Implications for practice. *Social Work with Groups, 20*(3), 3–19.

Schiller, L. Y. (2007). Not for women only: Applying the rlational model of group development with vulnerable populations. *Social Work with Groups, 30*(2), 11–26.

Schiller, L. Y. (2003). Women's group development from a relational model and a new look at facilitator influence on group development. In. M. B. Cohen & A. Mullender, *Gender and group work* (pp. 16–31). New York: Routledge.

Schultz, D. (2004). Cultural competence in psychosocial and psychiatric care: A critical perspective with reference to research and clinical experiences in California, US and in Germany. In A. Metteri, T. Krôger, A. Pohjola, & P. Rauhala (Eds.), *Social work visions from around the globe* (pp. 231–247). Binghamton, NY: Haworth.

Schneider, R. L. & Lester, L. (2001). *Social work advocacy*. Belmont, CA: Brooks/Cole.

Schwartz, W. (1961). *The social worker in the group*. The Social Welfare Forum, 146–177.

Sebold, J. (2011). Families and couples: A practical guide for facilitating change. In G. J. Greene and M. Y. Lee, *Solution-oriented social work practice* (pp. 209–236). NY: Oxford University Press.

Seligman, M. & Darling, R. B. (2007). *Ordinary families, special children: A systems approach to childhood disability* (3rd ed.). New York: The Guilford Press.

Shakya, H. B., Usita, P. M., Eisenberg, C., Weston, J., & Liles, S. (2012). Family well-being concerns of grandparents in skipped generation families. *Journal of Gerontological Social Work, 55*, 39–54.

Shalay, N. & Brownlee, K. (2007). Narrative family therapy with blended families. *Journal of Family Psychotherapy, 18*(2), 17–30.

Shebib, B. (2003). *Choices*. New York: Allyn and Bacon.

Shelton, M. (2012, May 7). Tornado recovery offers Joplin students new lessons. *NPR*. Retrieved from http://www.npr.org/2012/05/07/151950143/tornado-recovery-offers-joplin-students-new-lessons

Sherraden, M. (1993). Community studies in the baccalaureate social work curriculum. *Journal of Teaching in Social Work, 7*(1), 75–88.

Shields, G. & Kiser, J. (2003). Violence and aggression directed toward human service workers: An exploratory study. *Families in Society, 84*(1), 13–20.

Shier, M. L. (2012). Work-related factors that impact social work practitioners' subjective well-being: Well-being in the workplace. *Journal of Social Work, 12*(6), 402–421.

Shin, J., Taylor, M. S., & Seo, M-G. (2012). Resources for change: The relationships of organizational inducements and psychological resilience to employees' attitudes and behaviors toward organizational change. *Academy of Management Journal, 55*(3), 727–748.

Shulman, L. (2009a). Developing successful therapeutic relationships. In A. R. Roberts (Ed.), *Social worker's desk reference* (pp. 573–577). New York, NY: Oxford University Press.

Shulman, L. (2009b). Group work phases of helping: Preliminary phase. In A. Gitterman & R. Salmon (Eds.), *Encyclopedia of social work with groups* (pp. 109–111). New York: Routledge.

Siebold, C. (2007). Everytime we say goodbye: Forced termination revisited, a commentary. *Clinical Social Work Journal, 35*(2), 91–95.

Simmons, C. S., Diaz, L., Jackson, V., & Takahashi, R. (2008). NASW Cultural Competence Indicators: A new tool for the social work profession. *Journal of Ethnic and Cultural Diversity in Social Work, 17*(1), 4–20.

Simon, B. (1990). Re-thinking empowerment. *Journal of Progressive Human Services. 1*(1), 29.

Sims, P. A. (2003). Working with metaphor. *American Journal of Psychotherapy, 57*(4), 528–536.

Singh, A. A. & Salazar, C. F. (2011). Conclusion: Six Considerations for Social Justice Group Work. In A. A. Singh & C. F. Salazar, *Social justice in group work*. Practical interventions for change. New York: Routledge.

Slade, E., McCarthy, J. F., Valenstein, M., Visnic, S., & Dixon, L. B. (2012). Cost savings from Assertive Community Treatment services in an era of declining psychiatric inpatient use. *Health Services Research*. doi: 10.1111/j.1475–6773.2012.01420.

Smith, B. D. (2005). Job retention in child welfare: Effects of perceived organizational support, supervisor support, and intrinsic job value. *Children and Youth Services Review, 27*(2), 153–169.

Sohng, W. S. L. (2008). Community-based participatory research. In T. Mizrahi & L. E. Davis (Eds.), *Encyclopedia of social work* (pp. 1:368–370). Washington DC and New York: NASW Press and Oxford University Press.

Sormanti, M. (2012). Writing for and about clinical practice. In W. Green and B. L. Simon, *The Columbia guide to social work writing* (pp. 114–132). NY: Columbia University Press.

Sowers, K. M. & Rowe, W. S. (2009). International perspectives on social work practice. In A. R. Roberts (Ed.), *Social workers' desk reference* (2nd ed.) (pp. 863–868). New York: Oxford University Press.

Specht, H. (1990). Social work and the popular psychotherapies. *Social Service Review, 64,* 345–357.

Speer, P. W. & Christens, B. D. (2011). Local community organizing and change: Altering policy in the housing and community development system in Kansas City. *Journal of Community & Applied Social Psychology, 22*(5), 414–427.

St. Anthony's Medical Center. (2010). *Family Intervention and Planning.* St. Louis, MO

Stempel, J. (2013). *Supreme Court to hear same-sex marriage cases in late March.* Retrieved from: http://www.reuters.com/article/2013/01/07/us-usa-court-gaymarriage-idUSBRE9060N820130107

Steger, M. B. (2009). *Globalization.* New York: Sterling Publishing.

Stevenson, M. (2010). Flexible and responsive research: Developing rights-based emancipatory disability research methodology in collaboration with young adults with Downs Syndrome. *Australian Social Work, 63*(1), 35–50.

Strand, V., Carten, A., Connolly, D., Gelman, S. R., & Vaughn, P. B. (2009). A cross system initiative sup- porting child welfare workforce professionalization and stabilization. A task group in action. In C. S. Cohen, M. H. Phillips, & M. Hanson (Eds.), *Strength and diversity in social work with groups* (pp. 41–53). New York: Routledge.

Streeter, C. (2008). Community: Practice interventions. In T. Mizrahi & L. E. Davis (Eds.), *Encyclopedia of social work* (pp. 1:355–368). Washington DC and New York: NASW Press and Oxford University Press.

Strom-Gottfried, K. J. (2000). Ensuring ethical practice: An examination of NASW Code violations, 1986–97. *Social Work, 45*(3), 251–261.

Strom-Gottfried, K. J. (2003). *Managing risk through ethical practice: Ethical dilemmas in rural social work.* Presentation at the National Association of Social Workers Vermont chapter, Essex, VT.

Strom-Gottfried, K. J. (2008). *The ethics of practice with minors.* Chicago, IL: Lyceum Books, Inc.

Swenson, C. R. (1998). Clinical social work's contribution to a social justice perspective. *Social Work, 43*(6), 527–537.

Tebb, S. C. (1995). An aid to empowerment: A caregiver well-being scale. *Health and Social Work, 20*(2), 87–92.

Tebb, S. C., Berg-Weger, M. & Rubio, D. M. (2013). The Caregiver Well-Being Scale: Developing a short-form rapid assessment instrument. In press, *Health and Social Work.*

Thomas, H. & Caplan T. (1999). Spinning the group process wheel: Effective facilitation techniques for motivating involuntary client groups. *Social Work with Groups, 21*(4), 3–21.

Thyer, B. (2008). Evidence-based macro practice: Addressing the challenges and opportunities. *Journal of Evidence-based Social Work, 5*(3/4), 453–472.

Thyer, B. A. (2009). Evidence-based practice, science, and social work. An overview. In A.R. Roberts, *Social workers' desk reference* (2nd ed.) (pp. 1115–1119). New York: Oxford Press.

Tolbert, P. S. & Hall, R. J. (2009). *Organizations structures, processes, and outcomes.* Upper Saddle River, New Jersey: Pearson Prentice Hall.

Tomasello, N. M., Manning, A. R., & Dulmus, C. N. (2010). Family-centered early intervention for infants and toddlers with disabilities. *Journal of Family Social Work, 13,* 163–172.

Toseland, R. W. & Horton, H. (2008). Group work. In T. Mizrahi & L. E. Davis, *Encyclopedia of social work* (20th ed.) (pp. 2:298–308). Washington, DC and New York: NASW Press and Oxford University Press.

Turner, H. (2011). Concepts for effective facilitation of open groups. *Social work with groups, 34,* 146–156.

UAW Global Organizing Institute. (2012). *Homepage.* Retrieved from http://www.uaw.org/page/uaw-global-organizing-institute–0

Uken, A., Lee, M.Y., & Sebold, J. (2013). The Plumas Project: Solution-focused treatment of domestic violence offenders. In P. De Jong & I.K. Berg, *Interviewing for solutions* (4th ed.) (pp. 333–345). Belmont, CA: Brooks/Cole.

United Nations. (1997). *Human rights at your fingertips*. United Nations Department Of Public Information, New York: Author. Retrieved from http://www.un.org/rights/50/game.htm#60

U.S. Census Bureau. (2010b). *Valentine's Day 2011: February 14*. Available at: https://www.census.gov/newsroom/releases/archives/facts_for_features_special_editions/cb11-ff02.html

U.S. Census Bureau. (2011a). *Current Population Survey, 2011 Annual Social and Economic Supplement*. Washington, D.C. Government Printing Office

U. S. Census Bureau. (2011b). *Census bureau releases estimates of same-sex married couples*. Retrieved from http://www.census.gov/newsroom/releases/archives/2010_census/cb11-cn181.html

U.S. Census Bureau. (2012a). *Current Population Survey, 2012 Annual Social and Economic Supplement*. Washington, D.C. Government Printing Office

U.S. Census Bureau. (2012b). *Most children younger than age 1 are minorities*. Retrieved from http://www.census.gov/newsroom/releases/archives/population/cb12-90.html

U.S. Department of Housing and Urban Development. (n.d.). *Connecting to success: Neighborhood networks asset mapping guide*. Retrieved from http://www.hud.gov/offices/hsg/mfh/nnw/resourcesforcenters/assetmapping.pdf

Van Den Bergh, N. & Crisp, C. (2004). Defining culturally competent practice with sexual minorities: Implications for social work education and practice. *Journal of Social Work Education*, 40(2), 221–238.

Van Hook, M. P. (2008). *Social work practice with families: A resiliency-based approach*. Chicago: Lyceum Books.

Van Soest, D. (2008). Oppression. In T. Mizrahi & L. E. Davis, *Encyclopedia of social work* (20th ed.) (pp. 3:322–324). Washington, DC and New York: NASW Press and Oxford University Press.

Van Treuren, R. R. (1993). Self-perception in family systems: A diagrammatic technique. In C. Meyer, *Assessment in social work practice* (p. 119). New York: Columbia University Press.

Van Wormer, K. (2009). Restorative justice as social justice for victims of gendered violence: A standpoint feminist perspective. *Social Work*, 54(2), 107–116.

Vinter, R. D. (1974). Program activities: An analysis of their effects on participant behavior. In P. Glassner, R. Sarri, & R. Vinter (Eds.), Individual change through small groups (pp. 233–243). New York: The Free Press.

Vodde, R. & Giddings, M. M. (1997). The propriety of affiliation with clients beyond the professional role: Nonsexual dual relationships. *Arete*, 22(1), 58–79.

Vodde, R. & Gallant, J. P. (2002). Bridging the gap between micro and macro practice: Large-scale change and a unified model of narrative deconstructive practice. *Journal of Teaching in Social Work*, 38(3), 439–458.

Wagner, E. F. (2008). Motivational interviewing. In T. Mizrahi & L. E. Davis, *Encyclopedia of social work* (20th ed.) (pp. 3:273–276). Washington, DC and New York: NASW Press and Oxford University Press.

Wahab, S. (2005). Motivational interviewing and social work practice. *Journal of Social Work*, 5(1), 45–60.

Walker, L. (2013). Solution-focused reentry and transition planning for imprisoned people. In P. De Jong & I. K. Berg, *Interviewing for solutions* (4th ed.) (pp. 318–328). Belmont, CA: Brooks/Cole.

Walz, T. & Ritchie, H. (2000). Gandhian principles in social work practice: Ethics revisited. *Social Work*, 45(3), 213–222.

Warde, B. (2012). The Cultural Genogram: Enhancing the cultural competency of social work students. *Social Work Education*, 31(5), 570–586.

Warren, R. L. (1978). *The community in America*. Chicago: Rand McNally.

Wayne-Metropolitan Community Action Agency (2007). *Wayne-Metropolitan Community Action Agency: Community Needs Assessment 2007*. Retrieved from http://infopeople.org/sites/all/files/past/2007/needs/needs_waynemetro_survey.pdf

Weick, A. (1999). Guilty knowledge. *Families in Society*, *80*(4), 327–332.

Weick, A., Kreider, J., & Chamberlain, R. (2009). Key dimensions of the strengths perspective in case management, clinical practice, and community practice. In D. Saleebey (Ed.), *The strengths perspective in social work practice* (5th ed.) (pp. 108–121). Boston: Pearson.

Weil, M. & Gamble, D. N. (2009). Community practice model for the twenty-first century. In A. Roberts (Ed.), *Social workers' desk reference* (pp. 882–892). New York: Oxford University Press, Inc.

Weil, M. (2013). Community-based social planning. In M. Weil (Ed.), *The handbook of community practice* (pp. 265–298). Thousand Oaks, CA: Sage Publications.

Weil, M., Gamble, D. N., & Ohmer, M L. (2013). Evolution, models, and the changing context of community practice. In M. Weil (Ed.), *The handbook of community practice* (pp. 167–193). Thousand Oaks, CA: Sage Publications.

Weil, M., & Ohmer, M. L. (2013). Applying practice theories in community work. In M. Weil's (Ed.), *The handbook of community practice* (pp. 123–161). Thousand Oaks, CA: Sage.

Weil, M., Reisch, M., & Ohmer, M. L. (2013). Introduction: Contexts and challenges for 21st century communities. In M. Weil's (Ed.), *The handbook of community practice* (pp. 3–26). Thousand Oaks, CA: Sage.

West Virginia Board of Social Work Examiners. (n.d.). *Level D: LICSW: (Licensed Independent Social Worker) license*. Retrieved from http://www.wvsocialworkboard.org/licensinginfo/regular/licswlicense.htm

Wharton, T. C. (2008). Compassion fatigue: Being an ethical social worker. *The New Social Worker*, *15*(1),4–7.

Wharton, T. C. & Bolland, K. A. (2012). Practitioner perspectives of evidence-based practice. *Families in Society: The Journal of Contemporary Social Services*, *93*(3), 157–164.

Whitaker, T. & Arrington, P. (2008). *Social workers at work. NASW Membership Workforce Study*. Washington, DC: National Association of Social Workers.

Whitaker, T., & Wilson, M. (2010). *National Association of Social Workers 2009 compensation and benefit study: Summary of key compensation findings*. Washington DC: NASW.

Wheeler, W. & Thomas, A. M. (2011). Engaging youth in community development. In J. W. Robinson Jr. & G. P. Green (Eds.), *Introduction to community development: Theory, practice and service-learning* (pp. 209–227). Los Angeles, CA: Sage Publications.

Williams, N. R. (2009). Narrative family interventions. In A. C. Kilpatrick & T. P. Holland, *Working with families. An integrative model by level of need* (5th ed.) (pp. 199–223). Boston: Pearson.

Winship, K. & Lee, S. T. (2012). Using evidence-based accreditation standards to promote Continuous Quality Improvement: The experience of San Mateo County Human Services Agency. *Journal of Evidence-based Social Work*, *9*(1–2), 68–86.

Wise, J. B. (2005). *Empowerment practice with families in distress*. New York: Columbia University Press.

Witkin, S. L. (2000). Ethics-R-Us. *Social Work*, *45*(3), 197–212.

Wood, G. G. & Tully, C. T. (2006). *The structural approach to direct practice in social work: A social constructionist Perspective* (3rd ed.). New York: Columbia University Press.

Wood, G. G. & Roche, S. E. (2001). Representing selves, reconstructing lives: Feminist group work with women survivors of male violence. *Social Work with Groups*, *23*(4), 5–23.

Work Group for Community Health and Development at the University of Kansas. (2012). *The Community Tool Box*. Retrieved from http://ctb.ku.edu/en/tablecontents/chapter_1033.aspx

World Health Organization. (2012). *Global democracy deficit*. Retrieved from http:// www.who.int/trade/glossary/story037/en/index/html

Yalom, I. D. & Leszcz, M. (2005). *The theory and practice of group psychotherapy* (5th ed.). New York: Basic Books.

Young, S. (2013). Solutions for bullying in primary schools. In P. De Jong & I. K. Berg, *Interviewing for solutions* (4th ed.) (pp. 308–318). Belmont, CA: Brooks/Cole.

Zandee-Amas, R. R. (2013). A good groups runs itself—and other myths. *The New Social Worker, 20*(1), 10–11.

Zur, O., & Lazarus, A. A. (2002). Six arguments against dual relationships and their rebuttals. In A. A. Lararus & O. Zur (Eds.), *Dual relationships and psychotherapy* (p. 3–24). New York, NY: Springer.

CREDITS

Photo 1-A: © Lisa F. Young

Ex 1.1: Copyrighted material reprinted with permission from the National Association of Social Workers, Inc.

Ex 1.2: Healy, L. M. & Link, R. J. (2012). Handbook of international social work: Human rights, developmen, and the global profession. Used by permission of Oxford University Press.

Photo 1-B: © Lisa F. Young

Ex 1.4: University Declaration of Human Rights used by permission of Human Rights Education Association.

Photo 2-A: © marekuliasz

Ex 2.1: Copyrighted material reprinted with permission from the National Association of Social Workers, Inc.

Ex 2.3: Copyrighted material reprinted with permission from the National Association of Social Workers, Inc.

Ex 2.4: International Federation of Social Workers (IFSW). (2012). Ethics in social work: Statement of principles. Retrieved October 14, 2012 from http://ifsw.org/policies/statement-of-ethical-principles/. Used by permission.

Ex 2.5: New Zealand Association of Social Workers (NZASW). (1993). Code of ethics. Used by permission.

Photo 2-B: © Mark Bowden

QG 3: From Dolgoff/Loewenberg/Harrington. Ethical Decisions for Social Work Praictce, 8E. © 2009 Wadsworth, a part of Cengage Learning, Inc. Reproduced by permission. www.cengage.com/permissions

Ex 2.7: From The Propriety of Affiliation with Clients beyond the Professional Role: Nonsexual dual relationships. Arete 22(1) by R. Vodde and M.M. Giddings. © 1997. Reprinted with permission.

Photo 3-A: © Yuri Arcurs

Ex 3.3: From Skills for Direct Practice in Social Work by R. R. Middleman and G.G. Wood. Copyright © 1990. Columbia University Press.

Ex 4.1: From Assessing strengths, Identifying acts of resistance to violence and oppression, by K.M. Anderson, C.D. Cowger and C.A. Snively. In The Strengths perspective in social swork practice (the d.), by D. Saleebey (Ed.). Copyright Allyn & Bacon, 2009.

Ex 4.2: From Assessing strengths, Identifying acts of resistance to violence and oppression, by K.M. Anderson, C.D. Cowger and C.A. Snively. In The Strengths perspective in social swork practice (the d.), by D. Saleebey (Ed.). Copyright Allyn & Bacon, 2009.

Photo 4-A: © fatihhoca

QG 8: Adapted from The Strengths perspective in social work (5th ed.), by D. Saleebey. Copyright © 2009, Allyn & Bacon.

Photo 4-B: © Lisa F. Young

QG 10: Kagle, J. D. & Kopels, S. (2008). Social work records (3rd ed.). Long Grove, IL: Waveland Press, Inc. Used by permission.

Ex 4.8: Adapted from St. Anthony's Medical Center, St. Louis, Missouri. Reprinted with permission.

Ex 4.9: Adapted from St. Anthony's Medical Center, St. Louis, Missouri. Reprinted with permission.

Ex 4.10: Adapted from St. Anthony's Medical Center, St. Louis, Missouri. Reprinted with permission.

QG 11: From Dejong/Berg. Interviewing for Solutions, 4E. © 2013 Wadsworth, a part of Cengage Learning, Inc. Reproduced by permission. Www.cengage.com/permissions

Photo 5-A: © Alexander Raths

Ex 5.1: Adapted from The structural approach to direct practice in social work: A social constructionist perspective (3rd ed.), by G.G. Wood and C.T. Tully. Copyright 2006, Columbia University Press. Reprinted with permission.

Photo 5-B: © Adam Gregor

QG 16: Sormanti, M. (2012). Writing for and about clinical practice. In W. Green and B. L. Simon, The Columbia guide to social work writing (pp. 114-132). NY: Columbia University Press.

Photo 6-B: © Rob Hainer

Ex 6.4: From Culture in special education, by M. Kalyanpur and B. Harry. Copyright 1999, Paul H. Brookes. Reprinted with permission.

Ex 6.5: Van Hook, M.P. (2008). Social work practice with families: A resiliency-based approach. Chicago: Lyceum Books.

Ex 6.6: Van Hook, M.P. (2008). Social work practice with families: A resiliency-based approach. Chicago: Lyceum Books.

Ex 6.7: From Self-perception in family systems: A diagrammatic technique, by R.R. Van Treuren. In assessment in social work practice, by C. Meyer. Copyright 1993, Columbia University Press. Reprinted with permission.

QG 18: Warde, B. (2012). The Cultural Genogram: Enhancing the cultural competency of social work students. Social Work Education, 31(5), 570-586. Used by permission.

Ex 6.8: From The Culturagram, by E. P. Congress. In Social Workers' desk reference (2nd ed.), by A.R. Roberts. Copyright 2009, Oxford Press. Reprinted with permission.

QG 19: Adapted from St. Anthony's Medical Center, St. Louis, Missouri. Reprinted with permission.

Ex 7.1: From Hull/Mather. Undertssanding Generalist Practice with Families, 1E. © 2006 Wadsworth, a part of Cengage Learning, Inc. Reproduced by permission. www.cengage.com/permissions

Ex 7.2: Sebold, J. (2011). Families and couples: A practical guide for facilitating change. In G. J. Greene and M. Y. Lee, Solution-oriented social work practice (pp. 209-236). NY: Oxford University Press.

Photo 7-A: © Lisa F. Young

Ex 7.3: Adapted from St. Anthony's Medical Center, St. Louis, Missouri. Reprinted with permission.

Ex 7.4: Adapted from St. Anthony's Medical Center, St. Louis, Missouri; Missouri Department of Social Services.

QG 22: From Enabling and empowering families: principles and guidelines for practice, by CX.J. dunst, C.M. Trivette and A.G. Deal. Copyright 2003, Brookline Books. Reprinted with permission.

QG 23: From Enabling and empowering families: principles and guidelines for practice, by CX.J. dunst, C.M. Trivette and A.G. Deal. Copyright 2003, Brookline Books. Reprinted with permission.

Photo 7-B: © Lisa F. Young

Photo 8-A: © Blaj Gabriel

Ex 8.6: From Teaching a methods course in social work with groups, by R. Kurland and R. Salmon. Copyright 1998, Council on Social Work Education.

Ex 8.7: Kurland, R. & Salmon, R. (1998). Teaching a methods course in social work with groups. Alexandria, VA: Council on Social Work Education.

Photo 8-B: © Yuri Arcurs

Ex 8.8: Adapted from St. Anthony's Medical Center, St. Louis, Missouri. Reprinted with permission.

Ex 8.9: Adapted from Women's Support and Community Services, St. Louis, Missouri.

Photo 9-A: © Glynnis Jones

QG 27: From Group Composition, diversity, the skills of the social worker, and group development, by T. Berman-Rossi and T.B. Kelly. Presented at the Council for Social Work Education Annual Meeting, Atlanta, February. Copyright 2003. Reprinted with permission.

Photo 9-B: © Blaj Gabriel

Ex 9.1: Comer, E. & Meier, A. (2011). Using evidence-based practice and intervention research with treatment groups for populations at risk. In G.L. Greif & P.H. Ephross (Eds.) Group work with populations at risk (3rd ed.) (pp. 459–488). New York: Oxford University Press

Ex 9.2: Greif, G. & Ephross, P.H. (Eds.). (2011). Group work with populations at risk (3rd ed.). New York: Oxford University Press.

QG 28: Berg, R.D., Landreth, G.L., & Fall, K.A. (2013). Group counseling concepts and procedures (5th ed.). New York: Routledge.

Photo 9-C: © vm

Photo 9-D: © Yuri Arcurs

QG 30: Berg, R.D., Landreth, G.L., & Fall, K.A. (2013). Group counseling concepts and procedures (5th ed.). New York: Routledge.

Ex 9.7: Berg, R.D., Landreth, G.L., & Fall, K.A. (2013). Group counseling concepts and procedures (5th ed.). New York: Routledge.

Photo 10-A: © vm

Ex 10.2: Adapted from Center of Organizational and Social Research, Saint Louis University.

Ex 10.3: Royse, D., Staton-Tindall, M., Badger, K., & Webster, J.M. (2009). Needs assessment. New York: Oxford University Press.

Photo 10-B: © CREATISTA

Ex 10.4: City of Seattle, Washington. (2012). A Community Assessment of Need for Housing and Services for Homeless Individuals and Families in the Lake City Neighborhood. Retrieved from http://seattle.gov/realestate/pdfs/Needs_Assessment_data_report.pdf

Ex 10.7: Kretzmann, J. P. & McKnight, J. L. (1993). Building communities from the inside out: A part toward finding and mobilizing a community's assets. Evanston, IL: Center for Urban Affairs and Policy Research. Used by permission.

Ex 10.8: McKnight, J. L., & Block, P. (2010). The abundant community: Awakening the power of families and neighborhoods. San Francisco, CA: Berrett-Koehler Publishers

Ex 10.9: McKnight, J. L., & Block, P. (2010). The abundant community: Awakening the power of families and neighborhoods. San Francisco, CA: Berrett-Koehler Publishers

Photo 10-C: © THEGIFT777

Ex 11.1: Netting, F. E., Kettner, P. M., McMurtry, S. L., & Thomas, L. (2011). Social work macro practice. Boston: Pearson Allyn & Bacon.

Ex 11.3: Source: 350.org

Photo 11-A: © 350.org

Photo 11-B: © 350.org

QG 35: Adapted from Organizing for social change, by K. Bobo, J. Kendall, and S. Max. Copyright 2010, The Forum Press. Reprinted with permission.

QG 36: Adapted from New Robert's Rules of Order by L. Rozakis. Copyright 1996, Smithmark Reference.

QG 37: Adapted from Consensus through conversation, by L. Dressler. Copyright 2006, Berrett-Koehler Publishers, Inc. All rights reserved. www.bkconnection.com

Ex 11.5: Kretzmann, J. P. & McKnight, J. L. (2005). Discovering community power: A guide to mobilizing local assets and your organization's capacity. Evanston, IL: Asset-Based Community Development (ABCD) Institute. Used by permission.

Ex 11.7: Ohmer, M.L. & DeMasi, K. (2009). Consensus organizing: A community development workbook. Thousand Oaks, CA: Sage Publications, Inc.

Ex 11.9: Ohmer, M.L. & Korr, W.S. (2006). The effectiveness of community practice interventions: A review of the literature. Research on Social Work Practice, 16(2),132–145. Used by permission.

Ex 11.10: From Localized needs and a globalized economy, by J. Ife in Social work and globalization (Special Issue), Canadian Social Work, 2(1). Copyright 2000.

Ex 11.11: From International social work: Issues, strategies and programs by D. Cox and M. Pawar. Copyright 2006, Sage Publications, Inc. Reprinted with permission.

Ex 11.14: Speer, P. W. & Christens, B. D. (2011). Local community organizing and change: Altering policy in the housing and community development system in Kansas City. Journal of Community & Applied Social Psychology, 22(5), 414-427. Used by permission.

Photo 12-A: © Digital Vision

Ex 12.1: National Association of Area Agencies on Aging. (2012). National aging services network. Retrieved from http://www.n4a.org/about-n4a/join/

Photo 12-B: © Chris Fertnig

Photo 12-C: © CandyBox Images

Ex 12.5: Gambrill, E. (2012). Social work practice: A critical thinkers guide. New York: Oxford University Press.

QG 39: From Locke/Garrison/Winship. Generalist Social Work Practice, 1E. © 1998 Wadsworth, a part of Cengage Learning, Inc. Reproduced by permission. www. Cengage.com/permissions

Ex 12.7: Larson, K., & McGuiston, C. (2012). Building capacity to improve Latino health in rural North Carolina: A case study in community-University engagement. Journal of Community Engagement and Scholarship, 5(1), 14-23.

QG 42: Plitt, D. L. & Shields, J. (2009). Development of the policy advocacy behavior scale: Initialreliability and validity. Research on Social Work Practice, 19(1), 83-92. Reprinted by permission.

Photo 13-A: © gosphotodesign

Ex 13.1: Evans, S. D., Hanlin, C. E., & Prillehensky, I. (2007). Blending Ameliorative and transformative approaches in human service organizations: A case study. Journal of Community Psychology, 35(3), 329-346. Used by permission.

Ex 13.2: Netting, F. E., Kettner, P. M., McMurtry, S. L., & Thomas, M. L. (2012). Social work macro practice. Boston: Pearson Allyn & Bacon.

Ex 13.4: Netting, F. E., Kettner, P. M., McMurtry, S. L., & Thomas, M. L. (2012). Social work macro practice. Boston: Pearson Allyn & Bacon.

QG 43: Manning, T. (2012). The art of successful persuasion: Seven skills you need to get your point across effectively.

Ex 13.6: O'Connor, M. K., & Netting, F. E. (2009). Organization practice: A guide to understanding human service organizations. Hoboken, NJ: John Wiley and Sons.

Ex 13.7: Winship, K. & Lee, S. T. (2012). Using evidence-based accreditation standards to promote Continuous Quality Improvement: The experience of San Mateo County Human Services Agency. Journal of Evidence-based Social Work, 9(1-2), 68-86.

GLOSSARY/INDEX

350.org, 465, 466

501(c)3 organizations are nonprofit organizations through which most social services are offered; they are designated this by the U.S. Internal Revenue Service (IRS). Nonprofit organizations are sanctioned by the law to meet specified public needs, are exempt from paying taxes on organizational income, and donors are allowed to deduct contributions from their taxes, 497

IFSW *Statement of Principles*, 45
international, 482
solution-focused practice is a specific therapeutic
    perspective that emphasizes brief interventions,
    narrowly defined specific problem areas, and
    cognitive support in identifying explicit solutions
    to pressing problems, 33, 34, 113–114, 124–125
    crisis intervention, 156, 158
    critical constructionist emphasis, 271
    family social work, 267–270, 295–298, 311–312
    group work, 343–344, 357, 373–374, 395–396
    intervention, 177–180
spatial communities are structures of connectedness
    based on a physical location, 415
Specht, Harvey, 14
spectator questions, 293, 294
spirituality, 5, 118, 166
stakeholders are those who have an interest in
    community affairs, such as neighborhood leaders,
    415, 437–438
standardized assessment, 143, 273, 313, 321, 354, 401
standards, ethical, 41, 42
Standards for Social Work Practice with Groups, 332, 351,
    378–379
Statement of Principles (IFSW), 43–44
stigma, 84, 143, 251
story development questions, 123
strategic plans are comprehensive, formal plans for
    the future direction of the organization, 540
strategy is an overall approach to a change effort,
    542–545
strengths perspective is an orientation that
    emphasizes client system resources, capabilities,
    support systems, and motivations to meet
    challenges and overcome adversity to achieve
    wellbeing, 20, 29–30, 34, 36, 98
    assessment, 105, 109–112, 121–122
    client's goals and dreams, 131
    clinical writing, 225
    community needs assessment, 438
    community practice, 421, 442, 446, 456, 486–488
    crisis intervention, 158
    cultural competence, 116, 117–118, 119
    dialogue skills, 71
    disability, 204, 255–256, 258
    empowerment practice, 201, 202
    evaluation of intervention's compatibility with,
        224–225
    evaluation tools, 313–315, 316–318
    exception questions, 269, 270

family social work, 245, 288–292, 299, 310,
    313–315, 316–318
gay, lesbian, bisexual and transgender parents, 251
group work, 342, 343, 370–372, 394–395
IFSW *Statement of Principles*, 45
international families, 261
intervention, 174–177, 231
logistics and activities, 86–87
motivational interviewing, 205
respectful stance, 83
shared power, 166
single parent families, 253–254
skills and methods, 84–86, 181
stress, 178–179
Strom-Gottfried, K. J., 56–57, 62
structural exclusion, 94
substance abuse, 20, 46–47
    assessment documentation, 146, 358
    case management, 191
    grandparents raising grandchildren, 248
    group work, 341
    intergenerational patterns, 246
    non-voluntary clients, 150
subsystems are a dimension of systems theory; they
    are components of a system that also have
    interacting parts, provide a mechanism for
    organizing relationships and planning ways to
    engage with them, 242–243, 245, 418, 425
suicide, 40, 208
    ethical dilemmas, 55
    risk assessment, 148, 158–163
Summarizing (part of the OARS pneumonic) allows
    the social worker to expand on the previous
    reflections and transition to the next phase of
    work. Summaries bring together all the aspects of
    the conversation and aid in the planning of the
    change process as well as the evaluation of
    change that has occurred, 207
summarizing is a way to confirm an understanding
    of the client's message and address assumptions,
    76–77, 296, 398
summative research is research conducted to learn
    about the outcome, or effect, of interventions, 11
supervision, 12, 169
    advocacy, 200
    ethical decision-making, 62–63
    social worker's own family issues, 278
    sustaining ethical practice, 167
    tips for effective, 168
support

NEW DIRECTIONS IN SOCIAL WORK

SERIES EDITOR: ALICE LIEBERMAN, UNIVERSITY OF KANSAS

New Directions in Social Work is an innovative, integrated series offering a uniquely distinctive teaching strategy for generalist courses in the social work curriculum, at both undergraduate and graduate levels. The series integrates five texts with custom websites housing interactive cases, companion readings, and a wealth of resources to enrich the teaching and learning experience.

Research for Effective Social Work Practice, Third Edition

Judy L. Krysik, Arizona State University and Jerry Finn, University of Washington, Tacoma

HB: 978-0-415-52100-0
PB: 978-0-415-51986-1
eBook: 978-0-203-07789-4

Social Work and Social Welfare, Third Edition

Anissa Taun Rogers, St. Louis University

HB: 978-0-415-52080-5
PB: 978-0-415-50160-6
eBook: 978-0-203-11931-0

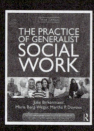

The Practice of Generalist Social Work, Third Edition

Julie Birkenmaier, Marla Berg-Weger, both at St. Louis University, and Martha P. Dewees, University of Vermont

HB: 978-0-415-51988-5
PB: 978-0-415-51989-2
eBook: 978-0-203-07098-7

Social Policy for Effective Practice: A Strengths Approach, Third Edition

Rosemary Chapin, University of Kansas

HB: 978-0-415-51991-5
PB: 978-0-415-51992-2
eBook: 978-0-203-79476-0